MW01620879

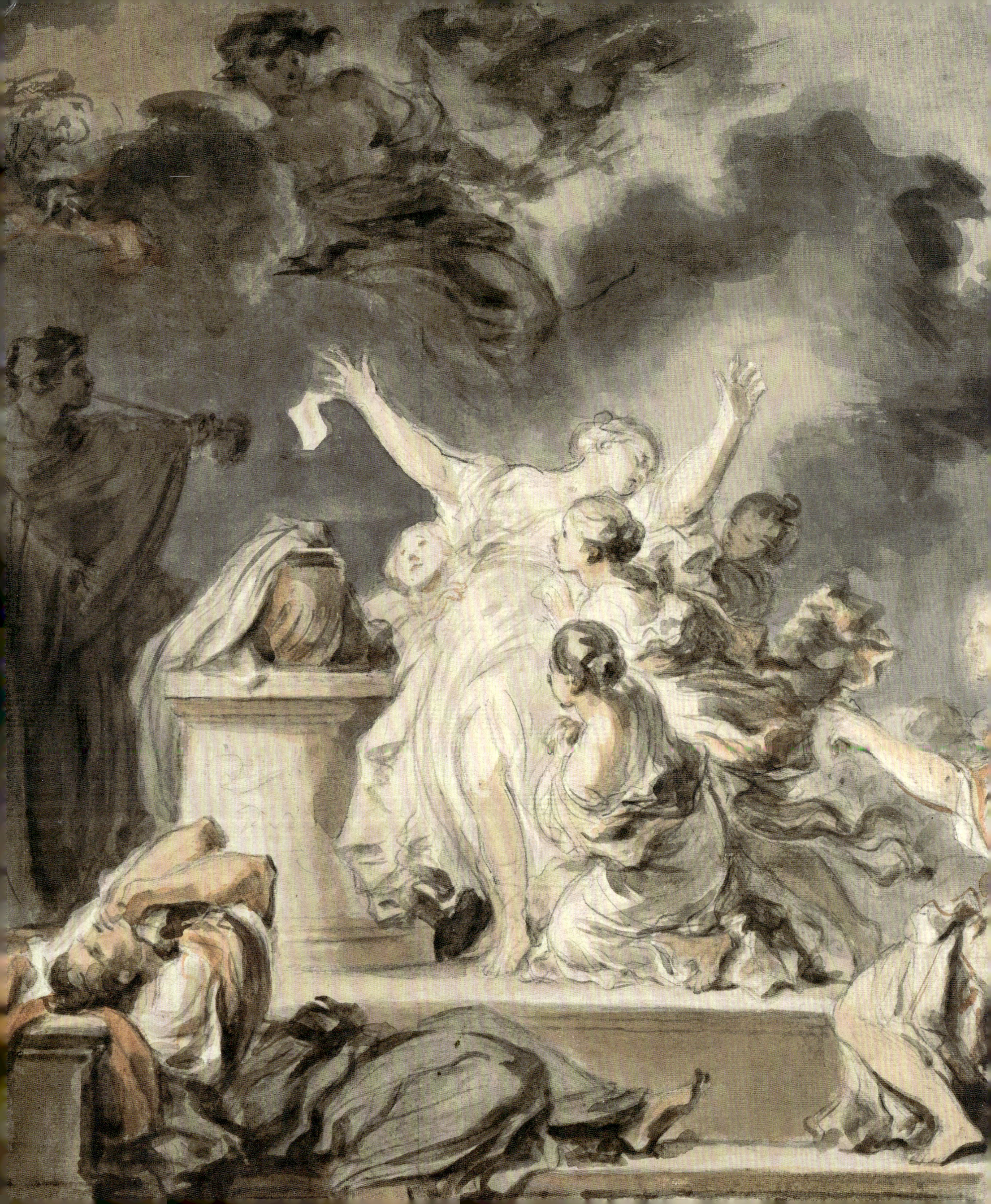

FRAGONARD
DRAWING TRIUMPHANT
Works from New York Collections

Perrin Stein

with contributions by

Marie-Anne Dupuy-Vachey

Eunice Williams

Kelsey Brosnan

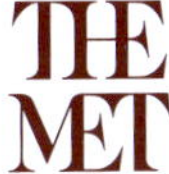

The Metropolitan Museum of Art, New York

Distributed by Yale University Press, New Haven and London

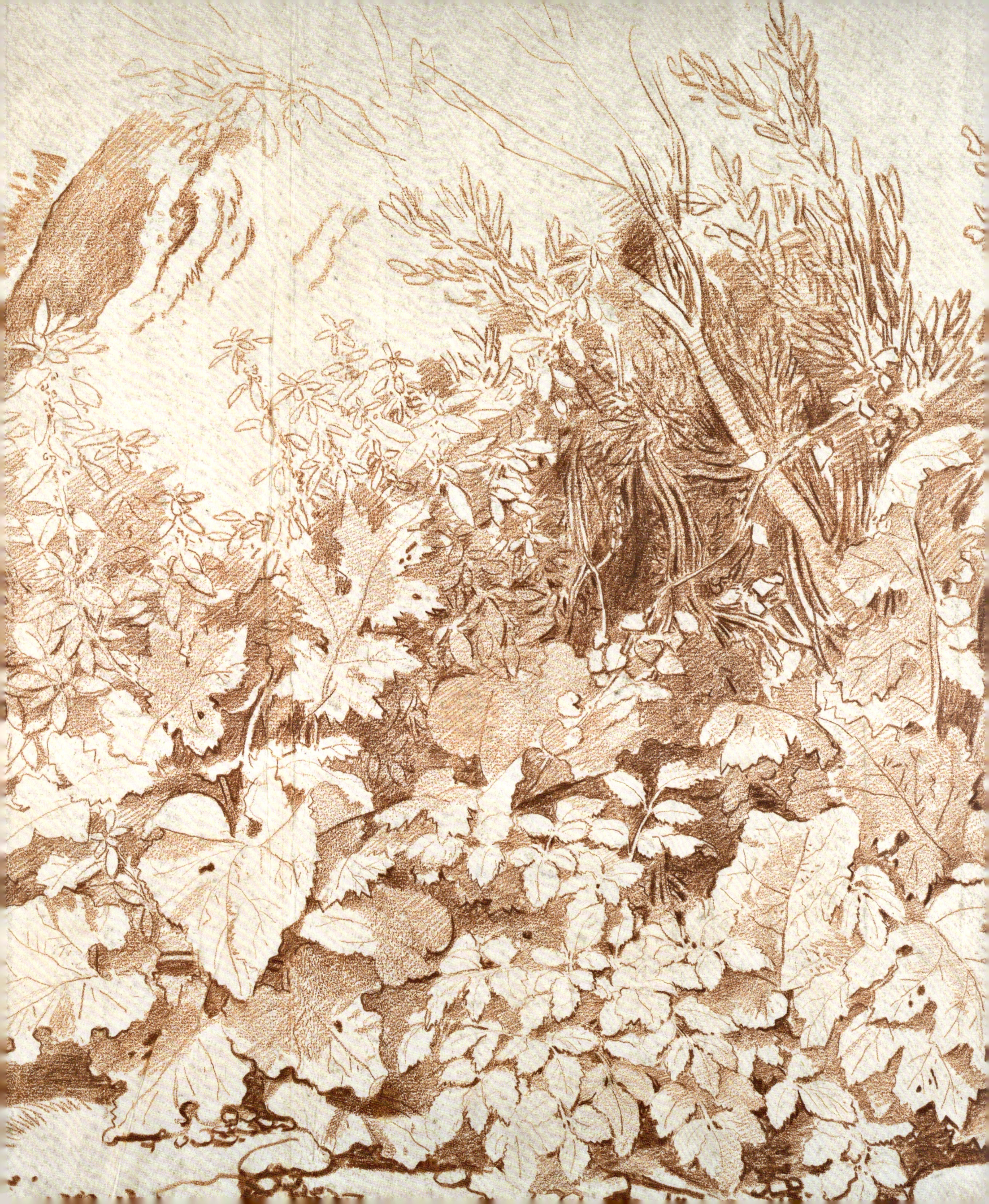

Contents

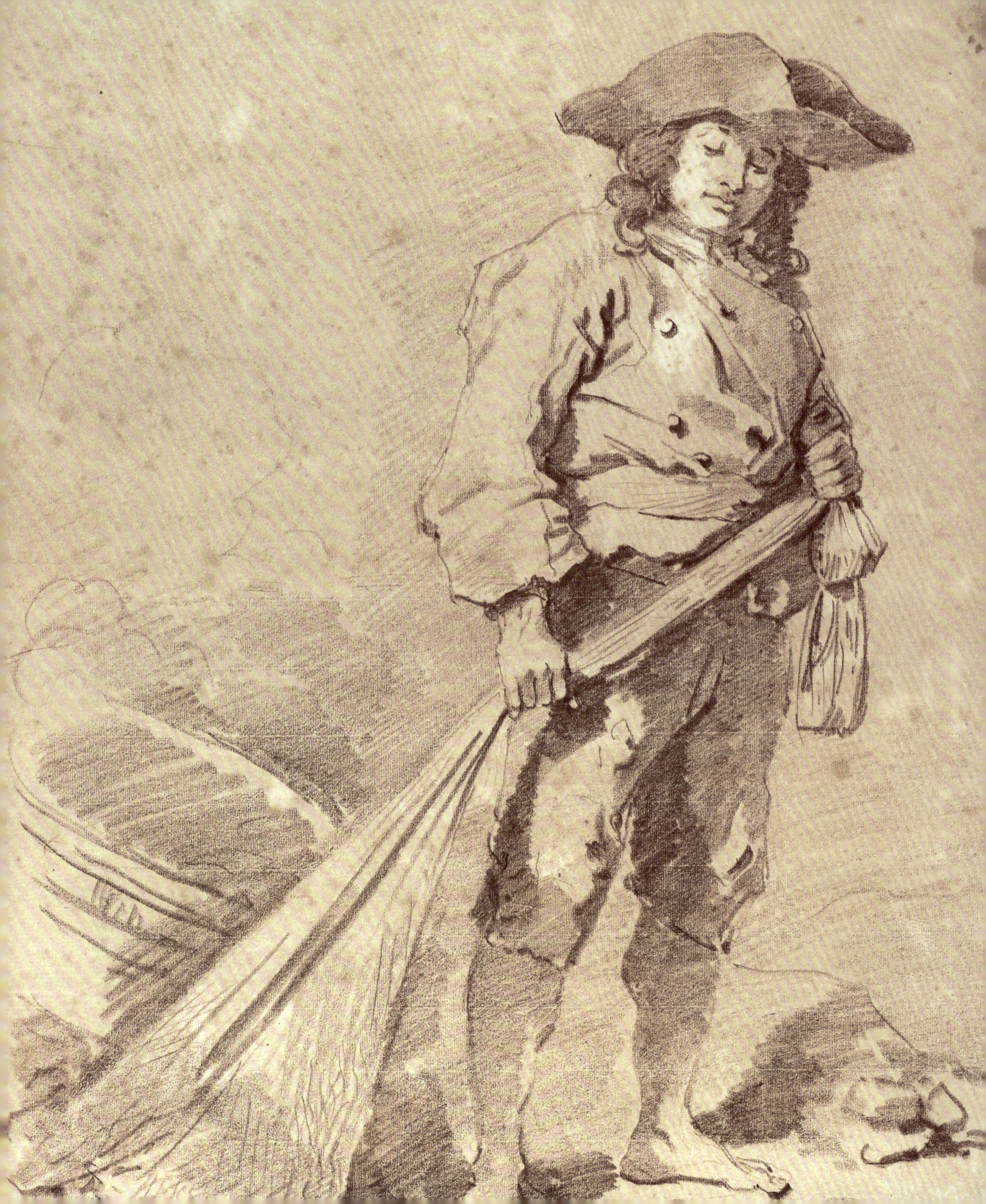

Director's Foreword

It has been almost thirty years since The Metropolitan Museum of Art organized, together with the Musée du Louvre in Paris, the groundbreaking retrospective of the work of Jean Honoré Fragonard, one of the masters of the French Rococo. Over the intervening decades our admiration for his work continued to grow and our understanding of his artistic process has deepened and evolved, aided in part by the study of newly discovered works on paper. Fragonard's drawings, once considered more narrowly in terms of their relationship to paintings and prints, are now better appreciated as independent forms of artistic expression—fully achieved works of art that inspire awe and delectation.

Born in 1732, Fragonard was a product of the age of the Enlightenment, a period of rapid change. As with many Rococo artists, his work was undervalued in the decades following the fall of the ancien régime. Unlike Francisco de Goya, he did not paint canvases to express moral outrage. He did not ally himself, as Giovanni Battista Tiepolo often did, with a religious institution or a great monarch. Nor did he, like Jacques Louis David, grab the harnesses of social upheaval. His heroes and heroines were commonplace, often fictional, their pursuits largely amorous or domestic. He was seen, in short, as more of a guilty pleasure than a noble taste.

But behind the lightness and familiarity of his subject matter lie a timeless appeal and a modern sensibility. With chalk and wash Fragonard found a certain liberation, a means to explore and experiment, and he would often return to the same subject multiple times in search of new effects and expressiveness. Modern audiences will marvel at the pure beauty that sprang from his hand, even as his sheets offer the means to reflect on a culture and artistic tradition at a moment of transition.

This catalogue and the exhibition it accompanies have been organized by Perrin Stein, Curator in the Department of Drawings and Prints, to advance our understanding of Fragonard's graphic oeuvre and its place in the society of his time and to celebrate several generations of collectors whose passion was instrumental in bringing his drawings to New York collections, where so many spectacular examples now reside.

The exhibition could not have been mounted without the generosity of many local collectors who have all lent precious works. We are also grateful to our colleagues at The Morgan Library & Museum, the Brooklyn Museum, and the New York Public Library who have made available Fragonard's works from their own holdings, which complement ours and help us tell the story of this gifted draftsman.

It is my pleasure to recognize the generous funders of this project, the Gail and Parker Gilbert Fund and the Diane W. and James E. Burke Fund, whose steadfast support of The Met has played a critical role in the realization of many exhibitions over the years. We also thank Mrs. Henry J. Heinz II for making this beautiful publication possible.

Thomas P. Campbell, Director
The Metropolitan Museum of Art

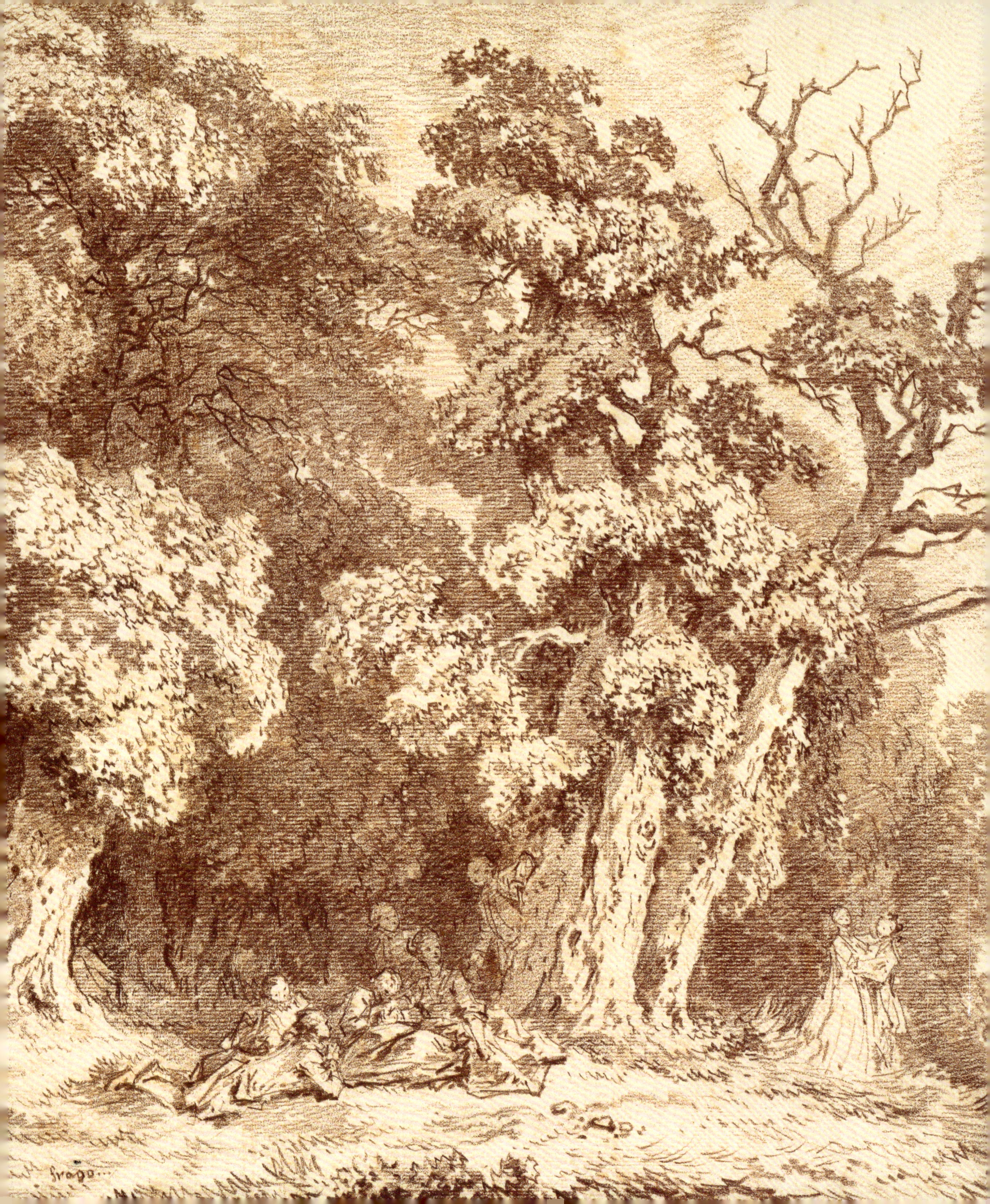

Acknowledgments

A project like this one benefits immensely from the thoughts, opinions, and assistance of others. Beyond the obvious value of pooled information, one is buoyed by shared enthusiasms. First and foremost I am grateful for the vast knowledge and expertise of my two collaborators in this project: Marie-Anne Dupuy-Vachey and Eunice Williams, both of whom have devoted a good portion of their professional lives to Fragonard's drawings. Kelsey Brosnan, a PhD candidate at Rutgers University, has been a most able research assistant, catalogue contributor, and, now, fellow *dix-huitièmiste*.

In addition, I am very cognizant that our work builds on the foundation of research done by previous scholars. From my first graduate school paper on Fragonard to the present day, I have kept close at hand the monographs by Jean-Pierre Cuzin and Pierre Rosenberg, as well as studies by my coauthors and others listed in the bibliography of this volume. To M. Rosenberg, whose writings on the artist span many decades, we owe a special debt of gratitude for generously making available to us his very rich documentation.

Part of the impetus for undertaking this project was the Museum's acquisition of a number of major drawings by Fragonard since I joined the Department of Drawings and Prints in 1995. For these acquisitions I have been fortunate to have had the support of past and present Directors, Philippe de Montebello and Thomas P. Campbell, and past and present department heads, George R. Goldner, former Drue Heinz Chairman, and Nadine M. Orenstein, Drue Heinz Curator in Charge, Department of Drawings and Prints. Our holdings have also been enhanced thanks to the bequests of the late Catherine G. Curran and Phyllis D. Massar. The support of the Drawings and Prints Visiting Committee, which takes many forms, has also been significant. Here I would like to acknowledge the encouragement and interest of two longtime members, Stephen A. Geiger and David T. Schiff. A true advocate of this Department, Mrs. Henry J. Heinz II was instrumental in the realization of this publication.

That it is possible to assemble a show highlighting all facets and periods of this important artist's career with loans drawn solely from New York holdings is a tribute to the passion of local collectors, in both private and museum settings. It is a passion that has deep historical roots and that continues to burn brightly into the present day. Our peer institutions have been most generous. We would like to thank our local colleagues: Richard Aste and Elizabeth Largi at the Brooklyn Museum; Madeleine Viljoen and Adrianne Rubin at the New York Public Library; and Colin B. Bailey, John Marciari, Jennifer Tonkovich, Giada Damen, Margaret Holben Ellis, and John D. Alexander at The Morgan Library & Museum. As for the private collectors whose gracious willingness to temporarily part with their drawings has greatly enriched the exhibition, we are indebted to Irene Roosevelt Aitken, Elizabeth and Jean-Marie Eveillard, Dr. Mary Tavener Holmes, and

Chronology

Kelsey Brosnan

1732

On April 4, Jean Honoré Fragonard is born in Grasse, in the south of France, to François Fragonard, a glove merchant, and his wife, Françoise Petit.

1738

The Fragonard family moves to Paris.

Ca. 1748–52

After several months in the studio of genre and still life painter Jean Siméon Chardin (1699–1779), Fragonard enters the studio of François Boucher (1703–1770).

1752

On August 26, Fragonard is awarded the Prix de Rome by the Académie Royale de Peinture et de Sculpture for his history painting *Jeroboam Sacrificing to the Idols*. Thereafter, Fragonard enters the Ecole des Elèves Protégés, led by painter Carle Vanloo (1705–1765).

1754

On March 4, paintings by students from the Ecole des Elèves Protégés, including Fragonard's *Psyche Showing Her Sisters Her Gifts from Cupid*, are presented to Louis XV at Versailles.

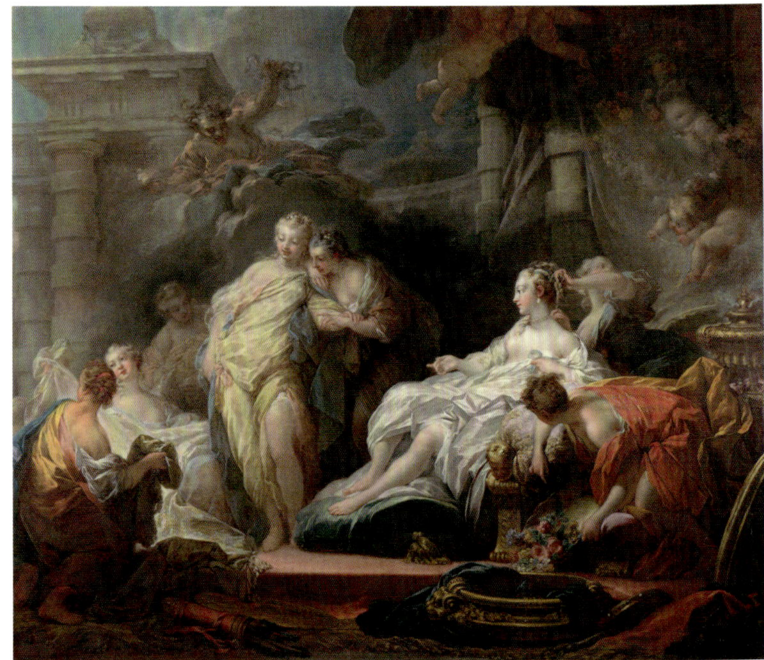

Jean Honoré Fragonard, *Psyche Showing Her Sisters Her Gifts from Cupid*, 1753. Oil on canvas, 66¼ × 75¾ in. (168.3 × 192.4 cm). National Gallery, London (NG6445)

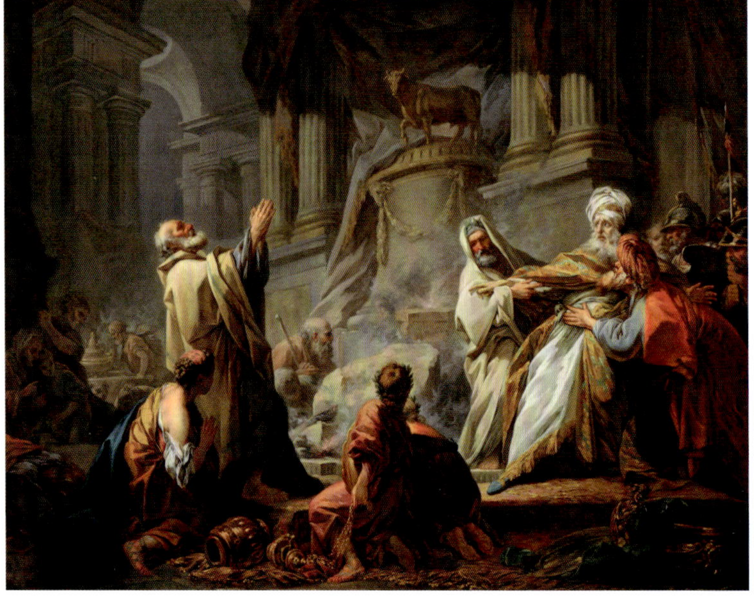

Jean Honoré Fragonard, *Jeroboam Sacrificing to the Idols*, 1752. Oil on canvas, 44 × 56½ in. (111.5 × 143.5 cm). Ecole Nationale Supérieure des Beaux-Arts, Paris (PRP 7)

1756–61

By December 22, 1756, Fragonard arrives at the Académie de France in Rome, directed by Charles Joseph Natoire (1700–1777). Fragonard is a pensionnaire there for nearly five years, studying the art of antiquity as well as Renaissance and Baroque works by Italian masters.

1760

Fragonard and *amateur* Jean Claude Richard, the abbé de Saint-Non (1727–1791), spend July and August in Tivoli, outside Rome, where the artist sketches the gardens of the Villa d'Este.

1761

After a brief visit to Naples, Fragonard departs Rome on April 14 in the company of Saint-Non. Fragonard copies works in various cities, including Florence, Bologna, Venice, and Genoa, before returning to Paris on September 26.

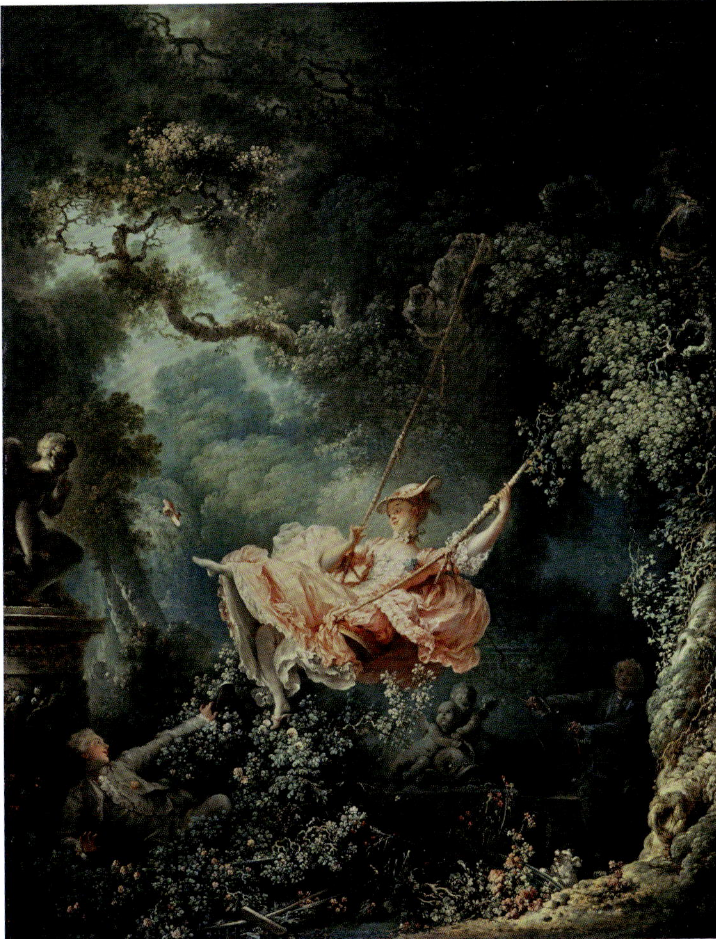

Jean Honoré Fragonard, *The Swing*, 1767. Oil on canvas, 31⅞ × 25¼ in. (81 × 64.2 cm). The Wallace Collection, London (P430)

1763–64

Fragonard produces a series of etchings, including four bacchanal scenes (cats. 26–29), and a group of sixteen etchings based on his copies after Italian masters (cats. 13–25).

1765

On March 30, Fragonard is accepted at the Académie. At the Salon in August, he exhibits his *morceau d'agrément* (acceptance piece), *Coresus and Callirhoë* (p. 139, fig. 85), as well as at least two drawings of the Villa d'Este.

Fragonard is given lodging at the Louvre, where he shares a studio with illustrator and miniature painter Pierre Antoine Baudouin (1723–1769), Boucher's son-in-law.

1766

For his *morceau de réception* (reception piece), Fragonard is charged with painting an allegory of Spring for a ceiling compartment of the Galerie d'Apollon at the Louvre. Ten years later, he acknowledges to the Académie that he will not complete this work.

1767

Fragonard participates in the Salon for the second and last time. He exhibits several drawings and two paintings, including *Group of Infants in the Sky*.

In October, Fragonard receives a private commission for *The Swing*.

In November, Fragonard and Baudouin receive permission to copy Rubens's Marie de Médicis cycle in the Palais du Luxembourg.

1769

On June 17, Fragonard marries miniaturist Marie Anne Gérard (1745–1823), also a native of Grasse. On December 16, their daughter, Rosalie, is born.

Fragonard paints portraits in Spanish dress (*à l'espagnole*) of Saint-Non and his brother, Louis Richard de la Bretèche (1722–1804), as well as sixteen other portraits traditionally referred to as *figures de fantaisie* (fantasy figures). The discovery in June 2012 of an annotated sheet of sketches (p. 8, fig. 5) has led to the re-identification of many of the subjects in the series.

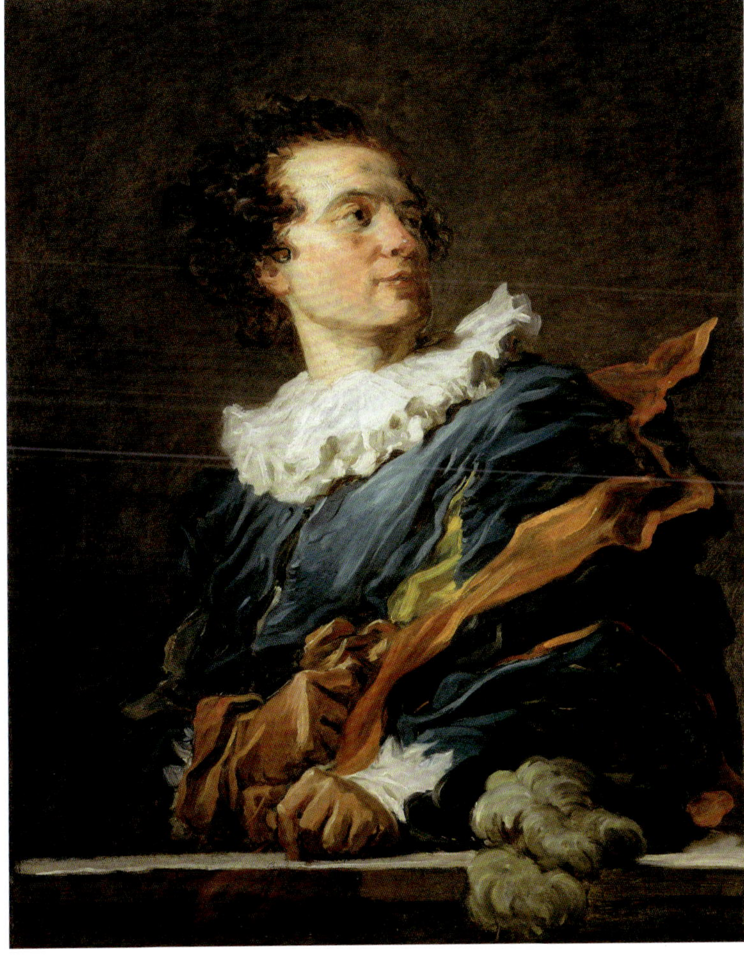

Jean Honoré Fragonard, *Abbé de Saint-Non*, 1769. Oil on canvas, 31½ × 25⅝ in. (80 × 65 cm). Musée du Louvre, Paris (MI 1061)

1770

Saint-Non publishes *Fragments choisis dans les peintures et les tableaux les plus intéressants des palais et des églises de l'Italie* (Fragments chosen from the most interesting paintings and canvases of the palaces and churches of Italy), the first of several suites of aquatints after drawings made in Italy, mostly by Fragonard. These volumes appear periodically through 1774.

On December 10, Fragonard and Jean-Baptiste Huet (1745–1811) receive a commission to produce paintings for the king's dining room at Versailles; these are never completed.

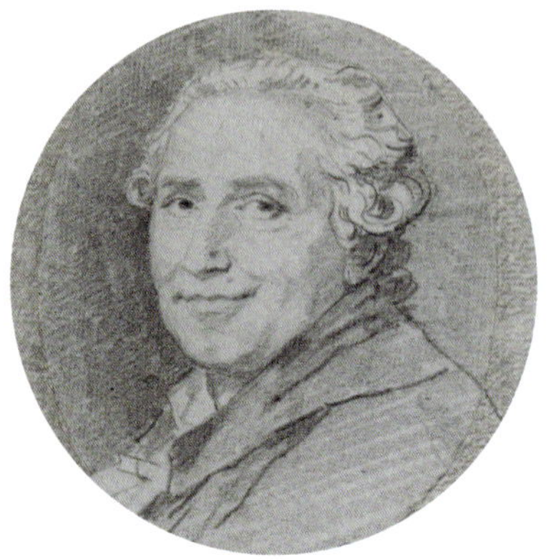

Jean Honoré Fragonard, *Self-Portrait*, ca. 1785. Black chalk, 5 × 4 in. (12.6 × 10.1 cm). Musée du Louvre, Paris (RF 41191)

1771

On February 18, Fragonard purchases numerous works of art, mostly by northern artists, from the estate sale of his teacher, François Boucher.

1771–72

Fragonard paints the Progress of Love series for the Louveciennes pavilion of the comtesse du Barry (1743–1793), a favorite of Louis XV. The four paintings are installed in 1772, but soon after they are taken down, returned to the painter, and replaced with panels by Joseph Marie Vien (1716–1809).

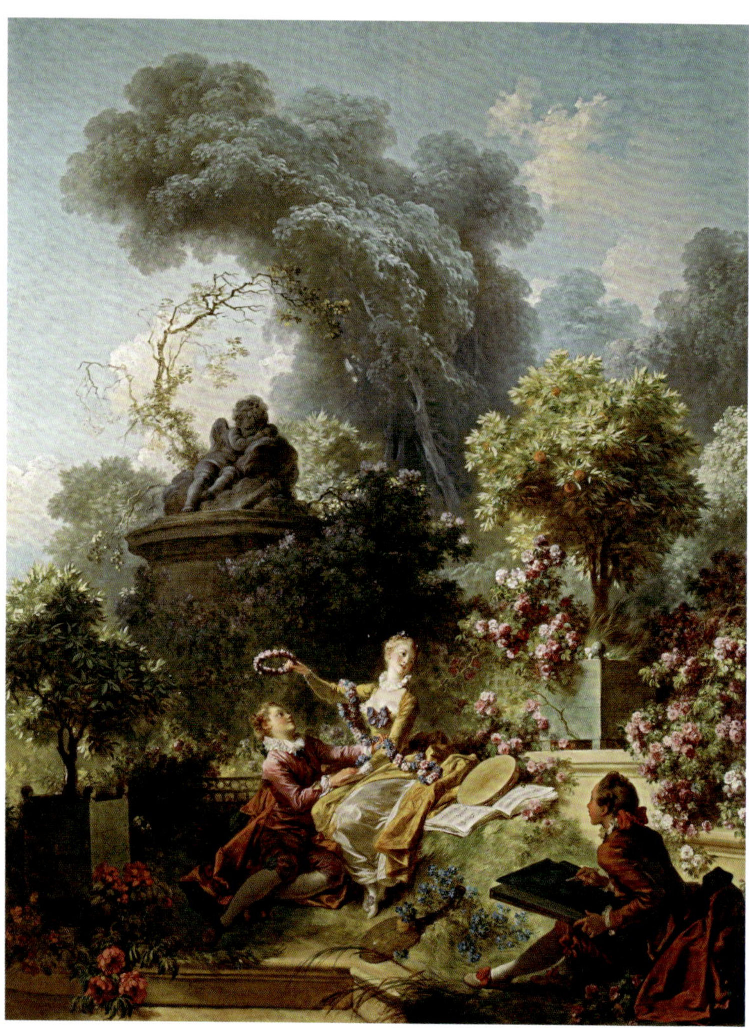

Jean Honoré Fragonard, *The Progress of Love: The Lover Crowned*, 1771–72. Oil on canvas, 125⅛ × 95¾ in. (317.8 × 243.2 cm). The Frick Collection, New York (1915.1.48)

1773–74

Fragonard travels abroad with patron Pierre Jacques Onésyme Bergeret de Grancourt (1715–1785). In the summer of 1773, they journey to Flanders and the Netherlands. After spending two weeks in October at Bergeret's château at Nègrepelisse, outside Toulouse, Fragonard and Bergeret (along with Fragonard's wife and Bergeret's mistress and son) travel throughout Italy.

1774

Louis XV dies on May 10 at Versailles; he is succeeded by his grandson, Louis XVI.

Fragonard, Bergeret, and the rest of the entourage return to Paris in September, by way of Vienna, Prague, Dresden, Leipzig, Frankfurt, and Strasbourg. Following their return, a dispute over the ownership of the drawings Fragonard created on the voyage leads to a lawsuit; accounts differ as to the resolution.

1775

By this time, Marguerite Gérard (1761–1837), the younger sister of Fragonard's wife, has come to live the with Fragonard family.

1778

Fragonard and Gérard produce a group of nine etchings based on Fragonard's brown wash drawings (cats. 80, 82–84). The *Journal de Paris* announces Gérard's *The Genius of Franklin* (p. 232, fig. 121) on November 15 and Fragonard's *The Armoire* (cat. 84) on November 27.

1779–86

Fragonard exhibits various etchings, drawings, and paintings at the Salon de la Correspondance, an alternative exhibition space organized

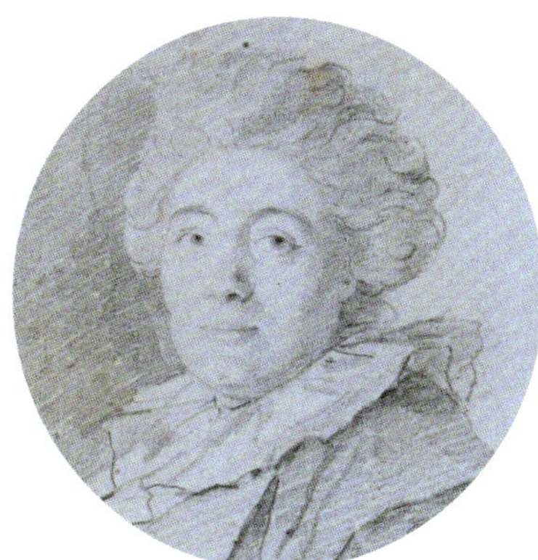

Jean Honoré Fragonard, *Portrait of Madame Fragonard*, ca. 1785. Black chalk, 5 × 5 in. (12.7 × 12.6 cm). Musée du Louvre, Paris (RF 41194)

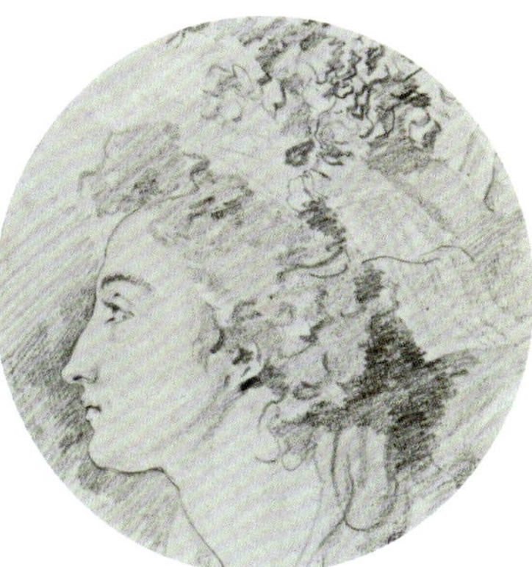

Jean Honoré Fragonard, *Portrait of Marguerite Gérard*, ca. 1785. Black chalk, 5 × 5 in. (12.6 × 12.6 cm). Musée du Louvre, Paris (RF 41197)

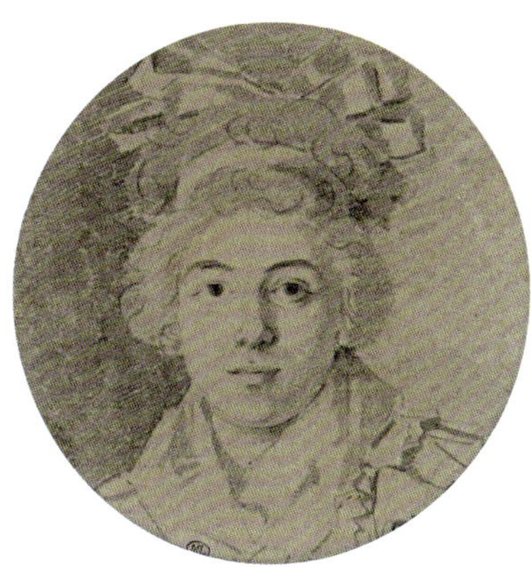

Jean Honoré Fragonard, *Portrait of Rosalie Fragonard*, ca. 1785. Black chalk, 5 × 5 in. (12.7 × 12.6 cm). Musée du Louvre, Paris (RF 41195)

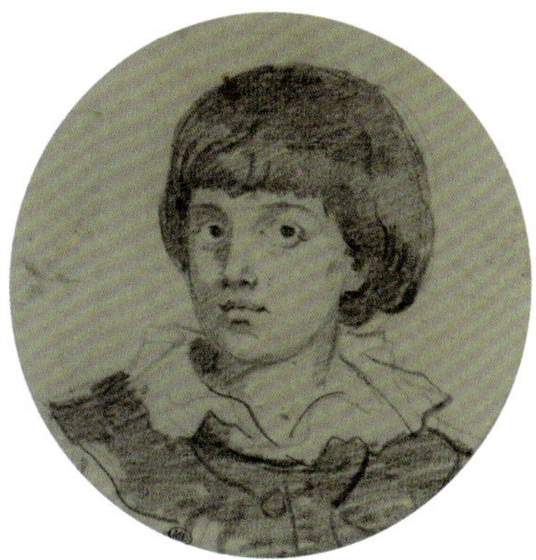

Jean Honoré Fragonard, *Portrait of Alexandre Evariste Fragonard*, ca. 1785. Black chalk, 5 × 5 in. (12.8 × 12.6 cm). Musée du Louvre, Paris (RF 41196)

by Pahin de la Blancherie (1752–1811). Madame Fragonard and Gérard occasionally exhibit works there as well.

1780

On October 26, Fragonard's son, Alexandre Evariste (1780–1850), is born in Grasse. He goes on to become a painter.

1788

On October 8, Fragonard's daughter, Rosalie, dies at the Bergeret family's château de Cassan near l'Isle Adam, outside Paris.

On December 23, Fragonard is censured by the Académie for his failure to produce a *morceau de réception*. His apparent lack of interest in full membership is attributed to his "capriciousness" and "irresponsibility."

1789

On July 7, Fragonard signs a certificate of authenticity attesting to the fact that two drawings, *The Lock* and *The Armoire*, bought at the Varanchan de Saint-Geniés sale (December 29–31, 1777), were indeed by his hand.

Following the storming of the Bastille on July 14, the National Assembly publishes the Declaration of the Rights of Man and of the Citizen on August 26.

On September 7, a group of daughters and wives of artists, including painters Marie Anne Fragonard and Marguerite Gérard, interrupts a meeting of the National Assembly to offer their jewelry as a patriotic gift to the nation.

1790

On January 12, Fragonard and his family travel to Grasse. They stay for at least fourteen months in the villa of Fragonard's cousin Alexandre Maubert, where Fragonard installs and expands the Progress of Love cycle.

1792

Fragonard returns to Paris by August. In September, Alexandre Evariste enters the studio of Neoclassical painter Jacques Louis David (1748–1825).

1793

Louis XVI is beheaded on January 21. Marie Antoinette follows him to the guillotine on October 16.

In August, the Académie Royale de Peinture et de Sculpture is dissolved by the National Convention.

In November, Fragonard becomes a member of the Commune des Arts, a Revolutionary body founded by David in opposition to the Académie Royale in 1790. Fragonard goes on to perform several administrative roles for the state, including curator at the newly founded Muséum Central des Arts (the future Musée du Louvre), a position he holds until 1800.

1799

Napoléon Bonaparte stages a coup d'état, overthrowing the Directoire and forming the Consulate.

1804

Napoléon is declared emperor of France on May 18.

1805

Napoléon evicts the artists remaining in their lodgings at the Louvre. Fragonard receives a yearly pension of 1,000 francs in compensation.

1806

On August 22, following a brief illness, Fragonard dies in his apartment at the Palais-Royal in Paris.

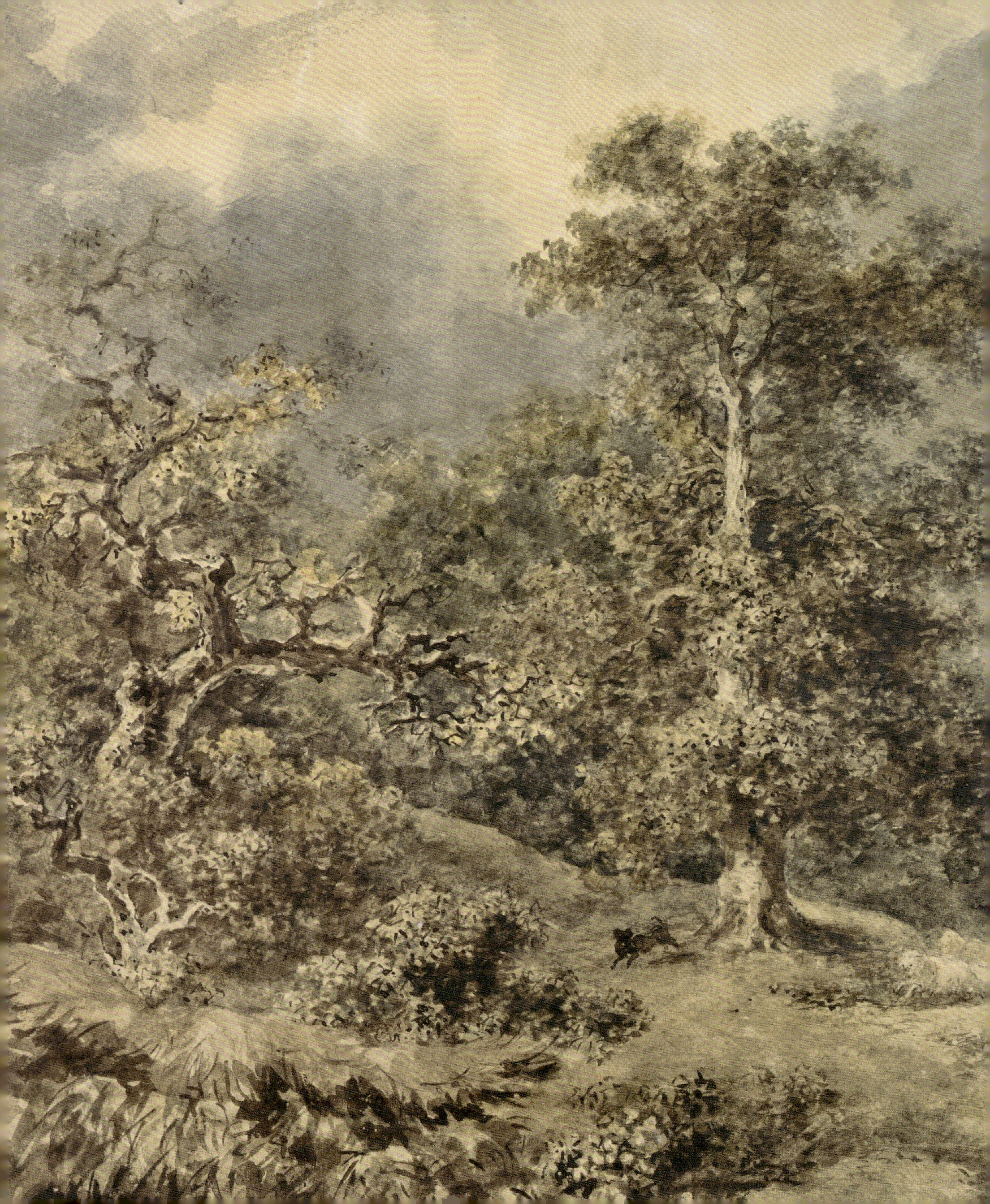

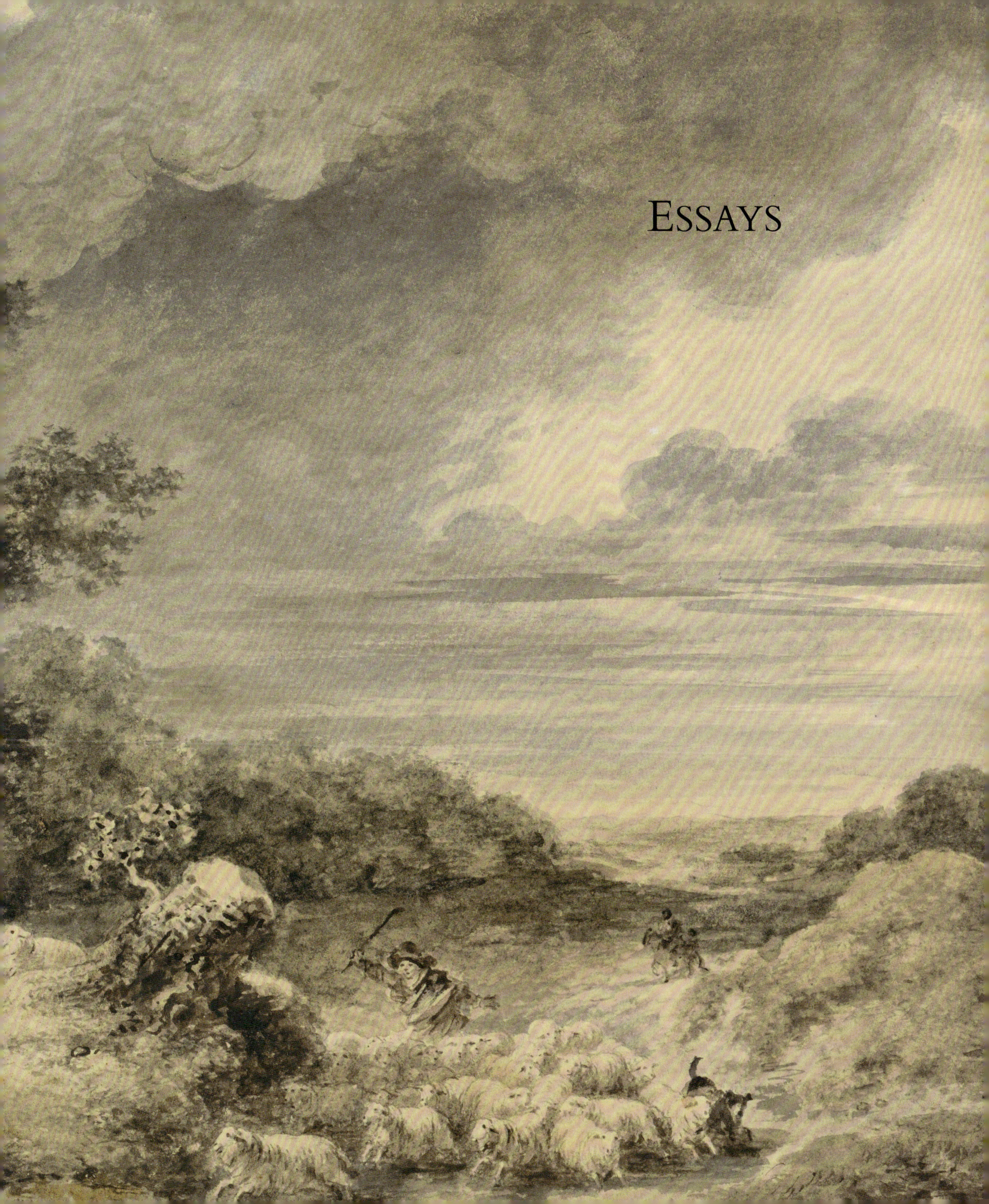

Essays

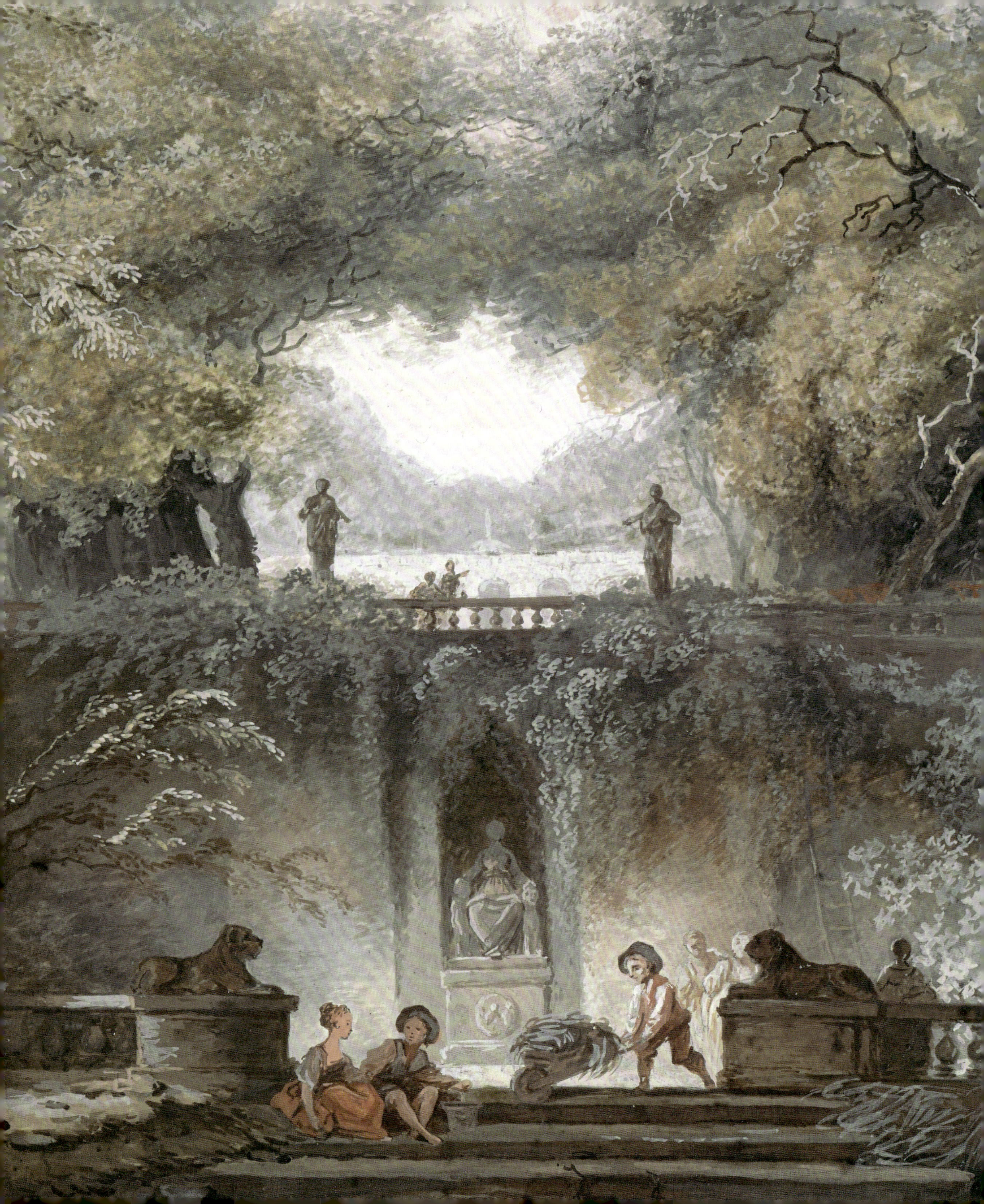

Fact, Fiction, Function, and Process
Toward a Modern View of Fragonard's Drawings

Perrin Stein

The modern view of Fragonard has only slowly taken shape, gradually emerging from an earlier literature dominated by the "Fragonard myth,"[1] a largely specious view of a painter born under the warm Provençal sun, at once indolent and imaginatively gifted. The building blocks of this myth date to both the artist's lifetime, when many early notices were penned by figures closely tied to the official academic path he chose to abandon, and to the years following his death in 1806, when he was regarded as complicit with the excesses of the then-disdained Rococo style and its aristocratic patrons.[2] The collectors and writers responsible for rehabilitating his artistic reputation in the second half of the nineteenth century did not reject this persona but instead embraced it, spinning out vivid evocations of a perfume-scented youth and a career spent producing lush and licentious scenes for a privileged clientele, continuing to confuse Fragonard's dreamlike pictures for his personal reality. It is not the intention of this essay to enumerate and counter the fallacies of this myth, which, in the past thirty years have been gradually put aside by modern scholars,[3] but rather to consider how the study and appreciation of Fragonard's drawings have evolved against the backdrop of an earlier tradition in which fiction had often proved more alluring than fact.

The discourse around Fragonard's drawings is as old as the work itself. Unlike Antoine Watteau, who kept his drawings close at hand for future use, Fragonard, whether for profit, fame, or friendship, chose to release his into circulation, where they elicited comment and acclaim from his early career onward.[4] During the years Fragonard was in Rome as an official pensionnaire of the French crown, his drawings were included in the shipments of student work sent back to Paris and were thus the subject of correspondence between Charles Joseph Natoire, the director of the Académie de France in Rome, and the marquis de Marigny, the director of the Bâtiments du Roi, who was in charge of the royal arts administration.[5] Natoire singled out for special praise the "very fine studies" Fragonard made of the gardens at Tivoli, where he spent the summer of 1760 in the company of his patron the abbé de Saint-Non, predicting that the sheets would not only be useful but also bring him much honor.[6] Indeed, upon the pair's return to France, Pierre Jean Mariette, the

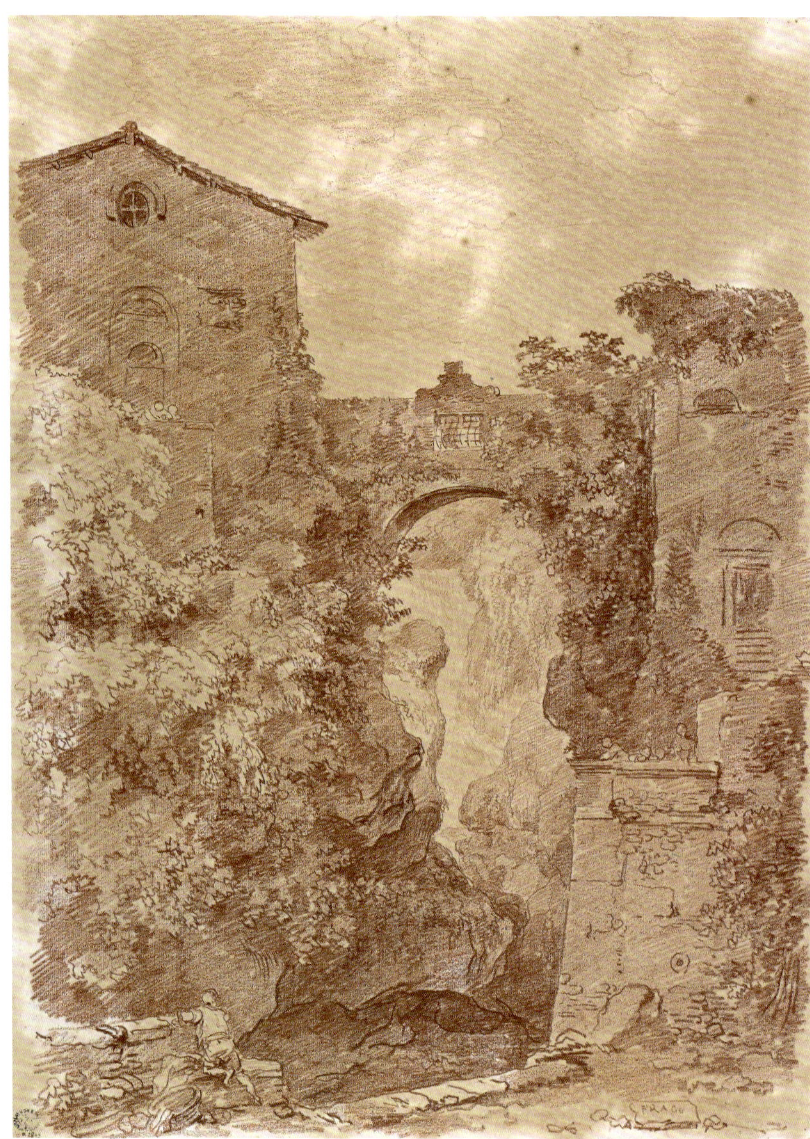

Fig. 1. Jean Honoré Fragonard, *The Grand Cascade at Tivoli*, 1760. Red chalk, 19¼ × 14¼ in. (48.8 × 36.1 cm). Musée des Beaux-Arts et d'Archéologie, Besançon (D.2843)

period's most admired collector and connoisseur of drawings, acquired by either purchase or gift a group of the sanguine landscapes, praising them as "done with much spirit and in which a great intelligence prevails."[7]

Fragonard's own assertion of the place of drawings within his oeuvre is evident in the fact that his submissions to the Salons of 1765 and 1767—the only two in which he participated—included both paintings and drawings (for example, fig. 1),[8] a practice that was far from typical at the time.[9] His decision not to exhibit in the following Salon set off a critical backlash. Louis Petit de Bachaumont attacked him in 1769 for "working for money" rather than for "posterity" and for treating subjects fit for the boudoir. In his critique of the Salon of 1781, Louis Carmontelle, a promoter of moralizing history paintings, declared that the public had rejected Fragonard's "indecent jokes."[10] These judgments were far from universal, however, and Fragonard's drawings continued to fetch high prices at auction in the years leading up to, and even in the decade following, the Revolution. Beginning in the second half of the 1770s his drawings appeared with frequency in sale catalogues, where they were commonly labeled as "superb," "excellent," and "beautiful," their technique most often described as "spirited" and "vigorous." As Anne Schroder has documented, if the market passed judgment on Fragonard, it was favorable; the sale of his work, and of the prints reproducing his compositions, allowed him to prosper and to leave a large estate to his family at his death.[11]

The notices published directly after Fragonard's death are laudatory, reflecting admiration for a man who contributed much, adapted to changing times, and trained two successful artists: his sister-in-law, Marguerite Gérard, and his son, Alexandre Evariste. Just two months after his death, Charles Louis François Lecarpentier, a professor of painting and drawing in Rouen, read a eulogy at the Société Libre des Sciences, Lettres, et Arts de Paris, an artistic society adjacent to the Louvre, in which he praised the variety and admirable effect of Fragonard's drawings, comparing his sketches to beautiful dreams. (For Lecarpentier's etched portrait of the artist, see fig. 2.) Charles Paul Landon, in a posthumous tribute published in his *Salon de 1808*, also addressed the appeal of Fragonard's works on paper, stating, "His drawings, which are numerous, were no less sought after than his paintings, and were dearly priced."[12] A different perspective on his life and work, containing the true roots of the Fragonard myth, can be found in Michaud's *Biographie universelle*, dating just ten years after the artist's death. Alexandre Lenoir's entry on Fragonard accused him of having been "seduced by the vicious influence of the school in which he studied," his work embodying "the frivolous taste of his century." To drive home this negative verdict of Fragonard as a victim of changing tastes and political circumstances, Lenoir made the claim, only recently proven erroneous, that in his late years the artist lost his fortune and "died unhappy."[13]

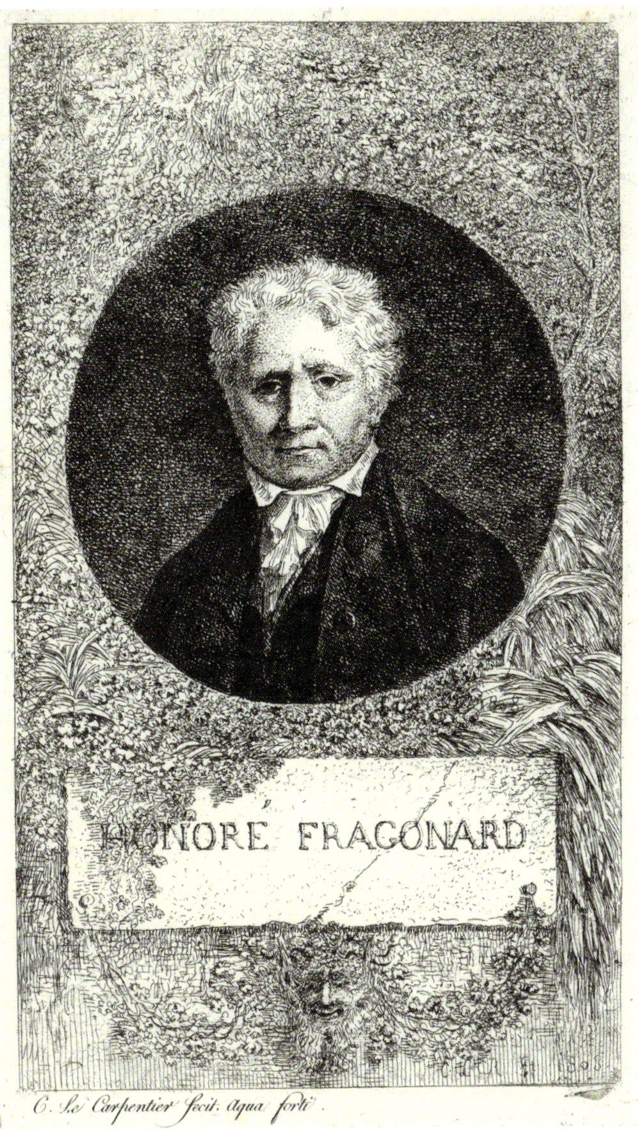

Fig. 2. Charles Louis François Lecarpentier (French, 1744–1808), after Marguerite Gérard (French, 1761–1837), *Portrait of Jean Honoré Fragonard*, 1808. Etching, sheet: 9¼ × 6⅛ in. (23.3 × 15.4 cm); plate: 7 × 4¼ in. (17.6 × 10.6 cm); image: 6½ × 3¾ in. (16.3 × 9.5 cm). The Metropolitan Museum of Art, New York, Gift of Madeleine Fidell-Beaufort, in memory of Samuel P. Avery, 2015 (2015.493.1)

The eclipse of Fragonard's reputation lasted only about fifty years. By the second half of the nineteenth century, his work was being rediscovered and eagerly sought by a number of collectors, including the brothers Edmond and Jules de Goncourt, as well as Hippolyte Walferdin, who alone amassed more than seven hundred sheets. Angered by the legacy of Lenoir's harsh and error-ridden biography, Théophile Fragonard, the artist's grandson, sent notes based on his family's recollections to a number of writers who incorporated them into publications dedicated to Fragonard's life and career. The abundant works, especially those on paper, collected by Walferdin and others provided an invaluable resource for Charles Blanc and other nineteenth-century biographers who sought to restore Rococo artists to the canon of French art.[14] Blanc saw in the burgeoning market appeal of Fragonard's work a better metric for judging his artistic merit than his failure to rise in the hierarchy of institutions of royal privilege.

For the Goncourt brothers, who published *L'art du dix-huitième siècle* in 1882, Fragonard's work provided rhapsodic transport to an earlier gilded era that they preferred to their own age of growing industrialization and social transformation. Their appreciation is framed through the lens of collecting (see, for example, fig. 3 and cats. 39, 56, and 66),[15] and one senses in their impressionistic readings of his art the intimate experience of contemplating works in the original. Their descriptions, which read as verbal counterparts to Fragonard's ribbons of flowing impasto and vaporous glazes, accord historical fact only the most minor role. The Goncourts had a special reverence for Fragonard's drawings, calling them "the diary of his imagination."[16] "Follow him," they suggest, "in the first flutter of an idea, when he flings upon the paper the elements of a composition, when he is searching and groping amid the mist which precedes the light."[17] Their discussion of his graphic output was organized by medium. In their redolent prose, Fragonard's compositions in brown wash became "exhalations" that "aroused the jealousy of daylight,"[18] while his sanguines were evoked as tactile performances featuring "wheelings and twistings" of chalk, carried out with a "feverish, desperate skill."[19]

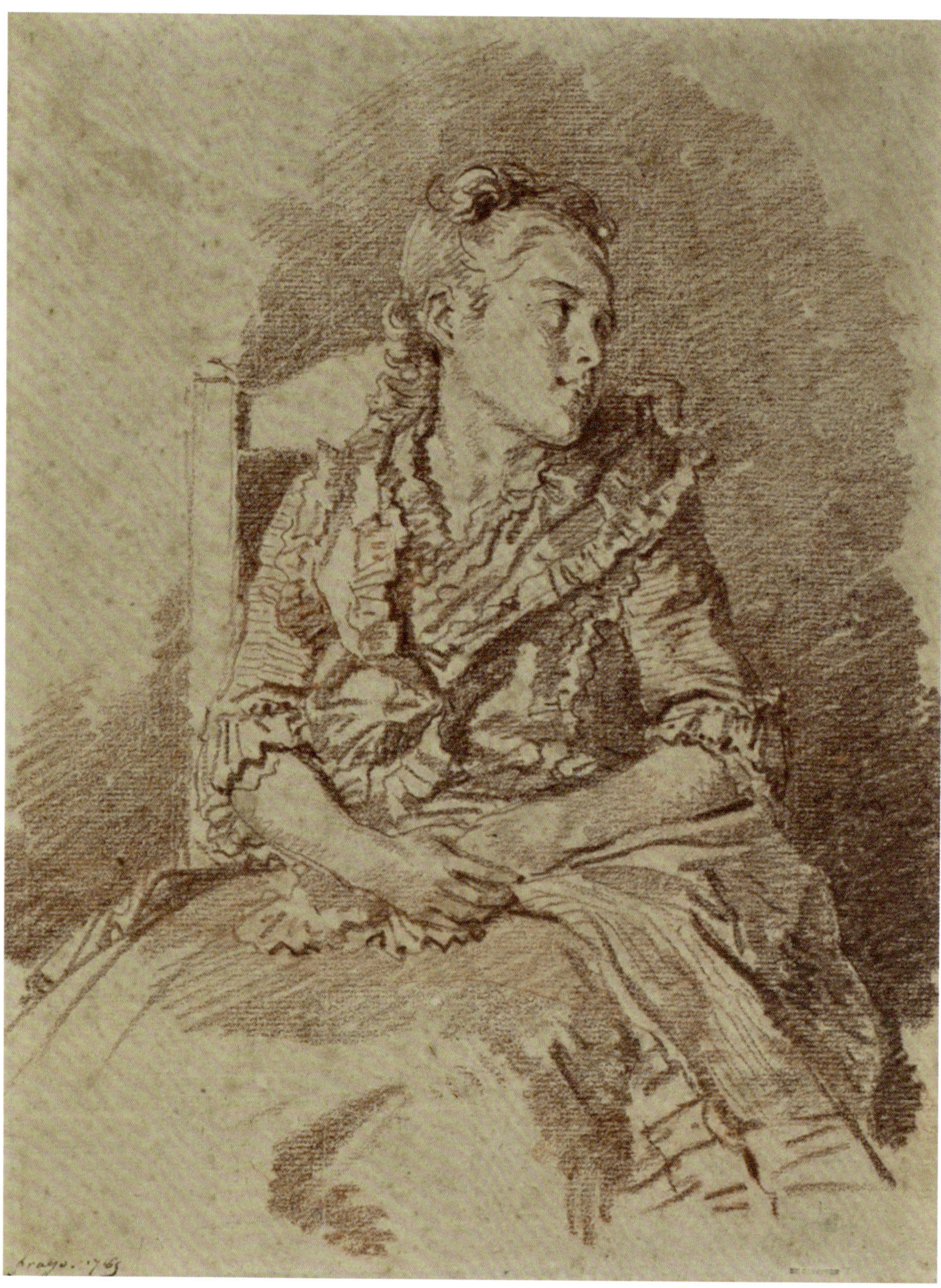

Fig. 3. Jean Honoré Fragonard, *Young Woman Seated*, 1785. Red chalk, 8⅞ × 6⅞ in. (22.3 × 17.2 cm). The Courtauld Institute of Art, London, Seilern, Antoine (Count); bequest; 1978 (D.1978.PG.229)

In 1889 Roger Portalis published the first real monograph on Fragonard, treating the artist's life and work in two volumes. He shed the poetic and nostalgia-infused language of the Goncourts and drew on a significantly larger base of primary source material, notably the *Correspondance* of the Académie Royale and the journal of Fragonard's patron Pierre Jacques Onésyme Bergeret de Grancourt, to assemble a more reliable and detailed picture of Fragonard's life, especially concerning his two trips to Italy. To be clear, Portalis marshaled these facts to supplement—rather than to challenge—the basic narrative framework constructed by the Goncourts, accepting a priori concepts such as Fragonard's sunny disposition, as determined by his birth in sun-drenched Provence. Declaring, "In drawing, there is the triumph of Fragonard,"[20] Portalis makes clear that he shared the Goncourts' veneration for Fragonard the draftsman, and accordingly his book features the first attempted catalogue of the artist's drawings.[21] However, by choosing to list the drawings in alphabetical order by title, the author tidily circumvented the difficulties posed by dating and stylistic development, problems that continue to challenge scholars to this day.

A small, unassuming booklet recorded the first exhibition to be devoted solely to Fragonard's drawings, which was on view for only three weeks in May 1931 at the premises of the dealer Jacques Seligmann & Fils at the Hôtel de Sagan, on the rue Saint-Dominique in Paris. The show boasted an illustrious roster of scholars as its organizing committee and featured loans from a long list of museums and private collectors on both sides of the Atlantic.[22] Louis Réau, who catalogued the works in the exhibition and was simultaneously preparing an ambitious study of the artist, clearly had a special admiration for Fragonard's drawings, which he referred to as his most "characteristic" work. "Fragonard," he wrote, "belongs to that category of artists who triumph in their first try, in sketches and in drawings."[23] The entries on individual sheets are richly documented, but, with the rare exception of those inscribed with a date or specifically linked with an Italian trip, Réau does not propose dates for the drawings, preferring to organize the catalogue by subject matter, beginning with religious scenes and ending with copies after earlier masters.

Although it would be decades before scholars began to address the problems of dating and stylistic development in Fragonard's graphic oeuvre, François Fosca's slim volume, *Les dessins de Fragonard*, which appeared in 1954, ventured into the previously unexplored territories of method and function. Raising questions that we continue to grapple with today, Fosca posited: "At first glance, it appears that there are two types of drawings, those drawn from nature, after an external model, and those drawn from memory, from an internal model, but in fact the distinction [between observation and invention] is difficult to discern."[24] In addition to the source of the imagery, he queried the function of the sheets, asserting that some were finished works made for other people and others were made for the artist himself.[25] Fragonard's greatest talent, according to Fosca, was his ability to represent movement, a skill that conferred upon him the role of precursor to Eugène Delacroix.[26]

The first catalogue raisonné devoted to the subject of Fragonard's drawings was the work of an unlikely figure, Alexandre Ananoff, a Russian-born astronautics enthusiast who eventually shifted his interests to the art of eighteenth-century France. Appearing in four volumes between 1961 and 1970, Ananoff's work is both essential and, at the same time, deeply flawed, not only in terms of its structure and methodology but also because the author is alleged to have been involved with the production and marketing of forgeries. Thus, his densely documented cataloguing interweaves historical references with duplicitous concoction.[27] The first volume begins with an introduction—ironically, almost wholly dedicated to the issues of fakes and forgeries—which is followed by catalogue notices organized in chapters according to subject (for example, "shepherds and washerwomen" and "parks and landscapes"). Only one quarter of the works are illustrated, and "accepted," "rejected," and "never

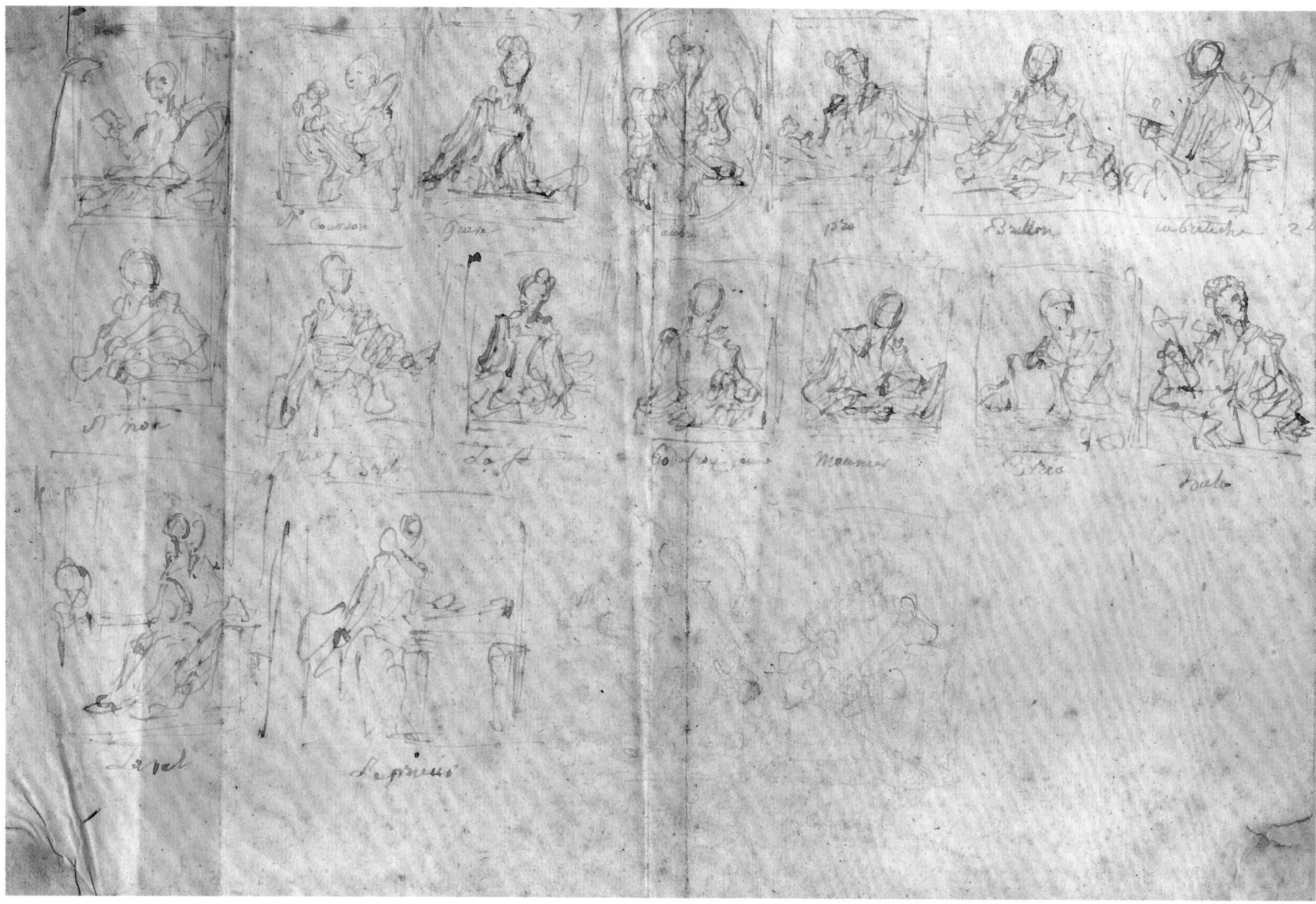

Fig. 5. Jean Honoré Fragonard, *Sketches of Portraits*, ca. 1769. Pen and brown ink over black chalk, 9¼ × 13⅞ in. (23.5 × 35 cm). Private collection, France

oeuvre. By quantifying the relatively small percentage of his works on paper that can be fairly considered preparatory for paintings, she provides a fresh appraisal of the function of drawing in Fragonard's oeuvre and creative process. As her essay in the present volume further demonstrates, drawing is at the center of Fragonard's artistic enterprise.

The story of Fragonard the printmaker, even more than that of Fragonard the draftsman, has been muddied by biographical innuendo and incorrect attributions, although this was not yet the case in the earliest sources. In Lecarpentier's eulogy, for instance, the artist's skill with the etching needle was singled out for praise: "Fragonard has ceased to live; but his paintings and his drawings dear to collectors will forever recall his rare talents. The charming etchings that he made in an exquisite taste will be placed alongside those of Benedetto [Castiglione], of Salvator [Rosa], and of the best artists in this genre."[46] The Goncourt brothers saw in Fragonard's etchings the signs of a disciple of Tiepolo. They couched their admiration in an analogy to drawing, describing them as "rapidly executed and resembling the sort of rough sketch that might serve to fix a memory or an impression on the page of a drawing book."[47] They must have had before them an impression of *The Little Park* (cat. 32) when they evoked

> a plate the size of a visiting card, [where] he would make a rapid record of the garden of some abandoned villa, a canopy of trees densely shadowed and pierced by a single shaft of daylight, or a terrace where slumbered the forgotten statue of a god caressed by overhanging foliage; and beneath the confusion of lines, the *grignotis*, as it would have been called at the time, the little landscape sparkles with light and life, with its cascades of branches and disordered mass of grass, its steps and balustrade guarded by two recumbent sphinxes.[48]

Problems arose, however, in the consideration of Fragonard's final phase of printmaking, which culminated in the ambitious *Armoire* (cat. 84). Because works of this period were closely connected to his training of his teenage sister-in-law, Marguerite Gérard, they bore the unsavory stain of speculation around the nature of their relationship. Baron Portalis wondered if Fragonard, in the "close proximity of the studio," might not have developed feelings that went beyond friendship for this beautiful young woman.[49] For the Goncourts, the closeness of their relationship cast doubt on the purported attributions of the prints made in 1778: "Now, the etchings by Miss Gérard—are they really by her? Are they not almost all completely by Fragonard?"[50] Even as the titillating specter of scandal gradually lost adherents in the second half of the twentieth century,[51] unease over the authorship of these prints persisted.

The first, and to this day only, comprehensive catalogue of Fragonard's prints was published by Georges Wildenstein in 1956,[52] building on information assembled one hundred years earlier by Prosper de Baudicour for his reference work on French *peintres-graveurs*—that is, painters who also made etchings.[53] Reflecting a thorough assimilation of the nineteenth-century skepticism of Gérard's abilities, Wildenstein absorbed her entire graphic oeuvre into a section of his catalogue titled "etchings executed in collaboration," which he qualified in his text, stating: "The hand of the professor dominates for the most part the delicate work of his young student."[54] Moreover, in the two cases where Fragonard and Gérard made etchings based on the same drawing, he confused the hands, in both cases illustrating Gérard's prints as works by Fragonard.[55]

Pierre Rosenberg's decision to not only include prints in the 1987–88 retrospective but also integrate them chronologically within the sequence of entries was a boon to the consideration of etchings as an integral part of Fragonard's oeuvre. We now believe that three of the prints included in that show were, in fact, the work of Marguerite Gérard,[56] but this does not diminish the endorsement of Fragonard's contributions to this sometimes neglected medium. Fragonard's oeuvre as a printmaker was further defined in 2012 when the fallacy of prints made in "collaboration" was challenged in an article by the present author and Rena Hoisington, in which we defined the artists' two distinct styles and attributed each of the nine 1778 prints to either one hand or the other.[57] In a 2013 publication, Fragonard's earlier engagement with etching (ca. 1763–64) was situated in terms of his relationship with the culture of *amateurs*, collectors who engaged in both the making of art and the practice of connoisseurship and who were closely tied to the vogue for collecting, and even imitating, the prints of the Italian *peintres-graveurs*. This valorization of their free and textured manner of etching would later be echoed in the aesthetic terms Lecarpentier

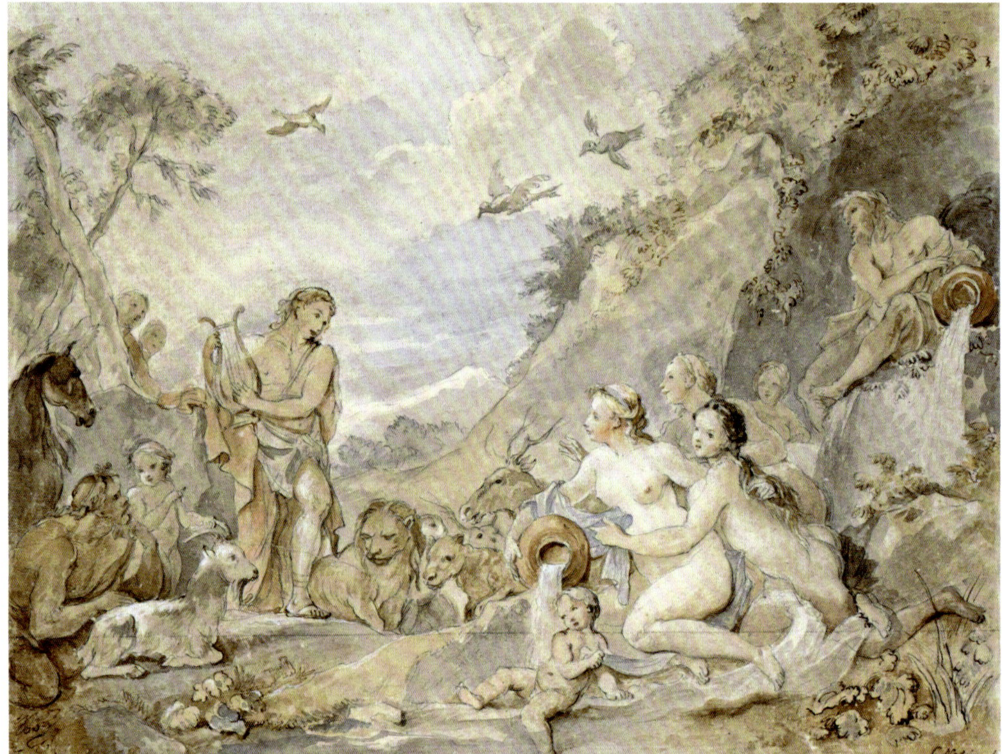

Fig. 6. Charles Joseph Natoire (1700–1777), *Orpheus Charming the Nymphs, Dryads, and Animals*, ca. 1757. Pen and brown ink, brown and gray wash, pale blue, yellow, and pink watercolor, and white heightening over preliminary drawing in pencil and black chalk, 16¾ × 32¼ in. (42.5 × 81.8 cm). The Metropolitan Museum of Art, New York, Robert Lehman Collection, 1975 (1975.1.676)

employed in his eulogy to frame Fragonard's contribution to printmaking.[58] In the present volume, we continue to make the case, implicit in the structure of the 1987–88 catalogue, for considering Fragonard's prints as an intrinsic part of his artistic method and achievement.

If modern scholars have finally put aside the "Fragonard myth," we still find ourselves in a terrain with few guideposts. In the analysis of his drawings more specifically, a clearer understanding of both their function and their role in Fragonard's creative process has often led to new questions. As we realize that the majority of the sheets were not made as preliminary works in the traditional sense—neither as studies for paintings nor as models for prints—their dating becomes less, not more, clear. More fruitful has been the attention paid to the social, artistic, and commercial milieus in which art was produced and displayed. Recent publications in the field of eighteenth-century art history have shown an increasing focus on major collectors of the period, often bringing close scrutiny to bear on specific commissions and relationships, while broader studies of the practices of collecting and display have made clear how Enlightenment culture buoyed the production of drawings, both as an activity and as a commodity.[59]

A greater awareness of the social and commercial venues for which Fragonard intended his drawings dovetails with a deepening knowledge of his self-referential working processes. The creative exploitation of a broad range of techniques—including copying, transfer, etching, and counterproofing—to create multiple versions of autonomous drawings aligns his methods with those of his teachers and contemporaries. Both François Boucher and Charles Joseph Natoire were lifelong copyists,

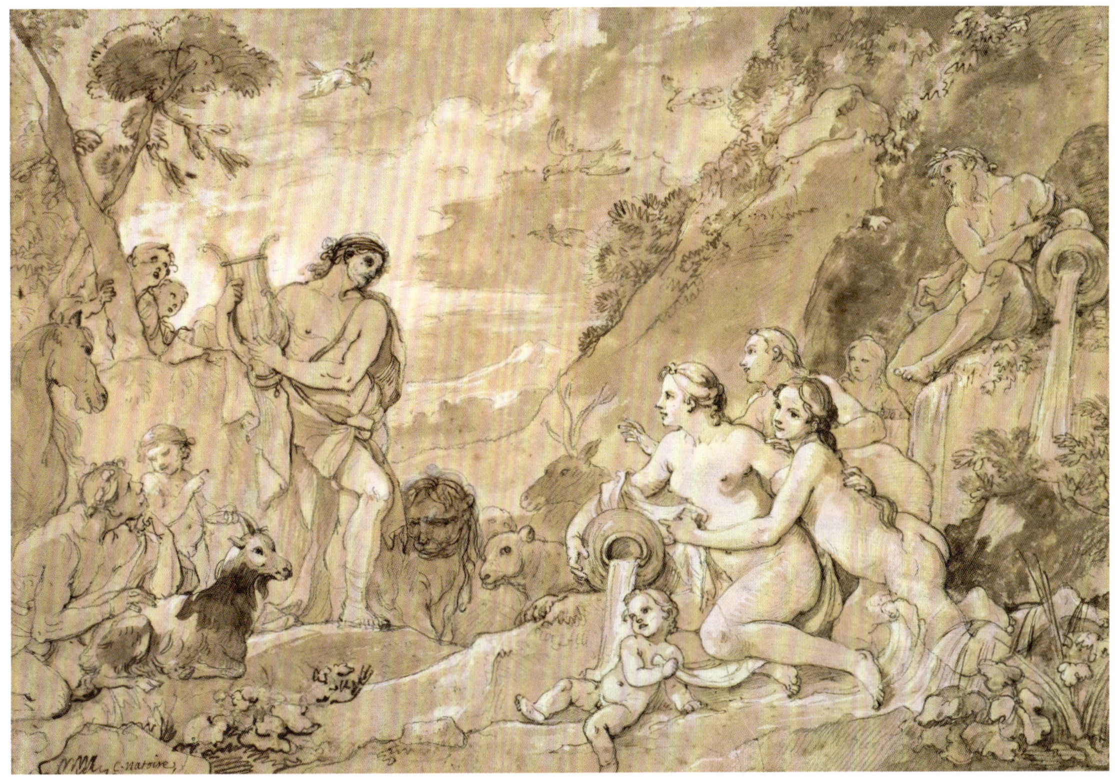

Fig. 7. Charles Joseph Natoire (French, 1700–1777), *Orpheus Charming the Nymphs, Dryads, and Animals*, ca. 1757. Pen and brown ink, brush and brown wash, heightened with gouache, over black chalk, 11⅞ × 17¼ in. (29.9 × 43.8 cm). The Horvitz Collection, Boston (D-F-208)

using the practice to merge their own styles with those of earlier masters whom they admired.[60] A ready precedent for Fragonard's predilection for multiples and iterations can be cited in the drawing practice of Natoire, who produced about 1757, shortly after the younger artist's arrival in Rome, no less than four drawn versions of *Orpheus Charming the Nymphs, Dryads, and Animals*, each exploring a different palette and mood (see, for example, figs. 6 and 7).[61] Strong parallels in the drawing methods of certain contemporaries have also emerged in recent studies, such as Jean-Pierre Cuzin's 2013 catalogue raisonné of François André Vincent[62] and Sarah Catala's research on Hubert Robert, who, like Fragonard, found inspiration in the production of versions and mirror images.[63]

New avenues of research are also enriching our conception of Fragonard's debts and influences. In 2015, Guillaume Faroult made the case for Pierre Antoine Baudouin, fellow pupil and son-in-law of Boucher, as Fragonard's mentor in libertine imagery. From 1765 until the elder artist's premature death four years later, Baudouin and Fragonard shared a studio in the Louvre and together copied the paintings of Peter Paul Rubens in the Palais du Luxembourg. Baudouin's salacious scenes, often small-scale works in gouache on paper, appear to have influenced, or at least validated, Fragonard in the years he first strayed from the path of the history painter.[64]

Progress can also be cited in the gradual reconstruction of Fragonard's late oeuvre, long a murky area for scholars, especially his production after the 1770s, when there are few dated works and he began to shift away from the brushy, improvisational style most associated with his genius.[65] A number of drawings datable to the 1780s have come to light in recent years; they typically represent domestic genre subjects and,

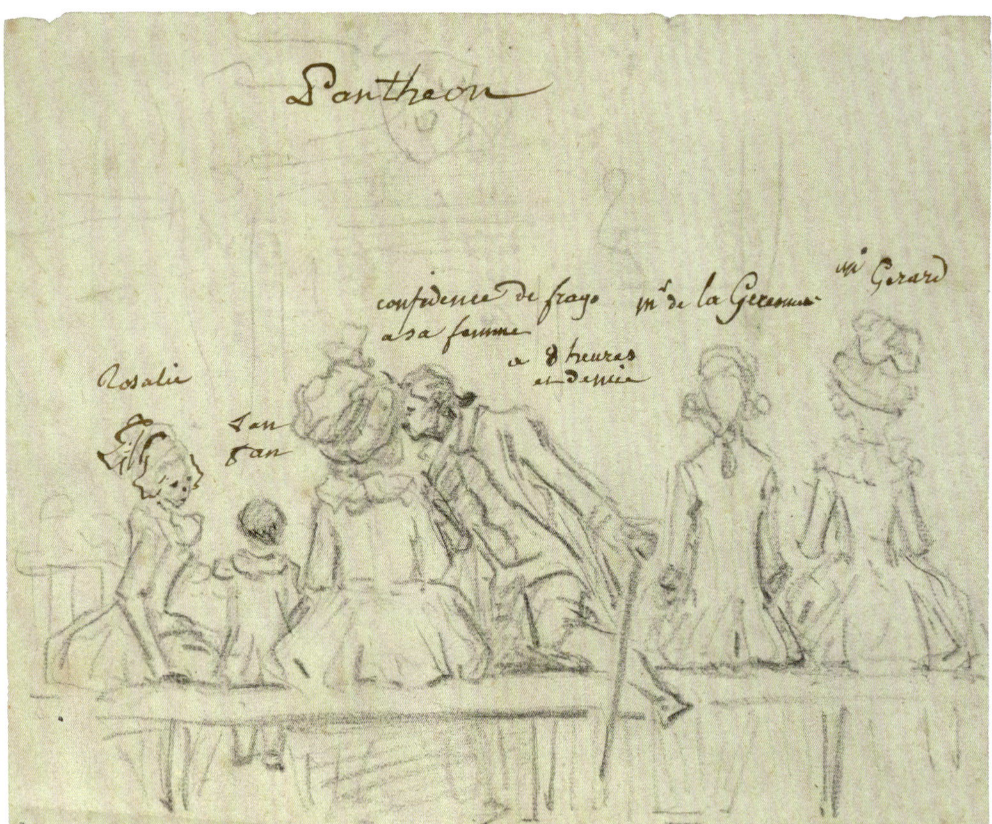

Fig. 8. Jean Honoré Fragonard, *Fragonard and His Family on a Bench*, ca. 1786. Black chalk with pen and brown ink, 7⅛ × 9⅛ in. (17.9 × 23.2 cm). Musée Jean-Honoré Fragonard, Grasse

in one case, a charming group of autobiographical caricatures (Musée Jean-Honoré Fragonard, Grasse).[66] These capture a happy moment in the family, shortly before the death of Fragonard's only daughter, Rosalie, at the age of eighteen. Pictured in the scene titled *Fragonard and His Family on a Bench* (fig. 8) are Rosalie on the far left, the artist's young son, Alexandre Evariste, labeled "fan fan," and, on the far right, his young sister-in-law, Marguerite Gérard.

Both Alexandre Evariste and Gérard went on to have successful careers as artists, their styles overlapping with Fragonard's late manner. Although he trained in the studio of Jacques Louis David and eventually specialized in troubadour subjects and costume design, Alexandre Evariste was indebted to the techniques and subjects of his father's late work, an affinity most visible in their shared interest in themes marked by early Romanticism.[67] Important insight into Fragonard's late career has also emerged from research on Marguerite Gérard conducted by Jean-Pierre Cuzin and Carole Blumenfeld, the latter of whom is preparing the catalogue raisonné. They have described an extended period of close collaboration between the two painters, during which they produced canvases featuring happy domestic scenes of mothers and young children, painted in a smoothly polished and descriptive technique.[68] One can also point to examples in which, as in their earlier etching collaboration, Fragonard provided designs in the form of drawings that Gérard used as models for paintings.[69]

The next hurdle in the field, and it is a daunting one, is the production of a modern catalogue raisonné of Fragonard's drawings, which Marie-Anne Dupuy-Vachey has valiantly embarked upon. The biggest challenge in producing such a work, and, indeed, in studying Fragonard generally, remains chronology. The task of assigning dates and imposing order is neither insignificant nor esoteric, but instead foundational to our understanding of the artist. Without the knowledge of when a work was made, as well as who owned it and who or what it depicts, interpretive constructions stand on unstable ground. Chronology is essential also to analyses of stylistic development and artistic influence. Comprehending the confluence of subject matter in the work of Fragonard and Baudouin, for instance, and determining the source of specific motifs and compositions require a firmer grasp of dating for Fragonard's production between his two Italian trips than has been established thus far. For example, our reading of works such as *Benevolent Women on Horseback Visiting a Village* (cat. 76), previously known under the more generic title *A Cavalcade*, gains rigor once the drawing is placed in chronological proximity to Jean-Baptiste Greuze's *Lady of Charity* (1775, Musée des Beaux-Arts, Lyon). Undated, works are untethered from their social context, and meaning ebbs away.

Fragonard's decision in the mid-1760s to stop exhibiting at the biannual Salons and to work primarily for private individuals has left us with a paucity of documentation relative to many of his contemporaries. As a result, progress toward the goal of better defining the authenticity, dating, and subjects of Fragonard's work has been slow, with the exception of an occasional discovery, such as the schematic labeled sketch of the *figures de fantaisie* portraits that recently emerged on the market (fig. 5).[70] Nonetheless, there remain many small areas that may yield a narrowing of uncertainty, if not precise dates. The evidence of reproductive prints, for instance, has been insufficiently examined, especially the chalk-manner etchings of Louis Marin Bonnet and Gilles Demarteau, which provide the *terminus ante quem* for a number of sanguine drawings (see cats. 54 and 69–71). Specialists in costume and the decorative arts may also shed more light on these questions. This is not to say that a good portion of Fragonard's oeuvre doesn't continue to resist specific dating and decoding of subject matter, as many of the entries in this volume make clear. One thing is for certain: while they each build on past scholarship, no one study of Fragonard's work can expect to be the last word.

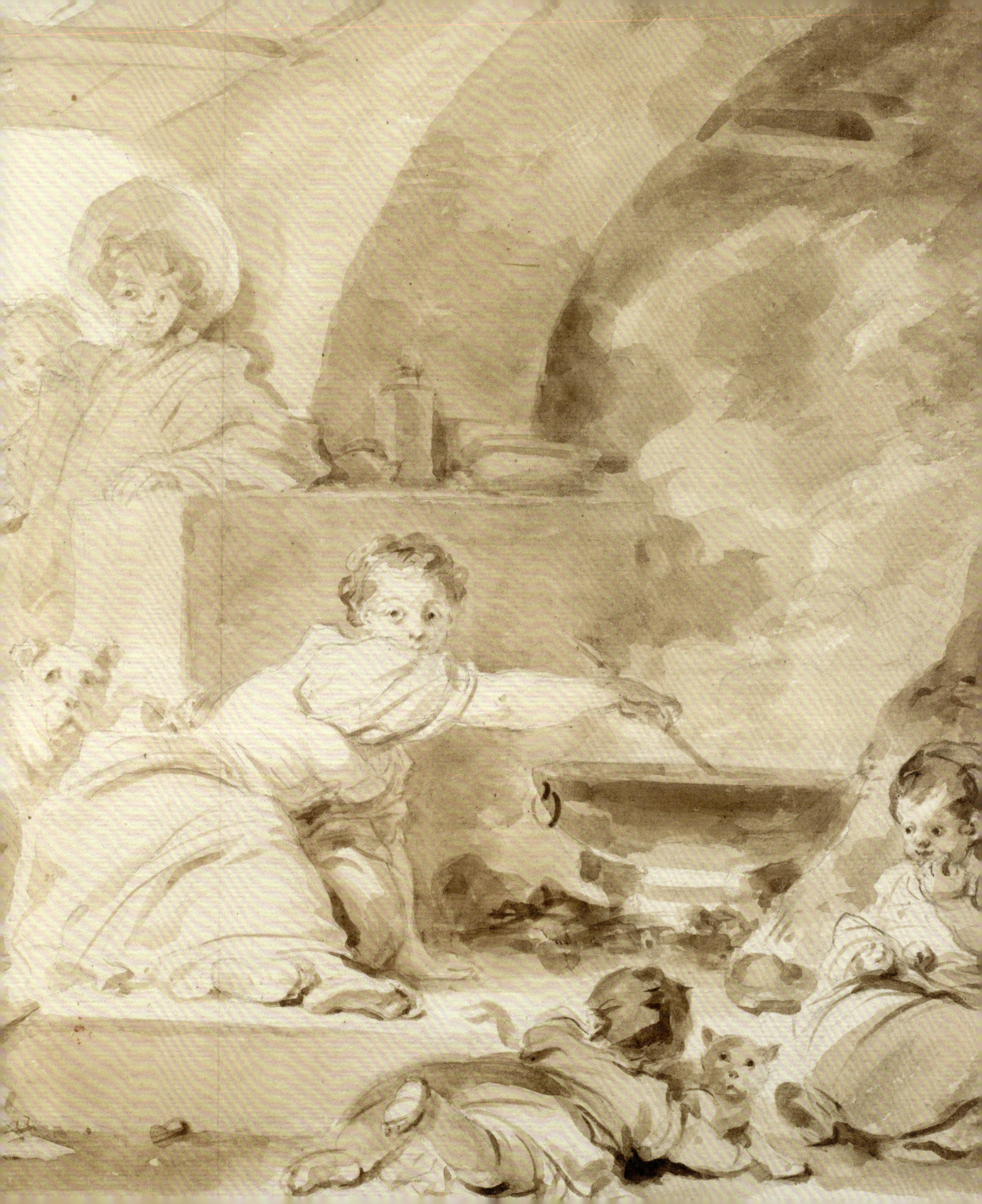

Every Possible Combination
Between Inspiration and Finish in Fragonard's Oeuvre

Marie-Anne Dupuy-Vachey

On September 7, 1753, at the end of the general meeting of the Académie Royale de Peinture et de Sculpture, medals were distributed for the prizes of the previous year. Fragonard led the pack, winning first place with his painting *Jeroboam Sacrificing to the Idols* (see p. xvi).[1] The meeting had begun with a reading of Claude Henri Watelet's "The Art of Painting."[2] It is not known if Fragonard appreciated this rather convoluted poem—Denis Diderot considered it worth throwing into the fire[3]—in which the author, following the tradition of Horace's *Ut pictura poesis*, strives to equate the arts of painting and poetry. But it is fitting to imagine the muse Erato presiding over the artist's debut. The verses from the first two cantos about "drawing" and "color" could be interpreted as an admonition to young artists like Fragonard: "The source of ennui is monotony: So change with respect to effect & harmony." Indeed, *ennui* and *monotony* are two words that Fragonard banished from his vocabulary. In tirelessly varying his style and constantly renewing his sources of inspiration over the course of his career, he would bequeath an oeuvre that is among the most original and seductive of his time.

When defining Fragonard's contribution, historiography has focused on this protean aspect but often only on the basis of his painted works. Beyond the few publications devoted solely to drawings, most monographs on the artist accord his graphic work only superficial attention, a secondary place. It was not so during his lifetime, when his drawings were as appreciated and sought after as his paintings.[4] "His good drawings cost their weight in gold and they are worth it," confirmed a connoisseur.[5] Indeed, one need only glance at the annotated auction catalogues of the day to observe this phenomenon. During the 1770s and 1780s, the prices at auction of certain sheets were comparable to those of paintings. Suggestive or risqué scenes were especially desirable. *The Armoire* (p. 240, fig. 125), showing the parents of a girl finding her lover's hiding place, even made 900 livres[6]—a substantial sum if we consider that *Le petit parc* (p. 134, fig. 84), a marvelous painting in the Wallace Collection, made only 520 livres in the same year.[7] But it was not only libertine subjects that whetted collectors' appetites. The watercolor *Visitation of the Virgin* was sold for the record amount of 1,200 livres in 1779.[8] By comparison, the price of 600 livres for the small-scale repetition of the painting *Coresus and Callirhoë*, a major composition, seems very modest.[9]

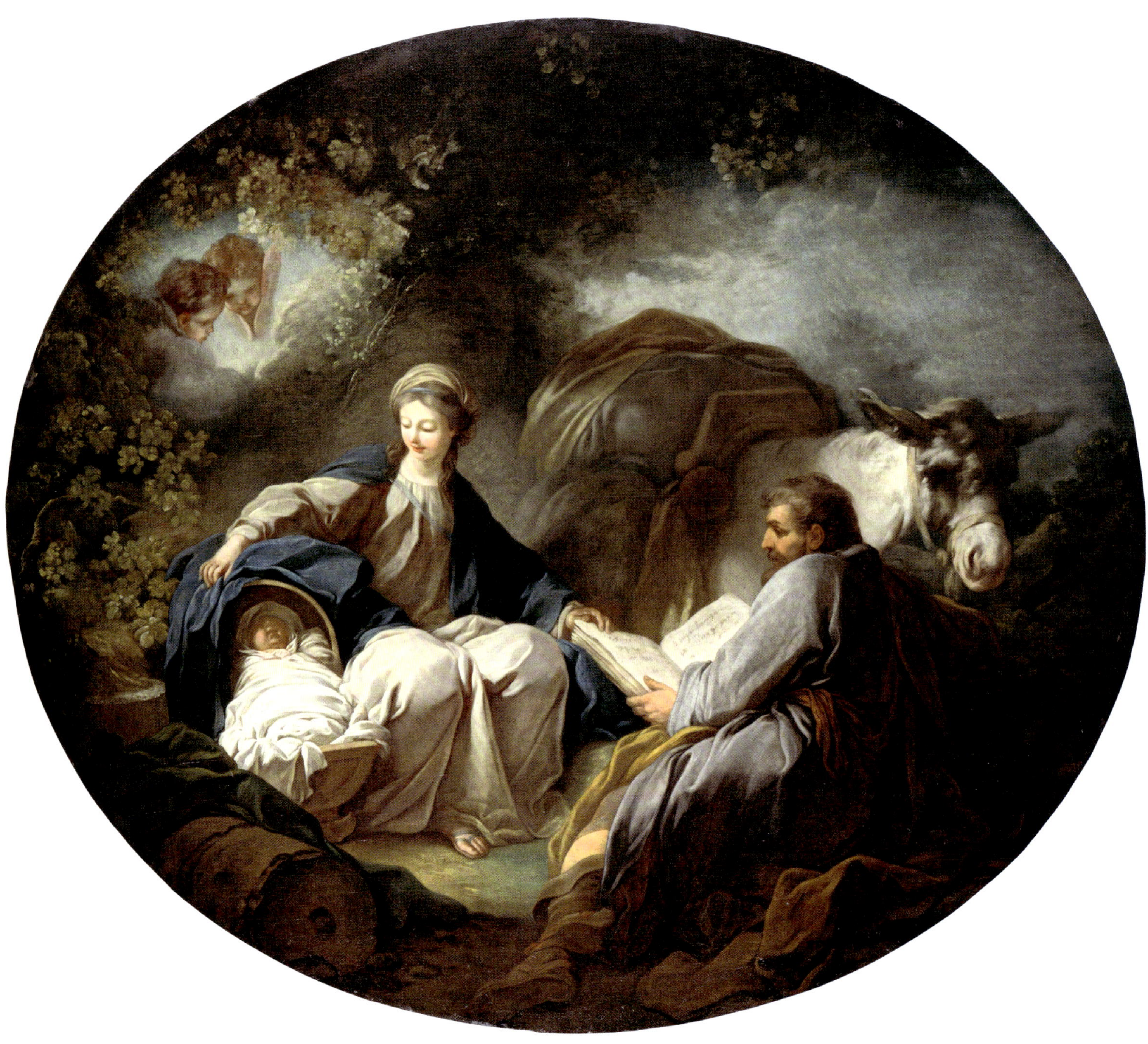

Fig. 10. Jean Honoré Fragonard, *The Rest on the Flight into Egypt*, ca. 1761–62(?). Oil on canvas, 74⅞ × 87 in. (190 × 221 cm). Private collection

baby Jesus has been shifted to the left, giving way to a tree trunk adorned with quickly scribbled branches. In the final painting, this dark mass melts into the background, and a donkey, bearing effects for the journey, appears on the right to provide more substance to the scene, now placed in an oval format.

The artist's quest for the ideal composition can also be seen in his habit of reversing the direction of a scene and the positions of figures. This occurs, for example, in *The Birth of Venus* (fig. 13),[37] for which the drawing in the Smith College Museum of Art is very likely a preparatory study (fig. 14).[38] In the drawing, the goddess's chariot is

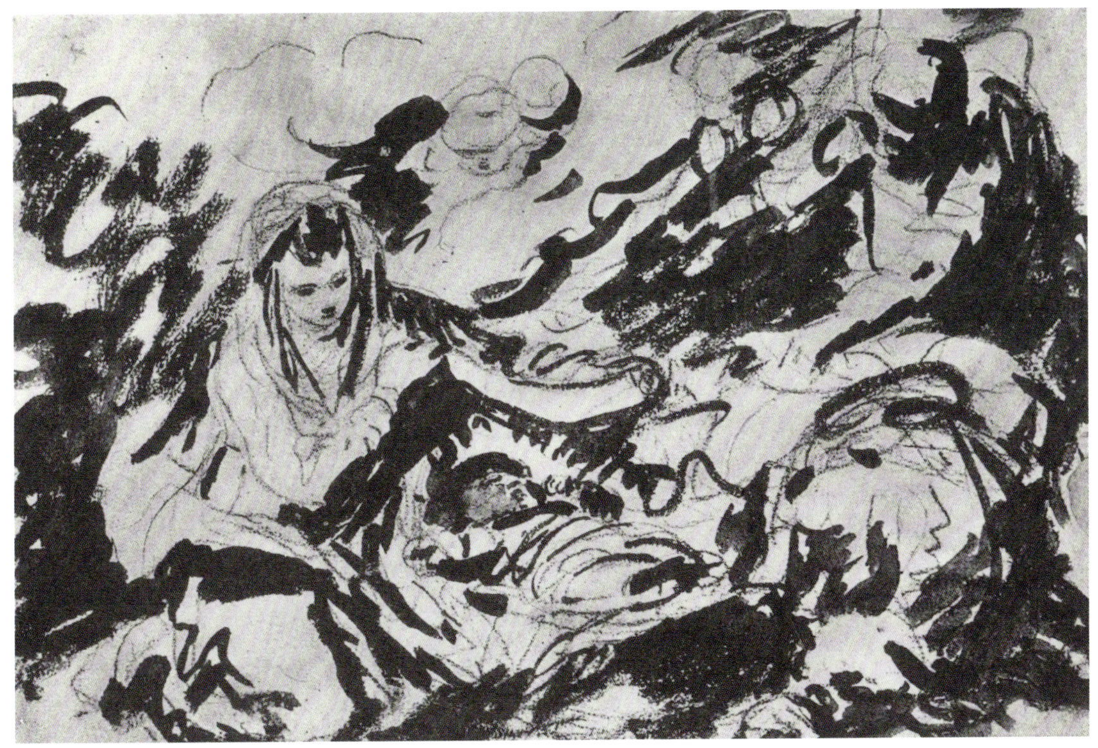

Fig. 11. Jean Honoré Fragonard, *The Rest on the Flight into Egypt*, ca. 1761–62(?). Red chalk, brown wash, 4⅝ × 6⅞ in. (11.5 × 17.3 cm). Location unknown

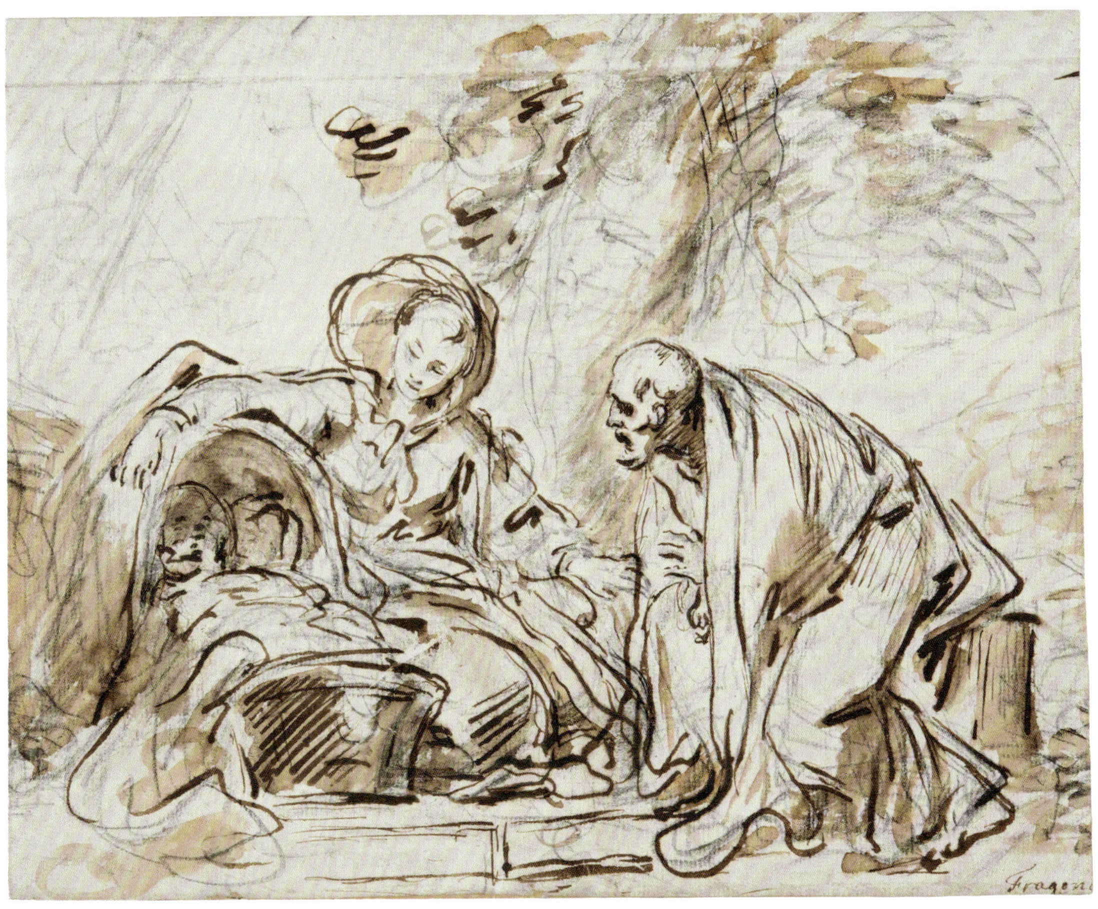

Fig. 12. Jean Honoré Fragonard, *The Rest on the Flight into Egypt*, ca. 1760–62(?). Black chalk, brown wash, pen and brown ink. 8½ × 10⅝ in. (21.5 × 27 cm). Nationalmuseum, Stockholm (NM 1/1930)

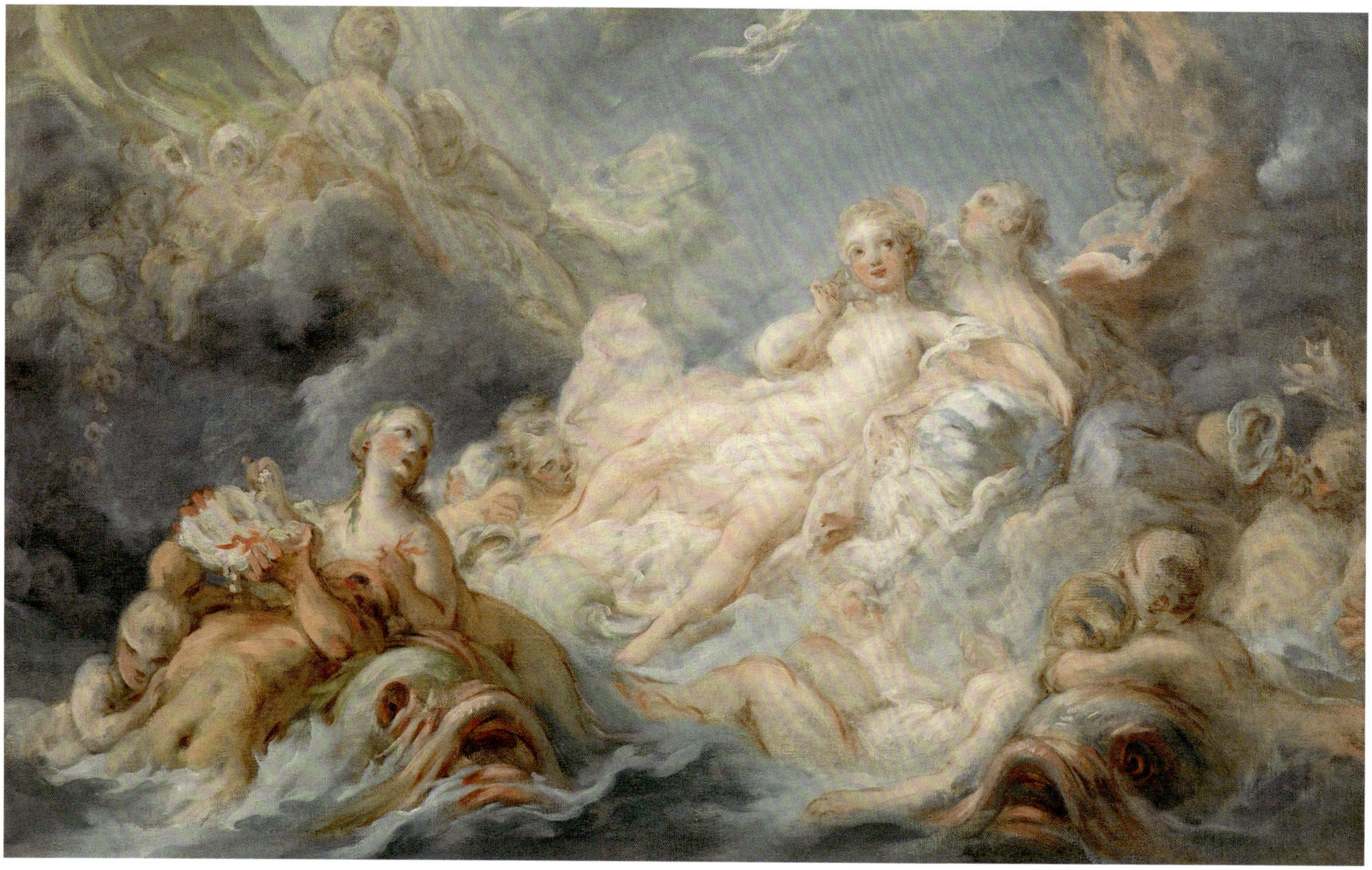

Fig. 13. Jean Honoré Fragonard, *The Birth of Venus*, ca. 1753–54. Oil on canvas, 21¼ × 32¾ in. (54 × 83 cm). Musée Grobet-Labadié, Marseille (GL 578)

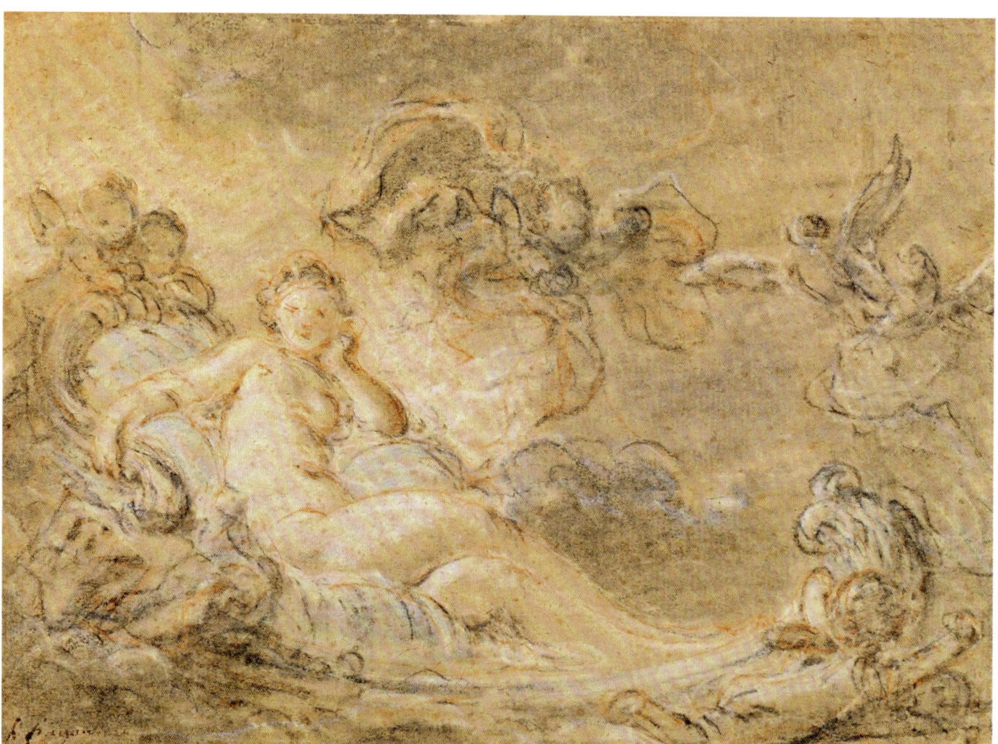

Fig. 14. Jean Honoré Fragonard, *The Birth of Venus*, ca. 1753–54. Black and red chalk with touches of blue and white chalk, 6½ × 9 in. (16.5 × 22.8 cm). Smith College Museum of Art, Northampton, Mass. (1992:29)

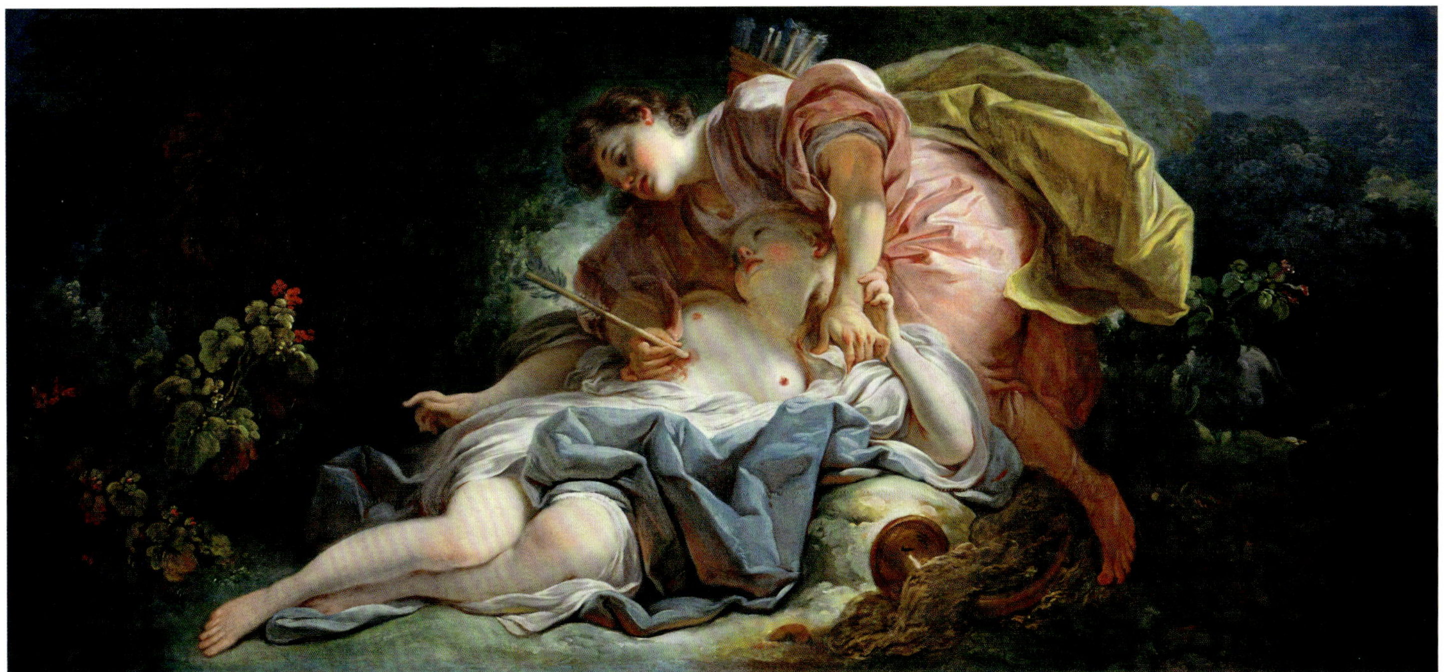

heading toward the right. White and blue highlights, added to the combination of black and red chalks, prefigure the colors of the later painting, in which tritons and naiads lead Venus, this time, toward the left. This method of reversal, perhaps developed from a set of counterproofs, certainly reflects the artist's preoccupation with the dynamic of the composition, to which the placement of the figures, light effects, and setting all contribute.

Dating to the same period—and corresponding to Fragonard's time in Boucher's studio—is *Cephalus and Procris* in the Musée des Beaux-Arts, Angers (fig. 15),[39] to which we can connect a small sketch (fig. 16). At first glance we see few affinities between the two works. They are quite different, not only in format but also in layout and style. The sharp pencil's stiff lines and contours, which are in some places quite angular, contrast with the smooth lines and rounded volumes of the painting. Nevertheless, it seems that Fragonard again developed his composition by experimenting with various combinations of techniques. This time he reversed the direction of only a part of the subject, not the whole composition. Procris, mortally wounded by Cephalus's arrow, underwent a few modifications, but the arrangement of her body, limply resting against a sort of knoll, remained the same in the painting. The left section of the drawing was transferred to the right side of the canvas, shedding two little putti who had been sharpening the hunter's arrows. In the painting, Cephalus still leans over his beloved, but he is positioned behind her in a more harmonious pose. His quiver is placed on his back, and his dog's head, seen on the extreme left of the drawing, appears in the painting on the opposite side, half hidden under foliage. A few very light touches of blue watercolor suggest the color that Procris's drapery will take on in the finished

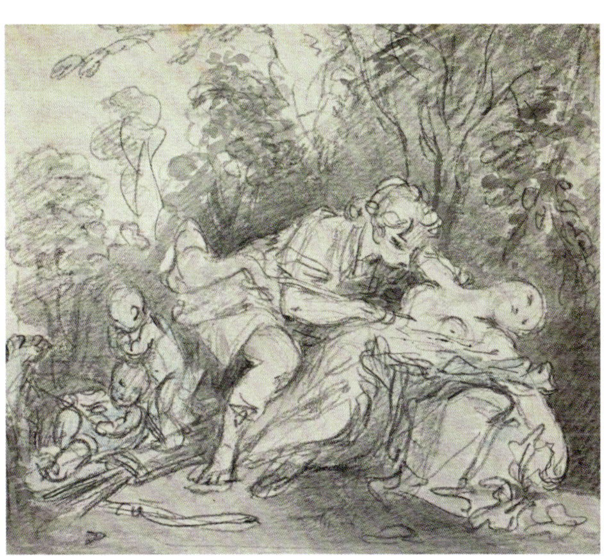

Fig. 15. Jean Honoré Fragonard, *Cephalus and Procris*, ca. 1755. Oil on canvas, 31⅛ × 68⅛ in. (79 × 173 cm). Musée des Beaux-Arts, Angers (MBA J 791 [J. 1887] P)

Fig. 16. Jean Honoré Fragonard, *Study for Cephalus and Procris*, ca. 1755. Black chalk, gray wash, watercolor highlights, 5⅝ × 6¾ in. (14.3 × 17 cm). Private collection

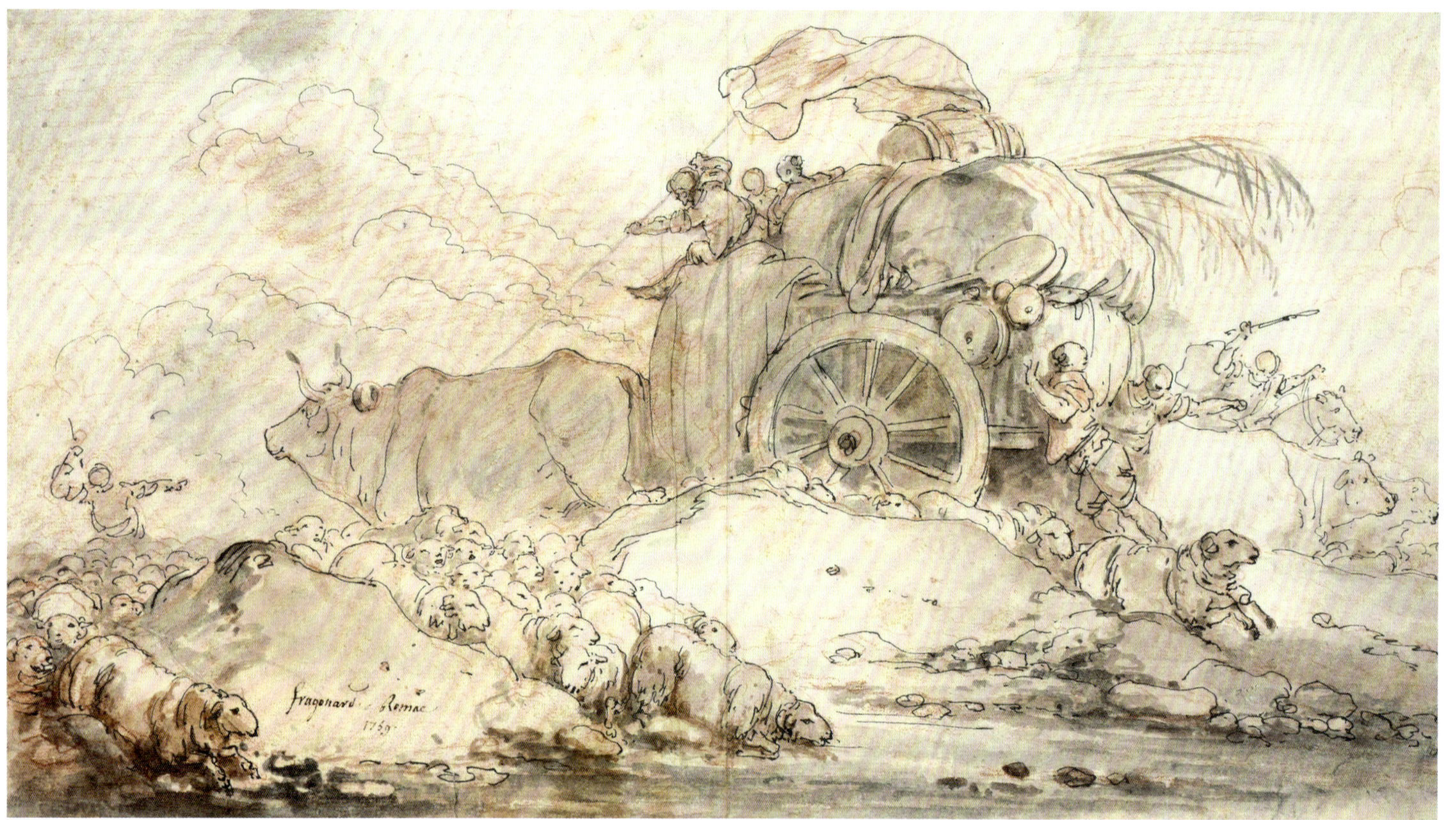

Fig. 17. Jean Honoré Fragonard, *The Stalled Cart*, also called *The Storm*, 1759. Red chalk, pen and brown ink, brown and gray wash, 8½ × 15⅝ in. (21.5 × 39.5 cm). Art Institute of Chicago (1936.4)

canvas. The drawing's format, almost square, supports its connection to the Angers painting. In fact, it must correspond to the original proportions of the canvas before it was cut down, as is proven by comparing it to the sketch for its pendant, *Jupiter and Callisto*.[40] Therefore, this drawing confirms what we had previously assumed: that at an unknown date the two canvases now in the Angers museum were cut down, mainly in the upper area, presumably to better fit into an architectural decor or boiserie. Another example of reversal, in a different genre but also dating from Fragonard's formative period, is *The Stalled Cart*, composed during his first stay in Rome. Studied initially in one direction in wash mixed with red chalk (fig. 17), this highly suggestive evocation of a threatening storm was translated into a painting in the opposite direction (fig. 18).[41] In my view, these few examples cannot be exceptions. They hint that Fragonard must have produced significantly more preliminary work, at least during his early years, than is suggested by the meager examples that survive today.

A VARIETY OF MEDIA

Although Fragonard ultimately reserved the use of red chalk on its own for autonomous drawings depicting landscapes (for example, cat. 65) and masterfully posed individual figures (for example, cats. 54, 59, 61, and 62), until the end of the 1760s he had also used it, mixed with other media, to sketch a few scenes that were later transferred to canvas, such as *The Birth of Venus* and *The Stalled Cart*. One finds

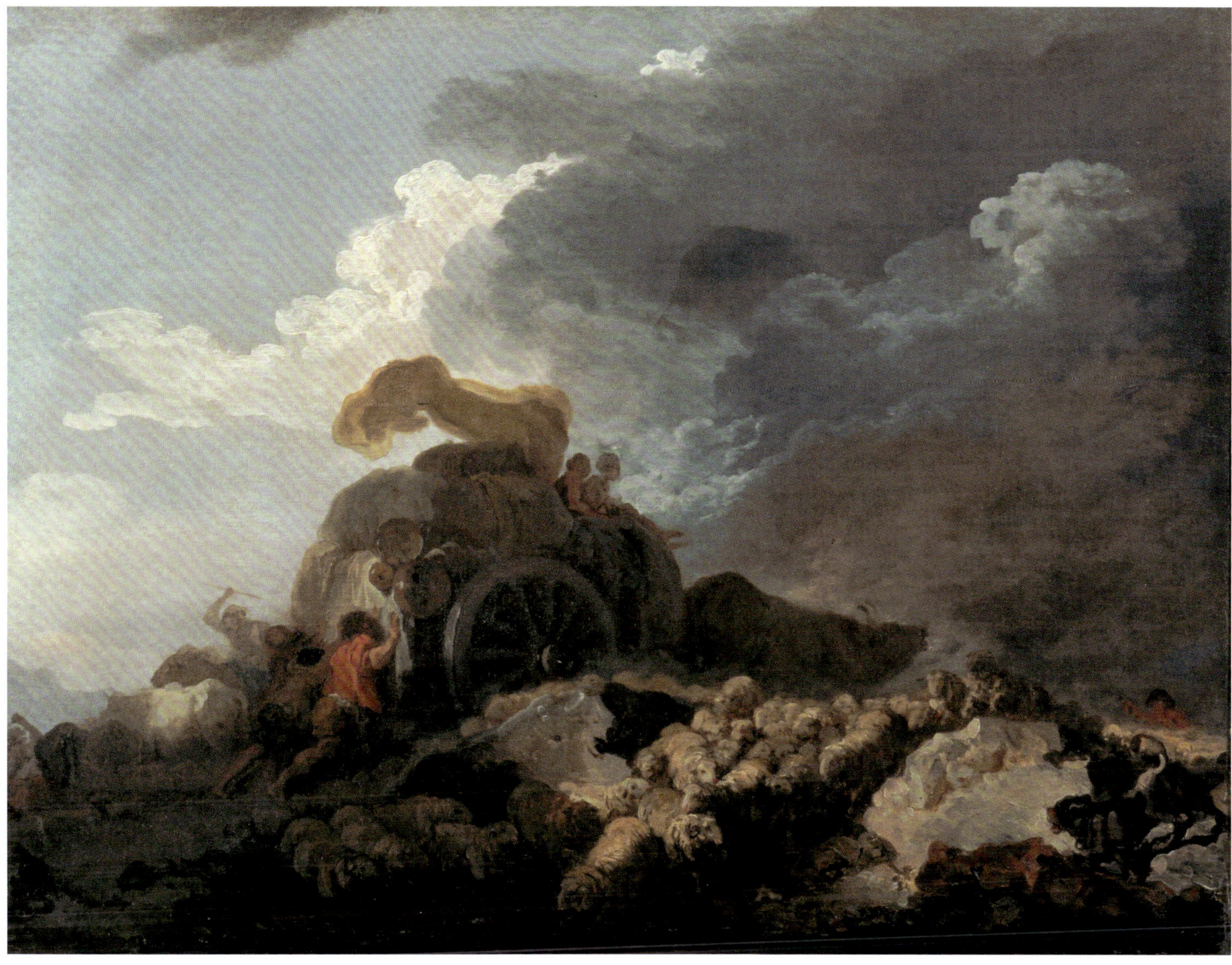

Fig. 18. Jean Honoré Fragonard, *The Stalled Cart*, also called *The Storm*, 1759. Oil on canvas, 28¾ × 38¼ in. (73 × 97 cm). Musée du Louvre, Paris (MI 1063)

the same combination of wash reworked in pen over a discrete sketch in red chalk in one of the drawn versions of the *The Bolt* (fig. 19).[42] The scene, its decor, and the youth of the models, as well as the artist's impulsive style, are reminiscent of Fragonard's second series of illustrations for La Fontaine's *Contes* (*Tales*), probably made in the early 1760s (cats. 85 and 86). The presence of red chalk could be an additional clue for dating this sheet about ten years earlier than the famous painted version (fig. 20).[43] He also put down his initial ideas for *Saint Louis Venerating the Crown of Thorns* (fig. 21) in a light sketch in red chalk.[44] The composition, undoubtedly intended to decorate an altar, was then further developed in pen and wash.

We have seen in the modest preparatory sketch for *Cephalus and Procris* that the watercolor highlights anticipate the colors of the painting. This is probably the case with *Saint Hubert Adoring the Cross*, a drawing highlighted with a few touches of yellow watercolor, although no equivalent painting is known.[45] In these

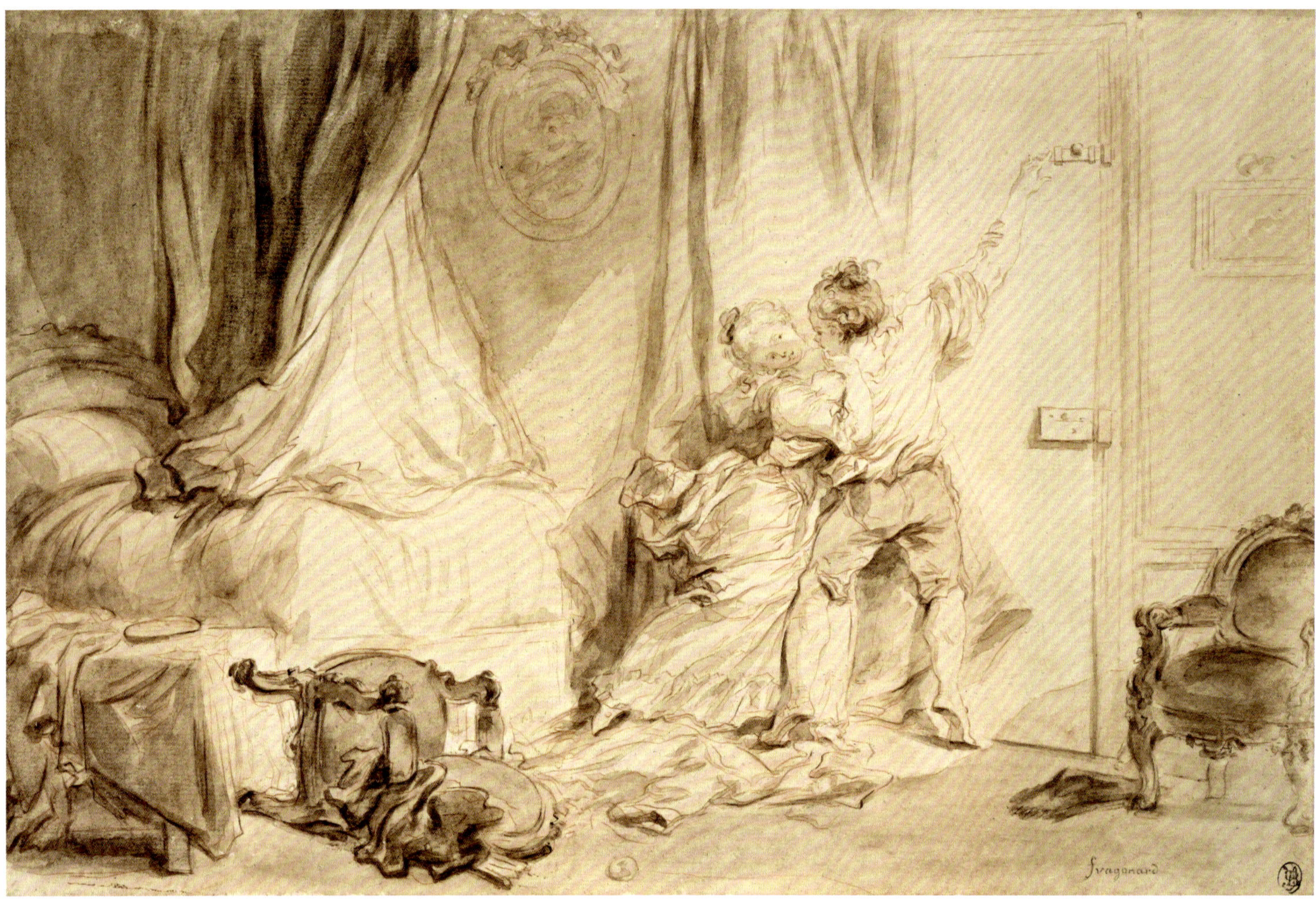

Fig. 19. Jean Honoré Fragonard, *The Bolt*, ca. 1765–69. Red chalk, brown wash, 9½ × 14½ in. (24 × 36.7 cm). Location unknown

two examples, the very pale, diluted shades serve less to color than to introduce nuance and contrast to the more generously distributed gray and brown washes. The artist thus accentuated one area or another while indicating the colors to be used on his palette. In some areas a lively pen and a pencil join in to organize the various elements of the composition a little more precisely. This mixed technique is observed in two other drawings for which the corresponding paintings are known only from descriptions in the catalogue of their sale in 1776.[46] They are pendants that show, on the one hand, a young man kneeling and embracing a statue of Friendship (fig. 22), and, on the other, an old man reaching his arms out toward an apparition.[47] Light touches of pinkish brown wash color the clothing of the former, while a very pale gray-blue tints the drapery and the surrounding clouds of the latter. In the only surviving preliminary study of *The Happy Moment* (fig. 23), a little pink watercolor delicately nuances the creases and folds of the bedclothes. We observe anew how the placement of the protagonists has been reversed, from an awkward embrace in the study, with the woman facing us and the man seen from the back, to a more telling configuration in the two canvases of the same composition (see, for example, fig. 24).[48]

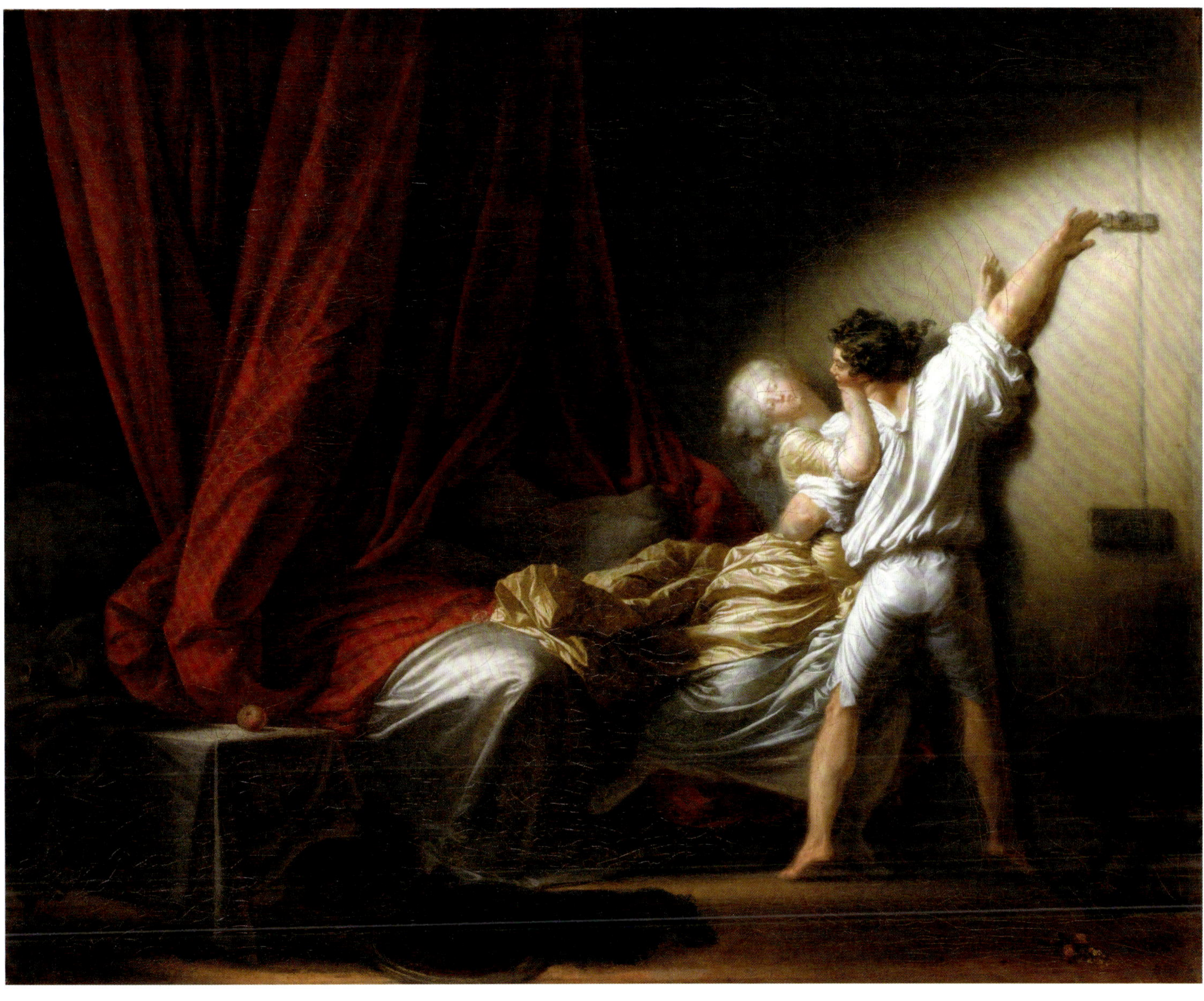

The color notes indicated here and there tend to corroborate the "preparatory" status of such sheets. Must we then systematically interpret all sheets with touches of watercolor, often distributed with little fuss against a tracery of black chalk, as a stage in the preparation of a painting? Interestingly, the version of *Competition* in Frankfurt,[49] brightened with quick touches of red, blue, and green, seems to have been made only for the purpose of preparing a more finished drawing, in gray wash alone. But we can speculate about *Children Dancing in a Park* (cat. 77 recto), which is also washed with patches of color in a more extensive manner than usual, especially in the vegetation that frames the composition on the left. This is a rare case in which we are able to observe the evolution of the same subject in three different versions (see also cat. 77 verso and p. 224, fig. 118), and it is tempting to see them as markers in the development of the large, magnificent canvas titled *La Fête à Saint-Cloud*.[50] The discrepancies between the

Fig. 20. Jean Honoré Fragonard, *The Bolt*, ca. 1777–78. Oil on canvas, 29⅛ × 37 in. (74 × 94 cm). Musée du Louvre, Paris (RF 1974-2)

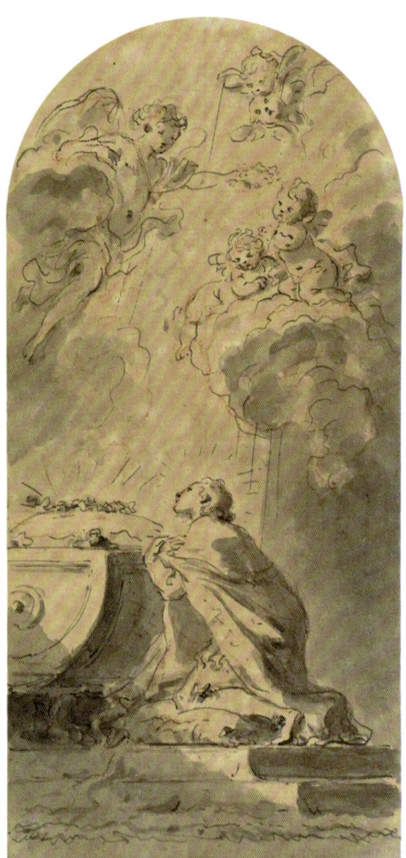

Fig. 21. Jean Honoré Fragonard, *Saint Louis Venerating the Crown of Thorns*, ca. 1756. Red chalk, gray wash, pen and black ink, 6⅝ × 3⅜ in. (16.8 × 8.4 cm). Musée des Beaux-Arts et d'Archéologie, Besançon (D.2856)

scenes described on paper and those painted on canvas demonstrate the amount of study Fragonard conducted over an extended period of time to compose this masterpiece, a project that could have encountered interruptions, as well as phases of maturation, before reemerging in a different form. As we have seen with *The Bolt*, certain subjects may have been developed over a relatively long period of time.

Drawings touched with watercolor are quite rare, however, and drawings related to paintings appear mainly in the form of wash over a black chalk sketch. Sometimes the rough sketch is especially vague, as in *The Pasha Receiving in His Harem* (cat. 90), in which the ink serves to organize the overall composition and make it more legible. The number of drawings currently recognized as being preparatory decreases over the course of Fragonard's career, which should be seen as a sign of the greater confidence gradually gained by the artist. Increasingly, his studies on paper became more highly finished scenes that were repeated almost exactly on canvas, as in *The Return of the Herd* (cat. 44). The style of these veritable *modelli* no longer has much to do with the trial and error of the early years. Nothing laborious or tense appears in these sketches, in which the suppleness of the line and the fluidity of the wash reflect the artist's free and fertile imagination. The contrast is especially striking if we compare two drawings with a similar theme, *The Rest on the Flight into Egypt* (fig. 11) and *The Adoration of the Shepherds* of about fifteen years later (fig. 25). The latter composition seems to have taken a hold on the artist, who introduced few changes in the painted version (fig. 26). However, the wiry, energetic draftsmanship in black chalk seen in works such as *The First Steps* (fig. 27)[51] demonstrates that even in the final phase of his career as a painter Fragonard was not averse to working out his compositions on paper.[52] In this case, the painting is one he created with his young sister-in-law, Marguerite Gérard (fig. 28). It is interesting to note that the right side of the painting, where scholars recognize the hand of the student, is not significantly different from the drawing, while the left side, which is more evidently the work of Fragonard, shows major changes, especially the addition of a figure.

A CRITICAL LINK IN THE CREATIVE PROCESS: THE STUDY OF THE MASTERS

One factor certainly played a part in the ease with which Fragonard mastered the arrangement of his compositions: his vast knowledge of art. Throughout his career he maintained a close connection to the work of earlier masters. Several hundred copies by Fragonard's hand are known; some are in brown wash and a few are in red chalk, but the majority are in black chalk. Many were counterproofed and retouched by the artist himself (for example, cat. 7). His almost innate sense of composition and his skill in placing figures and relating them to their surroundings probably benefitted from the many sessions he spent in the churches and palaces of Italy, Flanders, Austria, and Germany. His practice of copying made him an artist versed in Baroque perspective, Rubens's sense of movement, and the luminous contrasts seen in the work of Rembrandt and his followers. As a copyist he often sought to transpose details rather than entire works. By selecting especially striking motifs, he thus built a whole repertoire of poses that he could later deploy. The knowledge he gained from copying made him more audacious in working directly on the canvas,

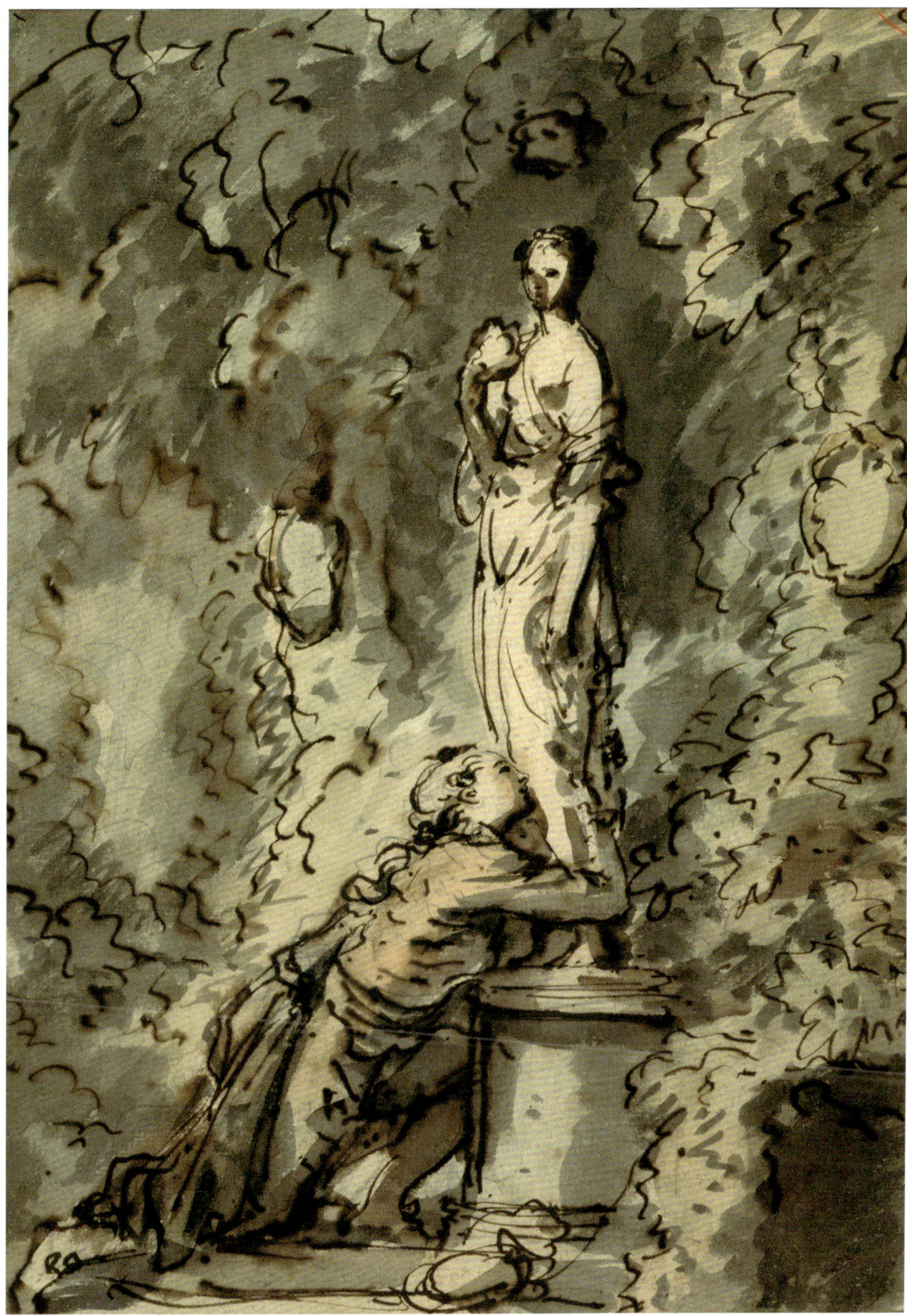

Fig. 22. Jean Honoré Fragonard, *Young Man Imploring a Statue of Friendship*, ca. 1770–72. Black chalk, brown and gray wash, pen and brown ink, watercolor, 13 × 9⅜ in. (33 × 23.8 cm). Private collection, London

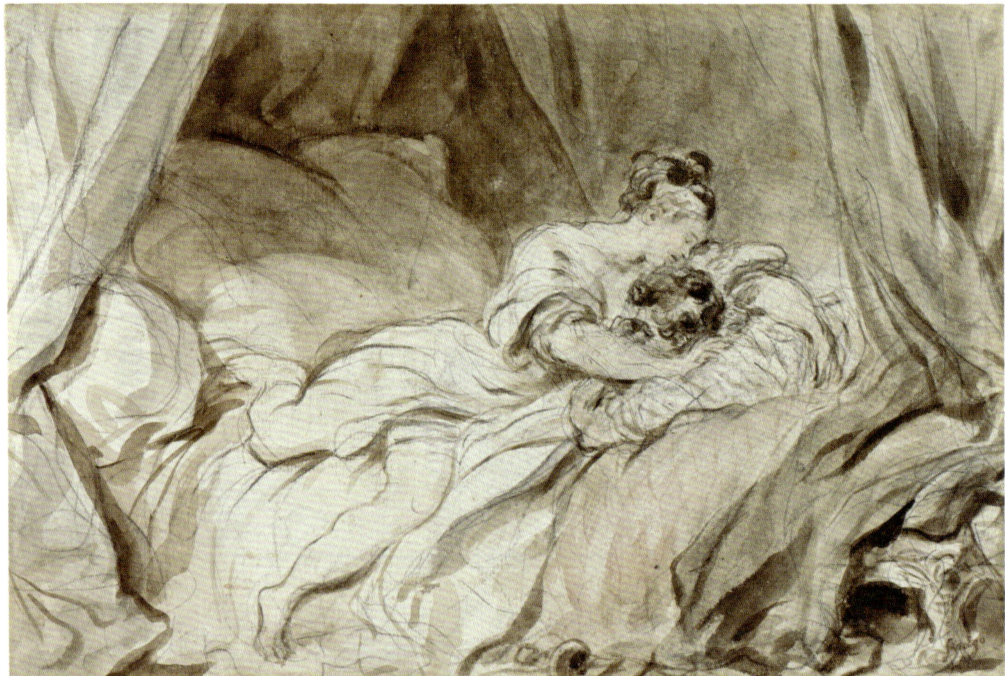

Fig. 23. Jean Honoré Fragonard, *The Happy Moment*, also called *The Useless Resistance*, ca. 1770–73. Black chalk, brown wash, watercolor highlights, 9⅛ × 13⅜ in. (23 × 34 cm). Philadelphia Museum of Art (201-210-2)

consequently sparing him the necessity of multiple preparatory sketches. As we see in his paintings, his practice was less a matter of direct borrowing from earlier masters than it was a certain way of appropriating their style, technique, and above all their spirit.

Many of Fragonard's paintings cannot be understood without the filter of his predecessors, and it is not uncommon to perceive their echoes in his work, even if it is impossible to determine if the borrowings were conscious. One example is the flamboyant *Portrait of a Sitting Cavalier*,[53] whose pose repeats, in reverse, that of Michelangelo's *Lorenzo de' Medici*, a marble sculpture that Fragonard copied when he passed through Florence.[54] Another example of this process, in which a copy provides the basis for a painting, can be observed with the subject of "The Education of the Virgin." After making copies of works by Tiepolo and Rubens,[55] Fragonard composed no less than six versions of this theme, some on canvas and others on paper.[56] But instead of repeating compositions by earlier artists he invented a new one, to which he introduced variations each time.[57] A painted version of the subject in San Francisco, originally very large in size and likely the first of the series,[58] shows affinities in its broad touch and acidic palette with the art of the Venetian painter Tiepolo. The two other versions on canvas (Amiens and Los Angeles), painted at a later date, are steeped in a harmony of golden browns and chiaroscuro worthy of Rembrandt. Fragonard's study of light effects is apparent in three related drawings, but can we thus deduce that the sheets are preparatory to the paintings? Close to the San Francisco canvas, a sheet in the Hammer collection,[59] executed in black chalk alone, could be evidence of the artist's intention to rework and correct the composition, given the harsh criticisms the painting had received.[60] The two other drawings (Saint Louis Art Museum and private collection) feature very similar compositions to those of the two little paintings, one of which is painted on a wood panel and shows the Virgin's face directed toward

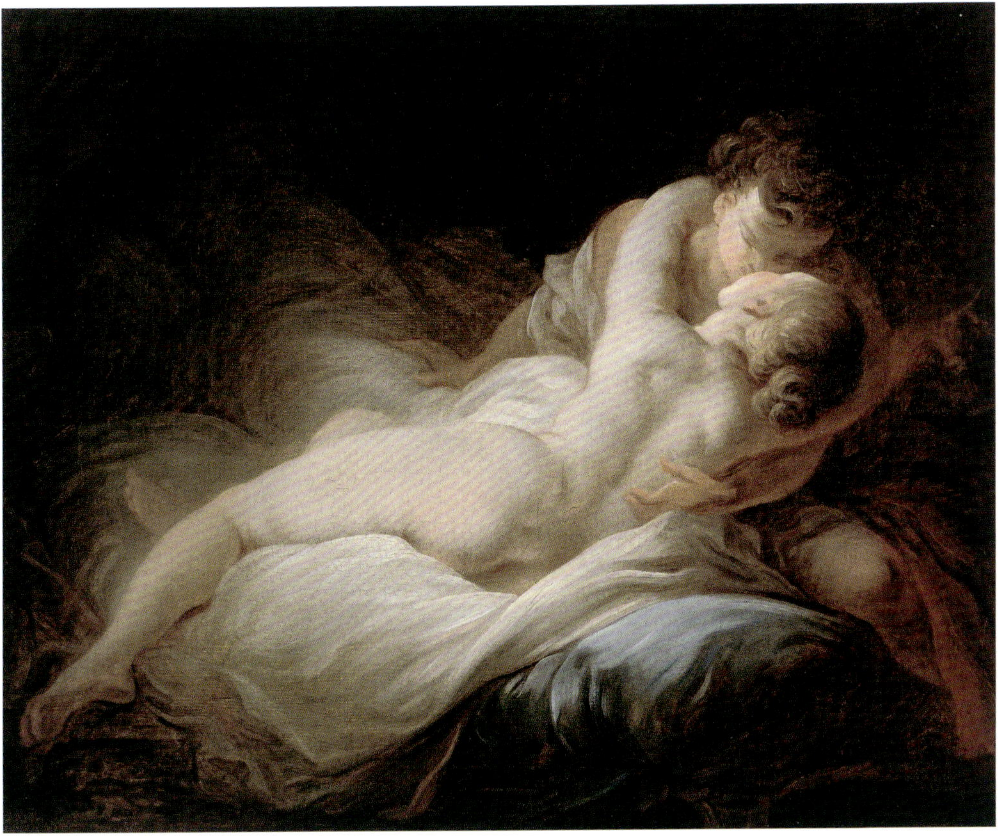

Fig. 24. Jean Honoré Fragonard, *The Happy Moment*, ca. 1770–73. Oil on canvas, 19¾ × 24 in. (50 × 61 cm). George Ortiz Collection, Switzerland

her mother rather than toward the book placed in front of them. But how do these works relate to one another? It is as if Fragonard reversed the usual process of creation by giving the paintings a sketchlike character, especially striking in the canvas now in Amiens (fig. 29), and by offering, with two black chalk drawings reworked in wash, versions that are much more precise and finished. The version that belonged to the collector Hippolyte Walferdin (fig. 30), produced in an exceptionally large format with carefully studied effects of sooty blacks moderated by stumping, appears to be the apotheosis of the series.

PAINTING FOR DRAWING

One of Fragonard's singularities was the practice of repeating his paintings on paper. Eunice Williams drew attention to this phenomenon with one of the earliest known examples, the wash drawing after *Coresus and Callirhoë* (cat. 37). The success of this large dramatic scene at the Salon of 1765 no doubt prompted the artist to duplicate it several times, according to the description in the sale catalogue when the drawing was sold in 1777.[61] The significant price of 720 livres that the drawing made at auction says a lot about the taste among *amateurs* for this type of *ricordo*. But profit does not seem to have been the only motive that led Fragonard to make copies after his own work, just as he had after earlier masters. Might he have sought to keep a record of his painted compositions in the form of an illustrated account book as, for example, Claude Lorrain had done? Such a working method hardly seems in accord with

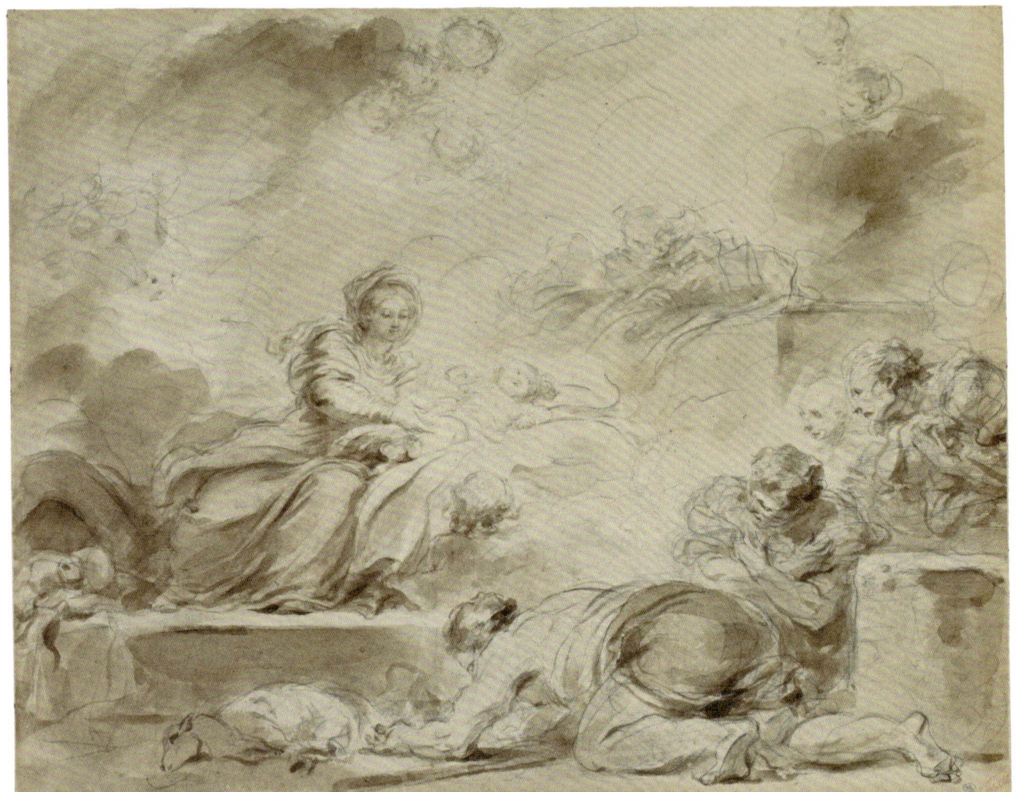

Fig. 25. Jean Honoré Fragonard, *The Adoration of the Shepherds*, ca. 1775. Black chalk, brown wash, 14 × 18¼ in. (35.6 × 46.3 cm). Musée du Louvre, Paris (RF 31875)

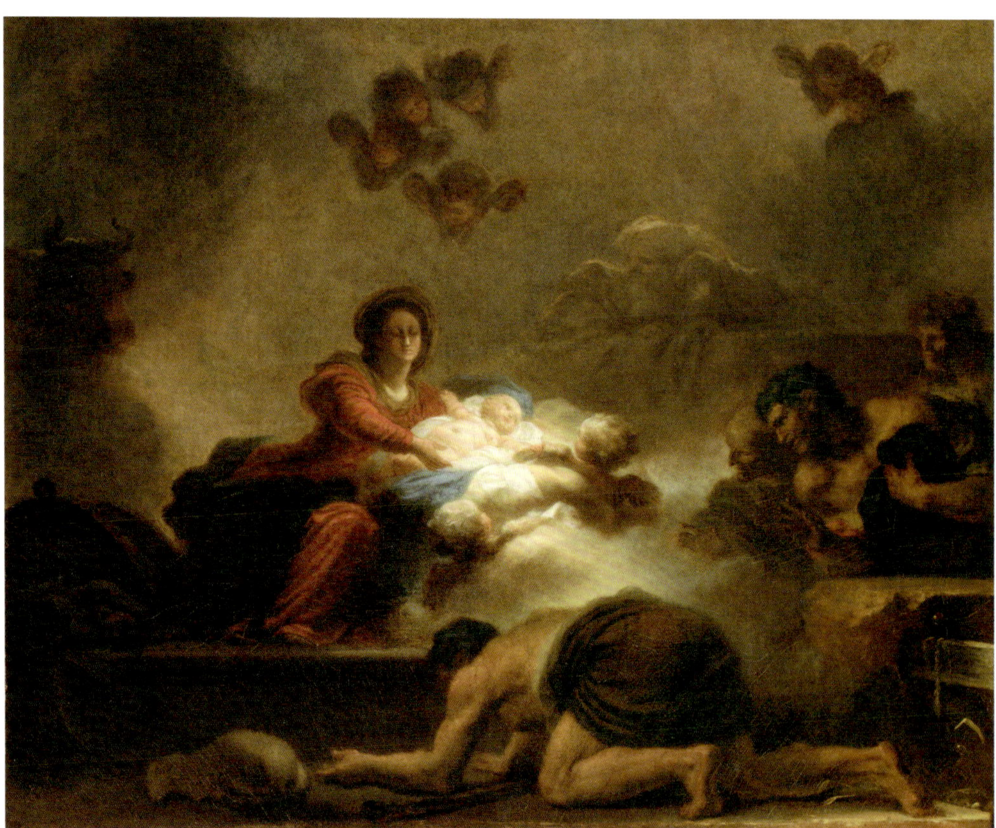

Fig. 26. Jean Honoré Fragonard, *The Adoration of the Shepherds*, ca. 1775. Oil on canvas, 28¾ × 36⅝ in. (73 × 93 cm). Musée du Louvre, Paris (RF 1988-11)

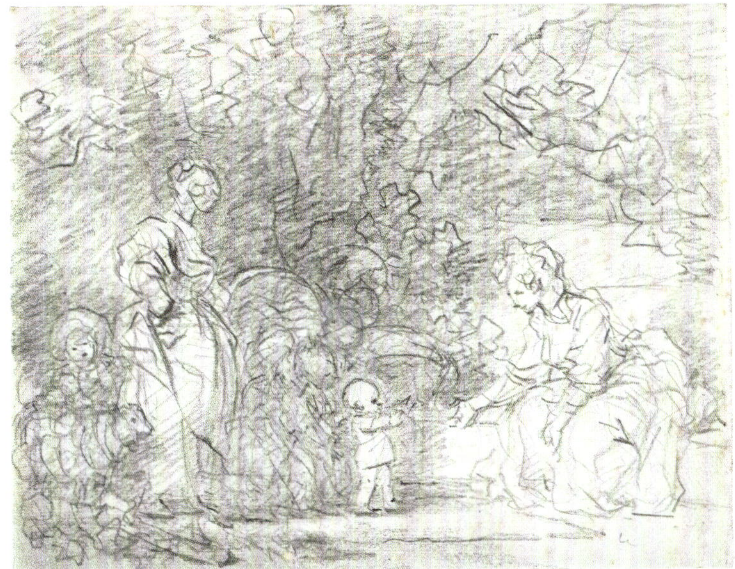

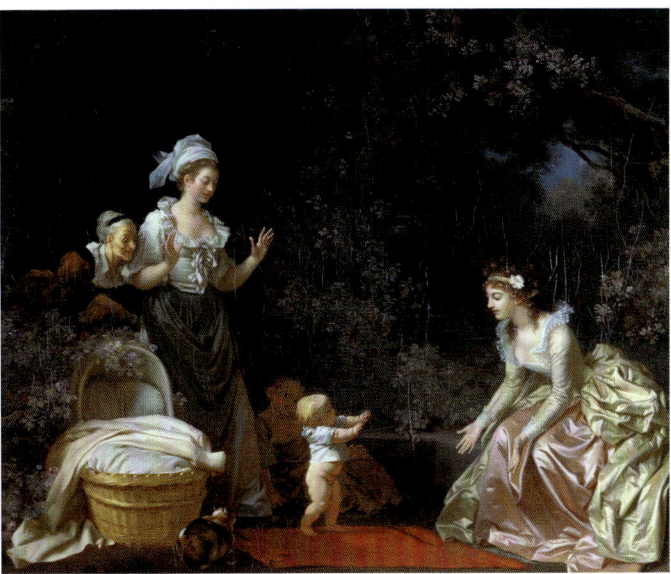

Fig. 27. Jean Honoré Fragonard, *The First Steps*, ca. 1780–85. Black and white chalk, 6¾ × 8⅞ in. (17.1 × 22.5 cm). Harvard Art Museums/Fogg Museum, Cambridge, Mass. (1992.2)

Fig. 28. Jean Honoré Fragonard, assisted by Marguerite Gérard, *The First Steps*, ca. 1780–85. Oil on canvas, 17⅜ × 21¾ in. (44 × 55 cm). Harvard Art Museums/Fogg Museum, Cambridge, Mass. (1961.166)

what we know of the artist's temperament, which was more improvisational than painstaking. He even seems to have taken a certain pleasure in *repeating*—I prefer this term to *reproducing*—his paintings in another medium. Far from having the cold and mechanical qualities of copies, Fragonard's repetitions are endowed with the spirit of originals.

Typically, the subject of the painting was transposed onto paper in black chalk with a quick and supple hand. Less messy than certain preparatory drawings, this light and free sketch nevertheless gives the impression that the artist has just invented it. The wash was adapted to the new size of the support and tonality of the scene. Fragonard's goal was not so much to repeat a composition as to transpose from one technique to another its charming ambience, effervescent spirit, and spontaneity. The disparities between the two versions were thus quite deliberate. The reductions on paper often necessitated a certain amount of simplification, without which the compositions would appear overcrowded and the desired effect would be undermined. Thus the parchment under the feet in *The Little Preacher*[62] and the large reed between the paws of the docile dog on the right in *Education Does it All* (fig. 31)[63] do not appear in the wash versions of each of these paintings.[64] Whereas the painting contains certain areas that disappear into the chiaroscuro, the wash offers greater legibility. The artist seems to have played the role of theater director, adjusting the light effects and colors depending on the support and technique. As in the case of *The Education of the Virgin*, mentioned above, one wonders if the painted composition served as a preparatory study for the version drawn in wash. This reversal of roles may also be the case with *Reading in the Kitchen* (cat. 75). Fragonard created the general mood of the canvas (p. 220, fig. 115) by applying paint in a range of light brown shades with almost the transparency of wash, upon which he placed the figures, which are treated with great delicacy. Although we do not know if it is an initial sketch, the painted canvas shows an intermediary stage, a sort of indefinable midway, to which the wash drawing offers a culmination. The presence of figures, which are barely sketched on the canvas, is much more evident on the paper. Likewise, in the wash

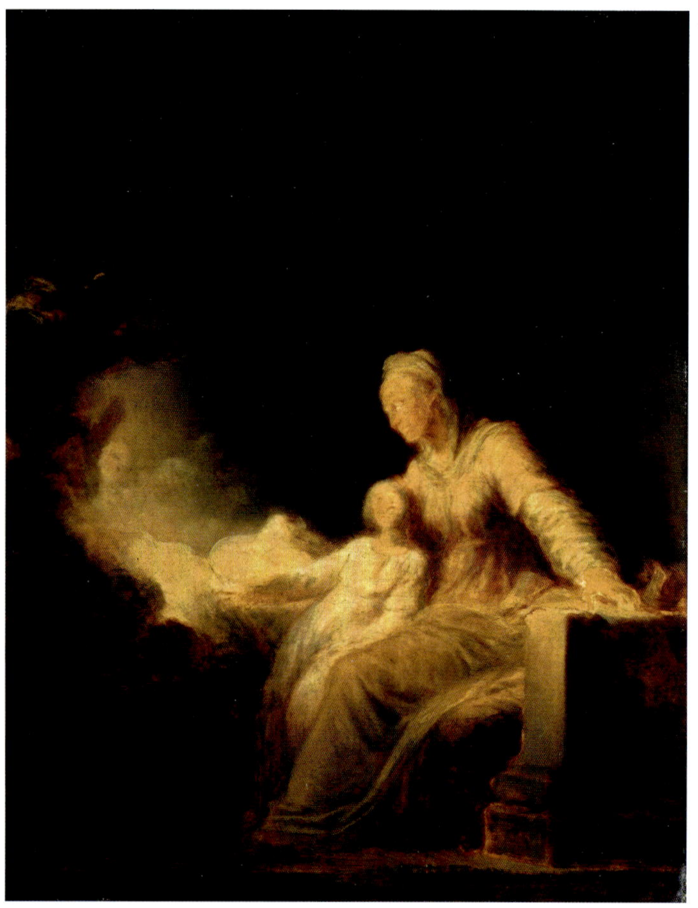

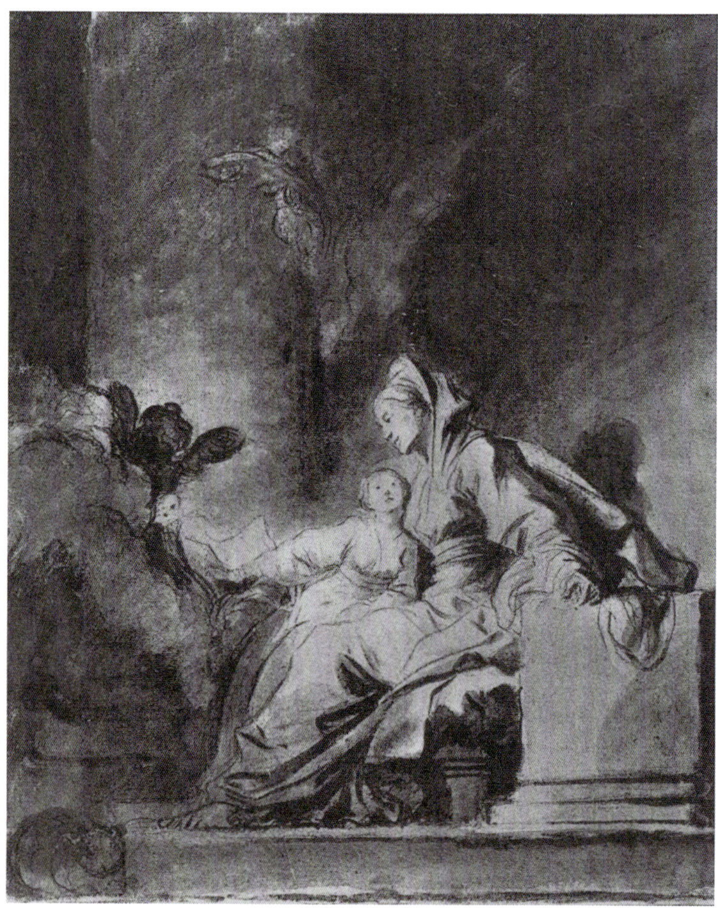

Fig. 29. Jean Honoré Fragonard, *The Education of the Virgin*, ca. 1775(?). Oil on canvas, 36¼ × 28¾ in. (92 × 73 cm). Musée de Picardie, Amiens

Fig. 30. Jean Honoré Fragonard, *The Education of the Virgin*, ca. 1775(?). Black chalk, brown and gray wash, charcoal, stumping, 21⅝ × 17⅝ in. (54.8 × 44.8 cm). Private collection

drawing one can better make out the exchange of glances that reinforce the poses and thus give a more intriguing structure to the scene. What is the svelte young woman reading that has attracted so much attention and curiosity, even from the dog who stares intensely at her?

Fragonard's practice of transposing his painted creations into the graphic universe continued through his late career. The superb sheet *The Vow to Love*[65] (fig. 32) repeats with uncommon skill a painting from the years 1780–85 (fig. 33).[66] The squaring—the only known example in the artist's entire oeuvre—which is visible to the naked eye under (and not over) the various shades of brown wash, provides additional proof of his proclivity for repetition and all the care he brought to it. Was this practice intended to make up for the relatively limited circulation of the artist's oeuvre in the form of reproductive prints? Unlike artists such as Boucher and Greuze, Fragonard did not have a strategy for the diffusion of his works, other than perhaps to keep it under his control. His paintings were engraved only sporadically and often quite late. He was probably not satisfied to see his compositions, which were known for their color and animation, stiffen and darken under the engraver's burin. Is it a coincidence that a certain number of paintings repeated on paper by the artist correspond to those engraved by printmakers such as Nicolas de Launay, the creator of prints after *The Little Preacher*, *Education Does it All*, *The Happy Family*, and *The Good Mother*? The latter two compositions,[67] dating from the years 1770–72, each led to the production of a beautiful watercolor by Fragonard (fig. 34). In this medium he attained a degree of fidelity to the model, a fact that is all the more remarkable given that no trace of black chalk can be seen under the light layers of wash, watercolor, and gouache highlights. Indeed, these very precise transpositions also raise the question of processes used by the artist, about which more study is needed.

The exchange of roles between painting and drawing is even more surprising when the latter is produced in dimensions equal to or larger than the former. In 1979, Eunice Williams described the magnificent landscape *Shepherd and Sheep on a Sunny Hillside* (cat. 45) as "the wash equivalent of an oil painting."[68] A similar landscape has recently reappeared, painted on a canvas that is about a dozen centimeters smaller in each dimension (p. 160, fig. 97).[69] A relatively early date, about 1763–65, seems possible, placing the painting at a time when the artist was beginning to take an interest in Dutch and Flemish landscape.[70] The fact that the later wash drawing, which is of dazzling virtuosity, follows the composition of the painting does not in the least diminish its status. In the drawing, the artist was not content to repeat and enrich the setting described on the canvas; instead he transcended it, using carefully studied light effects to express the "Dutch" character of the landscape. We see the opposite order of progression with *A Shaded Avenue*. The large, majestic wash drawing, usually dated to Fragonard's second journey to Italy, conveys the flickering light of a long allée planted with trees (fig. 35).[71] The small painting, which seems to be later, displays warm shades and "Ruisdael-like" effects, emphasized by the panel support (fig. 36).[72] With both *Shepherd and Sheep on a Sunny Hillside* and *A Shaded Avenue*, the second version, whether on paper or wood, displays less concern

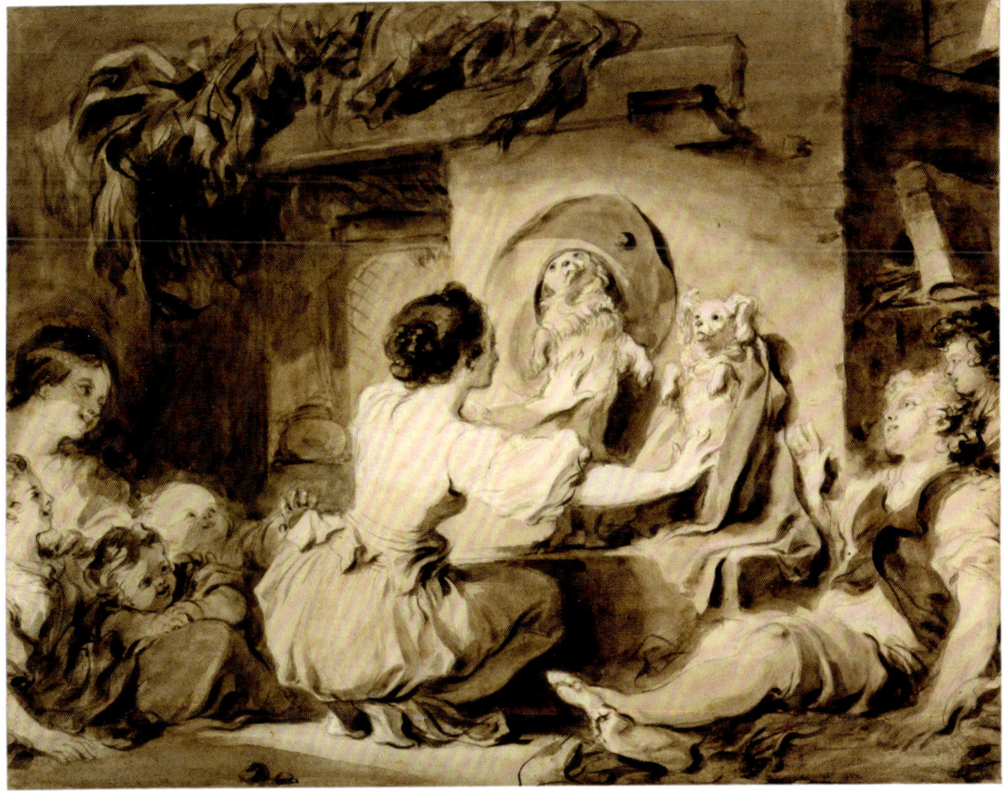

Fig 31. Jean Honoré Fragonard, *Education Does it All*, ca. 1776. Black chalk, brown wash, 13⅜ × 17¾ in. (34 × 45 cm). The Rothschild Collection, Waddesdon Manor, Aylesbury

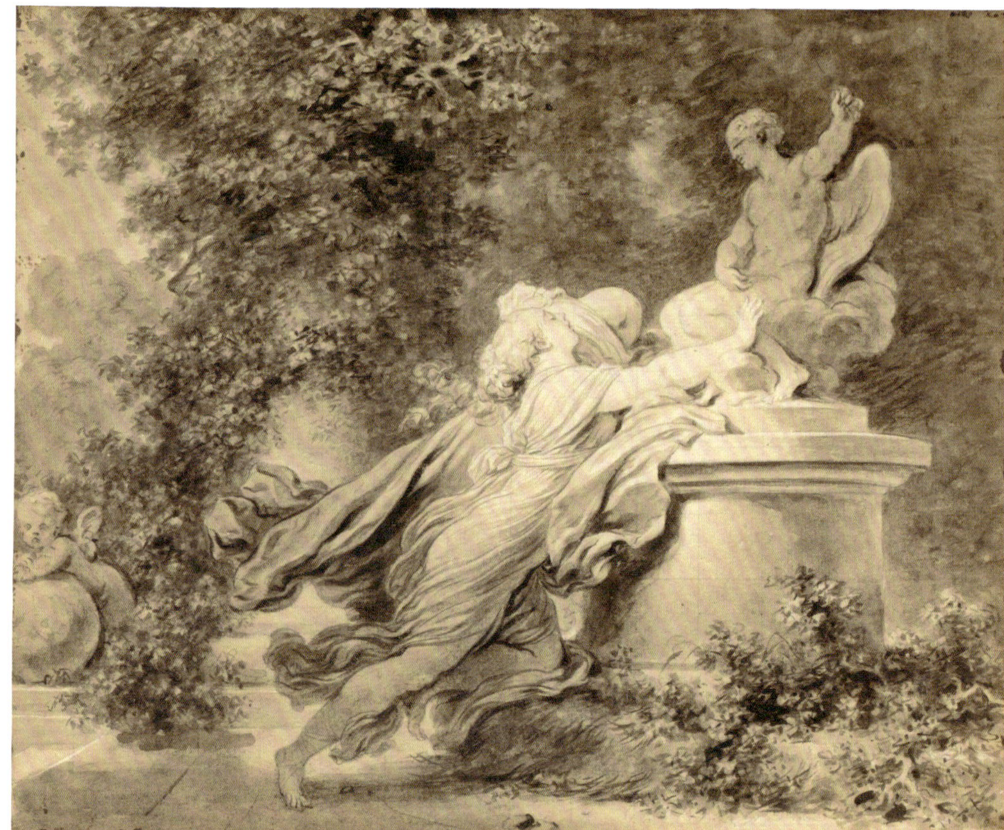

Fig. 32. Jean Honoré Fragonard, *The Vow to Love*, ca. 1780–85. Black chalk, brown wash, 13¼ × 16⅜ in. (33.5 × 41.6 cm). Cleveland Museum of Art (43.657)

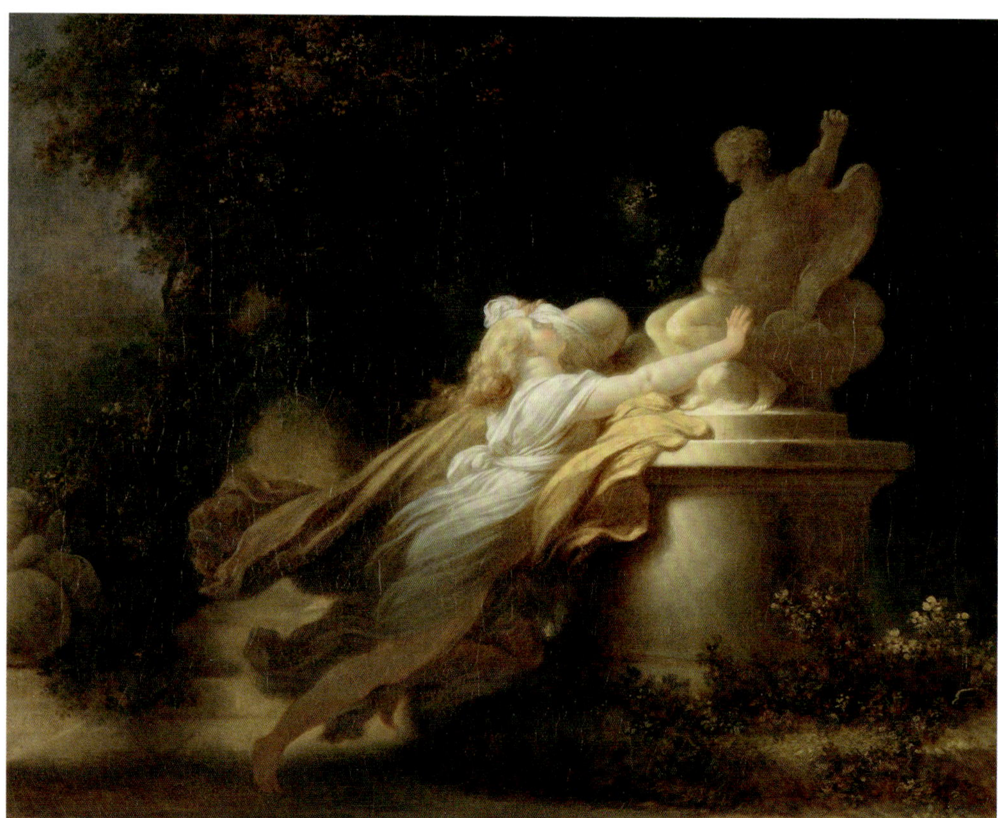

Fig. 33. Jean Honoré Fragonard, *The Vow to Love*, ca. 1780–85. Oil on canvas, 20½ × 24⅞ in. (52 × 63 cm). Private collection, New York

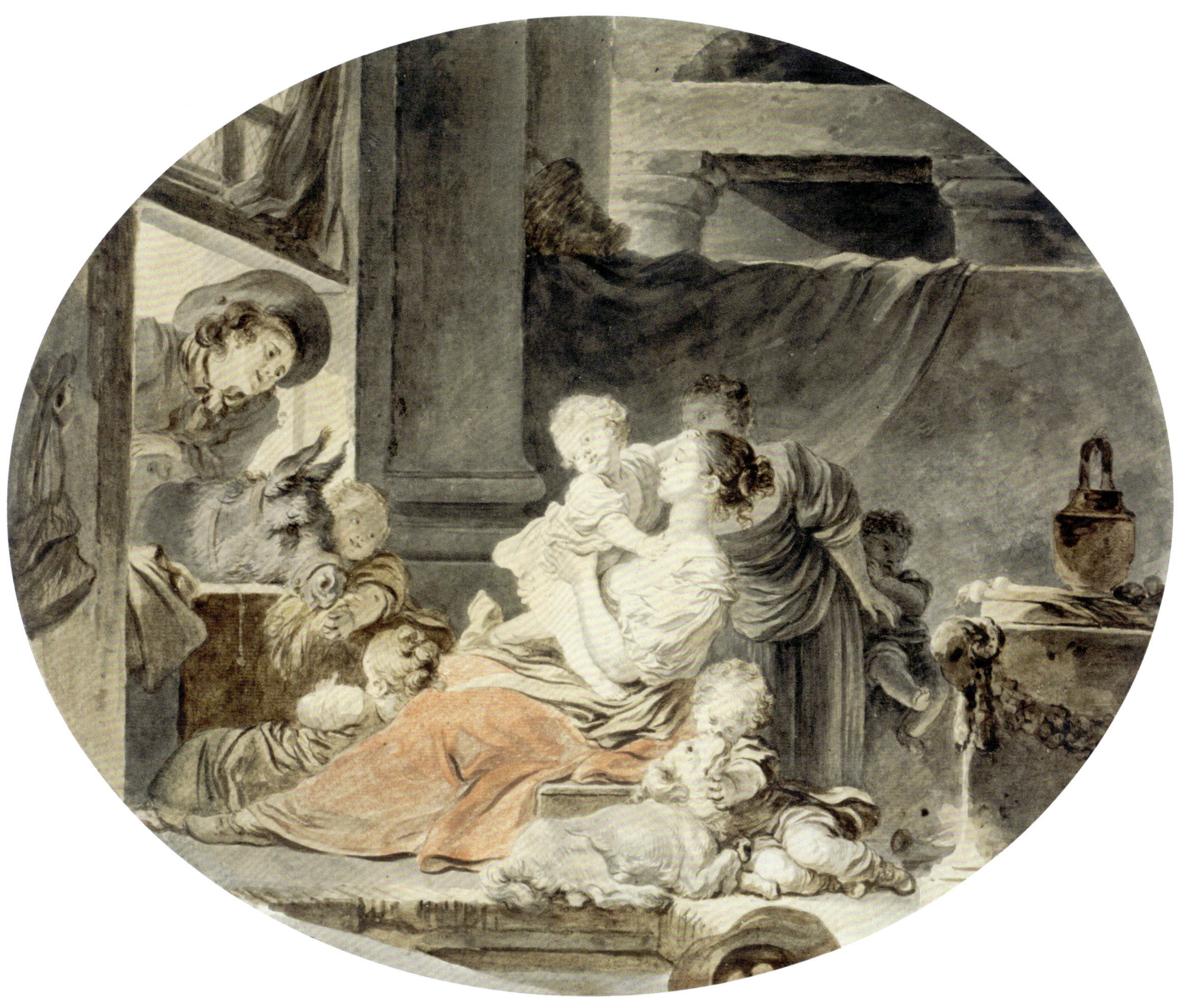

with overall harmony than with increased naturalism, especially noticeable in the depiction of the branches and foliage. The masses of trees, like the light on the vegetation, are studied with particularly remarkable precision. Many independent drawings and many more in a sketchbook in the Rijksmuseum in Amsterdam—one of only two such volumes by the artist to have survived intact—show the exercises in which the artist engaged, almost obsessively, making plein air sketches of trees, branches, and foliage. Although several pages depict the motif of an avenue vaulted with trees, it may not be possible to make a direct connection linking these sketches to a specific painting, nor even to *A Shaded Avenue*.[73] Yet, again, these studies run counter to the idea of a painter more preoccupied with virtuosity and rapidity than with careful preparation.

Fig. 34. Jean Honoré Fragonard, *The Happy Family*, 1770 or 1777. Black chalk, gray and brown wash, watercolor, gouache, 14 × 16⅜ in. (35.5 × 41.5 cm). Musée Cognacq-Jay, Paris (J. 146)

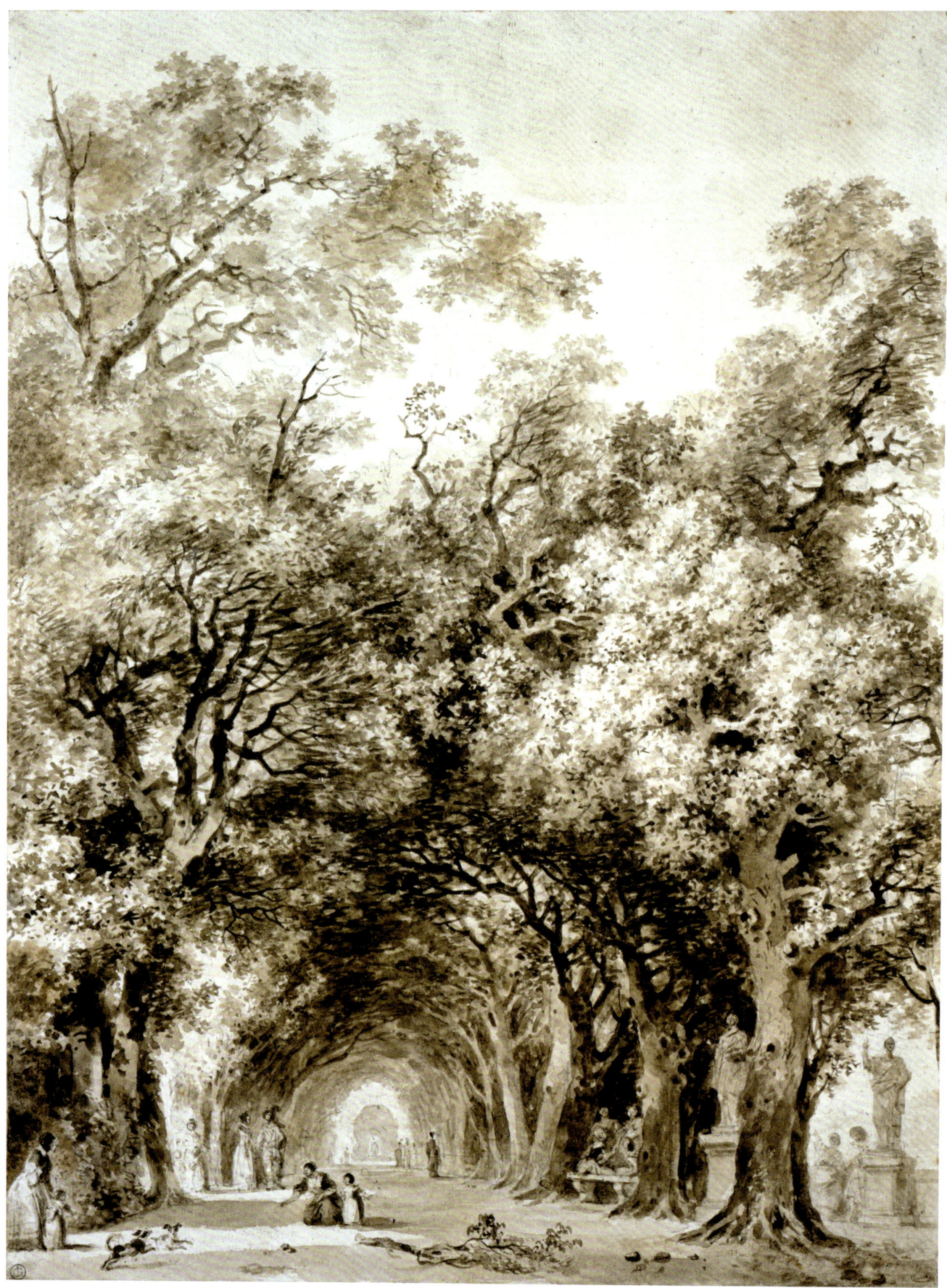

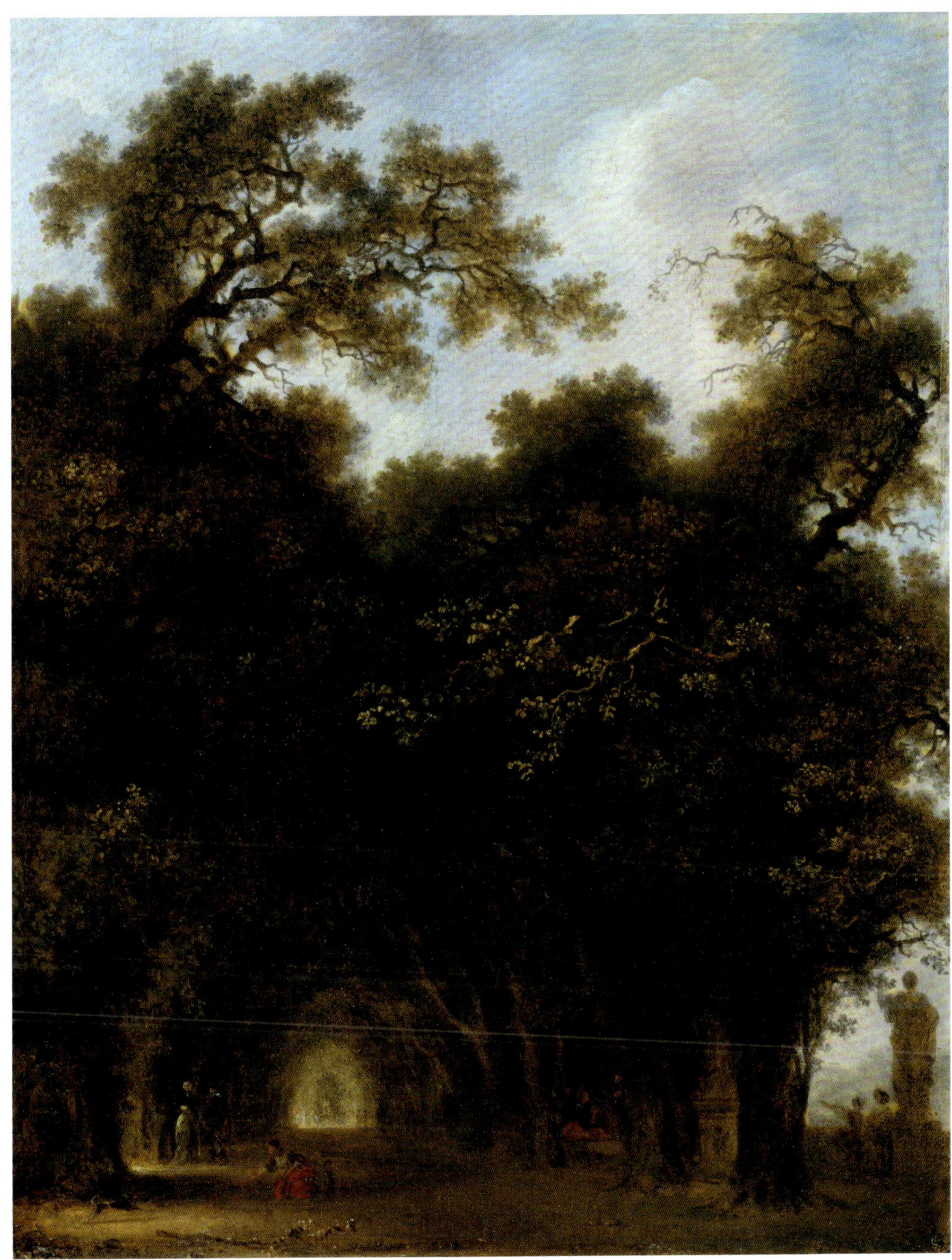

OPPOSITE: Fig. 35. Jean Honoré Fragonard, *A Shaded Avenue*, ca. 1773–75. Brown wash, 18 × 13¾ in. (45.7 × 34.7 cm). Petit Palais, Musée des Beaux-Arts de la Ville de Paris (Dutuit 966)

Fig. 36. Jean Honoré Fragonard, *A Shaded Avenue*, ca. 1773–75. Oil on wood, 11½ × 9½ in. (29.2 × 24.1 cm). The Metropolitan Museum of Art, New York, The Jules Bache Collection, 1949 (49.7.51)

TOWARD THE AUTONOMY OF DRAWING

Considering Fragonard's multiple techniques and methods, what we observe is less an orderly evolution than a desire to experiment with new solutions, particularly in the area of landscape. The six versions of *The Little Park* (cats. 30–34 and p. 134, fig. 84) offer an outstanding illustration of this. In the convincing sequence proposed in this volume by Perrin Stein, the gouache is the final work in the series, which begins in red chalk and continues on a canvas of the same dimensions. The counterproof reworked with pen and wash seems to be a key stage in the process of transposing the subject to canvas, notably with the addition of the two trees on the far right. Five other sanguine drawings made in the gardens of the Villa d'Este at Tivoli have also led to counterproofs reworked by the artist in wash and with a pen (see, for example, cat. 35).[74] However, for these, we do not know of any corresponding paintings. The auction catalogues of the period mention several large canvases depicting scenes of Tivoli, but the descriptions are too vague to allow comparisons.[75] Yet, it is not unreasonable to suggest that these reworked counterproofs also explore the pictorial effects of the wash with an eye toward the development of a painting, as in *The Little Park* series. Four of the five original Tivoli drawings that were the basis for the counterproofs belong to a magnificent group of ten red chalk drawings, now in Besançon.[76] Among these, *Great Cypress Trees* was also repeated later in wash over a very light initial sketch in black chalk.[77] *The Grand Staircase* led to a painting generally dated to the end of Fragonard's first Italian trip,[78] like the reworked composition of another red chalk drawing from the same group, *The Great Cascade at Tivoli*.[79] No counterproof of this last view is known, but it is possible that intermediary stages have been lost. As in the case of *The Little Park*, comparing the sanguines and paintings of Tivoli shows that the drawings cannot be considered preparatory studies in any traditional sense, even if they preceded the paintings. In the Besançon series, the monochrome chalk is exploited with remarkable dexterity, allowing the artist to achieve effects—luminous, poetic, and atmospheric—that are distinct in character from the more robust effects of paint on canvas.

These masterpieces of draftsmanship show that Fragonard began quite early in his career to develop a rich and solid graphic oeuvre that was parallel, rather than subordinate, to that of his paintings. As Pierre Rosenberg claims with respect to the Besançon series, they are "works of art in their own right: rarely, before Fragonard, had drawing been taken so seriously, and had it occupied such an important place."[80] The *Little Park* series is especially informative because it shows, on the one hand, that the artist repeated the same composition without great changes, the counterproof of one of the two red chalk versions being used, in a way, as a step to arrive at the painted version. On the other hand, the series demonstrates how a subject inspired by the artist's Italian sojourn was treated in various reprises over a period of several years. This instance is perhaps not unique, and I have sought to identify some analogous examples in order to better understand Fragonard's methods.

Consider two beautiful chalk drawings showing young people amusing themselves in landscape settings, presumably composed from motifs seen in Italy: *Le jeu de la palette* (*The Paddle*) (fig. 37) and *Le jeu de la bascule* (*The Seesaw*), now in the Städel Museum in Frankfurt.[81] Richard Rand has drawn attention to the existence of two pairs of paintings showing the same subjects but in different formats.[82] The smaller pair is apparently the same that was sold after Bergeret's death,[83] while the larger pair may correspond to two paintings mentioned in the posthumous inventory of the abbé de Saint-Non.[84] Only a fragment from the larger version of *Le jeu de la palette* has survived, now in the Musée des Beaux-Arts in Chambéry (fig. 38).[85] However, despite the damage it has suffered,[86] it constitutes a major clue in understanding the relationship of painting and drawing for Fragonard, as noted below. In the case of *Le jeu de la bascule*, a red chalk counterproof reworked in pen and wash is also known.[87] Its condition unfortunately does not allow precise analysis of the transformations made with respect to the original composition, but its existence suggests that the pendant scene, *Le jeu de la palette*, was also counterproofed and retouched. To this sequence of works also belongs an aquatint by Saint-Non that bears the date 1766 (fig. 39). It reproduces in reverse, as one expects for a print, the landscape that served as the setting for *Le jeu de la palette*, although with major changes, for the group of young suitors in the foreground of Fragonard's drawing does not appear. This is perhaps a choice made by Saint-Non in the interest of simplifying the layout, as he also did for his etching after *The Little Park*, from which the motif of the central fountain seems to have vanished.[88] However, other changes—the more compact masses of trees, the arbor pruned in the form of arches in the background—suggest that the model for Saint-Non's aquatint was not the red chalk drawing in Frankfurt but another sheet. A little sketch by Gabriel de Saint-Aubin in the margin of the catalogue of the Gros sale in 1778[89] appears to be the only record of this smaller version, of which the medium is not known.[90] The fact that Saint-Non translated this composition into aquatint, a printmaking technique that imitates the effects of wash, is not a sufficient argument to resolve the question of the medium of the drawing that served as his model.

The group detailed above, comprised of at least ten works associated with the pair formed by *Le jeu de la palette* and *Le jeu de la bascule*, is too incomplete to propose a chronological order.[91] However, the fine and descriptive manner of the Frankfurt pair of red chalk drawings suggests that they date later than the red chalk series in Besançon. In addition, comparing the Chambéry fragment of *Le jeu de la palette*, dated about 1757–59, to its equivalent in red chalk shows that in the drawing the cypress trunks were pushed to the left, thus opening up the composition. This improvement tends to confirm that the painting preceded the drawing. As Jean-Pierre Cuzin has suggested, the red chalk drawings could have been made after Fragonard's return to France.[92] It is therefore tempting to consider a date of a few years after his return, perhaps about 1765, when the artist's views of Italy were still very much in the spotlight. At least two such views, belonging to Saint-Non, were exhibited at the Salon that year.[93] It was also about this time that the last three versions of *The Little Park* were made, if we follow Stein's reasoning. Finally, as we have seen, in 1766 Saint-Non etched the expansive and airy version of the landscape that serves as the setting for *Le jeu de la palette*. But here we have a different order of progression than that proposed for the *Little Park* series, the last word going this time to the red chalk drawings. The fact that the owners of the two pairs of paintings were two of the artist's principal patrons, with whom he traveled throughout Italy—joining Saint-Non in 1761 and Bergeret twelve years later—is not without significance. Their closeness—they were brothers-in-law—could have been a factor in the repetition of the pair. The canvases in the smaller pair are not a priori the sketches for the larger pair, given their relatively large size (79 × 97 cm). Rather, they could be reductions, made about 1765, of the larger versions executed in Italy. It is worth reiterating here that these *amateurs*, and specifically Saint-Non, played a role that went well beyond that of a loyal client, making an essential contribution to the development and evolution of the artist's work.

Although Italy maintained a hold on Fragonard even after his return to France, the discovery of other horizons led him to explore new modes of representation.

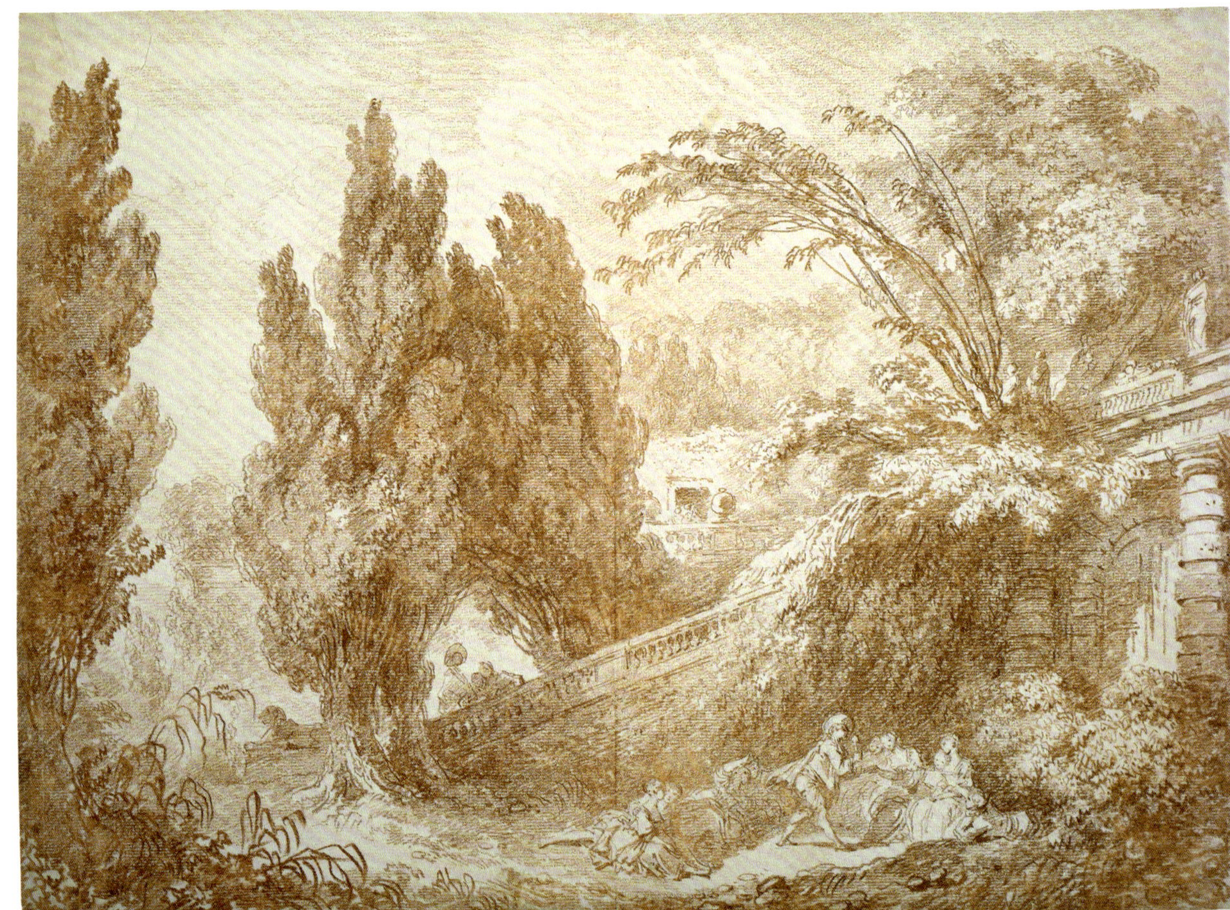

Fig. 37. Jean Honoré Fragonard, *Le jeu de la palette*, ca. 1761–65. Black and red chalk, 13⅜ × 18½ in. (33.9 × 46.8 cm). Städel Museum, Frankfurt (1234)

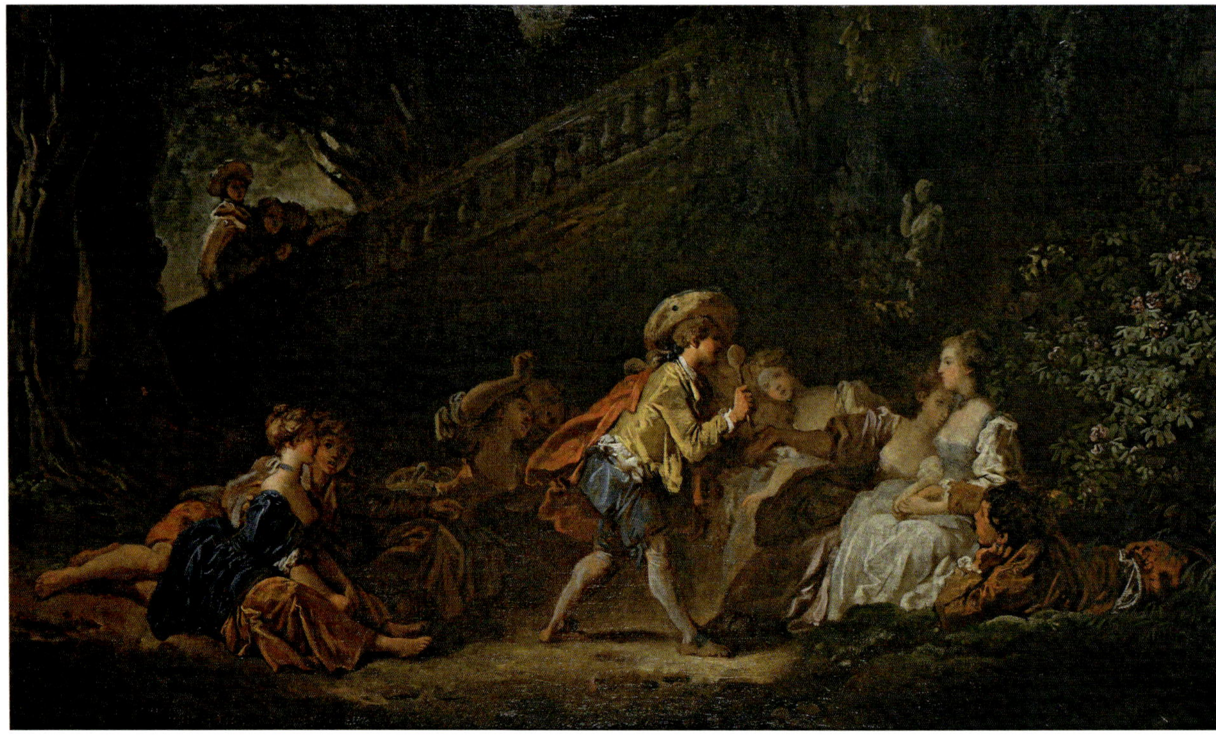

Fig. 38. Jean Honoré Fragonard, *Le jeu de la palette*, ca. 1757–59. Oil on canvas, 26⅜ × 44⅞ in. (67 × 114 cm). Musée des Beaux-Arts de Chambéry (M. 1033)

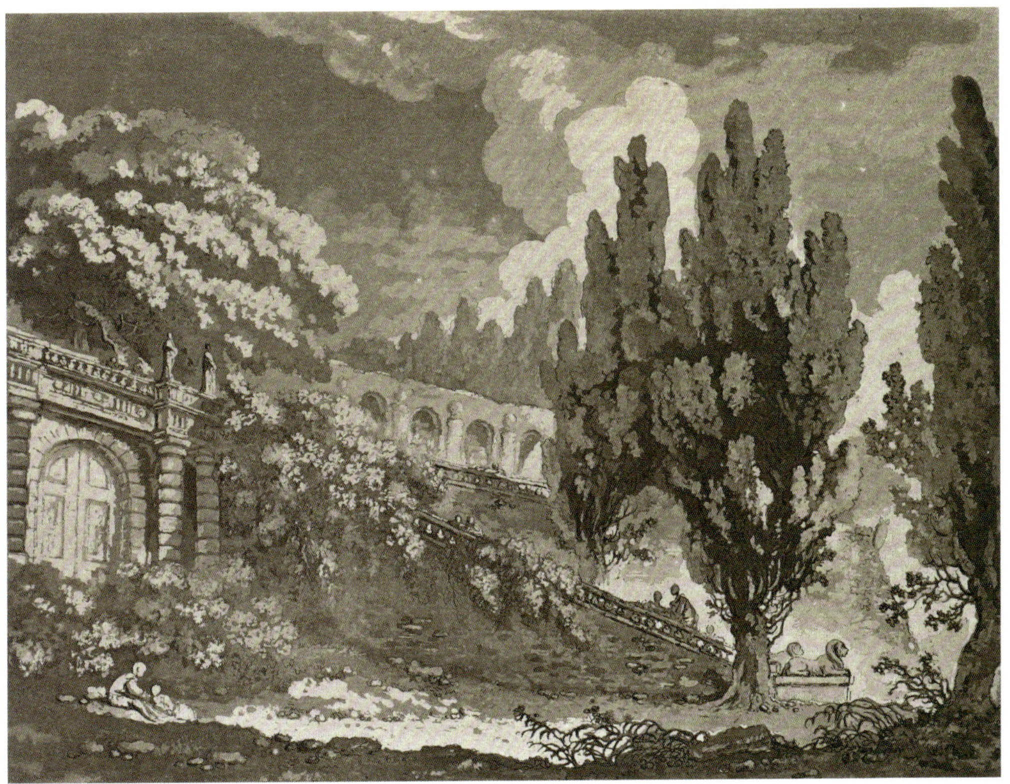

Fig. 39. Jean Claude Richard, abbé de Saint-Non (French, 1727–1791), after Jean Honoré Fragonard, *Le jeu de la palette*, 1766. Aquatint printed in brown ink, 8⅝ × 11⅛ in. (21.7 × 28.3 cm). The Metropolitan Museum of Art, New York, A. Hyatt Mayor Purchase Fund, Marjorie Phelps Starr Bequest, 2001 (2001.441.1)

His interest in the Dutch and Flemish schools is well known, as are his copies after Rembrandt, Ruisdael, Carel Fabritius, and Adrian van Ostade.[94] However, Fragonard was not content to study the paintings that adorned the homes of wealthy Parisian collectors. His knowledge was supplemented by travel; to date only one journey, in 1773, is documented (see, for example, cat. 52), but it was probably preceded by at least one other. Such a trip was not only an occasion for the artist to admire the works of these masters in their home country. It also enabled him to observe and experience firsthand the vast Dutch panoramas, with their low skies full of heavy clouds, their bronze-tinted vegetation, and their changing light. Many of these elements were so thoroughly assimilated by Fragonard that we see them expressed in numerous pastiches, some of which even had the honor of being hung as pendants to the paintings of his northern predecessors.[95] The attraction to Dutch landscape, pervasive among artists and collectors during this period, led him to experiment with new media and supports, passing easily from one to the other, in versions that were often uniform in size. For example, we know of three versions of *The Torrent*: an oil on paper (27 × 37 cm), an oil on canvas that is five centimeters larger in both dimensions, and a gouache that is slightly larger still.[96] In this category of landscapes in the Dutch style, we can point to only two cases of drawings that could possibly be considered preparatory. They relate to two paintings that were for a time kept together as pendants and are known under the titles *Stormy Weather* and *The Drinking Trough*.[97] For each painting there is a wash drawing over a light sketch in black chalk, in an oblong format (see, for example, cat. 46, titled *Sketch of "Landscape with Stormy Sky"*).[98] The styles of the two studies and probably their dates differ. But each one essentially focuses on the

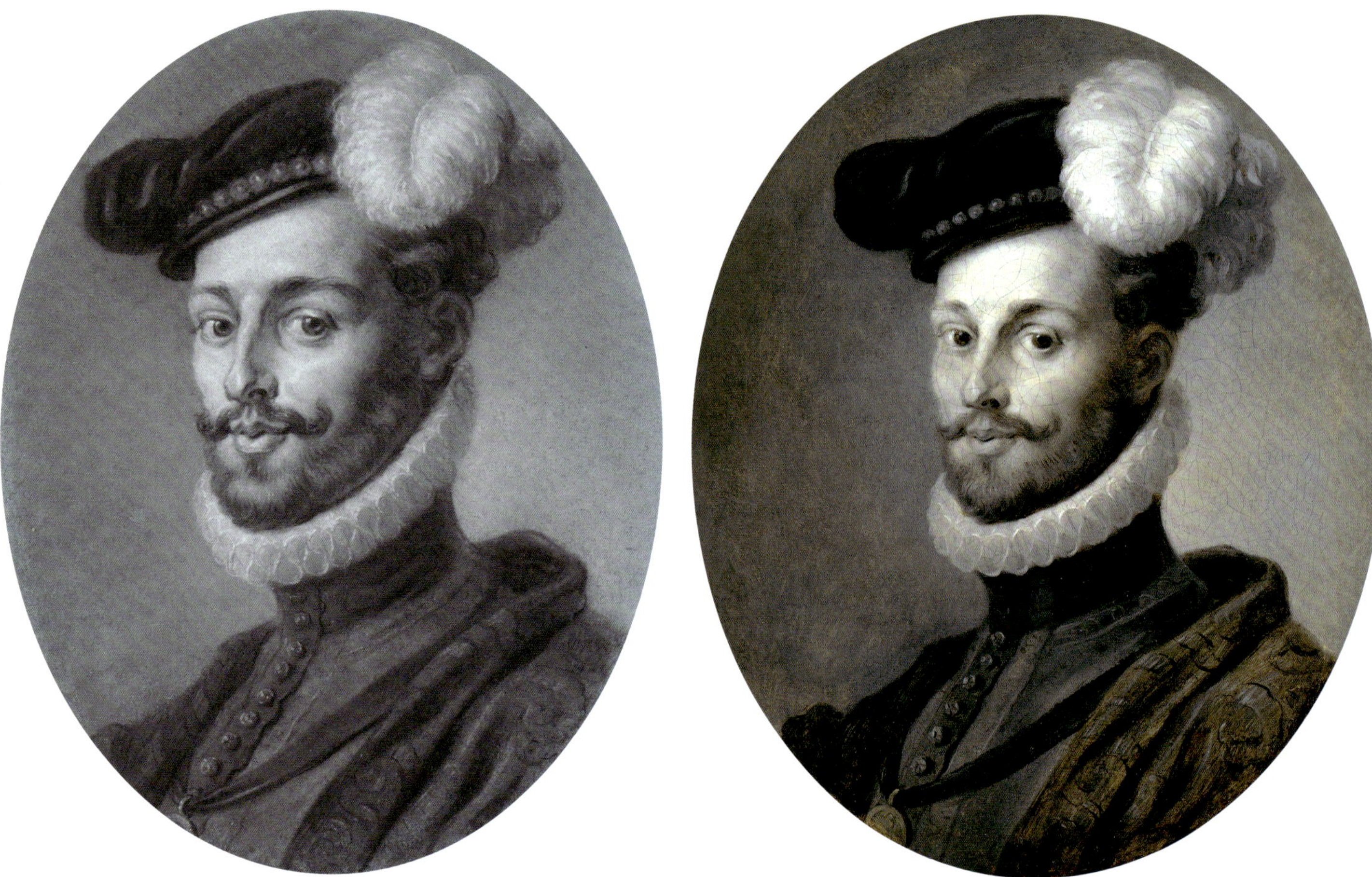

Fig. 40. Jean Honoré Fragonard, *Portrait of François de Bourbon, Comte d'Enghien*, ca. 1770–73. Pastel, 11½ × 9⅛ in. (29.2 × 23.2 cm). Private collection

Fig. 41. Jean Honoré Fragonard, *Portrait of François de Bourbon, Comte d'Enghien*, ca. 1770–73. Oil on canvas, 16⅝ × 14¼ in. (42 × 36 cm). Musée Jean-Honoré Fragonard, Hélène and Jean-François Costa Collection, Grasse

description of nature, with less attention paid, in comparison to the paintings, to the little, indistinct figures and the flocks of sheep that blend into the landscape. The mix of subtly nuanced brown and gray washes gives the sketch of *Landscape with Stormy Sky* the character of a watercolor. Indeed, it was in the medium of watercolor that the artist chose to make repetitions of the two finished paintings (see, for example, cat. 47). In both cases—oil and watercolor—he moved away from the more horizontal format of the wash versions, opting instead for proportions closer to square, which is reminiscent of Northern models. Despite the similarity of the compositions of the painted and watercolor versions, the change in medium yielded quite different results. While the heavy gray clouds and dark wooded areas in the painted version of *The Drinking Trough* are reminiscent of Ruisdael, the light shades and the feeling of coolness that emerge from the watercolor prefigure artists such as Thomas Gainsborough or Richard Parkes Bonington.[99]

In this survey of Fragonard's various methods, mention should be made of pastel, a technique in which he indulged alongside painting. Only a handful of his pastels are known today, making them difficult to discuss, but contemporary sources inform us that several had subjects identical to those of his recorded paintings. One example is the pastel version of *Les petites curieuses*,[100] the description of which, when it was sold at auction in 1780, tells us that it was larger than the little picture of the same subject painted on wood.[101] The discovery of fifteen grisaille portraits in pastel on blue paper, relating to the publication *L'histoire de la maison des Bourbon* by Joseph Louis Ripault Désormeaux, opens new perspectives for study. This previously unknown series comprises five portrait drawings that were the basis for prints reproduced in the publication, as well as ten others that were never engraved.[102] That the artist should have chosen this medium for portraits is not insignificant. The pastel version of *François de Bourbon, Comte d'Enghien* rivals its painted version in finesse and subtlety, the one seeming to be the mirror of the other (figs. 40, 41).[103]

In case after case, the various links between Fragonard's drawings and paintings are revealed to be ever more puzzling and complex. Just as we often hesitate to declare whether a painting is a sketch or a finished work, it is difficult to affirm whether a particular drawing precedes or follows a related painting in execution. The drawings that precede his paintings are not systematically preparatory; likewise, the terms *copy* and *repetition* seem ill suited and overly reductive for describing those made after paintings. It is preferable to speak of correspondences, a term that obviates the need to define precisely the status of individual works. As Jean-Pierre Cuzin has rightly observed, Fragonard enjoyed "being at odds with the typical process of the development of a work," proceeding instead "in a series of rebounds, by varying dimensions and employing techniques ranging from traditional to unconventional."[104] The liberties that the artist took seem to be as much a consequence of his independent character as of his completely exceptional mastery of different techniques. In the same way that he freed himself from the constraints of the Académie by abandoning the reception piece that would have made him a full member of the institution, he liberated himself from traditional studio practices. Playing with techniques, formats, and supports, he established a form of parity between drawings and paintings. Each work was an occasion to experiment, and this multiplicity of approaches is, in a way, his trademark. An analysis of the few sheets connected in one way or another to his paintings sheds some light on Fragonard's studio and his methods. From this emerges the image of an artist who is much more preoccupied with the development of his works than we might have thought. Nor should we mistake the feverishness of his chalk or the speed of his brush for carelessness. Despite the incomplete evidence available to us, we can follow the artist's progression and imagine the considerations that presided over each new composition, as well as the attention paid to how they would be received. His aim was less to complete a drawing or painting than to apply his talent and techniques toward extracting each subject's full expressive and poetic potential. Thus we grasp why his oeuvre feeds on itself, how his paintings and drawings repeat, reproduce, and engender each other. This play of echoes and correspondences reveals the curiosity of an artist in search of new experiences, exploring every possible combination to surprise and enchant his audience.[105]

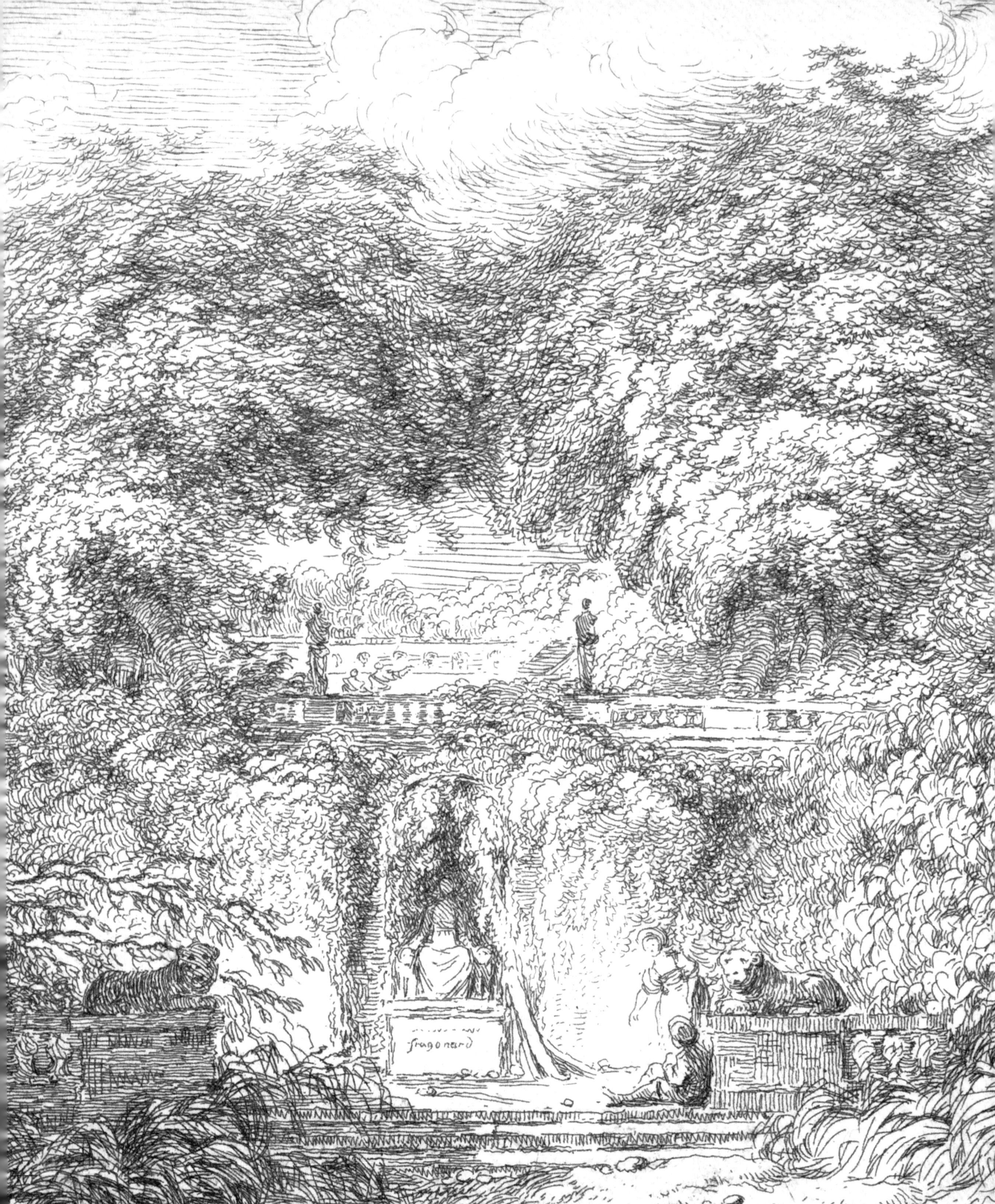
fragonard

Originals, Copies, Mirrors, and Multiples

Perrin Stein

The words *original* and *copy*, when applied to drawings by Fragonard, are both red herrings, concepts that have served to cloud rather than illuminate our understanding of his creative process. As Jean-Pierre Cuzin and Marie-Anne Dupuy-Vachey have articulated in recent years,[1] Fragonard was a nonlinear artist. If conventional academic practice dictated a methodical progression—from *première pensée* (initial sketch), to compositional study, to figure studies based on posed models, to a finished canvas whose composition might later be recorded and disseminated through reproductive prints—Fragonard's working method followed an entirely different model. An apt analogy is to the musical composer whose inventiveness finds expression in the reprise and variation of themes,[2] creating an ever more rich and layered universe where a work is neither truly original nor truly a copy.

The majority of Fragonard's drawings, as Dupuy-Vachey argues in "Every Possible Combination" in this volume, were not made as means to an end, as disposable steps in the creation of a painting. Works treating the same subject in a range of media and techniques should be seen as a series or a constellation of works exploring pictorial effect, rather than as a methodical progression toward a painted canvas. Cuzin described this lifelong bent for variation and mutability as "un processus de rebonds" (a series of rebounds or process of revisiting) and proposed using the term *series* more expansively to encompass the practice of repetition and the creation of multiples. His phrase "reprises en écho" (versions as echoes) captures the amorphous connections among certain works that have long confounded attempts to establish firm chronologies.[3] This essay will elaborate upon these perspectives, building on the work of Cuzin and Dupuy-Vachey to present Fragonard's works on paper—especially those from the traditionally marginalized categories of copy, counterproof, and etching—not as footnotes, secondary to his painted oeuvre, but as vital components of an artistic enterprise in which iteration and invention were closely intertwined concepts.

One implication of this notion of series as exploration, rather than sequence, is that it opens the door to a new understanding of the place of etching in Fragonard's oeuvre. Throughout his career, he was driven to plumb the pictorial possibilities of his compositions by reprising them in different scales, media, and techniques. Prints were an integral component of this method of working, not simply the records of finished works in other media. On only one occasion did he market a print for sale (cat. 84);

the others can be situated in noncommercial contexts—either in the atelier as part of the pedagogical relationship between artist and student or in the milieu of the *amateur*, where the practice of etching was a pursuit embedded in friendship and closely tied to connoisseurship and collecting.[4] Over the course of three decades, Fragonard made three distinct forays into printmaking: first, as a student of François Boucher; second, as part of an extended collaboration with his friend and patron Jean Claude Richard, the abbé de Saint-Non; and third, as the teacher of his young sister-in-law, the aspiring artist Marguerite Gérard.

The idea of a creative model that draws inspiration from revisiting compositions while introducing adjustments and changes also prompts us to re-evaluate Fragonard's copies after other artists. His copies, whether in oil paint, chalk, brown wash, or etching, span in date from his student years to his maturity. Almost none are straightforward records. They express, through the artist's choices, excerpts, omissions, and revisions, an engagement with art of the past that often went beyond emulation toward something closer to a dialogue or rivalry. He copied what he admired and what he thought he might later find useful, but he could rarely refrain from introducing "improvements," thereby making the work his own. Altering the compositions of earlier masters led to a deeper assimilation of their styles and motifs to the point where borrowing elided with invention. In this way, we often perceive mature works by Fragonard as steeped in the manner of a Tiepolo or a Ruisdael, without being able to point to a specific borrowing. The traditional hierarchy of dominant original and subservient copy was thus subverted, even overturned, as Fragonard absorbed and then subsumed the manners of the painters he admired. It is telling that the collector and author Edmond de Goncourt, in describing how Fragonard asserted his control over earlier masters, adopted the language of sexual conquest:

> Having once discovered the more accessible charms of these decadents, Fragonard lived in their company. He studied, questioned, copied, penetrated them. He entered into their works and might almost be said to have despoiled them. From Tiepolo, he took his cleverness and his scintillation; from Solimena he borrowed the sensuousness of his brushwork; from Pietro da Cortona, his trembling sunbeams, his uncertain, dancing light; and from Baroccio, his miraculous dabblings and the floating vagueness of his paint. [In this] passionate labour . . . he held the masters he loved in the close embrace of his emulation.[5]

One of the most basic methods of experimenting with variations on a composition was to reverse it. Reversals typically had their origin in a mechanical process such as printmaking or counterproofing, in which a fresh sheet of paper was pressed against an inked plate or chalk drawing and, when the elements were separated, the transfer naturally mirrored the original. There were many uses for such mirror images. By reversing chalk studies, a painter could multiply his repertoire of studies, poses, and compositions for future reference or have extras to sell or give as gifts. For printmakers, too, reversed images were useful to anticipate the mirroring nature of the printing process, especially when it was desired for the print to be in the same direction as the original. As a way to see a composition with fresh eyes, a counterproof might play a critical role in the genesis of a painting,[6] or it might simply become the basis for a new version, as in Fragonard's sanguine counterproofs richly reworked in brown wash to create sheets that not only mirror but build on the original. Fragonard was not alone in seeing the benefits of mirror images; indeed, for both his friend and fellow student Hubert Robert and their teacher in Rome, Charles Joseph Natoire, the practice of exchanging and reworking counterproofs was closely linked to friendship, pedagogy, and profit.

Both etching and counterproofing are, at their essence, mechanical processes that transfer a medium, chalk or ink, from one support to another, creating either a new variant or a base for a reworked version. This mode of generating works may well have spurred Fragonard to explore other means of transfer, from incising to the use of the pantograph, which seem to have entered his technical repertoire beginning in the mid-1770s.

ETCHING AND ASSIMILATION: PRINTMAKING IN BOUCHER'S STUDIO

The key to understanding how copying became, for Fragonard, the springboard of invention is to be found in the working methods of his master, François Boucher. Only in recent decades have scholars begun to piece together the vast underpinning of borrowing that fueled Boucher's artistic hegemony as the leading painter of the high Rococo. In my research I have discovered a consistent practice of adapting motifs from Chinese prints, ceramics, and objets d'art for his chinoiserie production,[7] and Françoise Joulie has documented a steady habit of copying and adapting motifs from Northern European paintings, drawings, and prints.[8] Alastair Laing and Jamie Mulherron are at work on a catalogue raisonné that will no doubt reveal many more such cases. Boucher's contribution, of course, is not diminished by this tendency to absorb and assimilate a broad range of influences and motifs; his appropriations are entirely consistent with the Rococo's voracious appetite for otherness, taking elements of exotica, the natural world (shells, plants, animals), and seventeenth-century art, both northern and southern, and spinning them all into an aesthetic of gilt and arabesques.[9]

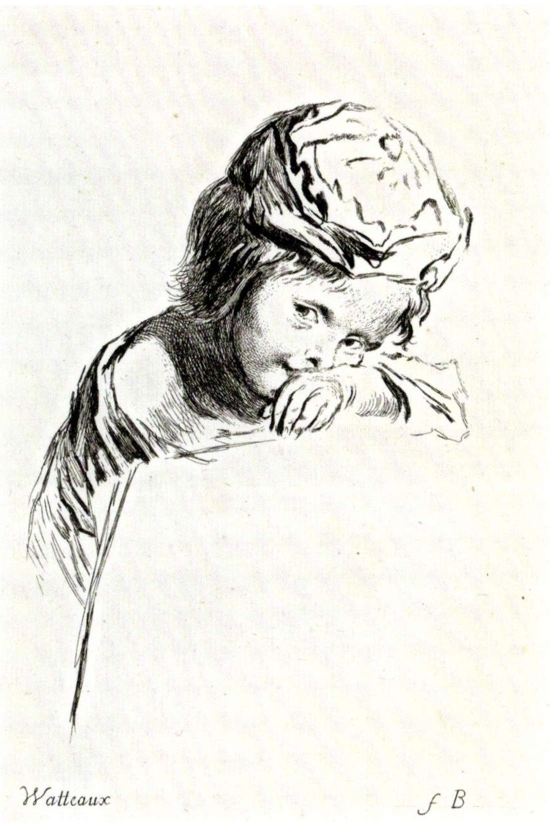

Fig. 42. François Boucher (French, 1703–1770), after Antoine Watteau (French, 1684–1721), *Bust of a Child Wearing a Hat*, ca. 1722–26. Etching, plate: 6⅞ × 4¾ in. (17.3 × 12 cm). The Metropolitan Museum of Art, New York, Harris Brisbane Dick Fund, 1928 (28.100.1[83])

Financial need had first introduced Boucher to the etching needle, when he was hired in his youth by Jean de Jullienne to make etchings—more than one hundred—after the drawings of Antoine Watteau.[10] In these, Boucher's touch is light and unlabored, as one sees in his etching (fig. 42) of Watteau's quickly drawn red and white chalk sketch of a playful child, one of two studies on a sheet (ca. 1715–16, Musée du Louvre, Paris).[11] In contrast to the highly faithful reproductive prints of this period, Boucher's etchings after Watteau suggest themselves as studies, interpretations, and homages—evidence of a young artist learning through emulation just as he would have from a living master.

Years later, during the period when Fragonard was associated with his studio—about 1748–56—Boucher was well aware of the power of reproductive prints to

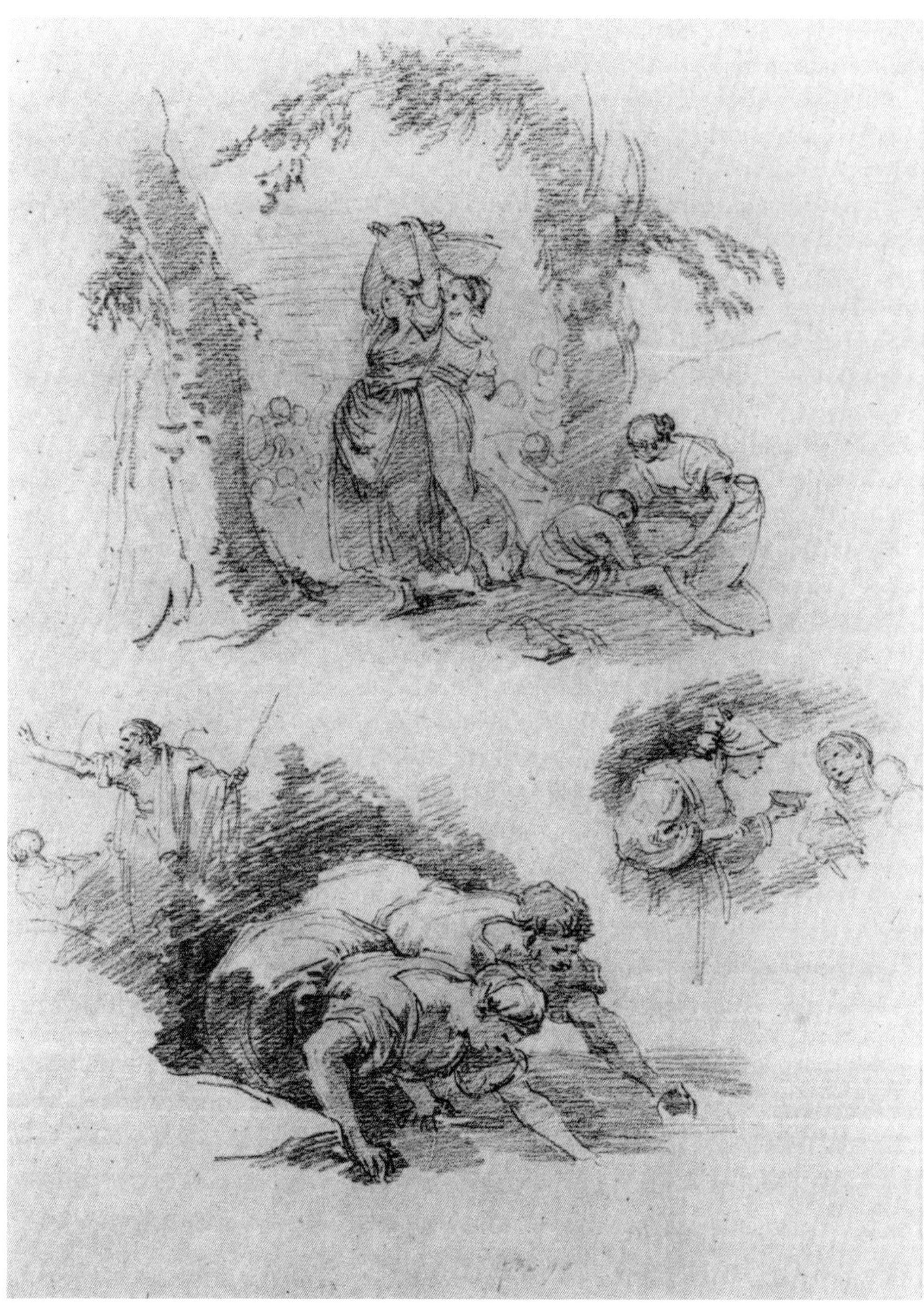

Fig. 43. Jean Honoré Fragonard, after Sebastiano Ricci (Italian, 1659–1734), *Studies of Washerwomen,* 1761. Black chalk, 11⅛ × 8⅛ in. (28.3 × 20.4 cm). Private collection, France

dynamic was, the fact that a true collaboration developed is evident in the complex afterlife of the drawings in the form of counterproofs, etchings, and aquatints, as the two artists, working either together or separately over a number of years, explored the copies' potential for regeneration through many iterations of reversal and reworking.

The counterproofing of the drawings must have begun not long after Fragonard's return to Paris in September of 1761. This process, whereby a damp sheet of blank paper was laid on the drawing and then run through a printing press, resulting in

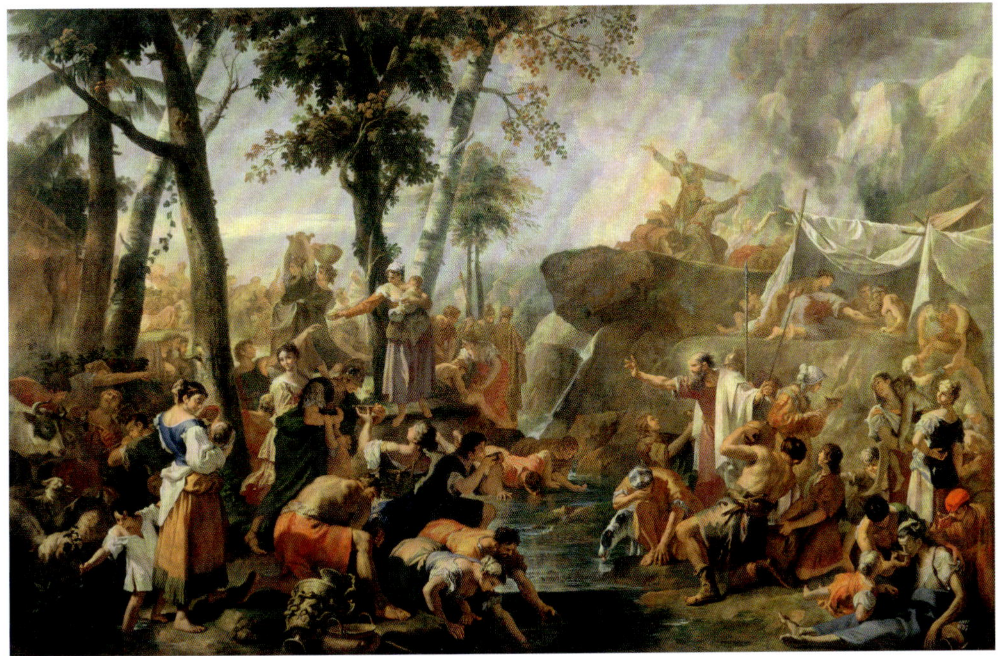

Fig. 44. Sebastiano Ricci (Italian, 1659–1734), *Moses Striking the Rock*, ca. 1727–29. Oil on canvas, 17 ft. 4¼ in. × 27 ft. 2⅜ in. (53 × 83 m). Fondazione Giorgio Cini, on deposit at the Gallerie dell'Accademia, Venice (952)

the transfer of a paler image in the opposite sense of the original, presumably took place under the supervision of Saint-Non, as he owned a press,[32] and it is in his hand that the chalk annotations identifying the source or location of each copy, illegible in reverse, were rewritten in ink.[33] The counterproofs were then reworked in black chalk to freshen and strengthen the designs (see cat. 7). Scholars have hesitated to claim who was responsible for the reworking,[34] although, for the most part, there is little reason to doubt that it was done by Fragonard himself.

Presumably the impetus for the counterproofing, a considerable task given the number of copies, was for Fragonard and Saint-Non to each have a set of the drawings. Even if Saint-Non had great plans to publish the series, Fragonard was the first to make etchings inspired by the Italian copy drawings, albeit in an informal and experimental vein (see cats. 13–25). His interest in returning to the technique he had learned in Boucher's studio must have been piqued by Saint-Non, who had made prints after Boucher and Le Prince before departing for Italy and took up etching again shortly after returning to Paris—this time choosing as models drawings by Hubert Robert and Fragonard, such as the *The Stubborn Donkey*, dated 1762 (fig. 45).[35]

We have no evidence that Fragonard intended the sixteen etchings after his Italian copies to be a commercial venture. Only ten of the sixteen are signed, and only one with the artist's full last name; the nine others bear only the playful abbreviation "frago," suggesting the casual milieu in which *amateurs* made and exchanged etchings as gifts.[36] The plates selected for etching were not of uniform dimensions, and the direction of the image, whether the same as the original or the reverse, seems to have been of little concern, as there are examples of each in the group.

With his own copy drawings as models, and the compositions therefore already established, Fragonard seems to have reveled in the possibilities of the etching needle. Unlike the black chalk sketches, which were made with the straightforward

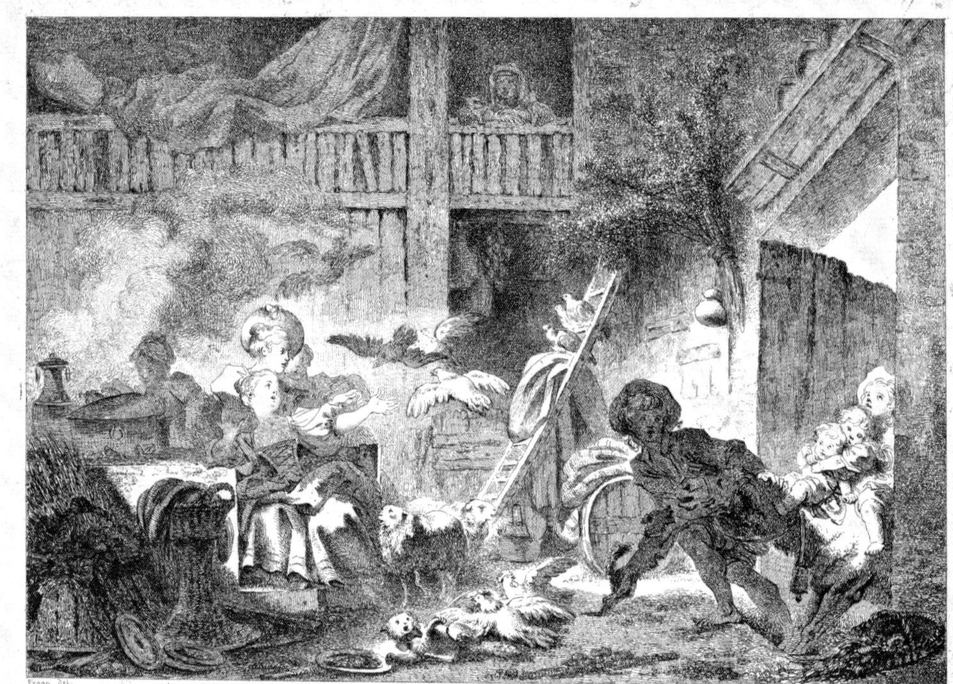

Fig. 45. Jean Claude Richard, abbé de Saint-Non (French, 1727–1791), after Jean Honoré Fragonard, *The Stubborn Donkey*, 1762. Etching, plate: 8 × 11⅜ in. (20.2 × 28.8 cm). The New York Public Library, New York, Purchase, 1994, with funds given in memory of Lucien Goldschmidt

technique of drawing the contours of the figures and then adding areas of tone with parallel hatching, the etched copies of Italian masters are richly textured and tactile. Hatching lines are rarely straight; instead, they bend and wiggle to follow the forms of the shapes they shade. The ease with which he drew with a stylus on a prepared copperplate is fully evident in the energized web of staccato marks, manifesting, even on a tiny scale, the qualities of "fire" and brio much admired by Fragonard's contemporaries. Although some of this taste for varied patterns of etched lines perhaps came from Saint-Non's technique, in the eyes of his contemporaries, Fragonard as a printmaker was closest to the Italian etchers of the seventeenth century. Charles Louis François Lecarpentier, a professor of painting and drawing in Rouen, declared in a eulogy to Fragonard read on October 16, 1806: "The charming etchings that he made in an exquisite taste will be placed alongside those of Benedetto [Castiglione], of Salvator [Rosa], and of the best artists in this genre."[37] Lecarpentier's admiration for this aspect of Fragonard's oeuvre is expressed also in his portrait of the artist (see p. 3, fig. 2). Etched in 1803 after a likeness by Marguerite Gérard, the portrait is framed by an abundance of foliage, simultaneously quoting Fragonard's *Bacchanal* prints (cats. 26–29) and the Italian etchers who inspired them.

Undertaken a full decade later, Saint-Non's project of etching the Italian copies was more orderly. He must have used the original drawings, rather than the counterproofs, as his models, and he made no effort to reverse them; for the most part, his prints tend to be in reverse of the original Italian paintings even when the models were well known.[38] He chose to use the newly developed technique of aquatint, an etching process that replicated the effects of wash drawings (see p. 86, fig. 66). Translating Fragonard's chalk sketches to wash-manner prints must have had a certain playful

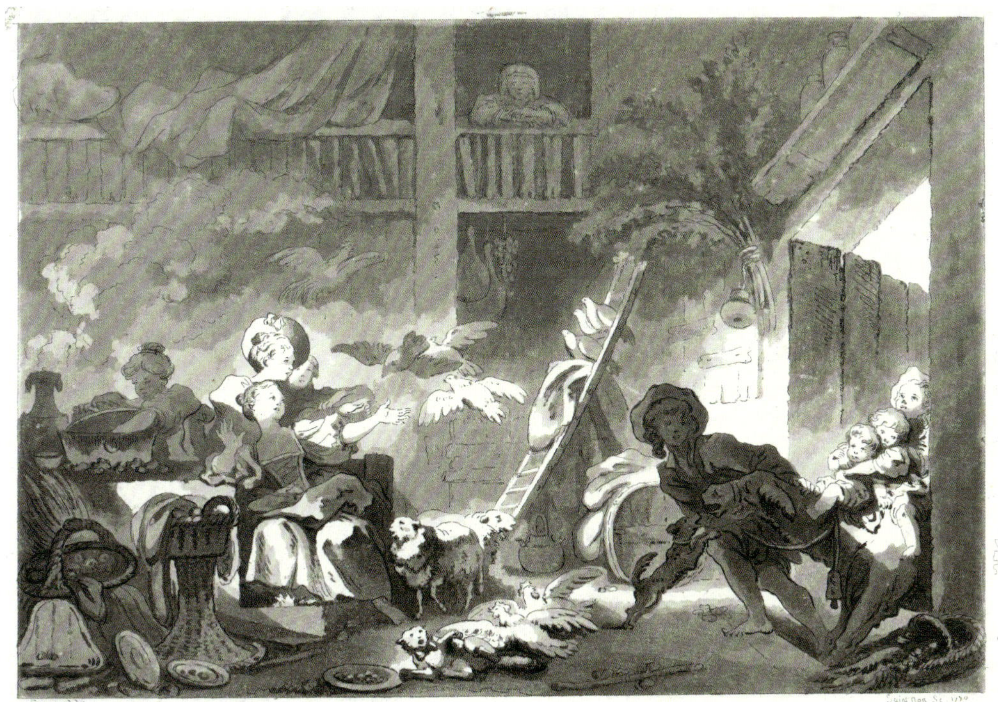

Fig. 46. Jean Claude Richard, abbé de Saint-Non (French, 1727–1791), after Jean Honoré Fragonard, *The Stubborn Donkey*, 1770. Etching and aquatint, plate: 7¾ × 11 in. (19.5 × 27.8 cm). The Metropolitan Museum of Art, New York, The Elisha Whittelsey Collection, The Elisha Whittelsey Fund, 1969 (69.574.13)

appeal. An appreciation for the mutability of a composition as it is both echoed and transformed by an iteration in a new medium must also account for the impulse behind Saint-Non's second treatment of *The Stubborn Donkey*, this time in aquatint (fig. 46).[39] The inherent whimsy of the suites of prints comes across as well in their unprepossessing titles: *Griffonis* (scribbles) and *Fragments* (fragments).[40] Far more conventional in format was Saint-Non's sumptuous four-volume travel guide, *Voyage pittoresque, ou description des royaumes de Naples et de Sicile* (1781–86), for which he hired professional reproductive printmakers to illustrate the works of art. For this publication, which featured engravings of whole compositions, Saint-Non even had to commission intermediary draftsman to rework Fragonard's drawings to the expected high level of finish.[41] Yet, the seemingly lighthearted *Griffonis* and *Fragments* would have resonated with *amateurs* in Saint-Non's circle. A variant of the word *griffoni* was used by the writer and collector Antoine Joseph Dézallier d'Argenville in his "Discours préliminaire sur la connoissance des desseins et des tableaux" (1762), which distinguished true connoisseurs, who could appreciate all drawings, including, "griffonnemens faits de rien" (scribbles made of nothing), from the "demi-connoisseurs," who appreciated only finished drawings.[42]

REVERSALS AND REVISIONS: REWORKED COUNTERPROOFS

The production of mirror images was not solely the purview of printmakers but a regular activity for draftsmen as well. Natural red chalk, also known as sanguine, reached its apogee as a drawing medium in the second half of the eighteenth century. A greasy and friable material, it produced a powder that, if not "fixed," could be easily smudged. The most expedient means to avoid smudging was to take a counterproof, that is, to place a dampened sheet of white paper directly on the drawing and run the two sheets together through an intaglio printer's press. The process not only removed excess powder from the original drawing but also created a slightly paler mirror image, referred to as a counterproof. Contemporary treatises such as Charles Antoine Jombert's *Méthode pour apprendre le dessein* (1755) and Antoine Joseph Pernety's *Dictionnaire portatif de peinture, sculpture et gravure* (1757) stated the necessity for counterproofing red chalk drawings and offered clear instructions.[43] The result, a mirror-image twin, was not a throwaway but a valued byproduct. For Jombert, the soft, even tones of the counterproof were "even more agreeable in appearance" than those of the original; and Pernety pointed out that the process not only prevents smudging but also generates "two for one."[44] This appreciation for counterproofs as aesthetic objects was shared by the major collectors of the day. One finds a framed counterproof by the sculptor Edme Bouchardon hanging among Jean de Jullienne's best paintings and drawings in his gallery.[45] Pierre Jean Mariette, whose collection focused on drawings and prints, owned a great many counterproofs of sanguines by Bouchardon and often presented them on the same ornate, hand-decorated mounts as other highly valued drawings in his collection (see, for example, fig. 47).[46] Fragonard, who was an infrequent buyer at art auctions with the exception of Boucher's 1771 sale, attended Mariette's sale on November 15, 1775, where he purchased lot 1150: a set of sixty counterproofs after Bouchardon's *Cris de Paris*.[47]

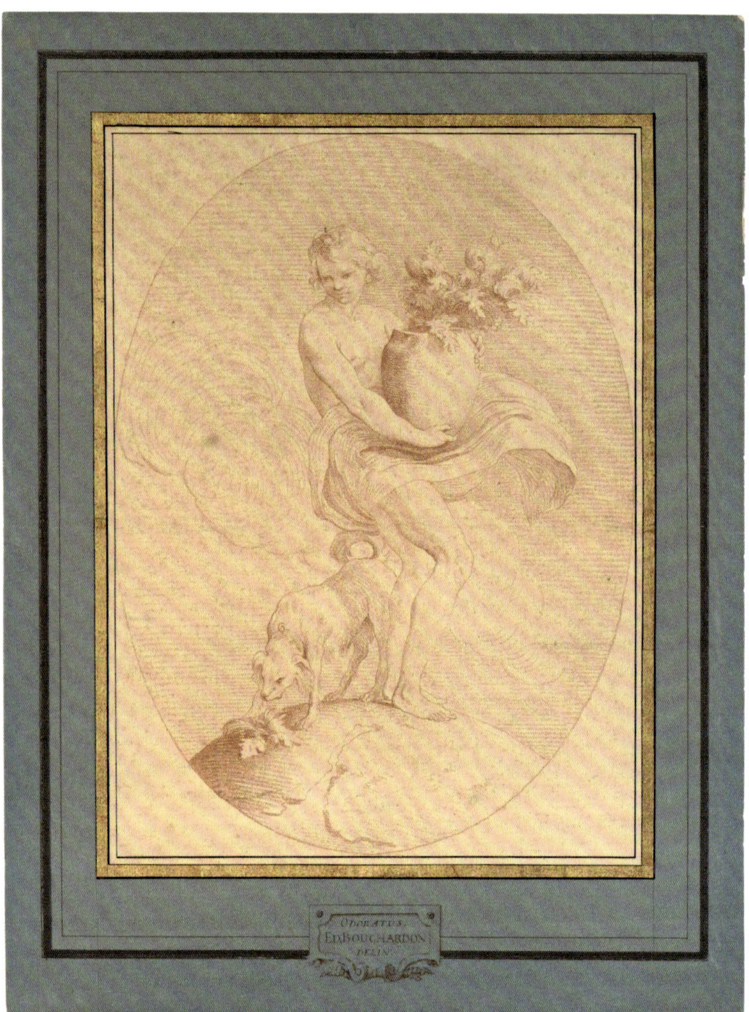

Fig. 47. Edme Bouchardon (French, 1698–1762), *The Sense of Smell*, ca. 1740–50. Red chalk counterproof, 15½ × 11⅝ in. (39.2 × 29.5 cm). The Metropolitan Museum of Art, New York, Harry G. Sperling Fund, 1973 (1973.317.1)

In addition to fixing the powdery red chalk of the original drawings and providing delicate offsets that were prized by contemporary collectors, counterproofs were valuable components of artistic practice for other reasons. They could serve as records of works that had been sold or given away, and they had the potential, by virtue of their reversed direction, to double the number of useful studies in an artist's portfolio. Dézallier d'Argenville noted in 1745 that Watteau had favored red chalk on white paper for his studies in order to have counterproofs, which enabled him to see his subjects from both sides.[48] Counterproofs could also be reworked, either in the same medium (cat. 7) or by adding wash or watercolor to a chalk counterproof (cats. 33 and 35). Modern scholarship has struggled to characterize, and has often devalued, these hybrid works, which straddle the divide between the multiple and the unique. Sarah Catala, in discussing Robert's practice of using counterproofs as the basis for new drawings, makes the case that, though born of a mechanical process of transfer, counterproofs regained their status as autonomous drawings when reworked by the artist's hand.[49]

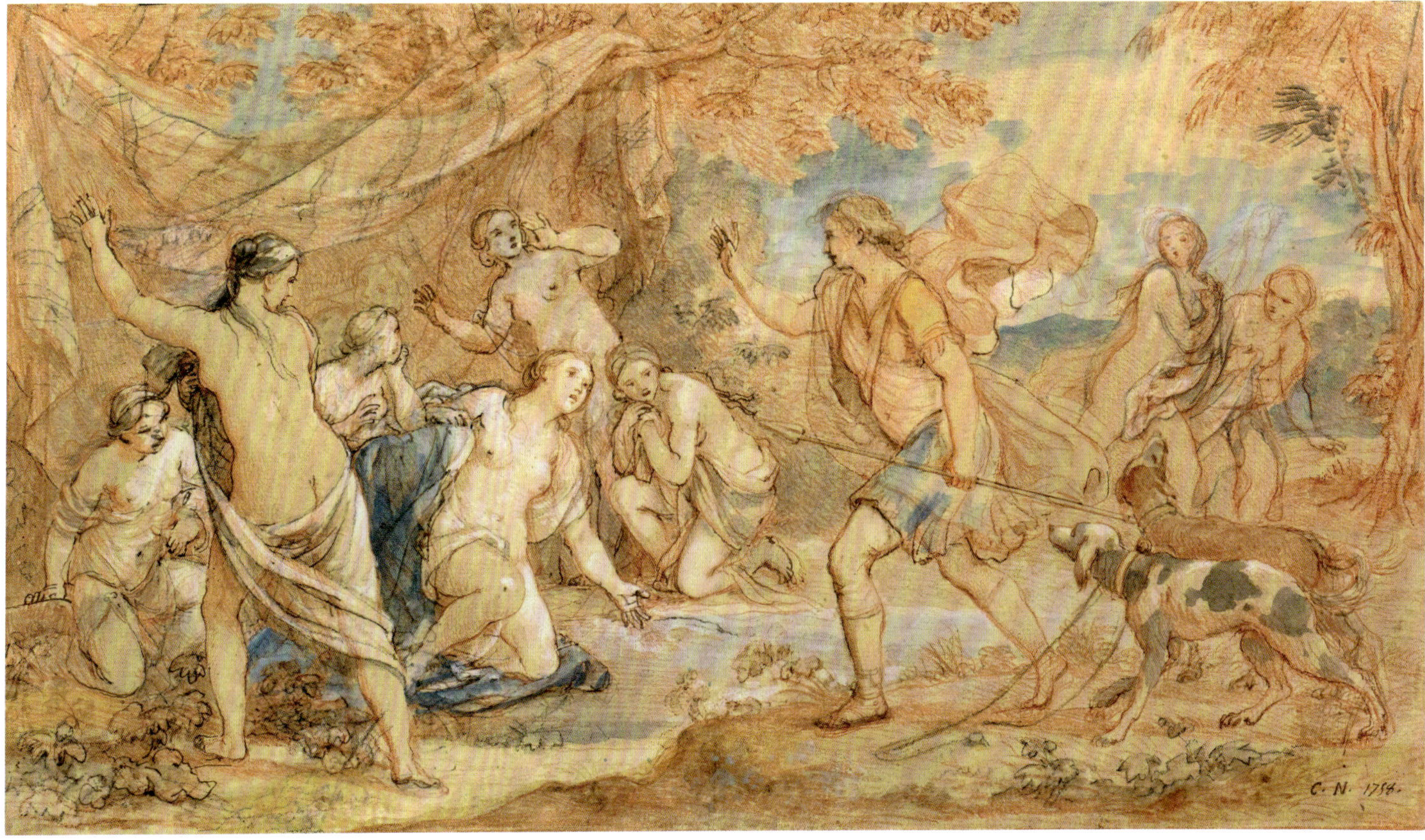

Fig. 48. Charles Joseph Natoire (French, 1700–1777), retouched counterproof of *Diana and Acteon* by an anonymous artist, 1758. Red chalk, pen and brown ink, watercolor, and white gouache over a red chalk counterproof, 10¼ × 14 in. (26 × 35.6 cm). Formerly private collection, New York

Although counterproofs after the drawings of many artists from the second half of the eighteenth century survive—one thinks first of Bouchardon, but also of Jean Simon Berthélemy, François André Vincent, and Louis Roland Trinquesse, among others—only a few artists made the reworking of counterproofs a regular part of their creative process. Fragonard, like Robert and other artists who were pensionnaires at the Académie de France in Rome during Natoire's directorship (1752–75), was exposed to a wide range of possible uses for the technique. From surviving examples, one can deduce that correcting students' drawings and counterproofs by reworking them was a central pillar of Natoire's teaching methods.[50] Their landscape drawings and copies after Italian masters were run through the press, and Natoire drew directly on the resulting counterproofs in pen and ink, brush and wash, and sometimes watercolor or gouache. The nature of these interventions leads us to imagine a number of purposes they may have played. Some were simply a teacher's revisions: moving limbs, correcting anatomy, and so forth.[51] In other instances, Natoire seems to have been demonstrating how one might elaborate a red chalk drawing, or, in the case of a counterproof, its pale mirror image, into a painterly, autonomous sheet. A vivid illustration of these practices can be seen in his elaborate reworking in chalk, pen and brown ink, and watercolor of a counterproof of an anonymous drawing of Diana and Acteon (fig. 48).[52] That he saw fault in the original is evident in his numerous corrections, especially to the poses and proportions of the figures, but the final painterly result must have met his approval, for he initialed and dated the sheet "CN 1758"—

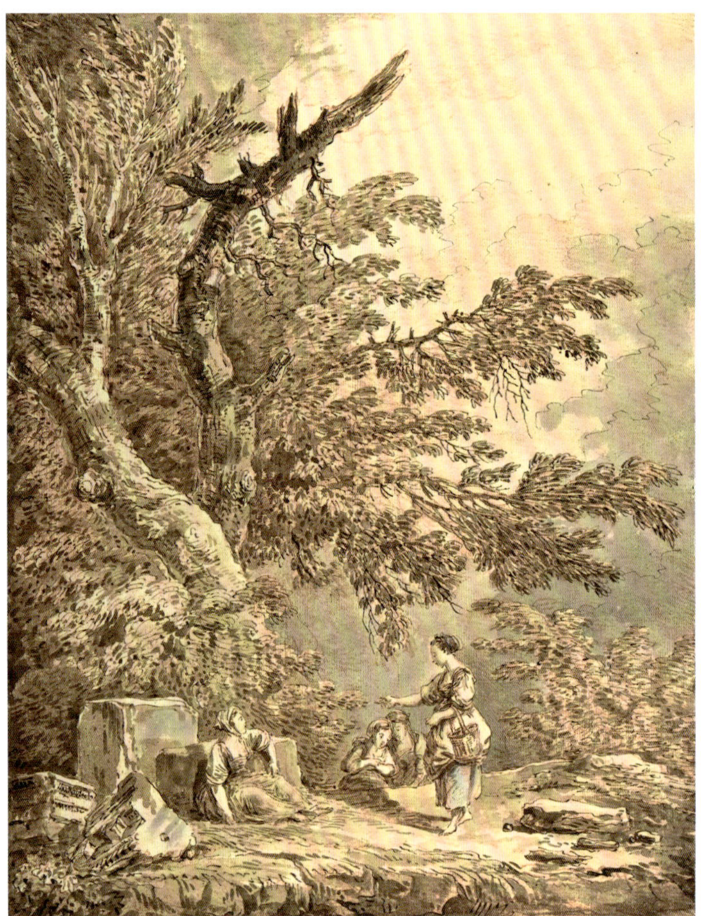

Fig. 49. Hubert Robert (French, 1733–1808), *Young Women in a Landscape with Architectural Fragments*, ca. 1773. Pen and brown ink, with brush and brown, gray, and blue wash, over a red chalk counterproof, 14½ × 11⅜ in. (36.6 × 28.7 cm). The Metropolitan Museum of Art, New York, Bequest of Alexandrine Sinsheimer, 1958 (59.23.70)

evidence that Natoire employed reworked counterproofs as part of his pedagogical practice during the period when Fragonard was a pensionnaire at the Palais Mancini. The fact that he signed and dated it also supports Catala's argument that reworked counterproofs had the stature of finished, autonomous drawings.

The ready availability of a printing press on the premises facilitated a growing role, both social and practical, for the counterproof at the Académie de France.[53] In this setting, which often attracted visiting or expatriate collectors, counterproofs were part of a cultural practice of gift and exchange associated with shared artistic activities, ranging from sketching trips in and around Rome to the drawing of caricatures. Pierre Adrien Pâris, an aspiring architect who often went on expeditions with the painting and sculpture students during his stay in Italy, described in his journal entry for September 19, 1771, drawing landscapes at Tivoli with Berthélemy and then exchanging counterproofs.[54] In this milieu of camaraderie, Vincent made counterproofs of a large number of his caricatures of fellow artists, presumably for similar purposes. Two decades earlier, counterproofs had played an important role in Robert's apparent friendship and collaboration with Jean Robert Ango, a shadowy figure in the orbit of the Académie who seems to have supported himself selling sanguine copies to visiting collectors.[55]

Even in this environment, where French artists in Rome routinely made counterproofs, and put them to myriad uses, Robert's example must have made a particular impression on Fragonard. To record compositions and expand his stock of imagery, Robert counterproofed studies of figures and individual motifs as well as finished drawings, producing hundreds of sheets, many of which survive today. A rich resource, these counterproofs allowed him to dip into the well of his Italian drawings for inspiration throughout his career. Mirror images became the basis, figuratively and literally, for endless variants, as Robert often returned to them, sometimes years later, to rework them with wash or watercolor, generating new compositions. A case in point is *Young Women in a Landscape with Architectural Fragments* (fig. 49), one of a pair of Italianate views—counterproofs reworked in brown ink and watercolor—dated about 1773.[56] And yet, to view this practice with cynicism, as merely a commercial expedient, is perhaps anachronistic. For Catala, this self-referential working method, rooted in repetition and revision, was less a means to exploit a successful formula than a natural result of an ingrained affinity for the fecundity of variation.[57] It is this tendency to see mutability as a springboard for creative regeneration that allies the methodologies of Robert and Fragonard.

In comparison to Robert, whom Marianne Roland Michel dubbed "the champion of the counter-proof,"[58] Fragonard produced reworked counterproofs (aside from those after his Italian copies or illustrations for La Fontaine)[59] that are fewer in

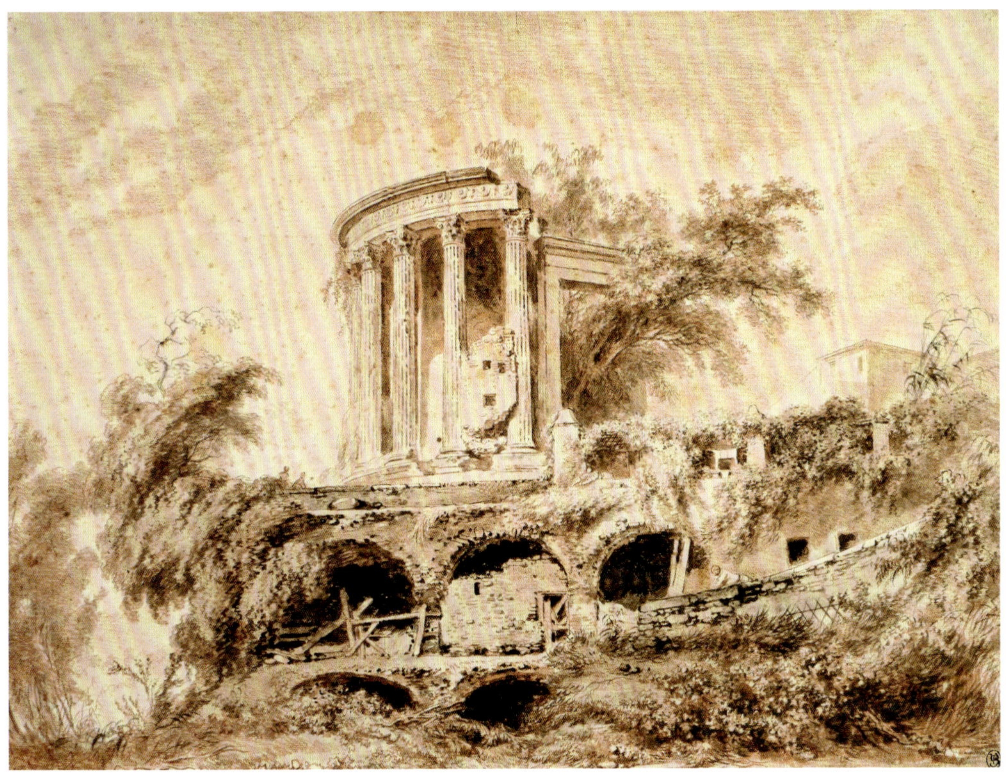

Fig. 50. Jean Honoré Fragonard, *Temple of Vesta at Tivoli*, ca. 1765. Brush and brown wash over a red chalk counterproof, 13½ × 17⅝ in. (34.1 × 45.8 cm). Indiana University Art Museum, Bloomington, Evan F. Lilly Memorial, Gift of Thomas T. Solley (77.54.2)

number but equivalent in ambition and sensibility. For these works, undoubtedly intended for collectors, Fragonard took as his starting point the series of sanguines of Italian gardens made in and around the Villa d'Este in Tivoli. He had exhibited at least two of the original drawings at the Salon of 1765, the first he took part in.[60] According to Saint-Non's biographer, Gabriel Brizard, at this point the collector realized that Fragonard's drawings were greatly admired and fetched extraordinary prices, and he therefore returned to the artist the ones he still had in his possession so that his friend could "benefit from their favor with the public."[61] It may well have been around the same time that Fragonard began to use bister to draw over the counterproofs of this famous group, allowing the rich tones of brown wash to play off the paler chalk armature and achieving a painterly effect unparalleled in his graphic oeuvre. Works such as *View of the Temple of Vesta at Tivoli* (cat. 35) and *The Little Park* (cat. 33) show the artist using pen and brush and two shades of ink to layer all manner of washes, hatching, zigzags, flecks, and dots, creating an animated range of tones and textures; the result is ultimately more sculptural and atmospheric than the original sanguine. If modern audiences have not always embraced this body of work—none were included in the 1987–88 retrospective—Fragonard's contemporaries undoubtedly did. Counterproofs and reworked counterproofs by the artist began to appear in auction catalogues in the 1770s and 1780s. The catalogue entry for lot 170 in the Chabot-Desmarets sale (December 17, 1787), for instance, describes with accuracy and appreciation what may be the version of the *Temple of Vesta at Tivoli* that is today at the Indiana University Art Museum in Bloomington (fig. 50): "a counterproof of a red chalk landscape, vigorously retouched in bister, offering ruined arcades surmounted by a circular temple."[62] Transcending their origins in a mechanical process of transfer, the counterproofs reworked in brown wash are painterly reinventions. As with his copies after Italian masters, Fragonard could not resist making changes, additions, and improvements with every iteration. The process of reversal ultimately set into motion the artist's critical faculties and became the catalyst for a new stage of creativity.[63]

EMULATION AND VIRTUOSITY: COPIES AFTER OLD MASTERS, PART 2

In 1773–74 Fragonard returned to copying with gusto, a mature artist at the height of his powers. Unlike Boucher, for whom copying the drawings of earlier masters was largely a Parisian pastime, a reflection of the pleasure and profit he derived from his access to the great collections of drawings owned by Pierre Crozat and Pierre Jean Mariette,[64] Fragonard tended to embark on campaigns of copying while he traveled. Indeed, his later copies in rich brown wash, often after Northern Baroque paintings, have provided essential clues in the reconstruction and dating of certain journeys.

Beginning with Roger Portalis in 1889, scholars have postulated that Fragonard made one or more trips to the low countries to study Dutch and Flemish masters, an idea supported by surviving sheets and mentions in early sale catalogues, but it was Sophie Raux's identification of an inscription on the verso of a copy after *Crucifixion* by Anthony van Dyck in Mechelen that definitively placed Fragonard in Flanders in the company of his patron Pierre Jacques Onésyme Bergeret de Grancourt in July 1773.[65] Such trips were not uncommon. The admiration for Dutch and Flemish art, having taken root in the 1730s and 1740s, burned bright in the 1760s and 1770s, and many French dealers and collectors made the trip north.[66] Also feeding this burgeoning taste was the painter and dealer Jean-Baptiste Descamps's *La vie des peintres flamands, allemands et hollandois*, which appeared in four volumes between 1753 and 1764.

Fragonard had been steeped in the art of the north from his earliest formation. His teacher, Boucher, collected northern paintings, drawings, and prints, and he made a lifelong habit of copying and adapting them for his own purposes.[67] Fragonard was an active buyer at Boucher's estate sale in 1771, acquiring not only drawings by his former master but many northern works as well, including a painting attributed to Van Dyck and a group of drawings by Rembrandt van Rijn and his school.[68] But perhaps the best evidence of their shared affinity for northern art of the seventeenth century is the painted copy Fragonard made, presumably while still in Boucher's studio, after Rembrandt's *Holy Family*, which was then in the Crozat collection (today in the State Hermitage Museum, Saint Petersburg). From Boucher's posthumous sale, we know Fragonard's early copy remained in Boucher's collection until his death.[69]

Knowing that Fragonard's journey north, or at least his most recent one, had taken place just before he and Bergeret de Grancourt set off for Italy casts the drawings of that more famous trip in a new light. Indeed, their Italian stay can now be seen as bookended by two periods of copying Northern Baroque paintings, first in Holland and Flanders in the summer of 1773 and then in cities such as Vienna and Dresden on their return in 1774. Perhaps these choices reflect Bergeret's taste, but the force of Fragonard's admiration is clearly visible in the gestural brio of sheets such as his copy

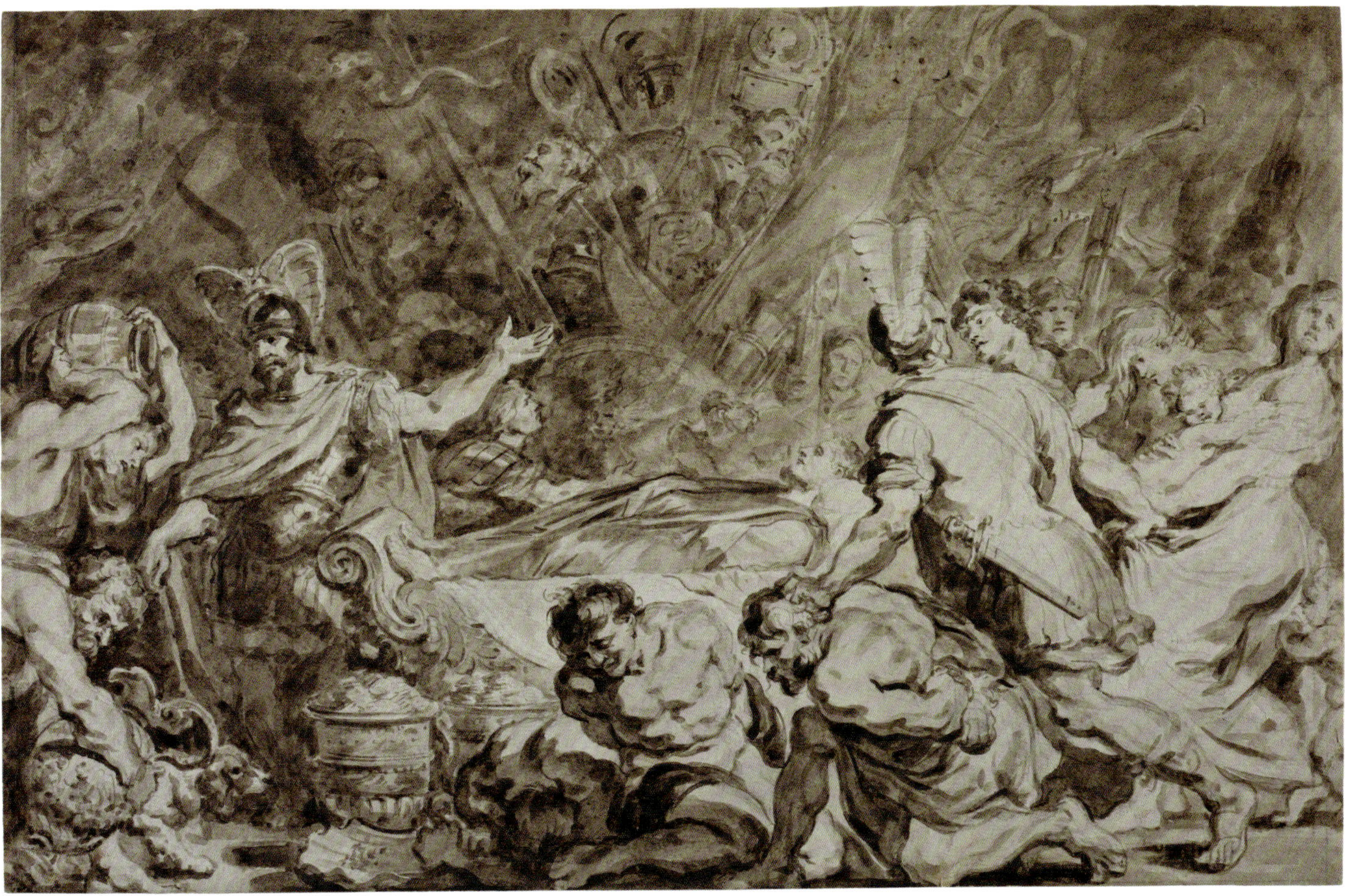

Fig. 51. Jean Honoré Fragonard, after Peter Paul Rubens (Flemish, 1577–1640), *The Funeral of Decius Mus*, 1774. Brush and brown wash over black chalk, 9½ × 14⅞ in. (24 × 37.6 cm). Cleveland Museum of Art, John L. Severance Fund (1980.17)

after Peter Paul Rubens's *The Funeral of Decius Mus* (fig. 51). This time on Italian soil, it seemed that the streets and gardens held more appeal than the interiors of churches and palaces.[70] The artist's medium of choice had also changed since his first visit. His copies were now in freely worked layers of brown wash over black chalk under-drawing, instead of the more easily portable chalk. Their virtuoso handling clearly transcends the goals of simply recording a composition and creating an aide-mémoire. They do not so much capture as re-create the painterly technique of artists known for free brushwork and brilliant color and contrast.

Fragonard's quest to emulate and match the talents of earlier masters—a kind of aesthetic sparring—reflects the milieu of contemporary collecting, in which an *amateur* seeking to promote the French school might commission a contemporary artist to paint or draw a pendant for an existing work in his collection.[71] A related example of this shared level of sophistication between an artist and his patron is the marquis de Véri's famous commission from Fragonard of *The Bolt* (ca. 1777–78, p. 27, fig. 20) to pair with his earlier canvas *The Adoration of the Shepherds* (ca. 1775, p. 32, fig. 26). While most earlier writers remarked on the daring disparity of subjects—the pairing of a lustful boudoir scene with the birth of Christ—Colin Bailey has seen the dichotomy through the lens of connoisseurship, as a contrast between the painterly chiaroscuro of Rembrandt and the smooth, polished facture of Gerard ter Borch or Gabriel Metsu.[72]

The clear contrast in technique between the black chalk copies after earlier masters made in the company of Saint-Non in 1761 and the painterly brown wash copies made while traveling with Bergeret in 1773–74 cannot be accounted for solely by stylistic evolution. For one thing, on his second Italian trip Fragonard was no longer excerpting figures and vignettes for future use. Nor is there any indication that the later copies were intended as models for prints. Instead, they give the impression of autonomous, finished works, their painterly manner emulating the brio of Rubens's brushwork and the strong contrast of light effects favored by painters of the Northern Baroque. Confirmation of the status of these copies as objects of delectation for *amateurs* and collectors can be found in early auction catalogues. The 1778 sale of the miniaturist Jean Antoine Gros, the father of the painter Baron Gros, included seven of Fragonard's wash copies after Northern Baroque masters, suggesting that they must have gone from the artist's portfolios to the art market quite quickly. Moreover, they were all described as framed "under glass," suggesting that, despite their status as copies, they were deemed fit for display on the wall.[73]

REPRODUCTION AND REINVENTION: PRINTMAKING WITH MARGUERITE GÉRARD

Fragonard's third and final foray into printmaking came relatively late in his career. This time he chose for models not his black chalk studies but his large, finished brown wash drawings, often of rustic family scenes.[74] Echoing his initiation as a student in Boucher's studio (cat. 1), his etchings of 1778 can be situated in the context of

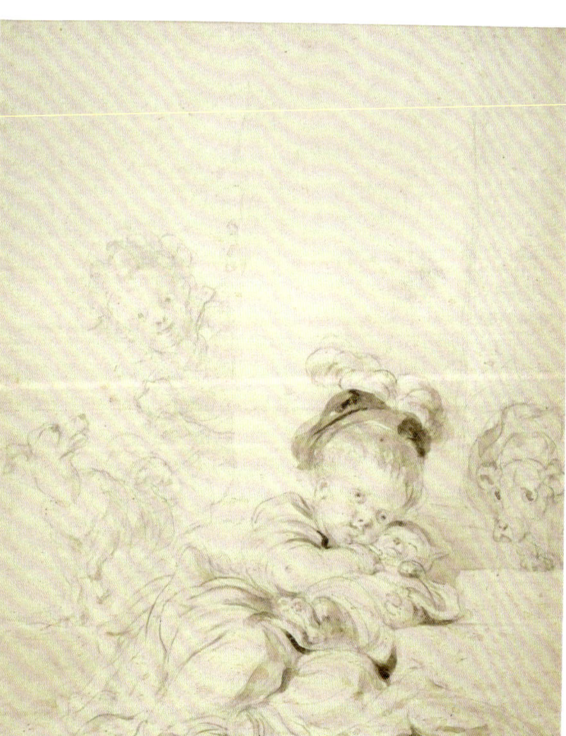

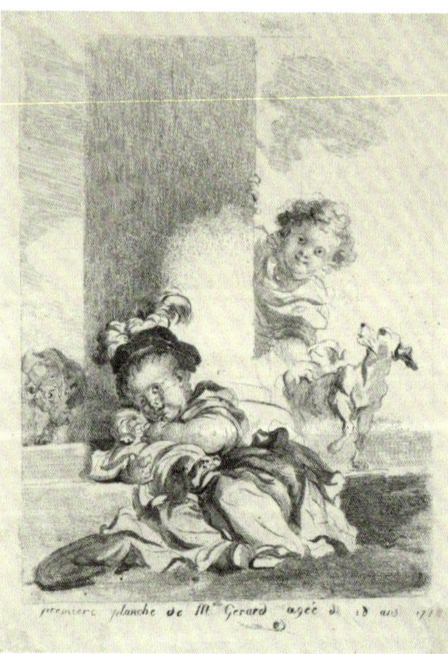

Fig. 52. Jean Honoré Fragonard, *The Swaddled Cat*, ca. 1777. Brush and brown wash over black chalk underdrawing, 17⅞ × 13⅝ in. (45.4 × 34.5 cm). Musée du Louvre, Paris (RF 42670)

Fig. 53. Marguerite Gérard (French, 1761–1837), *The Swaddled Cat*, 1778. Etching, 10⅜ × 7½ in. (26.1 × 19.1 cm). Art Institute of Chicago, Gift of Dorothy Braude Edinburg to the Harry B. and Bessie K. Braude Memorial Collection (2013.543)

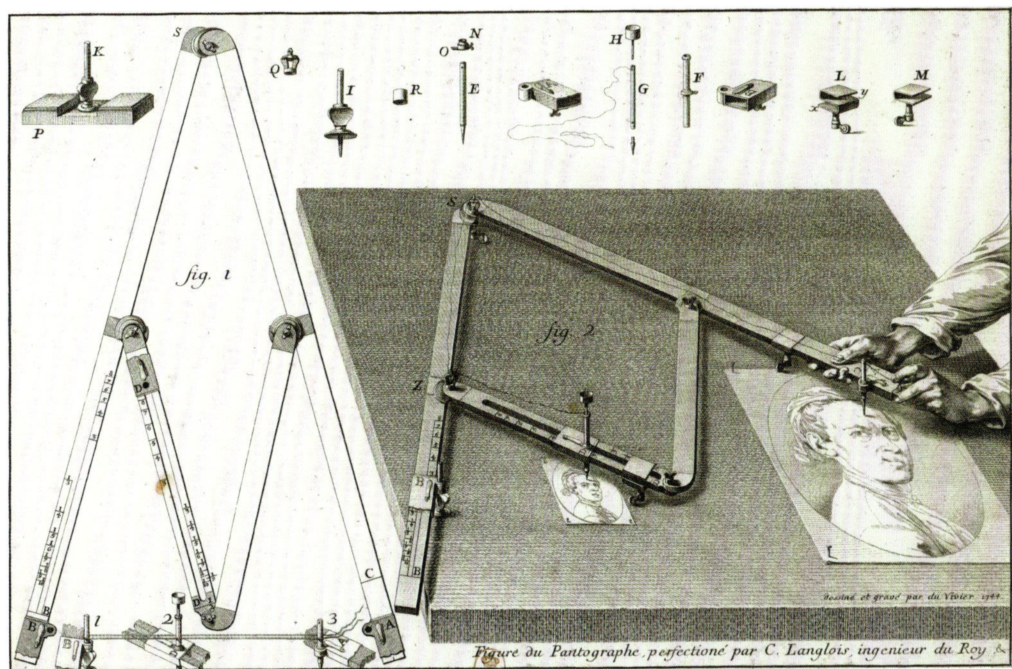

Fig. 54. Jean Duvivier, *Figure du pantographe*, 1744. Engraving. Bibliothèque nationale de France, Paris (Estampes, AA3 Duvivier)

artistic training, although this time Fragonard was the teacher and his sister-in-law, Marguerite Gérard, was the student. In a brief but intense joint project, lasting just under a year, Fragonard made four prints and Gérard five. In two cases, they treated the same subject. Although they clearly worked together, the long-held idea that certain plates were collaborations worked by two hands has been rejected by me and my colleague Rena Hoisington.[75]

These late prints deserve our attention not only as spectacular examples of the aesthetic and expressive potential of the medium in the hands of a mature artist but also for the light they cast on Fragonard's evolving style and working methods, an insight that comes in part from the opportunity to see his prints in conjunction with the initially naïve, but increasingly accomplished, etchings made by the teenage Gérard. It is revealing, for instance, that in the two cases where the artists worked, presumably in tandem, after the same model drawing (both of which are now lost), the placement and contours of the forms on the plate are exactly aligned (see cat. 83). Moreover, in two cases where Fragonard's original drawing survives, Gérard's print accurately replicates its forms and proportions but at a distinctly reduced scale (see figs. 52, 53, and p. 234, fig. 122). One way this may have been achieved is through the use of a pantograph (fig. 54), a tool trademarked and sold by Claude Langlois that could mechanically copy a design while either enlarging or reducing the scale.[76] Such a device, essentially a wooden parallelogram with movable joints and attachments for holding chalk, was described as useful for just this purpose in a 1745 printmaking manual, in which it was called a *singe* (ape). If Fragonard himself did not own one, he certainly had access to the one listed in Saint-Non's inventory as a "grand pantographe méchanique pour la reduction du dessein."[77]

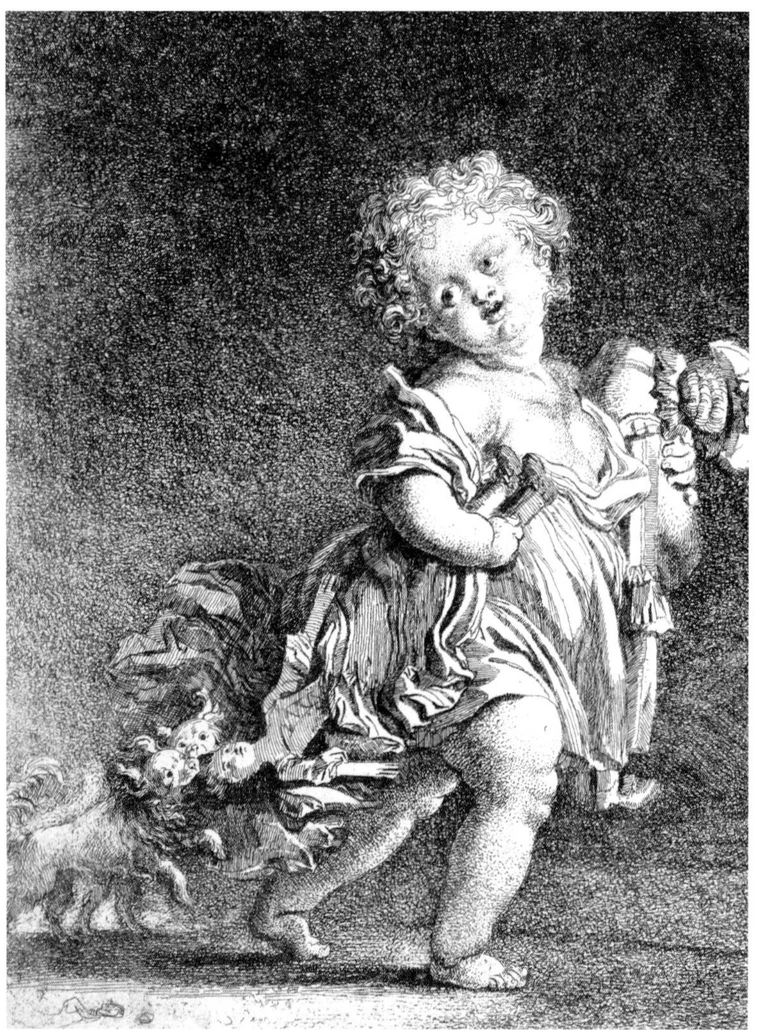

Fig. 55. Detail of *Fanfan*, cat. 83

If the two artists did indeed use a pantograph to reduce and transfer the contours of Fragonard's brown wash drawings to their prepared copperplates, their techniques otherwise diverged dramatically. In terms of her approach, Gérard was essentially a reproductive printmaker. She used simple etched lines to transcribe the black chalk marks of Fragonard's underdrawing and then created undulating shapes, ending in points, which she filled in with hatching, thus mimicking the exact placement and form of Fragonard's brown wash brushstrokes. For Fragonard, as evident in a multitude of instances, there was no such thing as a simple copy. Every iteration was imbued with invention.

In works such as *Fanfan* (fig. 55, detail of cat. 83), for example, an etching presumably based on a brown wash drawing,[78] even if he had the aid of a mechanical process to transfer the composition to the copperplate, he did not simply transcribe or reproduce it, he redrew it. Wielding the etching needle with fluidity, he put down an inventive array of marks, letting a tangle of scribbles create an inky backdrop against which the pale flesh is modeled with dots and dashes, thus creating a luminous and tactile image of a golden-faced child running across a dimly lit space, trailing clothing, toys, and pet dogs.

It is worth noting in this context that the practice of printmaking had witnessed a number of technological advances since Fragonard had last engaged with the medium. The 1770s, in fact, saw a remarkable flourishing of new intaglio techniques that successfully imitated popular drawing materials. Aquatint, practiced by his friend Saint-Non and by his contemporary in Boucher's studio, Le Prince, mimicked the effects of brush and brown wash. Chalk-manner engraving, employed by professional printmakers such as Gilles Demarteau and Louis Marin Bonnet, who had both reproduced drawings by Fragonard in the early 1770s, produced impressive facsimiles of sanguine drawings. Despite the ready availability of these technical innovations, with their capacity for replicating his drawing technique, it was the potential for variation and mutability rather than mimesis that attracted Fragonard to etching.

Thus, the style of Fragonard's 1778 etchings can be characterized as utterly distinct from his handling of chalk, pen, or wash. Consistent with his proclivity for echoes and versions throughout his oeuvre, his prints do not have as their primary goal the reproduction of his compositions; they are better characterized as autonomous variants, showcasing his graphic virtuosity and range across media. Like the seventeenth-century *peintres-graveurs* that he and many fellow artists and *amateurs* of the period admired, Fragonard found in printmaking a form of creative generation, even, remarkably, in an era when innovations in reproductive printmaking had achieved unprecedented levels of fidelity to the original. While reproductive printmakers turned out marvels of realism, not only simulating brown wash and colored chalks but also printing trompe l'oeil mats and faux collectors' marks,[79] Fragonard went in the opposite direction, choosing graphic techniques unrelated to the medium of the original—just as Saint-Non's *Griffonis*, published at intervals beginning in 1772, translated Fragonard's black chalk drawings of the early 1760s into aquatints evocative of drawings in rich brown wash.

TOOLS AND GENIUS: DRAWINGS INCISED FOR TRANSFER

If we accept the assertion that Fragonard's etchings are not primarily a means of simple reproduction, a pursuit apart from the rest of his oeuvre, but rather another avenue by which to explore iterations of his favored themes and compositions, then we might reflect on the broader implications of the shift in technique observed in his prints of 1778. As discussed above, it seems likely that Fragonard used a pantograph to reduce and transfer the design of his model drawings in brown wash to the varnished copperplate, but once the placement and the basic contours were established, he apparently felt liberated to execute the composition freehand, unleashing the potential of the new medium. Interestingly, at about the same time a parallel phenomenon seems to have emerged in his drawing methods: the use of incising to physically transfer the outlines of compositions from free preliminary sketches to new sheets, which were then worked up, presumably for collectors, in a more highly finished technique.

Three such examples of preliminary studies dating from 1775 to 1785 are included in this volume: *Children Dancing in a Park* (cat. 77 verso), *Benevolent Women on Horseback Visiting a Village* (cat. 76), and *A Boy Carried into a Salon* (cat. 99). All three are large in format (about fourteen by seventeen inches) and sketched broadly in black chalk with, in the last drawing, some transparent veils of added wash. Essentially, they are *premières pensées* writ large. In all three cases, a highly finished wash drawing of identical dimensions survives. Visible patterns of indentations across the surface document Fragonard's reason for making these exceptionally large sketches. These traces (see figs. 56 and 57), made by pressing a stylus with a blunt or rounded tip firmly along the contours of the figural and architectural elements, indicate that the artist physically transferred the placement of the forms directly to another sheet underneath, which he then worked up into a finished, salable drawing.

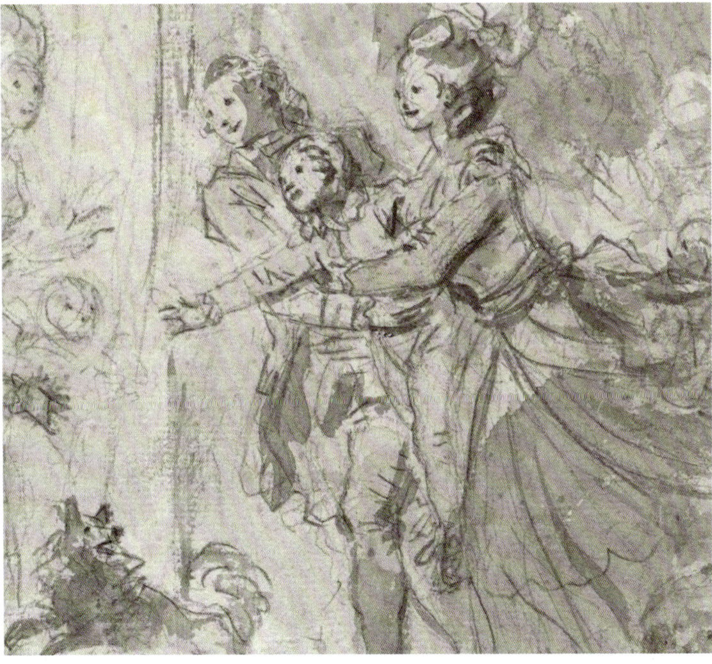

Fig. 56. Detail of *Benevolent Women on Horseback Visiting a Village*, verso, cat. 76

Fig. 57. Detail of *A Boy Carried into a Salon*, cat. 99

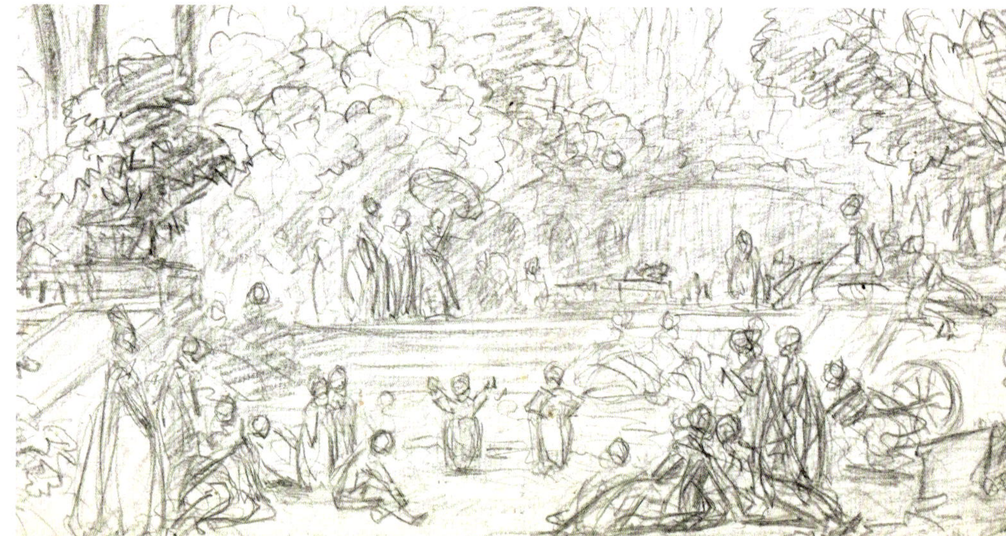

Fig. 58. Detail of *Children Dancing in a Park*, verso, cat. 77

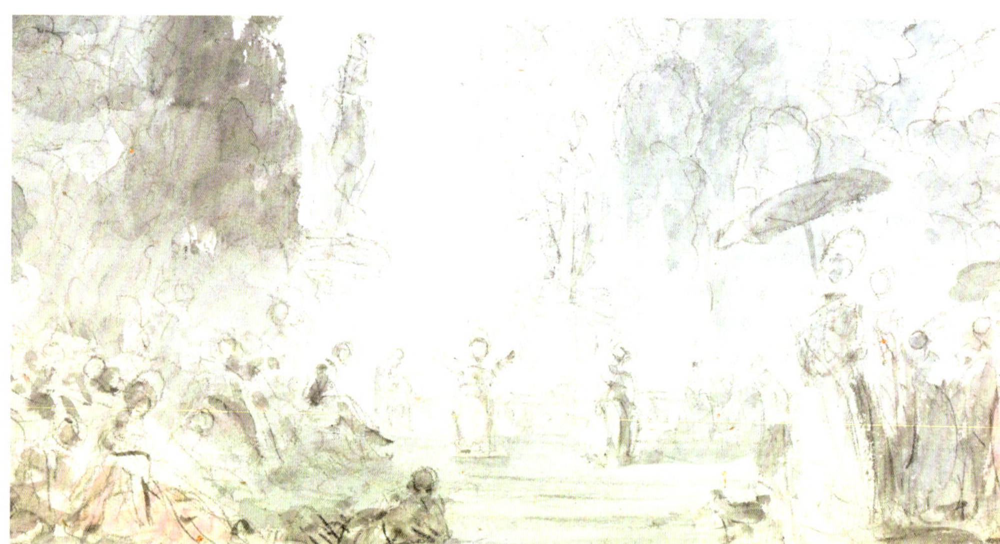

Fig. 59. Detail of *Children Dancing in a Park*, recto, cat. 77

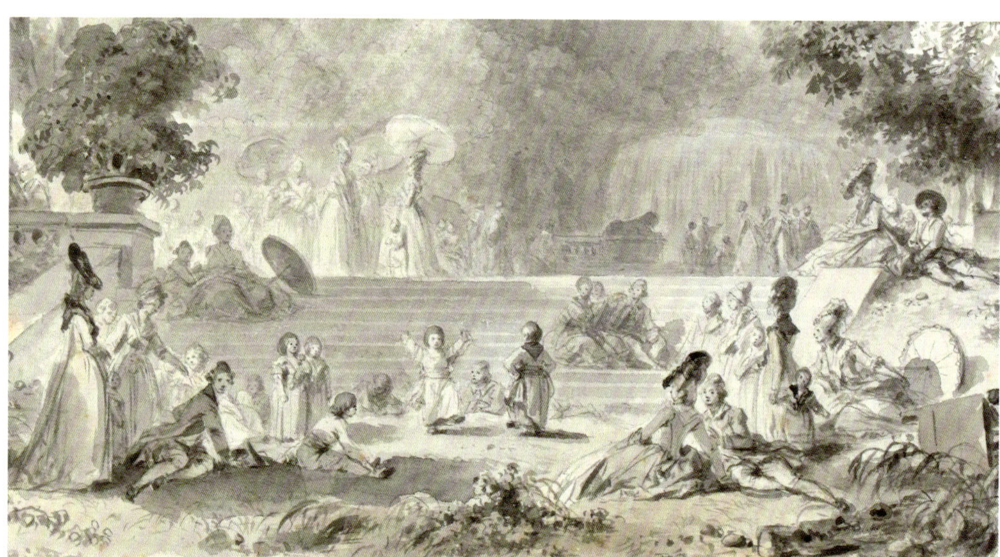

Fig. 60. Detail of *Children Dancing in a Park*, fig. 118

Should we be surprised to find Fragonard using such methods of transfer? That copying and tracing were commonplace studio practices for many eighteenth-century artists is evident in Jombert's popular 1755 treatise, *Méthode pour apprendre le dessein*, which featured an entire chapter with detailed accounts of the different methods and tools for copying drawings and paintings, including squaring, pouncing, transferring with tracing paper (paper made translucent with oil), counterproofing, using a pantograph, and tracing against a window.[80] These techniques, also found in a host of other eighteenth-century drawing manuals, are presented simply as skills useful in artistic production, without judgment or critique.[81]

It is important to stress that, for Fragonard, the ability to accurately transfer the basic armature of a composition from one support to another was not a cynical process of duplication aimed at a gullible market. Instead, each iteration provided a stage for a new performance. In the black chalk version of *Children Dancing in a Park* in the Lehman Collection (fig. 58, detail of cat. 77 verso), for instance, the scale of the sketch allowed a free, gestural handling that liberated the artist from the need for specificity. Much in the vein of Watteau's *fêtes galantes*, the focus of Fragonard's park scenes is on mood, not narrative. With figures dwarfed by nature, there is little need for individualization or expression; elegance and leisure are evoked through the repetition of simple motifs: oval hats perched on oval heads, the curved sweep of fabric falling from tiny waists, and rounded forms echoing from parasols to bushes, fountains, and clouds. In terms of sequence, the recto of the Lehman sheet (fig. 59, detail of cat. 77) may well have preceded the verso. The black chalk underdrawing is even looser and more amorphous, and watery veils of tinted watercolor unify the scene, imbuing the natural world with a dreamlike quality. The version at the Rijksmuseum in Amsterdam (fig. 60), which carries over the layout of the Lehman verso and the subtle washes of the Lehman recto, is not a preparatory work on the path toward the execution of a painting. It is an autonomous picture in a constellation of related works that includes examples on paper and canvas, ranging from sketchy to more finished, all exploring the potential and effects of their particular medium and scale.[82] The mutability of the subject across its many variants aligns with our notion that the garden represented is an imaginary one; indeed, scholars, despite attempts over the years, have generally had little success in their quest to identify specific locations in Fragonard's later landscapes. As appears to be the case with his most celebrated canvases—*The Island of Love* (ca. 1768–70, p. 206, fig. 109), *The Progress of Love* (1771–91, p. xviii), *Blindman's Buff* (ca. 1775–80, National Gallery of Art, Washington, D.C.), *The Swing* (ca. 1775–80, p. xvii), and *La Fête à Saint-Cloud* (ca. 1775–80, Banque de France, Paris)—the Lehman sheet is ultimately about the possibilities for leisure, play, and love in the welcoming setting of a lush, overgrown garden. According to Richard Rand, such works can be situated within the contemporary vogue among landscape designers and painters alike for the concept of the picturesque garden, which enticed the visitor with its hidden parts to be discovered and experienced.[83]

Ultimately, in the context of Fragonard's working process, incising and transferring were not tools along a linear path toward a single final end product. They are, in this case, and in countless other examples throughout his career, part of a creative process based on generating variants and multiples, in which the preexisting elements, carried over from one version to the next, liberated the artist from certain aspects of invention and the need for methodical preparation, allowing him to explore the expressiveness of technique and medium with greater freedom.

REPRISE AND REINVENTION: RECLAIMING THE MARGINAL IN FRAGONARD'S OEUVRE

"A little water, a little bistre, a wave of the hand—and the trick is done," so goes the description of Fragonard's drawing technique offered by the Goncourt brothers in 1880.[84] It was intended not as glib but as complimentary, an evocation of the unlabored spontaneity of genius. Yet, many of the examples discussed above do not fit into this nineteenth-century vision of artistic creation. We have seen copies, sometimes with compositions reprised in multiple iterations, like so many ripples in a pond: a quick sketch made of a painting in an Italian church or palace, reversed in a counterproof pulled later and reworked in black chalk, and reappearing, later still, in a version redrawn with an etching needle on a copperplate. Red chalk drawings were likewise run through the printing press to create counterproofs, pale twins to be drawn over and elaborated in a new medium. The early 1770s saw a new campaign of copying, this time not as artistic training but as a virtuoso exercise, which yielded sheets destined not for the painter's portfolio but for the collector's wall. In the later 1770s, painterly scenes in brown wash were reborn in reduced form as etchings, introducing effects of texture and chiaroscuro unattainable with the brush. Finally, large, sketchy drawings bear traces of incising, evidence of the artist's methods of transferring compositions to fresh sheets, their imagery reinvented in a new medium or technique. The "trick," it turned out, often required more than a wave of the hand.

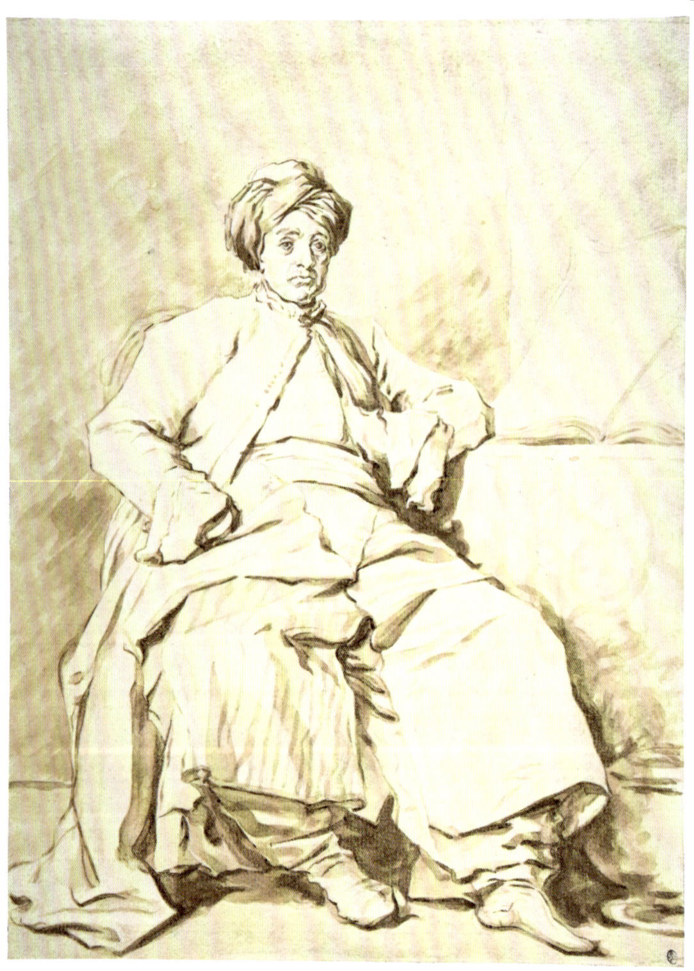

Fig. 61. After Jean Honoré Fragonard, *The Sultan*, 20th century. Brush and brown wash over traces of graphite, 14⅝ × 10⅞ in. (36.9 × 27.6 cm). The Metropolitan Museum of Art, New York, Bequest of Walter C. Baker, 1971 (1972.118.213)

The idea of the great artist as more genius than craftsman is a legacy of the nineteenth century that still informs our biases around eighteenth-century artistic practice and has contributed to the devaluation of multiples and variants. Negative associations with the processes of copying, tracing, and transfer are unfortunately reinforced by the prevalence of forgeries, a particular problem in the oeuvre of Fragonard, as first publicly exposed in a series of articles by Geraldine Norman in 1978.[85] Ironically, some of the methods used by twentieth-century forgers are not so different from the practices observed here.[86] Alexandre Ananoff, whose four-volume catalogue raisonné of Fragonard's drawings is liberally sprinkled with glowingly described fakes (for example, fig. 61), had published an article in 1956 asserting that Fragonard had traced his own drawings "à la vitre," or at the window, using transmitted light.[87] While that particular technique seems to have been used by forgers and not, as far as we know, by the artist himself, it was the very fact of Fragonard's own habitual creation of multiple versions that gave cover to copyists of ill intent.

What were the benefits of working this way? For Fragonard, the lifelong habits of copying and transfer nourished a self-referential working process, which in turn enabled a free and experimental technique. As Marie-Anne Dupuy-Vachey has justly observed, it was the extended engagement with the art of the past, recorded in the hundreds of black chalk copies made on the return from his first voyage to Italy, that accounted for the assimilated knowledge of figural types and compositional principles that later allowed Fragonard to dispense with systematic preliminary studies. The act of copying instilled in the artist an internalized sense of Baroque movement, mass, and light that enabled him to approach the blank canvas or sheet with audacity. His mature oeuvre is rich in reference and homage, but rarely, if ever, does one find exact quotation.[88]

There is a connection between the idea of working in series and variations, as articulated here, and other readings built around the repetition of signature motifs. For instance, Ewa Lajer-Burcharth characterizes the archway of foliage opening onto a distant or interior space, as one sees in *The Island of Love* or *The Little Park* (Wallace Collection, London), as a response not to observed reality but to an "internal mold" in which certain landscape forms correspond to feminine morphology, more specifically, drawing a connection between uterine imagery and the concept of creative generation.[89] Whatever the underlying motivation, working in echoes and iterations drew Fragonard further away from the direct observation and recording of reality but did not dull his inventiveness. On the contrary, his revisiting of compositions displays critical engagement and experimentation. The proliferation of versions, in different directions, in different sizes, and in different techniques, was part and parcel of Fragonard's creative enterprise, which comes into better focus when these forms of expression are no longer relegated to second-tier status.

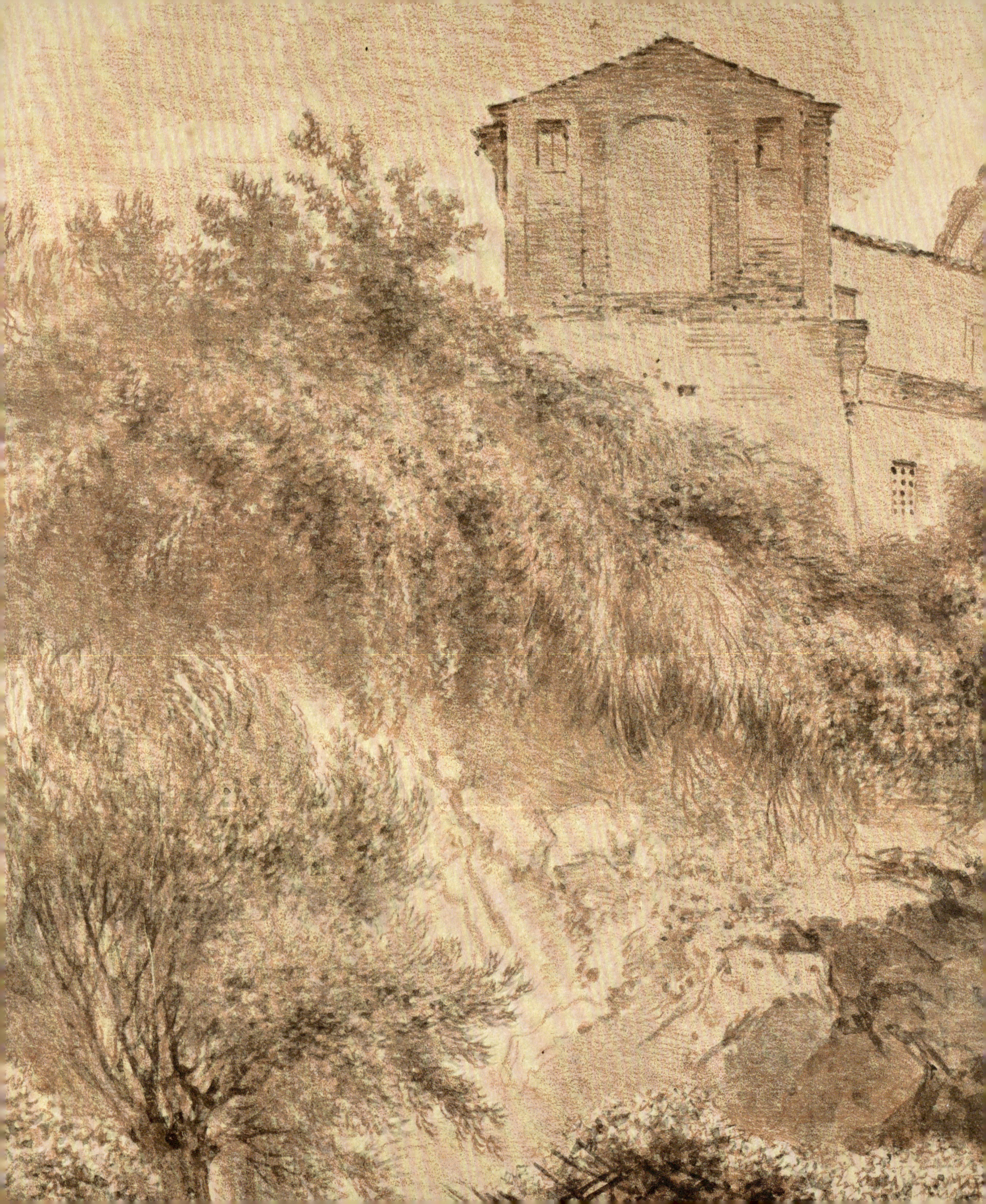

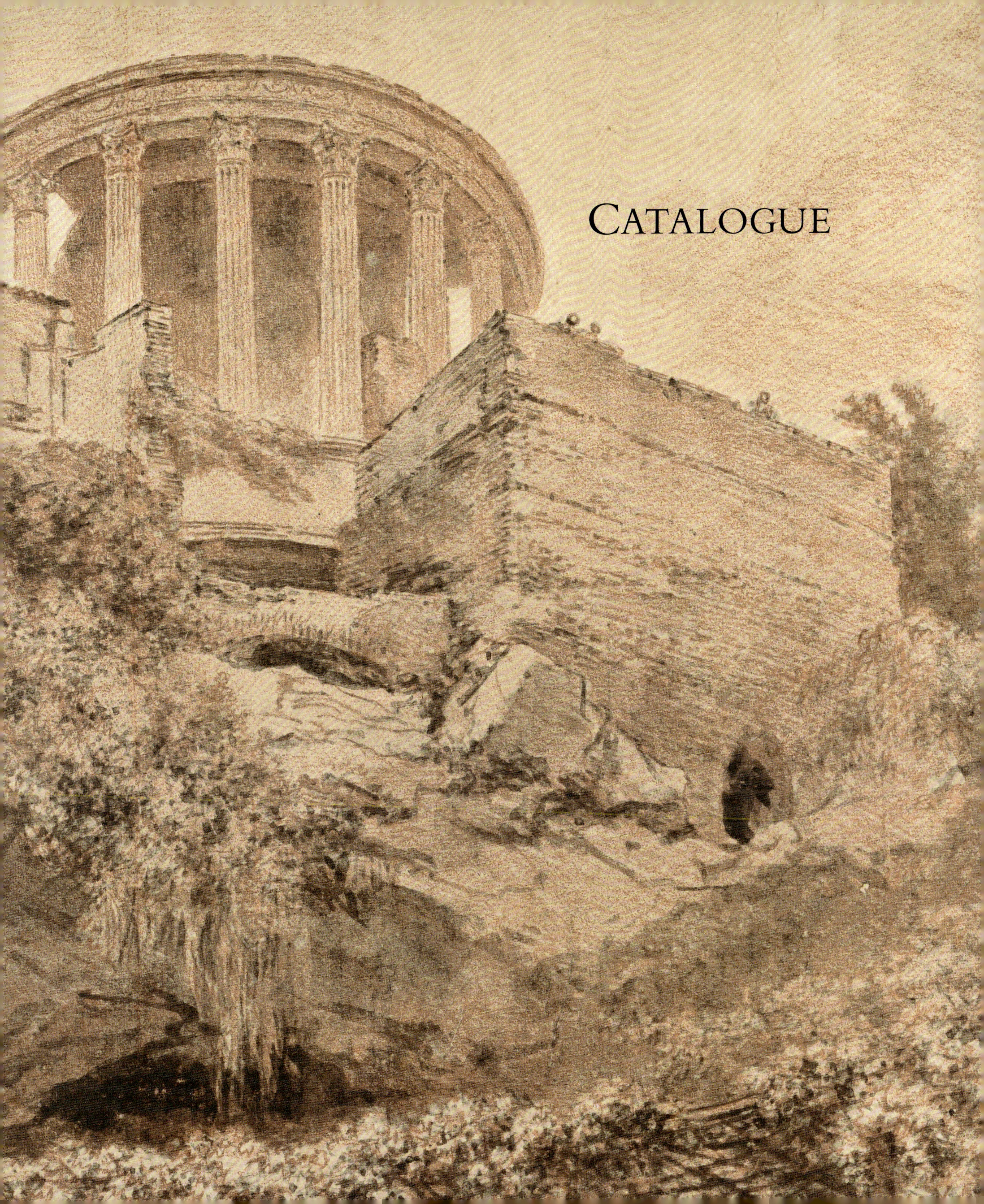

CATALOGUE

Early Years: Paris to Rome

Fragonard, born in Grasse, grew up in Paris from age six. With few biographical dates, plotting his development is a challenge. At about age sixteen, he was apprenticed unsuccessfully to a notary; according to his grandson Théophile, he spent his time at work sketching.[1] His mother brought him to François Boucher's busy studio, but he was rejected because of his lack of training. He then went to Jean Siméon Chardin's studio, where his color sense won him a place and where he learned the rudiments of painting and mixing pigments. When the aspiring artist presented himself to Boucher a second time, he was accepted.

Two major Parisian artists were responsible for Fragonard's early formation, first Boucher and then Carle Vanloo. In Boucher's studio, his initial responsibility was making cartoons for tapestry commissions; doing so, he learned to interpret Boucher's complex compositions, dense with multiple figures, foliage, and ornament. Boucher's personal approach to figures and landscape, basing both on imagination rather than observation and designing for decorative purposes, did not serve as a role model for Fragonard. However, he learned certain formal and abstract ideas for organizing compositions both figurative and landscape. In scenes with multifigural groups, for example, Fragonard adapted a favorite device of Boucher's, the *profil perdu* (in which the subject's face is turned more than halfway from the viewer), which can be seen in two drawings in this exhibition, *Coresus and Callirhoë* (cat. 37) and *Young Athenian Women Drawing Lots* (cat. 38), made after his return from Rome in 1761.

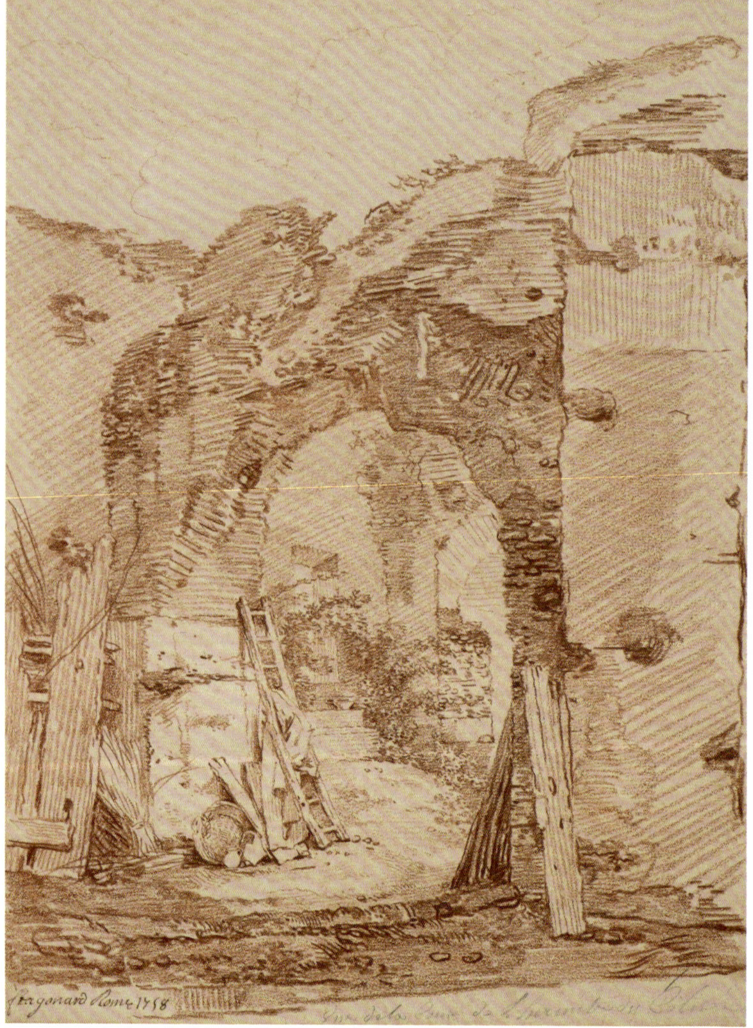

Fig. 62. Jean Honoré Fragonard, *The Hermit's Court in the Colosseum*, 1758. Red chalk, 14 × 10½ in. (35.3 × 26.5 cm). The Clark Art Institute, Williamstown, Mass., Acquired by the Clark, 2003 (2003.9.30)

Fragonard's early independent landscape drawings reflect lessons from Boucher in their formal design and manipulation of space, if not the Rococo richness of his teacher's work. The black chalk and wash *View of a Park* (cat. 2), with its compressed space and feathery trees, could easily be transformed into a tapestry design. In another example, *A Park Landscape* (cat. 5), Fragonard intelligently appropriated Boucher devices such as the diagonal counterpoint between leaning trees and structural balustrades.

Beyond teaching artistic practice, Boucher was important to Fragonard's career because he recognized his natural talent and sponsored him in the Prix de Rome competition of 1752. Fragonard had not been able to study at the Académie Royale, and Boucher's confidence in his gifted pupil allowed him to bypass the requirement of formal academic study.

The second definitive influence on Fragonard's formation was Carle Vanloo, director of the Ecole des Elèves Protégés. After winning the Prix de Rome, Fragonard entered the Ecole, where he learned drawing from posed models, along with a rigorous academic curriculum designed to prepare the young artists for their trip to Rome. Vanloo, Michel François Dandré-Bardon, and Nicolas Bernard Lépicié were the principal professors. None of the life studies Fragonard made there survive, but in later examples one can see the imprint of Vanloo's vigorous handling of red chalk, combining forceful outlines and systematic hatchings. *Life Study: Deacon Carrying a Book* (cat. 3), made later in Rome, reflects Fragonard's experience with Vanloo, as does the confident clarity of line he used to record the appearance of a Roman acanthus plant (cat. 4) in 1759. Similarly, the subjects of ancient history mentioned above, *Coresus and Callirhoë* and *Young Athenian Women Drawing Lots*, were informed by Vanloo's preference for formal compositions clearly defined by architecture and dramatic light.

Independent landscapes are Fragonard's personal triumph as a draftsman, but nothing he produced before he left for Italy would suggest that. Neither Boucher nor Vanloo could be called innovators in this genre. From them he learned the rudiments of drawing and its media—black chalk and red chalk—along with perspective and use of light.

When Fragonard finally arrived in Rome in December 1756, he brought impressive credentials for a promising career in history painting. However, his career ultimately took another path. His hard work and independent approach to style won the approval of Charles Joseph Natoire, director of the Académie de France in Rome. Natoire was both a history painter and a gifted landscape draftsman who believed in close observation of nature. He restored landscape drawing to the Académie curriculum and regularly took the pensionnaires on sketching trips around the Roman countryside to visit villas and gardens. In the Roman sunlight, Fragonard's genius flourished (see, for example, fig. 62), and he elevated landscape drawings to a new status.

EW

1. *An Angel Bringing Food to a Hermit*

After François Boucher (French, 1703–1770)
Ca. 1750–56
Etching
Sheet: 10¼ × 9½ in. (25.8 × 24.1 cm); plate mark: 9⅛ × 6¼ in. (23 × 15.8 cm); image: 8½ × 5⅞ in. (21.5 × 14.7 cm)
Inscriptions: below image, at left, "F Boucher Inv. & delinea"; below image, at right, "Fragonard Sculps"

Fragonard's initiation into the art of etching came during the period he was associated with Boucher's studio, generally considered to be about 1748 to 1756. Although this instruction yielded only a single plate, one should not underestimate the significance of Boucher as the source of transmission, for he was one of the first Rococo painters to embrace printmaking and certainly the first to truly understand and exploit its potential.[1] Thus, it is hardly a coincidence that many of the most creative *peintres-graveurs* of the second half of the eighteenth century have his tutelage in common.

An Angel Bringing Food to a Hermit reveals that Fragonard had an intuitive virtuosity to rival that of his teacher. The drawing by Boucher that was his model survives today in the National Gallery of Canada (fig. 63).[2] Executed in soft black chalk with a dull tip to allow for broad, atmospheric shading, the scene has a subdued, smoky quality with little textural differentiation. The line in Fragonard's etching is, by its nature, sharper and more defined. To suggest the amorphous clouds and shadows expressed by parallel hatching in Boucher's sheet, Fragonard invented a panoply of patterns and textures. Wiggling, overlapping lines flowing in irregular streams and flecks and dashes applied in a staccato fashion evoke the roughness and variety of organic surfaces. The density of these seemingly random lines is carefully calibrated to create a range of tones, while the areas of the plate left untouched sparkle with light.

The effect is freer than that of the etchings Boucher made for the market in 1756, *La petite repose* and *La blanchisseuse*,[3] and more akin to the loose execution seen in works such as *Andromeda*, for which Boucher etched a first state for a professional printmaker to complete in engraving.[4] However, the real inspiration for Fragonard's manner as a printmaker seems to have been Boucher's art collection, which included a large number of prints by the Italian etchers so admired by French collectors and *amateurs* at the time. The catalogue of Boucher's estate sale lists 175 prints by Pietro Testa, 137 by Giovanni Battista Tiepolo, 67 by Salvator Rosa, and 40 by Giovanni Benedetto Castiglione.[5] The availability of such examples makes it less surprising that Fragonard's first etching displays a sensibility analogous to Tiepolo's, whose free handling of the etching needle scattered flecks and dots across the plate and boldly left expanses of white paper untouched. PS

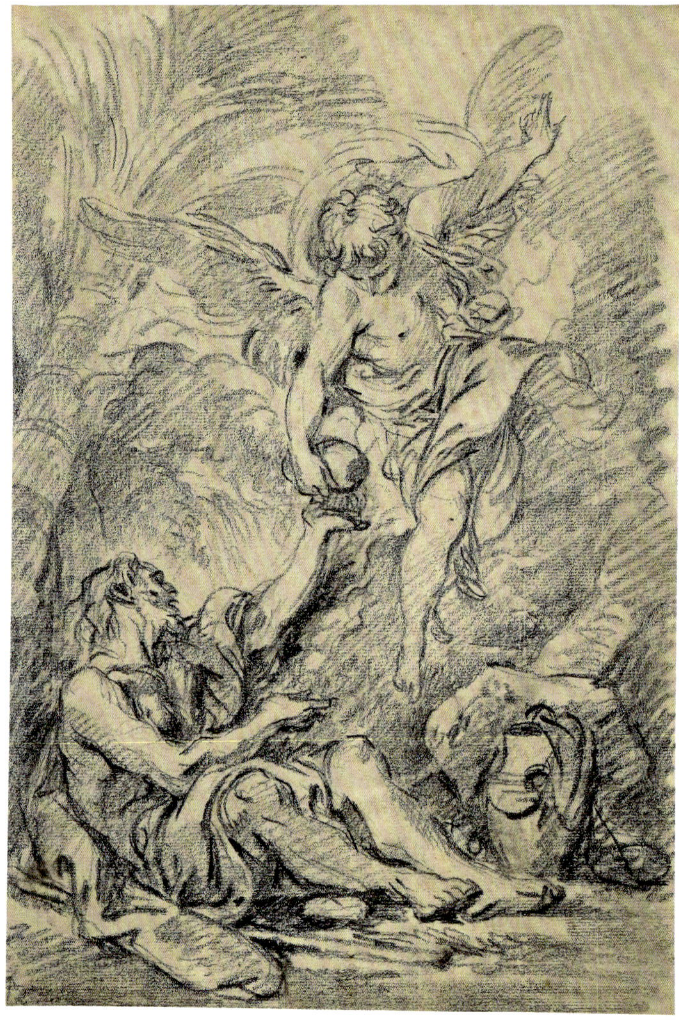

Fig. 63. François Boucher (French, 1703–1770), *An Angel Bringing Food to a Hermit*, ca. 1730–35. Black chalk, 12½ × 8½ in. (31.6 × 21.6 cm). National Gallery of Canada, Ottawa, Gift of Mrs. Samuel Bronfman, Montreal, 1957 (6888)

PROVENANCE: [L'Art Ancien, Zurich]; The Metropolitan Museum of Art, New York, The Elisha Whittelsey Collection, The Elisha Whittelsey Fund, 1949 (49.36.8)

SELECTED EXHIBITION: Stein et al. 2013, pp. 31–32, 187, 204, cat. no. 10.

SELECTED REFERENCES: G. Wildenstein 1956, p. 7, no. I; Paris 1987, cat. no. 1; Couturier 2004, pp. 60–61, cat. no. 20, fig. 31; Hoisington and Stein 2012, p. 143.

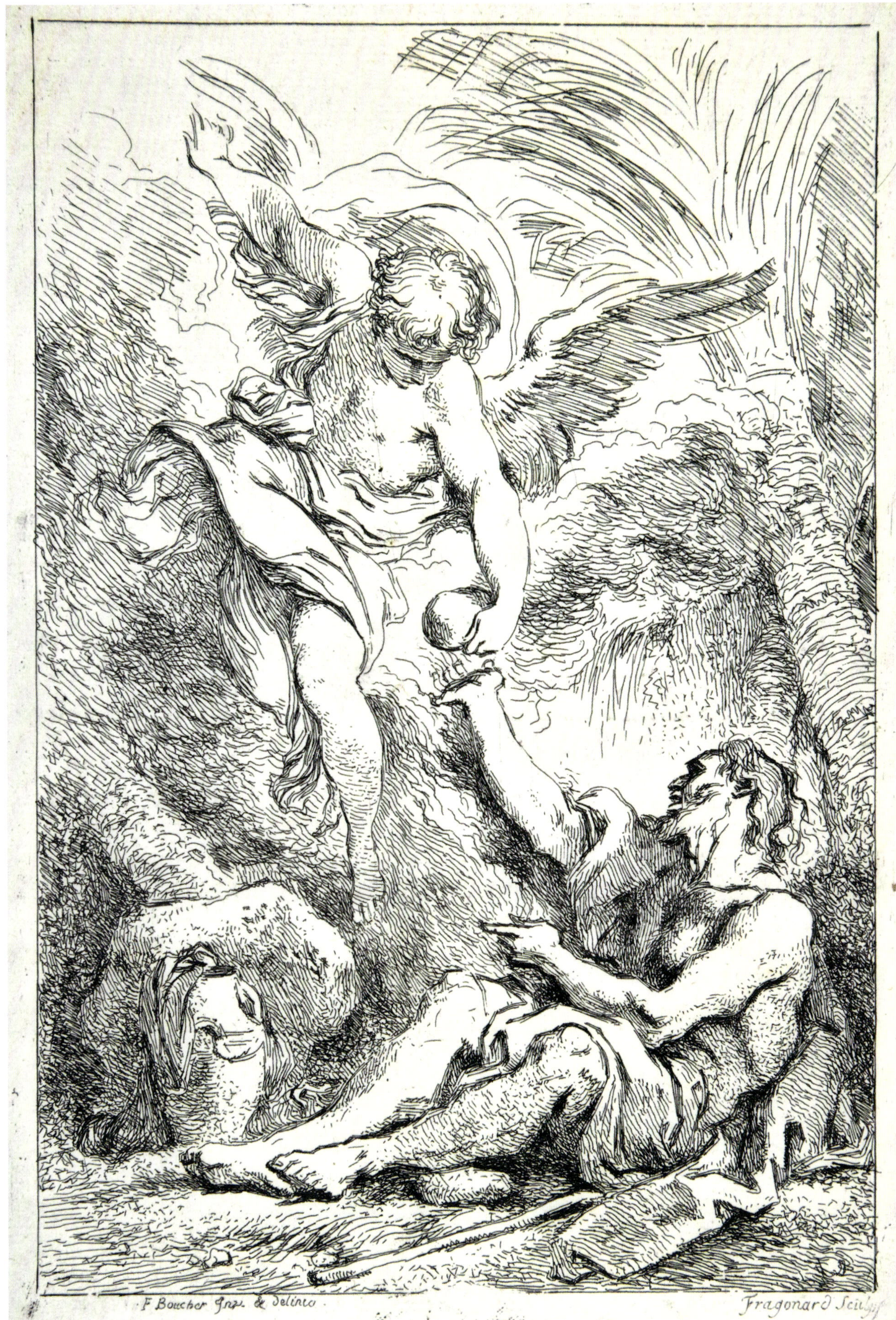
F Boucher Inv. & delineo
Fragonard Sculp

2. *View of a Park*

Ca. 1757–59
Black chalk, gray wash, touches of black and brown wash, framing lines in pen and black ink
10¾ × 15½ in. (27.3 × 39.4 cm)

This is an early drawing by Fragonard, before he found his voice, as it were, when he was self-consciously appropriating ideas from Boucher. The fledgling artist adopted Boucher's feathery trees and genre figures, such as the woman with a wheelbarrow on the right and the young man who observes her from the left. It is a theatrically composed landscape dominated by large trees in full foliage, where chalk underdrawing and wash unite to suggest movement from a breeze. The present work was probably drawn in Rome but it anticipates some aspects of style and handling of a similar *View of a Park* in Oberlin, to which it traditionally has been compared.[1] Separated by four or five years, the two represent Fragonard's decorative landscape aesthetic. Both combine the unreality of Boucher's Rococo style with unconventional perspective and sculptural motifs that Fragonard learned in Rome. Such a mixture betrays the youth of an artist still defining his style.

The arbor is off-center and shelters the statue of a seated female goddess, a trope of ancient Rome. The park is defined by the kind of false perspective associated with stage sets. To the far left, Fragonard introduces a palatial staircase and round temple, something clearly observed in Rome. The distant view is drawn in detail using quick, nervous lines. Fragonard uses the same linear schemata in red chalk to indicate distance in another early work, *Landscape with a Villa* (cat. 12). In contrast, the arbor and statue are boldly drawn in chalk, then deftly and precisely painted with several saturations of cool gray wash. The washes are modulated to suggest spatial depth yet are still transparent enough to let the chalk show. Chalk and wash are integrated into a decorative tapestry, another nod to Boucher's Rococo precedent.

It is this cool gray wash that has attracted attention and questions from writers who have doubted that Fragonard applied the wash.[2] They believe that the gray wash was added by another hand and at a later date. But their suspicions are based neither on close visual examination of this sheet nor on an understanding of wash drawing procedures. The gray wash is integrated into the design. Furthermore, I believe Fragonard experimented with gray wash deliberately because it was the preferred medium of Jean-Baptiste Greuze, whom he met in 1756 when he arrived in Rome.[3] From his early works, Greuze created a pictorial style using several densities of gray wash. In later years, Fragonard developed his own style of systematic monochrome drawings in brown wash. EW

PROVENANCE: Comte de Montesquiou; Otto Wertheimer (1878–1972), Paris, by 1951; [Knoedler & Co., New York]; The Metropolitan Museum of Art, New York, Harris Brisbane Dick Fund, 1952 (52.14)

SELECTED EXHIBITIONS: Williams 1978, cat. no. 6, ill.; Near 1981, cat. no. 8, ill.; Rosenberg 1988, cat. no. 38, ill.

SELECTED REFERENCES: Ananoff 1961–70, vol. 4 (1970), no. 2215; Bean and Turčić 1986, no. 115, ill.

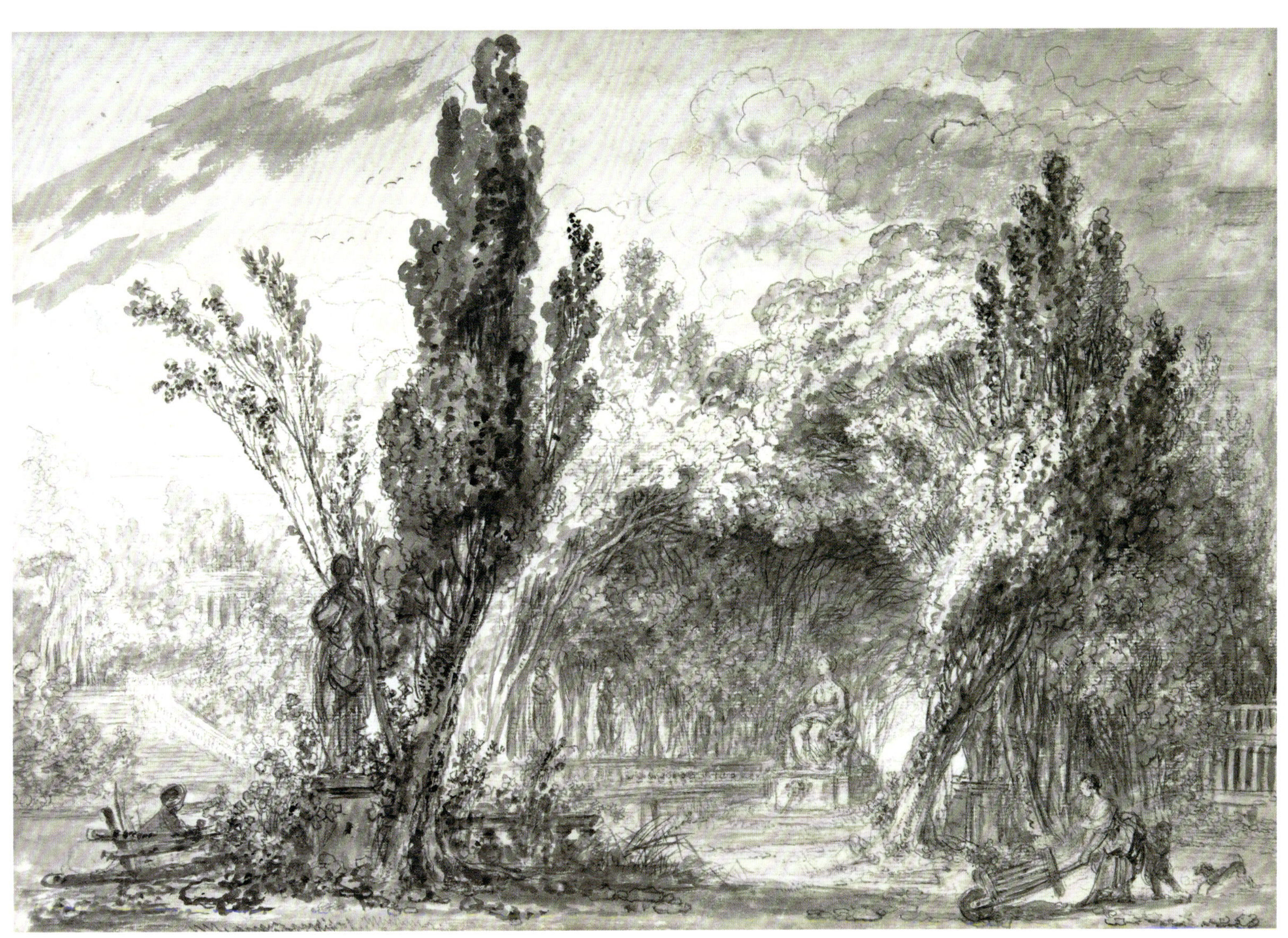

3. *Life Study: Deacon Carrying a Book*

Ca. 1758–59
Red chalk
21½ × 14¾ in. (54.6 × 37.3 cm)
Inscriptions: at lower right, in pen and brown ink, partially illegible due to a tear in the paper, "frago[nard]"; at lower left, in pencil in a modern hand, "DR 170"

In 1752, Fragonard won the Prix de Rome, a prize that was the first step for any artist who had ambitions for a brilliant career. Contrary to the rules, he entered the competition without having previously attended classes at the Académie. "It doesn't matter, you are my pupil," Boucher reputedly remarked,[1] apparently deeming his young student sufficiently prepared to compete. Consequently, Fragonard was able to benefit from an education as complete and codified as that provided by the Académie, where drawing, and more specifically sketching from the living model, was the foundation of instruction. The exercises would have followed a very precise order, as Claude Henri Watelet states in the article on drawing in Diderot and d'Alembert's *Encyclopédie*: "When the artist has succeeded in drawing a nude figure well, he can drape it."[2] Some of the first drawings that can be attributed to Fragonard show the mark of these years of apprenticeship, spent from 1752 to 1756 at the Ecole des Elèves Protégés under the authority of Carle Vanloo, and then, from 1756 to 1761, at the Académie de France in Rome, directed by Charles Joseph Natoire.

Fragonard's *académies*, or studies from the nude model, are known to us from a handful of engravings. Two such prints accompany Watelet's *Encyclopédie* article (plates XVII and XVIII). However, several sanguines survive in which the artist practiced drawing models clothed in ample draperies falling in deep and geometrical folds, similar to a monk's habit. These studies[3] have typically been connected to Fragonard's time in Rome. However, even before he left for Italy, he had mastered the art of drapery, as can be seen by comparing the figures in *Jeroboam Sacrificing to the Idols*,[4] the painting that won him the Prix de Rome in 1752, with those in *Christ Washing the Feet of the Apostles*, painted two years later for the cathedral of Grasse.[5] In that large canvas, the cloth follows the bodies' forms simply and naturally without any superfluous folds, thus contributing to the composition's nobility and authority.

Nevertheless, it seems beyond doubt that the sheet exhibited here belongs to the artist's Roman period. The subject corresponds to the next level in this type of study. The model is no longer draped in simple fabric but is clothed in precisely described liturgical vestments. This exercise had been instituted by Nicolas Vleughels when he directed the Académie de France in Rome (1725–37). Natoire, who occupied the post later, when Fragonard was a student there, reintroduced the practice because, as he wrote in October 1758, the "costumes of the church . . . produce such beautiful folds."[6]

This red chalk study with its monumental effect can probably be situated to about that date. Seen in profile, the model poses like a deacon carrying the scriptures in procession during a religious ceremony. The artist's facility is evident in his ability to render the different types of fabric. The thick and ample dalmatic with its silky effects is worn above a long white robe, or alb, in a lighter, more fluid cloth; its folds echo the bend in the deacon's right leg. The stole embroidered with a cross follows this movement, while heavy tassels anchor the cords of the alb.

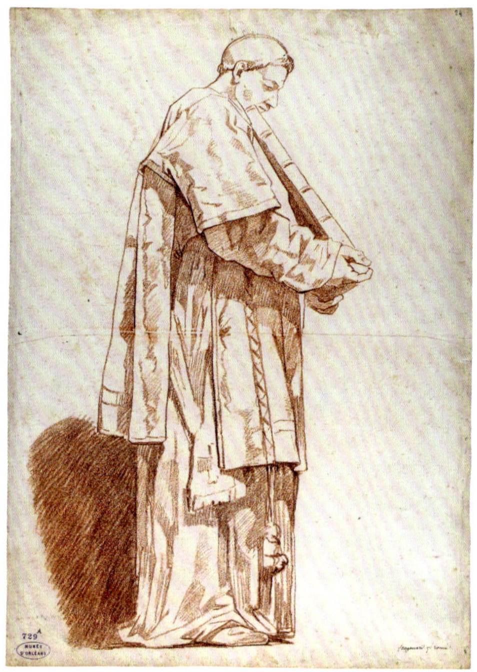

Fig. 64. Jean Honoré Fragonard, *Life Study: Deacon Carrying a Book*, ca. 1758–59. Red chalk, 21⅜ × 15⅜ in. (54.1 × 39.1 cm). Musée des Beaux-Arts, Orléans (729.A)

A red chalk drawing in the Musée des Beaux-Arts, Orléans, shows a model wearing an identical costume (fig. 64); it is annotated "fragonard f. roma."[7] In addition to the fixed pose, the position of the face and the slightly different manner of holding the book suggest that the study was created during a separate session. It could be earlier than ours, which shows greater subtlety and delicacy, notably in the treatment of the shadows. MADV

PROVENANCE: Sale, Christie's, London, April 3, 1984 (lot 85, repr., as "attributed to"); [Galerie Cailleux, Paris]; private collection, Paris; sale, Palais des Congrès (Poulain–Le Fur), Paris, June 25, 2002 (lot 19), unsold; sale, Hôtel Drouot (Rémy Le Fur), Paris, April 27, 2012 (lot 118); private collection

SELECTED EXHIBITION: Paris 1987, cat. no. 5.

SELECTED REFERENCES: Cuzin 1987, p. 251 n. 14; Pagliano 2005, p. 59 n. 77.

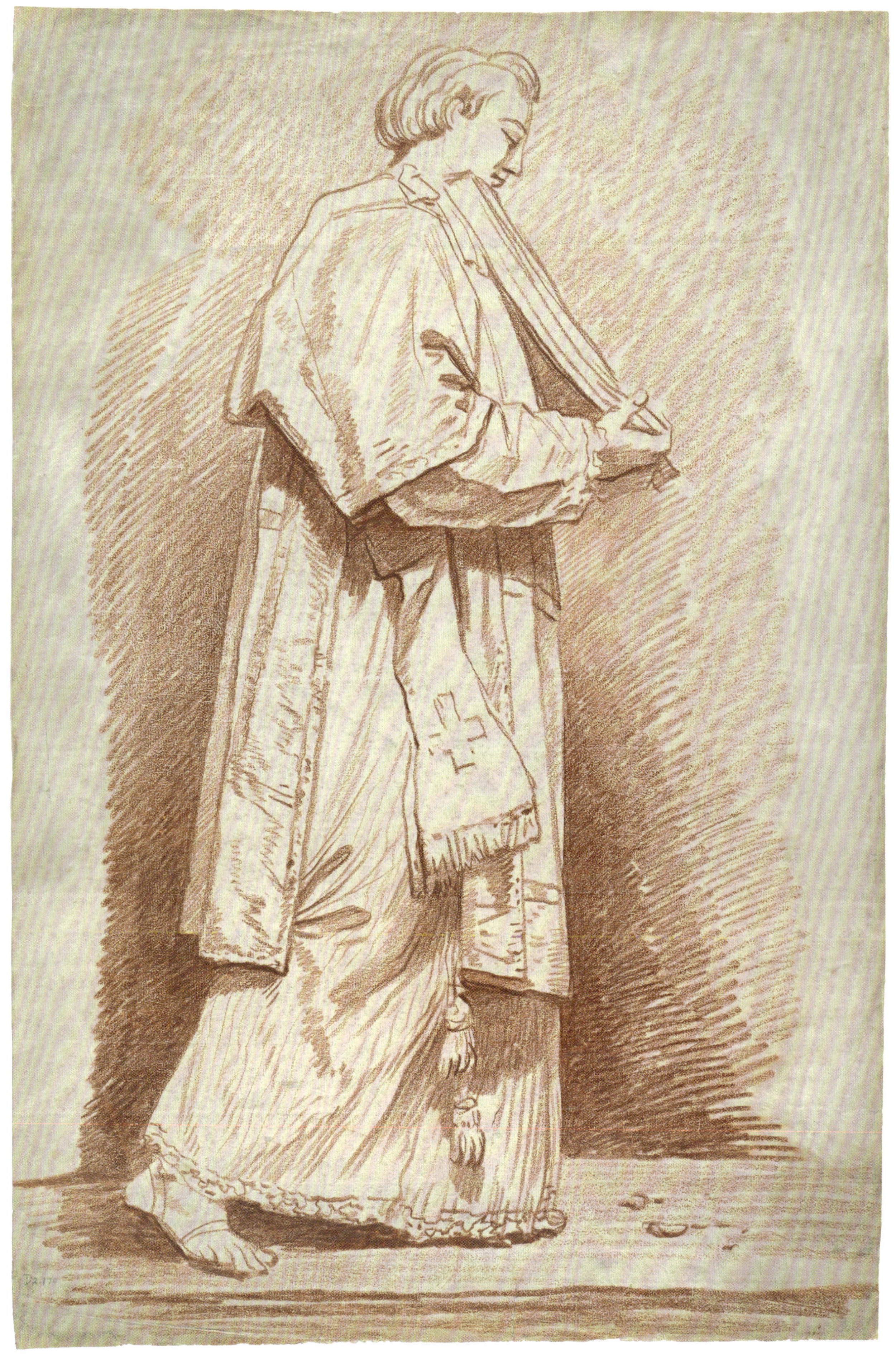

4. *Study of Plants, Including Acanthus*

Ca. 1759
Red chalk on white antique laid paper
15¾ × 20⅞ in. (40 × 53 cm)
Inscription: at lower left, in brown ink, "fragonard"

Natoire, as director of the Académie de France in Rome, regularly took the pensionnaires, their drawing tools in hand, on excursions in the Roman countryside. These plein air sessions were both exploratory and instructional. Natoire believed landscape should be part of the academic curriculum. The present study of plants, where the acanthus is prominent, was made during one such expedition. It belongs to a series of at least four large-scale formal plant studies Fragonard made in 1759 and confirms both his command of red chalk technique and talent for *mise-en-page* design. It is a precise close-up study, where delicate lines define individual leaves against the white background. One suspects that he was less interested in the acanthus as emblematic of ancient decorative art than in capturing its reflective leaves in strong sunlight.

For such an ambitious and focused work, surprisingly little is known about its history. The 1773 sale of Jean Denis Lempereur's collection included three lots with plant studies. One of them (lot 736) might describe the sheet exhibited here: "A study of different plants, grouped, very brilliant drawing in red chalk."[1] The name of the buyer was "françois," an unidentified collector who was also a buyer in the Gros sale in 1778.[2]

Ananoff's catalogue lists the Lempereur drawing, along with three other studies of plants, one of which (AA.964) can be connected to a known work, *A Study of Brambles*, in a Paris private collection (fig. 65). The ink inscription on this sheet, "fragonard Roma 1759," provides an important clue not only to when Fragonard made the plant studies, but also to the purpose of several highly finished red chalk landscape scenes with the same inscription.

In 1759 Fragonard was a third-year pensionnaire at the Académie de France in Rome. Natoire routinely sent reports about the young artists in his charge to the marquis de Marigny in Paris, whose responsibilities as director of the Bâtiments du Roi included oversight of the Académie. With an artist's instinct, Natoire recognized not only Fragonard's immense talent, but also his need for discipline. He appealed to Marigny, suggesting that all pensionnaires would benefit from a fourth year at the academy. Marigny granted this request in September 1759.[3]

In August and October 1759, Natoire dispatched to Marigny two sets of *envois de Rome* (including painted *académies*, or nude studies, and unidentified drawings) to demonstrate Fragonard's progress. The two exchanged lengthy letters that reveal how closely the arts administrators in Rome and Paris supervised the pensionnaires. Unfortunately, their correspondence fails to list individual drawings and paintings sent to Paris. Fragonard's *académies* have been lost, but we know at least seven red chalk drawings inscribed with the date 1759, of which four are large, finished landscapes.[4]

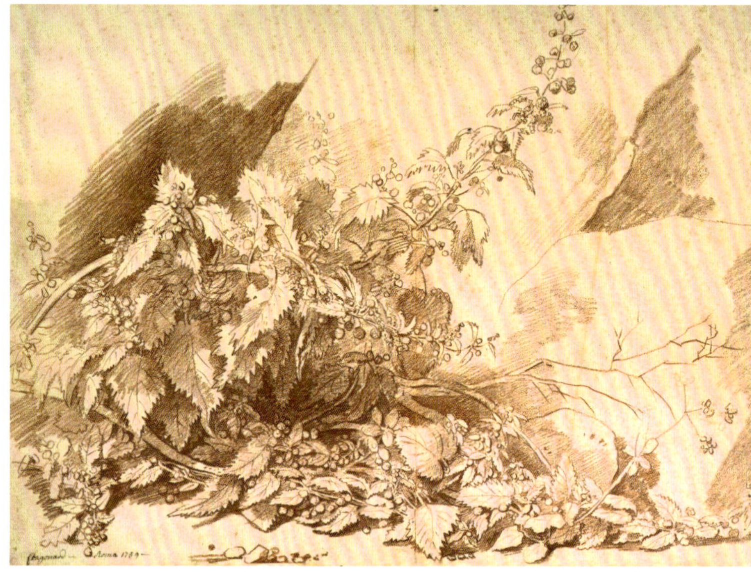

Fig. 65. Jean Honoré Fragonard, *A Study of Brambles*, 1759. Red chalk, 14¼ × 19¼ in. (36.2 × 48.9 cm). Private collection, France

Could some of these represent the unidentified *envois de Rome* mentioned in the correspondence? Fragonard did not usually sign or inscribe his works at any stage of his career. Therefore, it is suggestive of official purpose that several drawings display the date 1759. Further, it is significant that these sheets, whether inscribed by the artist or by Natoire, should depict landscape scenes and nature studies, because Natoire had argued in favor of featuring landscape in the curriculum.

Hubert Robert may have been on one of the drawing excursions when he made a drawing of an acanthus plant, today in the Musée de Valence. However, being more interested in architecture than botany, he added details symbolic of the Roman Forum to his drawing.[5] EW

PROVENANCE: Jean Denis Lempereur (1701–1779); his collection sale (Lugt 2171), Chariot, Boileau, and Joullain, Paris, May 24, 1773 (possibly lot 736); private collection, France; [Galerie de Bayser, Paris]; private collection

SELECTED REFERENCE: Ananoff 1961–70, vol. 4 (1970), no. 2368 (*Etude de Plantes Groupées*).

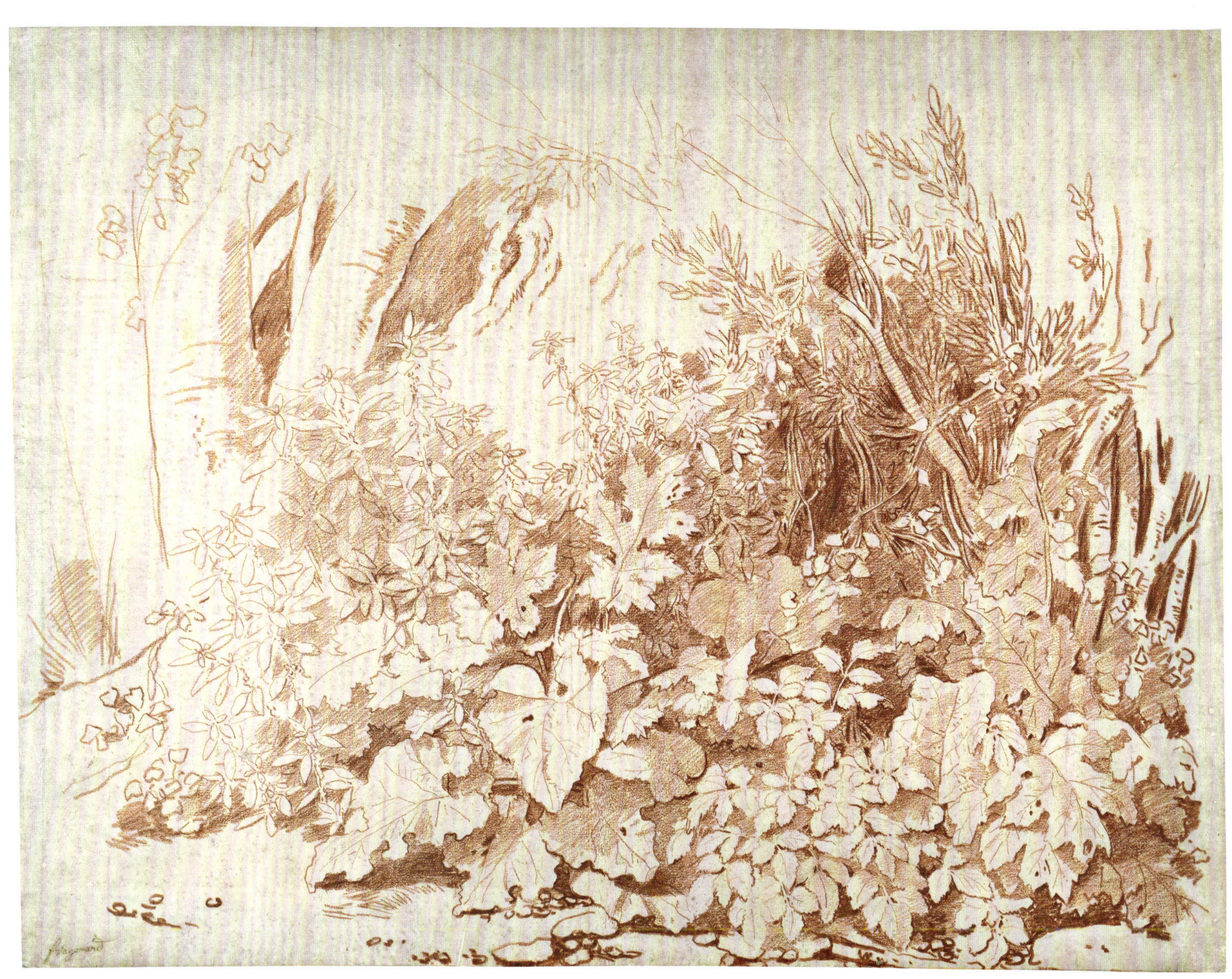

5. *A Park Landscape*

Ca. 1759–60
Two colors of red chalk
12¼ × 15¼ in. (30.9 × 38.7 cm)

Fragonard designed his landscapes to appear natural and inviting. Here, in a composition defined by dramatic vegetation and a strong diagonal, he creates a quiet scene in an overgrown garden. Small figures seated on the ground suggest scale rather than narrative. The compositional design is related to the conspicuous diagonals in two large red chalk landscapes in Frankfurt, *Le jeu de la bascule* (*The Seesaw*) and *Le jeu de la palette* (*The Paddle*) (p. 42, fig. 37).[1] At the same time, the description of foliage as silhouetted patterns signals a connection to another early work, *View of a Park* (cat. 2), in gray wash.

If the scene here is quiet and the figures are unaware of outsiders, the vegetation is exuberant, as Fragonard's uninterrupted chalk lines meander and bend to depict twisted trunks, errant foliage, and bushy shrubs. The central leaning tree with a forked trunk is, like *View of a Park*, another example of Fragonard saluting Boucher, this time in a medium he is making his own. The broken branch hanging down is one of Fragonard's favorite devices to direct the viewer's eye in another direction. Another device evident upon close examination is the exploitation, even augmentation, of the vertical fold in the paper, which he uses as a guide to organize the composition. This procedure is discussed in other entries (see cats. 48 and 49).

For coloristic and spatial effects, Fragonard deliberately introduced a second tone of red chalk, a brownish variety called *sanguine brûlée* or *sanguine foncé* because of its burnt hue. It was popular in academic figure drawing in the mid-1700s and a favorite of Boucher's. Here the two colors are mingled in the foliage and grass, but, to isolate the trunk of the forked tree, brown chalk is used alone. An analogous coloristic use of *sanguine brûlée* occurs in the mature red chalk landscape *Two Cypresses in an Italian Garden* (cat. 65).

The formal connection between the present work and the two large red chalk landscapes in Frankfurt reflects Fragonard's evolving personal interpretation of nature and landscape as emotional vehicles that resonate within the viewer. His depiction of space, along with development of signature markings and hatchings, contributes to the emotional impact of a composition.[2] The presence of a strong diagonal emerging from vegetation unites the present work and the Frankfurt drawings. Here and in *Le jeu de la palette*, it is a balustrade; in *Le jeu de la bascule*, the board itself is a corresponding diagonal.

The balustrade is likewise a key motif in an early painting in Chambéry, also titled *Le jeu de la palette*, in which it serves as background to elegant figures playing the paddle game.[3] According to Rosenberg's chronology, the two red chalk drawings in Frankfurt are preparatory to the Chambéry painting, which he places in about 1758.[4] However, the two red chalks display a mastery of execution that suggests they are autonomous works, perhaps even later than the painting (see also "Every Possible Combination" in this volume, pp. 15–45). The painting in Chambéry, and presumably the Frankfurt drawings, are connected to the abbé de Saint-Non's early patronage of Fragonard.[5] EW

PROVENANCE: Possibly in the collection of Hippolyte Walferdin (1795–1880) (according to the catalogue of the Decloux sale); Léon Decloux (1840–1929); his collection sale (Lugt 55952), Hôtel Drouot, Paris, February 14–15, 1898 (lot 65, repr. in color); acquired at the sale by Arthur Veil-Picard, Paris; by descent to his daughter, Jeannette Veil-Picard; by descent to the consignor to the sale, Artcurial, Paris, June 19, 2007 (lot 30, repr. in color); private collection

SELECTED REFERENCE: Ananoff 1961–70, vol. 2 (1963), no. 887, fig. 233.

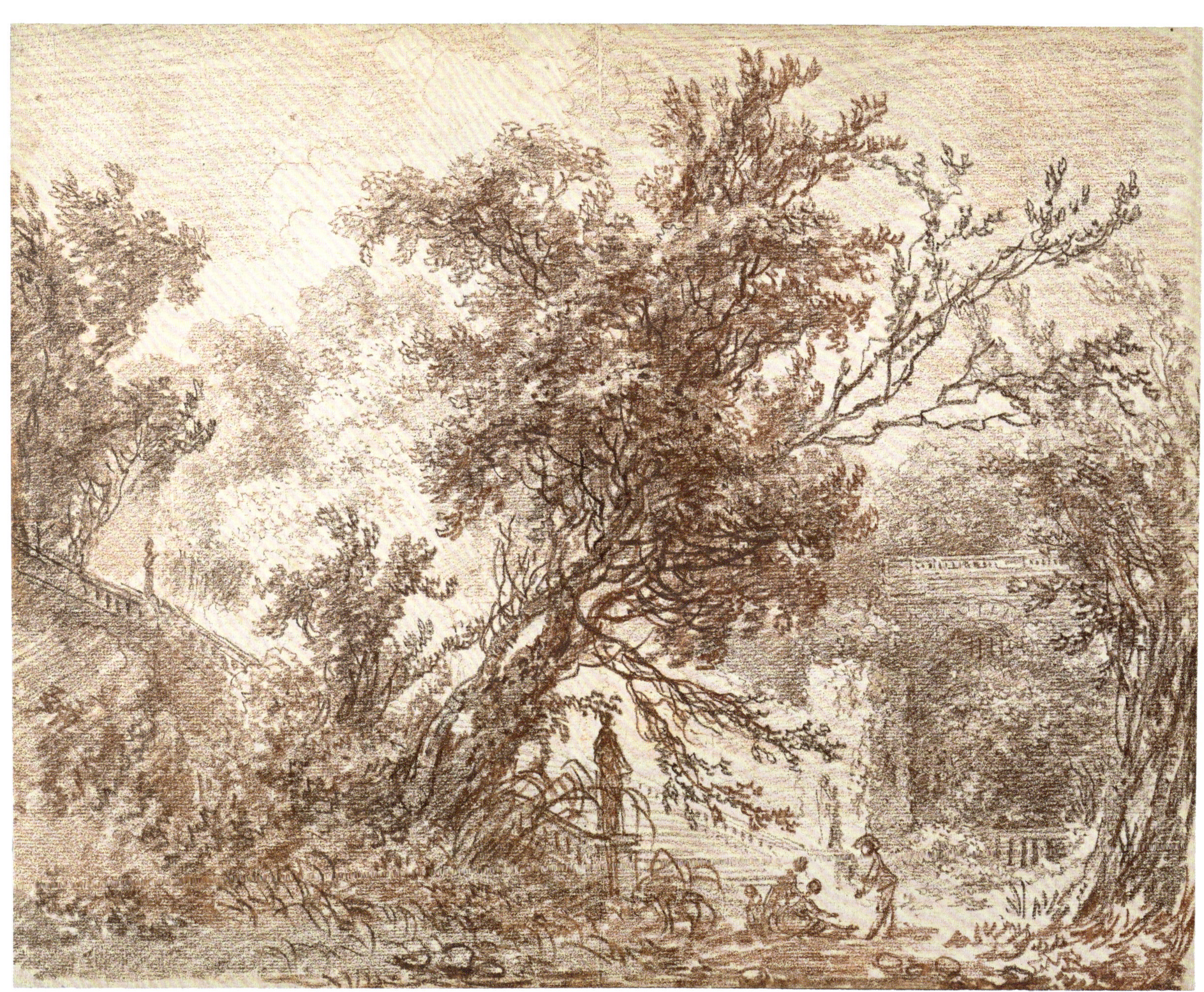

6. *Capriccio: Excavation of Roman Ruins*

Ca. 1760–62
Brush and brown and gray wash and watercolor over black chalk on antique laid paper
10⅜ × 12⅜ in. (26.2 × 31.3 cm)
Stamp: at lower right, blind stamp of the mount maker, François Renaud (Lugt 1042)

As a pensionnaire at the Académie de France in Rome, Fragonard had the opportunity to meet living artists in addition to studying masters of the past. Established artists such as Charles Joseph Natoire, Giovanni Battista Piranesi, and Giovanni Paolo Panini visited or were connected to the Académie, which was then housed in the Palazzo Mancini. Panini, a specialist in *vedute* (detailed cityscapes or vistas) and architectural capriccios, taught perspective at the Académie; his influence on the young Hubert Robert has been acknowledged.[1] Fragonard in the present work demonstrates that he could interpret the styles of both his friend Robert (nicknamed "Robert des ruines" for his many depictions of ruins) and the celebrated Panini.

The composition is a romantic meditation on past grandeur, as revealed during an excavation of picturesque Roman ruins. Since the Renaissance, regular excavations in Rome permitted students and connoisseurs to study relics of ancient Roman culture. The present composition depicts an imagined excavation, with workers actively digging and carrying fragments. Architectural elements and sculptural reliefs are displayed casually around the area, and on the right is a statue of a seated, draped female deity. In the background, overgrown with vegetation, are the ruins of a temple with a curved entablature and Corinthian columns. The structure recalls the temple dedicated to Vesta in the Roman Forum. In this context, could the statue represent Vesta, Roman goddess of the hearth?

This watercolor stands in contrast to Fragonard's typical compositions, where elegant or pastoral figures visit ruins in landscapes for pleasure or contemplation. Such figures, or staffage, are usually included for decorative reasons or to indicate scale or space. In this exceptional work, Fragonard has created an homage to Panini, even emulating the Italian's manner of depicting the subtle patina of weathered stone. As in Panini's works, the staffage figures can be interpreted as both ancient and eighteenth-century observers.

As an early work, *Excavation of Roman Ruins* can be compared to architectural capriccios from the same years, about 1760–62. *Temple in a Garden* (Peabody Art Collection, Baltimore Museum of Art) and *Scene in a Park* (Cleveland Museum of Art) share the same technique, beginning with cursive black chalk, pen and ink, brush with brown and gray wash, and finishing with accents of watercolor.[2]

The blind stamp of François Renaud (Lugt 1042), the mount maker and dealer, establishes the work's eighteenth-century provenance. Subsequent owners include Etienne Arago, a mayor of Paris, journalist, author, and archivist to the Ecole des Beaux-Arts; and Maurice Fenaille, a French pioneer in the petroleum industry and a dedicated amateur art historian and collector. EW

PROVENANCE: Etienne Arago (1802–1892), Paris, by 1884; Mme Charras; her estate sale (Lugt 76647), Galerie Georges Petit, Paris, April 2–3, 1917 (lot 53, repr.); Maurice Fenaille (1855–1937); private collection, France; sale, Couturier & Nicolay, Paris, March 30, 1979 (lot 5); sale, Sotheby's, London, July 2, 1997 (lot 69, repr.); sale, Sotheby's, New York, January 26, 2000 (lot 95); [W. M. Brady & Co., Inc., New York]; private collection

SELECTED EXHIBITIONS: Paris 1921, cat. no. 113; Paris 1931, cat. no. 78; Paris 1934, cat. no. 463; Copenhagen 1935, cat. no. 367.

SELECTED REFERENCES: Réau 1956, p. 227 (as Fenaille Collection); Ananoff 1961–70, vol. 1 (1961), no. 363, fig. 127.

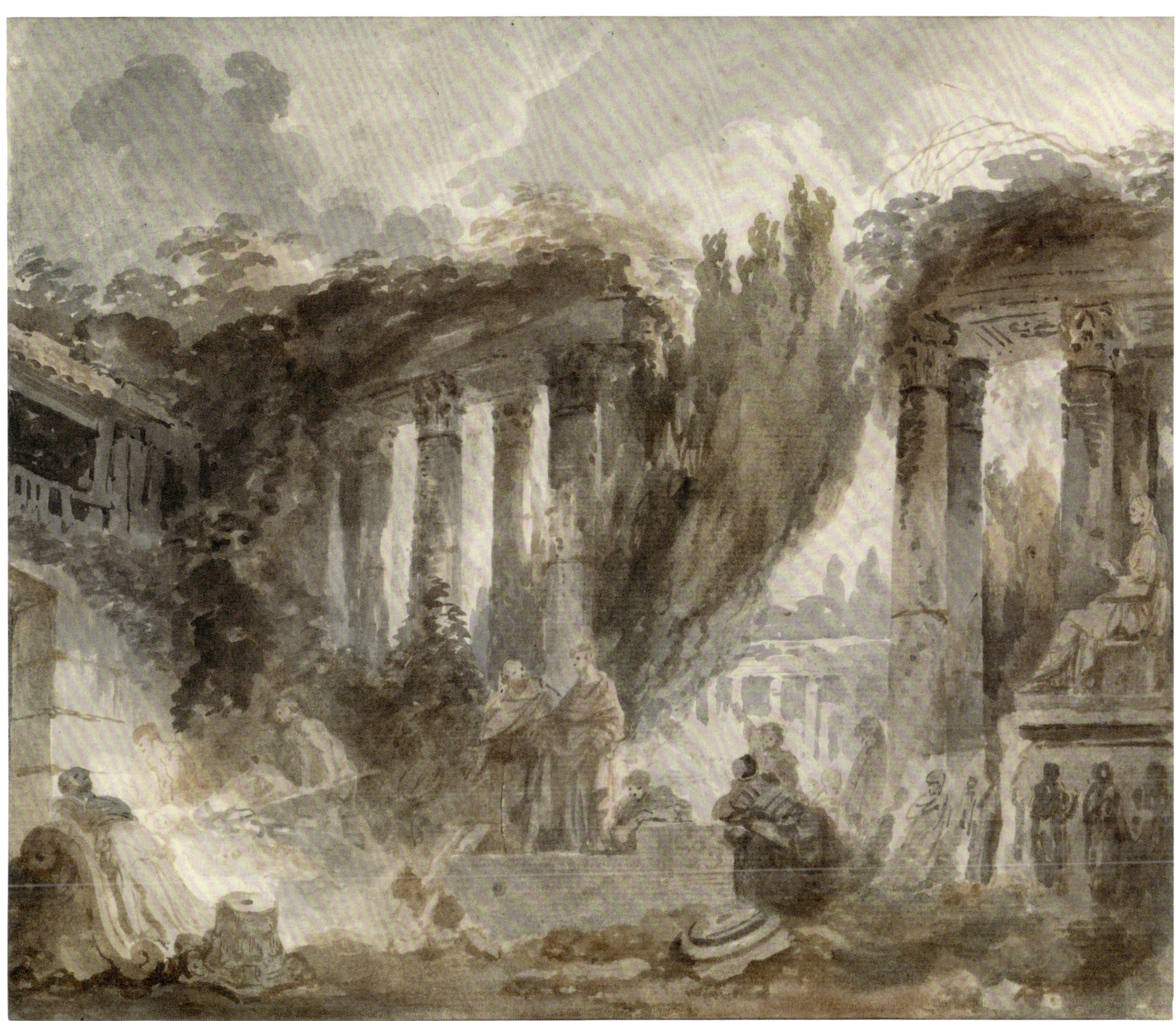

Fragonard and the Abbé de Saint-Non

The benefits of the Italian sojourn, for Fragonard, as for other young pensionnaires sent by the French crown to study in Rome, extended far beyond the structured curriculum of the Académie de France. The artistic growth of the French students often owed as much to the informal activities and commissions that grew out of friendships with visiting *amateurs* and local expatriates. Fragonard's good fortune came in the form of his relationship with Jean Claude Richard, the abbé de Saint-Non, who arrived in Rome in 1759. Expected by his family to go into the priesthood, Saint-Non preferred to devote himself to the arts—not surprising, perhaps, as his maternal grandfather was Louis de Boullogne, who had been first painter to the king. Saint-Non's stay in Rome lasted two years, longer than expected. During this time he went on a number of side trips, including one to the Villa d'Este in Tivoli with Fragonard in summer 1760, and employed several artists to make drawings on his behalf. Fragonard and Saint-Non made the trip back to Paris together, stretching the journey to more than five months as they wended their way through various Italian cities and sought out beautiful things to see and record.

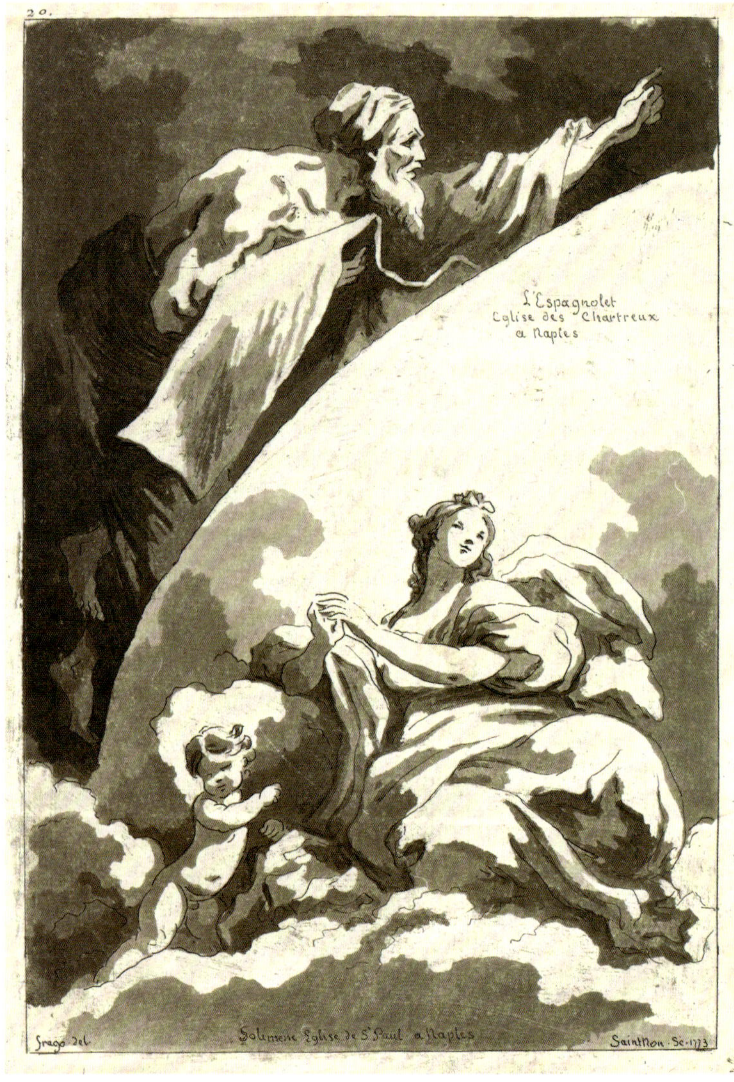

Fig. 66. Jean Claude Richard, abbé de Saint-Non (French, 1727–1791), *Copies after Giuseppe Ribera and Francesco Solimena*, 1773. Etching and aquatint, plate: 7⅞ × 5½ in. (20 × 14 cm). The Metropolitan Museum of Art, New York, Gift of Harry G. Friedman (56.648.17[17])

Fragonard's quickly sketched copies made over the course of their travels stayed in his patron's possession, and many of them were eventually translated into print: various suites of aquatints, etched by Saint-Non's own hand and published under the titles *Fragments* and *Griffonis* (scribbles), beginning in 1770 (see, for example, fig. 66); and the five-volume luxury publication *Voyage pittoresque, ou description des royaumes de Naples et de Sicile* (1781–86), with illustrations by professional reproductive printmakers. Although Saint-Non's *Journal*, first published in 1986, sheds considerable light on the sequence and precise dating of Fragonard's drawings, it leaves certain questions about the collaboration unresolved.[1] To what extent were plans for these projects already formed in Saint-Non's mind during the trip, and who directed the choices of works and details for Fragonard to copy? Despite these lacunae in our knowledge, the surviving visual evidence provides strong support to Jean-Pierre Cuzin's claim that, for Fragonard, the copying of old masters before, during, and after his return trip from Italy constituted a critical act of learning and, ultimately, proved to be an influence that vied in importance with the lessons of his flesh-and-blood teachers: François Boucher, Carle Vanloo, and Charles Joseph Natoire.[2]

Many contemporaries remarked on the trove of drawings in Saint-Non's possession when he returned to Paris in late September 1761. The collector Pierre Jean Mariette, who had a special interest in copy drawings,[3] quipped that Saint-Non had brought back both Fragonard himself and a large quantity of sheets the young painter had made for him. The German expatriate printmaker Johan Georg Wille noted that Saint-Non proposed to etch some of the works.[4] And Anne Claude Philippe de Tubières, the comte de Caylus, a writer, antiquarian, and *amateur honoraire* of the Académie, described the fruits of the trip in less prosaic terms, proclaiming that Saint-Non had amassed a stockpile that would nourish him for the rest of his life and commenting that the seedlings one acquires in Rome and other Italian cities can take root and live on in those who carry them.[5]

The drawings were done quickly, on a small scale and without belabored detail. Some represent entire compositions, but many pick out small vignettes, individual figures, or heads. Such "excerpts" often share the sheet with unrelated sketches. Thus, Saint-Non's titles for his suites of aquatints, *Fragments* and *Griffonis*, are well suited to the subjective and selective nature of the copies. Numbering in the hundreds, the drawings are now dispersed among many collections, with the largest holdings in the Norton Simon Museum in Pasadena and the British Museum in London. The vast majority are in black chalk, although one occasionally finds examples in sanguine.[6] The annotations they bear, typically giving the artist and the location of the work copied, are in Saint-Non's hand. Most of the drawings appear to have been counterproofed, presumably so Fragonard could have a record as well.[7] The two men stayed close friends for the remaining three decades of the abbé's life. His biographer, Gabriel Brizard, related the anecdote that when Saint-Non, years later, learned of the high prices that Fragonard's drawings had begun to command, he returned to the artist all of the drawings from their Italian trip so that he might derive the profit he deserved from them.[8]

In the end, we cannot know who chose each painting to copy or view to record, but we can be sure that the two young men were friends who enjoyed traveling and working together. Fragonard's copy drawings were not dutifully executed assignments but rather the physical record of a shared adventure, the spirit of which shines through in Saint-Non's account to his brother, "Fragonard is all fire; he draws constantly, one after the other; I find them charming. There is magic in them."[9] PS

7. *Saint Celestine V Renouncing the Papacy, after Mattia Preti*

After Mattia Preti (Italian, 1613–1699)
1761
Black chalk, over a black chalk counterproof
$7\frac{5}{8} \times 7\frac{5}{8}$ in. (19.5 × 19.3 cm)
Inscriptions: at lower left, in pen and gray ink, "Naples / Eglise de St. Pierre / de Calabrese"; at lower right, in black chalk, in reverse, "de Calabrese"

Before embarking together on their return journey to Paris, Saint-Non sent Fragonard to Naples "to see beautiful things," as reported by Charles Joseph Natoire in a letter to the marquis de Marigny dated March 18, 1761.[1] In addition to this altruistic aim, the abbé also had a more personal interest in sponsoring the trip, as a great many of Fragonard's copies after the oil paintings and frescoes found in Neapolitan churches would eventually be translated into illustrations for his sumptuous travel guide, *Voyage pittoresque, ou description des royaumes de Naples et de Sicile*, published beginning in 1781.[2]

Saint Celestine V Renouncing the Papacy is one of five compositions copied by Fragonard after paintings by Mattia Preti on the ceiling of San Pietro a Maiella.[3] The Metropolitan's sheet, however, is not the copy Fragonard drew in the church but rather a counterproof of that copy reworked in black chalk. Saint-Non's black chalk inscription specifying the place and the artist, illegible in reverse, has been rewritten in pen. Such reworked counterproofs, which exist for many of the copies made for Saint-Non, have been the subject of much speculation. Was the counterproofing done to produce images in reverse direction that could be used as models for etching? Apparently not, as neither Fragonard nor Saint-Non seems to have taken any special care to have their prints after Italian masters appear in the correct orientation. It seems likely that the entire set of Italian copies must have been counterproofed so that both men—Fragonard and Saint-Non—could each have a set. That the value of the counterproofs was not seen as strictly utilitarian is apparent in the aesthetic quality of the reworking.

Previous authors have hesitated to see Fragonard's own hand in these reworkings.[4] However, in examples like this sheet one sees not only the discontinuous angular contours associated with his early style but also a characteristically bold confidence in the crosshatching, which focuses on broad effects of light and shade while suppressing unnecessary detail. Fragonard's original copy drawing in the Norton Simon Museum (fig. 67) significantly alters and simplifies Preti's composition (fig. 68), omitting a chair on the left and a man's head on the right and turning the head of the foreground putto inward. In reworking the counterproof, Fragonard took this reductive sensibility one step further, leaving out the second chair (now on the left) and letting the architectural details of the setting dissolve into pure sky. PS

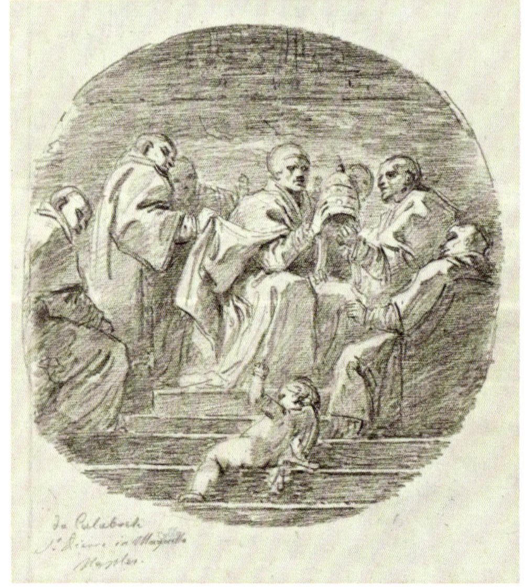

Fig. 67. Jean Honoré Fragonard, after Mattia Preti (Italian, 1613–1699), *Saint Celestine V Renouncing the Papacy*, 1761. Black chalk, $17\frac{3}{4} \times 13$ in. (45.1 × 33 cm). The Norton Simon Foundation, Pasadena

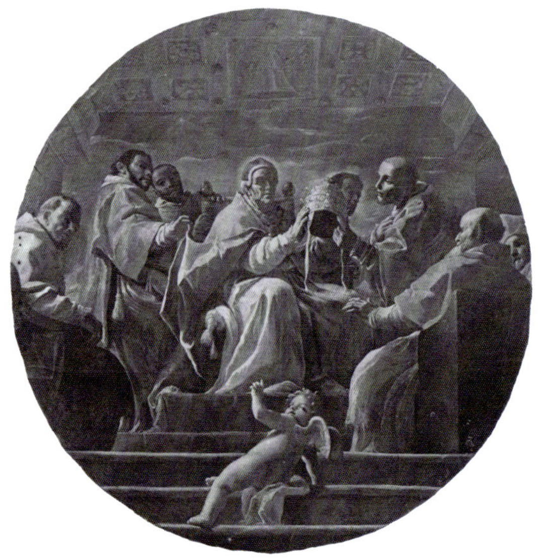

Fig. 68. Mattia Preti (Italian, 1613–1699), *Saint Celestine V Renouncing the Papacy*, ca. 1657–58. Oil on canvas, diam. $141\frac{3}{4}$ in. (360 cm). Church of San Pietro a Maiella, Naples

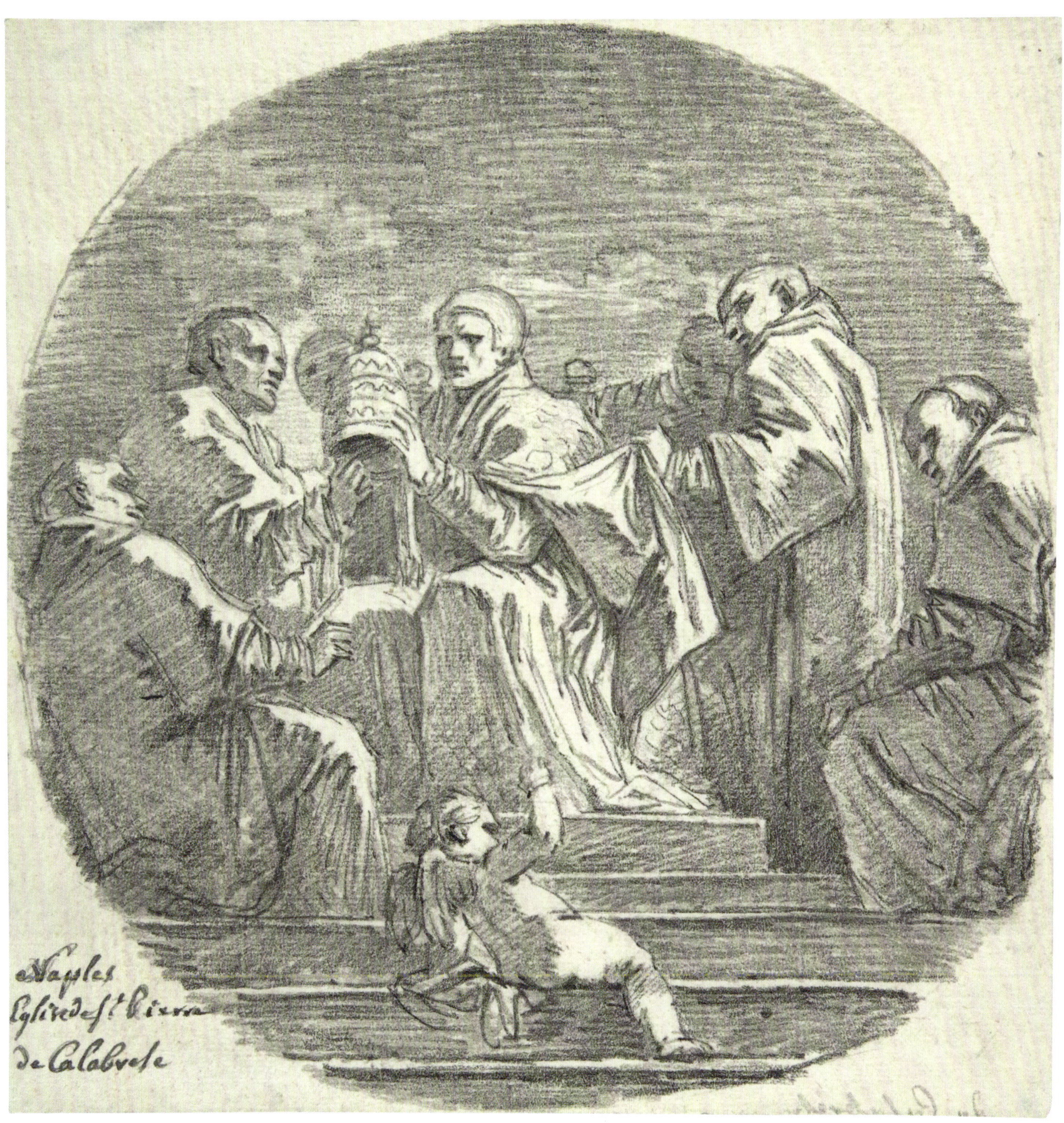

PROVENANCE: Sale, Hôtel Drouot, Paris, November 13, 1986 (lot 52); [Galerie Cailleux, Paris]; The Metropolitan Museum of Art, New York, Gift of Dr. and Mrs. John C. Weber, 1987 (1987.239)

SELECTED EXHIBITION: Stein and Holmes 1999, pp. 96–98, cat. no. 42.

SELECTED REFERENCES: Lamers 1995, p. 87, under no. 56; Rosenberg and Brejon de Lavergnée 2000, p. 344, under no. 38.

8. *Saint Rita Surrounded by Bees*

After Pietro Locatelli (Italian, ca. 1634–1710)
Ca. 1761
Black chalk
10¼ × 7⅜ in. (26 × 18.7 cm)
Inscription: at bottom center, in black chalk, "fragonard 1780"

This charming drawing of cherubs bathed in heavenly light spilling into a shadowy scene of rustic domesticity emerged on the art market only after the first edition of Pierre Rosenberg and Barbara Brejon de Lavergnée's *Panopticon* was published in 1986.[1] It was not initially recognized as a work from Fragonard's first trip, owing to the apocryphal date in the inscription and to the fact that the work copied is not a famous one.[2] The source, a painting by Pietro Locatelli in a Roman church (fig. 69), was discovered by the present author when the drawing was exhibited in New York in 1999 but, unfortunately, only after the catalogue had gone to press.

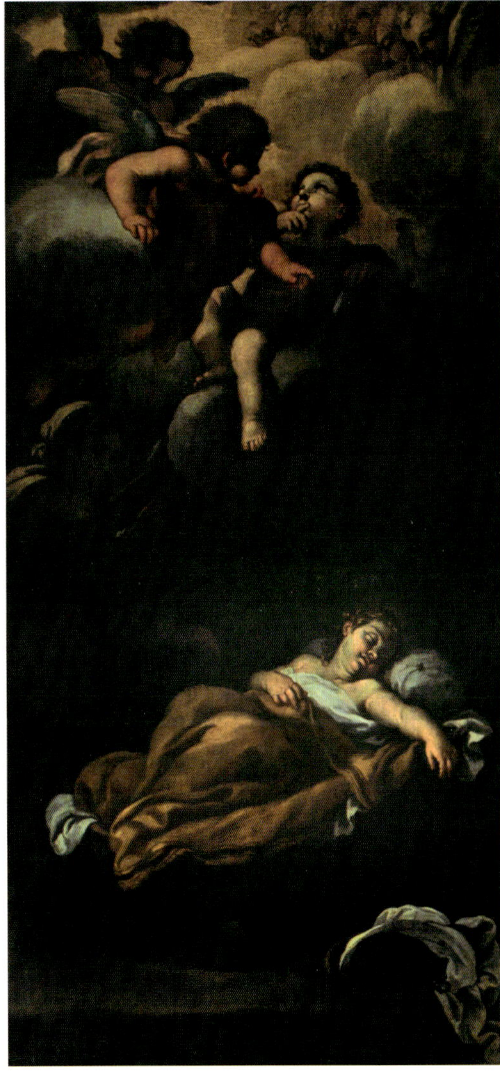

Fig. 69. Pietro Locatelli (Italian, ca. 1634–1710), *Saint Rita Surrounded by Bees*, ca. 1686. Fresco. Sant'Agostino, Rome

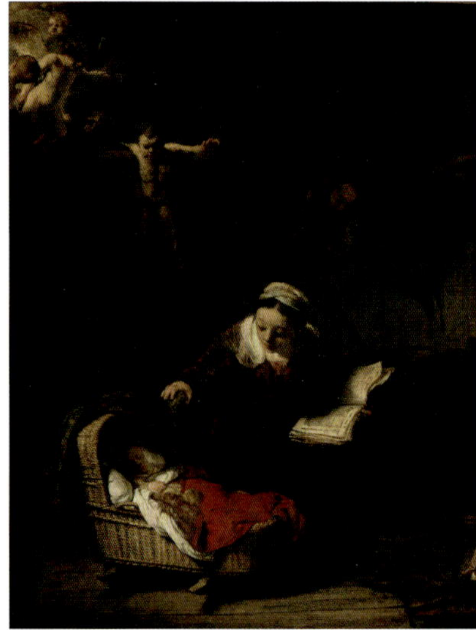

Fig. 70. Rembrandt (Dutch, 1606–1669), *The Holy Family with Angels,* 1645. Oil on canvas, 46⅛ × 35⅞ in. (117 × 91 cm). State Hermitage Museum, Saint Petersburg (741)

The chalk copies Fragonard made in Rome for Saint-Non, numbering more than seventy, record many visits to the Vatican and to a broad range of churches and palaces. This sheet is the sole extant record of a visit to the fifteenth-century church of Sant'Agostino, where in the 1680s the Roman Baroque painter Pietro Locatelli had decorated a chapel with a series of frescoes devoted to the life of the Augustinian nun Rita of Cascia.[3] The composition copied by Fragonard depicts the legend that on the day after her baptism, as she slept in her cradle, a swarm of white bees circled around her without causing her harm.

Of the copy drawings Fragonard executed in Rome, the majority of which highlight vignettes or figures from well-known works by major artists, this one stands apart. Was it Fragonard or Saint-Non who wanted an image of this relatively obscure painting, which few tourists would have lingered over? The particular iconography of Saint Rita's infancy does not seem to have been the attraction, as Locatelli's swarm of bees is omitted from Fragonard's sketch. One guesses that Fragonard may have been struck by the fresco's similarity to a painting by Rembrandt (fig. 70) that he had copied more than once while a student in Paris.[4] It remained his lifelong preference, when treating religious subjects, to gravitate toward those that featured domestic scenes of familial tenderness, which were close in sensibility to his genre paintings of peasant families in timeless rustic settings. PS

PROVENANCE: Private collection, Paris; [David and Constance Yates, New York]; Roberta J. M. Olson and Alexander B. V. Johnson, New York

SELECTED EXHIBITION: Stein and Holmes 1999, pp. 106–7, cat. no. 47.

SELECTED REFERENCES: Laing 1999, pp. 379–80; Rosenberg 2000a, p. 189; Rosenberg and Brejon de Lavergnée 2000, p. 441, fig. 9.

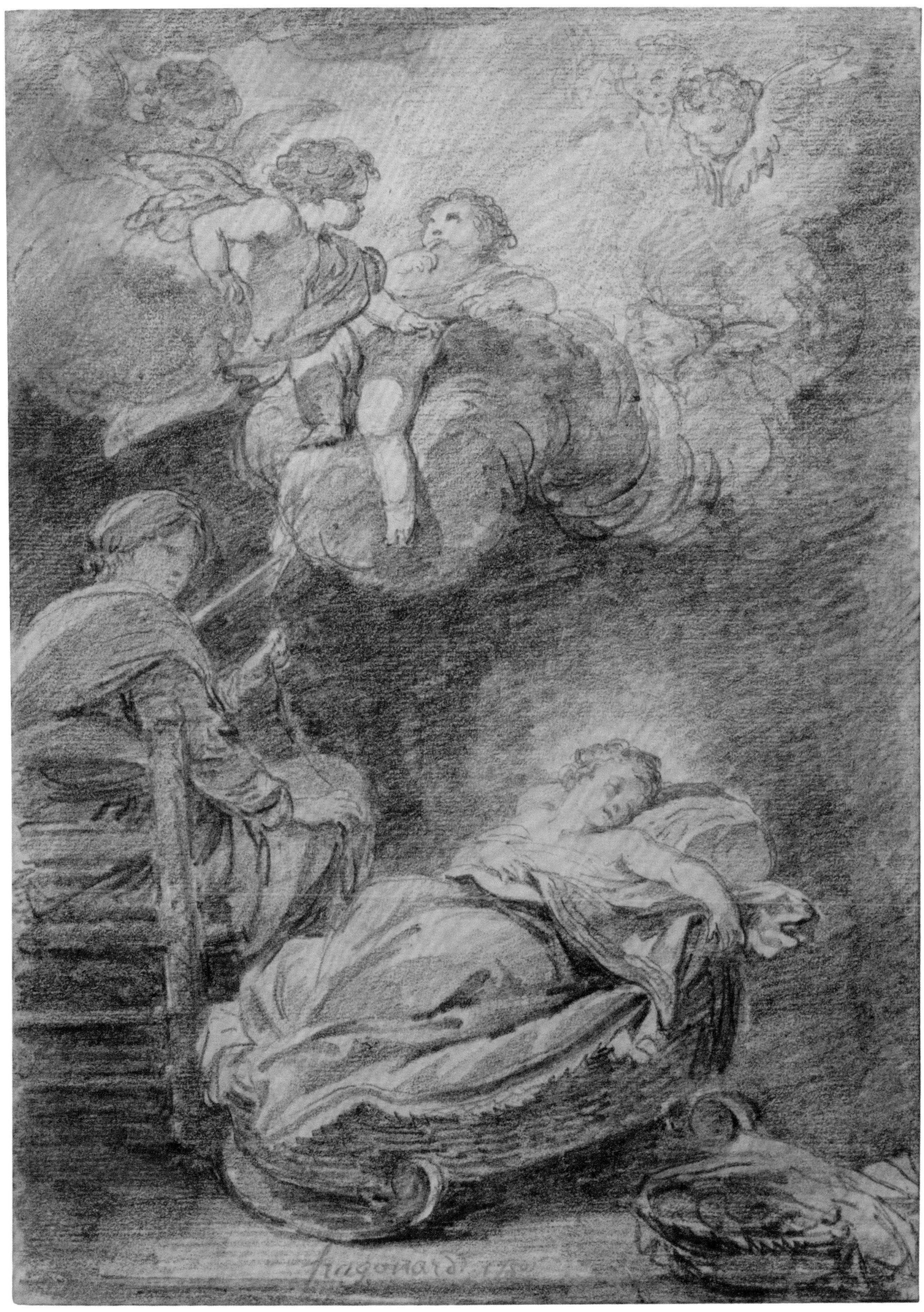
fragonard

9. *The Virgin and Child Appearing to Saint Hyacinth*

After Ludovico Carracci (Italian, 1555–1619)
1761
Black chalk
11½ × 8¼ in. (29.3 × 21 cm)
Inscription: at lower right, in black chalk, "Louis Carrache / à san domenico. Bologne"

This crisp and accomplished drawing, recorded at an exhibition in Vichy in 1943, was out of the public eye for about sixty years and is here reproduced for the first time. It captures with ease the central elements of Ludovico Carracci's *The Virgin and Child Appearing to Saint Hyacinth*, an altarpiece of 1594 that was then in the church of San Domenico in Bologna (fig. 71).[1]

Bologna was, after Rome, one of the most important stops on the itineraries of visitors to Italy in the eighteenth century. On their return trip to Paris in 1761, Fragonard and Saint-Non spent almost the entire month of July in Bologna, seeking out the works of the great seventeenth-century Emilian masters. Saint-Non had visited the church of San Domenico two years earlier, on his way to Rome in 1759, noting in his journal that it contained many superior things.[2] In addition to Ludovico's altarpiece, Fragonard drew Guido Reni's *Massacre of the Innocents* (1611, Pinacoteca Nazionale, Bologna) and sketched some of the angels playing music in the foreground of Reni's ceiling fresco, *Saint Dominic's Glory* (1613), in the main chapel.[3] Charles Nicolas Cochin's *Voyage d'Italie* (1758), which Fragonard and Saint-Non may well have consulted, called attention to Ludovico's canvas, noting that it contained both the beauties and the faults in color that one expected from the artist.[4] For Saint-Non, Ludovico embodied genius and *terribilità*.[5]

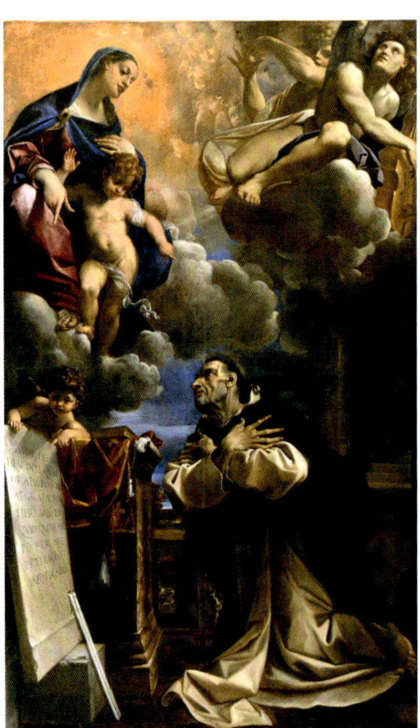

Fig. 71. Ludovico Carracci (Italian, 1555–1619), *The Virgin and Child Appearing to Saint Hyacinth*, 1594. Oil on canvas, 147⅝ × 87⅞ in. (375 × 223 cm). Musée du Louvre, Paris (186)

However, all of these qualities in the original painting largely fall away in Fragonard's copy, where the gently modulated hatching knits the figures and the atmosphere into a harmonious whole. Scholars have often remarked that Fragonard took liberties with the compositions he copied, and that is certainly the case here. At the upper right, he suppressed the musical instruments and the heads of angels in the clouds; in the earthbound part of the composition, he glossed over details of architecture and still life; and he minimized certain anatomical elements, such as the hands of the saint and the Virgin, which must have struck him as disproportionate or inelegant. This type of simplification, so often seen in Fragonard's Italian copies, is, on the one hand, a natural result of the drastic reduction of scale that was necessary to record in a sketchbook the composition of an altarpiece measuring more than twelve feet high. On the other hand, the distillation of the composition into its most essential forms and its translation into a graphic language that was personal and undisguised speak to the nature of the project as one of homage and assimilation.

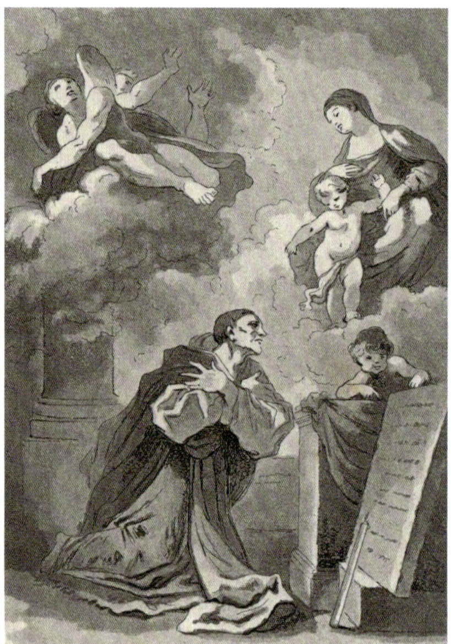

Fig. 72. Jean Claude Richard, abbé de Saint-Non (French, 1727–1791), *The Virgin and Child Appearing to Saint Hyacinth*, 1772. Aquatint, image: 7½ × 5⅛ in. (19 × 12.9 cm). The Metropolitan Museum of Art, New York, Harris Brisbane Dick Fund, 1945 (45.47.4 [73])

A parallel sensibility can be seen in the approach Saint-Non used to translate Fragonard's chalk drawing into aquatint eleven years later (fig. 72). Unlike the professional printmakers of the day, Saint-Non took no steps to avoid the reversal of the composition by the printing process,[6] nor did he make an effort to evoke the style and handling of the painter; rather, he embraced the ability of the recently invented technique of aquatint to imitate Fragonard's soft tonal hatching. His print is as much after Fragonard as it is after Ludovico. PS

PROVENANCE: [Galerie Sévigné, Vichy, in 1943]; [sold at Hôtel Drouot, Paris, ca. 2001–6, per Galerie de Bayser, Paris]; Olivier Scherberich (b. 1960), Colmar; [Galerie de Bayser, Paris]; private collection

SELECTED EXHIBITION: Vichy 1943, cat. no. 14.

SELECTED REFERENCE: Rosenberg and Brejon de Lavergnée 2000, p. 401, under no. 276 (as unlocated).[7]

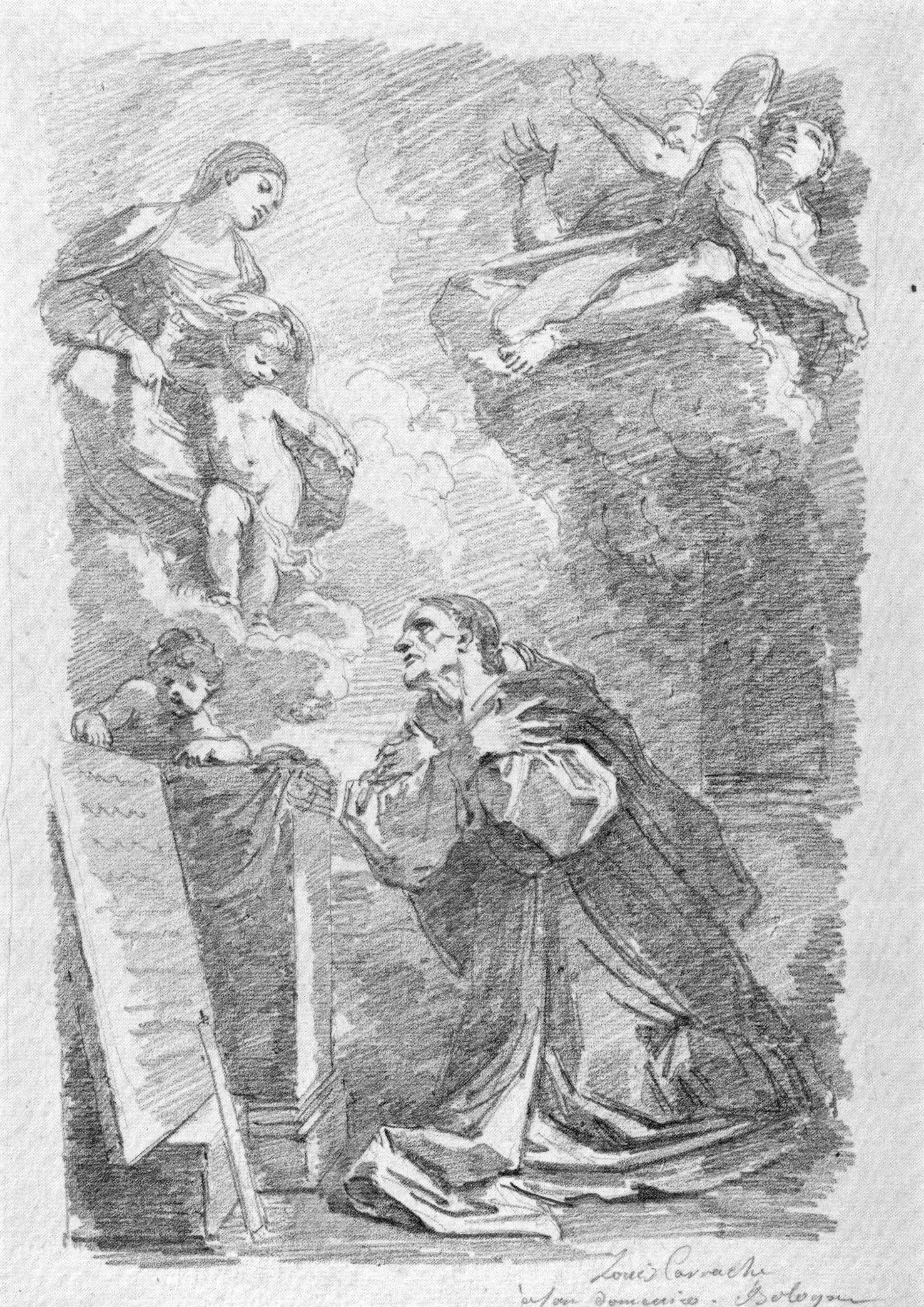
Louis Carrache
à San domenico · Bologne

10. *Hercules and Cacus, after Annibale Carracci, and the Destruction of Enceladus, after Agostino Carracci*

After Annibale Carracci (Italian, 1560–1609) and after Agostino Carracci (Italian, 1557–1602)
1761
Black chalk, framing lines in pen and brown ink
8 × 11½ in. (20.4 × 29.3 cm)
Inscriptions: at lower left, in black chalk, "augustin Carrache"; at lower center, in black chalk, "Palais Sampieri / Bologna"; at lower right, in black chalk, "Annibal Carrache"

In addition to its richly embellished churches, Bologna boasted a great many palaces that figured on the itineraries of visiting *amateurs* and artists. Among them, the Palazzo Sampieri, according to Saint-Non's journal, contained the most interesting collection of paintings in Bologna. The decor featured works by Agostino, Annibale, and Ludovico Carracci, although distinguishing their hands proved a challenge for both Saint-Non and Charles Nicolas Cochin, who had catalogued the highlights of the palace's interior in his *Voyage d'Italie* (1758).[1] In the Metropolitan's sheet, Fragonard chose to combine two figure studies done after the two over-chimney frescoes. The inscriptions in Saint-Non's handwriting attribute the source of the group copied on the left to Agostino and that of the figure on the right to Annibale, attributions since reversed by modern scholars.[2]

The frescoes depict the defeat of two giants, Cacus at the hands of Hercules and Enceladus crushed by boulders. In both cases, Fragonard treated the figures as "excerpts," leaving no indication of the irregularly shaped surrounds that, in the frescoes, barely contain the struggling figures. The massive scale of the giants, as well as their pained expressions and exaggerated musculature—what Saint-Non would have referred to as their *terribilità*—have all been toned down. The hands and the feet are less oversize in proportion to the bodies, and the faces are less obscured and less monstrous. PS

PROVENANCE: Mrs. Paul Moore, New York; The Metropolitan Museum of Art, New York, Gift of Mrs. Paul Moore, 1960 (60.53)

SELECTED EXHIBITION: Williams 1978, pp. 48–49, cat. no. 11.

SELECTED REFERENCES: Ananoff 1961–70, vol. 2 (1963), no. 1052, fig. 281, vol. 3 (1968), p. 335; Bean and Turčić 1986, pp. 107–8, no. 111; Rosenberg and Brejon de Lavergnée 2000, pp. 81, 82, 265, 267, 398, no. 263.

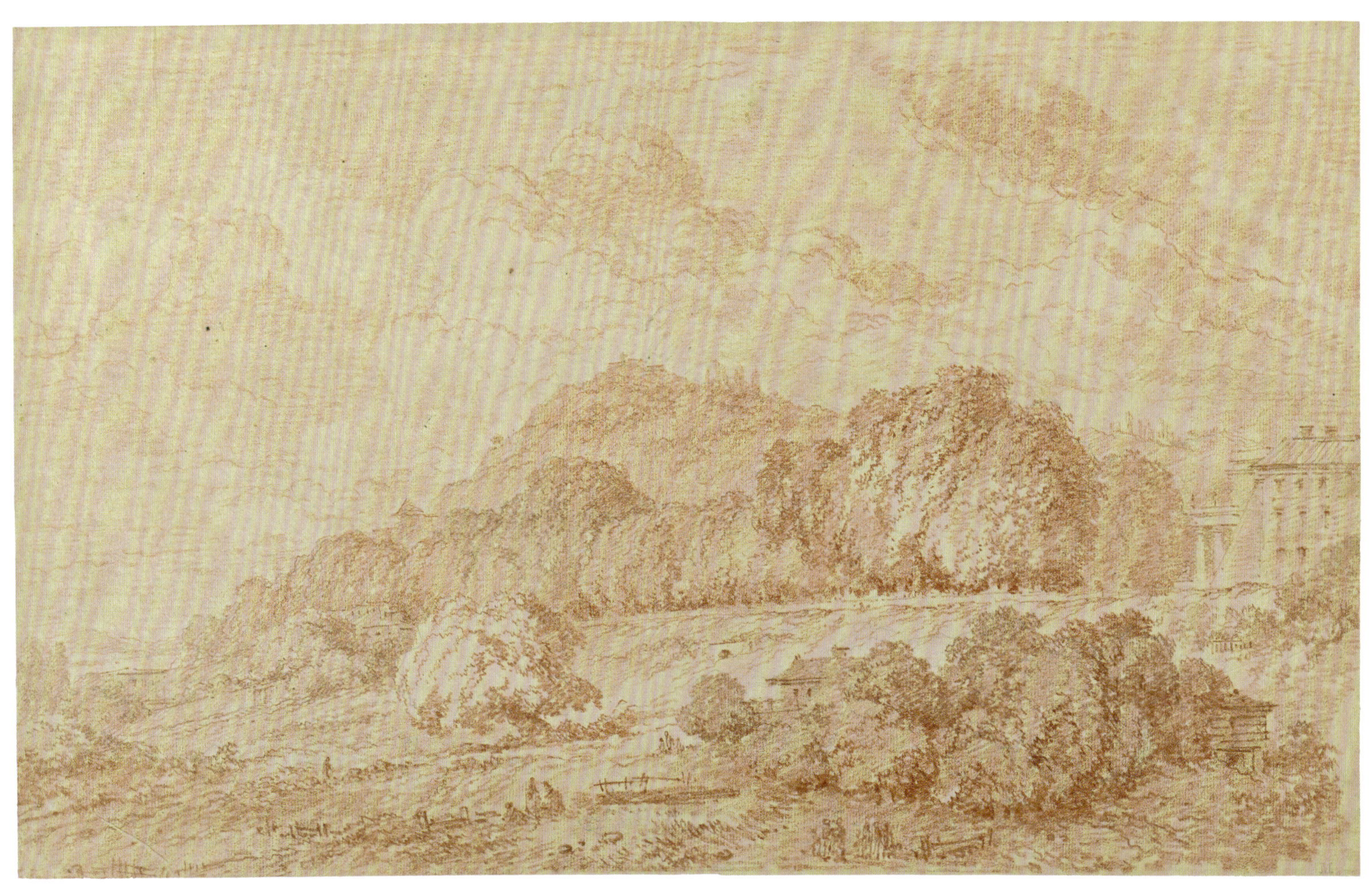

Etchings Inspired by Italy

Fragonard returned to Paris from Italy in September 1761, having spent more than five months traveling with his patron the abbé de Saint-Non. He would achieve great acclaim with the immense and powerful painting *Coresus and Callirhoë* (p. 139, fig. 85), his *morceau d'agrément* (acceptance piece) presented to the Académie Royale in March 1765 and exhibited at the Salon later that year, but his activities during the intervening years remain something of a mystery. Among the few works that can be assigned with certainty to this period are a group of etchings produced about 1763–64, which were inspired by the landscape, paintings, and antiquities of the Italian peninsula. Small in scale, they are nonetheless true treasures of Rococo printmaking, virtuoso exercises in freedom and inventiveness. As a group, they make clear that Fragonard stayed close to Saint-Non after the two returned to Paris, was attracted to the abbé's fascination with etching, and continued to draw inspiration from the works of Italian masters and the gardens that they had studied in each other's company.

Of the twenty-one prints resulting from this campaign, Fragonard's second foray into printmaking, sixteen were based on the black chalk copies after Italian masters that he had drawn for Saint-Non.[1] To understand their character, we might begin by asking why he made them. Despite the tradition of referring to the prints as a group, their copperplates were not of uniform dimensions. They were not advertised for sale and are not printed with a publisher's address (which is how prints were typically marketed in the eighteenth century); many do not even bear the artist's name, and the ones that do are typically signed casually "frago," in the informal handwriting of a *peintre-graveur*, not the legible inscription of a professional printmaker. These

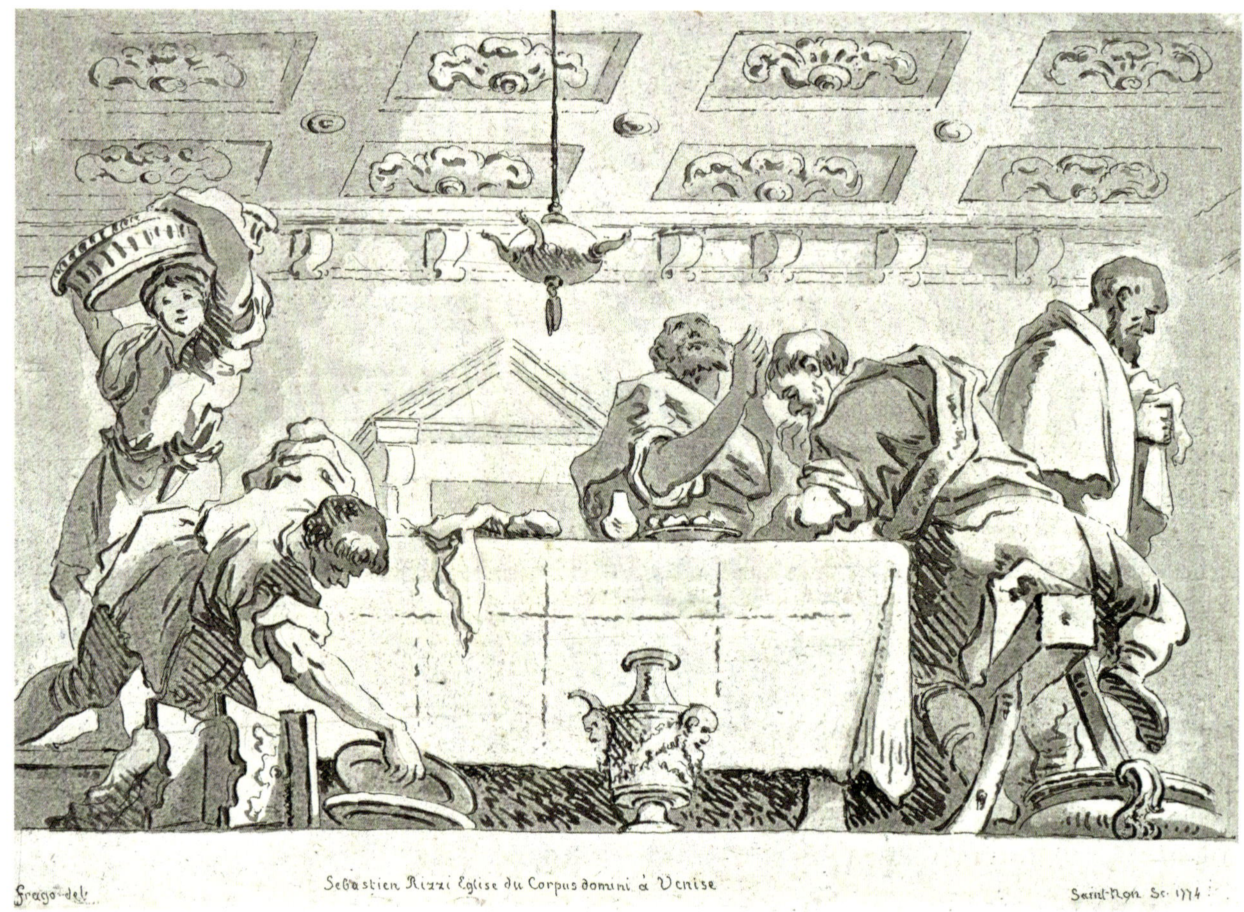

Fig. 74. Jean Claude Richard, abbé de Saint-Non (French, 1727–1791), *The Last Supper*, pl. 130 from *Recueil de griffonis, de vues, paysages, fragments antiques et sujets historiques*, ca. 1780. The Morgan Library & Museum, New York (PML 140102)

are all hallmarks of prints made not for the commercial print market but within the milieu of the *amateur*, in which artistically inclined members of the upper classes pursued etching as a cultivated activity related to sociability and connoisseurship.[2]

In many ways, Fragonard's sixteen etchings after Italian masters presage Saint-Non's *Fragments*, the suites of aquatints that Saint-Non began to publish in 1770 (see, for example, fig. 74).[3] Saint-Non's prints would diverge from Fragonard's most visibly in his use of the aquatint technique, a new process with which he had first experimented in 1767, according to Jean de Cayeux.[4] In 1764, assuming one assigns the whole group of Fragonard's etchings after Italian masters to the date that appears on two of the prints (cats. 18 and 24), it would not have been surprising to find Fragonard choosing the etching needle, as it was Saint-Non's preferred technique at that time. Indeed, Saint-Non had already begun making etchings after drawings by Fragonard (see p. 54, fig. 45) and Hubert Robert in the two years since his return to Paris.[5] It was with his guidance and encouragement—and presumably his tools and printing press—that Fragonard was reinitiated into the printmaking technique that he had first learned in Boucher's studio years earlier.

With hundreds of copy drawings to choose from, one assumes that Fragonard's selection of which sixteen to etch was a wholly subjective one. Etchings based on Venetian paintings predominate, accounting for ten of the sixteen compositions,[6] a clear illustration of an affinity to which Pierre Rosenberg has long drawn our attention.[7] Beyond the preference for Venetian art, distinctions outnumber commonalities. Seven are in the same direction as the original source and nine are in reverse, suggesting that Fragonard used as his models either original drawings or counterproofs, respectively, with little concern for the fidelity of the print in terms of orientation.[8] He sometimes chose to etch whole compositions, remaining relatively faithful to the original source, while in other cases he based the etchings on quick studies of figures or groups of figures lifted from their original context. Just as he had freely made adjustments to the compositions in the course of drawing the copies, Fragonard often continued to tinker with poses and details as he translated his drawings to print. In addition to these divergences, one observes an inconsistency in finish within the group. Some work the design to the borders of the plate, while others adopt a sketchier manner, leaving large swathes of white paper. In terms of technique, the etchings after Italian masters are more complex and varied than the chalk drawings on which they were based. Whereas the drawings are characterized by quick and broken contours that are filled in with soft parallel hatching to create a range of tones, the etchings display a great variety of marks, the needle, in Fragonard's hand, improvising squiggles, dashes, flecks, and dots to evoke a wide spectrum of textures as well as tones. In its flickering and variegated effect, the handling of this group references the etching technique of the Italian eighteenth-century *peintre-graveur*, a graphic manner that was admired by both Fragonard and the *amateurs* of the day who passionately collected this material.[9] PS

13. *Saint Luke*

After Giovanni Lanfranco (Italian, 1582–1647)
Ca. 1764
Etching, first state of two
Sheet: 9⅛ × 6¾ in. (23 × 17.3 cm); plate mark: 4⅞ × 3⅝ in. (12.2 × 9.2 cm); image: 4½ × 3⅛ in. (11.5 × 8 cm)
Inscriptions: at lower left, below image, "Lanfranc a naple aux St Apotre"; at lower right, just inside the framing line, the traces of a largely burnished-out signature, "frago."

14. *Saint Mark*

After Giovanni Lanfranco (Italian, 1582–1647)
Ca. 1764
Etching, second state of two
Sheet: 7¾ × 4⅝ in. (19.5 × 11.6 cm); plate mark: 4⅝ × 3⅝ in. (11.8 × 9.2 cm); image: 4⅜ × 3⅛ in. (11.1 × 8 cm)
Inscriptions: at lower left, "lanfranc aux Sts Apotres a Naples"; signed at lower right, "frago."

In the second half of the eighteenth century, Naples increasingly became an important stop on the Italian itinerary of French visitors, artists and *amateurs* alike. Saint-Non made his first trip there almost immediately after arriving in Rome in 1759 and returned in 1760 in the company of Hubert Robert, who made many drawings for him, often after antiquities. In March 1761, on the eve of his return to France, Saint-Non sent Fragonard and Jean Robert Ango to Naples to make drawings after the major paintings in the city's churches and palaces, many of which would later be used as models for prints.

It is not known whether Fragonard and Ango were given instructions on what to copy, but we know from Saint-Non's journal that he considered the church of Santi Apostoli to be one of the most beautiful in Naples, describing the vault by Giovanni Lanfranco as painted with a stunning ardor and audacity.[1] Cochin, in his *Voyage d'Italie*, used similar language to evoke the power and genius of the frescoes.[2] The pendentives of the church's dome each featured a depiction of one of the four apostles, but Fragonard seems to have drawn only Saint Mark and Saint Luke. His drawings make little reference to the original shape and setting of the frescoes, and, in the case of *Saint Luke*, he simplified the composition by omitting the cow in the foreground and half of the putto at the upper left. While the two drawings are similar in style and lightness of touch,[3] the two etchings they inspired diverge. However, Georges Wildenstein's description of the first state of *Saint Mark* as having a white background[4] suggests that Fragonard may have begun the two etchings in tandem, but took only *Saint Mark* to a higher level of finish, with a second round of etching to add clouds and fill in the composition up to the framing lines. PS

CAT. 13. PROVENANCE: [Paul Prouté, Paris]; The Metropolitan Museum of Art, New York, The Elisha Whittelsey Collection, The Elisha Whittelsey Fund, 1957 (57.581.32)

SELECTED REFERENCES: G. Wildenstein 1956, p. 26, no. XVII; Rosenberg 1988, p. 121, cat. no. 39; Rosenberg and Brejon de Lavergnée 2000, p. 338, under no. 12.

CAT. 14. PROVENANCE: [Paul Prouté, Paris]; acquired in 1950, Kennedy Fund, Print Collection, Miriam and Ira D. Wallach Division of Art, Prints and Photographs, The New York Public Library, Astor, Lenox and Tilden Foundations (MESG [91548])

SELECTED REFERENCES: G. Wildenstein 1956, p. 16, no. VII; Rosenberg 1988, pp. 122–23, cat. no. 40; Rosenberg and Brejon de Lavergnée 2000, p. 342, no. 27.

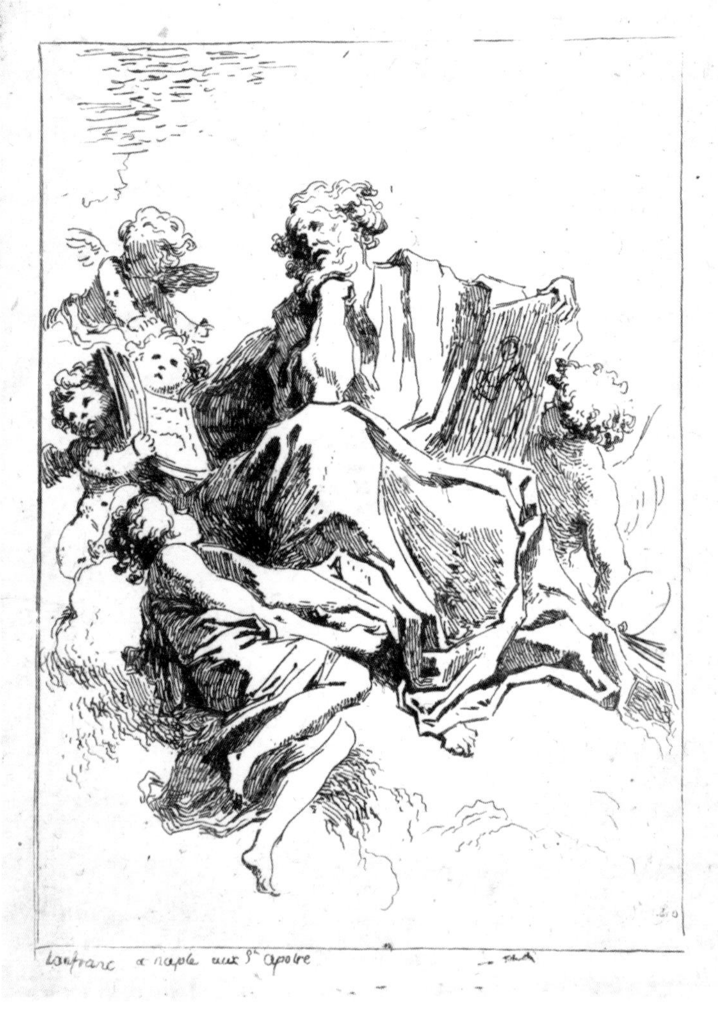

CAT 13

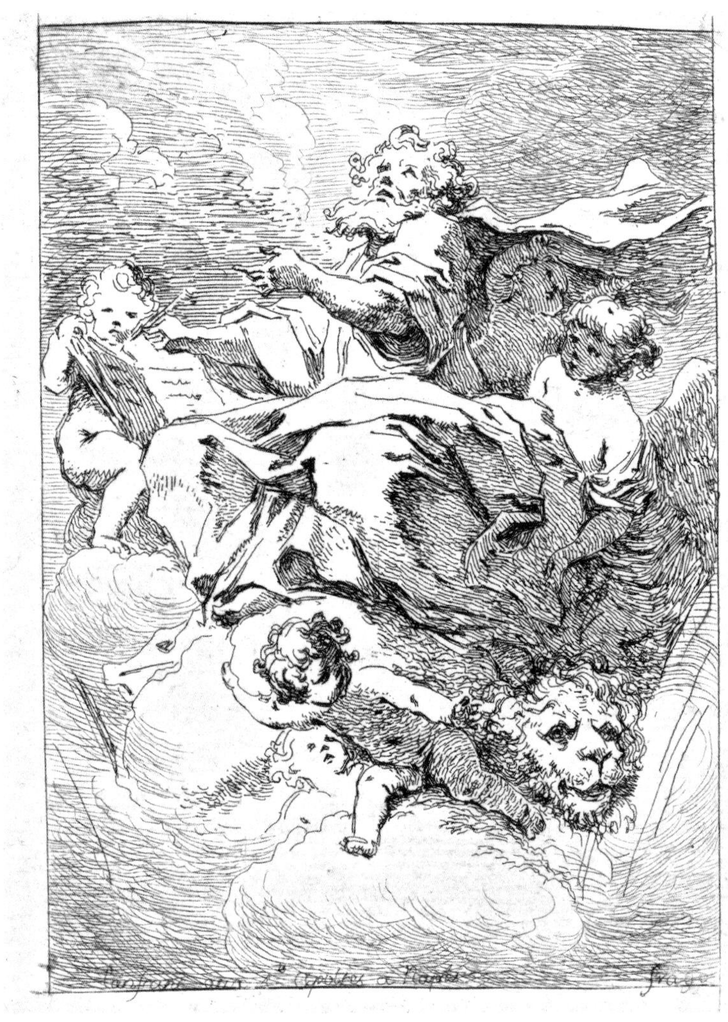

CAT 14

15. *Saint Catherine of Alexandria*

After Mattia Preti (Italian, 1613–1699)
Ca. 1764
Etching, first state of two
Sheet: 8½ × 5⅞ in. (21.5 × 15 cm); plate mark: 5¾ × 3¾ in. (14.5 × 9.6 cm); image: 5⅜ × 2¾ in. (13.7 × 7 cm)

Like *Saint Luke* and *Saint Mark* (cats. 13, 14), this etching was based on a drawing Fragonard made in March 1761 during a visit to Naples, where he was sent by Saint-Non to record major works of art. This scene, of Saint Catherine touched by divine love, is one of five compositions recorded by Fragonard after paintings by Mattia Preti for the ceiling of San Pietro a Maiella (see also cat. 7). Saint-Non was interested in the whole series; he made aquatints after the group in 1773 and had Nicolas Bernard Lépicié draw reworked versions for his *Voyage pittoresque . . . de Naples et de Sicile*, published in four volumes (1781–86).[1] However, Fragonard chose to etch only this one image, the least busy and most poetic of the group.

Fragonard's etching differs from his drawing[2] in characteristic ways. He made subtle adjustments throughout, cropping the upper margin to emphasize the dove of the Holy Spirit, giving the standing putto a second leg, and amplifying Saint Catherine's drapery. The soft parallel lines of chalk hatching in the drawing, which produced areas of even tone, were replaced in the etching by distinct lines of crisp black ink, densely applied in short and staccato strokes that follow in direction the form of the objects they shade, building a strong tonal contrast and suggesting a broad range of textures. PS

PROVENANCE: [Paul Prouté, Paris]; The Metropolitan Museum of Art, New York, The Elisha Whittelsey Collection, The Elisha Whittelsey Fund, 1959 (59.599.31)

SELECTED REFERENCES: G. Wildenstein 1956, p. 24, no. XV; Rosenberg and Brejon de Lavergnée 2000, p. 344, no. 34.

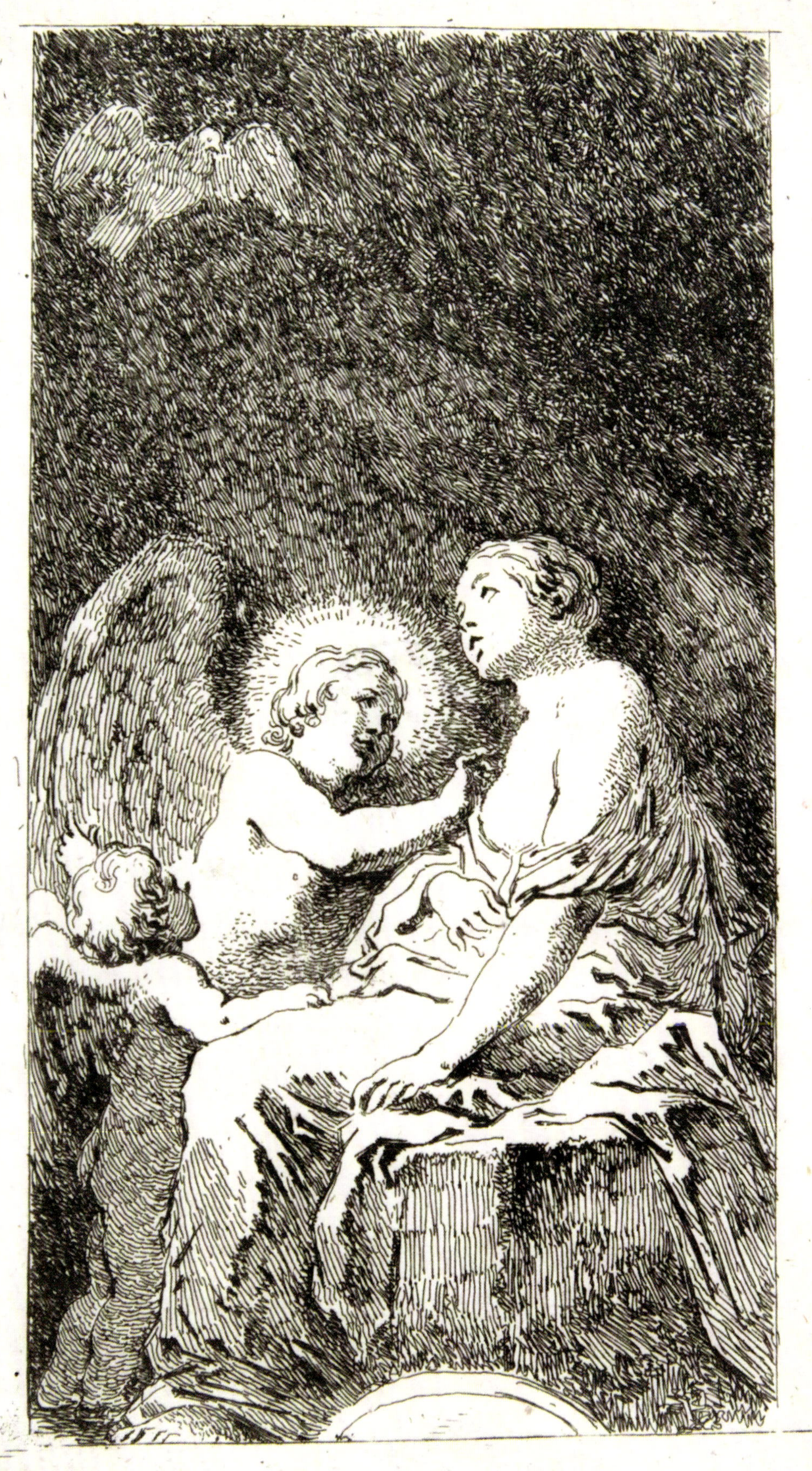

16. *The Flight of Cloelia*

After Livio Mehus (Flemish, active in Italy, ca. 1630–1691)
Ca. 1764
Etching
Sheet: 3¾ × 5⅞ in. (9.6 × 14.9 cm); plate mark: 3⅝ × 5¾ in. (9 × 14.4 cm); image: 3½ × 5⅛ in. (8.7 × 12.9 cm)
Inscription: at lower right, "frago"

The first extended stop for Fragonard and Saint-Non, following their departure from Rome, was Florence, where they stayed from April 17 to May 6, 1761. From that three-week period, thirty-nine drawings survive, which include studies after sculpture, architecture, antiquities, and paintings. The majority show details excerpted from their original context, and many have multiple sketches to the sheet. Fragonard's choices reveal that although he was not immune to the charms of Raphael, Michelangelo, and Andrea del Sarto, it was the Baroque masters who most captivated him or at least seemed the most suitable as models.

Saint-Non's inscription on the drawing upon which this print was modeled tells us that it was based on a painting then in the Villa Corsini by the Flemish-born painter Livio Mehus. It is difficult to know how faithful Fragonard's copy was to the original painting, which is untraced, although what was likely a variant was exhibited in Venice in 1947 with an attribution to Luca Giordano.[1] The subject, taken from the early history of Rome, is from the story of Cloelia, a young Roman girl taken hostage by Porsenna, King of Clusium. She staged a nighttime escape on horseback, crossing the Tiber and returning to Rome, only to be recaptured and returned to Porsenna. Impressed with her bravery, he agreed to free some of the remaining hostages.[2] PS

PROVENANCE: Robert Dumesnil collection (per inscription on the mat); [Paul Prouté, Paris]; acquired in 1950, Kennedy Fund, Print Collection, Miriam and Ira D. Wallach Division of Art, Prints and Photographs, The New York Public Library, Astor, Lenox and Tilden Foundations (MESG [91544])

SELECTED REFERENCES: G. Wildenstein 1956, p. 19, no. X; Chiarini 2000, pp. 10–11, fig. 3; Rosenberg and Brejon de Lavergnée 2000, pp. 178–79, 372, no. 155.

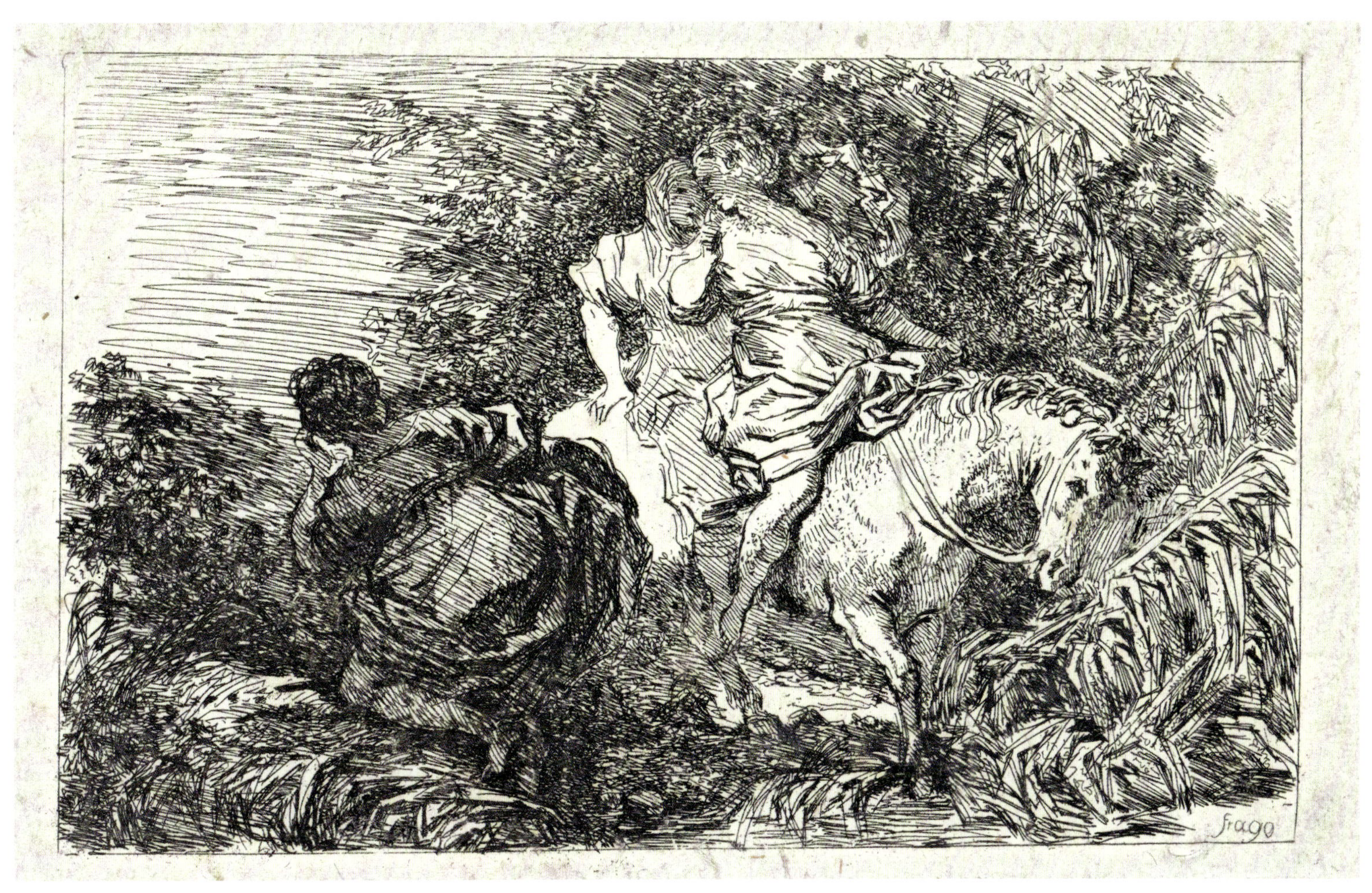
frago

17. *The Circumcision*

After Jacopo Tintoretto (Jacopo Robusti) (Italian, 1519–1594)
Ca. 1764
Etching, second state of two
Sheet: 3⅝ × 5⅜ in. (9.3 × 13.7 cm); image: 3⅜ × 5⅛ in. (8.5 × 12.9 cm)
Inscription: at lower left, on the step, "frago"

18. *The Disciples at the Tomb*

After Jacopo Tintoretto (Jacopo Robusti) (Italian, 1519–1594)
1764
Etching, first state of two
Sheet: 5½ × 3⅝ in. (14 × 9.3 cm); image: 5⅜ × 3⅝ in. (13.8 × 9.3 cm)
Inscriptions: at lower left, on the plinth, "Eglise St Roch a Venise / Tintoret"; at lower center, "frago Sculp 1764" [numeral 6 reversed]

Lasting from May 8 to June 23, 1761, Fragonard and Saint-Non's stay in Venice was the longest of any stop along their route from Rome to Paris. Saint-Non wrote in his journal on the day of their departure that he was leaving "without regret,"[1] reflecting, presumably, the thoroughness of their exploration of the city and its treasures. There is no doubt that the experience left an indelible mark on Fragonard, who made sixty-five copy drawings over the course of the six weeks spent studying the Venetian masters. His stylistic affinities are most evident with painters of the Rococo period, but the copies also reveal a strong interest in the Venetian art of the sixteenth and seventeenth centuries. Whether the initial selection of works to copy was Saint-Non's or Fragonard's, it is interesting to note that the sixteen copies Fragonard later chose as subjects to etch included two after Tintoretto, a prolific painter whom Saint-Non criticized for his discordance and

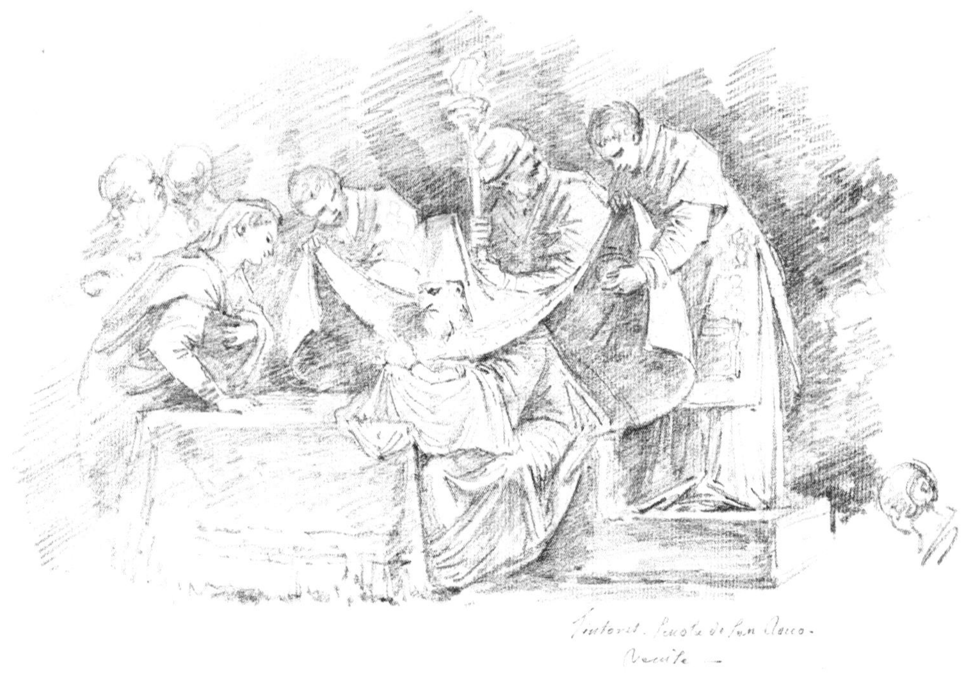

Fig. 75. Jean Honoré Fragonard, *The Circumcision, Study after Tintoretto*, 1761. Black chalk, 13 × 17¾ in. (33 × 45.1 cm). The Norton Simon Foundation, Pasadena (F.1970.03.120.D)

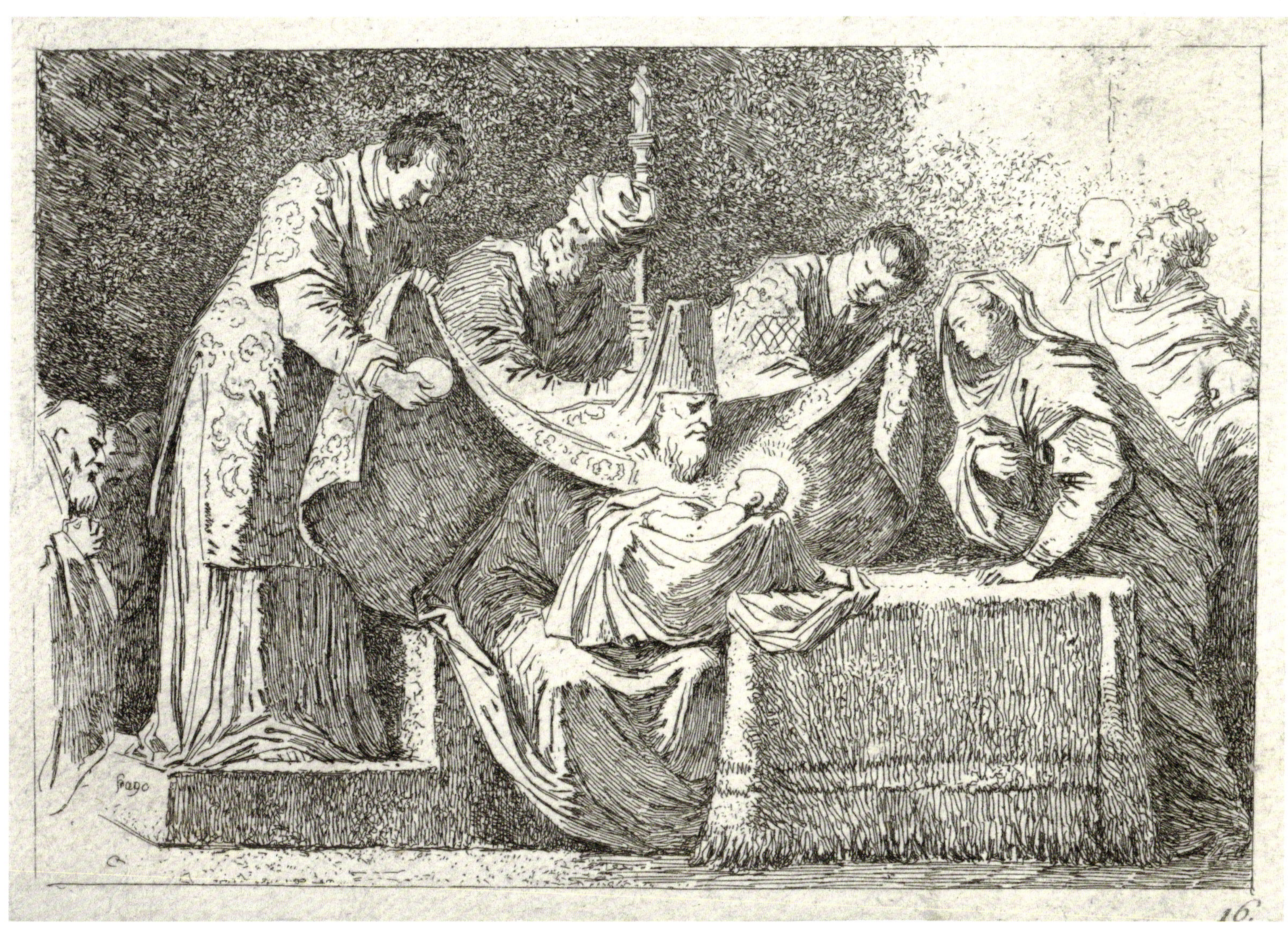

CAT 17

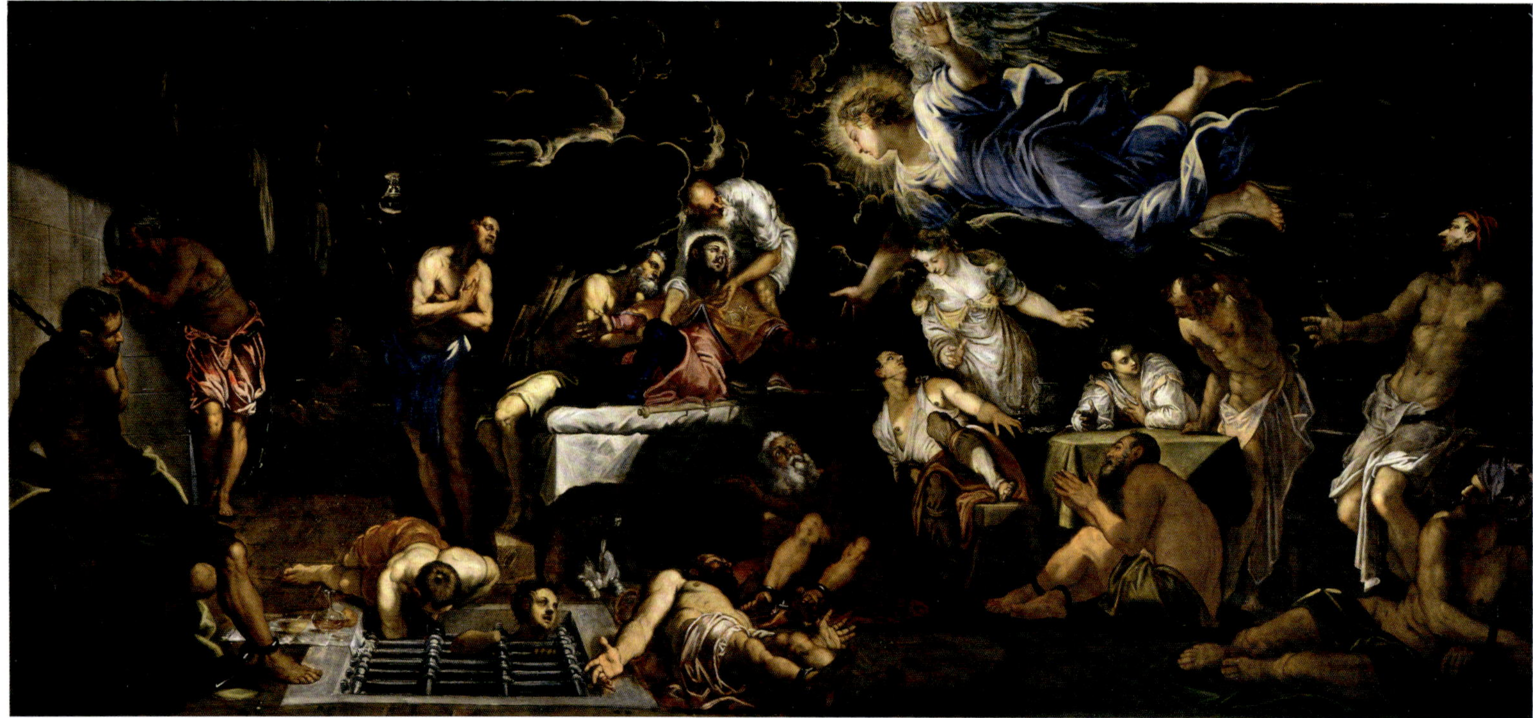

Fig. 76. Jacopo Tintoretto (Jacopo Robusti) (1519–1594), *Saint Roch in Prison, Visited by an Angel,* 1567. Oil on canvas, 9 ft. 10⅛ in. × 35 ft. 1⅞ in. (3 × 6.7 m). San Rocco, Venice

darkness, while praising his "fire" and enthusiasm.[2] According to Pierre Rosenberg, it was the liberty of Tintoretto's brush, the vigor and visibility of his touch, that attracted Fragonard.[3]

As usual in his practice of making copies after Italian masters, Fragonard felt free to pick and choose the elements that appealed to him in Tintoretto's paintings. Copying the *Circumcision* from the Scuola Grande di San Rocco,[4] Fragonard transformed Tintoretto's vast and cold interior into a more intimate space, with a reduced cast of characters emerging from shadows. While the irregular edges of the drawing (fig. 75) make clear that the image is an excerpt from a larger composition,[5] the etching (cat. 17) is worked to the edges of the plate, its right and left margins repopulated with figures either invented or dimly remembered. *The Disciples at the Tomb* (cat. 18) is a vignette of four figures lifted from a much larger composition, *Saint Roch in Prison, Visited by an Angel* (fig. 76).[6] Chains, shackles, and barred windows all fall away in Fragonard's copy, which focuses on the angel and conveys the hope that his arrival heralds. PS

CAT. 17. PROVENANCE: [Phyllis Massar, New York]; The Metropolitan Museum of Art, New York, Bequest of Phyllis Massar, 2011 (2012.136.210)

SELECTED REFERENCES: G. Wildenstein 1956, p. 31, no. XXII; Rosenberg and Brejon de Lavergnée 2000, p. 377, no. 176.

CAT. 18. PROVENANCE: [Paul Prouté, Paris]; The Metropolitan Museum of Art, New York, The Elisha Whittelsey Collection, The Elisha Whittelsey Fund, 1957 (57.581.34)

SELECTED REFERENCES: G. Wildenstein 1956, p. 25, no. XVI; Rosenberg and Brejon de Lavergnée 2000, pp. 192, 194, 378, no. 179.

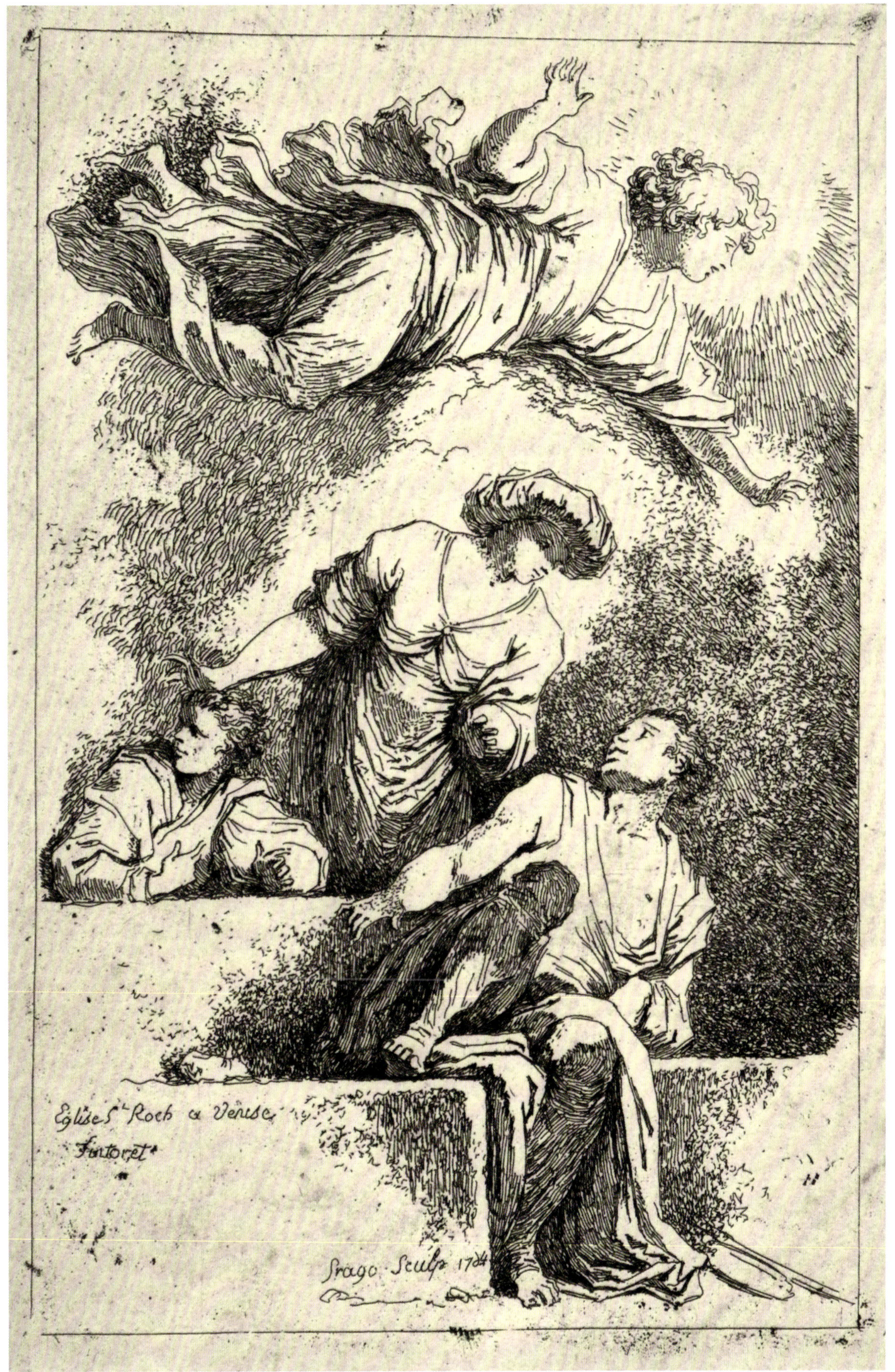

CAT 18

20. *Fabius Maximus before the Senate at Carthage*

After Giovanni Battista Tiepolo (Italian, 1696–1770)
Ca. 1764
Etching, first state of two
Sheet: 9⅛ × 7⅛ in. (23.3 × 18.2 cm); plate mark: 6½ × 4½ in. (16.5 × 11.5 cm); image: 6⅛ × 4 in. (15.4 × 10.1 cm)
Inscriptions: at lower left, below image, "Tiepolo. Palais Delphino Venise"; at lower right, "frago"

21. *The Banquet of Anthony and Cleopatra*

After Giovanni Battista Tiepolo (Italian, 1696–1770)
Ca. 1764
Etching, first state of two
Sheet: 9⅛ × 6⅞ in. (23.3 × 17.5 cm); plate mark: 6½ × 4½ in. (16.5 × 11.3 cm); image: 5⅞ × 4⅛ in. (14.8 × 10.6 cm)

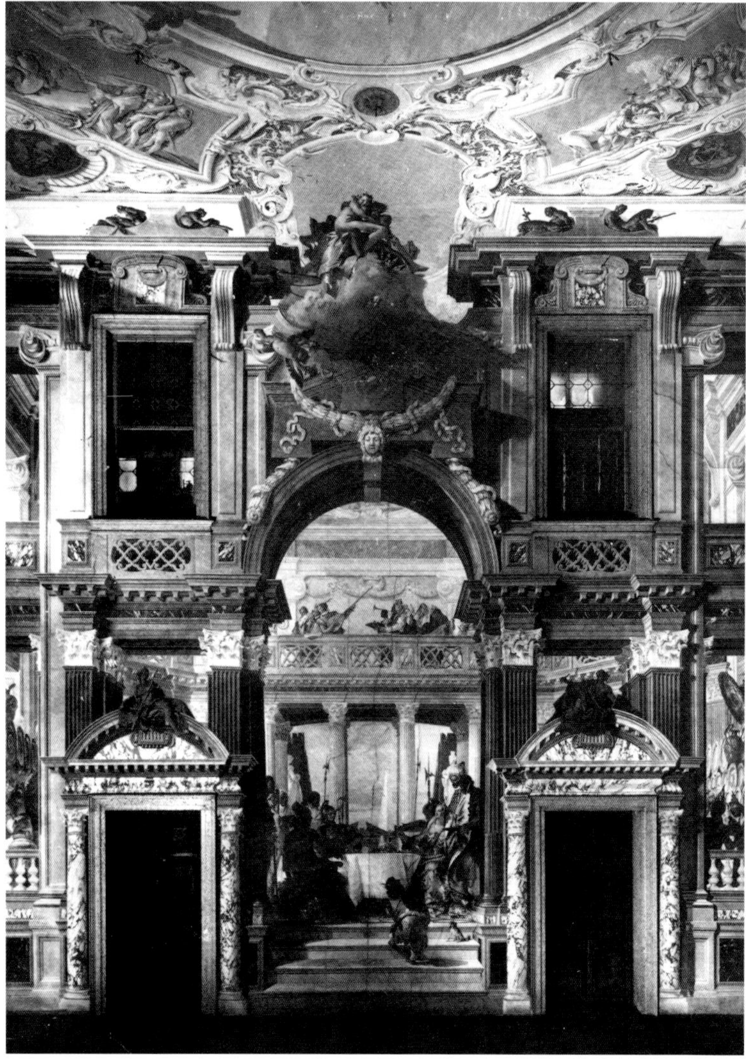

Fig. 77. Giovanni Battista Tiepolo (Italian, 1696–1770), *The Banquet of Anthony and Cleopatra*, ca. 1744. Fresco. Palazzo Labia, Venice

Of the many Italian masters Fragonard copied on his travels through Italy in 1761, only one was a living artist: Giovanni Battista Tiepolo, whose fame, by that time, had spread throughout Europe. He made five studies alone based on Tiepolo's series of ten paintings for the main room of the Ca' Dolfin, a group singled out by Saint-Non in his journal as having the most beautiful color and composition and as producing a most seductive effect.[1] That Fragonard shared this admiration is evident in the fact that three of the sixteen works he chose to etch, from almost four hundred copies, were after his Venetian contemporary.[2] His approach to the five drawings from the Ca' Dolfin cycle was far from methodical; some sheets combine figures and vignettes from different canvases, while others, like *Fabius Maximus before the Senate at Carthage* (Norton Simon Museum, Pasadena), capture an entire composition, albeit in simplified form.[3] As in other cases, the sketchy treatment of the drawing, wherein the composition does not extend to the edges of the sheet, was replaced in the print (cat. 20) by a more finished effect, achieved through a variety of marks and textures carried up to the framing lines.

In *The Banquet of Anthony and Cleopatra* (cat. 21), Fragonard used the medium of etching not to transcribe but to reinvent the composition. When sketching Tiepolo's fresco in the Palazzo Labia, Venice, he focused on the elegant figures at the table, leaving out the soldiers, the musicians, and the elaborate trompe l'oeil architecture. He used the upper portion of the sheet to quickly note the figural group of Pluto abducting Persephone painted on the ceiling above the fresco. Sharing neither time nor space in Tiepolo's dizzyingly elaborate decor (fig. 77), the two elements are knit together in a unified composition in the etching; the columns are transformed into cypress trees, and white clouds from behind the trees billow into the foreground to support the mythological pair, hovering, it would seem, just above the table.[4] PS

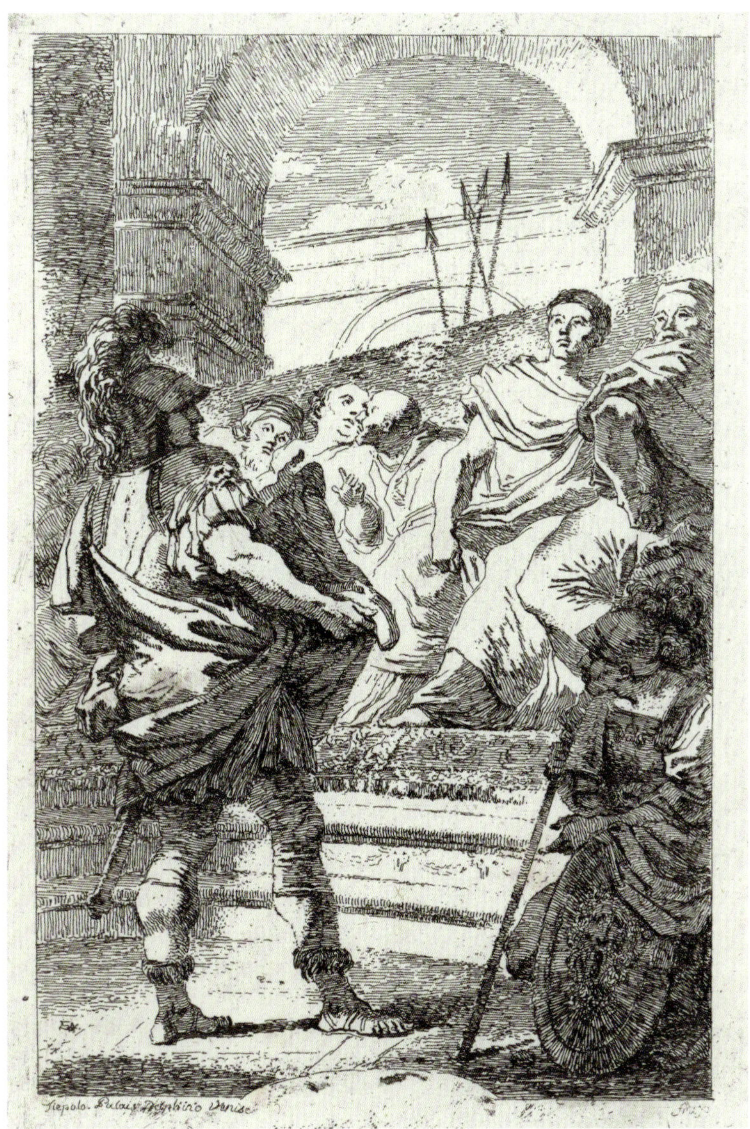

CAT 20

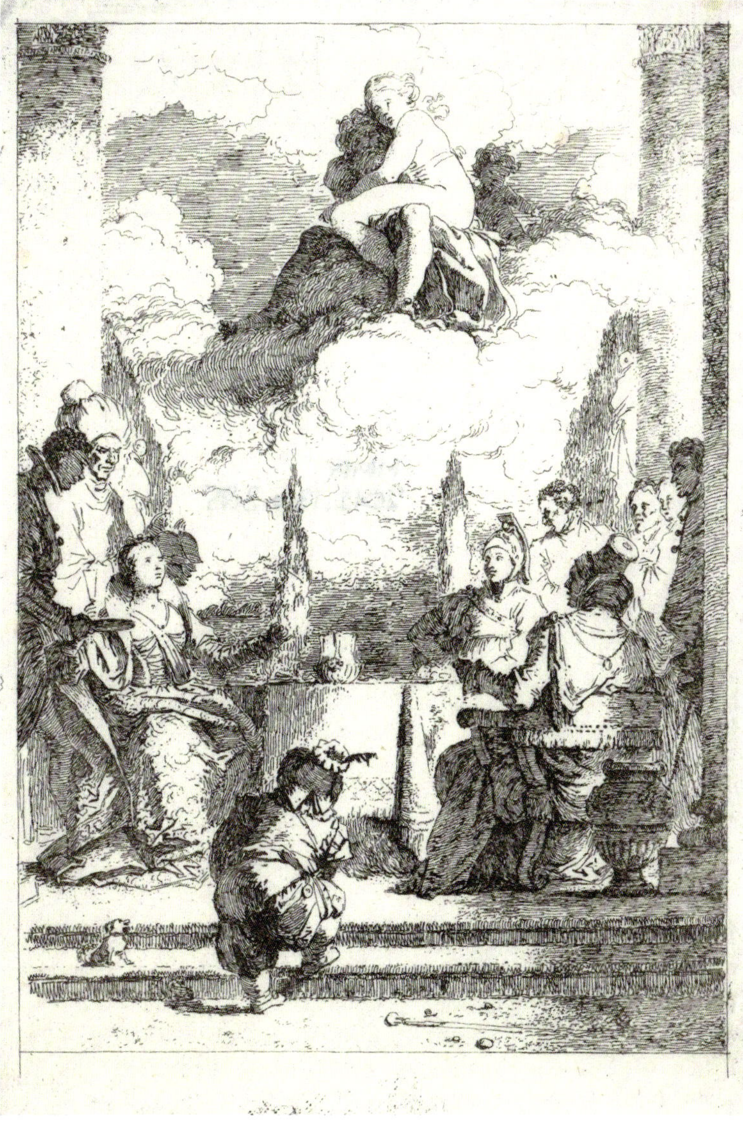

CAT 21

CAT. 20. PROVENANCE: [Paul Prouté, Paris]; acquired in 1950, Kennedy Fund, Print Collection, Miriam and Ira D. Wallach Division of Art, Prints and Photographs, The New York Public Library, Astor, Lenox and Tilden Foundations (MESG [91550])

SELECTED REFERENCES: G. Wildenstein 1956, p. 22, no. XIII (as "Mucius Scevola"); Rosenberg and Brejon de Lavergnée 2000, p. 385, no. 210.

CAT. 21. PROVENANCE: Phyllis Massar, New York; The Metropolitan Museum of Art, New York, Bequest of Phyllis Massar, 2011 (2012.136.385)

SELECTED REFERENCES: G. Wildenstein 1956, p. 21, no. XII; Rosenberg 1988, pp. 132–33, cat. no. 51; Rosenberg and Brejon de Lavergnée 2000, p. 386, no. 212; Stein et al. 2013, pp. 163–64, 166–67, 198, cat. no. 98.

22. *The Vision of Saint Jerome*

After Johann Liss (German, ca. 1595/1600–1631)
Ca. 1764
Etching, first state of three
Sheet: 9 × 6⅞ in. (22.9 × 17.5 cm); plate mark: 6½ × 4½ in. (16.5 × 11.5 cm); image: 6⅛ × 4¼ in. (15.4 × 10.6 cm)

To judge from the works Fragonard chose to copy, his admiration for Venetian painting focused more on figural works than on landscape; but in terms of period and style, his selection was broad, including a range of artists from Tintoretto to Tiepolo. Of the seventeenth-century Venetian masters, one of the most admired was Johann Liss, whose altarpiece for the church of San Nicolò da Tolentino was often singled out for praise in eighteenth-century guidebooks. Charles Nicolas Cochin, who spent a month in Venice in 1751, lauded the canvas's free and painterly quality.[1] The warm palette and sketchlike aesthetic must have appealed to Fragonard as well. Although his original drawing is untraced, the etching he made from it a few years after returning to France is the most successful of the plates he derived from his Italian copies. By varying the spacing and direction of his etched lines, Fragonard not only imbued the print with sparkling energy but also successfully replicated the strong contrasts and tonal range of the painting. Beyond the subtraction of extraneous detail that is common to this group of etchings, the most notable tweak Fragonard gave to Liss's composition was to turn the head of the uppermost angel, whose gaze is cast downward in the painting but directly engages the viewer in the print. This alteration derives its logic from the dramatic shift in format; we now see the angel not far above our heads in the upper margin of a lifesize altarpiece but in the intimate, hand-held scale of an etching. PS

PROVENANCE: [Paul Prouté, Paris]; acquired in 1950, Kennedy Fund, Print Collection, Miriam and Ira D. Wallach Division of Art, Prints and Photographs, The New York Public Library, Astor, Lenox and Tilden Foundations (MESG [91549])

SELECTED REFERENCES: G. Wildenstein 1956, p. 23, no. XIV; Rosenberg 1988, p. 135, cat. no. 53; Rosenberg and Brejon de Lavergnée 2000, p. 386, no. 216; Stein et al. 2013, pp. 163–65, 198, 220, cat. no. 97.

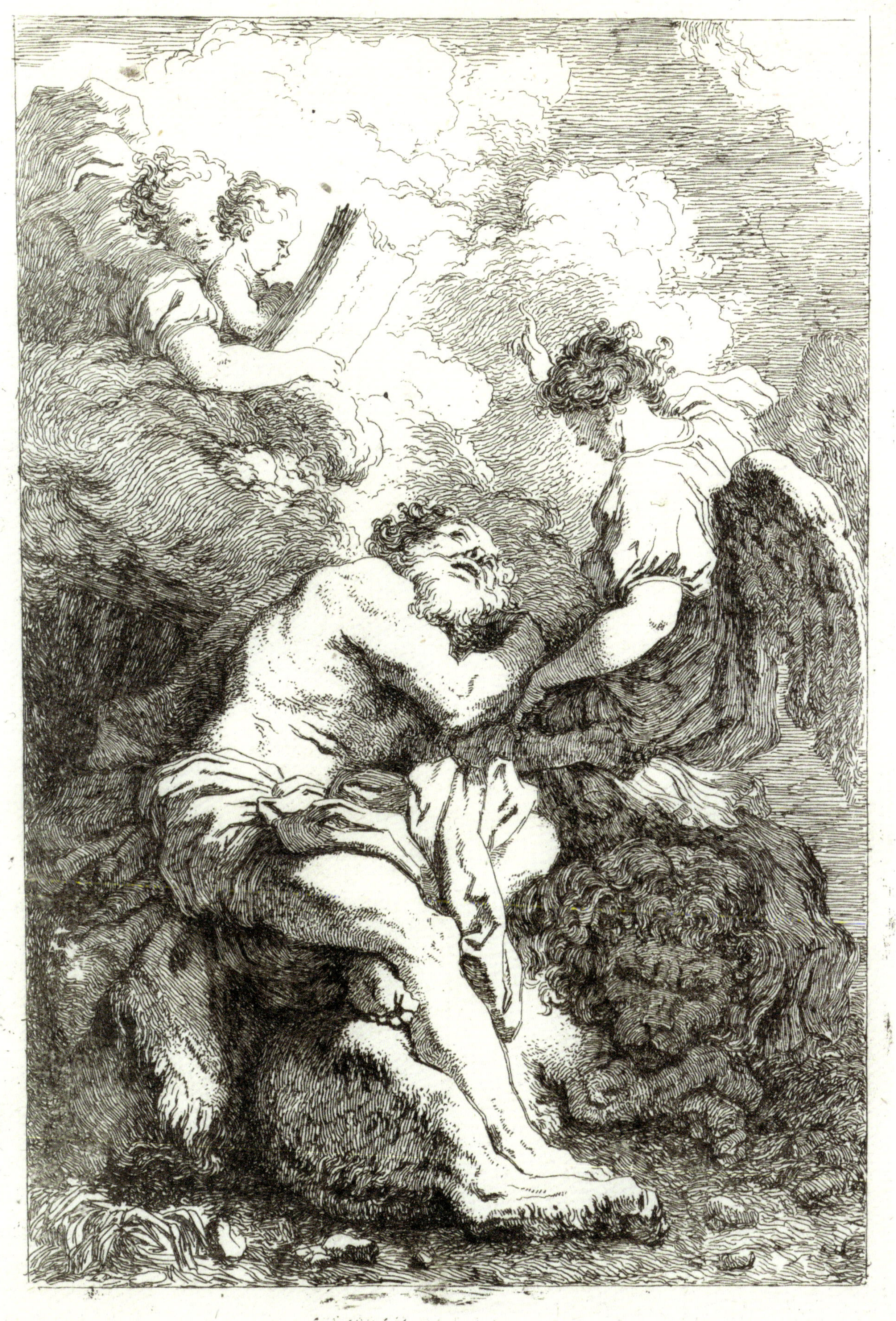

23. *Mythological Scene, possibly Diana Seducing Callisto*

After Pietro Liberi (Italian, 1605/1614–1687)
Ca. 1764
Etching, first state of two
Sheet: 6⅜ × 4⅜ in. (16.1 × 11 cm); image: 5⅞ × 4⅛ in. (14.9 × 10.5 cm)
Inscription: at lower left, below image, "Cav libris palais Resonico a Venise"

A seventeenth-century painter influenced by sixteenth-century masters such as Titian and Veronese, Liberi found success with his erotic, libertine subjects. His painting of two intertwined female figures floating in the clouds (fig. 78) must have originally had a mythological subject, but by the time it was in the collection of Consul Smith in the eighteenth century, its identification had been lost.[1] In hindsight, given our knowledge of Fragonard's later development, his choice of this painting to draw and then later etch is not surprising. He was lucky to have seen it, however, for in 1762, the year after his visit to Venice, it was acquired by George III of England. Given the format of Fragonard's version, one might assume that the canvas had been cut down after leaving Italy, but this does not seem to be the case; Liberi favored closely cropped compositions for his mythological scenes, and a replica of this painting with nearly identical dimensions, painted by his son Marco, survives in a private collection. Fragonard's "improvement" was to endow the airborne lovers with a sunny expanse of billowing clouds. PS

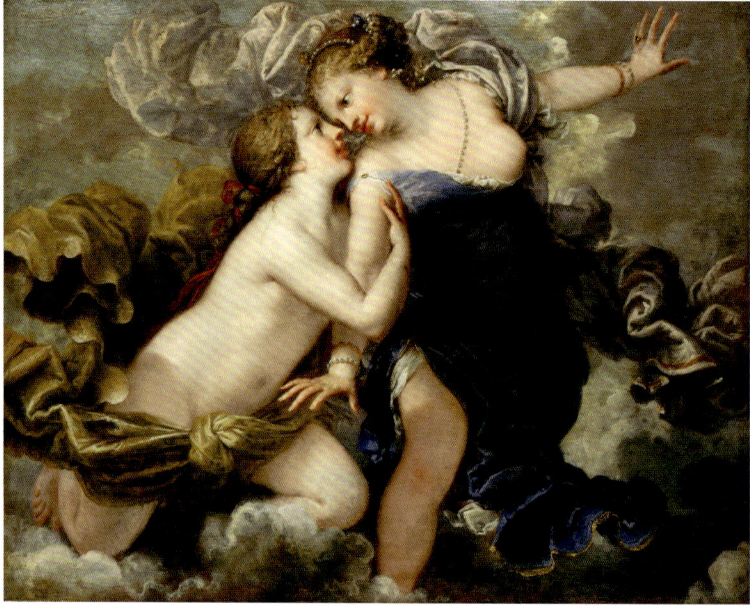

Fig. 78. Pietro Liberi (Italian, 1605/1614–1687), *A Mythological Subject, possibly Diana Seducing Callisto*, ca. 1660–65. Oil on canvas, 46¾ × 59½ in. (118.6 × 151 cm). Royal Collection Trust (RCIN 405705)

PROVENANCE: Leo Steinberg, New York; [Susan Schulman, Printseller, New York]; The Metropolitan Museum of Art, New York, The Elisha Whittelsey Collection, The Elisha Whittelsey Fund, 2011 (2011.283)

SELECTED REFERENCES: G. Wildenstein 1956, p. 20, no. XI; Rosenberg and Brejon de Lavergnée 2000, p. 390, no. 230.

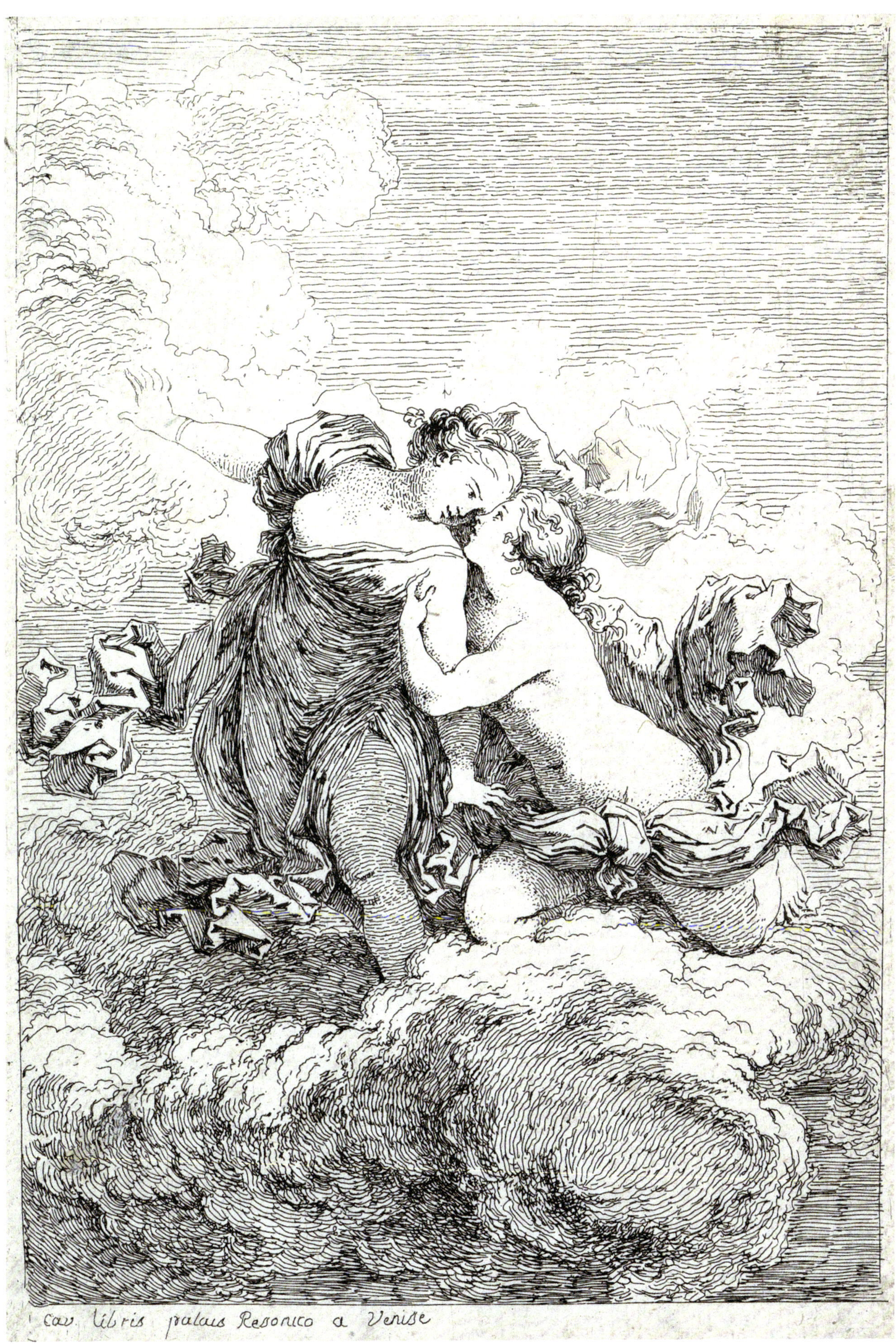
Cav. libris palais Resonico a Venise

24. *Moses and Hur*

After Ludovico Carracci (Italian, 1555–1619)
1764
Etching, first state of two
Sheet: 6⅞ × 9⅜ in. (17.3 × 23.6 cm); plate mark: 3⅞ × 5½ in.
(9.8 × 13.9 cm); image: 3⅜ × 5⅛ in. (8.7 × 12.9 cm)
Inscriptions: at lower left, below image, "annibal Carache Coupole de la Cathedrale de Plaisance"; at lower right, on the arch, "frago 1764 [with the numeral 6 in reverse] fevrier."

25. *Angel Holding a Palm and a Crown*

After Ludovico Carracci (Italian, 1555–1619)
Ca. 1764
Etching, first state of two
Sheet: 7⅞ × 9¼ in. (20 × 23.4 cm); plate mark: 3½ × 5⅝ in.
(8.9 × 14.2 cm); image: 3½ × 5⅛ in. (8.9 × 13 cm)
Inscriptions: at lower left, below image, "Annibal Carrache. Coupole de la Cathedrale de Plaisance"; at lower right, on the arch, "frago. Sc."

Just before turning south to Genoa, the abbé de Saint-Non and Fragonard stopped for two days in Piacenza, where there was little to see, according to Saint-Non, besides the cathedral.[1] Fragonard must have spent much of the limited time he had with his head craned upward, studying the powerful multifigured frescoes that covered the ceilings of the church, cherry-picking figures or vignettes that he found particularly striking to quickly sketch in black chalk. Indeed, the inspiration for this pair of etchings came from two distinct studies from different parts of the ceiling, which are juxtaposed on a single sheet in the Norton Simon Museum, Pasadena.[2] Excerpted from their

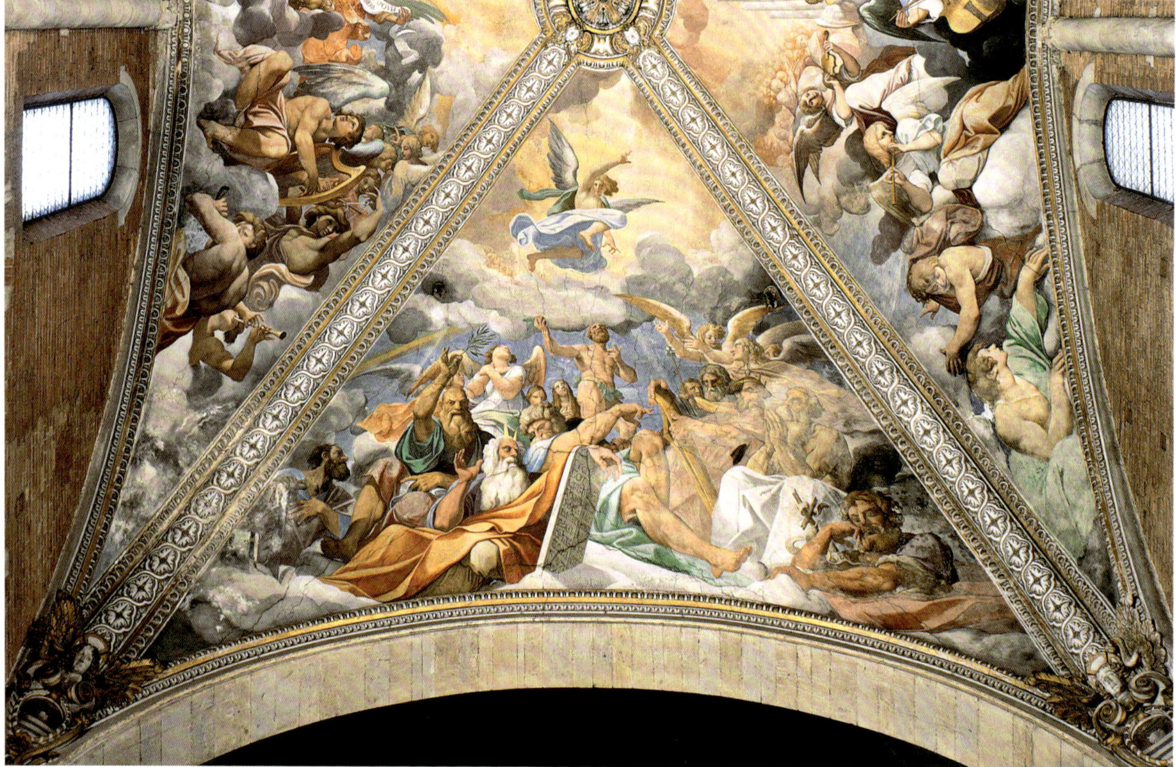

Fig. 79. Ludovico Carracci (Italian, 1555–1619), *The Limbo of the Patriarchs*, 1607–8. Fresco. Cathedral, Piacenza

frago 1764 fevrier
annibal Carache Coupole de la Cathedrale de Plaisance

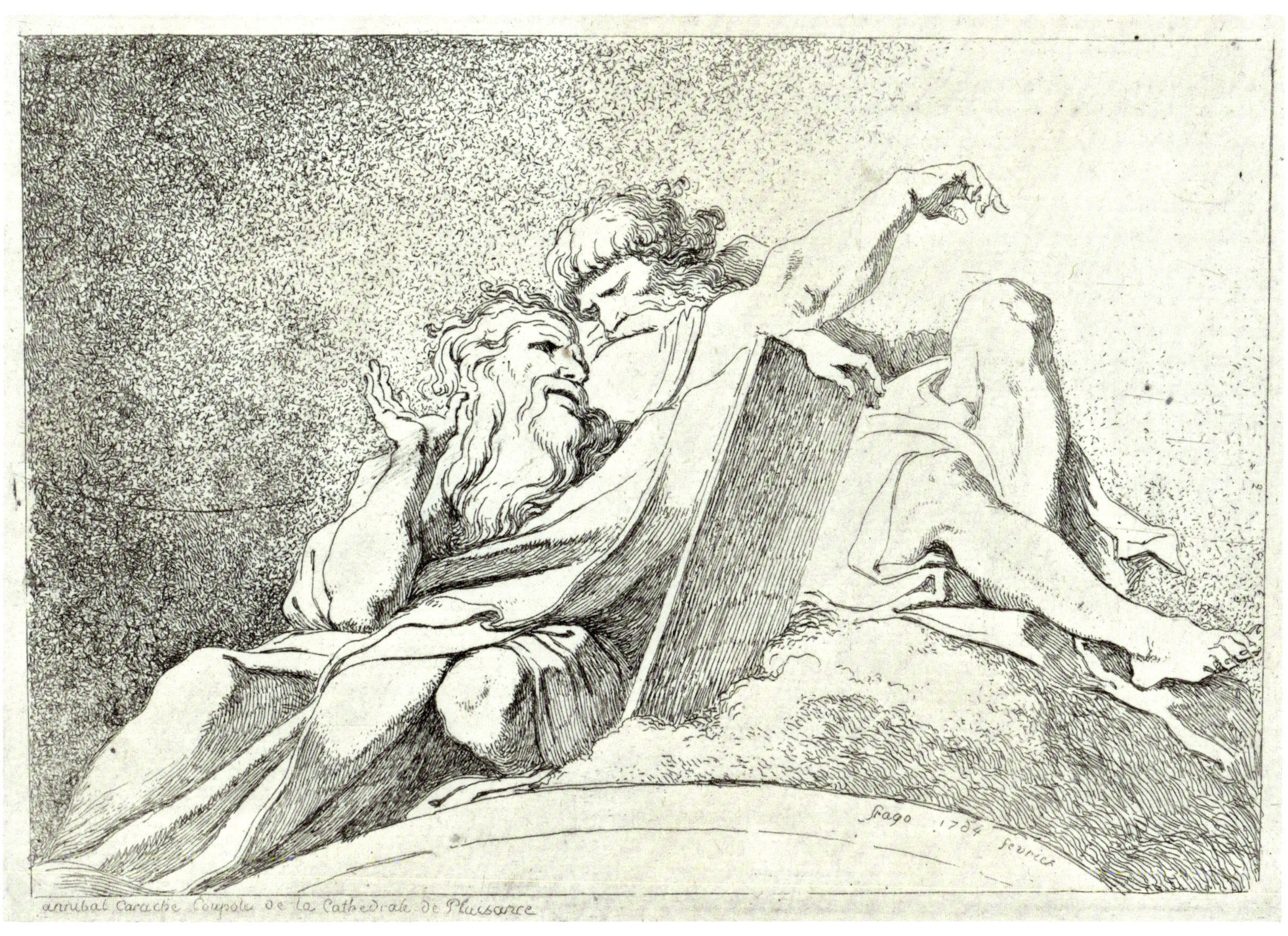

CAT 24

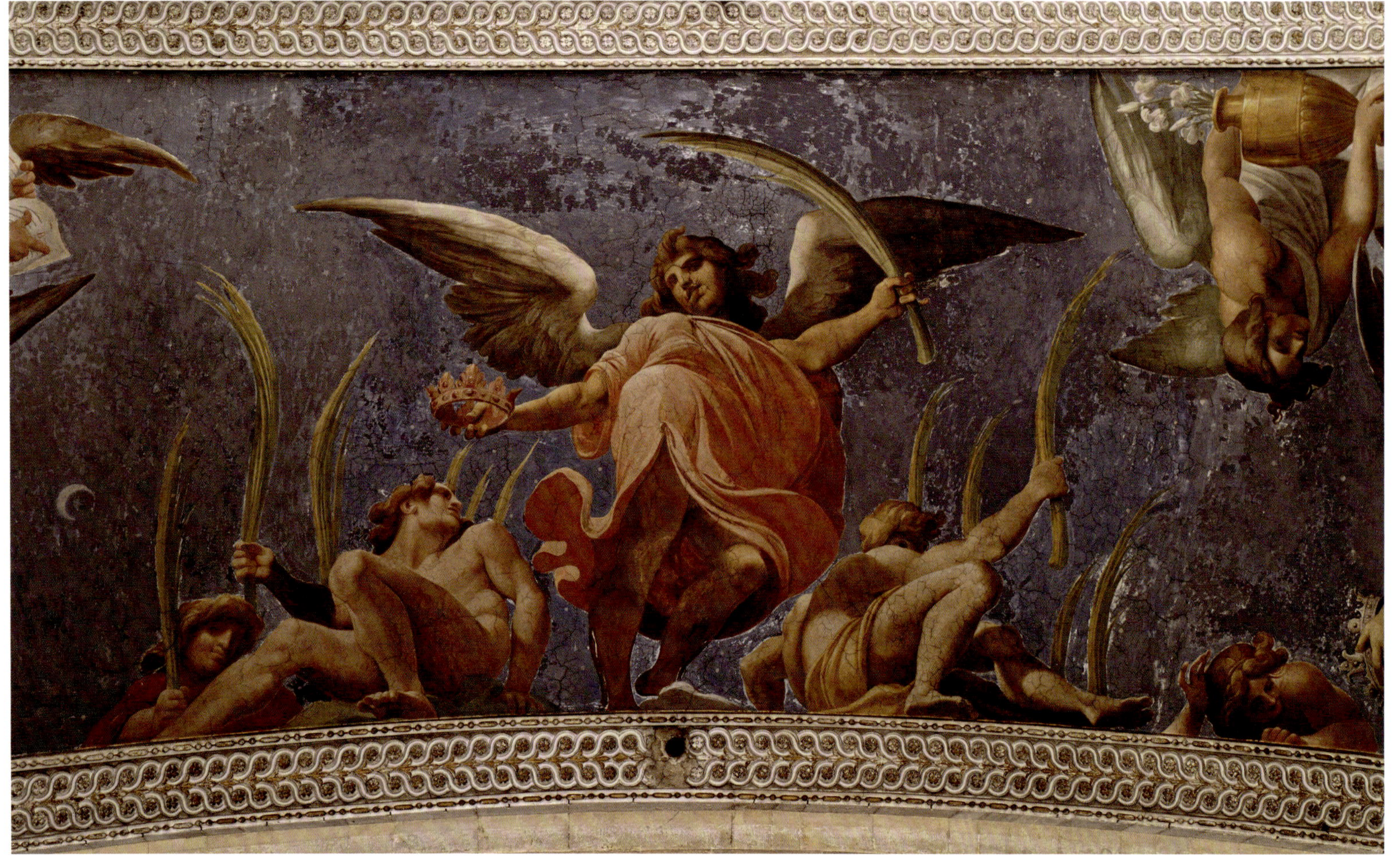

Fig. 80. Ludovico Carracci (Italian, 1555–1619), *Triumphant Angels with Symbols of the Virgin Mary*, 1607–8. Fresco. Cathedral, Piacenza

busy compositions and set against an open background marked only by scattered flecks, the figures in the prints take on a monumentality and elegance. The original sources of Fragonard's borrowings were two frescoes by Ludovico Carracci: for *Moses and Hur* (cat. 24),[3] *The Limbo of the Patriarchs* (fig. 79), a dense pyramidal pile of Old Testament figures; and for *Angel Holding a Palm and a Crown* (cat. 25), *Triumphant Angels with Symbols of the Virgin Mary* (fig. 80), with its foreshortened angels set against a blue background.[4] From the inscription on the sheet in Pasadena, it appears that Saint-Non believed the frescoes to be by Annibale Carracci. However, Charles Nicolas Cochin, who had passed through the city ten years prior, accurately described them in his 1758 *Voyage d'Italie* as by Ludovico and praised them highly, especially *Triumphant Angels with Symbols of the Virgin Mary*, which was located in the barrel vault of the presbytery.[5] PS

CAT. 24. PROVENANCE: [Paul Prouté, Paris]; acquired in 1950, Kennedy Fund, Print Collection, Miriam and Ira D. Wallach Division of Art, Prints and Photographs, The New York Public Library, Astor, Lenox and Tilden Foundations (MESG [91545])

SELECTED REFERENCES: G. Wildenstein 1956, p. 28, no. XIX; Rosenberg and Brejon de Lavergnée 2000, p. 411, no. 315.

CAT. 25. PROVENANCE: [Paul Prouté, Paris]; The Metropolitan Museum of Art, New York, The Elisha Whittelsey Collection, The Elisha Whittelsey Fund, 1957 (57.581.33)

SELECTED REFERENCES: G. Wildenstein 1956, p. 29, no. XX; Rosenberg and Brejon de Lavergnée 2000, p. 411, no. 315.

Frago. Sc.
annibal Carrache. Coupole de la Cathedrale de Plaisance

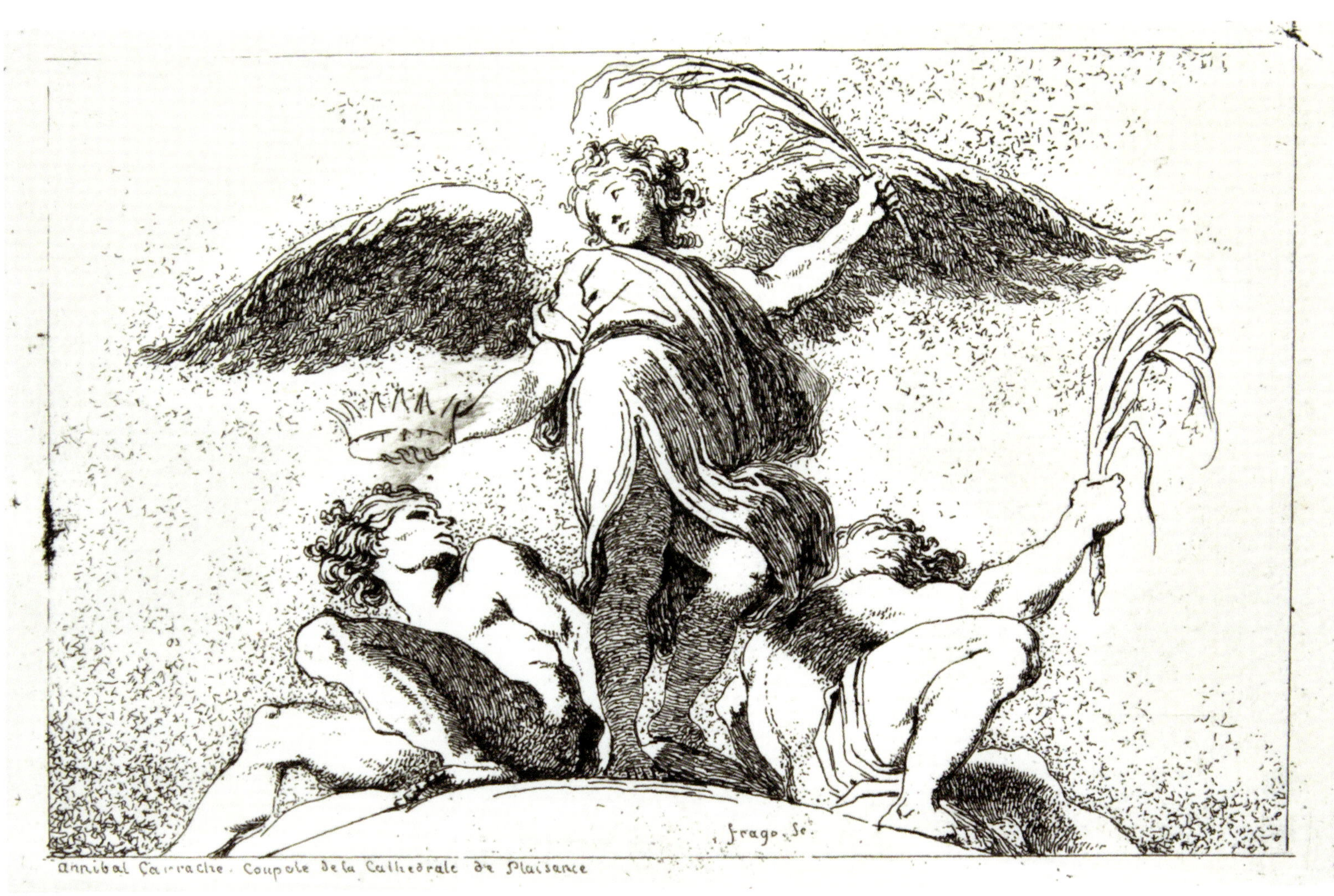

CAT 25

BACCHANALS

26. *Nymph Supported by Two Satyrs*

1763
Etching
Sheet: 9⅛ × 12⅛ in. (23 × 30.8 cm); plate mark: 5¾ × 8⅜ in. (14.8 × 21.1 cm); image: 5¼ × 7⅝ in. (13.2 × 19.4 cm)
Inscriptions: on rock in center foreground, "1763" [numeral 6 printed in reverse]; at lower right, below image, an effaced inscription

27. *The Satyr's Family*

1763
Etching
Sheet: 9¼ × 12 in. (23.3 × 30.5 cm); plate mark: 5¾ × 8⅜ in. (14.4 × 21.3 cm); image: 5¼ × 8 in. (13.3 × 20.3 cm)
Inscription: at lower left, "FRAGO"

28. *Nymph Astride a Satyr*

1763
Etching
Sheet: 9¼ × 11⅞ in. (23.5 × 30.2 cm); plate mark: 5⅞ × 8⅜ in. (14.8 × 21.1 cm); image: 5¼ × 7⅞ in. (13.4 × 20 cm)
Inscription: at lower edge of relief, "FRAG9O" [with the numeral 9 between the G and the O]

29. *The Satyrs' Dance*

1763
Etching
Sheet: 9¼ × 11⅞ in. (23.3 × 30.1 cm); plate mark: 5¾ × 8¼ in. (14.4 × 21 cm); image: 5⅜ × 8 in. (13.6 × 20.2 cm)
Inscription: on rock at lower left, "Frago"

These four prints of bacchanalian subjects, arguably the most beautiful etchings of the French Rococo, abound in mystery. It has always been assumed that the central scenes derived from ancient bas-reliefs that Fragonard copied near the end of his first Italian trip, although their sources have never been satisfactorily identified.[1] It is also possible, however, that the motifs do not reflect actual antiquities, but rather are pseudo-antique products of the artist's imagination. In either case, the prints were presumably based on drawings, the location of which, too, is a lacuna in our knowledge. What seems clear, though, is that Fragonard shared the drawings that had served as models for his etchings with the abbé de Saint-Non, who four years later made aquatints based on three of them, in addition to others with similar motifs.[2] Drawings and counterproofs closely related to Saint-Non's etchings survive in Cambridge, Massachusetts; Besançon; and Warsaw.[3] Although these sheets are sometimes attributed to Fragonard, they anticipate the *mise-en-page* of Saint-Non's etchings, which often combined sketches of antiquities from various locations into orderly layouts; therefore, they more likely represent intermediary models drawn by Saint-Non, based on motifs culled from the sketchbook pages of other artists.[4] Unless or until new drawings or information comes to light, this debate over Fragonard's sources will remain in the realm of connoisseurship.

More important is Fragonard's presentation of the subjects on the copperplate. The conceit of setting the satyrs' games into lush, overgrown greenery, at once timeless and suggestive of the passage of time, puts the viewer in intimate proximity to a lustful, pagan past. In their playful, almost Pygmalion-like way of breathing life into ancient sculpture set in neglected gardens, the *Bacchanal* compositions recall the often whimsical approach of Hubert Robert, Fragonard's

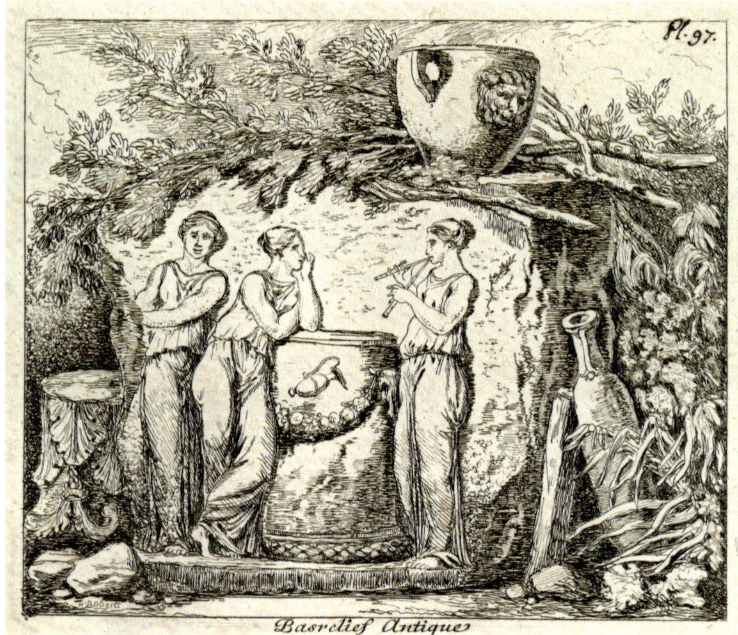

Fig. 81. Hubert Robert (French, 1733–1808), *Ancient Bas-relief*, ca. 1760–63. Etching, 5½ × 6½ in. (13.8 × 16.5 cm). The Metropolitan Museum of Art, New York, Rogers Fund, 1952 (52.519.88[160])

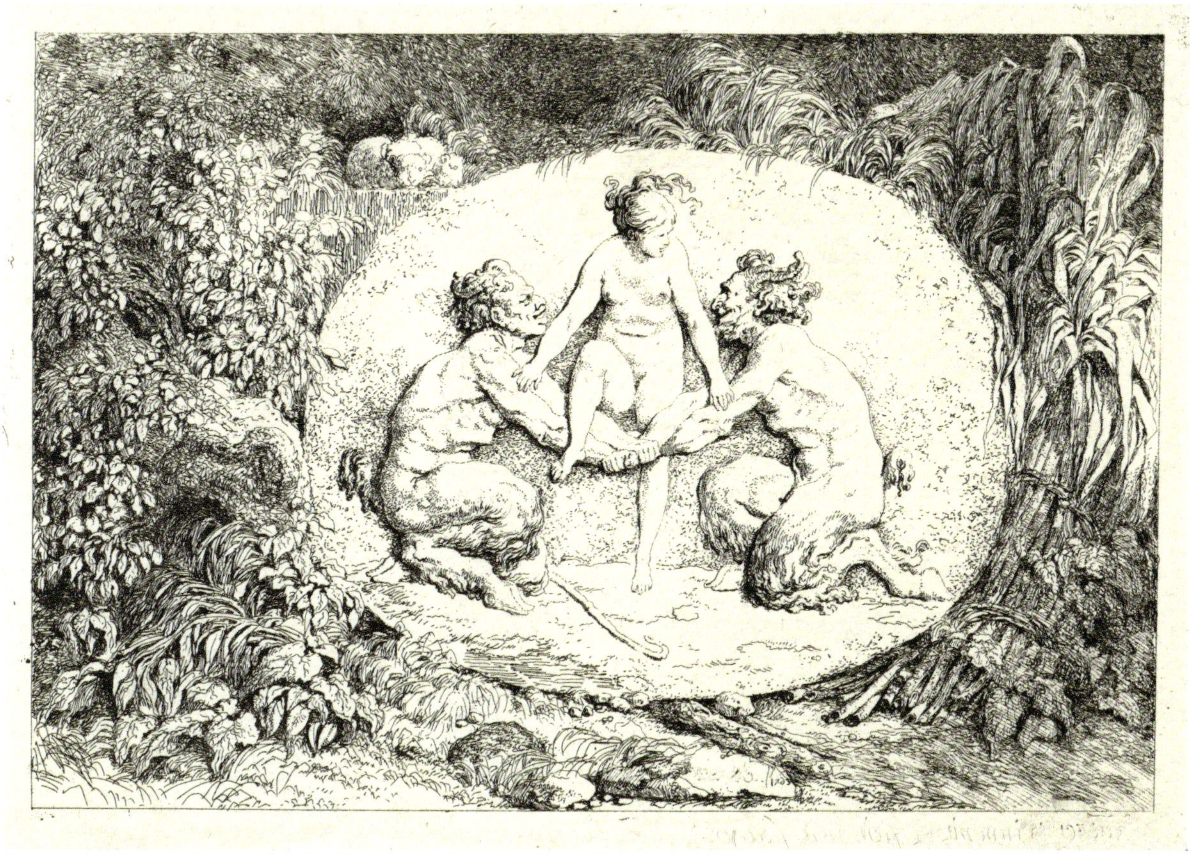

CAT 26

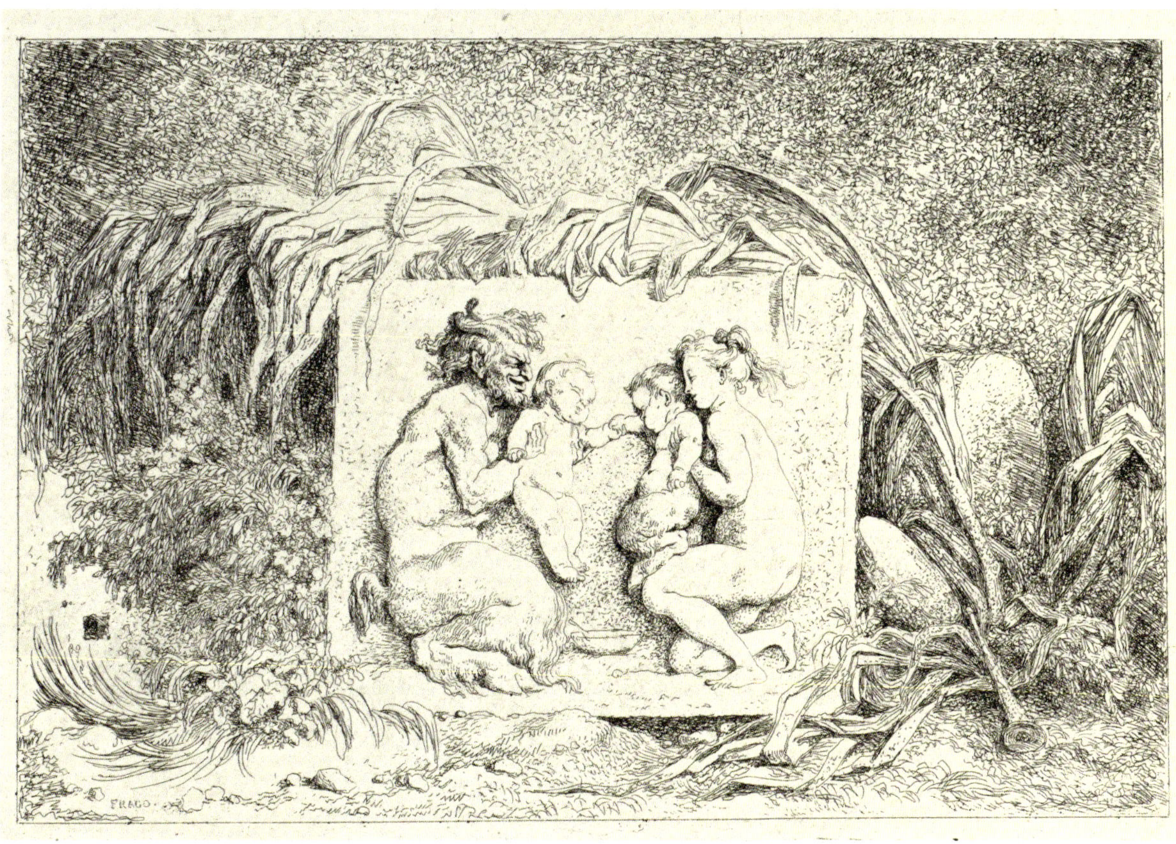

CAT 27

LE PETIT PARC: A GARDEN AND ITS ITERATIONS

30. *The Little Park*

Ca. 1761–63
Red chalk
14 × 18¼ in. (35.6 × 46.4 cm)

31. *The Little Park*

Ca. 1761–63
Red chalk
14⅛ × 17⅜ in. (35.7 × 44.2 cm)
Beurdeley mark (Lugt 421) in black ink at lower left

32. *The Little Park*

Ca. 1763
Etching
Sheet: 5¾ × 8¼ in. (14.6 × 20.8 cm); plate mark: 4⅞ × 6⅝ in. (12.3 × 16.7 cm); image: 4⅛ × 5⅝ in. (10.4 × 14.2 cm)
Signed in the plate on the pedestal of the statue at center, "fragonard"

33. *The Little Park*

Ca. 1763–65
Pen and brown ink, with brush and brown and gray wash and some white gouache (at lower left), over a red chalk counterproof
13⅝ × 17⅜ in. (34.6 × 44.1 cm)
On the mount, the blind stamp of mount maker François Renaud (Lugt 1042)

34. *The Little Park*

Ca. 1765
Gouache on vellum
7¾ × 9½ in. (19.7 × 24.1 cm)

"A marvel among marvels" was how *The Little Park* (cat. 31) was described when it sold at auction in 1883.[1] This lovely, nearly symmetrical composition, featuring a peasant boy finding respite in the verdant surroundings of an overgrown Italian park, ultimately inspired Fragonard to create six distinct variants: three drawings, a gouache, an etching, and a painting now in the Wallace Collection, London.[2] Rather than classifying them according to the conventional categories of study, finished work, and replica, they are best seen as a constellation of individual works, variations exploring how shifts in medium, direction, and scale can inflect the same subject with different moods. The title, *Le petit parc* (*The Little Park*), first appeared in the nineteenth century, linked to the etching.[3] Earlier references were just to *Le parc* or *Intérieur d'un parc*, and one wonders if the adjective *petit* initially referred to the scale of the etching rather than the subject, as the scene depicted is constructed like a stage set, in layers of planes, in which dense foliage frames a central vignette with a terraced balustrade and tiny, distant stairs, suggesting, on the contrary, a vast space that dwarfs its human inhabitants.

Among the questions that have long vexed scholars is the extent to which *The Little Park* depicts or recalls the gardens of the Villa d'Este in Tivoli, where Fragonard spent the summer of 1760 in the company of the abbé de Saint-Non.[4] The sanguine landscapes he drew there won him considerable acclaim upon his return to Paris, and two of them were included with his submission to the Salon of 1765.[5] The early literature on the artist tended to link the *Little Park* composition

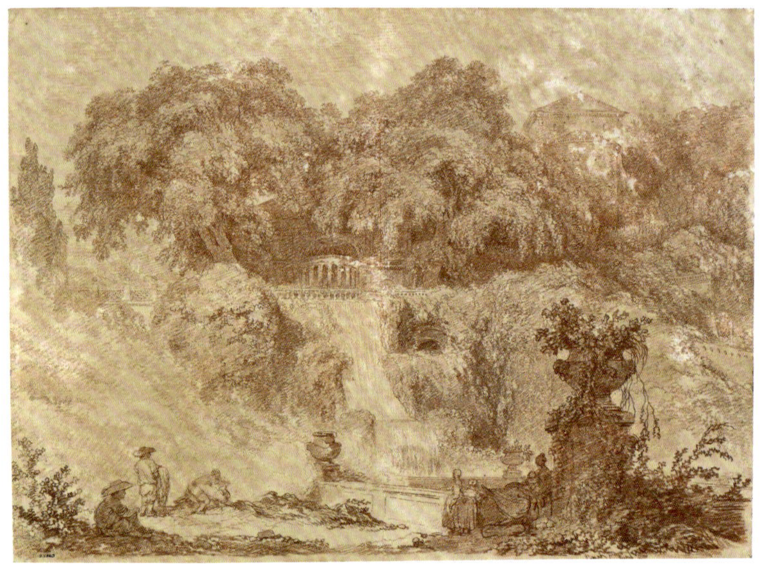

Fig. 83. Jean Honoré Fragonard, *The Garden and Terraces of the Villa d'Este from the Foot of the Fountain of the Water Organ*, 1760. Red chalk, 14 × 19⅛ in. (35.6 × 48.5 cm). Musée des Beaux-Arts et d'Archéologie, Besançon (D.2840)

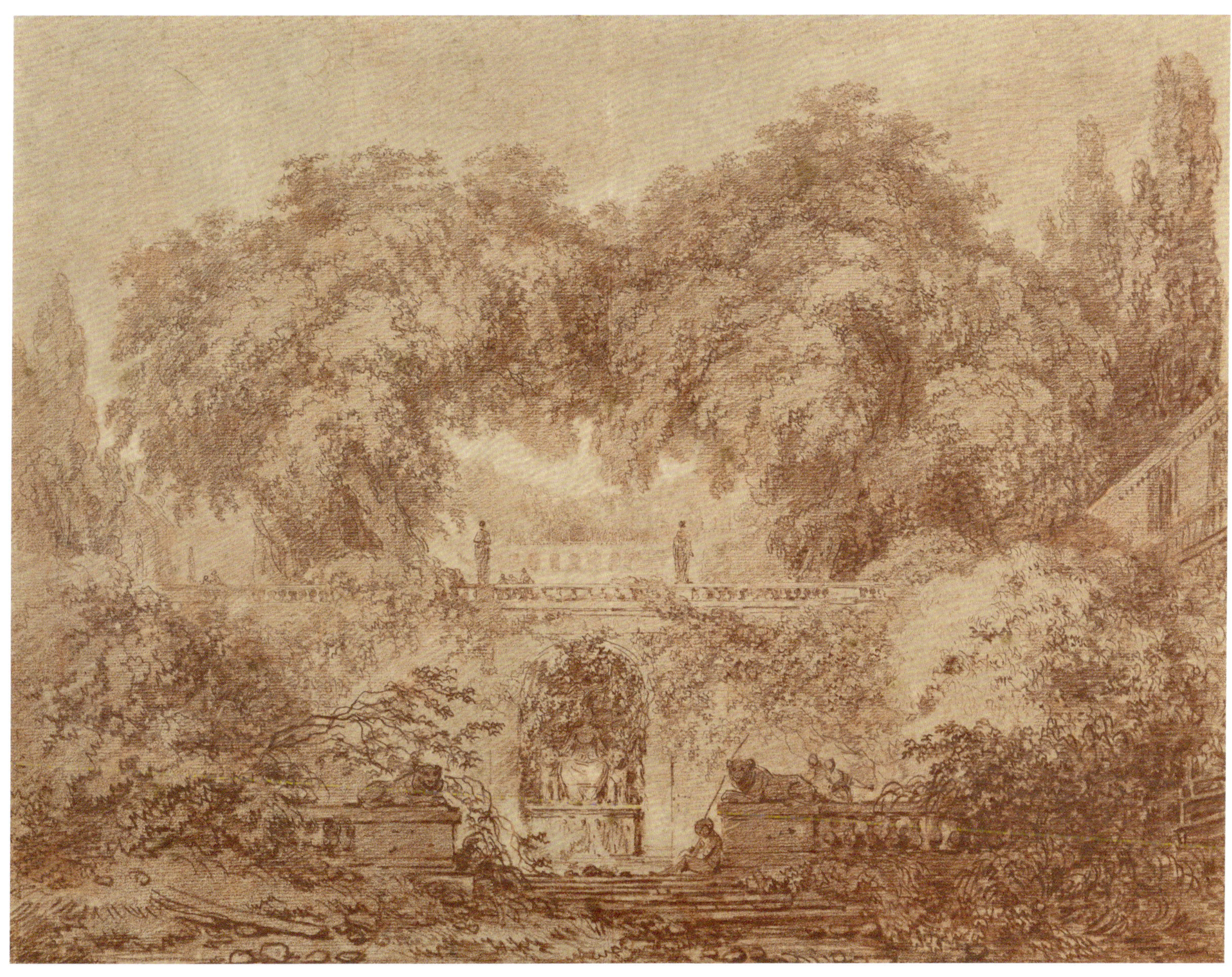

CAT 30

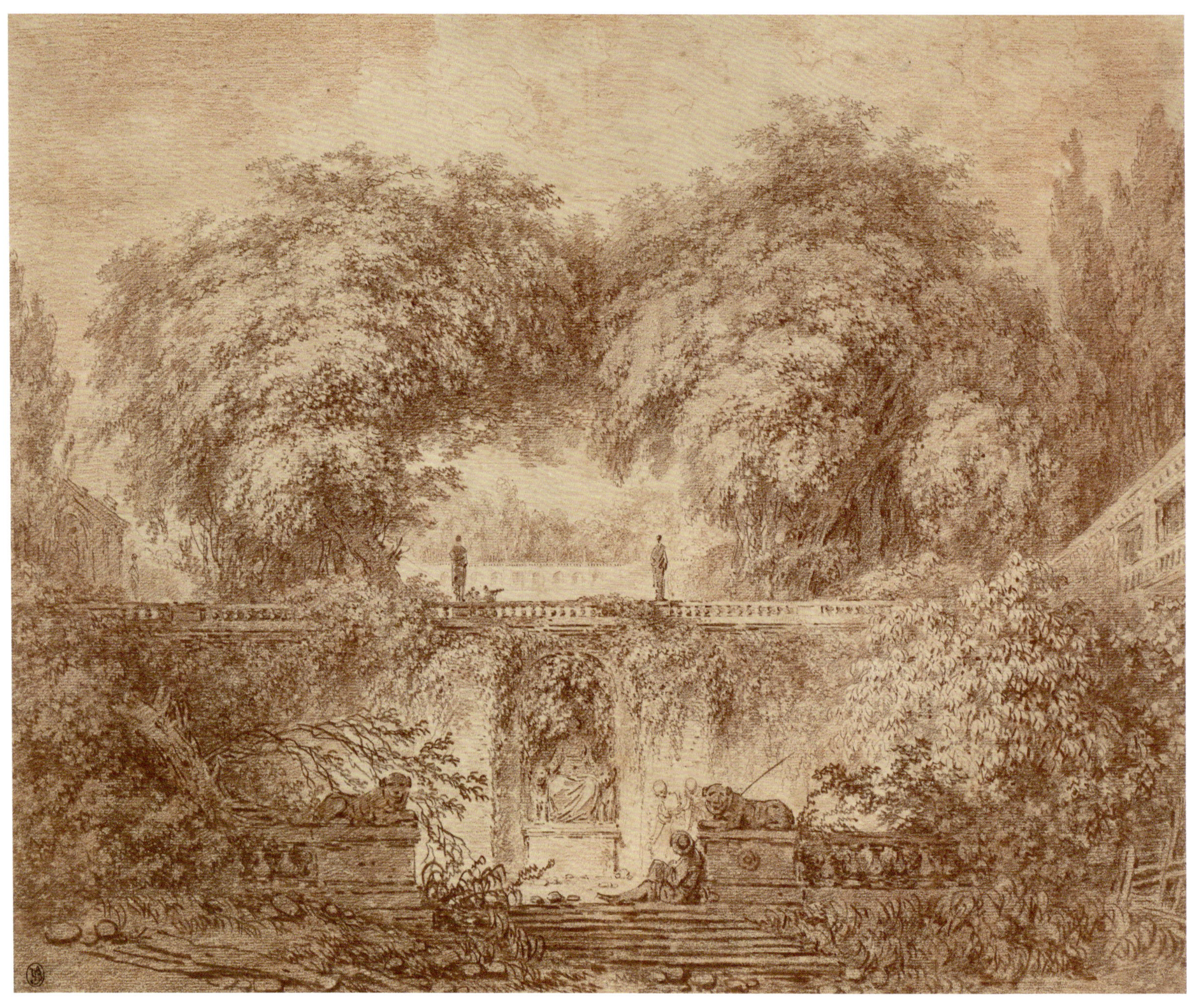

CAT 31

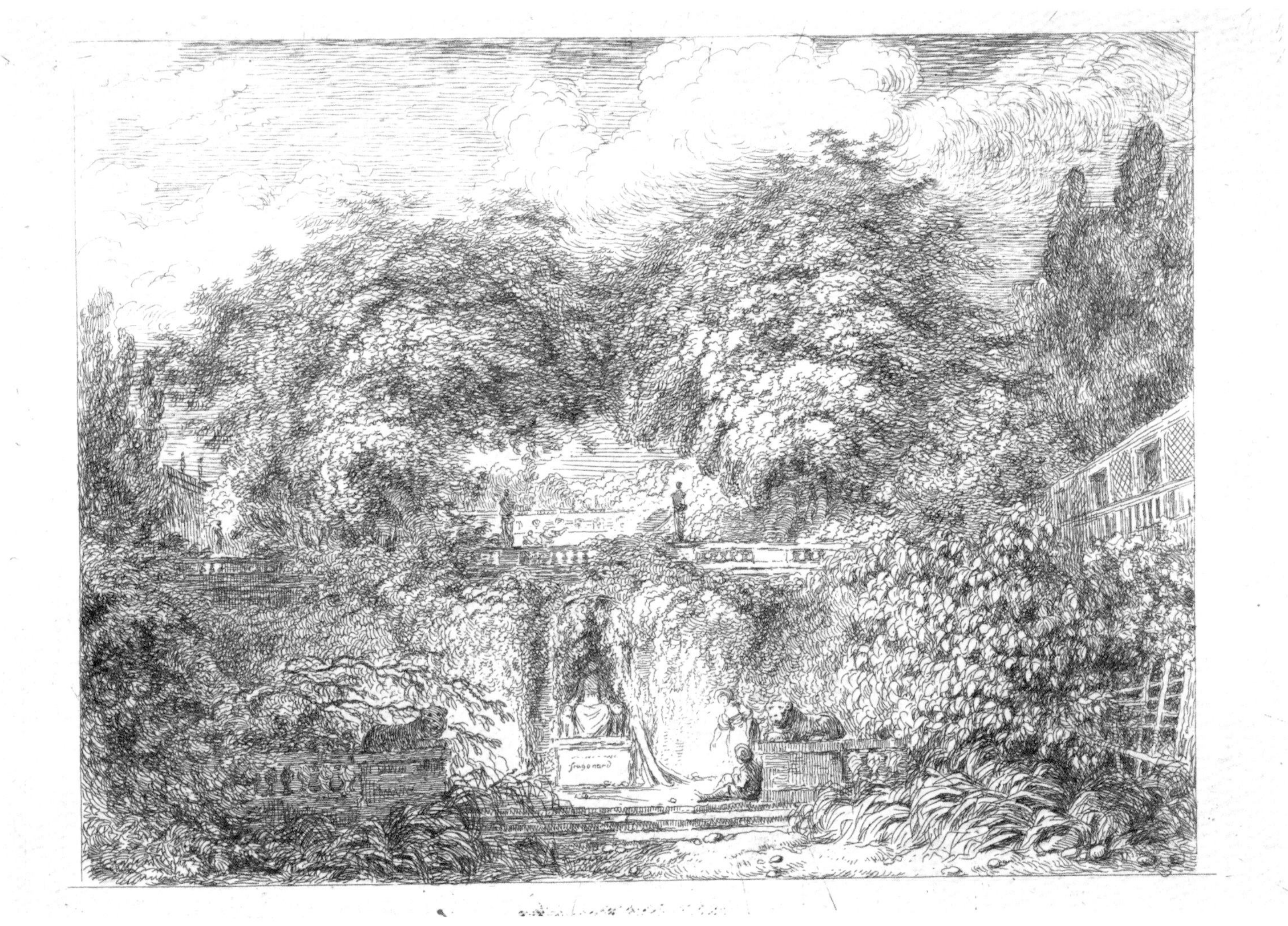

CAT 32

with these works and assume it was done at the same time, but Victor Carlson in 1984 described the scene as Fragonard's "own invention" and a "*souvenir d'Italie*," pointing out that it lacked any specific correspondence to the architectural features of the Villa d'Este gardens.[6] Others have since concurred. In 1988, Philip Conisbee deemed the subject "an artistic fancy, strongly reminiscent though it may be of the celebrated Italian park."[7] Eunice Williams, in 1990, pointed to the rapid notations made in a sketchbook (today in the Harvard Art Museums) as the seed of the artist's interest in certain broad compositional ideas.[8]

While it is true that none of the man-made architectural elements in *The Little Park* correspond in any precise way to the fountains, statues, stairs, and buildings of the Villa d'Este gardens, there is one borrowing that other scholars have overlooked: the two central trees that fill the upper half of the composition—their forms and contours, their massing of foliage, the angle of their trunks as they tilt away from the center—and the placement of the balustrade in front of them, as well as the location of the cypresses and the building to their left, are all lifted, with great fidelity, from one of Fragonard's plein air drawings made in Tivoli, where their arboreal progenitors frame the Fountain of the Water Organ (fig. 83).[9] The artist even carried over the clumped foliage that obscures our view of the balustrade in places. Perhaps we should not be surprised that Fragonard, in creating *The Little Park*, a composition aptly described by Pierre Rosenberg as one of his "most vibrant homages to nature,"[10] would prove more entranced with the lush canopy created by these irregular and stately old trees than with the man-made elements of the garden. Even in the drawings made on the spot, in the gardens of the Villa d'Este, Fragonard had, again in the words of Rosenberg, "privileged nature to the detriment of architecture."[11]

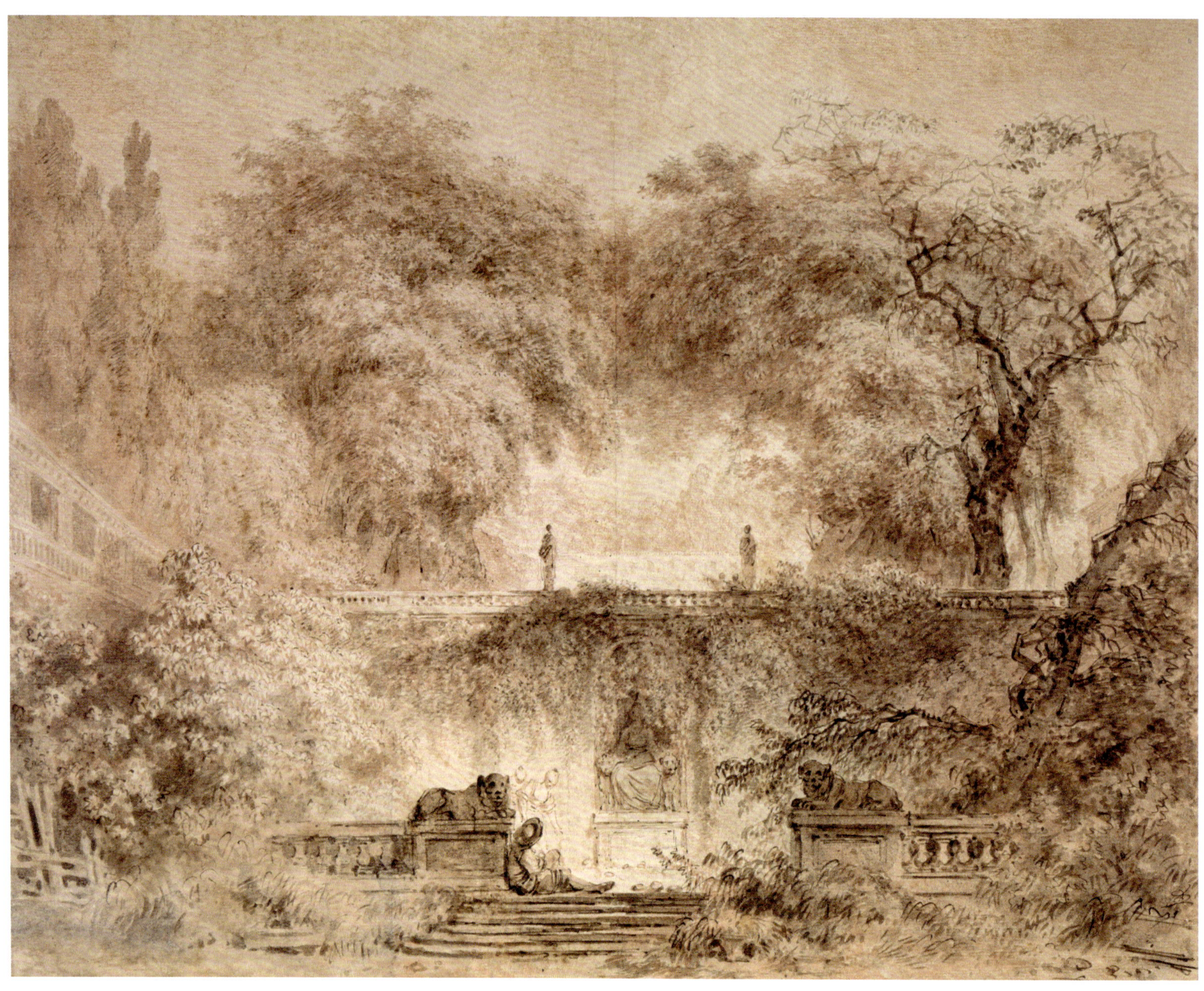

CAT 33

Other thorny issues include the dating and order of the group. The etching (cat. 32), assumed to be part of, and likely the first of, Fragonard's printmaking campaign of 1763–64,[12] is generally considered to date from about 1763 and provides an anchor around which the other *Little Park* works can be situated. Whether the six versions were made within a short or more extended period of time is less certain, but a tentative sequence can be proposed. Given that it has the closest correspondence to the Tivoli drawing in its placement of the tree trunks and the particular irregular forms of the massed foliage, the sanguine formerly in the Doucet collection (cat. 30) was the first in the sequence, made between his return to Paris in 1761 and 1763, the presumed date of the etching.[13] Drawn with textured marks over a soft, even layer of hatching, it has an ethereal, dreamlike quality, with spatial recession ordered through planes of ever paler tonality. The second in the sequence, dating from the same period, was the other sanguine version, formerly in the Beurdeley collection (cat. 31), rendered in a darker, more brick-colored shade of red chalk. With the scheme of the layout established, Fragonard put his virtuoso handling of the red chalk on display; instead of relying on a more generalized abstraction, he treated the foliage with much greater specificity and variation, making the contrast between dark and light areas more pronounced and sparkling. This is especially evident around the base of the seated statue, where he recessed the archway around the niche and gave the base of the wall a general pallor, suggesting the play of light reflected off of a pool of water. He also fine-tuned the placement and poses of the figures to add narrative interest. One of the figures behind the balustrade gestures dramatically, and the group of women near the seated shepherd has been moved to a more prominent area. Introduced into the lower left quadrant is a craggy, broken tree trunk, a motif that would assume even greater importance in subsequent versions, aligned with Fragonard's growing predilection in the 1760s for highlighting natural cycles of growth and decay in his wooded scenes. Nature overgrowing man's temporal constructs was a favored theme of eighteenth-century landscape; one thinks not only of Fragonard's friend Hubert Robert but also of the earlier generation of artists who sketched in the neglected gardens at Arcueil, outside Paris.[14]

At this point, a counterproof (which would later be reworked) was made of the second red chalk drawing, and that counterproof was used as a model for the etching (cat. 32), which, reversed as a result of the printing process, is in the same direction as the original drawing. The etching, despite its considerably reduced scale, follows its model closely and shares its interest in exploring how deliberately varied mark-making can suggest the inviting lusciousness of a sun-dappled Italian garden, from the heavy grasses bent over in the right foreground, to the profuse pointed leaves of the bush just above, to the gnarled branches behind the lion on the left. The etched lines of the copperplate were not very deeply bit, producing in the printed impressions a delicate effect, often described as silvery. Significantly smaller than the two sanguines, and truly deserving of the adjective *petit*, the print must be admired for its ability to draw us into an entrancing world, at once intimate and expansive.[15]

The next three versions may have followed in short succession but more likely were made after a period of time had passed, for their mood is slightly different. This second phase was initiated by Fragonard's return to the counterproof of his second drawing. A counterproof, made by running a damp piece of paper through a press over a red chalk drawing, transfers a paler imprint of that drawing onto a new sheet, reversing its direction. There are many reasons why an artist would make a counterproof: to remove extra chalk dust, to have a record of a drawing, or to see a composition mirrored (see "Originals, Copies, Mirrors, and Multiples" in this volume, pp. 47–69).[16] Reworking a counterproof—that is, drawing anew on the sheet, either in the same medium or a different one—might be done to create a finished, saleable work of art or possibly to experiment with changes to a composition. In the case of *The Little Park* (cat. 33), Fragonard used pen and brown ink and brush and brown and gray wash, a technique he increasingly favored, and to great effect, in the mid-1760s. The reworking in wash imbued the sheet with a painterly effect, lending a vaporous quality to the sunshine and its reflection in the unseen water at the base of the fountain. Fragonard also added elements not present in the original sanguine: terra-cotta pots in the foreground and, most notably, two dark and craggy trees, either dying or losing their leaves for the winter. Emphatically drawn in zigzag patterns, the trees interject a contrasting element, perhaps intended as melancholic, into the idyllic serenity of the earlier versions.

The reworking of the counterproof clearly represented a rethinking of the subject, and the new elements introduced became essential components of the painted version (fig. 84).[17] In the canvas, the terra-cotta pots—signs of human presence—increased in number, spreading from the foreground to the balustrade above the fountain. The broken tree trunk at the lower left and the silhouetted, mostly bare tree trunk rising above it were carried over from earlier versions. Their leaves, picked out in gold and ocher impasto, serve to not only distinguish the spatial layers of the composition but also to add a note of impending autumn to the already crepuscular tones of the picture.

The dimensions of the canvas are exactly the same as those of the three drawings. The only work in the series that is smaller, with the exception of the etching, is the gouache (cat. 34), generally considered to be a reduction of the Wallace Collection painting. In this final iteration, the composition is essentially unchanged, but the difference in the medium allowed for a new palette of grayed pastels, accented with touches of rust and salmon. Fragonard exploited the opaque and fluid nature of the medium, layering the crisply delineated foreground elements over the more blended forms in the distance. He also further emphasized the craggy, bare tree on the terrace at the upper right, which bends back toward and echoes the larger one on the left. Here, as in each of the six variations, Fragonard, like a composer, circled around and repeated his formal themes of mirroring and reflection, always retaining elements of irregularity within the overall symmetry. PS

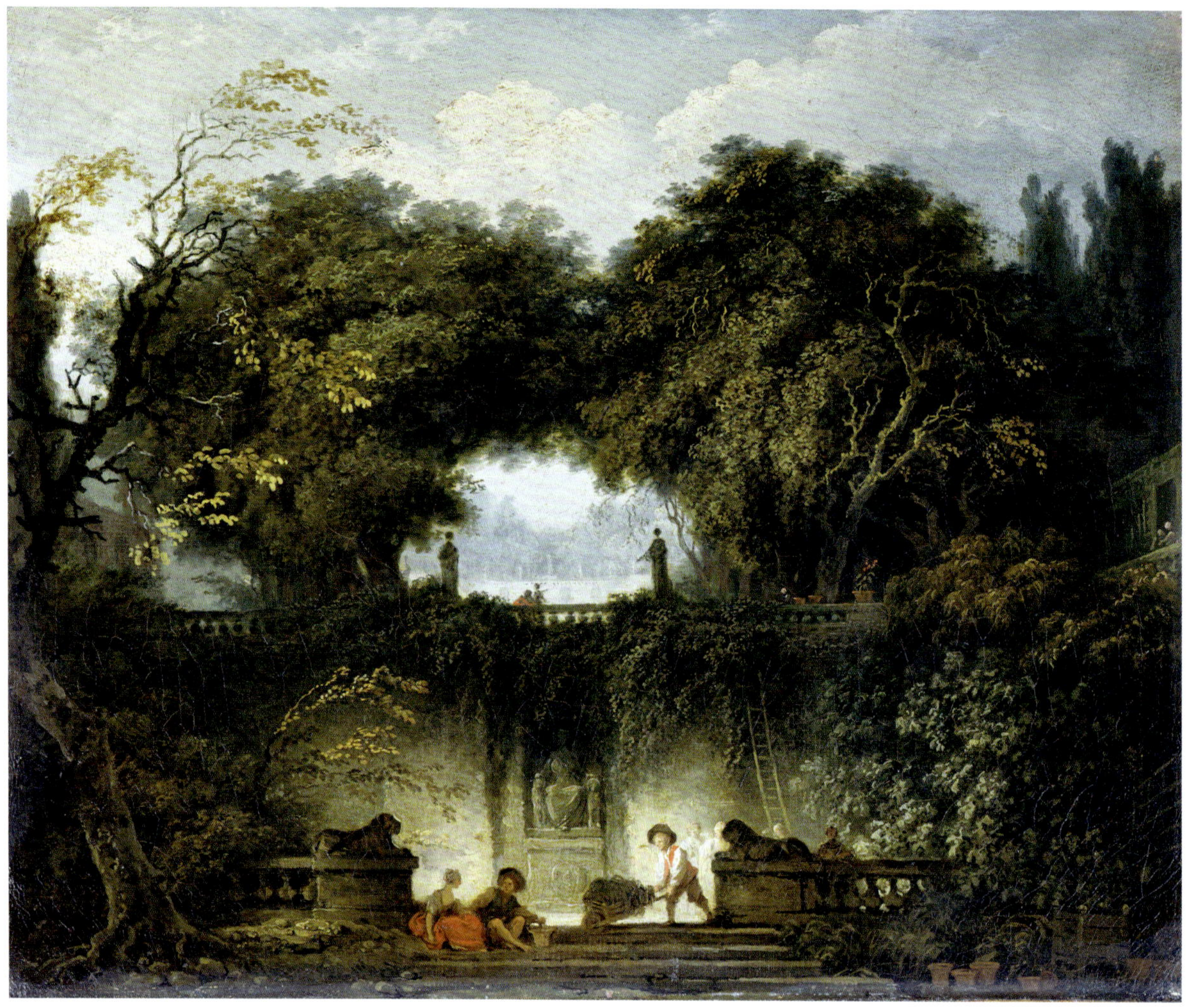

Fig. 84. Jean Honoré Fragonard, *Le petit parc*, ca. 1765. Oil on canvas, 14½ × 17¾ in. (36.6 × 45 cm). The Wallace Collection, London (P379)

CAT. 30. PROVENANCE: Possibly Jean Denis Lempereur (1701–1779); his collection sale (Lugt 2171), Chariot, Boileau, and Joullain, Paris, May 24, 1773 (lot 729, "[u]n superbe dessein à la sanguine; c'est une vue de jardin où l'on remarque une statue dans une niche, & sur le premier plan un escalier décoré de deux lions."), purchased by François;[18] possibly Hippolyte Walferdin (1795–1880); his estate sale, Hôtel Drouot, Paris, April 12–16, 1880 (lot 188), to Lauverjat;[19] Jacques Doucet (1853–1929); his collection sale, Galerie Georges Petit, Paris, June 5, 1912 (lot 13), to Seymour de Ricci (1881–1942); private collection, Switzerland; [Rosenberg & Stiebel, New York]; acquired in 1983 by a private collection

SELECTED EXHIBITION: Wintermute 1990, pp. 186, 188, cat. no. 35, pl. 35 (entry by Eunice Williams).

SELECTED REFERENCE: Ananoff 1961–70, vol. 1 (1961), p. 154, no. 351, fig. 125.

CAT. 31. PROVENANCE: Possibly Jean Denis Lempereur (1701–1779); his collection sale (Lugt 2171), Chariot, Boileau, and Joullain, Paris, May 24, 1773 (lot 729, "[u]n superbe dessein à la sanguine; c'est une vue de jardin où l'on remarque une statue dans une niche, & sur le premier plan un escalier décoré de deux lions."), purchased by François;[20] Marie-Joseph-François Mahérault (1795–1879); his estate sale (Lugt 40241), Hôtel Drouot, Paris, May 27–29, 1880 (lot 51), to Lacroix; Jacques Victor, comte de La Béraudière (1819–1885); his collection sale (Lugt 42893), Hôtel Drouot, Paris, April 16–17, 1883 (lot 114), to Roblowsky (per Ananoff); Alfred Beurdeley (1847–1919); his collection sale (Lugt 63070), Galerie Georges Petit, Paris, March 13–15, 1905 (lot 66), to Pierre Decourcelle; Pierre Decourcelle (1856–1926), Paris; [Galerie de Bayser, Paris]; private collection

SELECTED REFERENCE: Ananoff 1961–70, vol. 1 (1961), pp. 154–55, no. 352, fig. 126.

CAT. 32. PROVENANCE: [R. S. Johnson Fine Art, Chicago]; The Metropolitan Museum of Art, New York, The Elisha Whittelsey Collection, The Elisha Whittelsey Fund, 2011 (2011.91)

SELECTED EXHIBITIONS: Carlson and Ittmann 1984, pp. 150–51, cat. no. 46; Stein et al. 2013, pp. 33–34, 187, cat. no. 11.

SELECTED REFERENCES: G. Wildenstein 1956, pp. 8–10, no. II; Rosenberg 1988, pp. 153–54, cat. no. 66.

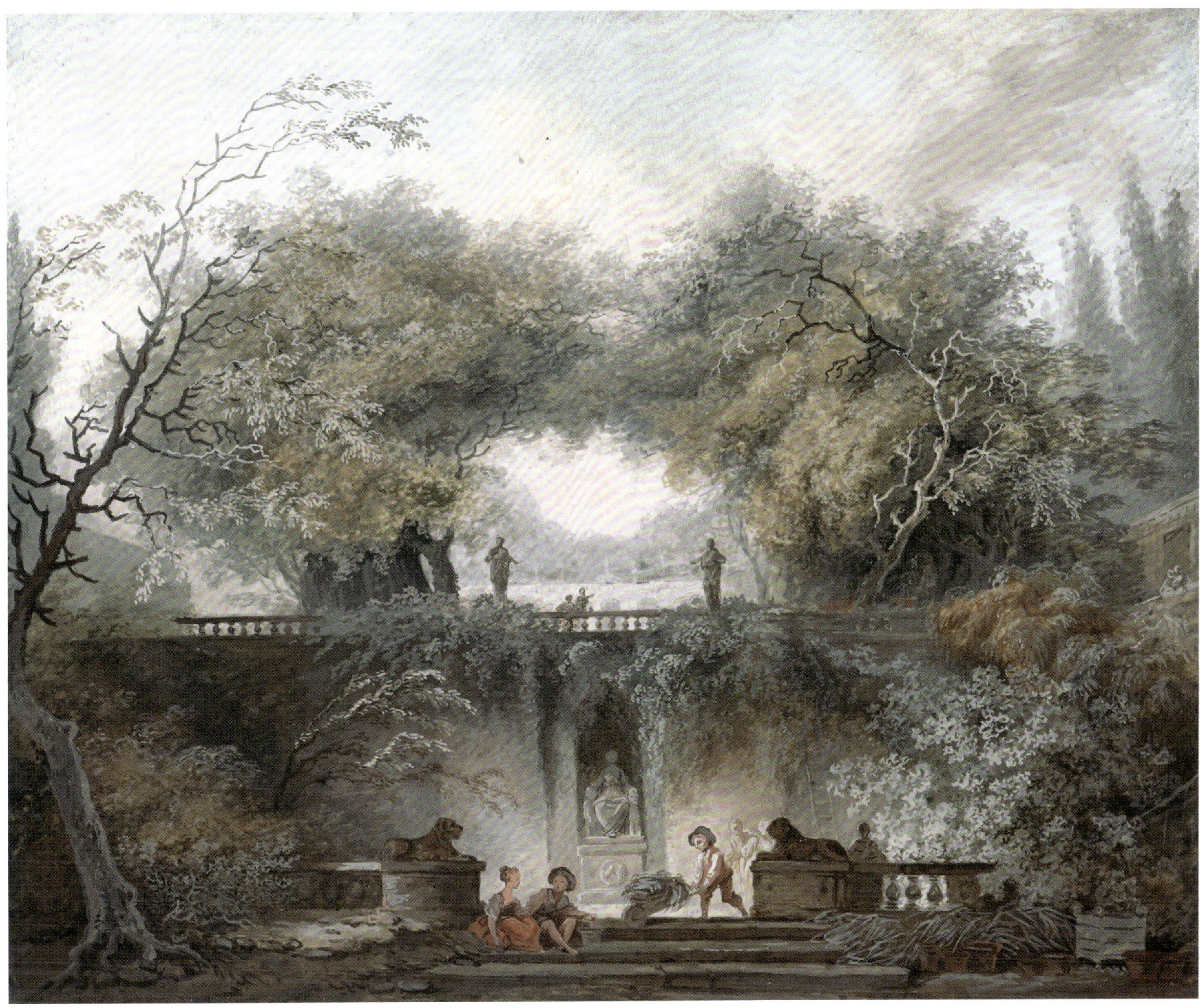

CAT 34

CAT. 33. PROVENANCE: Lemarié collection, sale, Desvouges and Baudoin, Hôtel Drouot, Paris, April 25–27, 1912 (lot 579); Baron de Vaux (per Ananoff); Mrs. William H. Crocker (Ethel Willard Crocker [1861–1934]); sale, Christie's, New York, January 28, 1999 (lot 139); [W. M. Brady & Co., Inc., New York, 2000]; private collection

SELECTED EXHIBITIONS: New York 1914, pp. 56–57, cat. no. 34; New York 2000, cat. no. 31 (entry by Eunice Williams); Grasselli et al. 2007, pp. 152–53, cat. no. 59 (entry by Margaret Morgan Grasselli); Brooks et al. 2012, pp. 8, 78, cat. no. 72.

SELECTED REFERENCES: Ananoff 1961–70, vol. 4 (1970), pp. 91–92, no. 2148, fig. 578; Grasselli 2009, pp. 200–201, 287–88, under cat. no. 88.

CAT. 34. PROVENANCE: Jacques de Bryas; his sale (Lugt 56156), Galerie Georges Petit, Paris, April 4–6, 1898 (lot 55), to Stettiner [or Wildenstein?[21]]; Berenice C. Bowles (b. 1895) (per Sotheby's); Sotheby's, January 14, 1987 (lot 181); Mr. and Mrs. Eugene V. Thaw, New York; The Morgan Library & Museum, New York, Thaw Collection (1997.85)

SELECTED EXHIBITIONS: Rosenberg 1988, *hors catalogue*;[22] Denison et al. 1996, pp. 52–53, cat. no. 26 (entry by Cara D. Denison).

SELECTED REFERENCE: Ananoff 1961–70, vol. 3 (1968), p. 121, no. 1575.

35. *View of the Temple of Vesta at Tivoli*

Ca. 1760–65
Red chalk counterproof, reworked by the artist in brown ink, brown and gray wash
13⅜ × 18¼ in. (33.8 × 46.2 cm)
Inscription: at lower right, in ink, in the hand of Josef Camesina de Pomal, "H.fragonard f"

During the summer of 1760, the abbé de Saint-Non invited Fragonard for an extended stay at the Villa d'Este in Tivoli. The journey is well documented in the correspondence between Natoire, director of the Académie de France in Rome, and the marquis de Marigny, director of the Bâtiments du Roi in Paris,[1] and in Saint-Non's travel diary. There he described the gardens of the Villa d'Este as "the most delicious thing in the world" while acknowledging their dilapidated condition.[2]

It was precisely this state of disrepair and ruin that appealed to artists who visited the villa. Fragonard was no exception. For Saint-Non, he produced ten large, highly finished drawings in red chalk depicting scenes of villa architecture, fountains, and gardens. Each work was conceived as a formal composition worthy of display. In fact, Fragonard exhibited at least two at the Salon of 1765.[3] These red chalk landscapes, now in the Musée des Beaux-Arts et d'Archéologie, Besançon, are considered paragons of eighteenth-century French red chalk technique.[4]

Fragonard made at least two highly finished red chalk drawings of the Temple of Vesta, also in the town of Tivoli, during that summer with Saint-Non. The circular temple dates from the first century B.C. and, although sometimes called the Temple of the Sibyl, was in fact dedicated to Vesta. In each drawing the artist playfully manipulates the scene and perspective to transform the emotional power of the historic site. The drawings pull together complex perspective with archaeological details and dramatic local scenery.

The better known of the two temple drawings, which is in Besançon, presents a classic image of the temple observed from an improbably close range at the level of the masonry foundations.[5] Even the frieze is described in detail. Fragonard makes the architectural scene more theatrical by dividing the temple into two symmetrical sections, with columns on the right and structural fragments on the left. He interprets nature as an intrusive and destructive force, causing large trees to explode through the temple wall. Behind the originality of Fragonard's interpretation is an echo of Piranesi's bizarre views of ruins that date from the 1750s. In 1761, Piranesi etched the temple showing the same opposing vertical sections.[6] These similarities suggest that Fragonard and Piranesi must have known each other and been aware of Roman archaeological circles. Piranesi frequented the Palazzo Mancini, met many pensionnaires, and became a friend of Hubert Robert.

The drawing exhibited here, a richly reworked counterproof of the second temple drawing, utilizes another tool of stagecraft to achieve its dramatic power. Space and perspective differ dramatically from the Besançon sheet. Here, the height of the steep precipice is exaggerated and pushed to the top of the sheet without diminishing details. Crumbling foundation stones are held in place by a jungle of vines and hanging branches. A mysterious small figure is almost obscured within the carefully tended arbor or vineyard that fills the foreground. For Fragonard to record realistically the present composition, he would have been seated deep in the ravine below the steep cliff. In fact, there was such a position where artists stood on rocks protruding from the cliffs. The Austrian artist Albert Christoph Dies etched the view, which he published in *Collection ou suite de vues pittoresques de l'Italie* (1798).

The original from which the present counterproof was pulled is lost, but, based on the handling of red chalk, it was made on the same visit to Tivoli in 1760. Fragonard's light black chalk preparations are detectable beneath the maze of original red chalk and his reworkings. One wonders if he worked from memory or from informal sketches. The serious work in red chalk covers the sheet with a variety of lines—flowing, zigzagging, serrated. Red chalk drawings contained a powdery residue of chalk dust that, if not removed, would discolor the sheet. Therefore, a counterproof was routinely made, producing as a dividend a second image in reverse, which Fragonard used to create a new composition. Any date for the reworking is speculative, but it most likely happened when Fragonard was back in Paris. With critical success at the Salon of 1765, he was no longer a pensionnaire but an artist eager to meet potential collectors. He turned to drawings and counterproofs made in Rome. In the present drawing, he used pen, ink, and two colors of wash to rework the scene. Brush and wash expanded the range of textures and definition of foliage. The final result, as seen here, is a visually rich tapestry of coloristic layers and confident strokes. EW

PROVENANCE: Josef Camesina de Pomal (1765–1827), Vienna (Lugt 429); Heinrich August Mauser; his sale, Leipzig, May 10, 1820 (lot 15); J. Grünling; his sale, Vienna, February 25–March 19, 1823 (lot 388); State Hermitage Museum sale, C. G. Boerner, Leipzig, April 29, 1931 (lot 80, pl. VII); Robert Treat Paine, Brookline, Mass., by 1929; Sotheby's, London, July 4, 1988 (lot 70); private collection

SELECTED EXHIBITION: Boston 1939, p. 100, cat. no. 64, pl. LXXVI.

SELECTED REFERENCE: Ananoff 1961–70, vol. 2 (1963), pp. 112 and 114, nos. 866 and 871, vol. 3 (1968), p. 329, no. 866, vol. 4 (1970), p. 381, no. 871a, fig. 707.

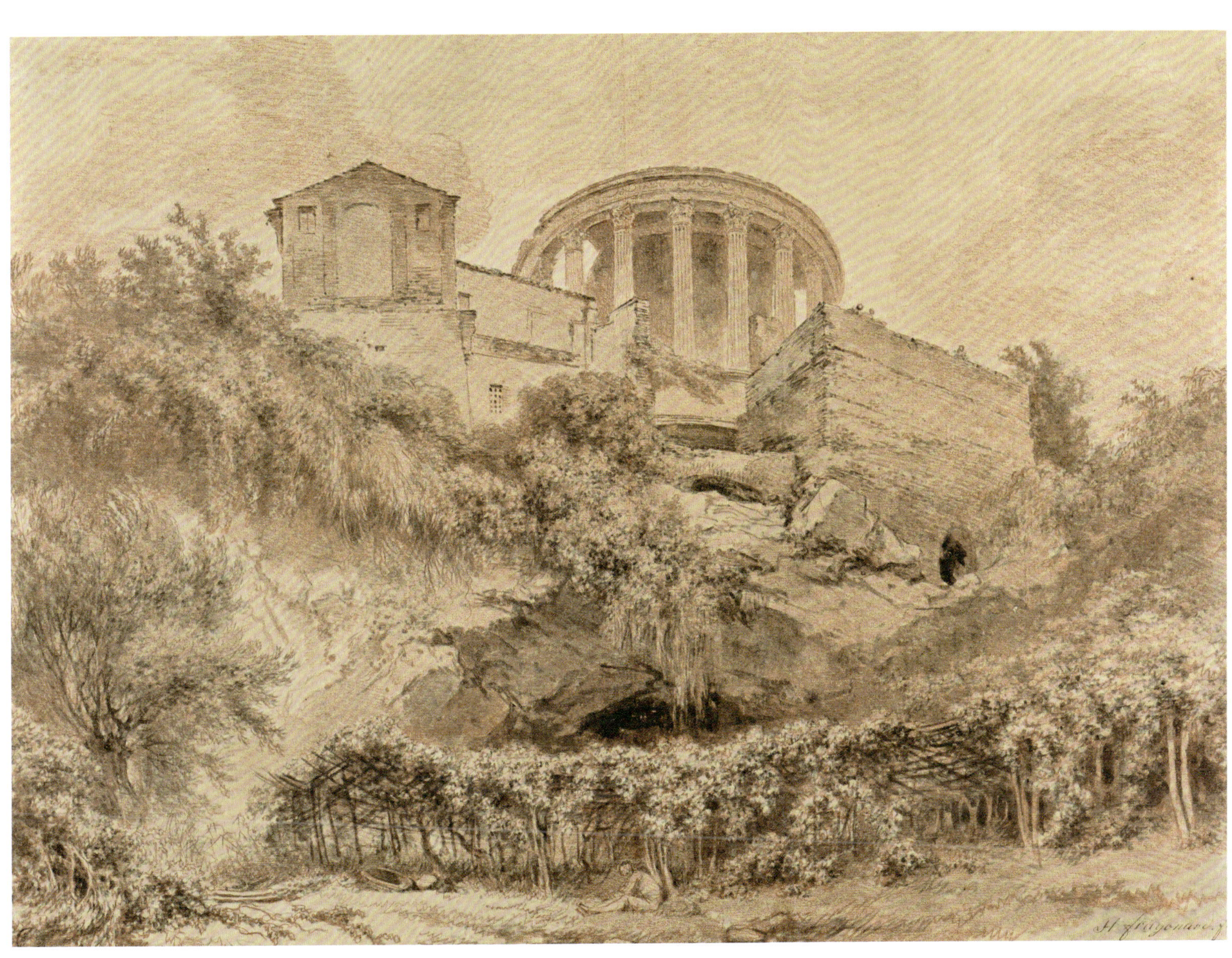

Fragonard and the Académie Royale

During the ancien régime, the Académie Royale de Peinture et de Sculpture, founded in 1648, was an institution of critical importance for any artist seeking official recognition and prestigious commissions from the court. In this context, Fragonard's conduct might seem surprising, but it is also likely revealing of his personality and highly independent character. On his return from Italy, he did not show any great eagerness to join the artistic elite of his time. It was only after three and a half years that he presented his *morceau d'agrément* (acceptance piece), the work that represented the first step toward admission to the Académie. Nor were incentives lacking to encourage him to reach the status of full academician. His acceptance piece, *Coresus and Callirhoë* (fig. 85), was hailed and greeted with unanimous acclaim upon its presentation to the Académie on March 30, 1765. The king immediately bought it to have a version woven at the Gobelins factory. In the wake of this success, a pendant was commissioned from the artist, who was assigned lodging and a studio at the Louvre. By way of a *morceau de réception* (reception piece), necessary for full membership in the Académie, Fragonard was asked to paint one of the compartments in the Galerie d'Apollon in the Louvre, the decoration of which had been left unfinished by Charles Le Brun in the preceding century. In spring 1766, he received two further royal commissions: first for two overdoors for the château de Bellevue and, not long after, for a pair of paintings for the king's dining room at Versailles. But Fragonard did not seize any of these opportunities, which would have permitted him to establish himself as one of the leading artists of his time. The pendant for the *Coresus* would remain at the stage of a sketch (see cat. 37), and the commissions for the Louvre, Bellevue, and Versailles were never fulfilled.

Like others who had achieved the status of *agréé* (accepted) at the Académie, Fragonard was allowed to exhibit at the biennial Salons, a practice that offered young artists the possibility of making themselves better known and expanding their clientele. Fragonard, however, would participate only twice, in 1765 and 1767. The difficulties he encountered in receiving payment for the *Coresus* do not alone explain his lack of interest in the Académie. In 1788, this institution attributed Fragonard's failure to submit a reception piece to his "capriciousness" and "irresponsibility."[1] Abandoning the career of a history painter, Fragonard preferred to devote his energies to a more varied range of subject matter intended for private clients. If his case is exceptional, his attitude also coincides with the intensification of criticisms of the Académie, which would lead to the institution's suppression by the Revolution in 1793. MADV

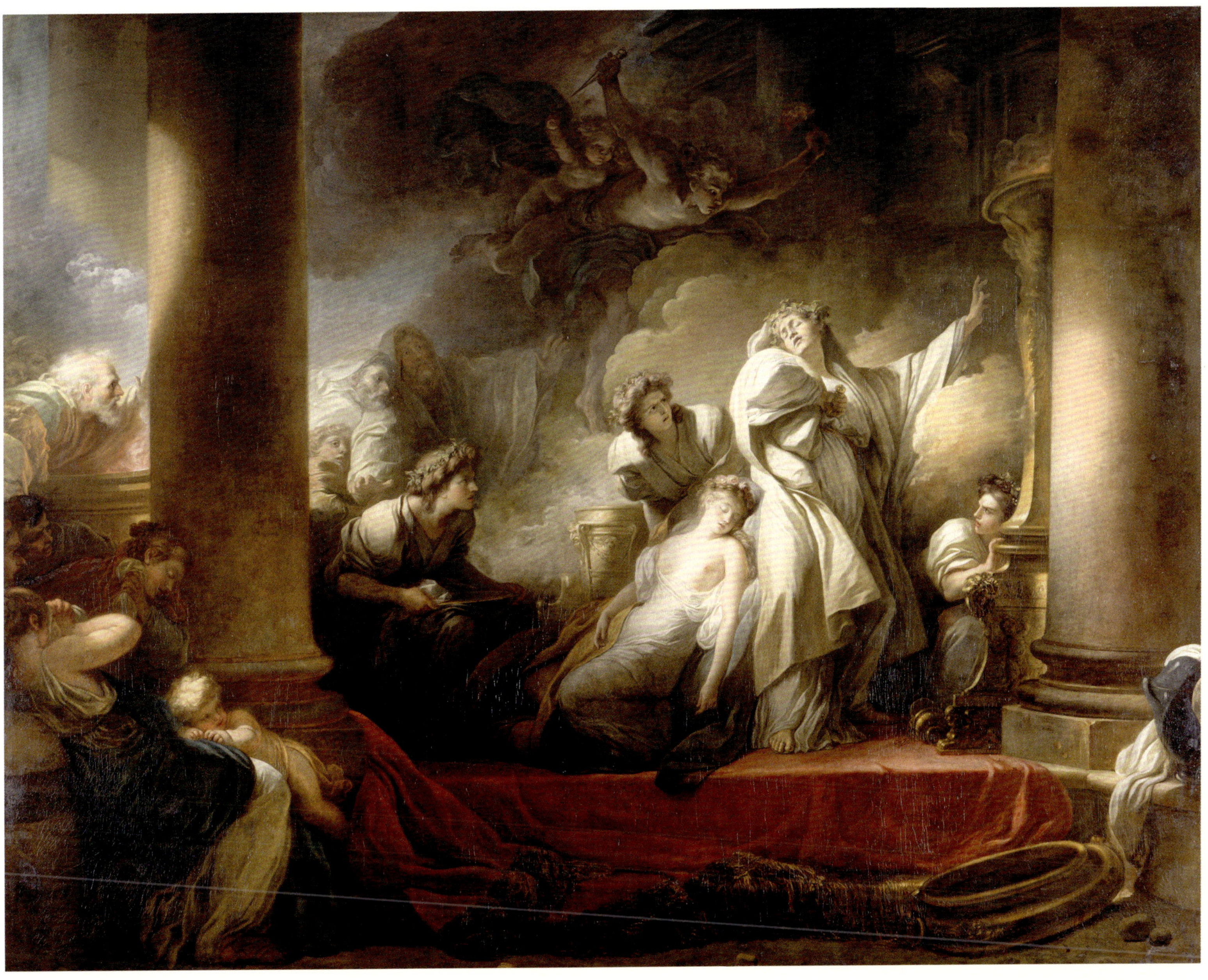

Fig. 85. Jean Honoré Fragonard, *Coresus and Callirhoë*, 1765. Oil on canvas, 10 ft. 2½ in. × 13 ft. 1½ in. (3.11 × 4 m). Musée du Louvre, Paris (4541)

36. *Rinaldo in the Enchanted Forest*

Ca. 1763
Brown wash over very light black chalk underdrawing
13¼ × 18 in. (33.5 × 45.7 cm)

Jerusalem Delivered, a highly romanticized tale of the First Crusade (1096–99), has continually inspired painters, illustrators, and composers since its publication in 1581. But very few have ventured to interpret the episode chosen by Fragonard, that of the antepenultimate canto (XVIII, 17–37) of Torquato Tasso's epic poem. There the author describes how the knight Rinaldo, resisting the charms of the sorceress Armida, overcomes the evil spells that envelop the forest where the Christians must take the wood needed to lay siege to Jerusalem. This noble act inspired Fragonard to create a pair of compositions, each interpreted in two ways: one drawn, the other painted. In the first set, Armida attempts in vain to seduce Rinaldo as he enters the forest.[1] In the second, illustrated by the magnificent wash drawing in the Metropolitan Museum, the knight, brandishing his weapon, prepares to strike the enchanted tree. But the felling of the tree by the iron of his sword was already well along, and the trunk falls to the ground, Armida's specter escaping from it in a final contortion. In the poem, her monstrous acolytes disperse before disappearing forever. But in this wash version, two sphinxes surround the knight as if to distract him from his mission, while dragons and serpents, grouped on the right, menace him with their howls and wide-open maws. Several figures with fierce expressions, including a giant with a shock of hair that is as thick as his beard and moustache, come to take part in the attempt to prevent Rinaldo's act.

The painting illustrating the same episode (fig. 86) has major variants, which offer a slightly different reading.[2] In it, Rinaldo is presented not as besieged but as victorious over the infernal creatures. Caught by a force that sweeps them beyond the picture frame, they flee backward or creep along the ground. These changes, which more closely adhere to the text, lead us to think that the wash drawing preceded the painting. In the drawing, the artist's imagination manifests itself more freely, especially in the description of a fantastical universe. His humor is also at work in the evocation of the earth trembling and cracking at the moment when the knight slices into the tree: toward the center of the foreground, in a manner more comic than dramatic, only the protruding hands can be seen of a poor creature swallowed up into a fissure. A small abandoned trumpet recalls the musical festivities that a few moments earlier had celebrated Rinaldo's arrival in the forest. On the right a figure is thrown backward, legs in the air, like the peasant girl who has fallen from her donkey (see p. 151, fig. 92). So many delicious details, but they are at odds with the nobility of the hero and the philosophical tenor of the story, which celebrates courage and control of the passions. By contrast, the drawing relating to the earlier episode, in which Rinaldo enters the enchanted forest, conforms strictly to the painted version. For that reason, should it be considered a repetition of that painting, which could explain the difference in handling between the two sheets? It seems to us, rather, that these stylistic differences are indicative of the intelligence with which Fragonard has interpreted the poem. The first scene is treated in shades of bister, suited to evoking an enchanting place with multiple sources of illumination. For the Metropolitan's sheet, depicting a later episode, Fragonard has chosen a very dense wash in a more subdued tone, tending toward gray, which, laid down in broad areas, forms a strong contrast with the parts left in reserve. In this way he succeeded in suggesting a sort of lunar illumination for this scene, which Tasso describes as plunged in darkness. In all likelihood, both drawings preceded the creation of the paintings. MADV

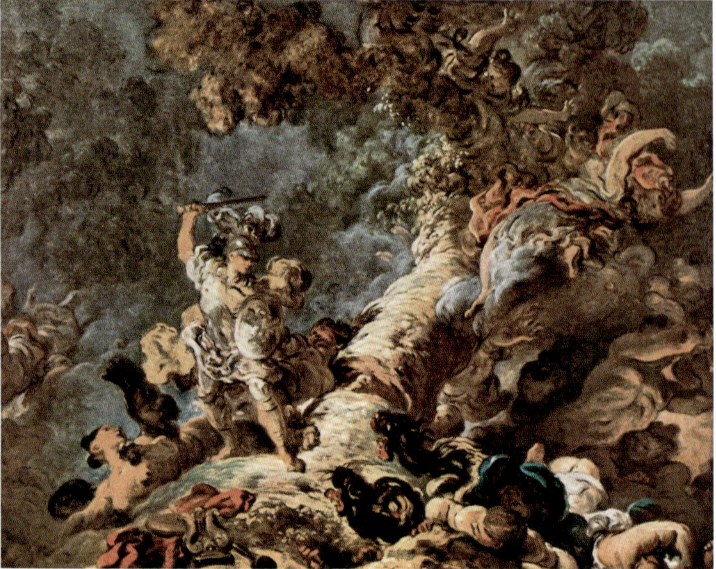

Fig. 86. Jean Honoré Fragonard, *Rinaldo in the Enchanted Forest*, ca. 1763. Oil on canvas, 28⅜ × 35⅞ in. (72 × 91 cm). Private collection, Paris

PROVENANCE: Sale (Lugt 34819), Hôtel Drouot, Paris, April 27–28, 1874 (lot 75, "Guerrier combattant des monstres. Très beau et vigoureux dessin au bistre"); Alfred Le Ghait; his collection sale (Lugt 37158), Hôtel Drouot, Paris, February 28–March 1, 1877 (lot 64, "Guerrier combattant des monstres. Scène tirée probablement de la *Jérusalem délivrée*. Vigoureux dessin à la sépia [33 × 46 cm]"), 230 francs; Guiraud brothers, according to Ananoff; [Jacques Guerlain]; [Galerie de Bayser, Paris]; The Metropolitan Museum of Art, New York, Purchase, Louis V. Bell, Harris Brisbane Dick, Fletcher, and Rogers Funds and Joseph Pulitzer Bequest; Guy Wildenstein Gift; The Elisha Whittelsey Collection, The Elisha Whittelsey Fund; Kristin Gary Fine Art Gift; and funds from various donors, 2009 (2009.236)

SELECTED EXHIBITION: Rosenberg 1988, cat. no. 71bis (exhibited in Paris only).[3]

SELECTED REFERENCES: Ananoff 1961–70, vol. 3 (1968), no. 1703, vol. 4 (1970), p. 432; Cuzin 1987, p. 252 n. 6; Louis 1994, p. 191 n. 3; Beresford and Raissis 2003, pp. 84–87, fig. 22.3 (entry by Peter Raissis); Reuter et al. 2013, pp. 238, 240, fig. 18 (essay by Marie-Anne Dupuy-Vachey).

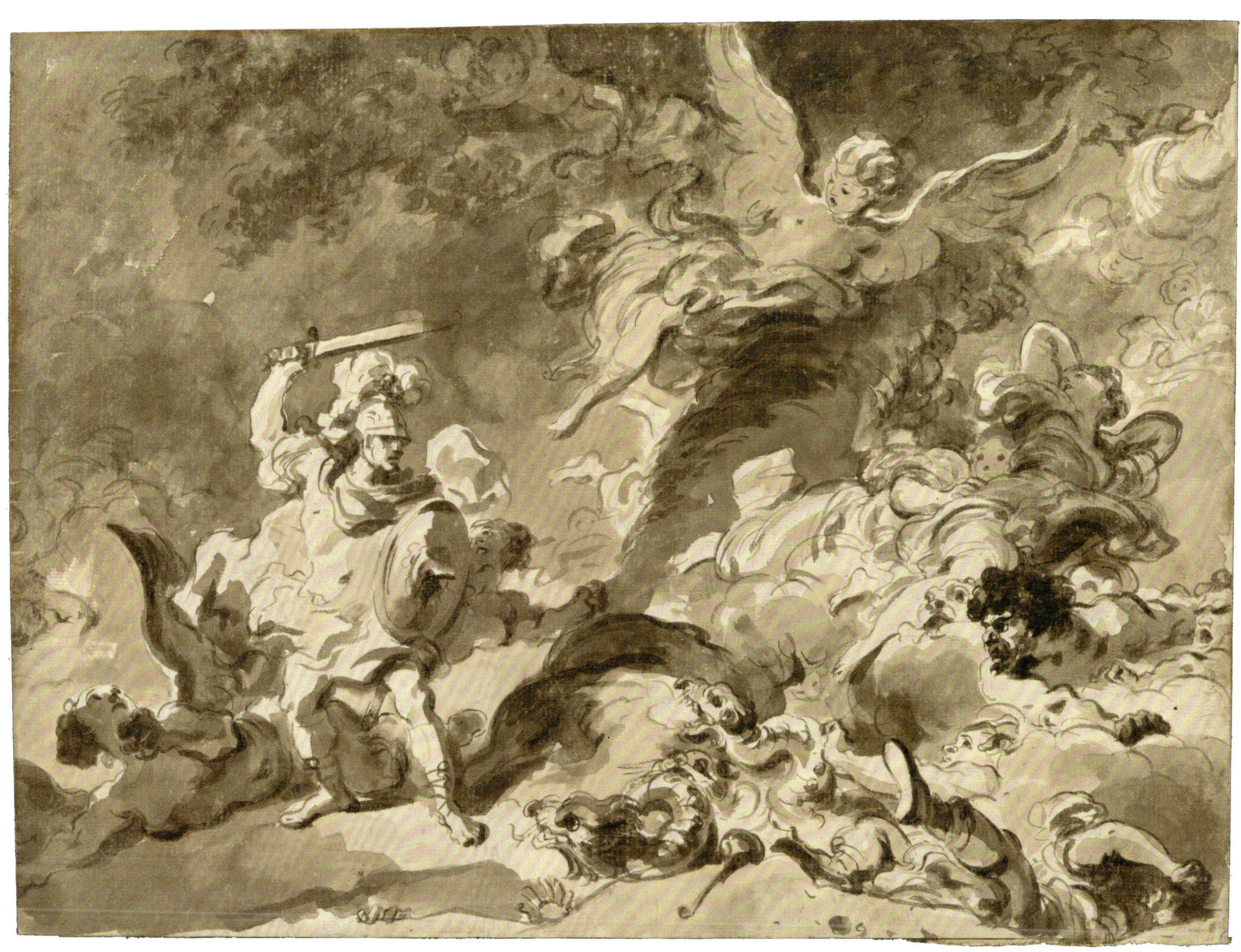

37. *Coresus and Callirhoë*

1765 or later
Brown wash over black chalk underdrawing
13⅝ × 18⅜ in. (34.6 × 46.5 cm)

Coresus, the high priest of the temple of Calydon, wounded by the indifference of the beautiful Callirhoë, seeks revenge by praying for Dionysus to intervene. The city thus finds itself plunged in total chaos, its inhabitants having become inebriated by the god's will. Only Callirhoë's death will appease the god. But rather than sacrificing the one he loves, Coresus chooses to stab himself, an act that triggers strong emotions in the crowd and causes Callirhoë to faint. Pausanias was one of the first authors to recount this dramatic story,[1] which is rarely depicted by artists. It inspired Fragonard's largest canvas (more than ten by thirteen feet) (p. 139, fig. 85),[2] the work that won him entry to the Académie on March 30, 1765, and earned him many accolades at the Salon of the same year. One would think a painting of such importance, both in terms of its size and its significance to the artist's career, would require numerous preparatory studies. But, to date, only a single sketch is known.[3] Given the many disparities between it and the final version, one assumes there were intermediary stages that allowed the artist to develop his composition. In addition, X-rays of the huge canvas have shown that the artist introduced significant changes, even at a late stage.[4]

Furthermore, it is accepted that the small painted version in the Real Academia de Bellas Artes de San Fernando, Madrid (fig. 87),[5] and the sheet exhibited here are repetitions rather than preparatory

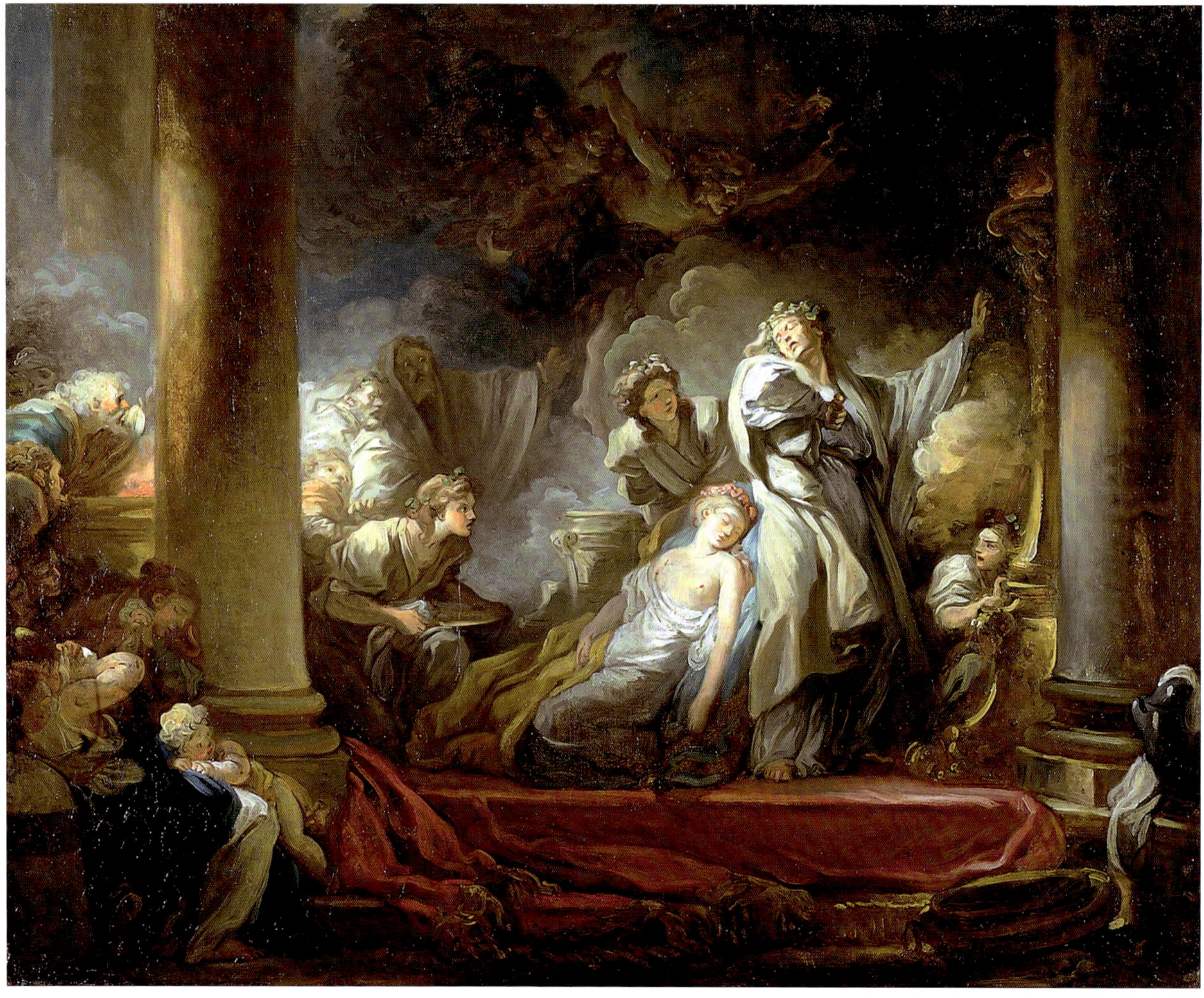

Fig. 87. Jean Honoré Fragonard, *Coresus and Callirhoë*, 1765. Oil on canvas, 25⅝ × 31⅞ in. (65 × 81 cm). Real Academia de Bellas Artes de San Fernando, Madrid (0710)

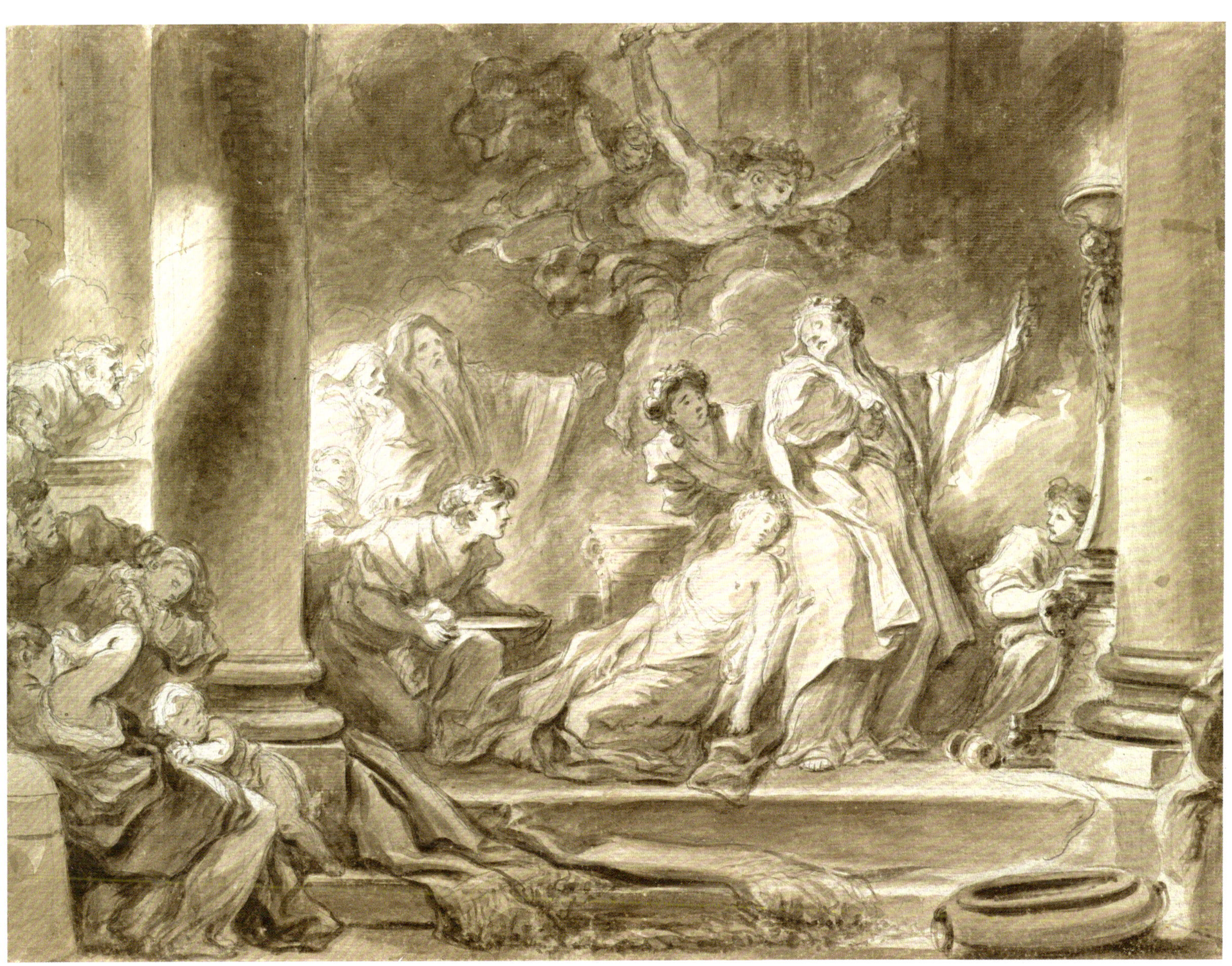

39. *The Indiscreet Bull*

Ca. 1763–65
Brown wash over black chalk underdrawing
9⅛ × 6⅞ in. (23.2 × 17.5 cm)

A remarkable painter of animals, Fragonard often depicted cattle, to the extent of making them the sole subject of a number of wash drawings and a painting, the superb *White Bull*.[1] The influence of the Dutch masters, revered by our artist, is obvious in the choice of this type of subject. But, transcending genres, Fragonard also enjoyed combining the livestock theme with that of the herders' amorous adventures. In these scenes, the brutal force of the animal in a way echoes that of a man seizing his companion, not without violence. However, humor and irony are never far away, as in *The Stable* (fig. 90), where a couple romps under the mocking eye of a beast.[2]

The Indiscreet Bull—a recent title, but one more evocative than *The Drinking Trough* or simply *The Bull*, the title of Jules de Goncourt's etching made after the drawing—again casts an animal as spectator to a somewhat risqué scene. This is very much in line with the spirit of the poet Jean de La Fontaine's *Contes* (*Tales*), for which Fragonard provided several dozen illustrations (see cats. 85 and 86). It seems to draw its inspiration directly from his illustration for the tale called "La Clochette" (The Bell) (fig. 91), in which a farm girl goes in search of a stray cow, guided by the animal's cowbell, which rings out from the depths of a dark wood. But the bell is in fact a trap laid by a scoundrel who covets the damsel and ends up raping her.[3] In the sheet here, which has a slightly larger format than the illustration for La Fontaine, the bulky mass of the beast is highlighted. A bell hangs pointedly from its neck and water escapes from its mouth, suggesting that it has just drunk from the fountain. As if dumbstruck, it stares ahead at the scene taking place. Precariously balanced on the edge of the drinking trough, a girl with a frightened expression tries to fend off the vigorous advances of the cowherd. Her resistance is probably in vain, if we are willing to see, in the manner of modern interpretations,[4] a thinly veiled metaphor for how the struggle will end in the water pouring into the basin. We note the staff resting in the foreground and the jug placed next to the basin, two accessories abandoned by the characters and attesting to the suddenness of their encounter. Fragonard has not omitted any detail, giving his composition all the qualities of a short story.

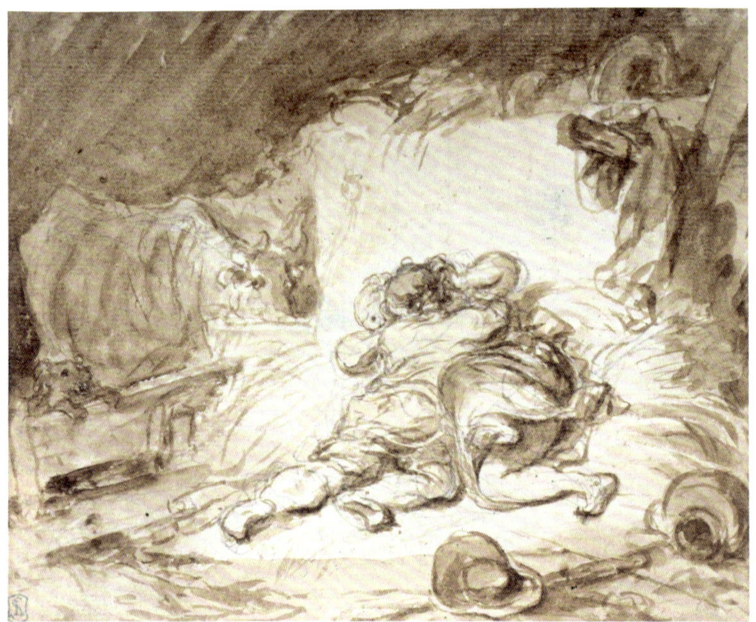

Fig. 90. Jean Honoré Fragonard, *The Stable*, ca. 1763–65. Brown wash over black chalk underdrawing, 5¾ × 7¼ in. (14.6 × 18.3 cm). Musée Cognacq-Jay, Paris (139)

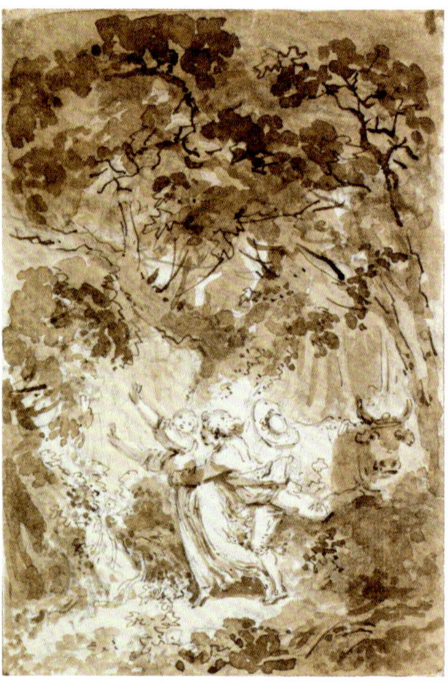

Fig. 91. Jean Honoré Fragonard, *The Bell*, ca. 1761–63. Black chalk counterproof, reworked in pen and brown ink, brown wash, 8⅛ × 5½ in. (20.5 × 14 cm). Petit Palais, Musée des Beaux-Arts de la Ville de Paris (L. Dut. 1173, vol. 1, 21)

The chalk twirls and zigzags, indicating in an allusive manner the essential elements of the composition. Then comes the work of the brush, just as jaunty, distributing here and there a few touches of ink, hanging a mysterious calligraphy from the branches of the tree. But there is no retouching with the pen as is seen in the retouched counterproofs of the *Contes* series. Even the tiniest details, such as the facial expressions, are indicated with only the point of the brush. The artist, no longer constrained by either the obligation to conform to the poet's verse or the need to maintain a stylistic homogeneity with other scenes, here expresses himself with absolute freedom. MADV

PROVENANCE: Edmond and Jules de Goncourt, their stamp (Lugt 1089) at lower center; their sale (Lugt 55024), Duchesne, Paris, February 15–17, 1897 (lot 92, repr.), sold for 7,500 francs to the comtesse de Péthion; [Sigismond Bardac (1856–1919), Paris, according to Ananoff]; Walter Burns (according to the present owner); acquired by Mortimer L. Schiff, New York, from Agnew's, London, in 1922; by descent to John M. Schiff, New York; private collection

SELECTED EXHIBITION: Paris 1879, cat. no. 589.

SELECTED REFERENCES: Ananoff 1961–70, vol. 1 (1961), no. 99, fig. 47, vol. 2 (1963), p. 298; Thuillier 1967, p. 114; Rosenberg 1988, p. 175, fig. 2; Launay 1991, pp. 106, 120, no. 97.

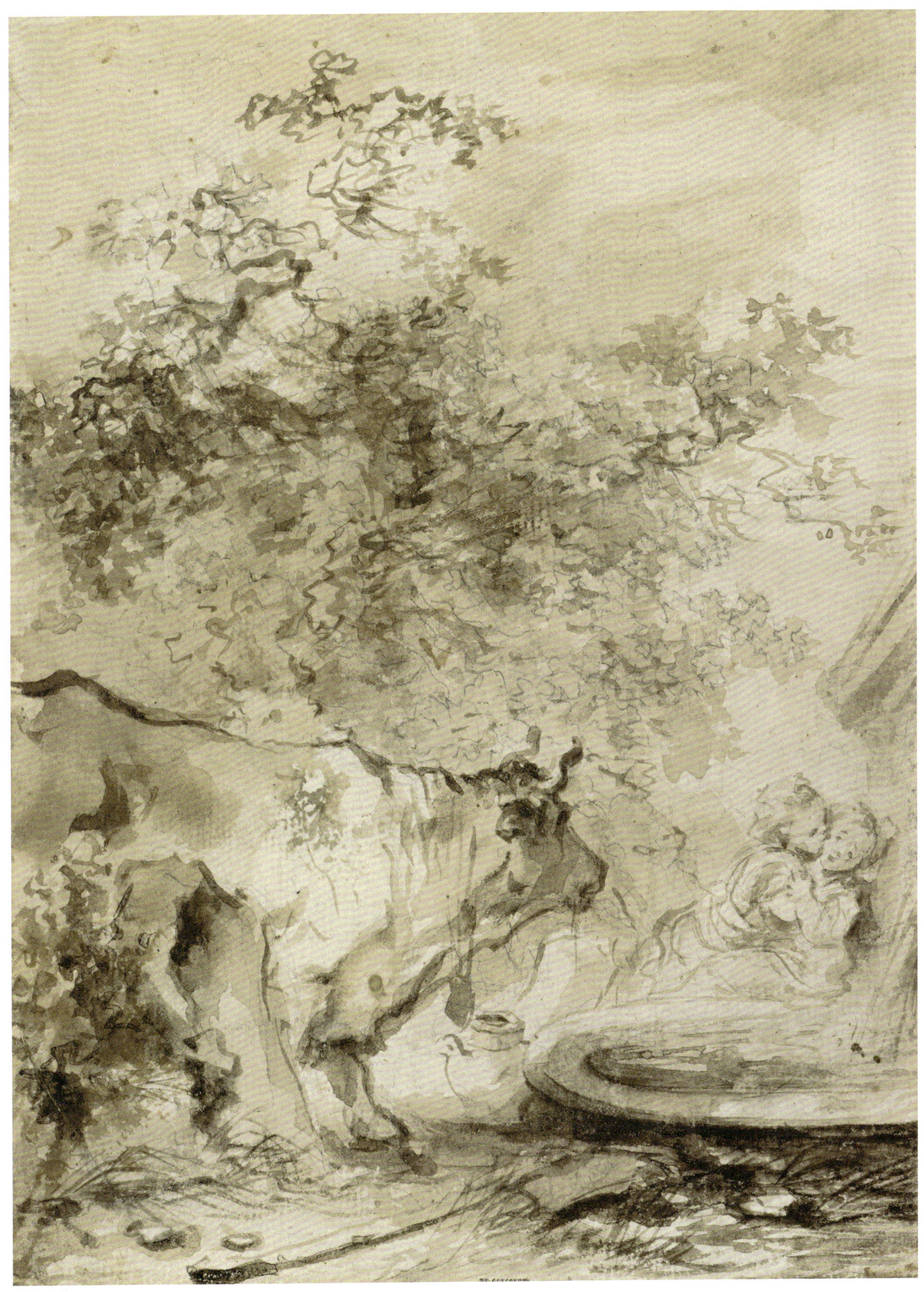

40. *The Frightened Flock*

Ca. 1765
Brush and brown and light gray wash over black chalk
9¾ × 15 in. (24.8 × 38 cm)
Inscriptions: on the milestone, in ink, "XII"; in black chalk, "VII"

Sheep occupy a significant place in Fragonard's bestiary. In contrast to his depictions of bulls, here it is not the isolated animal that captured the artist's attention but the way sheep gather, move, and cluster together, and the confusion that sometimes results from their herding instinct. The most famous example is the flock of sheep that hurtles into the foreground of *The Stalled Cart*, a painting made during the artist's first period in Italy (p. 25, fig. 18).[1] An inscription on the preparatory drawing for that painting allows the composition to be dated to 1759 (p. 24, fig. 17).[2] The sheet shown here displays much greater ease in both the arrangement of the composition and the use of the wash. The very light black chalk sketch and the equally sparing wash complement each other. Light and volume are indicated with precision, without any superfluous effects and without the pen being called in to reinforce details or to emphasize contours. The main focus is on the action, or rather the actions, animating the scene. On one side, the flock is captured in a sort of whirling movement around the milestone; on the other, the shepherd rushes forward, staff in hand, accompanied by his dog. His hat is thrown backward—or perhaps it is a hood billowing in the wind—a sign of his haste. We note with surprise that his gaze, like his steps, is not directed toward his flock but toward an objective beyond the borders of the sheet. Is he preparing to hunt a predator—a wolf or a bird of prey—whose presence would explain the panic that has gripped the flock? Whatever the case may be, the scene works perfectly this way, with the completion of the narrative left to the viewer's imagination.

However, it should be recalled that this drawing, at least since its appearance at auction in 1790 and until 2010, was associated with another one, *The Broken Strap* (fig. 92).[3] In the same dimensions and

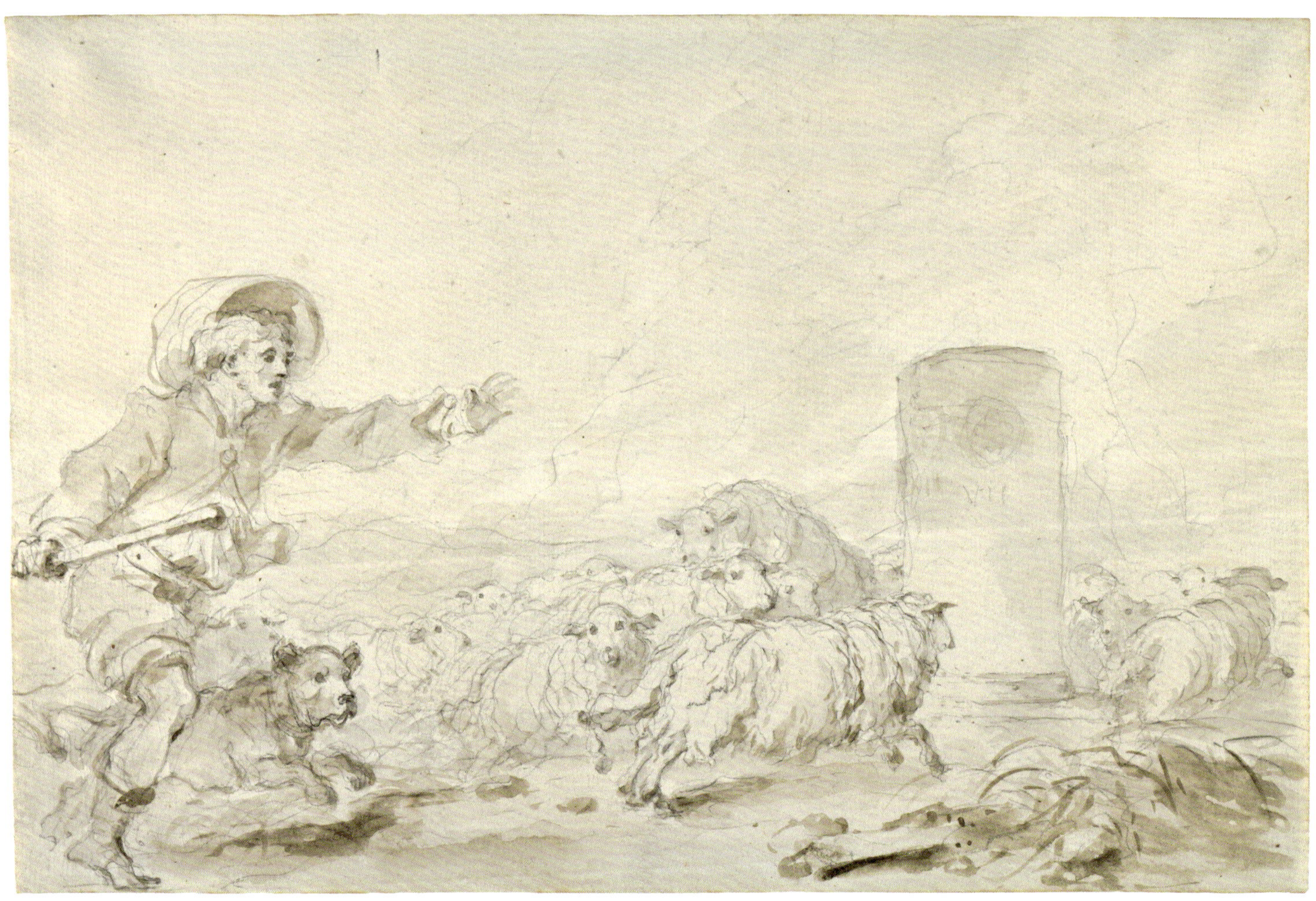

technique, it shows a comical scene in which two donkeys are the protagonists. One has just bitten the hindquarters of its companion, who has reacted with a violent kick, causing his saddle to loosen and his rider, a peasant girl, to be thrown to the ground. The girl finds herself flat on her back, her bare legs exposed to the mocking looks of passersby. Given the early association of the two drawings, we may wonder if the two share a narrative connection. The event that unfolds in *The Broken Strap* could very well have caused the sheep here to panic, and our shepherd may be rushing to the aid of the girl. His expression, like the gesture of his hand, seems to signify a desire to help. If a real danger had threatened the flock, it would have been more convincing to show him brandishing his staff to frighten off the predator. Although we cannot prove that these two sheets were intended to be seen side by side, there is a logic to their association. Were they, for all that, composed at the same time? The question is worth asking given the slight but notable disparities, both in form and content. The ribald subject of *The Broken Strap* corresponds to a vein that was greatly appreciated by a certain clientele. There is nothing bawdy, however, in the scene of *The Frightened Flock*. The slightly more lively and assured treatment of the wash in this second sheet could indicate that it was composed later. Since Fragonard was not short on witticisms, should we see an indication of its dating (December 7? July 12?) in the roman numerals (XII and VII) shown on the milestone, which presumably indicate in *lieues* (leagues) the distances that separate the place from neighboring towns? We will content ourselves by more prudently suggesting a date of about 1765. MADV

PROVENANCE: M. [François Georges Maréchal, marquis de Bièvre (1747–1789)] sale, Hôtel de Bullion, Paris, March 10 and following days, 1790 (part of lot 29, "un pâtre conduisant un troupeau de mouton"); Vicomte Beuret sale, November 25, 1924 (lot 18, repr.), sold for 42,000 francs to David David-Weill (1871–1952); David David-Weill; his collection sale, Sotheby's, London, June 10, 1959 (lot 81, repr.), sold for £1,600 to Slatkin; [Regina Slatkin/Charles Slatkin Gallery, New York]; Mr. and Mrs. Douglas Williams, New York; sale, Christie's, New York, November 3, 1977 (lot 102); [David Carritt, Limited, London]; private collection, London; [Leclaire Kunst, 2010]; acquired by the current owner on March 23, 2010; private collection

SELECTED EXHIBITION: London 1978b, cat. no. 8.

SELECTED REFERENCES: Henriot 1926–28, vol. 3 (1928), pp. 197, 199; Ananoff 1961–70, vol. 1 (1961), no. 300, fig. 110, vol. 2 (1963), p. 305, vol. 4 (1970), p. 353; Rosenberg 1988, pp. 176, 177, fig. 3.

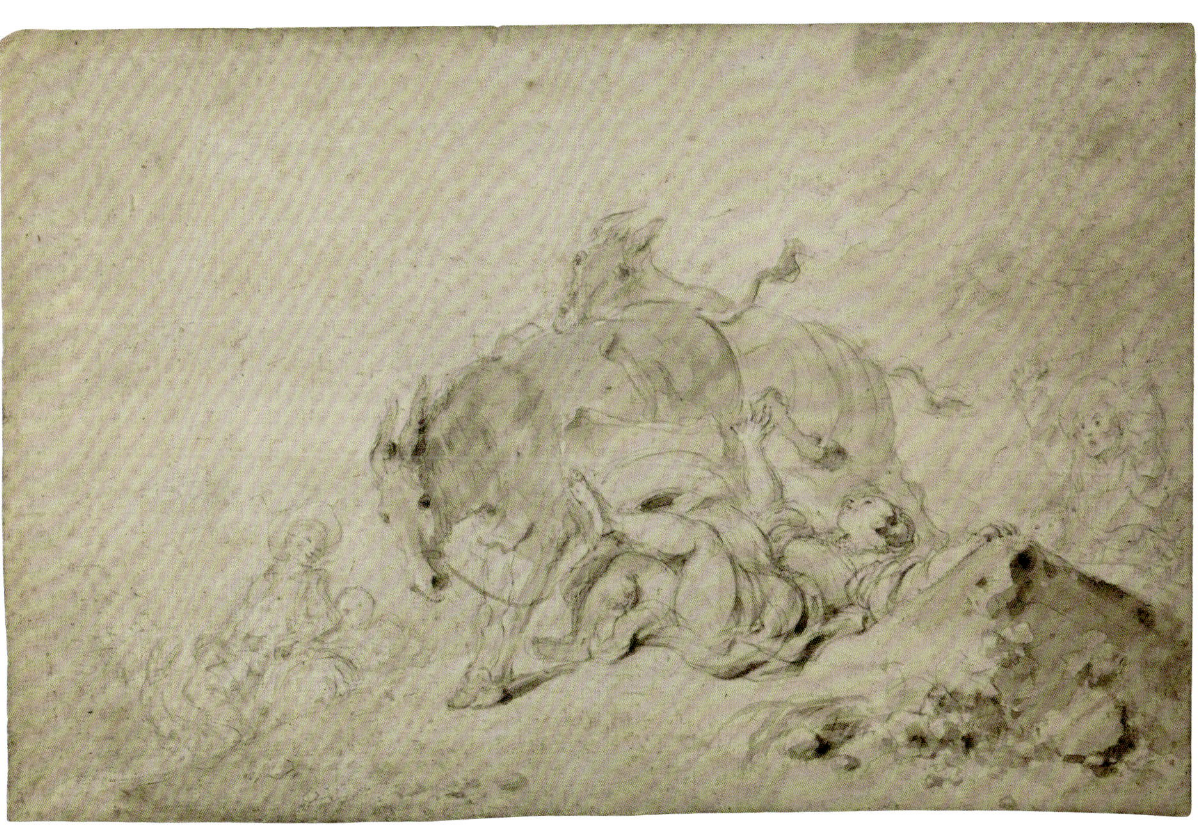

Fig. 92. Jean Honoré Fragonard, *The Broken Strap*, ca. 1763–65. Brown wash over black chalk underdrawing, 9½ × 14⅞ in. (24 × 37.6 cm). Private collection

41. *Foliage Study: Branches of a Chestnut Tree*

Ca. 1765(?)
Red chalk
12⅞ × 16⅛ in. (32.5 × 41 cm)
Inscription: on the mount, "fragonard"

Trees and foliage occupy an important place not only in Fragonard's landscapes but also as background elements in his narrative subjects. As he worked in the studio, he was able to summon from memory and draw individual trees or masses of foliage. This mastery was developed through informal studies, such as the present sheet, made outdoors, *sur le motif*, and the formally composed study of an acanthus (cat. 4).

This sheet records with spontaneity and objectivity branches of a chestnut tree heavy with leaves and nuts. The Christie's catalogue identified it as a European chestnut, *Castanea sativa*, which grew throughout southern Europe, including France and Italy. The foliage is naturalistic but in repetition becomes stylized, as branches cascade across the sheet with momentum from left to right. Initial analysis of the handling of red chalk seems to connect it to works from Fragonard's first stay in Italy, in 1760. Natoire's instruction and practice obviously inspired Fragonard to look closely at nature on his own time. He was more interested in textures, reflections, and patterns of light than botanical accuracy.

However, there is another dynamic within the image, one of an artist revisiting in later years the practice preached by Natoire. Fragonard developed his mastery by continued practice and observation of plants and trees. The present sheet exhibits the relaxed confidence of an artist's casual effort made spontaneously. It is worth comparing it to a rare sketch in gouache and watercolor in Grasse (fig. 93). Assembled on a single page are multiple studies of individual leaves; it reads like an academic exercise. Assigning a date to either sheet presents a conundrum. Fragonard used gouache in Paris in the 1760s. Perhaps the Grasse gouache and the present sheet both date from the mid-1760s. EW

PROVENANCE: Collection P. and N. Baur de Boer, Amsterdam; their sale, Christie's, London, July 4, 1995 (lot 90); private collection

SELECTED REFERENCE: Ananoff 1961–70, vol. 1 (1961), no. 343, fig. 122.

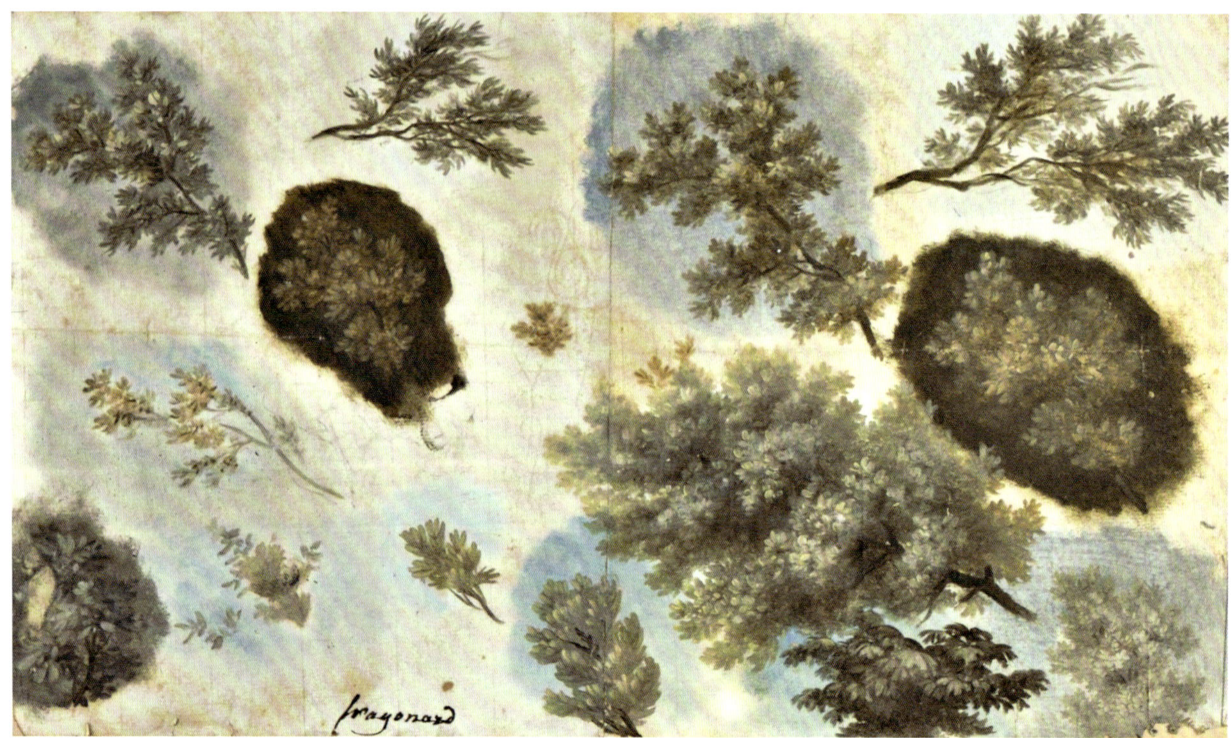

Fig. 93. Jean Honoré Fragonard, *Individual Studies of Leaves*, mid-1760s. Gouache and watercolor, 8⅞ × 15 in. (22.4 × 38 cm). Villa-Musée Jean-Honoré Fragonard, Grasse, Gift of François Carnot (659-T)

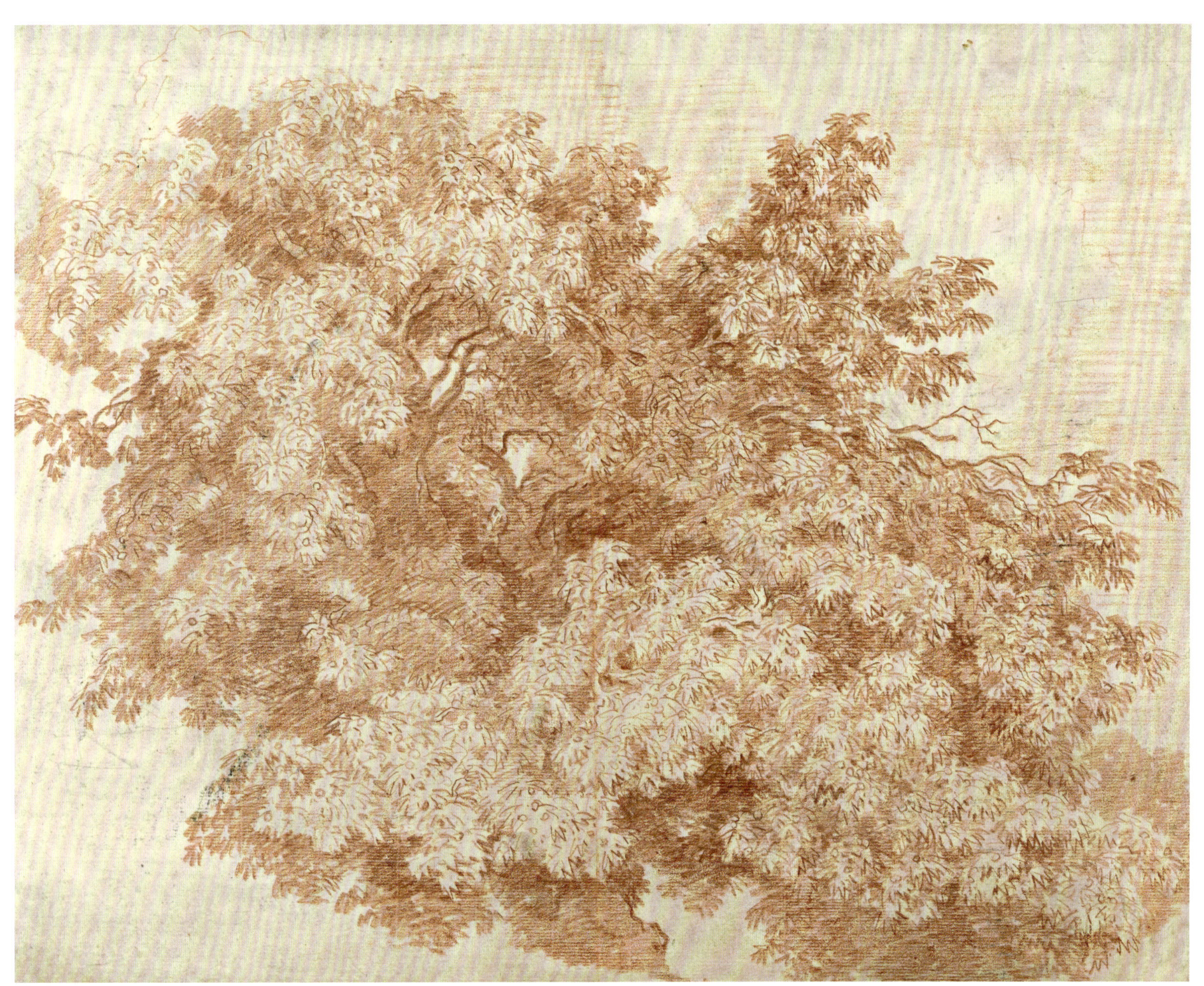

42. *Farm Buildings beside a Waterway*

Ca. 1765
Red chalk over traces of black chalk underdrawing
14¼ × 19⅜ in. (36.1 × 49 cm)

43. *Farm Buildings beside a Waterway*

Ca. 1765–70
Black chalk, pen and brown ink, brush and brown wash
13¾ × 18⅞ in. (35 × 47.8 cm)

A finished composition repeated in different media presents a rare opportunity to examine the works' commonalities and consider the order in which Fragonard may have executed them. Existence of two versions is also evidence of the important role played by his circle of patrons, the private collectors who knew each other and were in a position to make specific commissions, a possible explanation for the creation of close variants in different techniques. Each drawing confirms the artist's sharp observation of life and his personal command of media and technique.

The scene, although likely made up, was probably inspired by Fragonard's experience at rural estates owned by friends such as the abbé de Saint-Non and his elder brother, Louis Richard de la Bretèche.[1] The cluster of riverside buildings includes, in addition to cottages and sheds, a large fortified tower (a donjon) in the distance and a dovecote on the left. These buildings are typically part of an estate and represent French vernacular architecture that would have been familiar to Fragonard. Features such as high-pitched roofs, dormers, and half-timber construction could be found throughout provincial France and were not unique to Holland and the low countries.

The traditional title, *Village*, deserves review. The origin goes back to descriptions in early sale catalogues. When the duc de Rohan-Chabot's collection was sold at auction in 1787, the wash version of this composition was described by Jean-Baptiste Pierre Le Brun as a "village on the edge of a river inspired by Hobbema."[2] Later, when the same sheet appeared in an anonymous sale (May 31, 1790), the name of Ruisdael was invoked. Authors of sale catalogues used the names Hobbema and Ruisdael as marketing ploys to assure higher prices at a time when Parisian collectors were passionate admirers of seventeenth-century Dutch art.

Curiously, the red chalk version was described as a "réplique" of the wash drawing in the Bourgarel sale (1922), an opinion repeated by Wilhelm in 1957 and Ananoff in 1963.[3] On the contrary, the red chalk composition was probably the first and created by Fragonard in about 1765. The date is confirmed by an inscription on the verso of its red chalk counterproof, given by the artist to Aignan Thomas Desfriches: "Drawing after nature by Monsieur Fragonard, which he made a present to me, 15 September 1765—Desfriches."[4]

The red chalk creates a sunny atmosphere for the extensive scene that is organized in planes, from near to distant. Trees and hedges separate the background from human pursuits. In contrast, the foreground is filled with figures and descriptive details that allude to activities of rural life. Everything is drawn with clarity using a variety of graphic strokes. Lines are crisp and firm but vary in pressure on the white paper. The purely linear definition of architecture is complemented by a richly patterned spread of vegetation and foliage. Here Fragonard's chalk moves with the same flexibility and rhythm associated with the foliage created by his etching needle in the etchings dated about 1763 (see cat. 32).[5]

The large cottage at right anchors the scene in both versions. The red chalk composition includes numerous casks on the ground and in the small boat, suggesting, perhaps, cider production. Is this structure, which has no chimney, a pressing room or mill for cider or vinegar? As staffage, a woman and child standing in the door observe another woman rolling a barrel to the water. Behind, in mid-distance, is a half-timber house with another barrel and a ladder. These carefully integrated details hint at the activities of the inhabitants without being intrusive. A sense of authenticity pervades the scene.

In the wash version of the composition, the cottages show fewer details and, as a result, have lost the implied anecdotal reference to cider production. The season is vague, as are the activities. Are figures in the dinghy tying up or pulling a net? In contrast to the previous version, Fragonard began this one with a black chalk preparation. But he is not reproducing the first version, only reinventing it with layers of wash, from transparent to dark brown. Here, both foliage and architecture are drawn extensively with the point of the brush. At the right, blurred strokes of wash imply windblown trees, contrasting with the short, staccato brushstrokes for the dense grasses and the stand of trees behind the dovecote. This version, with its range of brown tonalities, might have inspired an eighteenth-century dealer, painter, and connoisseur such as Jean-Baptiste Pierre Le Brun to think of Hobbema or Ruisdael. EW

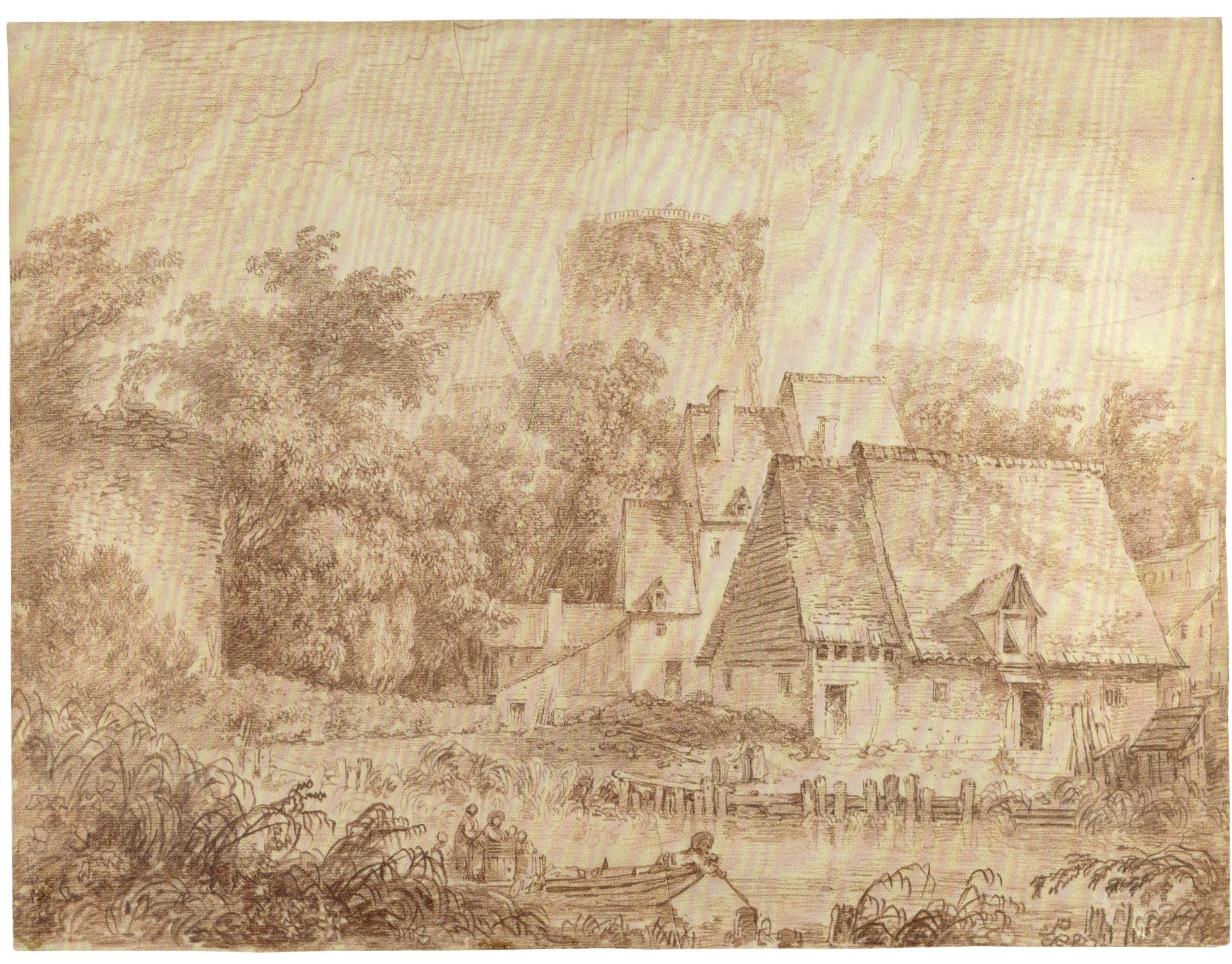

CAT 42

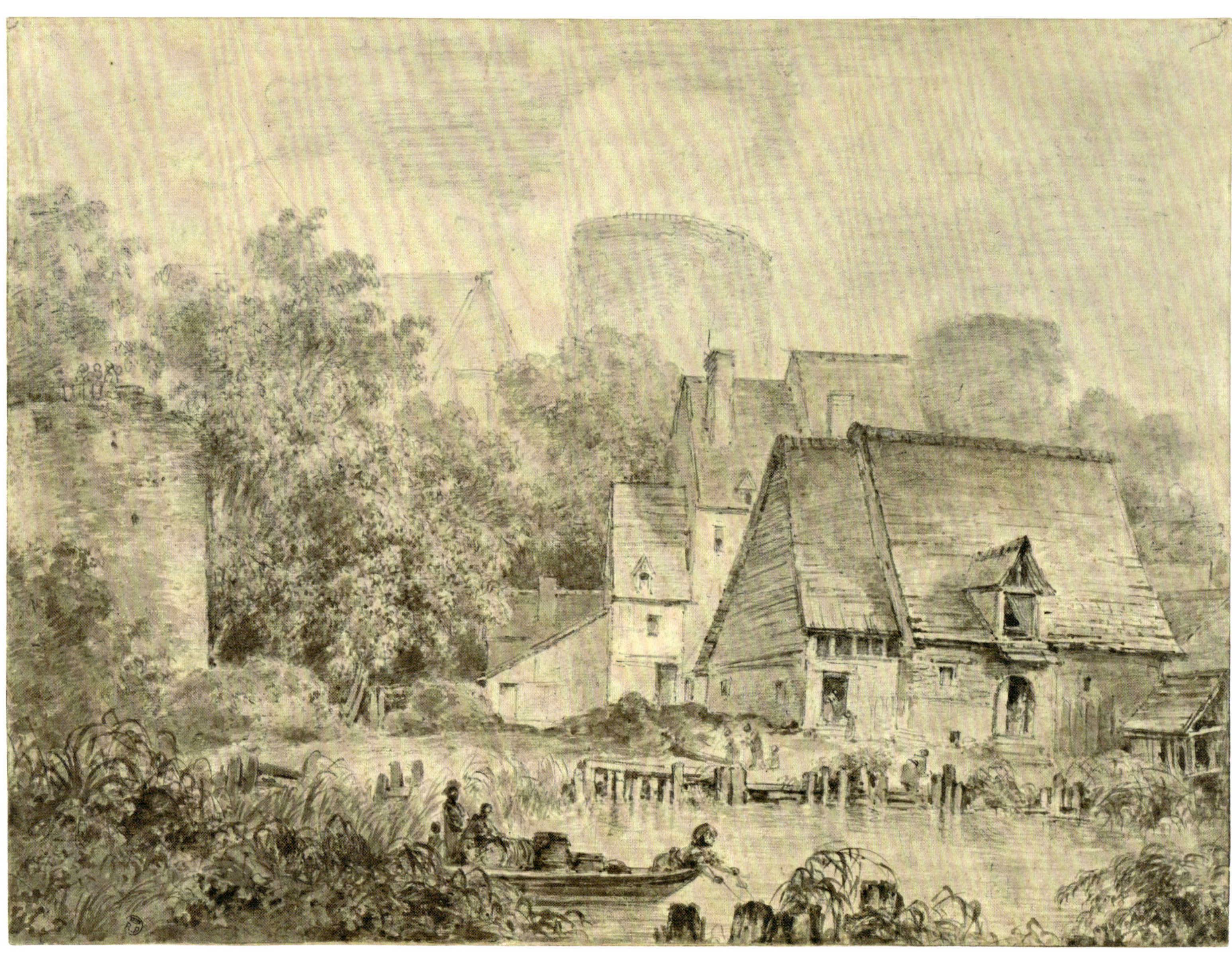

CAT 43

CAT. 42. PROVENANCE: Mathieu Guillaume Thérèse de Villenave (1762–1848); his sale (Lugt 16751), Paris, December 1–8, 1842 (lot 606), to de LaSalle; Henri Duval de Liège; his sale, Muller, Amsterdam, June 22–28, 1910 (lot 123); Georges Bourgarel; his sale (part two, Lugt 84218), Paris, November 13–15, 1922 (lot 84), to Esders; Armand Esders (1889–1940); his estate sale, May 28, 1941 (lot 1), to Dequoy; sale, Hôtel Drouot, Paris, December 15, 1994 (lot 54); private collection

SELECTED EXHIBITION: New York 1996, cat. no. 17, ill.

SELECTED REFERENCE: Ananoff 1961–70, vol. 2 (1963), no. 957, fig. 258.

CAT. 43. PROVENANCE: Louis Antoine Auguste, duc de Rohan-Chabot; his collection sale (Lugt 4230), Lebrun, Paris, December 10–15, 1787 (lot 211), expert Le Brun; anonymous sale, Paris, May 31, 1790 (lot 181); Baron Roger Portalis (1841–1912) (his stamp, Lugt 2232, at lower left), Paris; his collection sale (Lugt 46356), Hôtel Drouot, Paris, March 14, 1887 (lot 88), unsold; anonymous sale (Portalis), February 2–3, 1911 (lot 98); collection of John Postle Heseltine (1843–1929) and Dr. J. Paul Richter (1847–1937), their sale, Muller, Amsterdam, May 27–28, 1913 (lot 297, pl. 46); Alfred Strölin; his sale, June 30, 1922 (lot 3); Richard Owen to Countess Wachtmeister; her sale, Sotheby's, London, December 15, 1954 (lot 94), to Galerie Cailleux, Paris; to Walter C. Baker, New York; The Metropolitan Museum of Art, New York, Bequest of Walter C. Baker, 1971 (1972.118.212)

SELECTED EXHIBITIONS: Paris 1907, cat. no. 192; Virch 1962, cat. no. 78, ill.

SELECTED REFERENCES: Portalis 1889, vol. 2, p. 307, ill. opp. p. 166; Virch 1960, pp. 315–16; Ananoff 1961–70, vol. 2 (1963), no. 958, fig. 259, vol. 3 (1968), pp. 141–42; Bean and Turčić 1986, no. 114, ill.

44. *The Return of the Herd*

Ca. 1768–69
Brown wash over black chalk underdrawing
8⅜ × 13¾ in. (21.3 × 34.8 cm)

The recent reemergence of this sheet, which had been untraced since its appearance at auctions at the end of the eighteenth century, has allowed some clarification of the muddled provenances of the various versions of the composition catalogued by Ananoff. This drawing probably corresponds to the one that belonged to the writer Louis Jean François Collet.[1] The dimensions given in the catalogues of the 1787 Collet sale and the 1791 Lebrun auction are significantly larger, but it is possible, especially in the latter case, that they include the mount, as sometimes happens. It is also obvious that the present drawing has been reduced in size, as shown by the motifs cut off all around the edges of the sheet, especially the truncated branches of tree in the upper area. This reduction was probably done in the nineteenth century to make the work conform in format with a drawing by Jean-Baptiste Hilaire that was also in the Collet sale of 1787 and with which it reappeared in 2013.[2]

This association is surprising given that the two sheets have nothing in common except the blondness of the wash. Neither their subjects nor their styles are comparable. If Fragonard's drawing had to be connected to one by another artist, we would look to Jean-Baptiste Le Prince, in whose work we find echoes of Fragonard, in the pastoral, rustic inspiration of this type of scene, in the use of wash, and in the treatment of the foliage. Indeed, it was as "attributed to" Le Prince that another version of *The Return of the Herd*, which had not been trimmed, appeared at auction in 1957 (fig. 94).[3] It is unusual in Fragonard's work to encounter two versions with so few variants. This repetition likely attests to the success of a composition that the artist also interpreted on canvas (fig. 95)[4] and that was circulated in the form of an etching by Dominique Vivant Denon. With its expansive, cloudy sky, against which stands out the form of a tree with gnarled branches, its contrasting light effects, and its palette playing on hues of browns and greens, the painting possesses all the characteristics developed by Dutch landscape artists of the seventeenth century, down to the pair of white bulls and the windmill on the right.

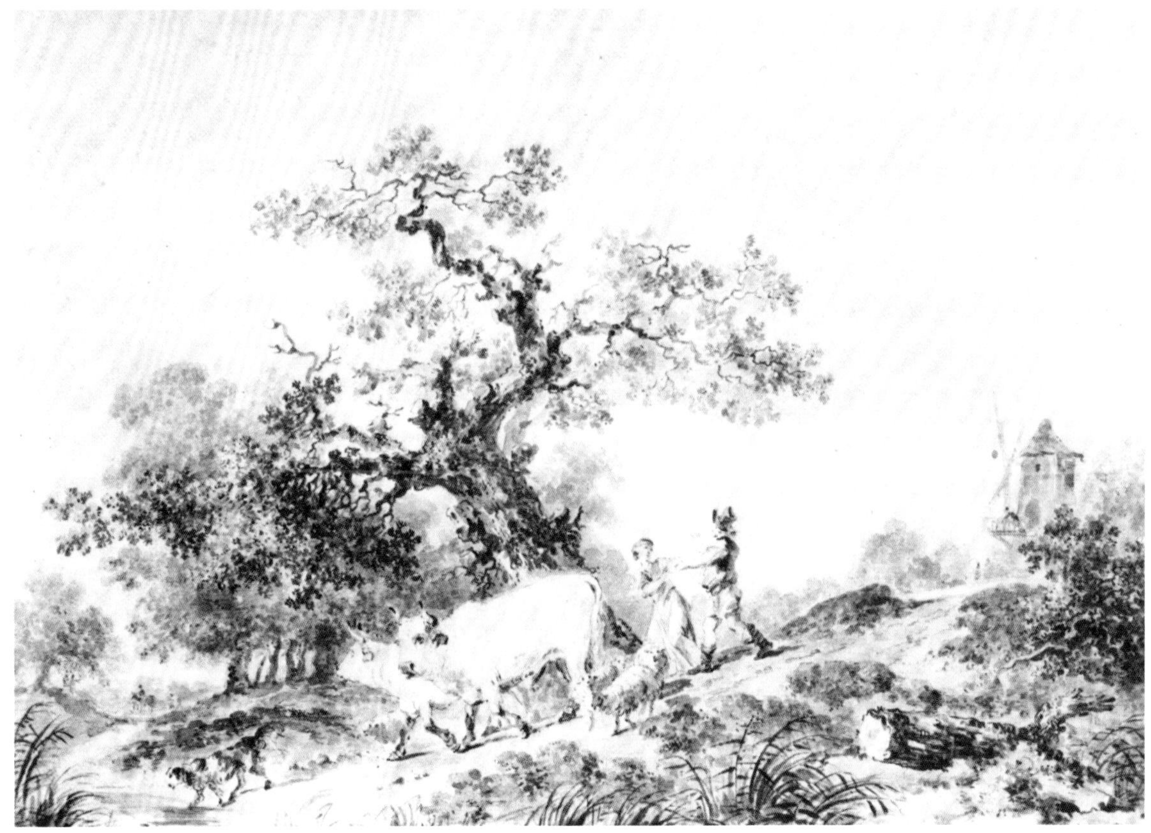

Fig. 94. Jean Honoré Fragonard, *The Return of the Herd*, ca. 1768–69. Brown wash over black chalk underdrawing, 10½ × 14⅜ in. (26.5 × 36.5 cm). Location unknown

45. *Shepherd and Sheep on a Sunny Hillside*

Ca. 1768–72
Brush and brown wash over graphite
13⅝ × 18⅜ in. (34.4 × 46.6 cm)

In this view of a wooded hillside, Fragonard again plays with light to create a luminous landscape, with only a few signifiers of subject, such as shepherds and a flock of sheep. His landscapes include many categories, often with minimal narrative, that explore natural elements such as storms, sky, sunlight, and, of course, earth. *Landscape with Stormy Sky* (cats. 46 and 47) is another example of how these elements repeatedly inspired him.

The lens through which Fragonard interprets nature in this drawing is that of seventeenth-century Dutch artists such as Jacob van Ruisdael, whose pictures Fragonard copied.[1] The present sheet references the Dutch master, from whom he freely appropriated formal ideas such as the diagonal slope of terrain, trees dramatically silhouetted like tracery against the sky, and the sharp ray of sunlight that divides the space. Fragonard adapted Ruisdael's foliage style to his personal pointillist manner of handling brush and wash. As a result, the surface vibrates with closely spaced daubs of wash that together create volumes of heavy foliage. Close examination reveals that the trees are constructed with a network of intersecting straight and angular brushstrokes wet with brown wash. Implicit in every stroke is the sense of organic growth and connectivity. In contrast to this precise brushwork, Fragonard's loose, loopy underdrawing can be seen along treetops and clouds.

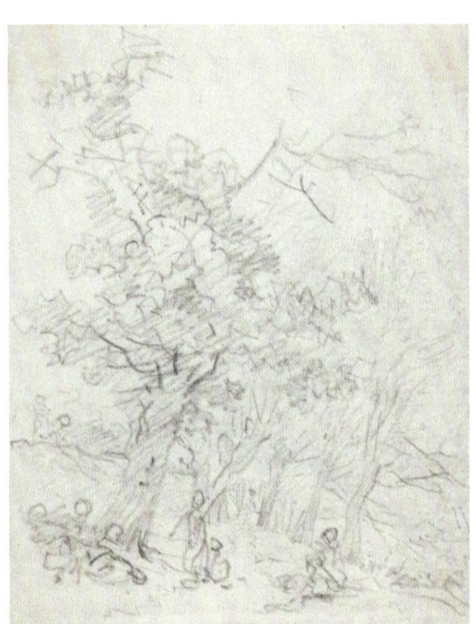

Fig. 96. Jean Honoré Fragonard, *Figures in a Landscape*, recto, ca. 1761–65. Black chalk, 8⅛ × 6⅜ in. (20.6 × 16.1 cm). Nationalmuseum, Stockholm (NM 260/1972)

The broad foreground is filled with Fragonard's typical devices of strategically placed logs and scruffy grasses that simultaneously invite and distance the viewer. The beam of light connects this area to the visible horizon in the distance, a formal device as well as a thematic element. Each detail provides evidence of Fragonard's deliberate approach to the composition of even the most "natural" scenes.

If Fragonard's composing seems effortless, it is because he had observed nature closely and made casual black chalk sketches in notebooks now dispersed. A double-sided sheet in Stockholm offers a clue to the reality that he transformed into art. Depicting similarly sturdy trees on a hill, *Figures in a Landscape* (fig. 96) is part of a group of similar landscape studies that might have belonged to a sketchbook.[2]

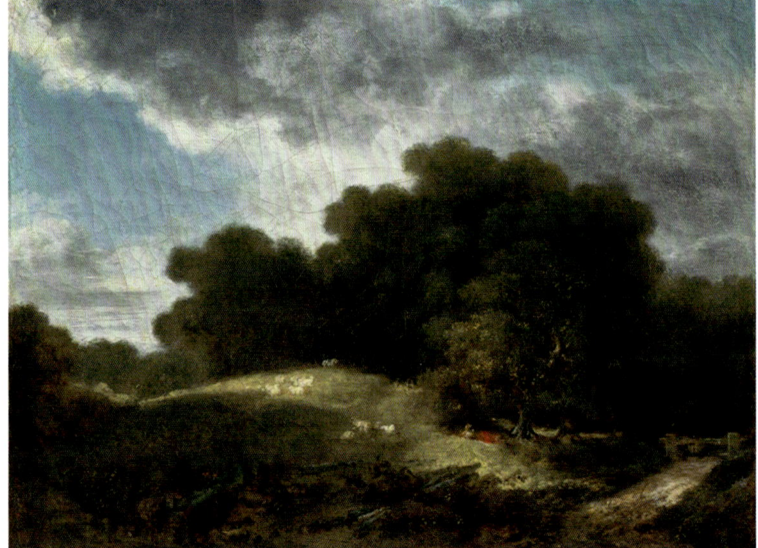

Fig. 97. Jean Honoré Fragonard, *Shepherd and Sheep on a Sunny Hillside*, ca. 1763–65. Oil on canvas, 9⅛ × 11⅞ in. (23 × 30 cm). Private collection

An oil painting of the same composition, but with reduced dimensions, was sold in Paris on December 19, 2014 (fig. 97).[3] There are minor differences, such as a shepherdess instead of the young man of the drawing. Scholars differ in assigning a date for the painting. Marie-Anne Dupuy-Vachey believes it is earlier than the drawing, about 1763–65, whereas Jean-Pierre Cuzin would put it later, about 1766–70, closer to the date of the drawing.[4] EW

PROVENANCE: Sir James Knowles; his estate sale (Lugt 66613), Christie's, London, May 27–29, 1908 (lot 238); Charles Fairfax Murray (1849–1919), London and Florence; from whom purchased in 1909 through Galerie Alexandre Imbert, Rome, by Pierpont Morgan (1837–1913), New York (no mark, but see Lugt 1509); his son, J. P. Morgan Jr. (1867–1943), New York; The Morgan Library & Museum, New York (III, 114)

SELECTED EXHIBITIONS: Williams 1978, cat. no. 49, ill.; Rosenberg 1988, cat. no. 95, ill.; Eitel-Porter et al. 2006, pp. 170–71, cat. no. 81, ill. p. 223.

SELECTED REFERENCES: Portalis 1889, vol. 2, possibly p. 309; Morgan Collection 1912, no. 114, ill.; Ananoff 1961–70, vol. 3 (1968), no. 1380, fig. 389.

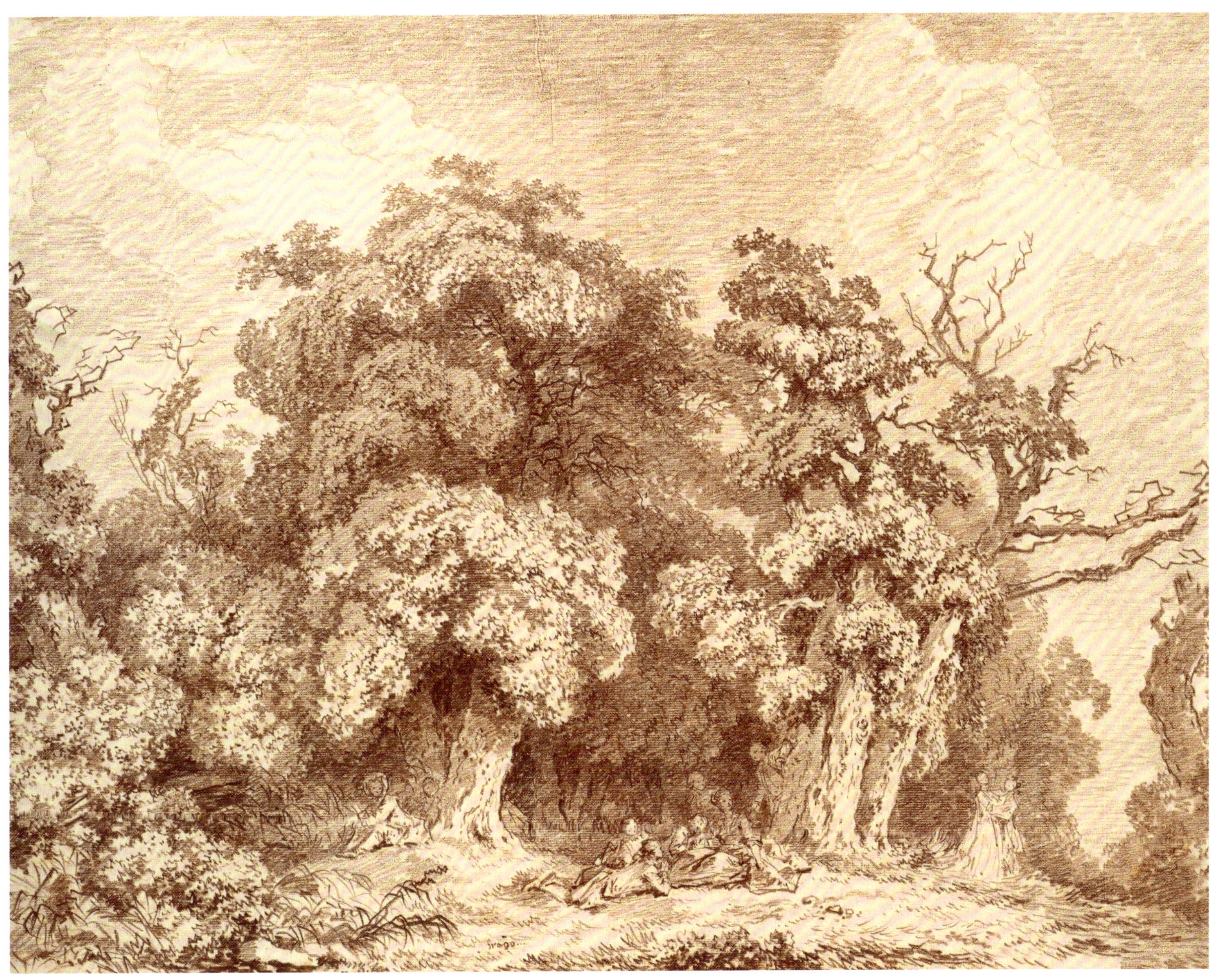

CAT 49

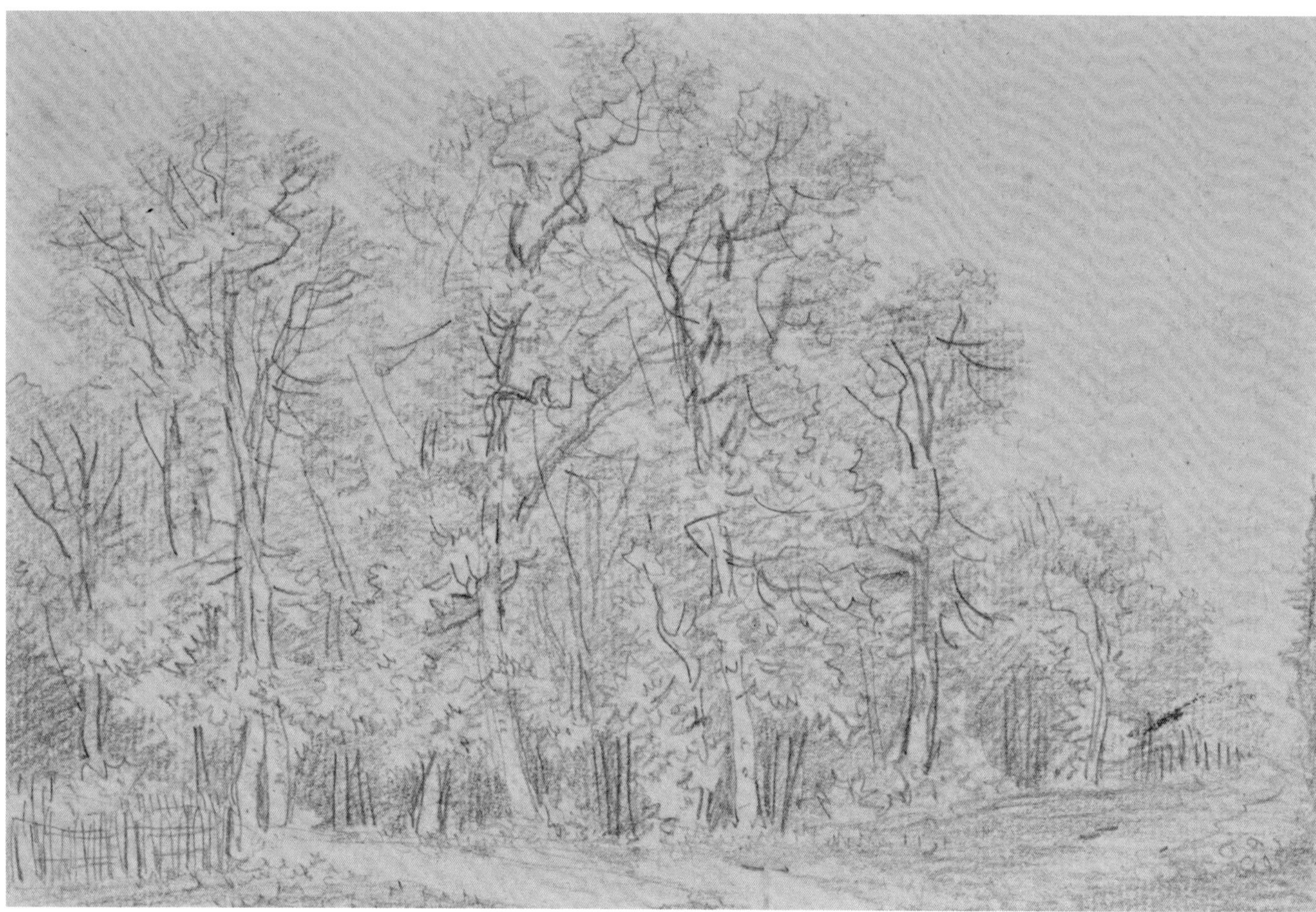

Fig. 98. Jean Honoré Fragonard, *Edge of a Wood*, ca. 1770. Black chalk, 6⅜ × 9⅝ in. (16 × 24.2 cm). Middlebury College Museum of Art, Vt. (1968.004)

the elegant figures in the foreground of the finished sheet. As social symbols, these staffage figures add a subtext to the composition, expanding it from pure observation of nature to a scene of aristocrats enjoying the countryside.

Fragonard understood that forests were an important natural resource for timber and hunting. He would not have had to travel far to find them in the vicinity of Paris, where old growth forests were hunting grounds for the king and the aristocracy, including the Forêt de Rouvray (now the Bois de Boulogne) and the Forêt de Marly in Yvelines, the latter just west of Paris and near Saint-Non la Bretèche, where the abbé de Saint-Non's family had estates.[1] The site is not as important as the fact that Fragonard's sustained friendships with patrons provided opportunities for him to develop his art.

The red chalk study exhibited here was probably drawn outdoors, en plein air, as a deliberate step leading to the more finished work executed in his studio. He began by lightly folding the sheet vertically at the center to form a subtle guide with which to design the composition. It is not a firm crease and is almost imperceptible.[2] Clumps of trees emerge from multiple sets of even, diagonal hatchings. Also in the study, he gave prominence to armlike anthropomorphic bare branches; in the finished work, he reduced their reach. On both drawings, Fragonard varies thickness and pressure of his chalk strokes, some very fine, others hard. The surfaces are uniformly vigorous, a synthesis of reality and imagination.

The finished composition is a direct continuation of the study, edited to enhance the internal formal structure of the foliage. In the center, a light vertical fold and chalk line repeat the fold line observed in the study. Over the years, red chalk dust collected in the crease, making it more visible. On the left, an irregular branch fills a gap in the foliage, while the bare branches at the right are cropped and contained. The viewer's eye is focused on the center, where darkness alludes to the mystery or danger of the forest. Fragonard elaborated the immediate foreground with his signature graphic patterns to describe various grasses. The artist creates a finished composition worthy of wall display.

Throughout his life, Fragonard returned to certain instinctive ideas and compositional themes. Making routine sketches provided continuity. Going around Paris or walking in the countryside, he probably had a sketchbook tucked in his coat. These "notes" are his handwriting and cannot be forced into a chronology. Unfortunately, his sketchbooks were broken up over the years and only two survive.[3] However, many rapidly executed, even scratchy, individual sheets exist and can be examined as seeds for compositions such as the present pair. Sketchbook sheets are difficult to date, but Fragonard, like any good artist, built on the work in which he had already invested. A black chalk sketch (fig. 98) depicts woodland similar to that shown in these two sanguine drawings, a stand of trees with heavy foliage and asymmetrical lines of recession at the sides.[4] EW

CAT 48. PROVENANCE: Anonymous sale, Sotheby's, London, April 27, 1977 (lot 17); [Galerie Cailleux, Paris]; Christie's, London, July 9, 2002 (lot 75); [C. G. Boerner, Artemis Fine Arts, New York]; private collection

SELECTED EXHIBITIONS: Cailleux et al. 1978, cat. no. 12; Paris 1987, cat. no. 48; New York 2003, cat. no. 32.

SELECTED REFERENCES: Massengale 1993, p. 31, fig. 41; Stein and Holmes 1999, p. 164, fig. 70.1.

CAT. 49. PROVENANCE: Jacques Doucet (1853–1929); his collection sale, Galerie Georges Petit, Paris, June 5, 1912 (lot 14, repr.); Marius Paulme (1863–1928) (per Ananoff); Maurice Fenaille (1855–1937); his daughter and son-in-law, M. and Mme François Panafieu; M. Panafieu's anonymous sale, Hôtel Drouot, Paris, June 23, 1959 (lot 6), to Georges Wildenstein; [Wildenstein & Co., New York]; The Metropolitan Museum of Art, New York, Purchase, Lila Acheson Wallace Gift, 1995 (1995.101)

SELECTED EXHIBITION: Stein and Holmes 1999, pp. 164–66, cat. no. 70, ill.

SELECTED REFERENCE: Ananoff 1961–70, vol. 1 (1961), no. 336, ill., and Pl. E, vol. 3 (1968), p. 298, vol. 4 (1970), p. 355.

50. *Draftsman in a Trellised Garden*

Ca. 1770–72
Black chalk; framing line in pen and black ink
15 × 9⅞ in. (38 × 25 cm)
Inscription: at lower right, on the mount, in pen and brown ink, "Fragonard"

This drawing shows a composition that is as charming as it is intriguing. We find ourselves in a place that is hard to define, a sort of garden partitioned on the left and partially overhead by trellises with square lattice. This structure is bordered on the right side by a building whose facade can just barely be made out and to which a few steps, visible at right, provide access. A statue, probably of Amor, as the eighteenth-century auction catalogues claim, constitutes the focal point of this space. In addition to a few boxes and planters, there are numerous pots of squat proportions, which are appropriate for holding shrubs. Without obeying a strict symmetry, they are distributed very artistically. In the middle distance two orange or bay trees in planters are arranged facing each other, raised high on very tall legs made of square posts. Other pots have been placed in between. Was this novel arrangement intended to provide a verdant view to the inhabitants of the second floor of the adjacent house? Garlands of jasmine or honeysuckle[1] escape from the elevated planters and are draped in festoons along the top of the trellises, lending a festive air to the scene. Open to the sky, the space is neither an orangery, nor a greenhouse, nor a winter garden. Nor do we have here an ephemeral decor, a setting designed for a temporary use.

Trellises constituted at the time a major element in garden design. In urban gardens, small rooms of trellises and porticoes were often used to cover unsightly walls or mask "unpleasant views."[2] They were also featured in trompe l'oeil decor for interiors.[3] Fragonard was familiar with this type of trompe l'oeil decor, as he participated alongside Boucher and Jean-Baptiste Huet in the decoration of a salon for the engraver Gilles Demarteau. He is even the author of the ornamentation of a door (fig. 99)[4] that depicts a stone sculpture framed with trelliswork and foliage, similar to that seen at the center of the garden in our drawing. However, these features in our drawing seem quite real, neither a fictive decor nor one born of the painter's imagination. It is also possible that a system of mirrors added to the effect of an enfilade, as the space seems to extend beyond the statue. Despite its exceptional character, the site shown has not yet been identified.[5] Given the fragility of these wooden structures and the cost of their maintenance, their lifespan was short, and few records have preserved their memory.

Fig. 99. Jean Honoré Fragonard, *Love Triumphant*, ca. 1769–70. Oil on canvas, 54 × 28⅜ in. (137 × 72 cm). Musée Carnavalet, Paris (CARP2100)

As Edgar Munhall has commented,[6] the profusion of greenery, the wooden crates, and even the sculpture evoke the decor designed by Fragonard for Madame du Barry's pavilion at Louveciennes in 1771–72, specifically the canvas titled *The Lover Crowned* (p. xviii),[7] where an artist at work appears, as in the present sheet, in the lower right corner. Without being directly connected to the commission, this drawing, which shows surprising mastery of perspective on Fragonard's part, could be dated to about the same time. MADV

PROVENANCE: Unidentified collector, previously thought to be Gabriel Huquier (1695–1772), his mark (Lugt 1285) stamped at lower left; sale, Paris, November 15–22, 1779 (lot 266, "la Vue d'un joli Bosquet, dans le fond duquel est la statue de l'Amour: on voit sur le devant un Dessinateur assis: ce Dessin est à la pierre noire 14 sur 10 de l. [37.9 × 27.1 cm]"), sold for 12 livres 1 sol, with lot 267, to J. Desmarets; possibly anonymous sale (Lugt 3260), Hôtel de Bullion, Paris, May 2, 1781 (lot 119, "Le Bosquet de l'Amour; on y voit sa statue dans le fond d'un treillage entourée de différens pots de fleurs; sujet en hauteur; à la pierre noire, d'un bel effet"); sale [Groult], Hôtel Drouot, Paris, March 26, 1953 (lot 90, repr.); [Galerie André Weil, Paris]; acquired from Weil by Robert Lehman in March 1953; The Metropolitan Museum of Art, New York, Robert Lehman Collection, 1975 (1975.1.626)

SELECTED EXHIBITIONS: Williams 1978, cat. no. 21; Sutton 1980, cat. no. 140; Rosenberg 1988, cat. no. 151.

SELECTED REFERENCES: Ananoff 1961–70, vol. 2 (1963), no. 650, vol. 4 (1970), p. 374, fig. 702; Munhall 1971, pp. 404, 406–7, fig. 9; Massengale 1979, p. 271, fig. 102; Cuzin 1987, p. 100; Haverkamp-Begemann 1999, no. 119 (entry by Mary Tavener Holmes and Donald Posner).

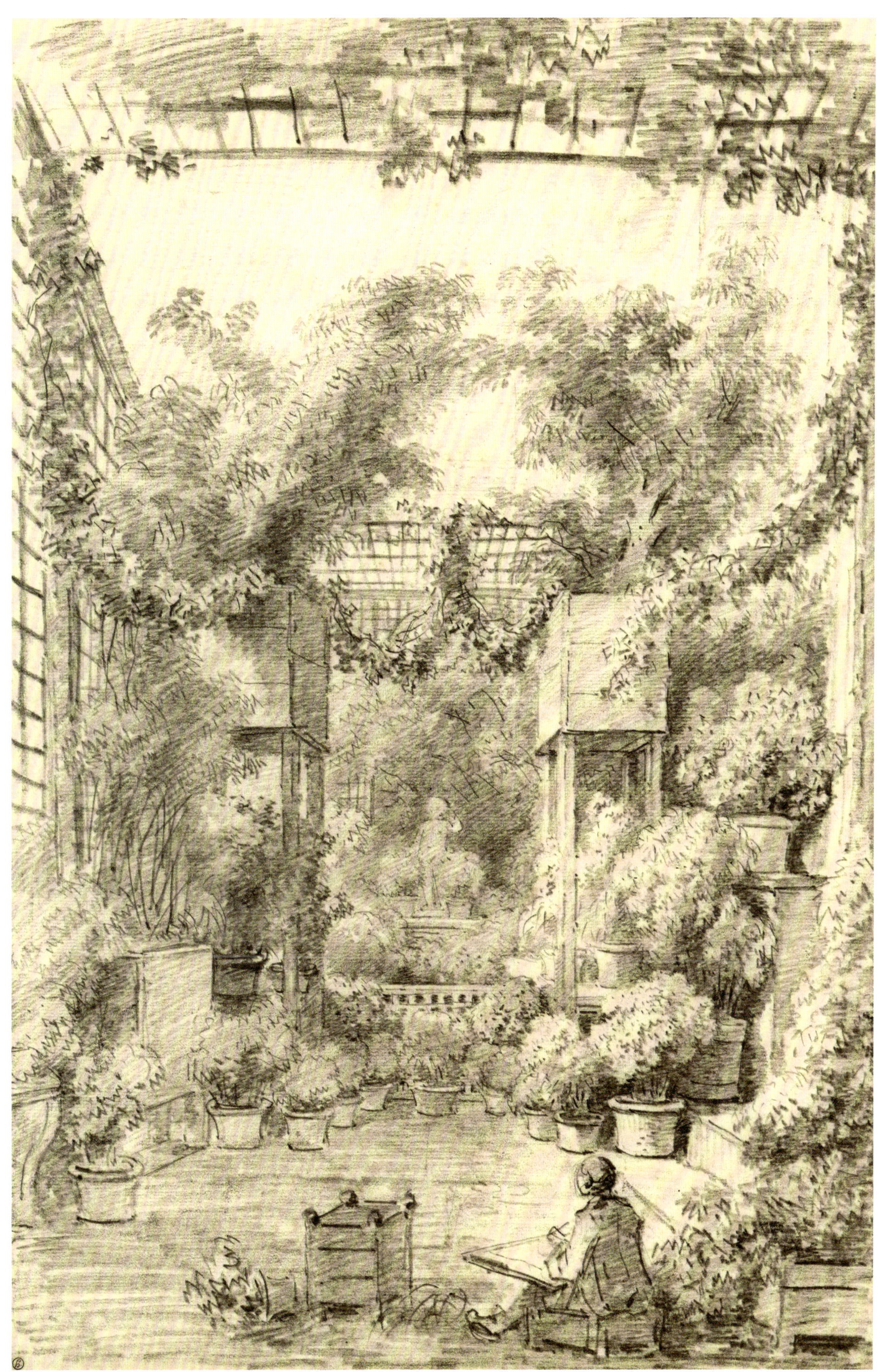

51. *The Service Yard of a Château, with Poultry*

Ca. 1770–73
Red chalk
13⅜ × 17⅞ in. (34 × 45.2 cm)

Fragonard, with curiosity and amusement, observes the lively service yard of an estate; the château's roofline, including its grand pediment, is visible through the trees. This drawing is evidence of his continued interest in everyday life, as shown also in *The Bread Oven at the Château de Nègrepelisse* (cat. 56) and the *Sketch of a Family of Farm Workers* (cat. 74).

Traditionally the service yard, or *basse-cour*, was the base of château productivity and had many functions. This was the part of the estate devoted to service, utility, and farm maintenance. It was distinguished from, but could be contiguous to, a formal courtyard (*cour de seigneur*), an arrangement almost unique to France. In addition to poultry, the *basse-cour* might include barns, stables, dovecotes, winepresses, and bakeries.[1]

It seems that Fragonard has quietly entered the yard unobserved except by the large dog in the foreground, whose eyes meet our own. There are turkeys everywhere, including on the raised roost hung from two central trees. Poultry, and especially turkeys, are not quiet birds, and even a few can produce a cacophony. Through his explosive draftsmanship, Fragonard conveys a sense of the discordant noises filling the poultry yard. Bold lines and wide gestures define the trees; broad hatchings and angular turns form zigzag patterns that evoke sounds rising into the foliage. There is no preparatory underdrawing. His forceful chalk almost digs into the paper from the speed and spontaneity of execution, suggesting that it was probably made *sur le motif.*

This is a real place, with a sense of life observed firsthand. The turkeys here are raised for the seigneur's table, not for display of decorative plumage or prestige, as they had been during the previous century in Queen Marguerite of Navarre's garden on the Left Bank of Paris.[2] Equipment such as a wheelbarrow and barrels suggests farm activities, including cider- or winemaking. Several figures, only lightly indicated, are at work to the left and on the right. Buildings on three sides define the perimeter of the courtyard, dominated in the left distance by a massive circular tower. This is a dovecote (*pigeonnier* or *colombier*), which was associated with important estates.[3]

It is tempting to connect this realistic scene to the château de Nointel in Val-d'Oise, the formal facade of which was centered by a large pediment similar to the one shown here. That château belonged to Pierre Jacques Onésyme Bergeret de Grancourt, a member of a family of wealthy tax farmers (*fermiers généraux*) who possessed titles and properties in several parts of France. They bought the *seigneuries* of Frouville and Nointel, as well as nearby Châteaupré, at Cassan.[4] Fragonard's cordial relationship with Bergeret, who was the brother-in-law of the abbé de Saint-Non, provided opportunities for the artist to visit one or another property. Nointel features a long allée of trees bordering steep steps that creates the illusion of immense distance. It has been claimed by recent owners of the property that the allée at Nointel was the inspiration for Fragonard's depictions of allées of trees.[5]

The prominent *pigeonnier* in the left distance occupies its typical location in the farmyard of an estate; the alternative placement was an open space away from the residence. However, maps and ground plans of Nointel from the eighteenth century and the present day show no evidence that such a structure stood in the farmyard. Perhaps this drawing was inspired by another château. Classical central pediments were popular features of many châteaux facades in the Val-d'Oise. And Fragonard's subject, after all, is not the architecture but the life on the estate.

A counterproof of this sheet is at the Rijksmuseum, Amsterdam.[6] EW

PROVENANCE: With Otto Wertheimer (1896–1972), Paris; private collection, Switzerland; Sotheby's, London, July 4, 2007 (lot 87); private collection

SELECTED REFERENCE: Ananoff 1961–70, vol. 3 (1968), no. 1339, fig. 385.

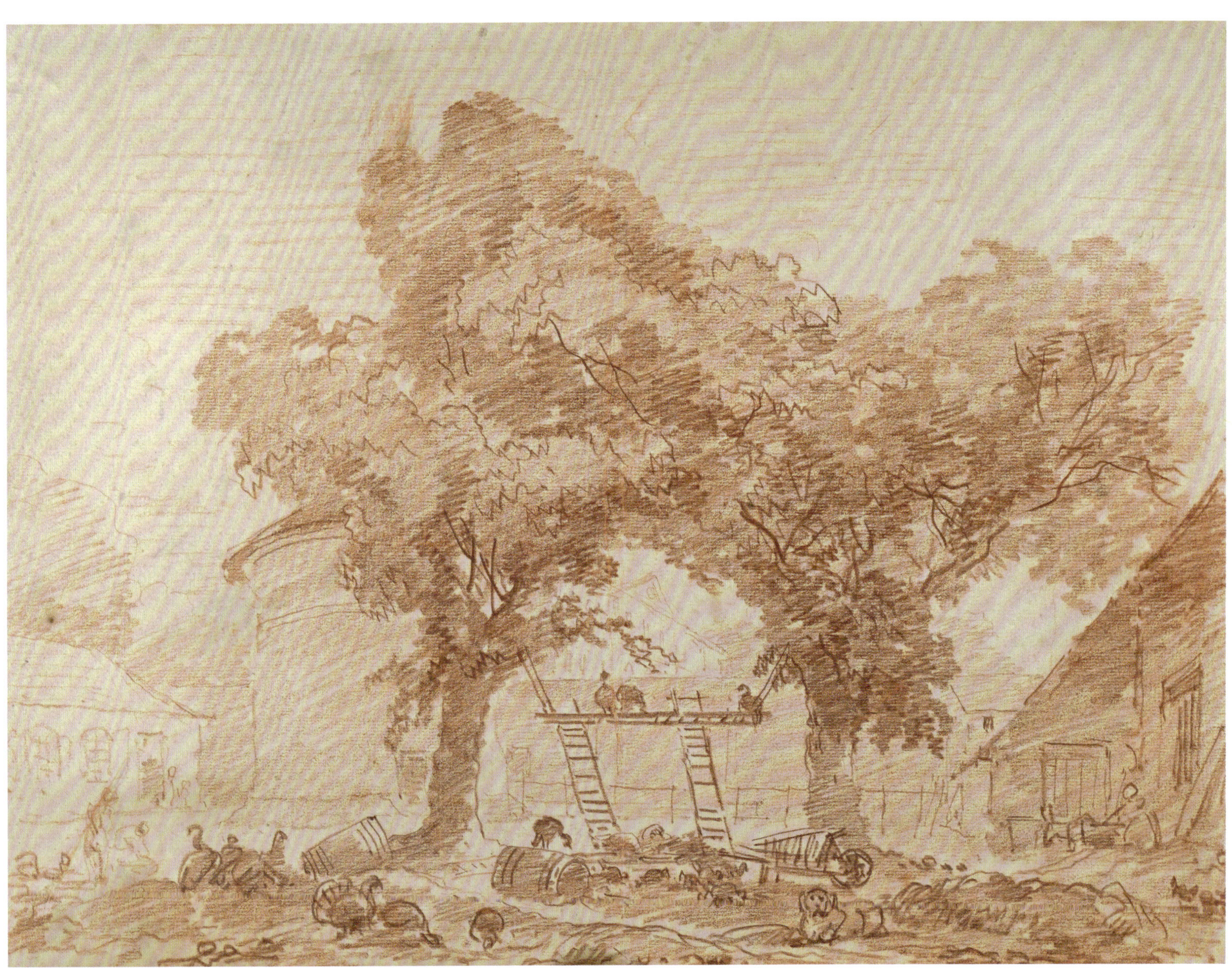

Travels with Bergeret, 1773–74

Fragonard had the exceptional good fortune to visit Italy a second time, twelve years after his stay as a pensionnaire at the Académie de France in Rome. The opportunity came in the form of a yearlong voyage organized by the collector and financier Pierre Jacques Onésyme Bergeret de Grancourt (see fig. 100), who had known Fragonard for at least a decade and probably longer.[1] He was a major patron of Fragonard's master, François Boucher, and was the brother-in-law of the abbé de Saint-Non, Fragonard's patron on his first Italian trip. The journey to Italy, it is now known, was not their first trip together, as the two had shortly before made a voyage north and are documented in Flanders in July 1773.[2] Bergeret had been to Italy only briefly, in 1762, but a decade later the wealthy fifty-eight-year-old *fermier général* had the means to sponsor a large group on a leisurely tour of Europe. Fragonard was permitted to bring his wife; Bergeret's entourage included Jeanne Vignier, a former maid who would become his third wife, Pierre Jacques, a son from a previous marriage, and a retinue of servants, including a cook, a valet, and two coachmen.[3]

Many details of the trip are chronicled in Bergeret's journal.[4] Their itinerary took them first to the south of France. They stayed for two weeks in Nègrepelisse, a town north of Toulouse where Bergeret had recently inherited a château,[5] before sailing from Antibes to Liguria and continuing on to Rome, where they remained for four months. According to the custom of the time, they were warmly welcomed into the daily life of the Académie. An enthusiastic band of students, including Pierre Adrien Pâris, François André Vincent, and François Guillaume Ménageot, functioned as guides and companions, assisting Bergeret as he saw the sites and built his collection. In the spring the group set off for Naples, a destination recently popularized by excavations at Herculaneum and Pompeii. At the beginning of the summer, they began their two-month return journey, passing through Bologna and Venice before looping eastward to take in the treasures of Vienna, Prague, Dresden, and Frankfurt. As Fragonard and Saint-Non had done years before, they paused for the artist to make drawings after the paintings that filled the churches and palaces along their route.

Although Fragonard's second journey was superficially parallel to his first, his aesthetic experience was markedly different. No longer in training to be a history painter, he was not so much studying the art, landscape, and people of Italy as he was reveling in it. The year was consumed with nothing but drawing. He was not compelled to make paintings or to earn money, and his drawings of this period exude an easy confidence. Most of his output was in either sanguine or brown wash, techniques in which he had achieved an unparalleled mastery. He made quick and sharply observed portraits of companions, friends, and colorful figures from the streets: dwarfs, fishermen, vendors, and entertainers. In landscapes, he was more drawn to the picturesque and the parkscape than to specific sites or monuments. In copies after earlier masters, the vigor and gusto of the Baroque held a stronger appeal than the more distant models of the Renaissance or the classical past. In short, he had strayed from the path of the history painter for which his early

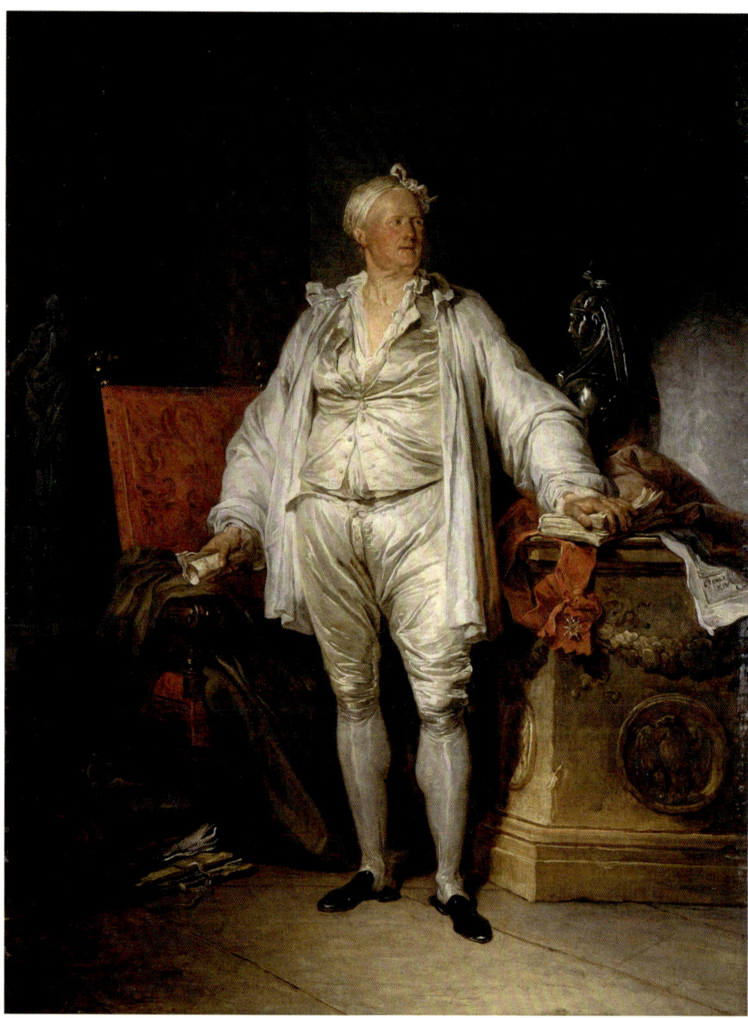

Fig. 100. François André Vincent (French, 1746–1816), *Portrait of Pierre Jacques Onésyme Bergeret de Grancourt*, 1774. Oil on canvas, 23⅝ × 18¾ in. (60 × 47.5 cm). Musée des Beaux-Arts et d'Archéologie, Besançon (843.1.27)

years had prepared him; it was the artist he had become—a painter of rustic families, lush gardens, and romantic idylls—that now colored his choices of what to study and record.

That Bergeret appreciated and took pleasure in Fragonard's drawings is beyond doubt. While still in Italy, either alone or with friends, he spent rainy evenings going through the portfolios of drawings. However, sometime around or shortly after their return to Paris, an illuminating dispute arose between the two men. Bergeret had assumed, as was common practice at the time, that the drawings made during the journey were his property. Fragonard, however, had assumed the opposite and was refused in his attempt to collect them. Their quarrel escalated into a lawsuit; nineteenth-century sources differ on the outcome. Théophile Fragonard, the artist's grandson, writing four decades after Fragonard's death, claimed that the *fermier général* was ordered to pay 30,000 livres if he wished to keep the drawings—which he did. According to Baron Portalis, writing in 1880, Bergeret preferred to return the drawings rather than pay that sum to Fragonard.[6] Although the resulting acrimony was enduring, Fragonard and Bergeret's son, Pierre Jacques, remained lifelong friends. The drawings made during this unusually well-documented year are among Fragonard's finest. Reinvigorated by renewed exposure to Italy and unencumbered by financial pressure, he turned his gaze to all that appealed to him in the labor and leisure that made up quotidian life on the Italian peninsula. PS

52. *Fragonard and His Companions aboard a Boat on the Rhine*

1773
Pen and brown ink, brush and brown wash over black chalk underdrawing
8⅛ × 12¾ in. (20.6 × 32.4 cm)
Inscriptions identifying the figures, in pen and brown ink: on the trunk on which the foreground figure is leaning, "Lubersa[c]"; in the center, on the bed in the background, "frago"; a little lower, toward the right, on a trunk, "motion"; a little higher, on the right, "Bergeret." Inscription on the mount, in pen and brown ink, in a different hand: "vue de l'intérieur d'un vaisseau battu par la tempête ou se trouvoit, Messrs Fragonard Bergeret Lubersac et Motion, 1773"

This drawing has long been connected to Fragonard's second trip to Italy, specifically to the short crossing by sea between Antibes and San Remo that took place on November 11, 1773. Bergeret de Grancourt, who had initiated that trip and invited the artist, indeed described in his diary how the storm, and the resulting seasickness, had forced them to abandon the sea route and continue their expedition on dry land.[1] However, the accommodations described here by Fragonard are hardly consistent with those of the Mediterranean felucca on which they would have traveled from Antibes. Moreover, the inscriptions on the present sheet name, in addition to the artist and his patron, two others who are not mentioned in Bergeret's account of the voyage. For these reasons, the traditional interpretation of the scene was regarded with some caution until a careful reading of the German weekly newspaper *Gülich und bergische wöchentliche Nachrichten* allowed the subject to be identified correctly. This gazette reported the arrival of four Frenchmen in Düsseldorf on August 23, 1773: "N. Bergeres, Mausion, Lubersalle and Fragonard in Zweibrückerhof."[2] Since Düsseldorf was the port through which travelers going to or coming from Amsterdam passed, we have here a crucial element that contributes to clarifying Fragonard's itinerary during the summer of 1773, the initial groundwork of which has been established by Sophie Raux.[3] We deduce that, after Brussels, Mechelen, Antwerp, The Hague, and Amsterdam, our travelers boarded the boat to go back up the Rhine as far as Düsseldorf. The journey then continued toward Spa, where Fragonard and his three companions are again mentioned on September 2.[4] We imagine that their stay in the spa town helped them to recover from the ordeal of the Rhine. Accounts of the period agree in describing the crossing of the river as particularly grueling despite the comfort of the boats, which Fragonard's drawing serves to confirm.[5] The precision of his reporting is all the more impressive since he seems not to have been spared: his habitually abbreviated name, "frago," designates the figure lying motionless on his back in the alcove on the right.[6] Sitting by his side, also in a bad way, we find a certain "Motion," whom we have every reason to believe is Bergeret's brother-in-law, Etienne Charles Maussion, seigneur de la Courtaujaye, who was at the time treasurer of Alençon. His death on October 15 of the same year could suggest that he never truly recovered from this voyage. In the foreground, lying on the floor and writhing in pain, is probably the abbé Charles François de Lubersac de Livron,[7] grand vicar of the diocese of Narbonne. Through the opening on the right, we glimpse Bergeret sitting at a table on the upper level, the only one not to have fallen ill, as he would recall with some pride when he took a boat again a few months later.[8] The setting, which gives pride of place to the chamber pot, seeks to transform the very trying nature of the situation into a comical farce. We can count on Fragonard to exaggerate and raise a smile at the memory of this distressing episode of the journey. MADV

PROVENANCE: Possibly W. G. Coesvelt Esq. collection, vicomte de Castelruiz sale (Lugt 18164), Christie's, London, April 27, 1846 (lot 13, "The artist and others on board ship"), but this provenance is not consistent with that given by Sigismond Bardac (1856–1919), Paris, from whom Mortimer L. Schiff acquired the drawing in the 1920s, and who mentioned a provenance, "Matirlan [perhaps for Malvilan, Fragonard's descendants and cousins], Grasse"; by descent to John M. Schiff, New York; private collection

SELECTED REFERENCES: Ananoff 1961–70, vol. 1 (1961), no. 272, fig. 91; Rosenberg 1988, p. 365, fig. 2, p. 375; Boulot et al. 1990, p. 218; Dupuy-Vachey 2012, fig. 2.

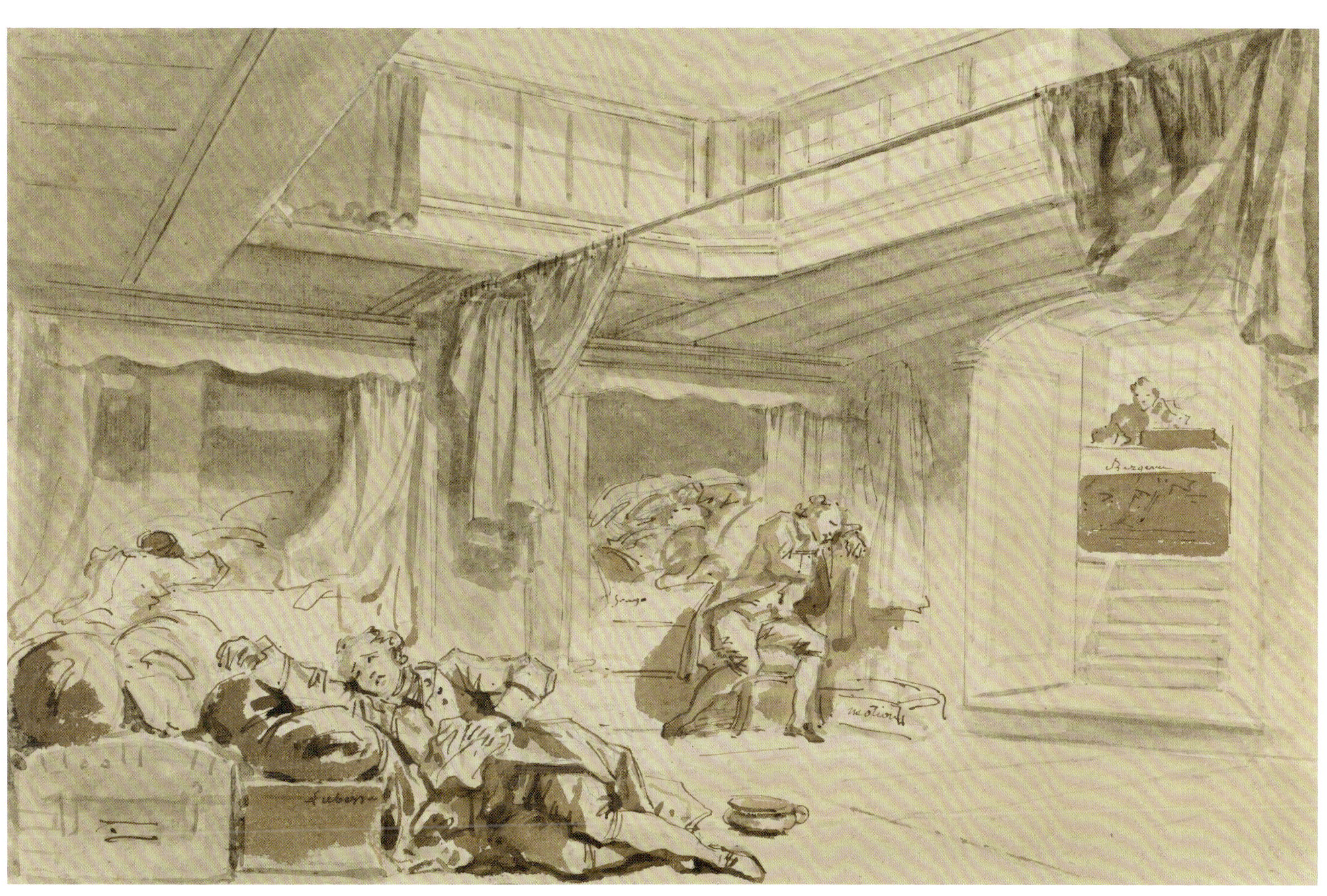

53. *The Château de Nègrepelisse*

1773
Red chalk
13¾ × 19½ in. (34.8 × 49.4 cm)

In October 1773, Bergeret and Fragonard set out on a long itinerary that is remembered for its transformative impact on Fragonard's style and, afterward, for Bergeret's litigation over the artist's brilliant drawings. From Bergeret's journal it is possible to follow the journey by date and place. Self-centered, he gives few details about Fragonard's activities or contributions to the trip. He does mention that the artist was always making drawings.

The party traveled a week before reaching Bergeret's château de Nègrepelisse, near Montauban, on October 12. They spent fourteen days there. The pause was planned so Bergeret could organize structural repairs and related business around the estate.[1] The château, which dates from the thirteenth century, was constructed as a central court surrounded by walls; towers mark the four corners. Bergeret's journal does not mention specific commissions, but Fragonard enjoyed the freedom to explore and observe the property. The drawings from Nègrepelisse in this exhibition (see also cats. 55 and 56) document his continued interest in both landscape and daily activities.

Bergeret writes that they arrived in summery weather, a factor in Fragonard's depictions of the château. Taking full advantage of the sun, Fragonard made two large finished views in red chalk and one in brown wash.[2] One of the former (fig. 101) is a formal view of the west elevation that provides a sense of its medieval bulk and grandeur. Fragonard includes a traditional formal device of a deep foreground with small figures to establish scale and to separate the viewer. The drawing is presented as a portrait of an imposing estate to flatter the owner.

In contrast, the drawing shown here is a more intimate view of life outside the fortification, as seen from the north elevation, with several sheds and a mill wheel. The composition spreads across the sheet as a deliberate and complex construct of geometric shapes and interlocking planes. However, Fragonard took liberties and collapsed real space and proportions between the round corner towers, the crenelated square tower, and the taller square donjon. The trees are lightly drawn as a balance to the enduring manmade domain.

Fragonard's composition again utilizes a foreground, but here the viewer is invited to experience the main subject. There is a canal or pond—the château was situated on the Aveyron River—where people gather to fish or enjoy the sun. For the structural verticals and horizontals Fragonard used firm, crisp lines and precise hatchings and allowed reserved spaces to emerge as elements of the sheds. They are echoed in the construction of the dock and its reflections in the water in the right foreground. EW

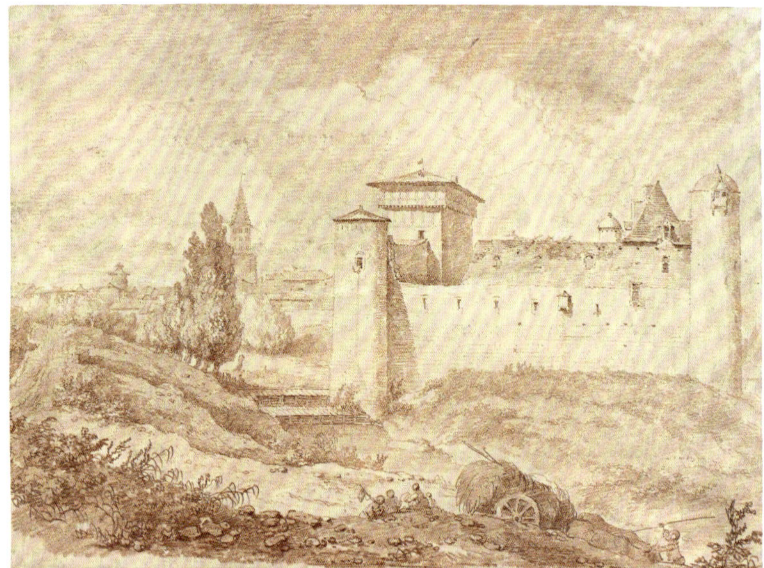

Fig. 101. Jean Honoré Fragonard, *The Château de Nègrepelisse*, 1773. Red chalk with traces of black chalk, 14¼ × 19½ in. (36.2 × 49.4 cm). Museum Boijmans Van Beuningen, Rotterdam (F-I-244)

PROVENANCE: Peter Kröler, Essen; [Ferdinand Wendl, dealer, Berlin (1930)]; Collection H. B. (not in Lugt); Johannes Goldsche, Berlin, his stamp (Lugt 1310a), verso; [Galerie Arnoldi-Livie, Munich]; private collection

SELECTED REFERENCES: Ananoff 1961–70, vol. 3 (1968), no. 1488; Rosenberg 1988, under cat. no. 171, fig. 2.

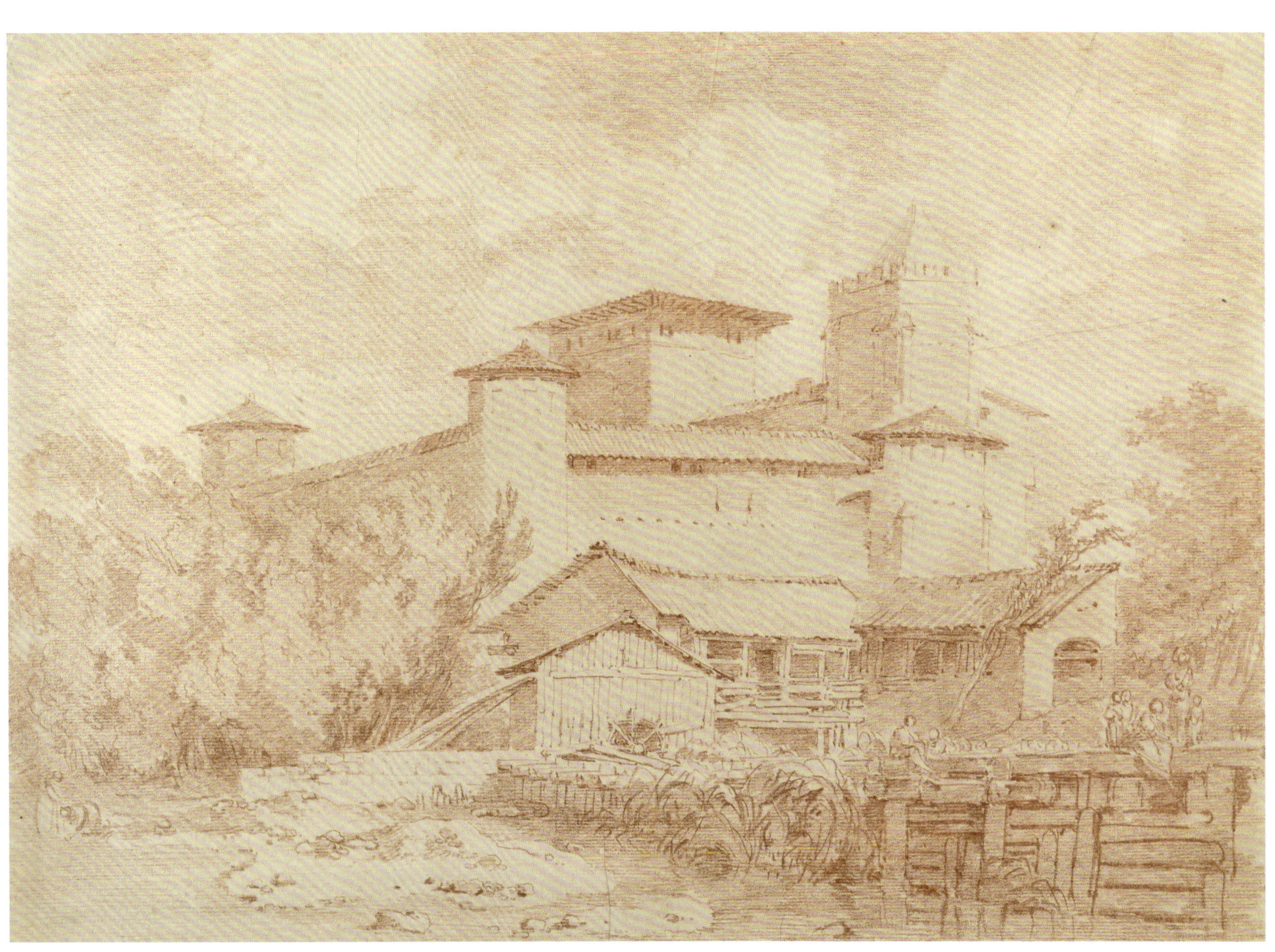

54. *Portrait of a Magistrate*

1773
Red chalk
18⅛ × 14⅜ in. (45.9 × 36.5 cm)
Inscriptions: at lower left, in black chalk strengthened with pen and brown ink, "Fragonard," and in a different shade of brown ink, "père fecit"; at lower right, in the hand of Xavier Atger, in another shade of brown ink, partly on the drawing, partly on the mount, "Est ne Canis aut vulpes / sub tabula positus"; at lower right, stamped with the blind stamp of the mounter François Renaud (Lugt 1042) and in black ink with the mark of the Galerie Cailleux, Paris (Lugt 4461)

Traditionally titled *Portrait of a Magistrate*, this impressive sheet belongs to a group of more than a dozen drawings of seated men, some in chalk and some in brown wash, that have been connected with Fragonard's second Italian trip. Associated, either securely or tentatively, with different stages of the journey and on variously sized sheets of paper, the group is, more properly, made up of several smaller groups. Many questions linger about whom they depict, for whom they were made, and how they should be interpreted.

The Magistrate can be linked to five related sheets in the Musée Atger in Montpellier,[1] all executed in sanguine on large sheets of paper,[2] and together comprising one of the more homogeneous and better documented subgroups. Based on the evidence of contemporary prints, the sitters for two drawings in the Montpellier group have been identified: one as Bergeret and one as Adam Malet, an "avocat en parlement, notaire royal et lieutenant de juge" in the city of Nègrepelisse. The drawing of Bergeret, however, long thought to be contemporaneous with the Italian trip, actually predates it by several years, a fact supported by Gilles Demarteau's system of numbering his prints, which suggests a date of about 1770–71 for his chalk-manner print of Bergeret, number 251 in his oeuvre.[3] It differs somewhat from the present sheet and others in the group: it is drawn on a slightly smaller piece of paper, and the design does not extend to the edges of the sheet. *The Magistrate*, so similar in its careful, almost dry technique to the portrait of Malet, is likely a portrait of another one of Bergeret's friends in Nègrepelisse. Like the drawings in the Montpellier group, it seems to have gone from the collection of Bergeret, the sponsor of Fragonard's trip, to that of Montpellier-born collector Xavier Atger, who had a fondness for adding humorous inscriptions on drawings or their mounts. In this case, his "Est ne Canis aut vulpes / sub tabula positus" playfully questions whether the animal under the table is a dog or a fox. For Fragonard, too, the dog peeking out from the shadows must have been intended as a note of levity to offset the sobriety of the portrait.

One must assume that the Nègrepelisse group was made at Bergeret's request and perhaps inspired by his own portrait in red chalk, as the men depicted would have been his friends and acquaintances, not Fragonard's. To commission or collect a series of portraits of one's social circle, rather than one's family, for instance, was a popular practice at the time, and one can point to countless examples of artists who created works in this vein, from Louis Carrogis, called Carmontelle, to Charles Nicolas Cochin II. However, the most immediate precedent might have been from Fragonard's own hand: his series of sketchlike paintings of people in pseudo-Spanish dress, traditionally known as the "fantasy figures" but recently understood as virtuoso portraits of contemporaries, perhaps members of a social circle connected to Bergeret's brother-in-law, the abbé de Saint-Non.[4]

In contrast to those flamboyant portraits, whose sitters seem animated by a shared devotion to the arts, the Nègrepelisse drawings are more gravity-bound. The three most similar to the New York sheet—those depicting Bergeret, Malet, and the man previously identified as Saint-Non[5]—all represent men ranging from middle aged to elderly, shown full-length and seated on simple chairs, with attributes of their professions nearby. They seem to breathe not the rarefied air of inspiration but that of ledgers, account books, and legal documents. In the present drawing, the ponderous authority of the sitter's face finds an echo in his weighty robes, their vertical folds firmly rendered in confident hatching with minimal effort. The tablecloth, too, falls in sharply defined folds, lit, apparently, by natural light pouring in from the left. PS

PROVENANCE: Probably Pierre Jacques Onésyme Bergeret de Grancourt (1715–1785); probably his estate sale (Lugt 4027), Baradelle, Paris, April 24–29, 1786 (part of lot 210); Xavier Atger (1758–1833); probably his estate sale (Lugt 13614), Derbanne and Defer, Paris, April 7–12, 1834 (part of lot 3); M. Dromont; his sale (Lugt 32752), Delbergue-Cormont and Vignères, Paris, December 6–9, 1871 (lot 759); M. Laperlier; his sale (Lugt 38972), Hôtel Drouot, Paris, February 17–18, 1879 (lot 67); Alphonse Kann; his sale, Galerie Georges Petit, Paris, December 6–8, 1920 (lot 99), to Baré (per Ananoff); anonymous sale [O. Lévy], Hôtel Drouot, Paris, May 25, 1962 (lot 33); [Galerie Cailleux, Paris]; from whom acquired in 1986 by a private collection, New York

SELECTED EXHIBITIONS: Cailleux et al. 1978, p. 39, cat. no. 14; Méjanès 1983, cat. no. 31; Rosenberg 1988, p. 411, cat. no. 200.

SELECTED REFERENCE: Ananoff 1961–70, vol. 1 (1961), p. 114, no. 231, vol. 2 (1963), fig. 356, vol. 3 (1968), p. 296, vol. 4 (1970), p. 351.

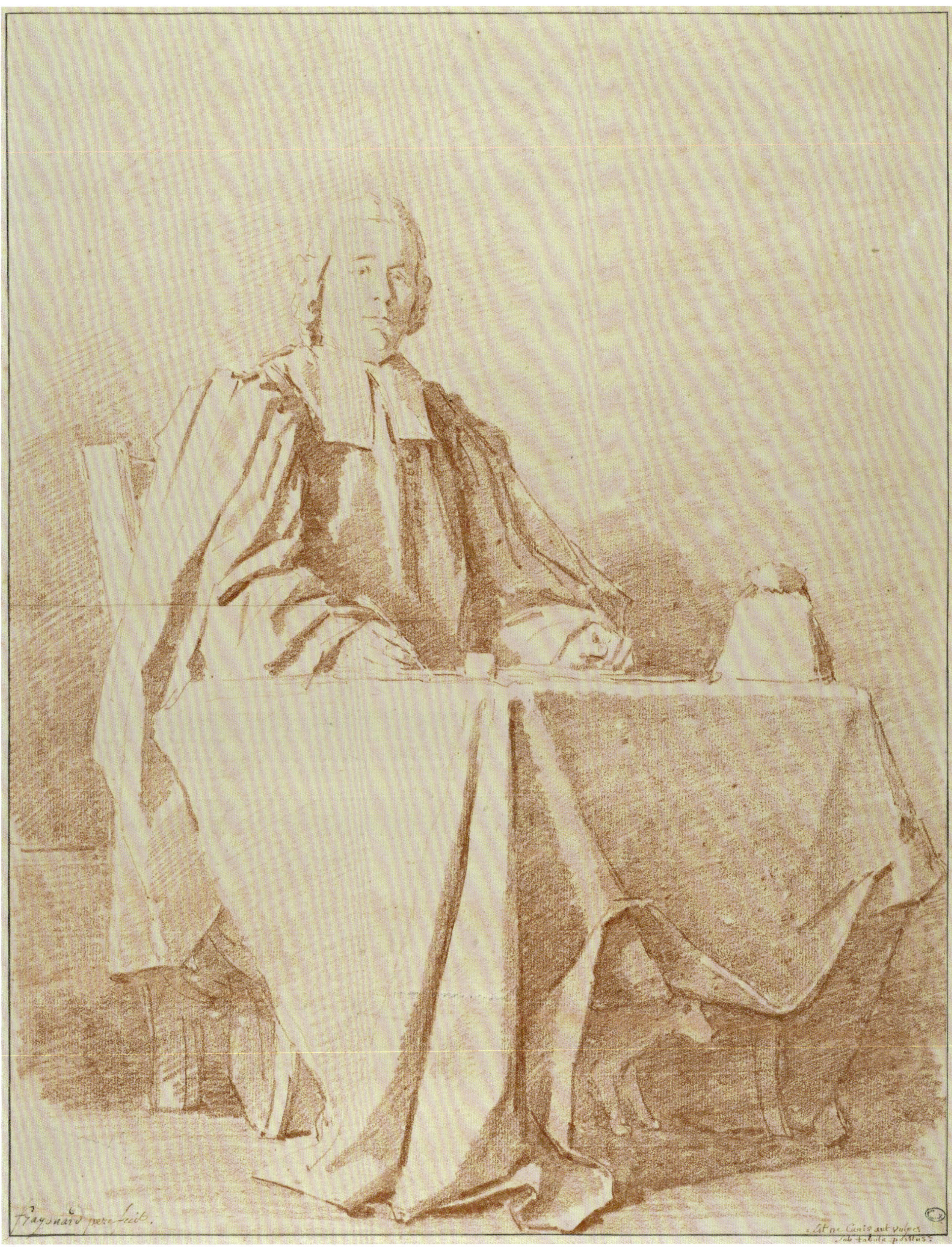
Fragonard pere fecit.
Est ne Canis aut vulpes
Sub tabula positus?

55. *Sketch of "The Bread Oven at the Château de Nègrepelisse"*

1773
Brush and brown wash over black chalk on tan paper
7¼ × 8⅞ in. (18.4 × 22.5 cm)

56. *The Bread Oven at the Château de Nègrepelisse*

1773
Pen and brown ink, brush and brown wash over black chalk
11¼ × 14¼ in. (28.6 × 36.2 cm)
Inscription: on the beam above the oven, by Bergeret, in ink, "Four banal de Nègrepelisse / 8bre 1773"

It is rare to have both a preparatory sketch and the finished drawing together. This is the second such pair in the exhibition (see cats. 46 and 47). Each represents a stage in the artist's creative process, but in both cases Fragonard's first draft, though simplified and generalized, is visually and aesthetically complete. If the larger version did not exist, the smaller composition would be prized as a spirited study.

In the sketch, Fragonard establishes the proportions of the room with a few rudimentary lines drawn freehand. It seems to be a vast hall with a beamed roof and capable of accommodating dozens of people. This is probably theatrical if not artistic license. A vertical fold can be detected in the center of the sketch. Fragonard typically employs this subtle, almost invisible marker in landscapes.[1] Here, it acts as a guide for organizing the figural groups across the respective compositions. It is a crowded, public spectacle, with women carrying loaves, bakers wielding bread paddles, and others observing the action. Fragonard's chalk follows broadly cursive paths, forming loops for heads and gestures, and is followed by a layer of wash. Broad strokes of brush and brown wash block out figures and define a darker frame in the foreground. The darker foreground is a visual device that Fragonard often used in both landscapes and genre scenes.

On the finished sheet, in addition to the fold, a faint vertical indentation at top marks the approximate center, enabling the artist to reinvent his composition. He works freehand without attention to spatial proportions. On the larger format, the figure groups come to life as individuals, defined by types of costume as much as by activity. Women carrying large round loaves ready for the oven are assembled much like an animated chorus line of dancers. Indeed, keeping the sequence moving between the women and the bakers involved a kind of choreography. Fragonard's spirited brush meets the challenge. Repeated outlines contribute to a sense of oppressive heat in the room and of anticipation among the spectators. Everyone is working together at the essential collaborative task of baking bread, men and women alike.

The oven at Nègrepelisse was a real place, although in the oven design Fragonard took liberties with scale, as he often did in the interest of pictorial illusion. The communal oven (*four banal*) was part of the seigneurial system; feudal lords, in this case Bergeret, operated large ovens, as private ovens in dwellings were banned for fear of fire. It was to this separate, solidly built structure housing large ovens that women brought their bread to be baked. It is natural that Fragonard should have visited the bakers. The aroma of freshly baked bread aside, the subject appealed to his interest in routine human activities rather than as social commentary. Later in the trip, he would depict beggars, street vendors (cat. 58), and fishermen (cats. 61 and 62) without condescension.

Bergeret's party arrived at Nègrepelisse on October 12, 1773. His journal never mentions the existence of such utilitarian labors as baking, but on the finished drawing he proudly inscribed the date on one of the ceiling beams. The historic importance of the oven at Nègrepelisse to the town and community is commemorated today by a new structure built as an educational center within the footprint of the old château. EW

CAT. 55. PROVENANCE: C. Loyeux; sale, Hôtel Drouot, Paris, April 18–19, 1898 (lot 42, "Four public. Esquisse au bistre du dessin qui figurait à la succession des Goncourt [18.5 × 22.5 cm]"); Sigismond Bardac (1856–1919), Paris; Jacques Seligmann, New York; private collection

SELECTED REFERENCE: Ananoff 1961–70, vol. 1 (1961), no. 269.

CAT. 56. PROVENANCE: Louis Antoine Auguste, duc de Rohan-Chabot (1733–1807); his estate sale (Lugt 7315), Paillet, Paris, December 8, 1807 (part of lot 60); Edmond and Jules de Goncourt, their blind stamp (Lugt 1089); their sale (Lugt 55024), Duchesne, Paris, February 15–17, 1897 (lot 98); Marius Paulme, Paris; Sigismond Bardac (1856–1919), Paris, 1907; Jacques Seligmann, Paris; Mortimer L. Schiff, 1917; by descent to John M. Schiff, New York; private collection

SELECTED REFERENCES: Ananoff 1961–70, vol. 1 (1961), no. 268, fig. 95; Rosenberg 1988, under cat. no. 171, fig. 4; Launay 1991, no. 102, fig. 22.

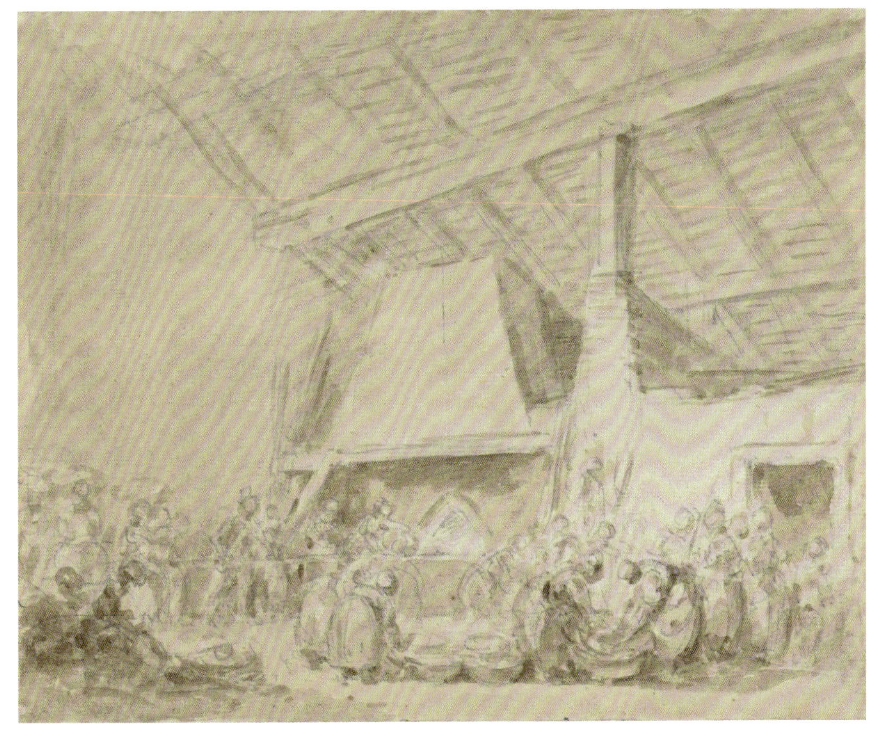

CAT 55

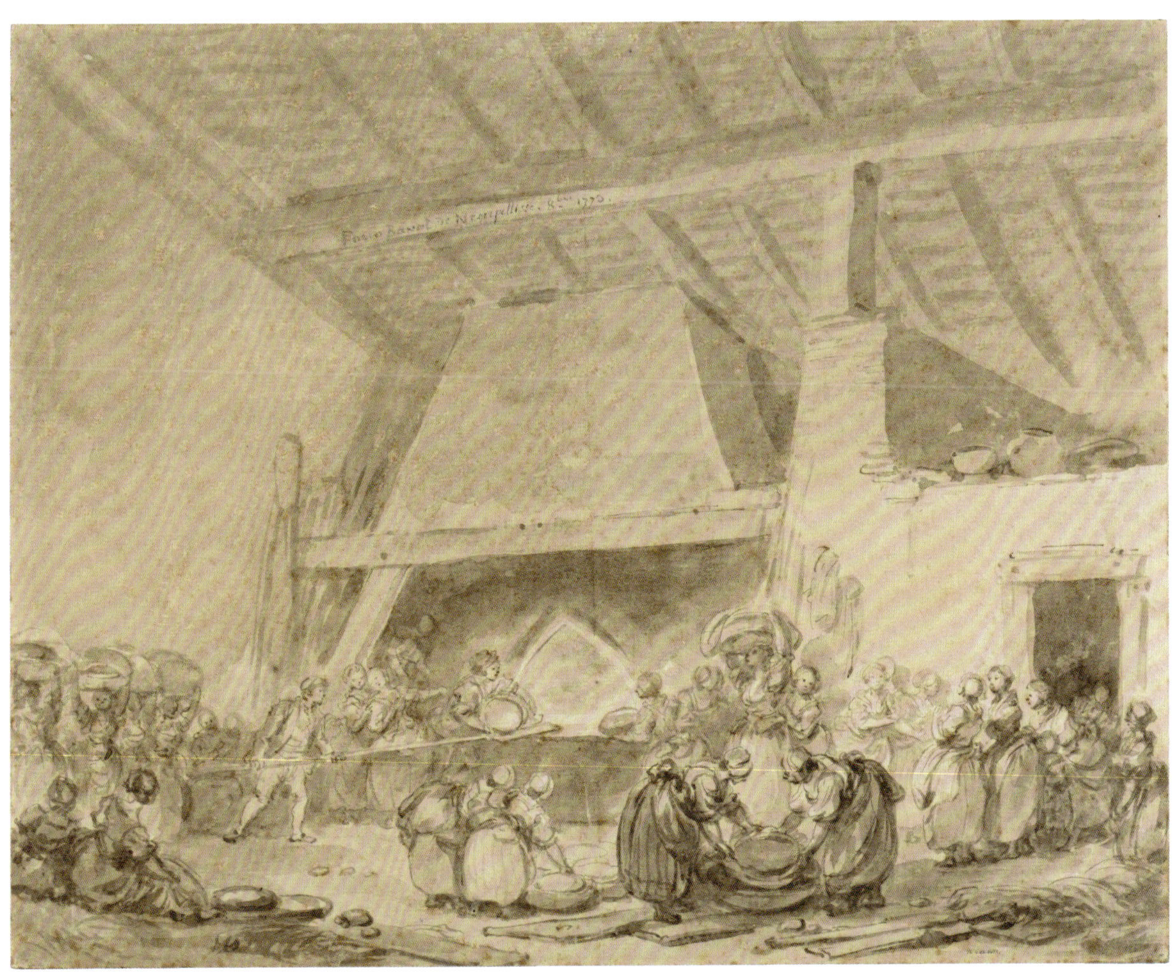

CAT 56

57. *The Sultan*

1774
Brush and brown wash over black chalk underdrawing
14¼ × 11¼ in. (36.2 × 28.6 cm)
Inscription: at lower right, in pen and brown ink, "Roma / 1774"; at lower right, stamped in black ink with the collector's mark of Baron Dominique Vivant Denon (Lugt 779)

What had once been one of the most published and feted Fragonard drawings in the Metropolitan's collection was recognized in the late 1970s as a modern fake.[1] Some decades would elapse, but the loss was eventually made whole in the form of the original, which arrived at the Museum as part of the bequest of Catherine Curran in 2008. Unlike the forgery, the Curran version bears an inscription in Bergeret's hand, "Roma 1774," and the collector's mark of Baron Dominique Vivant Denon, the artist, collector, diplomat, and first director of the Musée du Louvre. The authentic version is presented publicly here for the first time.

The traditional title of the sheet, *The Sultan*, dates only to the 1846 sale of Vivant Denon's nephew; in earlier sales in 1797 and 1826 it was referred to as "A Seated Turk."[2] In all probability, the sitter is neither a sultan nor a Turk but a model or someone in the circle of the Académie de France in Rome who posed in Turkish dress. The practice of making studies of such figures—which occurred frequently in history subjects, exotic genre paintings, and port scenes—traced its lineage to the Ottoman-themed masquerade staged by the pensionnaires in 1748.[3] Fragonard himself was later inspired to create *turquerie* scenes (for example, cat. 90), a popular form of exoticism in eighteenth-century France.

Fragonard's skills both as a painter and as a draftsman merge in the brown wash drawings of this period. First, he sketched the forms in loose, flowing marks, holding the chalk very lightly. Over this airy armature he built up the figure in layers of translucent gray-brown wash, convincingly evoking the weary and worn features of the sitter and the different layers of fabric while animating the whole with a naturalistic sense of daylight. A separate study (fig. 102), done either just before or just after the present sheet, treats only the sitter's head, focusing more on his facial features and expression.[4] The beauty of the pooling brown washes that flowed from Fragonard's brushes, sometimes limpid and golden and other times velvety and dark, was not lost on the young artists studying at the Académie. François André Vincent, in particular, sought to emulate the older artist's manner. His success was such that the attribution of certain sheets is still contested in the scholarly literature.[5] PS

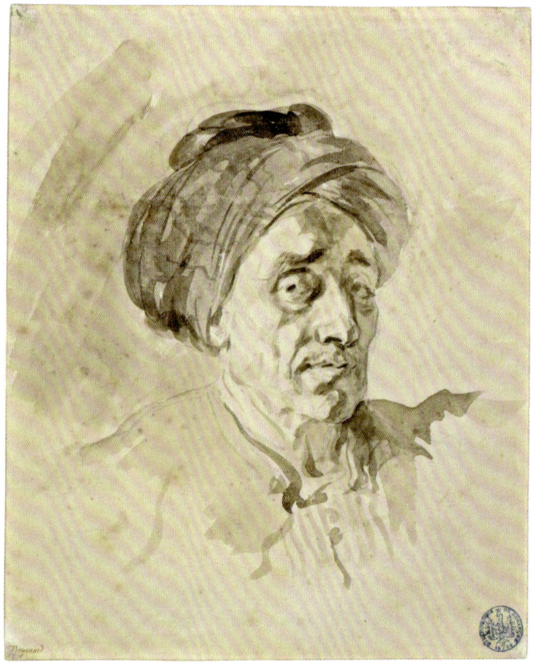

Fig. 102. Jean Honoré Fragonard, *Head of a Turbanned Man*, 1774. Brush and brown wash over black chalk underdrawing, 12¾ × 10⅜ in. (32.2 × 26.4 cm). Musée des Beaux-Arts et d'Archéologie, Besançon (D.2944)

PROVENANCE: [Desmarets, Paris]; his cessation of business sale (Lugt 5555), Paris, March 17, 1797 (lot 85, "[u]n turc assis, dessin lavé au bistre"); Baron Dominique Vivant Denon (1747–1825), his estate sale (Lugt 11164), A. N. Pérignon, Paris, May 1–19, 1826 (lot 729); Baron Brunet-Denon, his estate sale (Lugt 18011), Bonnefons de Lavialle, Hôtel des Ventes Mobilières, Paris, February 2–15, 1846 (part of lot 271); Lord Currie and Mrs. Bertram Currie; sale, Christie's, London, June 29, 1962 (lot 46); acquired at the sale by Mrs. Catherine G. Curran, London; The Metropolitan Museum of Art, New York, Bequest of Catherine G. Curran, 2008 (2008.437)

SELECTED REFERENCES: Ananoff 1961–70, vol. 2 (1963), p. 80, no. 758, fig. 209; Rosenberg 2006, p. 154, under cat. no. 84, fig. 85; Shelley 2009; Stein 2009, fig. 2.

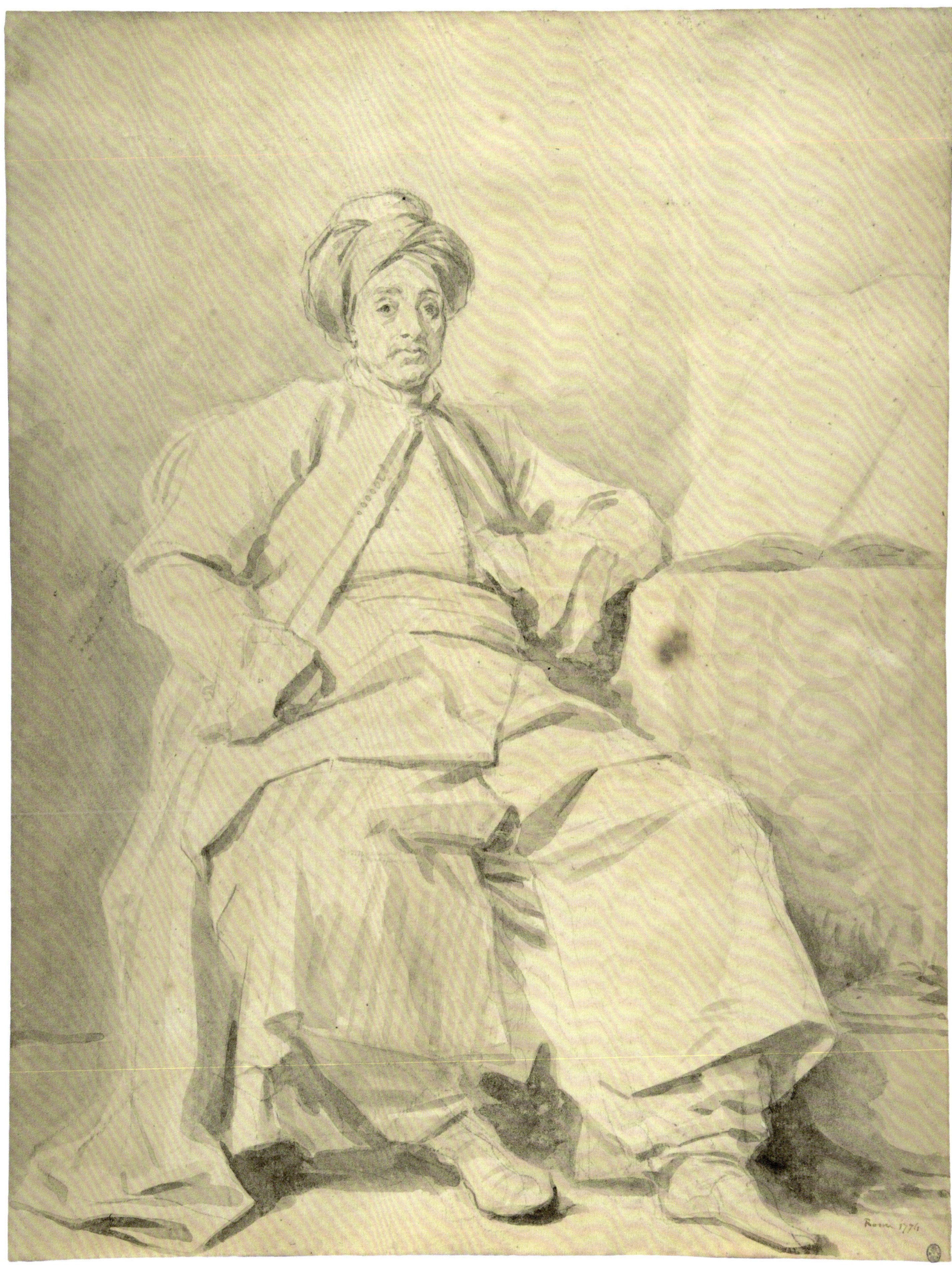
Rome 1776

58. *Man Displaying Birds*

1774?
Black chalk
13⅞ × 9¾ in. (35.1 × 24.8 cm)
Inscriptions: at lower left, below image, in pen and brown ink on mount, "fragonard"; at lower right, below image, in black chalk on mount, "Capital"

In this startlingly direct study, a man sits outdoors on a block of stone, holding a curved rod upon which two small birds perch, their cage on the ground by his feet. Presumably trained, the birds do not appear to be restrained, but it is unclear whether the man is a street entertainer hoping for coins from passersby or a bird seller displaying his wares. His unconventional attire suggests a warm climate: his upper body is bare, save a blanket or cloak draped across his shoulders, his breeches are unbuttoned, and his baggy stockings are paired with casual slip-on shoes. What appears to be his hat sits upside down on the ground behind his right foot. It is easy to imagine that Fragonard came upon this figure on the streets of Rome, or elsewhere in Italy, and was struck by his picturesque métier and wide-eyed gaze, as he looks not at the viewer but into the distance, as if lost in reverie. French artists in Rome had long produced drawings, paintings, and prints of picturesque Italian "types," which were sought after by collectors, especially those who had themselves traveled in Italy. This study of a man with birds, like the *Head of an Italian Peasant* (cat. 63), is distinguished by its sense of psychological exploration.

The drawing was unknown before Eunice Williams attributed it to Fragonard in 1990[1] and the Arnoldi-Livie gallery in Munich exhibited it in 1991. More difficult than its attribution is the question of dating. Black chalk was Fragonard's preferred medium in 1761, during his return trip from his first stay in Italy, but drawings from that period (cats. 2–6) were smaller in format and were either copies after earlier masters or landscape views. The figure studies from his first trip were larger than this sheet and rendered in red chalk; depicting figures draped and posed in the Palazzo Mancini, they were made as part of the regimented curriculum of the Académie de France in Rome (see cat. 3). It was on his second trip to Rome in 1773–74 that Fragonard had the freedom and inclination to draw figures from life, including acquaintances, members of his entourage, and models he may have encountered on the streets: fishermen, dwarfs, peasant women, and children.[2] These drawings, although similar in subject matter to *Man Displaying Birds* and of similar dimensions, are all executed in either red chalk or brown wash, making this sheet an anomaly. It has in common with the 1761 drawings a somewhat angular application of black chalk and contours that are sometimes gone over twice, but it fits comfortably with Fragonard's practices during his second trip, when he made large-scale, portraitlike studies of Italian street characters. Thus, we have opted to see this as a study made outdoors in the early summer of 1774, atypical in medium but characteristic in terms of subject. PS

PROVENANCE: [Arnoldi-Livie, Munich]; from whom acquired in 1991 by a private collection

SELECTED EXHIBITIONS: Munich 1991, cat. no. 3; Williams 1993, cat. no. 1.

SELECTED REFERENCE: Rosenberg 1993.

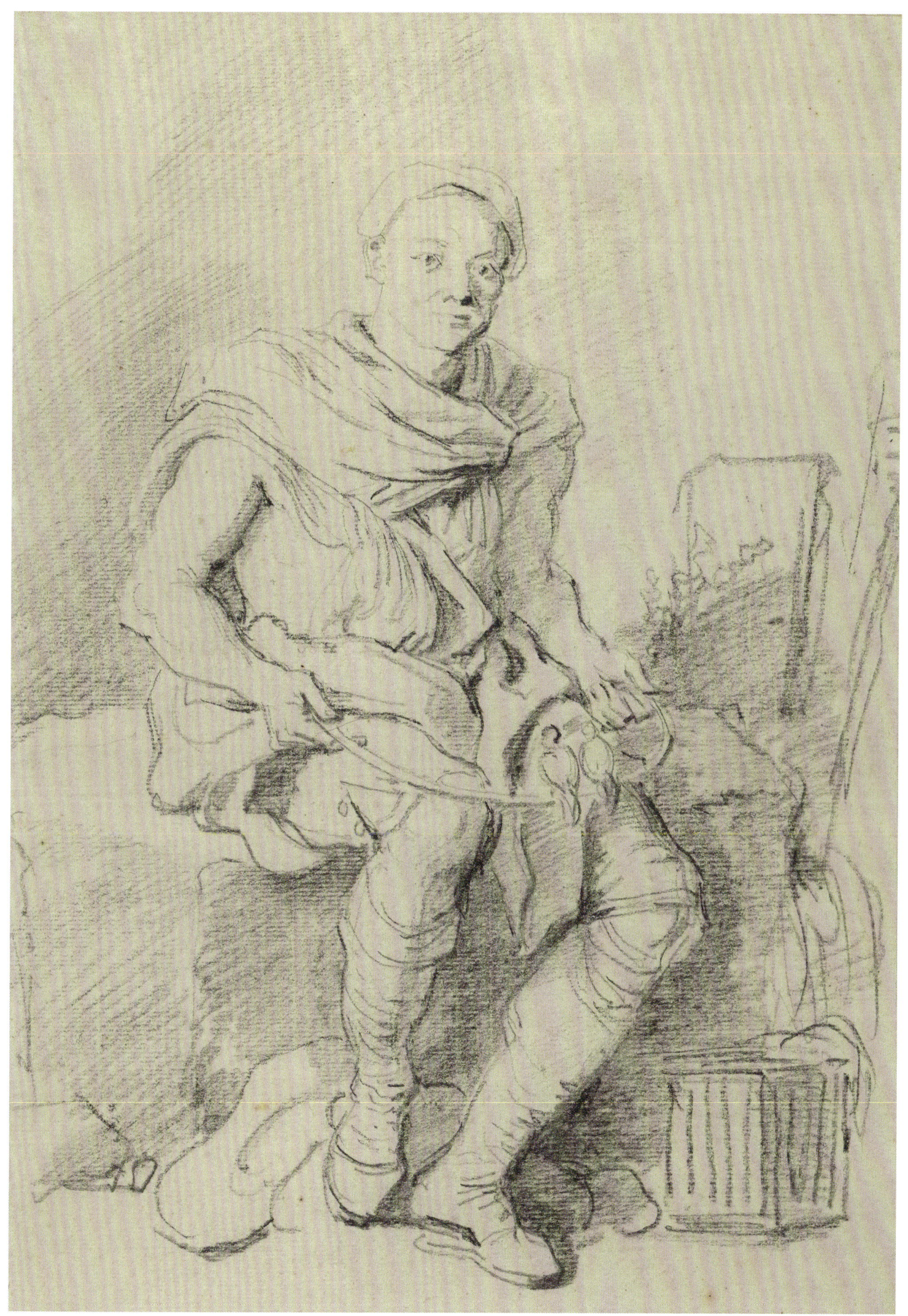

59. *Seated Man Reading*

1774?
Red chalk
13⅜ × 9¼ in. (34 × 23.3 cm)
Inscription: at lower right, in faint graphite, "Fragonard"; at lower right, the blind stamp of Francis Abbott (Lugt 970)

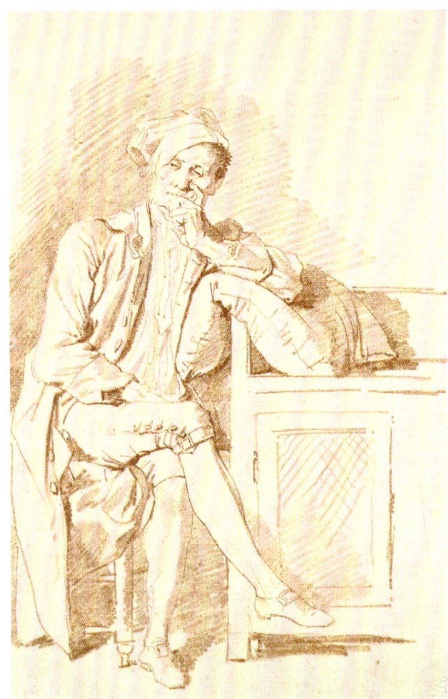

Fig. 103. Jean Honoré Fragonard, *Seated Man*, ca. 1773–75. Red chalk, 14⅜ × 9½ in. (36.5 × 24 cm). Musée d'Ixelles, Brussels

Fig. 104. Jean Honoré Fragonard, *Seated Man Holding a Book*, ca. 1773–75. Red chalk, 17¾ × 14⅝ in. (44.9 × 37 cm). The Horvitz Collection, Beverly Farms, Massachusetts

Bathed in sunlight and engrossed in a book, the man depicted here was perhaps unaware that he was being sketched. The sheet is executed with an admirable economy of means and gives us no clues as to the setting or identity of the sitter beyond the informality suggested by his head covering. Nervous but confident lines establish the contours, and quickly laid down hatching blocks in shadow and tone. Obscured by a horizontal form in the foreground, his feet and the bottom of his coat are hidden from view.

In the nineteenth century, when the sheet was in the collection of Francis Abbott in Edinburgh, it had a pendant of the same technique and dimensions (fig. 103). For Pierre Rosenberg, these were late drawings, done after Fragonard had returned from his second Italian trip.[1] However, it is equally possible that they were done abroad, as he frequently made drawings of his compatriots living or traveling in Italy. A drawing in the Horvitz collection (fig. 104), for example, which has been tentatively proposed as a portrait of François André Vincent,[2] suggests that Fragonard may have continued sketching red chalk portraits in Rome after making the more formally conceived series in Nègrepelisse, and that they were more varied in scale and technique.[3] Leaving aside the question of dating, the Metropolitan's drawing is a powerful display of Fragonard's ability to draw figures from life, harnessing his fluid and animated draftsmanship to a close observation of nature. As he rarely made figure studies for his paintings, this talent is most evident in independent sheets like this one.[4] PS

PROVENANCE: Francis Abbott (British, 1800–1893), his dry mark (Lugt 970) at lower right; his estate sale (Lugt 52191), Dowell's, Edinburgh, January 22–26, 1894 (part of lot 337, with another red chalk drawing of "a Man in the attitude of Meditation"); sale, collection of M. X . . . [Camille Groult (1832–1908), per Frick Art Reference Library], Galerie Georges Petit, Paris, June 21–22, 1920 (lot 153); [Wildenstein & Co., Inc., New York]; Miss Edith L. Sachs; The Metropolitan Museum of Art, New York, Gift of Mrs. Howard J. Sachs and Mr. Peter G. Sachs, in memory of Miss Edith L. Sachs, 1978 (1978.516.1)

SELECTED EXHIBITION: Rosenberg 1988, p. 437, cat. no. 207.

SELECTED REFERENCES: Ananoff 1961–70, vol. 1 (1961), pp. 112–13, no. 226, fig. 86; Bean and Turčić 1986, pp. 108–9, no. 112.

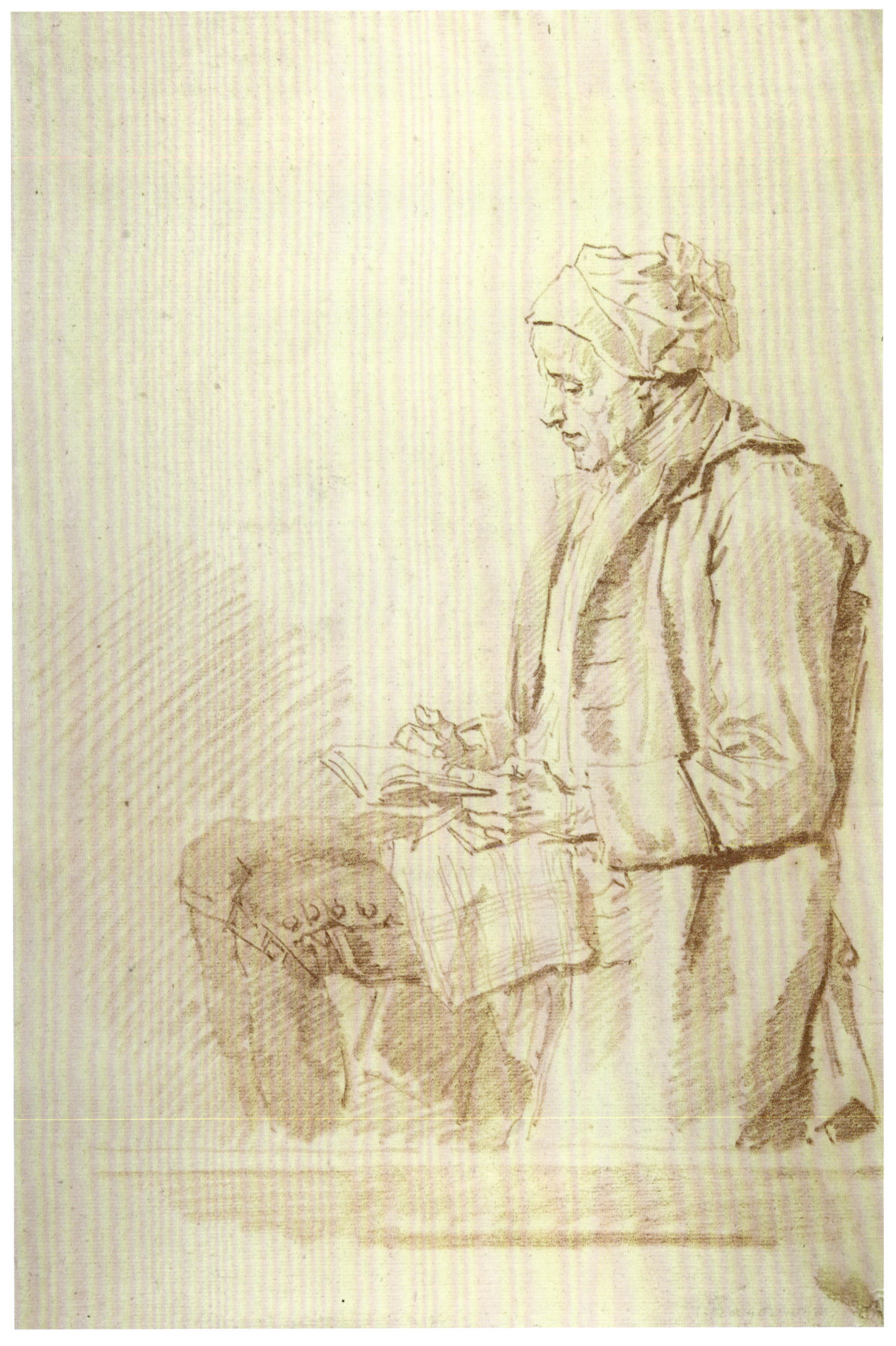

60. *Portrait of a Neapolitan Woman*

1774
Brush and brown wash over faint black chalk underdrawing
14½ × 11⅛ in. (36.7 × 28.2 cm)
Inscription: at lower right, in pen and brown ink, "Naples 1774-feme / S.. te Lu."

Fragonard, Bergeret, and their entourage spent two months in Naples, from April 15 to June 12, 1774. The distinctive inhabitants of this southern coastal city inspired some of the finest drawings of the entire trip, but none more famous than *Portrait of a Neapolitan Woman*. In a century when images of women were often idealized or coquettish, this candid and direct portrayal is one of startling modernity. Although the identity of the sitter is not known, the drawing is a searching portrait of disarming directness, transcending the long-established tradition of foreign artists sketching local women in their picturesque dress. The modeling of the young woman's features and sympathetic gaze, achieved through an unerring application of brown wash in a range of subtle gradations, is a testament to the mastery that Fragonard had attained at this point in his career, when he wielded the brush with such ease that exuberance and naturalism went hand in hand.

Inscribed on the sheet by Bergeret is an abbreviation for "femme de Sainte Lucie," a reference, as Eunice Williams has pointed out, to the Passeggiata di Santa Lucia, a popular thoroughfare for both pedestrians and carriages.[1] The sitter's elaborate garb, from the ornamental trim of her jacket to her dangling earrings and layered necklaces, suggested to Williams the holiday finery worn during the feast of Januarius, the patron saint of Naples, which took place in the first week of May.[2]

Whether the sitter was indeed a "fisherman's wife" dressed for a festival,[3] or a posed model, as suggested by Jean-Pierre Cuzin,[4] she inspired a constellation of related works, some by Fragonard and some by François André Vincent. That this talented young pensionnaire had accompanied the group to Naples is nowhere mentioned in Bergeret's journal; however, it is documented in the many pairs of drawings that he and Fragonard made side by side.[5] For the "woman from Santa Lucia" we have, in addition to this drawing, a full-length seated study by Fragonard, now in Frankfurt,[6] as well as a small canvas and two versions of full-length standing portraits, all attributed to Vincent by Cuzin, although he hesitates to some degree over the last two and other "fragonardesque" wash drawings.[7] These questions aside, it is clear that in 1774, when Vincent adopted this manner, which was so distinct from his earlier draftsmanship, it was in the spirit of emulation. PS

PROVENANCE: Possibly the M. [François Georges Maréchal, marquis de Bièvre (1747–1789)] estate sale, Hôtel de Bullion, Paris, March 10 and following days, 1790 (part of lot 34, "[t]rois belles études de têtes, dont un buste de femme vue de face et richement ajusté"); Martial Pelletier; his collection sale (Lugt 29763), Delbergue-Cormont, Paris, April 29–May 4, 1867 (lot 1315); Antoine-François Marmontel (1816–1898), Paris; his collection sales: (Lugt 30517), Hôtel Drouot, Paris, May 11–14, 1868 (lot 233); (Lugt 42554), Hôtel Drouot, Paris, January 25–26, 1883 (lot 103); and (Lugt 56122), Hôtel Drouot, Paris, March 28–29, 1898 (lot 24), repurchased by his family; E. M. Hodgkins; his collection sale, Galerie Georges Petit, Paris, April 30, 1914 (lot 28), unsold; Casimir I. Stralem (1886–1932), New York, in 1931; his wife, Edithe Alice (née Neustadt), Pleasantville and New York, from 1932; her son, Donald S. Stralem (1903–1976), New York and Palm Springs; his wife, Mrs. Donald S. Stralem (Jean Lehman Ickelheimer [1908–1994]), New York, until 1972; Mr. and Mrs. Eugene V. Thaw, New York; The Morgan Library & Museum, New York, Thaw Collection (2001.60)

SELECTED EXHIBITIONS: Williams 1978, pp. 94–95, cat. no. 33; Rosenberg 1988, pp. 398–99, cat. no. 192; Eitel-Porter et al. 2006, pp. 172–73, cat. no. 82.

SELECTED REFERENCE: Cuzin 2013, pp. 78–79, fig. 18.

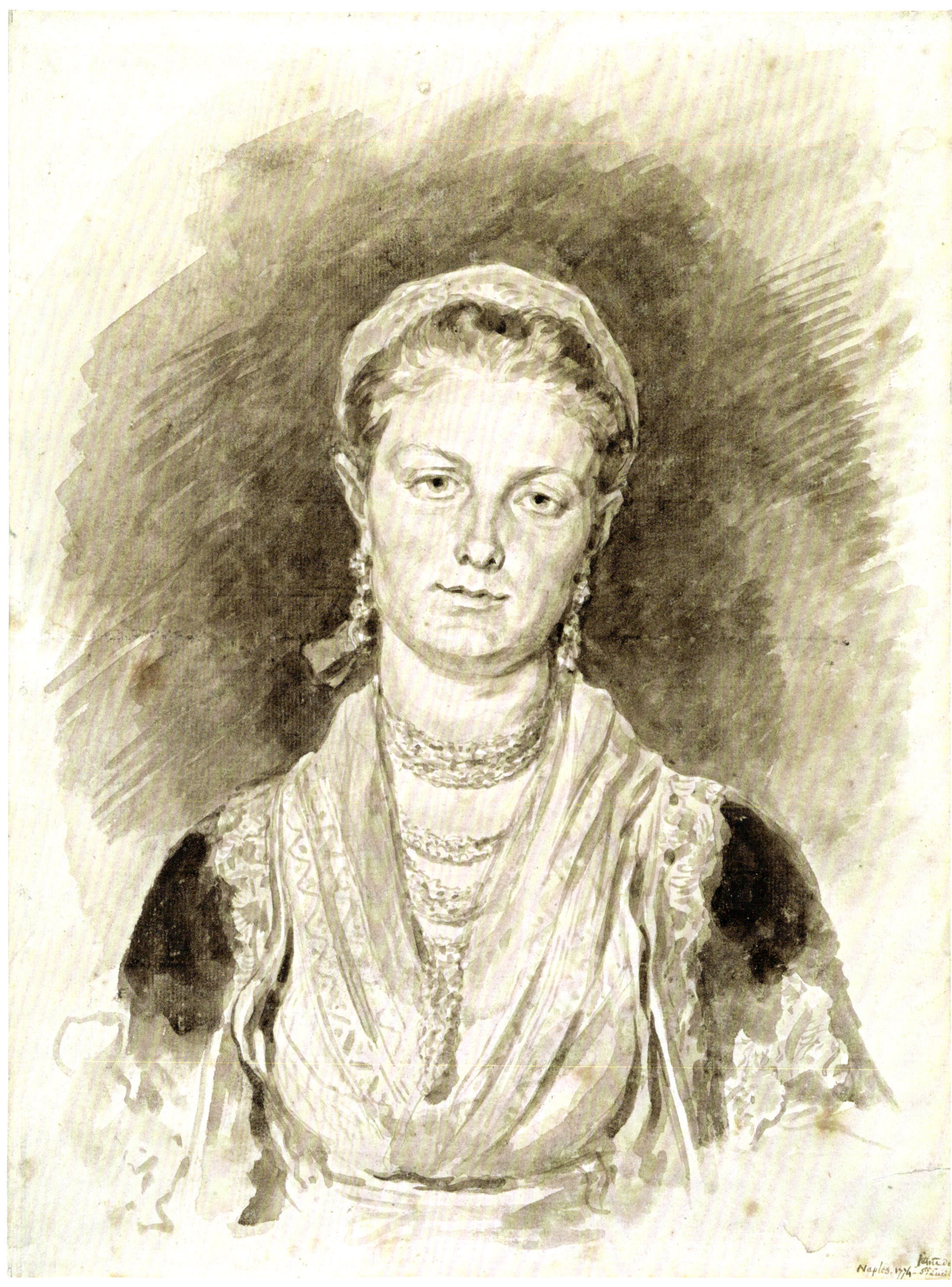
Naples. 1774

through the scale, brio, and candor of his presentation, endowing his barefoot subjects with an unprecedented monumentality and dignity. PS

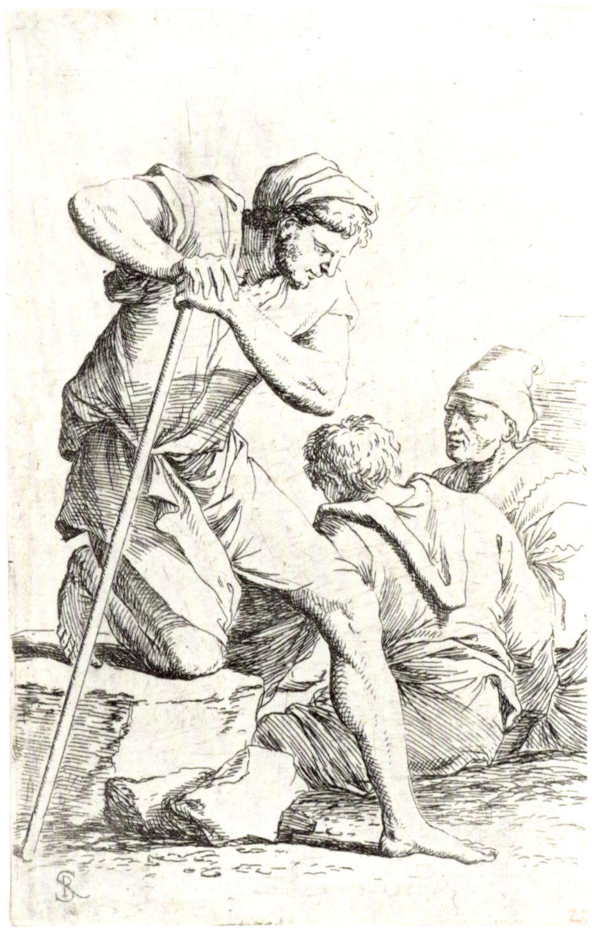

Fig. 106. Salvator Rosa (Italian, 1615–1673), *Three Peasants, One Kneeling on a Rock*, ca. 1656–57. Etching, 5⅝ × 3¾ in. (14.3 × 9.4 cm). The Metropolitan Museum of Art, New York, Purchase, Joseph Pulitzer Bequest, 1917 (17.50.17-116)

CAT. 61. PROVENANCE: Probably Pierre Jacques Onésyme Bergeret de Grancourt (1715–1785); possibly his estate sale (Lugt 4027), Baradelle, Paris, April 24–29, 1786 (part of lot 210), or to his son Pierre Jacques Bergeret (1742–1807); Xavier Atger (1758–1833); possibly his estate sale (Lugt 13614), Derbanne and Defer, Paris, April 7–12, 1834 (part of lot 3, "Bouchardon [Edme] / Soixante-neuf dessins au crayon rouge et à la sanguine, études de têtes et figures académiques; de ce nombre plusieurs par Fragonard père."); Hippolyte Walferdin (1795–1880); his estate sale (Lugt 40074), Hôtel Drouot, Paris, April 12–16, 1880 (lot 232), purchased for 140 francs by Baron Hottinguer; Hottinguer family, Zurich, by descent; [Salamander Fine Arts, London]; acquired in 2006 by The Metropolitan Museum of Art, New York, Purchase, Walter and Leonore Annenberg and The Annenberg Foundation Gift, 2006 (2006.353.1)

SELECTED EXHIBITION: *Paper Chase: Two Decades of Collecting Drawings and Prints*, New York, The Metropolitan Museum of Art, 2014–15 (no catalogue).

SELECTED REFERENCES: Portalis 1889, vol. 2, p. 310; Ananoff 1961–70, vol. 2 (1963), p. 81, no. 766; Stein 2007, fig. 12.

CAT. 62. PROVENANCE: Probably Pierre Jacques Onésyme Bergeret de Grancourt (1715–1785); possibly his estate sale (Lugt 4027), Baradelle, Paris, April 24–29, 1786 (part of lot 210), or to his son Pierre Jacques Bergeret (1742–1807); Xavier Atger (1758–1833); possibly his estate sale (Lugt 13614), Derbanne and Defer, Paris, April 7–12, 1834 (part of lot 3, "Bouchardon [Edme] / Soixante-neuf dessins au crayon rouge et à la sanguine, études de têtes et figures académiques; de ce nombre plusieurs par Fragonard père."); Hippolyte Walferdin (1795–1880); his estate sale (Lugt 40074), Hôtel Drouot, Paris, April 12–16, 1880 (lot 231), purchased for 140 francs by Baron Hottinguer; Hottinguer family, Zurich, by descent; [Salamander Fine Arts, London]; acquired in 2006 by The Metropolitan Museum of Art, New York, Purchase, Walter and Leonore Annenberg and The Annenberg Foundation Gift, 2006 (2006.353.2)

SELECTED EXHIBITION: *Paper Chase: Two Decades of Collecting Drawings and Prints*, New York, The Metropolitan Museum of Art, 2014–15 (no catalogue).

SELECTED REFERENCES: Portalis 1889, vol. 2, p. 310; Ananoff 1961–70, vol. 2 (1963), p. 81, no. 765; Stein 2007, fig. 13.

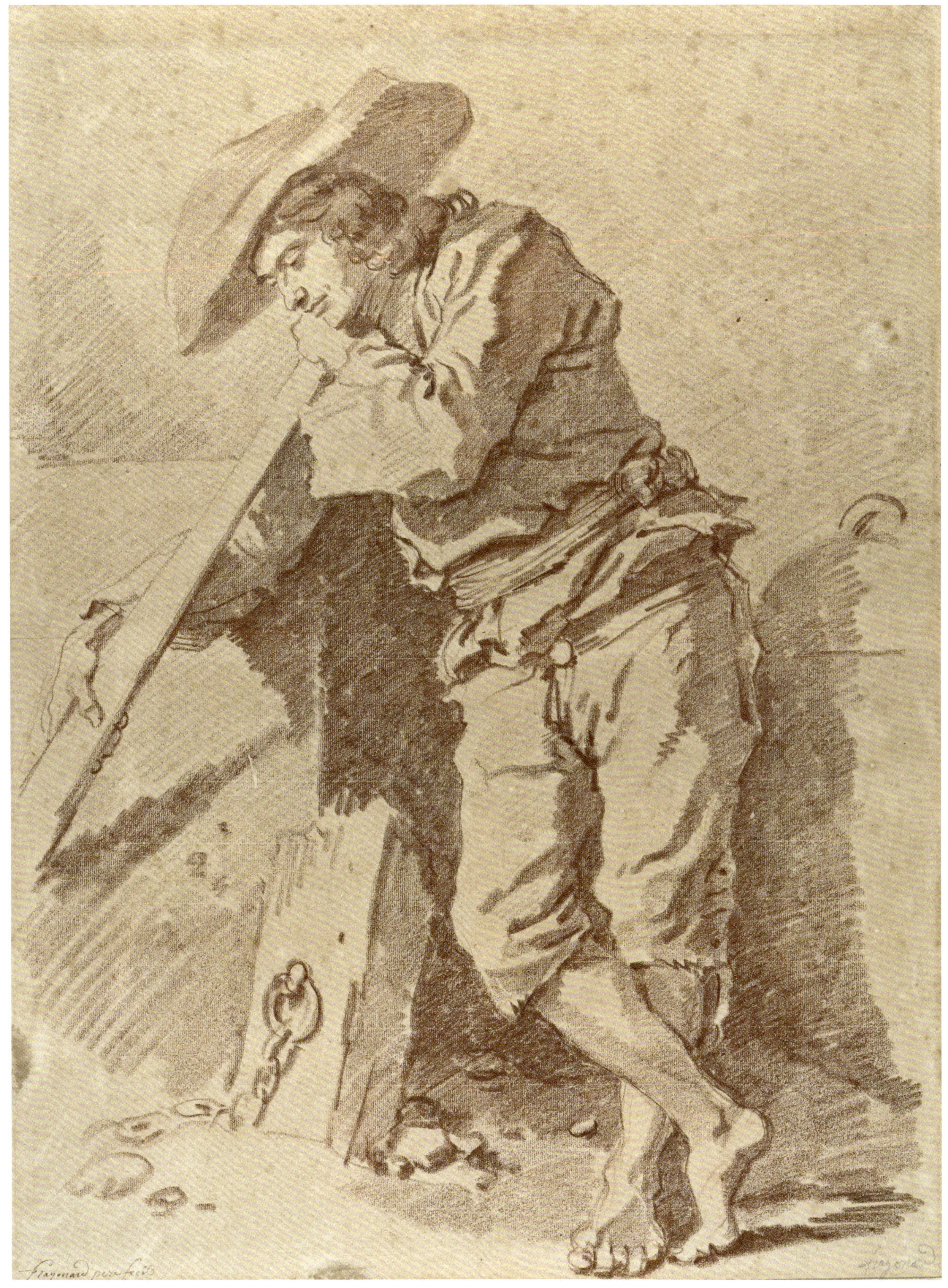

CAT 62

63. *Head of an Italian Peasant*

1774
Brush and brown wash over black chalk underdrawing
12¼ × 9½ in. (31 × 24 cm)
Inscription: at lower right, in pen and brown ink, "Rome 1774"

On his second Italian trip, Fragonard was drawn less to the art in the palaces and churches and more to the characters on the streets. Whether presented in full-length views or in portraitlike head studies, the figure drawings of 1773–74 often go beyond picturesque genre to become probing psychological explorations. Like the subject of *Portrait of a Neapolitan Woman* (cat. 60), this weather-beaten man of indeterminate age engages the viewer with a direct gaze. Gradually built up in layers of translucent wash, applied with a broad-tipped brush, the topography of his face comes into focus, with its chiseled cheekbones, deep eye sockets, and furrowed brow, all framed by his abundant curly hair and beard.

Although Fragonard invested time and effort in this intimate portrayal, there is no record of the sitter's identity. To Roger Portalis, in 1889, he was an "homme du Peuple italien," a man of the common Italian people. Alexandre Ananoff, in 1961, christened him a "Pêcheur italien." However, he lacks any specific attributes of a fisherman, and the inscription on the sheet states that it was drawn in Rome, not seaside Naples, making this supposition less likely. His vocation probably mattered little to Fragonard, who, like Tiepolo, had a great affinity for the richly textured faces of old men, whose gravitas enriched history and genre scenes alike. PS

PROVENANCE: Possibly the Desmarets sale (Lugt 2841), Hayot de Longpré, Paris, April 24, 1778 (lot 136, "Une tête de Vieillard, vue de face, avec une grande barbe, largement traitée au bistre"), bought by Robert Quesney; Marie-Joseph-François Mahérault (1795–1879); his estate sale (Lugt 40241), Hôtel Drouot, Paris, May 27–29, 1880 (lot 55); Baron Roger Portalis (1841–1912), Paris; his collection sale (Lugt 46356), Hôtel Drouot, Paris, March 14, 1887 (lot 89); Camille Groult (1832–1908), Paris; by descent to his grandson, Pierre Bordeaux-Groult (1916–2007) (per Wildenstein); [Wildenstein and Co., New York]; private collection

SELECTED EXHIBITION: Sutton 1980, cat. no. 138, ill.

SELECTED REFERENCES: Portalis 1889, vol. 2, p. 314; Ananoff 1961–70, vol. 1 (1961), p. 79, no. 128, vol. 3 (1968), p. 293, fig. 56.

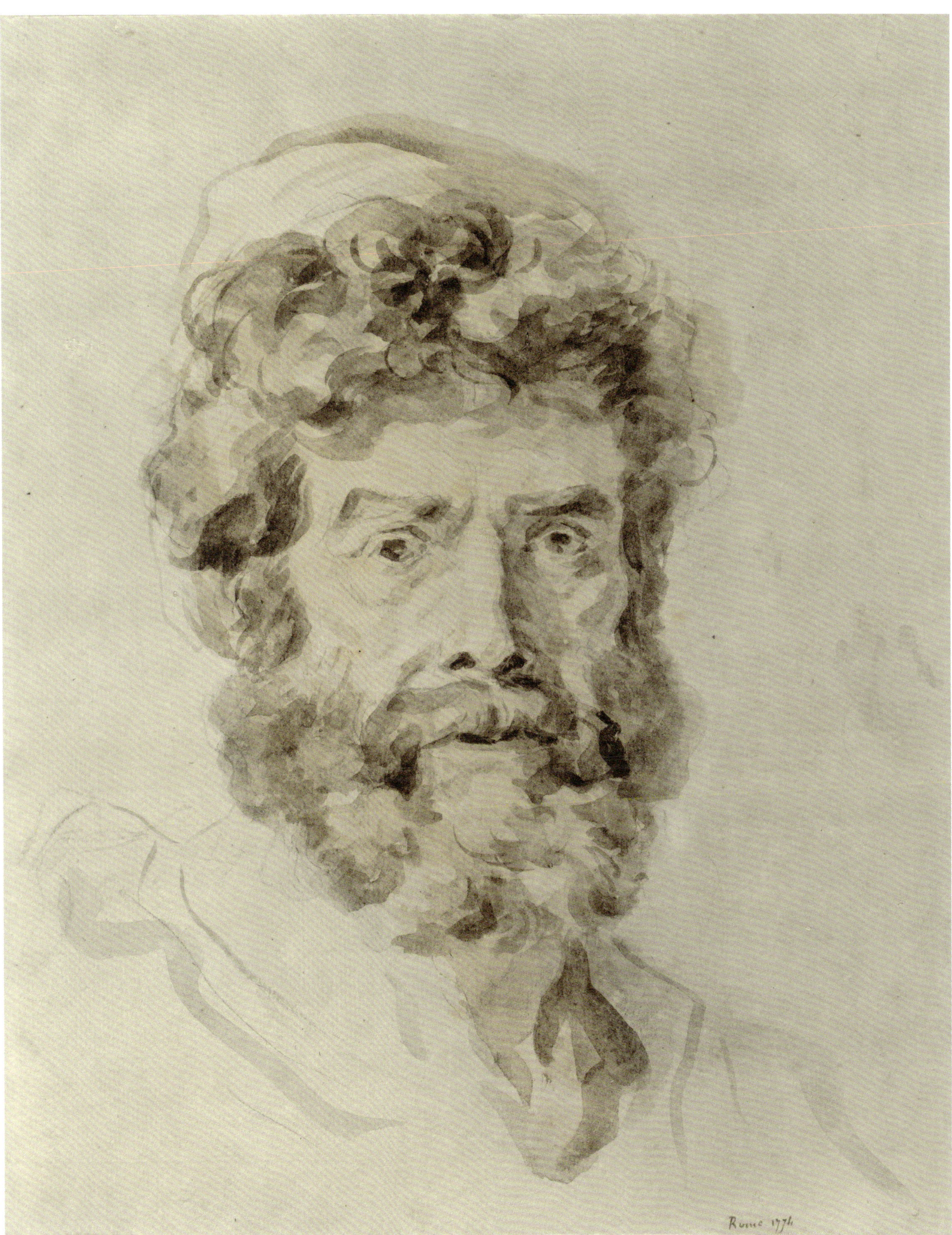
Rome 1774

64. *Diogenes*

1774
Brush and gray-brown wash over traces of black chalk underdrawing
14 × 11 in. (35.5 × 27.9 cm)
Inscription: at upper left, in pen and brown ink, effaced

Fragonard's return trip from Italy with Bergeret in 1774 was not as leisurely as his voyage home with Saint-Non in 1761, lasting a little over two months as opposed to a little over five, and the itinerary was different. Instead of circling back after visiting Venice, they took the eastern route around the Alps, passing through Vienna, Prague, Dresden, and Frankfurt before returning to Paris via Strasbourg. The picture galleries in these cities were rich in paintings by Rubens and other Baroque masters, and Fragonard's days were filled with absorbing the wealth of treasures before his eyes. To contrast the fruits of these two journeys, the copies made for Saint-Non were more numerous in number, but smaller in format and almost always in black chalk. Those made with Bergeret were fewer, but on larger sheets, and worked freely in brown wash, producing a very painterly effect.

From August 20 to August 30, Bergeret's party was in Dresden, where he had nothing but praise for the collections of the Elector of Saxony, whose princely generosity led him to open his galleries to visitors for the sake of progress in the arts.[1] From Bergeret's journal, we know that Fragonard was established in the galleries every morning by eight o'clock, and Bergeret himself, when he couldn't join the artist, went later by carriage to "collect the drawings."[2]

One canvas that attracted Fragonard's attention was the haunting, bust-length image of the Cynic philosopher Diogenes (died 323 B.C.), who eschewed the corruption of civilization. Painted by Jusepe de Ribera in 1637 (fig. 107), Diogenes is wrapped in a heavy mantle and bears only his attribute, a lantern, which he used in broad daylight while searching a busy marketplace for an honest man. By filling the background with a golden wash, Fragonard draws the eye to this detail, where the white of the reserved paper illuminates only the hand, the candle, and the reflective sheen of the lantern's lid. A number of eighteenth-century sales list drawings of this subject by Fragonard, although some are described as horizontal or as including multiple figures, suggesting that he copied at least one other version.[3] In this pared-down composition, which presents Diogenes as an unkempt man with a piercing gaze, Fragonard may have emulated Ribera's virtuoso brushwork and his tenebrist palette, but there is also an uncanny echo of a drawing he had made from life a few months earlier, before leaving Rome (cat. 63).[4] Whether it was simply a type he admired or had use for, or whether this copy unconsciously channels his memory of a man he had met on the streets of Rome, the parallels between the two illuminate the fluid and interconnected relationships between life study, copy, and invention in Fragonard's oeuvre. PS

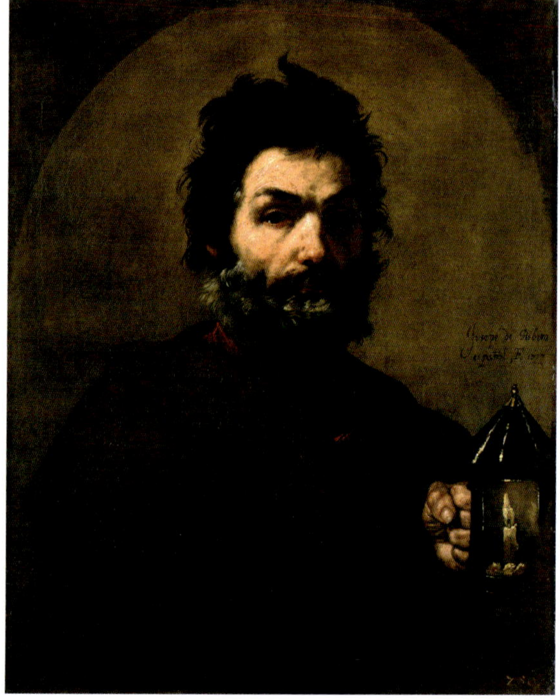

Fig. 107. Jusepe de Ribera (Spanish, 1591–1652), *Diogenes*, 1637. Oil on canvas, 30 × 24 in. (76 × 61 cm). Staatliche Kunstsammlungen, Gemäldegalerie, Dresden (Gal. no. 682)

PROVENANCE: Possibly in the anonymous sale (Lugt 4235) (presumably the collection of Louis Antoine Auguste, duc de Rohan-Chabot, per the Getty Provenance Index® Databases, sale catalogue F-A977[5]), Boileau, Paris, December 17–22, 1787 (part of lot 166, "Deux Bustes d'hommes, remplis de caractère & du plus grand effet, l'un qui porte une lanterne de sa main gauche, semble caractèriser un Diogêne. Ces études très terminées, sont faites de bistre au pinceau sur papier blanc"); purchased at the sale by Antoine-Charles Dulac; anonymous sale, Palais Galliera, Paris, December 3, 1966 (lot 6); S. Higgons, Paris (per Ananoff); anonymous sale, Palais Galliera, Paris, December 11, 1969 (lot 6); private collection; acquired in 2008 by private collection

SELECTED REFERENCE: Ananoff 1961–70, vol. 4 (1970), p. 63, no. 2056, fig. 557.

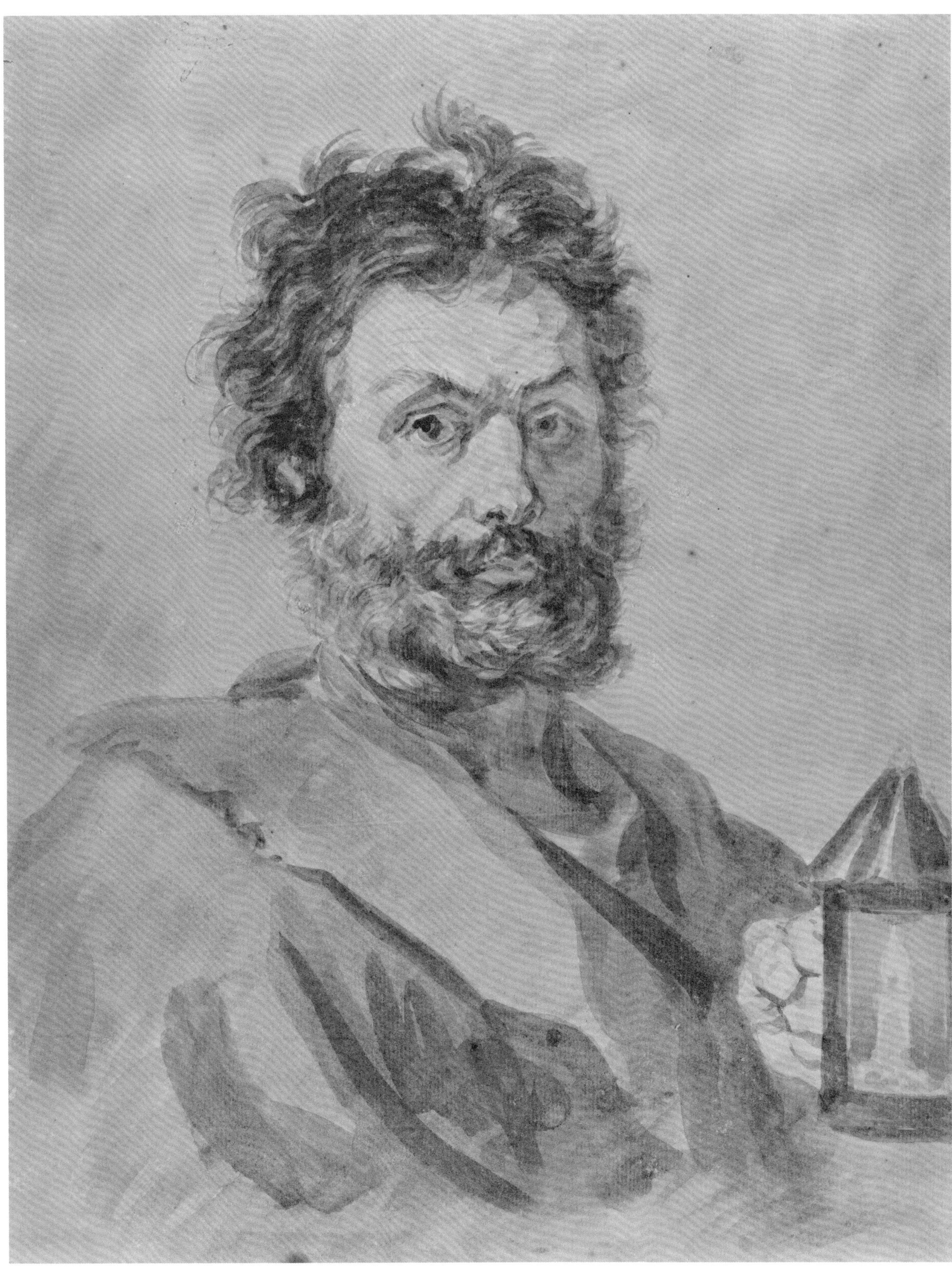

Late Career and Shifting Roles

Fragonard continued to draw and paint following his return in 1774 from his second Italian voyage, but despite the fact that his fame was well established—his works fetched high prices at auction and were frequently engraved—his output progressively slowed, and after the Revolution his activities shifted to museum administration. He exhibited occasionally at the Salon de la Correspondance but never submitted a reception piece to the Académie Royale, for which he was finally censured in 1788. Free to choose his own subjects, he gravitated toward landscape, genre, and literary scenes. Italy, in particular, loomed large in his imagination, its motifs so indelibly absorbed into his personal repertoire that scholars have difficulty separating drawings done in Italy from those made after his return (see cats. 65–67). Well into the 1780s, Fragonard's landscapes continued to feature towering cypresses, weathered stone stairs, parasol pines, and overgrown fountains, as if depicting a recurring dream set in a nonspecific, but clearly Italianate, garden. His figural subjects, too, have a dreamlike aspect, portraying allegories of inspiration and scenes of passion, longing, and emotional transport.

The universal joys of family life are also a frequent theme during this period, when Fragonard was increasingly occupied with his own family. Marguerite Gérard came to Paris from Grasse to live with her sister and brother-in-law about 1775. Soon after, Fragonard must have begun her artistic training. Her personal style, while influenced by that of her famous teacher, gravitated in the direction of the polished and highly detailed "Dutch manner" popular in these years. Fragonard himself had begun to experiment with a more refined technique in the second half of the 1770s, as we see in a work like *The Bolt* (p. 27, fig. 20), painted for Louis Gabriel, the marquis de Véri, about 1777–78. By the 1780s, the two artists were collaborating, and works such as *The First Steps* (p. 33, fig. 28) and *The Beloved Child* show a harmonious integration of the two hands.[1]

Fragonard's son, Alexandre Evariste, was born in 1780 and would also become an artist, entrusted, at the age of twelve, to the studio of Jacques Louis David. His earliest works were in a Neoclassical vein, but by about 1820 he began to favor subjects drawn from French history, executed in the troubadour style. Fragonard's wife, Marie Anne, was likewise a practicing artist, whose charming miniature portraits (see, for example, p. 7, fig. 4) were, until 1996, considered part of Fragonard's oeuvre.[2] If Fragonard's daughter, Rosalie, had artistic talent, we do not know; she died in 1788 at the age of eighteen, while at the Château de Cassan, a property owned by Pierre Jacques Bergeret, Fragonard's friend and the son of his late patron, Pierre Jacques Onésyme Bergeret de Grancourt.[3]

Fragonard himself became ill following Rosalie's death, and the entire family left Paris for Grasse, arriving in January 1790 and staying for approximately two years. Upon their return to the French capital, they were helped on several occasions by David, who was responsible for Fragonard being granted new lodgings at the Louvre and an administrative position in the Muséum Central des Arts (the future Musée du Louvre). David's most generous praise, in advocating for his friend, is oft-quoted: "He will devote his old age to the preservation of the masterpieces whose number he helped to increase in his youth."[4]

Fragonard's late drawings, dating from the late 1770s through the late 1780s, can be stubbornly resistant to precise dating and interpretation. Because few are studies for paintings, their chronology is mired in as much murkiness as those of earlier periods. Some are variations on painted compositions, while others are autonomous, finished works. A great many sheets were inspired by literary sources; if these were the result of a specific commission, no documentation has survived. Yet, even as his output as a painter gradually diminished, his graphic work continued to display a distinct vitality in the many informal black chalk sketches recording, and sometimes poking fun at, the day-to-day life of Fragonard, his family, and his social circle. Rapid studies, such as *Fragonard and His Family on a Bench* (p. 12, fig. 8), *A Boy Carried into a Salon* (cat. 99), and *Seated Man, His Elbow Resting on a Book* (cat. 100), are steeped in affection and whimsy. They were neither studies for paintings nor intended for the art market. Rather, they are further evidence of how drawings, for Fragonard, were often simply a cause for pleasure. It is tempting to read Fragonard's own thoughts on his legacy in a recently rediscovered work, dated 1797 and exhibited at the Salon in 1798, in which he is presented not as a painter but as a draftsman, holding his *porte-crayon* to his heart (fig. 108). PS

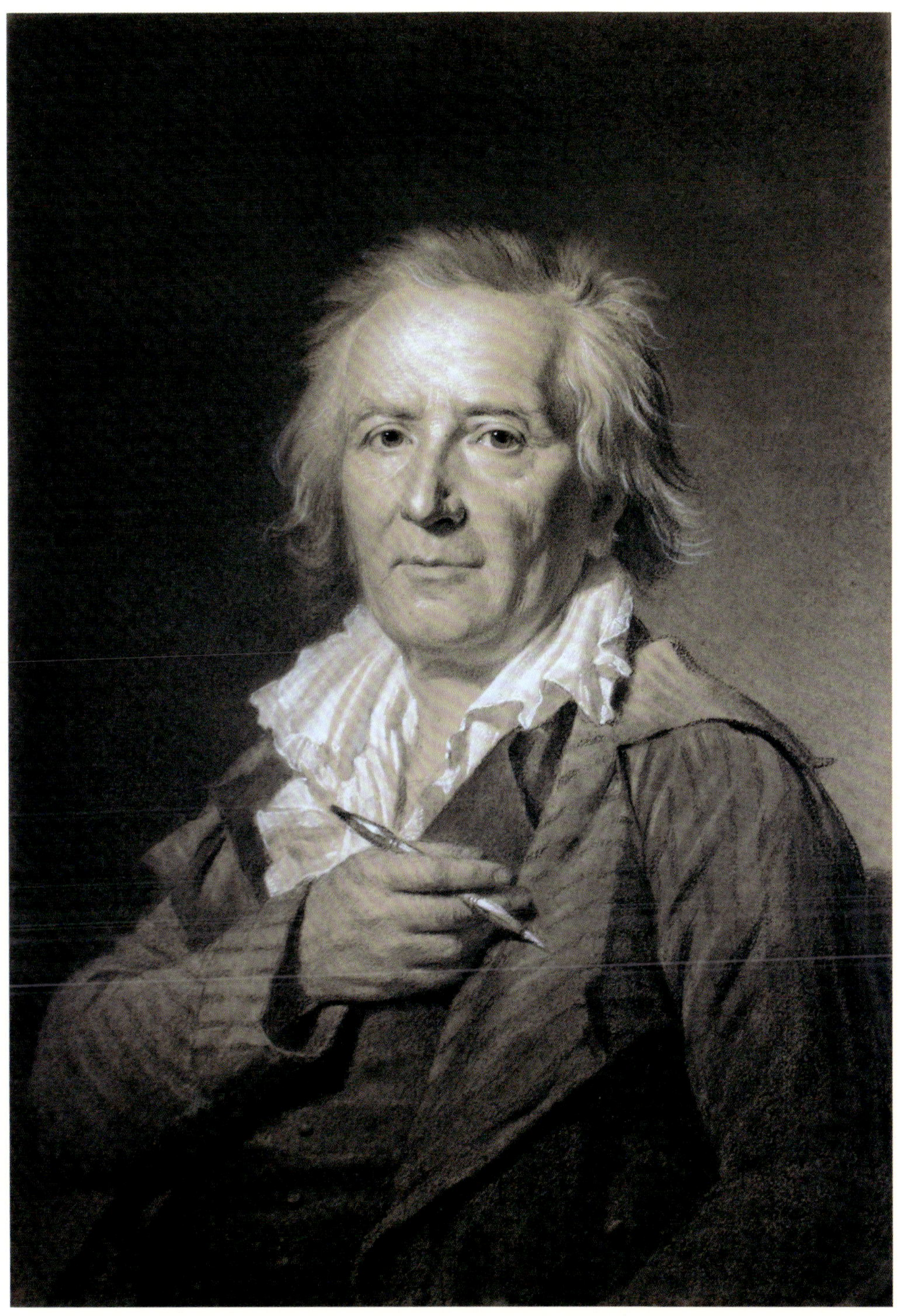

Fig. 108. Jacques Antoine Marie Lemoine (French, 1751–1824), *Portrait of Jean Honoré Fragonard*, 1797. Black chalk, stumped, and heightened with white chalk on beige paper, 12⅝ × 8⅞ in. (32 × 22.5 cm). Private collection

65. *Two Cypresses in an Italian Garden*

Ca. 1774
Two hues of red chalk with later framing lines in pen and brown ink
10⅝ × 12⅞ in. (26.9 × 32.5 cm)
Inscription: on verso of the mount, in graphite, "7"

Tall cypresses and classical gardens were the basic currency of Fragonard's formal landscape drawings in the early 1760s. They represent his mastery of red chalk. After his experience at Tivoli and the creation of the large red chalk views now in Besançon, Fragonard continued to develop personal variations or interpretations on the theme of parks and villas for another decade. The present composition is a distillation of that earlier experience and was made years later, during a second trip to Rome. This should set to rest the assumption that Fragonard consciously favored certain media during certain periods.

When this drawing was made, in about 1773–74, he was more interested in atmosphere and mood than in an encyclopedic vision of nature. It is comparable to the sheet in Rotterdam known traditionally as *Bergeret's Lunch*, where red chalk is applied as a veil of color through which the small figures and coaches appear silhouetted.[1] There are few contours defined by lines. Instead, boundaries and edges of foliage and objects result from variations in pressure on the chalk.

The composition is dominated by a pair of tall, full cypress trees recognizable from those depicted in Tivoli drawings such as *Cypresses at the Villa d'Este*.[2] The present garden is Fragonard's invention based on the deep store of visual memories from his first Roman years. To the standard elements of trees, broad sky, and garden ornaments Fragonard introduces a palpable silence in spite of the presence of small figures exploring the landscape. Red chalk of familiar hue is complemented by strategic and coloristic additions using brown chalk, perhaps *sanguine brûlée*, to the foliage that is further defined by nervous zigzag lines. The artist's decision to add brown details might have been motivated as much by experimentation as by desire to add a naturalistic note of dryness and decay to the otherwise verdant foliage. It implies the high heat and haze of a summer when rain has been scarce. It was not a new device for the artist. One finds accents of brown chalk in sheets dating more than a decade earlier, such as *Cypresses at the Villa d'Este* and *A Park Landscape* (cat. 5).

Further enhancing the sultry sense of summer (*la stagione estiva*)—and probably not something Fragonard intended—are passages of surface rubbing as a result of handling or manipulation when the counterproof was pulled. The present sheet is unquestionably the original drawing and not a counterproof. Lines in the latter would be flat and static, but here there is great variety in the pressure to apply the chalk lines, resulting in a range of tone. All hatching lines, even delicate ones, are in the correct direction for a right-handed artist. With such a richly textured surface of red chalks, an early counterproof was essential to prevent smears or discoloration. EW

PROVENANCE: [Galerie Cailleux, Paris, 1978]; private collection, New York; sale, Sotheby's, New York, January 13, 1989 (lot 3), unsold; Christie's, London, July 2, 1991 (lot 336), unsold; [W. M. Brady & Co., Inc., New York, 1998]; private collection

SELECTED EXHIBITIONS: Cailleux et al. 1978, cat. no. 13, ill.; Grasselli et al. 2007, pp. 154–55, cat. no. 60; Brooks et al. 2012, pp. 13–14, 78, ill.

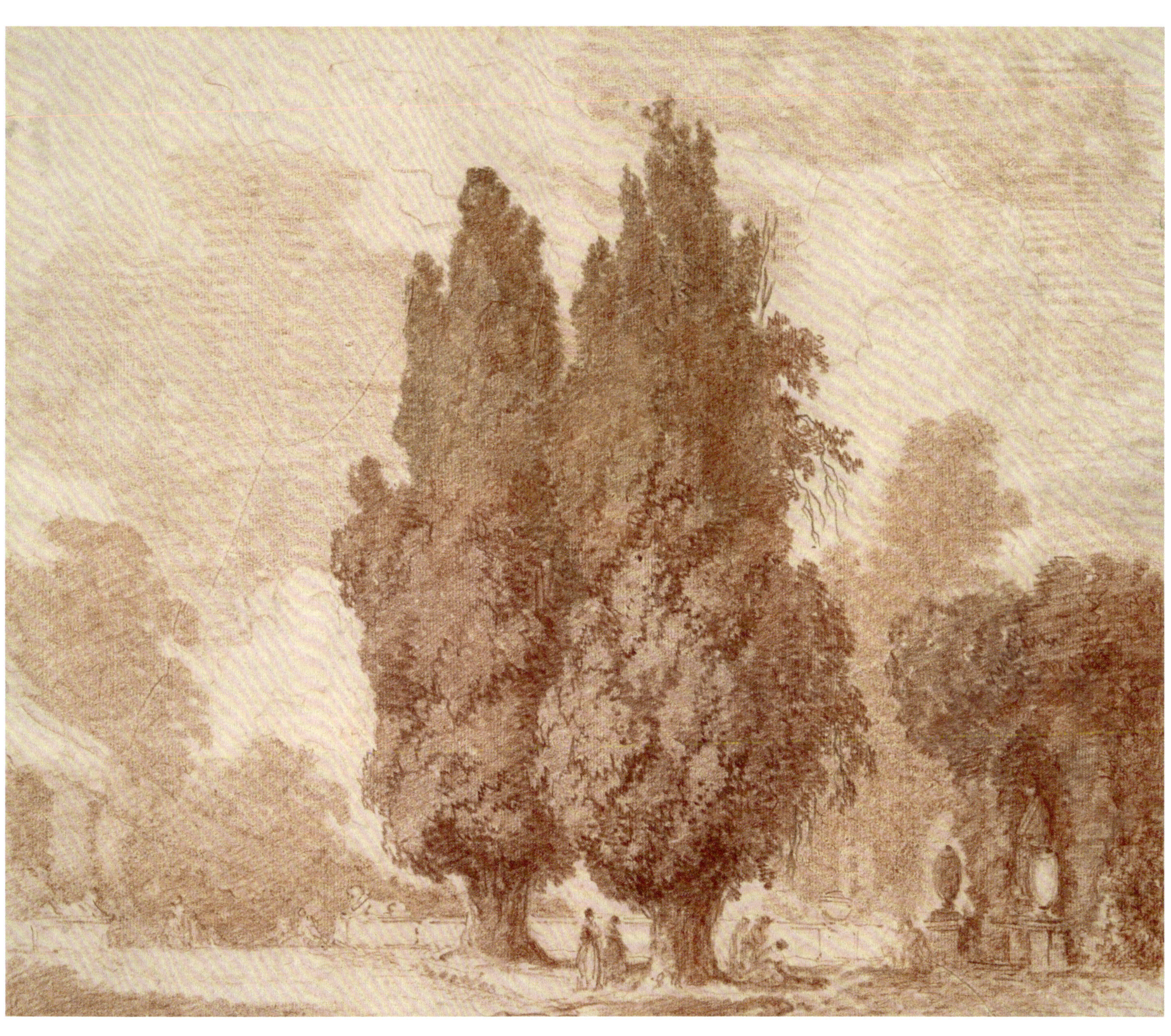

66. *Imaginary View of a Roman Villa with Parasol Pines*

Ca. 1774
Bister wash over black chalk
11⅜ × 15⅜ in. (28.8 × 39 cm)

Attempts to identify the villa and location of this animated scene have distracted from its real subject, the artist's poetic response to effects of dappled light and atmosphere. Unfortunately, the visual impact of the sheet before us is diminished by its faded condition. Perhaps, because of its beauty, it was continuously displayed and therefore exposed to sunlight, ironically the subtext of the composition.

Parasol pines (*Pinus pinea*) are ubiquitous in Rome, and Fragonard was obviously fascinated by them during both his stays there. Walking around the city, he made small sketches of the pines in chalk and wash. Later, in the studio, he composed finished drawings such as the present example. The sharp spiny branches gave him the opportunity to draw, with chalk or point of brush and brown wash, intricate linear patterns for the skeletal framework of his composition. Brown wash applied in numerous short strokes emulates the transformative effects of light flooding the ground below. The Goncourts, early owners of the present work, described Fragonard's process of creating "floating effects of light on the moistened paper which absorbed his contours."[1] This tranquil view of summer recreation is suddenly interrupted by the dramatically soaring diagonal of a single tall pine, which forms both a symbolic and literal umbrella over the scene.

Clusters of staffage figures of all ages, dwarfed in scale by the tall trees, occupy the garden. Their shapes and poses come from Fragonard's ensemble of players who populate other works from this second trip to Italy in 1773–74. They also are present in the busy kitchen at Nègrepelisse (cat. 56). Their liveliness is perceptible, almost audible, an impression achieved by Fragonard's freely drawn staccato pattern of curvilinear pen outlines and shapes. Attention to mood and the effects of light, achieved by using layers of brown wash, align this composition with Fragonard's preoccupations during this trip.

Fragonard is free of theory or historicism in evoking this festive scene. The villa is a generalized classical block with lateral wings, merely a dim background where details are suppressed in favor of pictorial unity. The composition is about diffused light and not about architecture. Past titles referenced the Villa Pamphili and the Villa Borghese, both of which had notable stands of parasol pines. Bergeret was impressed by important Roman families and their properties and included many on his itinerary. In his journal he mentions the vast tree plantings—pines, cypress, laurel—at the Villa Pamphili that are as green in winter as in summer. The party visited in December 1773 and again in June 1774.[2] EW

PROVENANCE: Possibly M. Bruun-Neergaard; his collection sale (Lugt 8580), Hôtel de Bullion, Paris, August 29–September 7, 1814 (part of lot 129, as "Vue de la villa Borghèse hors des murs de Rome," with five other drawings by Fragonard); possibly Maingot collection, Paris; his estate sale, Paris, November 11–13, 1850 (lot 32); Pierre Defer, Paris; his collection sale, Hôtel de Commissaires-Priseurs, Paris, February 28–March 1, 1859 (lot 367); Edmond and Jules de Goncourt, Paris, their stamp (Lugt 1089) at lower right, recto; their sale, Paris, February 15–17, 1897 (lot 100), to L. Behrendt for Camille Groult; Camille Groult (1832–1908), Paris; his sale, Galerie Georges Petit, Paris, June 21–22, 1920 (lot 149, ill.), to Wildenstein; Richard Owen, 1924; Philip Hofer, Cambridge, Mass.; acquired by Robert Lehman in 1957; The Metropolitan Museum of Art, New York, Robert Lehman Collection, 1975 (1975.1.630)

SELECTED EXHIBITIONS: Szabó 1980, cat. no. 11, ill.; Szabó et al. 1988, cat. no. 33, ill.

SELECTED REFERENCES: Ananoff 1961–70, vol. 3 (1968), no. 1441, vol. 4 (1970), fig. 736; Launay 1991, pp. 301–2, no. 104, colorpl. 14, fig. 149; Haverkamp-Begemann 1999, pp. 340–41, no. 122, ill.

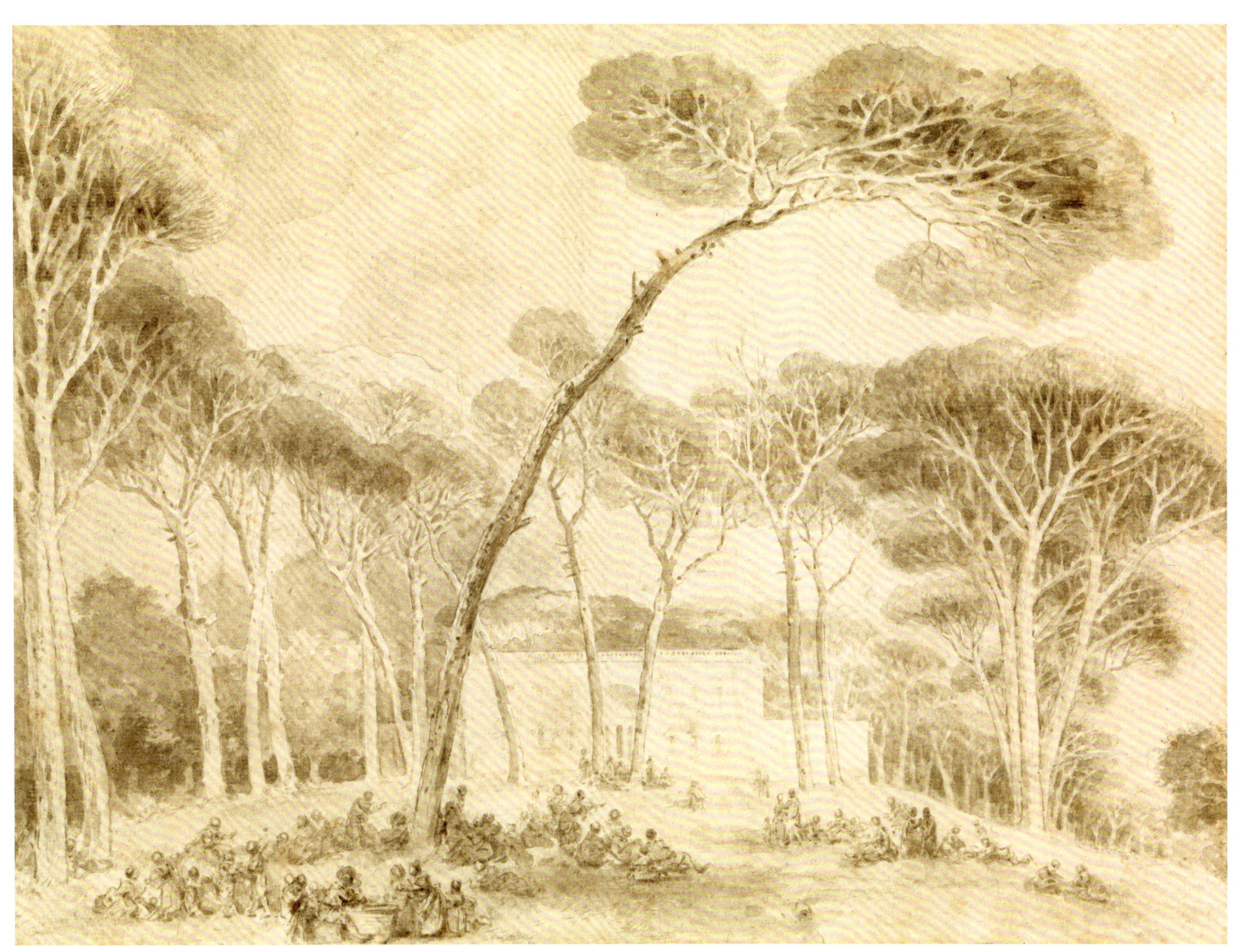

67. *Imaginary Italian Garden*

After 1774
Brush and brown wash over black chalk
11¾ × 16⅝ in. (29.8 × 42.2 cm)

On January 10, 1774, Bergeret recorded in his journal a visit to Piranesi's studio: "After dinner I spent an hour at the home of the famous Piranesi, a draftsman and printmaker who has a curious collection of all kinds of marble antiquities, vases, figures, tombs, and precious materials. He sells it for as much as he can. This is a man who has made immense and curious prints."[1]

This passage could describe the present composition, with its jumble of ancient statues and artifacts, architectural fragments, broken steps, and rampant vegetation. Small figures, perhaps treasure hunters and tourists, explore the area. If there is a subject beyond the assortment of ancient objects distributed so casually, it is the thrill of discovery enjoyed by antiquarians and collectors in Rome. Bergeret as a tourist if not as a treasure hunter frequently visited markets around Rome, such as the one on Piazza Navona.[2] He, and presumably his entourage, also visited artists such as Piranesi, who seems also to have been a dealer.

The connection between Piranesi and the French community of Rome, including that of the Académie de France at Palazzo Mancini, has not been studied adequately.[3] He lived across from the Académie on via del Corso, knew Giovanni Paolo Panini, who taught perspective there, and became friends with Hubert Robert. Therefore, the artistic community in Rome offered opportunities for Fragonard to see Piranesi's work when he was a pensionnaire and later, in 1773–74, as a mature, established artist.

The present drawing is a capriccio, an imaginary scene inspired by experiences in Rome. Fragonard had also seen the hallucinatory inventions of Piranesi's *vedute* (views) and *carceri* (prison scenes). Looking closely, one sees that Fragonard appropriated elements from Piranesi: a multilevel structure with arches and columns is connected by flights of steps and pierced illogically by the large tree in the center. The composition consists of strong opposing diagonals, against which large-scale sculpture and broken artifacts are juxtaposed, their dimensions exaggerated for dramatic effect. At the far right, a large Roman comedy mask (*oscillum*) fills the corner. Fragonard and Bergeret would have seen examples in Roman collections, including at the Vatican, as well as the example of the famous Bocca della Verità (Mouth of Truth) carving displayed on the church of Santa Maria in Cosmedin.

If the present work is an homage to Piranesi, it is also pure Fragonard at his most spontaneous. His broad, loose black chalk underdrawing by this time is a signature, his hand moving rapidly over the surface of the paper. Fragonard's complex layering of rich brown washes, varying from transparent to almost opaque, unifies the composition. A slightly smaller drawing from this same period, with a similar romantic assemblage of ruins and antiquities, is known as *Entrance to the Villa Adriana*.[4] Both drawings were probably made in Paris after 1774. EW

PROVENANCE: K. E. Maison, London; Otto Wertheimer, Paris; [Knoedler & Co., New York]; T. Edward Hanley, Bradford, Pa.; Mr. and Mrs. Eugene V. Thaw, New York; The Morgan Library & Museum, New York, Thaw Collection (2001.59)

SELECTED EXHIBITIONS: Stampfle and Denison 1975, cat. no. 36, ill.; Williams 1978, cat. no. 40, ill.; Near 1981, cat. no. 14, ill.

SELECTED REFERENCE: Ananoff 1961–70, vol. 1 (1961), no. 364, fig. 133.

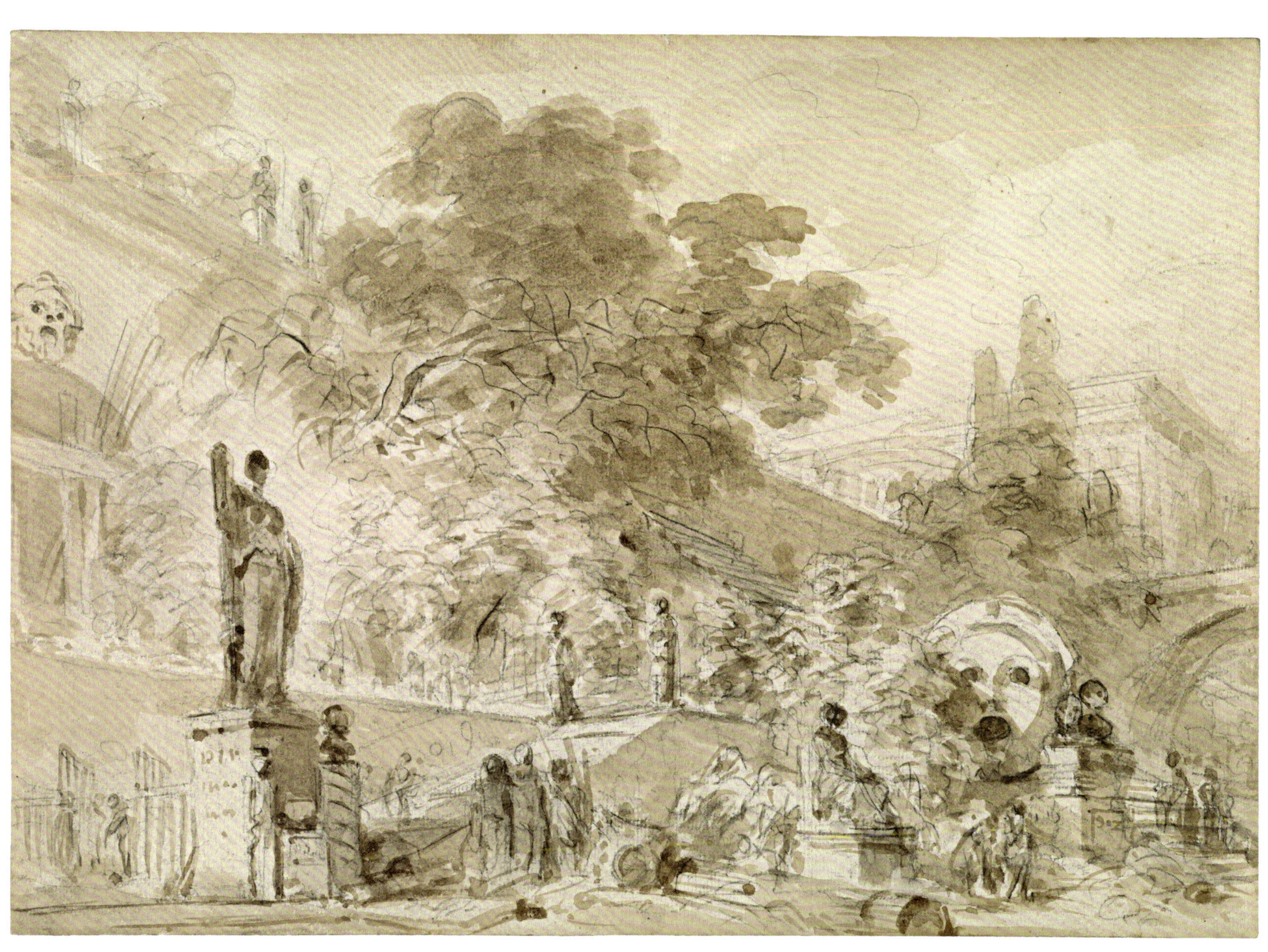

68. *The Island of Love*

Ca. 1770–80
Gouache over traces of black chalk underdrawing
11 × 14¼ in. (27.9 × 36.2 cm)

This spirited and moody gouache and the related canvas in Lisbon (fig. 109) are two of the most admired enigmas in Fragonard's oeuvre. The once traditional title (dating only to 1868), *The Fête at Rambouillet*, was abandoned by Pierre Rosenberg in 1987 in favor of *The Island of Love*, a title given in the auction catalogue when the painting was sold in 1795,[1] although Richard Rand has pointed out that it was described as a "vue d'un Jardin pittoresque" when it first appeared at auction in 1784.[2] This descriptive title is significant, according to Rand, as the first time the term had been applied to a landscape by Fragonard and as a recognition of the innovative nature of the composition, which was "deeply informed by the precepts of the picturesque garden,"[3] a novel aesthetic approach to both the design and experience of gardens pioneered in the 1760s and 1770s by theorists, patrons, and designers who were among the artist's close friends and associates.[4]

The idea that the composition depicts a specific garden, much less a specific event, has been thus largely supplanted by the broader reading that the artist's fictive garden, with its overgrown hedges, tumbling cascade, and elegant pleasure seekers, reflects the type of aesthetic experience that would have appealed to the connoisseurs and *amateurs* who were Fragonard's patrons. Liberated from the idea of *The Island of Love* as a topographical record, scholars have put forward various alternative interpretations. Ewa Lajer-Burcharth, for instance, interprets the composition in terms of female morphology, seeing the hollows in the dense foliage as womblike and related to the idea of creative generation.[5] Rand sees in the sinuous paths of the *jardin pittoresque* an analogy for movement within society, alluding to liberty combined with menace and instability.[6]

The oil painting to which this gouache is related was presumably a commission from Jean Benjamin Delaborde, at whose sale it appeared in 1784.[7] An amateur musician and composer, Delaborde was named *premier valet de chambre* for King Louis XV in 1762 and *fermier général* in 1774. He certainly would have known Fragonard by about 1770, when his mistress, the dancer Marie Madeleine Guimard, commissioned the artist to decorate her *hôtel particulier* on the rue de la Chaussée-d'Antin;[8] the painting has been dated to about this time or sometimes more broadly to about 1768–75.[9] As for the date and first owner of the gouache, we are left to speculate. Our assumption is that the gouache, like *The Little Park* (cat. 34), postdates the oil and was made not simply as a repetition but as a separate work with a different scale and medium, ultimately producing a different mood. While the predominant greens and yellows of the Gulbenkian painting evoke the late afternoon light of a summer's day, the gouache produces a mistier and more dreamlike effect with its grayed palette, often referred to as silvery, offset by touches of gold and ocher. For Etienne-François

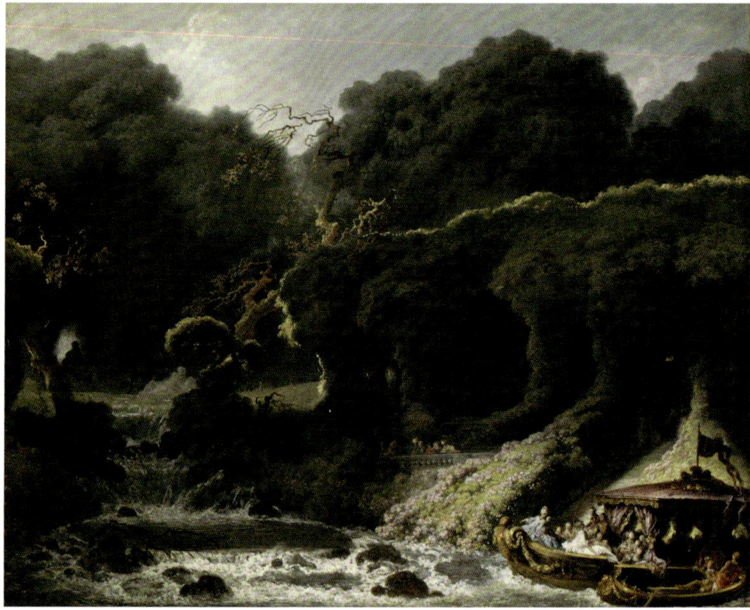

Fig. 109. Jean Honoré Fragonard, *The Island of Love*, ca. 1768–70. Oil on canvas, 27⅞ × 35½ in. (71 × 90 cm). Museu Calouste Gulbenkian, Lisbon

Haro, writing in the preface of the 1868 sale catalogue, the gouache was a "unique pearl in the master's jewel box."[10]

In 2000, Rosenberg drew attention to two eighteenth-century sale catalogues that listed gouaches with a description matching that of the *Island of Love* as "in the taste of" Fragonard. It appears that these are not two but a single gouache, which was acquired by Jean Antoine Hubert, Vassal de Saint-Hubert, at a sale in 1776, where it was catalogued as being by Nicolas Pérignon,[11] and then sold at his sale two years later with an attribution to Simon Mathurin Lantara.[12] Either this gouache of shifting attribution was an early copy, now lost, or perhaps it was the present drawing misunderstood as a copy. As Fragonard only rarely worked in this medium, there is a paucity of works with which to compare it. However, details such as the way the distinct, impastoed brush marks of the craggy tree overlay the thinly painted and blended mass of more distant foliage are similar to aspects of his landscapes on canvas. Eunice Williams has also likened the tiny dabs of highlights that lend texture to the hedges to the pointillist technique Fragonard developed for the landscapes in brown wash he made on his second trip to Italy.[13]

As with many of his landscapes of the 1770s, *The Island of Love* presents a garden as an imagined setting, not for pastoral or rustic scenes but for upper-class diversions. Also in keeping with his approach during this period, Fragonard seems to have preferred using

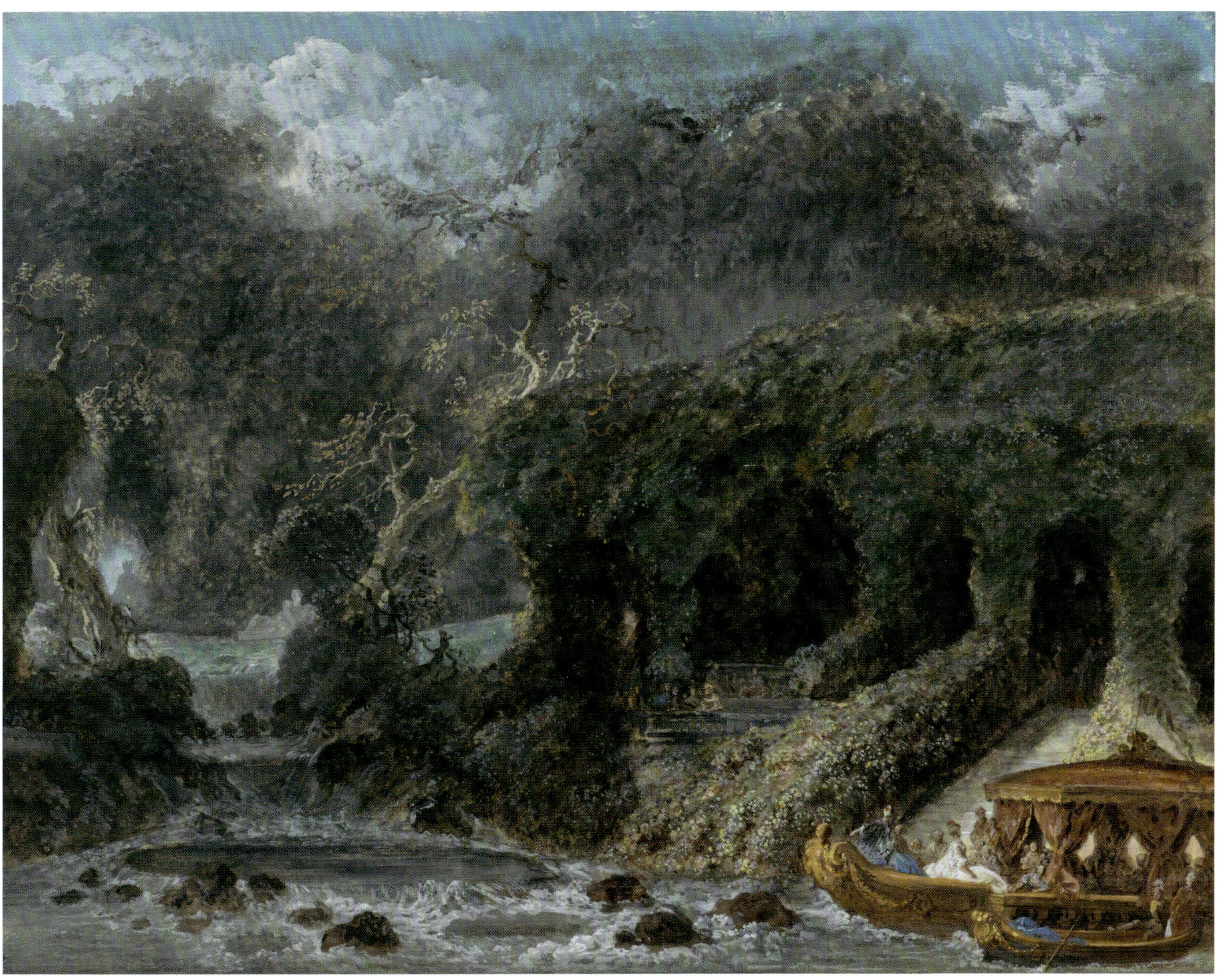

an assimilated vocabulary of motifs and forms as a creative springboard rather than describing an identifiable place. A gilded pleasure boat bearing fashionable company navigates perilously close to the rocky cascades. The shadowy interiors of the *cabinets de verdure*—outdoor rooms created with trimmed hedges—dwarf their inhabitants. Such elements, which were characteristic of picturesque garden design, retain the indelible imprint of Italy, recalling, on a tamer scale, the drama and mystery of the Villa d'Este garden at Tivoli, with its stepped cascades and shady grottoes.[14] PS

PROVENANCE: Daniel Saint (1778–1847), miniature painter; his collection sale, Hôtel des Ventes, Paris, May 7, 1846 (lot 287); Eugène Tondu; his estate sale (Lugt 28476), Hôtel Drouot, Paris, April 24–26, 1865 (lot 127); F. de Villars; his collection sale (Lugt 30318), Hôtel Drouot, Paris, March 13, 1868 (lot 37); Etienne-François Haro (1827–1897), the great-nephew of Hubert Robert, Paris; Mme Périer, Paris; Sigismond Bardac (1856–1919), Paris; by descent to Joseph Bardac, Paris; [Wildenstein & Co., New York]; acquired in 1926 by Mr. and Mrs. Herbert N. Straus, New York; by descent to Herbert N. Straus, New York; sale, Christie's, London, July 3, 2007 (lot 137); private collection

SELECTED EXHIBITIONS: Williams 1978, pp. 130–31, cat. no. 51; Rosenberg 1988, pp. 357–58, cat. no. 169; Stein and Holmes 1999, pp. 166–68, cat. no. 71 (entry by Mary Tavener Holmes).

SELECTED REFERENCES: Ananoff 1961–70, vol. 1 (1961), pp. 118–19, no. 246, vol. 2 (1963), p. 303; Cuzin 1988b, pp. 101, 253 n. 9; Rand 1995, pp. 196–203; Rand 2001.

69. *A Young Woman Seated on the Ground*

Ca. 1770–73
Red chalk over traces of graphite
8¾ × 11⅛ in. (22.2 × 28.1 cm)
Inscription: on mount, at lower left, below image, in pen and brown ink, "Fragonard"

70. *A Young Woman Standing with Her Hands on Her Hips (La Coquette)*

Ca. 1770–73
Red chalk over black chalk underdrawing
14⅜ × 8¼ in. (36.5 × 21 cm)

71. *A Young Woman Seated on a Chair*

Ca. 1770–75
Red chalk
13⅜ × 9 in. (34 × 22.9 cm)
Blind stamp of mount maker François Renaud (Lugt 1042) at lower right; "FR" and a blind stamp "PH" on the mount

These three sheets belong to a large, amorphous group of red chalk drawings of young women shown full length, either seated or standing and either indoors or out.[1] Stylish in their dress and at ease in their poses, the subjects elude easy categorization. They lack the specificity of either portraits or drawings made for *gravures de mode* (costume plates), and they do not display narrative genre elements. Scholars have long dated the group to the decade of about 1775 to 1785, following Fragonard's return from his second trip to Italy. This consensus has nourished, and has been nourished by, a continuing fascination with the identity of the sitters. During this period, Fragonard had at hand two young members of his family who could have modeled for him: his sister-in-law Marguerite Gérard and his daughter, Rosalie. Marguerite, whose legendary beauty had long been the basis for innuendo (see "Fact, Fiction, Function, and Process" in this volume, pp. 1–13), was living in Paris by at least 1775 and perhaps for some years before that.[2] Rosalie, whose death of consumption in 1788 devastated the family, would have been sixteen in 1785.

However, this charming scenario of the artist sketching his young daughter and sister-in-law in pretty dresses and carefree poses may not ultimately be borne out by the facts. One piece of evidence that has not been given sufficient attention is the dating of two prints related to this group of drawings. In the 1760s and 1770s, large-scale virtuoso chalk drawings enjoyed a great popularity that was closely tied to the invention of chalk-manner engraving in the late 1750s.[3] Seeing Gilles Demarteau's stunning facsimiles on view in the Salon of 1767, Diderot raved about how much they were like real drawings:

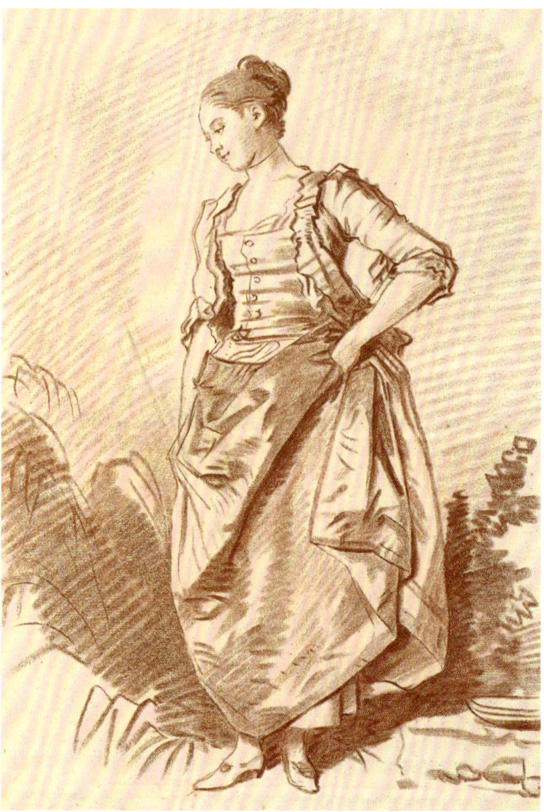

Fig. 110. Gilles Demarteau (French, 1722–1776), after Jean Honoré Fragonard, *Study of a Woman*, ca. 1772–73. Crayon-manner print, 14 × 9⅞ in. (35.5 × 25 cm). Bibliothèque Nationale de France, Paris (Ef. 9 rés.)

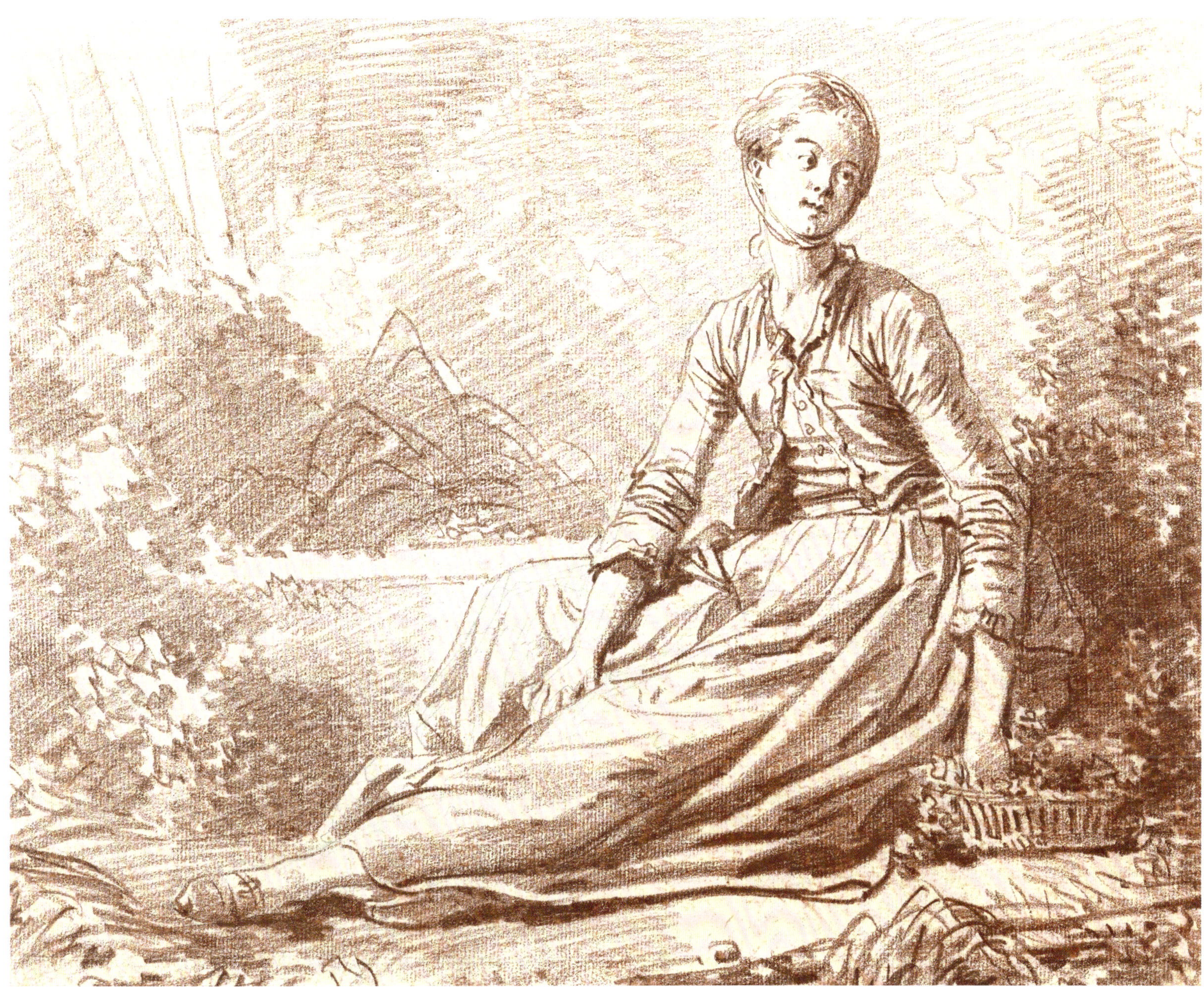

CAT 69

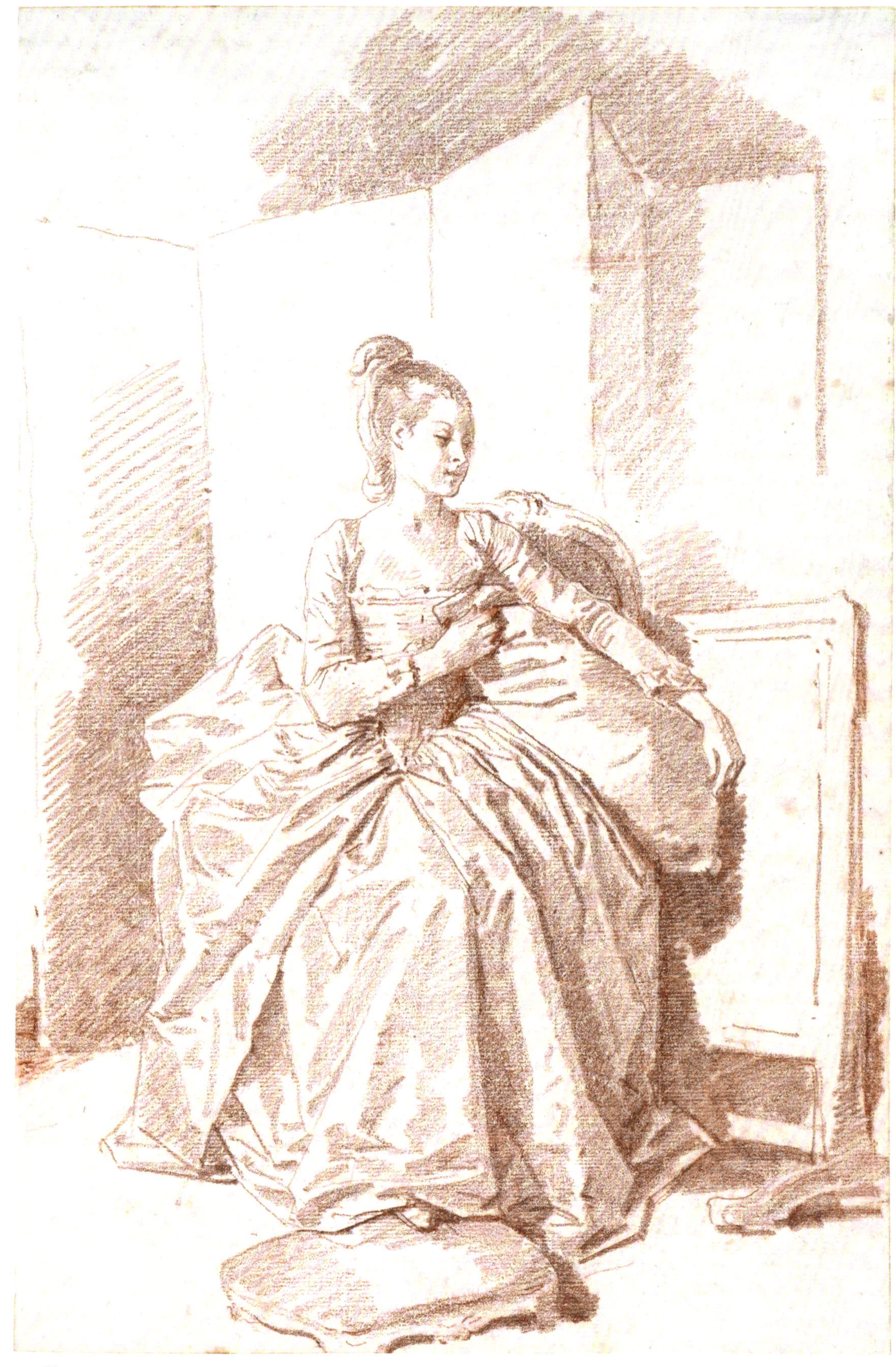

CAT 71

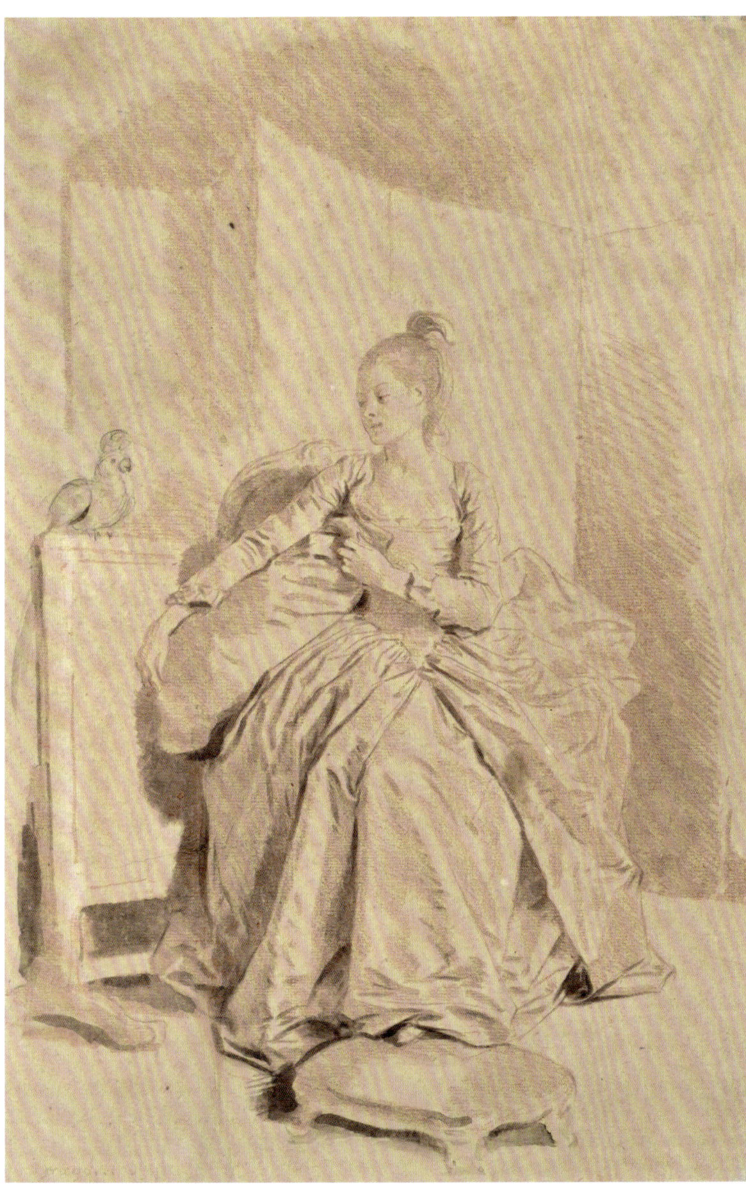

Fig. 111. Jean Honoré Fragonard, *Young Girl with a Parrot,* ca. 1770–73. Red chalk counterproof, reworked in brush and brown wash, 14 × 9¼ in. (35.4 × 23.4 cm). Fine Arts Museums of San Francisco, Achenbach Foundation for Graphic Arts, Bequest of Mrs. Henry Potter Russell (1966.54)

The admiration for this type of drawing among the nineteenth-century collectors who rediscovered Fragonard is best articulated in the tactile prose of Edmond and Jules de Goncourt:

> Still more vigorous are those studies in *sanguine* of women, drawn from the life, finished in a single rapid sitting, in which the red chalk, almost crushed under the artist's pressure, seeming to flog the backgrounds with its corkscrew markings, brutalizes the stuffs, the trimming of a dress, rumples triumphantly the fanciful fripperies and adornments of costume, attacks with the same force the features, hacking them with shadow, and performs the miracle of revealing, beneath such violent handling, the smile of a pretty woman.[13]

PS

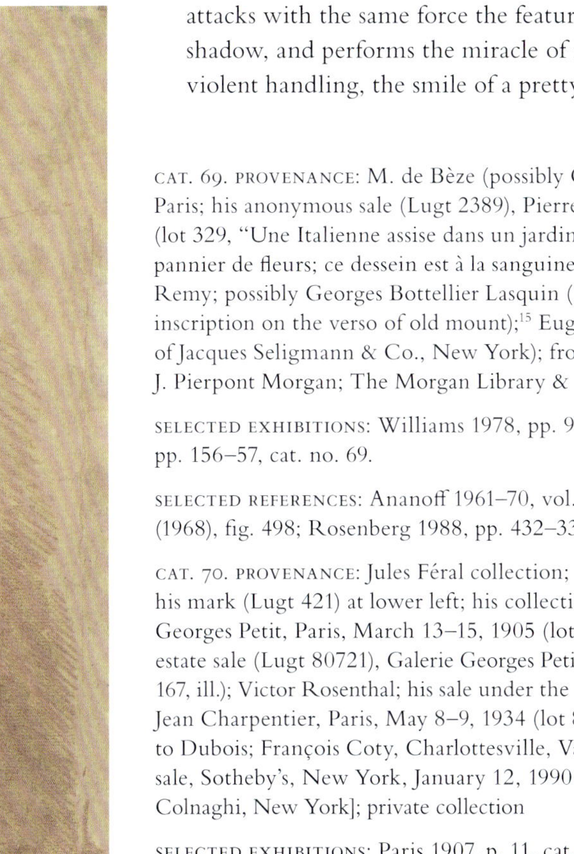

CAT. 69. PROVENANCE: M. de Bèze (possibly Claude Guillaume de Besse),[14] Paris; his anonymous sale (Lugt 2389), Pierre Remy, Paris, April 3, 1775 (lot 329, "Une Italienne assise dans un jardin; elle a sa main gauche dans un pannier de fleurs; ce dessein est à la sanguine"), sold for 40.2 livres to Pierre Remy; possibly Georges Bottellier Lasquin (1882–1932), Paris (according to inscription on the verso of old mount);[15] Eugene Glaenzer (d. 1923, manager of Jacques Seligmann & Co., New York); from whom purchased in 1907 by J. Pierpont Morgan; The Morgan Library & Museum, New York (I, 289a)

SELECTED EXHIBITIONS: Williams 1978, pp. 90–91, cat. no. 31; Denison 1993, pp. 156–57, cat. no. 69.

SELECTED REFERENCES: Ananoff 1961–70, vol. 1 (1961), p. 103, no. 197, vol. 3 (1968), fig. 498; Rosenberg 1988, pp. 432–33, under cat. no. 203, fig. 8.

CAT. 70. PROVENANCE: Jules Féral collection; Alfred Beurdeley (1847–1919), his mark (Lugt 421) at lower left; his collection sale (Lugt 63070), Galerie Georges Petit, Paris, March 13–15, 1905 (lot 69, ill.), unsold; Beurdeley estate sale (Lugt 80721), Galerie Georges Petit, Paris, June 8–10, 1920 (lot 167, ill.); Victor Rosenthal; his sale under the initials M. A. G . . . , Galerie Jean Charpentier, Paris, May 8–9, 1934 (lot 89, ill.), sold for 36,000 francs to Dubois; François Coty, Charlottesville, Va.; Mr. and Mrs. O. W. Smith; sale, Sotheby's, New York, January 12, 1990 (lot 123); [purchased at the sale by Colnaghi, New York]; private collection

SELECTED EXHIBITIONS: Paris 1907, p. 11, cat. no. 161 (as in the collection of A. Beurdeley); Ongpin 1997, cat. no. 40.

SELECTED REFERENCES: Portalis 1889, vol. 2, p. 305, ill. opp. p. 240 (as in the collection of M. Féral); Ananoff 1961–70, vol. 1 (1961), p. 92, no. 165, vol. 2 (1963), p. 300, fig. 343, vol. 4 (1970), p. 349; Rosenberg 1988, pp. 432–33, under cat. no. 203, fig. 3.

CAT. 71. PROVENANCE: Edmond Filleul; sale, Sotheby's, Monaco, June 21, 1991 (lot 13); [Galerie de Bayser, Paris]; The Morgan Library & Museum, New York, Purchased on the Sunny Crawford von Bulow Fund 1978 (1993.6)

SELECTED EXHIBITION: Denison et al. 1995, pp. 38–39, cat. no. 15.

72. *The Dreamer*

Ca. 1775–80
Brush and brown wash over black chalk underdrawing
12⅛ × 8½ in. (30.8 × 21.6 cm)

Sitting in front of her dressing table, a young woman has dozed off. The artist has captured her in a natural pose, sitting sideways in an armchair with one arm casually resting on the back of the chair and her hand supporting her inclined head. Her other hand holds an open book on her lap. The shape of her little flat hat embellished with feathers is reflected in the mirror on the dressing table. The fine, light brush-strokes describe, without dwelling on, a few details of her outfit, such as the gathers of the sleeve knotted at the elbow and the shawl with its ruffled edge enveloping her shoulders, its ends meeting over the bust. The darker color of the shawl contrasts with the satin dress, where all the light is concentrated. A rather generic costume, it would have been in style over a long period, from the 1760s to the 1780s. Except for the stripes on the upholstery covering the armchair and on the tablecloth, the decor is very plain. Is it to make it less austere that the artist has added two female figures on the left? Described with a broad and heavy brush, they form a contrast with the refinement of the dozing woman. The face of the onlooker to the right is almost a caricature.

It would be in vain to seek the identities of the figures shown here among the artist's intimates, as has been attempted. In our opinion, the scene is more likely a variation on the theme of the woman captured in a private setting, of which other examples by Fragonard contain comparable elements. In each case, the artist did not limit himself to the simple description of a model posing in costume; he sought to give a more narrative character to the exercise. *The Letter*[1] offers the most finished example of this type of mise-en-scène, showing a young man in Spanish costume surprising a young lady sitting on a sofa. Except for a small ruffle wrapped around the neck, she is dressed in the same way as the central figure in the present drawing and sports an identical hat, similarly adorned with dark feathers, her hair gathered into a chignon. In the Metropolitan sheet, the simple dress of the two women in the background suggests a lower social rank. By their gestures they hint at a little intrigue, one pointing to the sleeper mockingly while the other, a finger on her mouth, signals her to be silent. This second figure, with her bonnet and small dark cape, is found, but described with greater care, in *The Confidence*.[2] In that drawing she contrasts with her companion, who is dressed in a more sophisticated manner and wears a ribbon bracelet on each of her wrists, like our dreamer.[3] The beautiful young lady in *The Reading*[4] is shown sitting in a similar pose as the dreamer and in a comparable armchair, another element that connects these two works. It is difficult to determine the chronological order of the related sheets, to which another version of *The Dreamer* (fig. 112) should be added. Several factors encouraged Eunice Williams to place that one before the Metropolitan's version. However, the layout of the Boston version shows a better integration of the two standing women and less roughness in the application of the wash in the background, perhaps reflecting a more developed consideration of the composition. The term *replica* in any case is not appropriate for any of these versions, which might more accurately be characterized as variations on a theme. MADV

Fig. 112. Jean Honoré Fragonard, *The Dreamer*, ca. 1775–80. Brown wash and watercolor, 12⅛ × 8⅛ in. (30.8 × 20.6 cm). Museum of Fine Arts, Boston (65.2566)

PROVENANCE: Possibly anonymous sale (Lugt 5097), Paris, July 8, 1793 (part of lot 66, "Deux autres Dessins lavés au bistre; l'un représente une jeune fille tenant un livre à la main; l'autre deux femmes qui assises causent ensemble"); Baronne de Ruble, Paris (1889); Alfred Beurdeley (1847–1919), his stamp (Lugt 421) at lower right; his collection sale (Lugt 63070), Galerie Georges Petit, Paris, March 13–15, 1905 (lot 71), 20,000 francs to Cognacq; Ernest Cognacq until at least 1921; Gabriel Cognacq; his estate sale, Paris, May 14, 1952 (lot 1, repr.), 3,100,000 francs; [Mrs. Walter Feilchenfeldt, Zurich]; acquired by Robert Lehman from Feilchenfeldt in April 1965; The Metropolitan Museum of Art, New York, Robert Lehman Collection, 1975 (1975.1.627)

SELECTED EXHIBITIONS: G. Wildenstein 1921, cat. no. 145; Paris 1931, cat. no. 26; Daulte 1954, cat. no. 77, pl. XVII; Williams 1978, cat. no. 48; Rosenberg 1988, p. 559, cat. no. 271.

SELECTED REFERENCES: Portalis 1889, vol. 1, ill. opp. p. 140, vol. 2, p. 305; Ananoff 1961–70, vol. 1 (1961), no. 58, and no. 179 (for the drawing in the 1793 sale), vol. 2 (1963), p. 295, vol. 4 (1970), p. 347, fig. 682; Haverkamp-Begemann 1999, no. 120 (entry by Mary Tavener Holmes and Donald Posner).

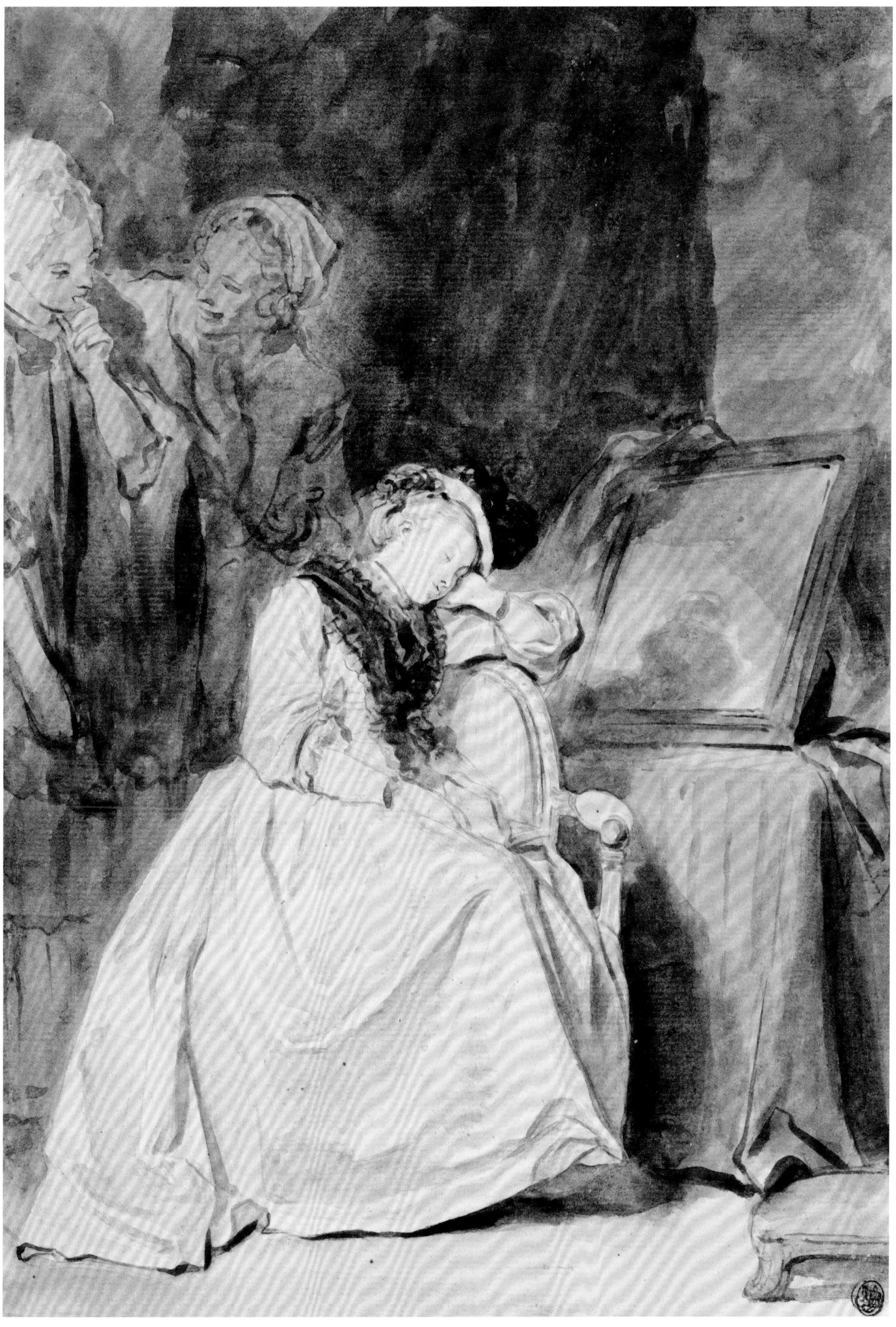

73. *The Bread Box*

Ca. 1775–77
Brown wash over black chalk underdrawing
10½ × 15⅜ in. (26.5 × 39 cm)

This particularly seductive sheet takes its title from the large wooden chest at its center, which serves to keep bread dry. An equally apt title would be "The Distribution of Bread." Two women preside over the scene. One, on the right, plunges her arm into the bin to take out the large loaves that the second passes out with one hand while keeping the bin's cover open with the other. The composition is built around this balanced movement in an especially skillful and harmonious way. On the left, very young customers press forward, accompanied by a bearded old man—a recurring figure in the artist's oeuvre—leaning on his cane and a young woman perched on a low wall, a basket resting on the ground behind her. Her attention is focused on two squabbling toddlers, whom she attempts to calm with a gesture of her hand. Another child restrains a dog as they both ardently covet the loaf a small girl cautiously grasps. On the right are two other dogs; the one standing upright, with two paws placed on the shoulders of his young master, who has already been served, seems to be demanding his share. The scene takes place in an indefinable setting; behind the figures are a clock and planks leaning against a wall. Branches fill the empty area of the wall above the bread box, while clothes and a hat hang on the right. It is not strictly speaking a bakery but rather a sort of storeroom where villagers come to stock up on bread. The brilliant radiance expressed by both the delicately nuanced blond wash and the intense lighting falling on the bin evokes a sunny region. Perhaps Fragonard observed a similar scene in his native Provence? One is struck by the naturalness of the poses. The slightest details ring true, even the folds on the purveyor's apron, part of which is pulled over the edge of the trunk and used to wipe off the surplus flour covering the loaves.

This version seems to precede, rather than prepare, a second one that is executed in wash with slightly more contrast over a similarly understated black chalk sketch (fig. 113). In this second version, the number of actors is reduced to eleven; the delightful group on the right formed by the little boy and his dog has disappeared. A muscular man has replaced the woman occupied with retrieving the loaves from the bin, while the young woman seated on the left now stands, holding the dog's leash, her basket on her left arm. But the main difference lies in the large format of the second sheet.[1] By treating it on a monumental scale, the artist has made this picture of rural daily life an inspiring subject, a tone in alignment with the treatment of the central female figure, at once imposing and full of nobility. Bread, the essential foundation of the peasant food supply in that period, was a constant preoccupation, rising prices or shortages being at the root of many revolts in pre-Revolutionary France. But Fragonard's intention was not to denounce poverty. If we note that the adults are barefoot, it is also true that the unruly children appear to be more gourmand than famished. The artist invites us, rather, to a celebration of country life at its simplest, joyous and full of human warmth. MADV

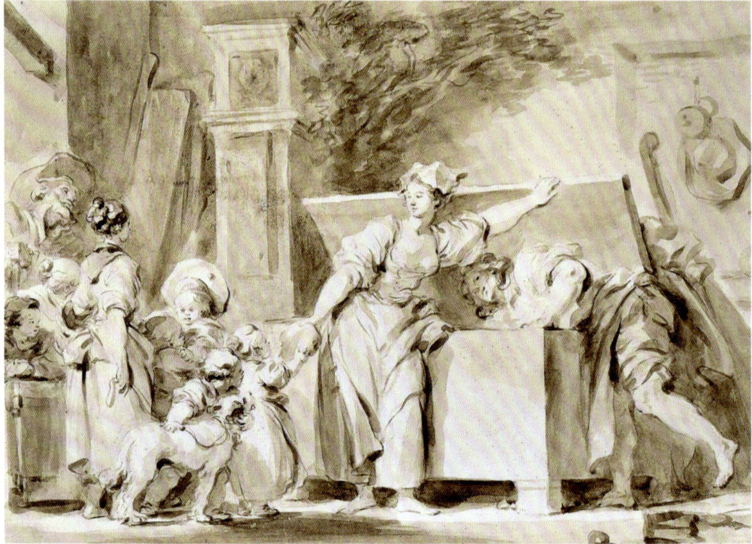

Fig. 113. Jean Honoré Fragonard, *The Bread Box*, ca. 1775–77. Black chalk and wash, 16⅝ × 23⅜ in. (42.1 × 59.3 cm). Private collection

PROVENANCE: Private collection, France, 1939 (according to the 1997 auction catalogue); sale, Paris, April 24, 1997 (lot 159, repr.); [Didier Aaron, Paris, London, and New York, 1998]; private collection

SELECTED EXHIBITION: Grasselli et al. 2007, cat. no. 64, ill. (entry by Margaret Morgan Grasselli).

SELECTED REFERENCE: Reuter et al. 2013, p. 120, fig. 1 (entry by Marie-Anne Dupuy-Vachey).

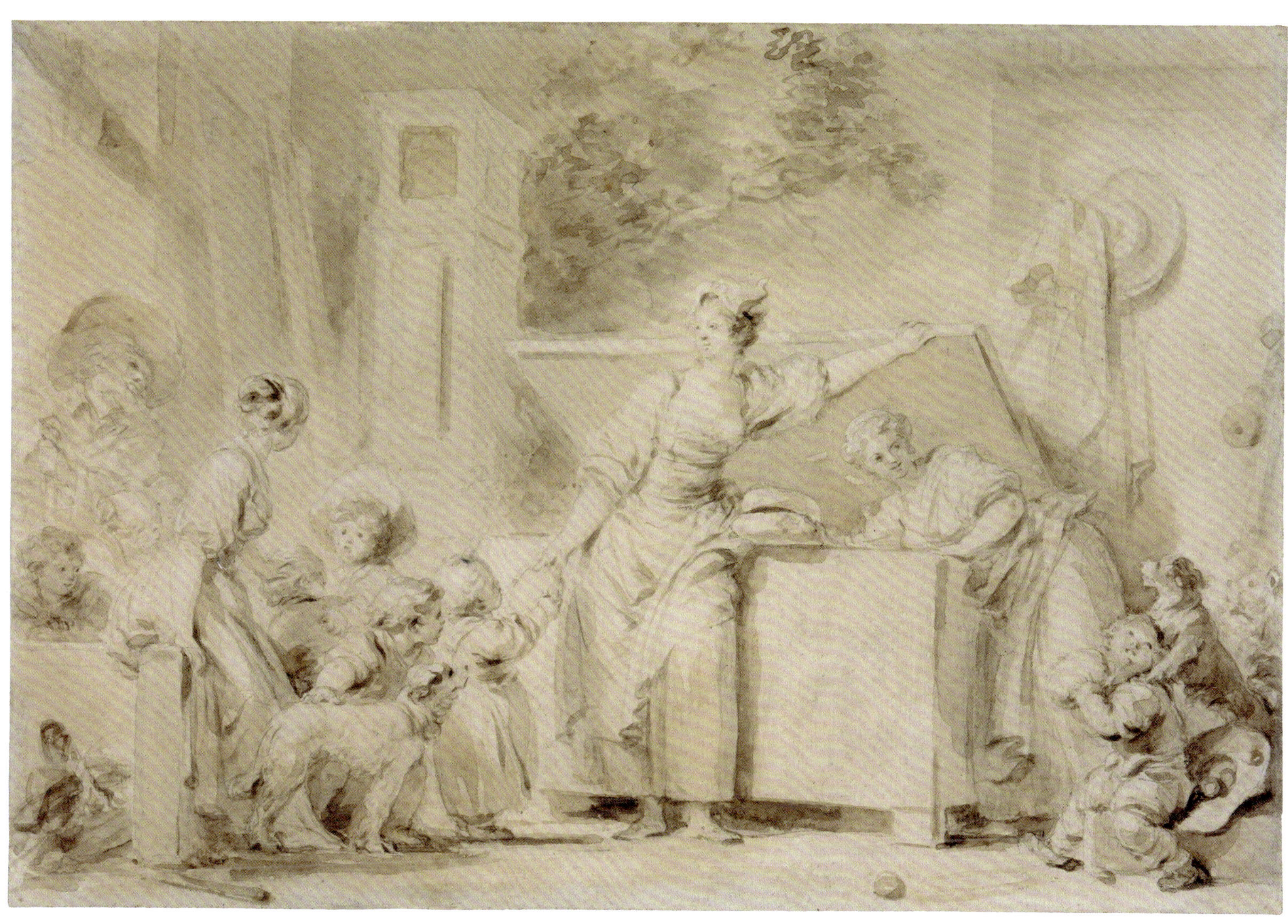

74. *Sketch of a Family of Farm Workers*

Ca. 1773–78
Black chalk
9⅜ × 7¼ in. (23.8 × 18.2 cm)

Fragonard's eye for the theater of human life, both comic and compassionate, brought him to parks and villas, to farms and kitchens, to bedrooms and salons. Here, on a sketchbook page, he made a schematic record of a family of estate workers posed near the gate to the yard where they live and work.[1] The real location is not as important as the sense of the quiet and seriousness of the figures, who are defined in a few lines. On the left, members of a family are seated in front of their dwelling, with children at their knees and chickens almost underfoot. On the opposite side of the entrance are other women with children. Through the open gates we can see a stand of trees and a road.

The location here is similar to that shown in *The Service Yard of a Château, with Poultry* (cat. 51), where turkeys rule the roost. This informal sketch captures the essentials—the sitters and setting—with a few strokes of black chalk. The date is difficult to determine because sketchbooks are tools of rapid notation instinctive to the artist. The page is evidence, however, of how Fragonard repeatedly observed scenes of everyday life. It might have been drawn on the visit to the château with the turkeys or to another, such as Nègrepelisse (cat. 53).

The drawing was attached at the corners to an important document, the printed announcement for Fragonard and Marguerite Gérard's etching *The Genius of Franklin*, published in 1778. The repurposed sheet served as a protective backing and was not visible to the viewer. A stylistically similar black chalk sketch of a coach and horses crossing a bridge (fig. 114), from the collection of I. Q. van Regteren Altena, was sold at Christie's, Paris, on March 25, 2015. It, too, was mounted on the back of the printed announcement for the 1778 etching. Both sheets were part of the same lot (114) in the Christie's 1972 sale, suggesting that these black chalk sketches have a long shared history, going back to Fragonard and his family. EW

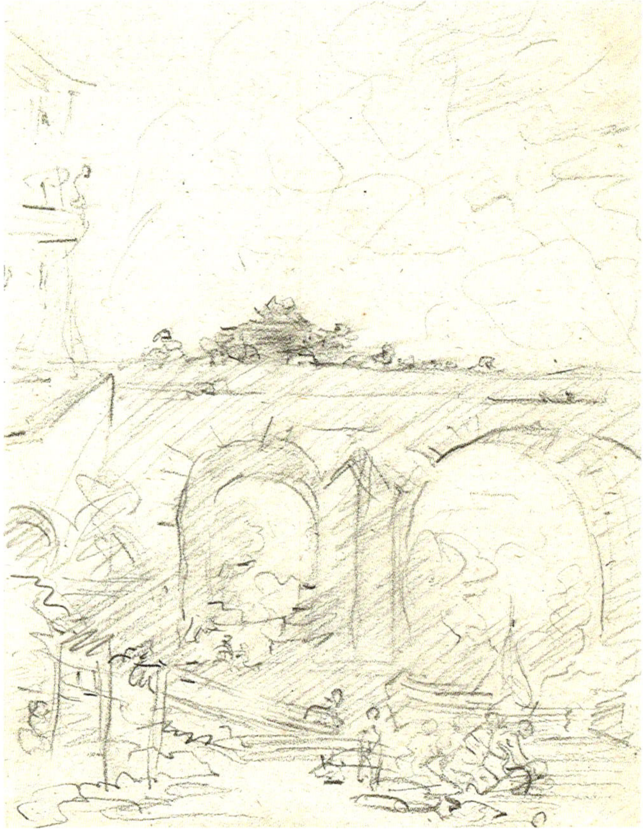

Fig. 114. Jean Honoré Fragonard, sketchbook page showing a coach and horses crossing a bridge, ca. 1775–80. Black chalk, 8⅛ × 6⅜ in. (20.5 × 16.2 cm). Private collection, New York

PROVENANCE: Private collection, France; sale, Christie's, London, March 28, 1972 (part of lot 114), purchased by Adolphe Stein, Paris and Lyon; by descent to Peggy Stein; sale, Christie's, Paris, March 22, 2007 (lot 296); private collection

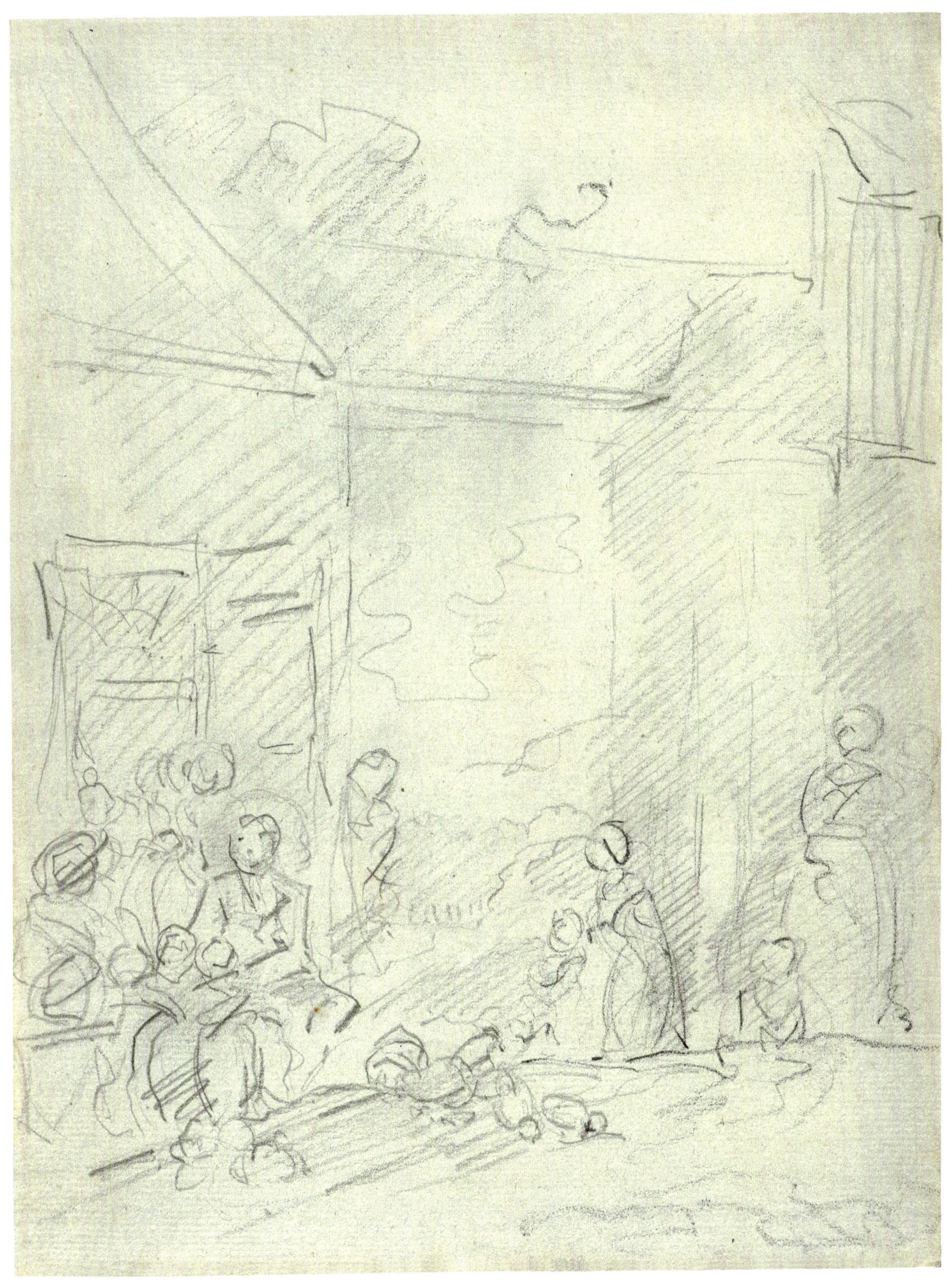

75. *Reading in the Kitchen*

Ca. 1775–80
Brown wash over black chalk underdrawing
13⅜ × 17⅞ in. (33.8 × 45.2 cm)

Given the number of drawings and paintings that Fragonard chose to set in a kitchen, we can surmise that this room was for the artist the equivalent of a sort of small theater where he sought inspiration. It is true that the kitchen was at the time the principal, and often only, room in many cottages. This essential gathering place is the setting for many little scenes that the artist transposes and interprets in his way, always retaining only their most cheerful elements. His humor and the tenderness of his vision are expressed more freely there than in the refined and constrained atmosphere of Parisian salons. This rustic theme punctuates his entire oeuvre, and many motifs are repeated from one sheet to another, proving that it is a matter each time of recombining elements rather than simply transcribing reality. The chimney, with its vaulted opening and deep hearth, constitutes the central focus. Around it, figures—sometimes up to a dozen, of all ages and invariably accompanied by animals—are distributed like actors in a play whose plot is left to the spectator's imagination. In these everyday dramas, one might find an old man sleeping while cooks stir the pot,[1] fritters being prepared for a toddler's feast day,[2] or listeners gathering around for a reading.[3]

The beautiful drawing exhibited here offers a sort of synthesis of the different scenes and motifs developed in the 1760s and 1770s. Here, the dozing old man can be found on the left, while at the center a young woman seated on the ground absentmindedly stirs the basin heating over the fire. Like the other figures, her attention is monopolized by the reading of the young woman who leans against a column shaft and rests a foot on the step. Her slim figure, plainly but elegantly attired, and her lovely little headdress with feathers denote her as a city person socially more elevated than her audience, which is simply dressed and probably illiterate. What can be the subject of her reading? Given the age of the very attentive little boy positioned behind her, it is probably not the local gazette, but rather a story or a captivating tale. The large volume abandoned in the foreground could indicate that a reading session during the meal preparation is perhaps not unusual. The slightly *di sotto in su* angle suggests that the artist placed himself on a low chair or perhaps even on the ground, like the two children on the right. Unlike other scenes of this type, in which the black chalk sketch is extremely evident and nervous, here it is calmer and more discreet. Rather than serve as an initial study, in this case the sketch provides indications or markers to guide the brush. The mastery and confidence with which the wash has been applied recall certain sheets from the second journey to Italy. The distribution of light in different areas is especially successful, as are the gradations of wash used to construct the space. The highly finished nature of this composition is perhaps explained by the existence of two directly connected drawings, both upright in format, which appear to be preparatory studies. One shows the reader, the little acolyte behind her, and the child on the far right;[4] the other features the central area of the scene, with the cook, the child with a cat, the dog, and the couple in the background.[5] Finally, a painting has recently reappeared that shows our composition with minimal variants (fig. 115). MADV

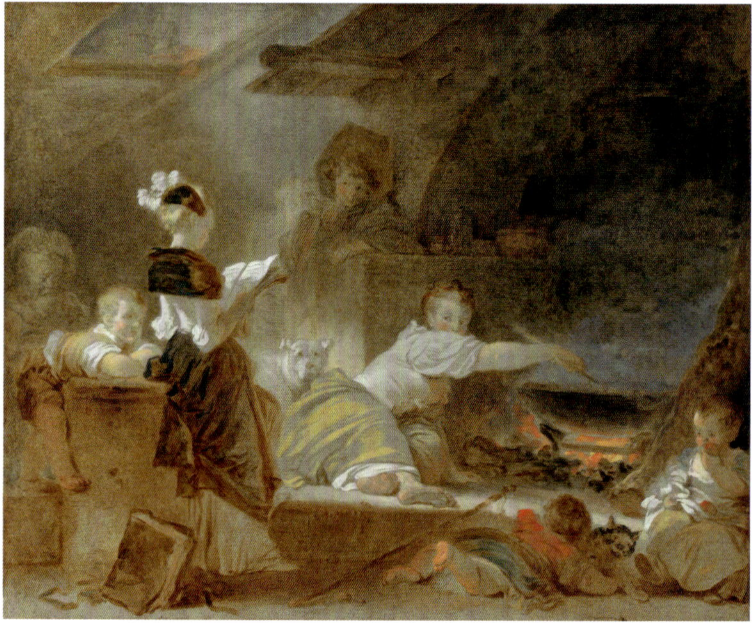

Fig. 115. Jean Honoré Fragonard, *Reading in the Kitchen*, ca. 1775–80. Oil on canvas, 23 × 29 in. (58.3 × 73.4 cm). Private collection, courtesy Etienne Bréton/Saint Honoré Art Consulting

PROVENANCE: In the same French family from the early 19th century until the late 1980s; private collection

SELECTED EXHIBITION: Rosenberg 1988, cat. no. 279.

SELECTED REFERENCES: Reuter et al. 2013, pp. 237–38, fig. 14 (entry by Marie-Anne Dupuy-Vachey); Wall 2014, p. 191 n. 25, fig. 203, pl. LXX.

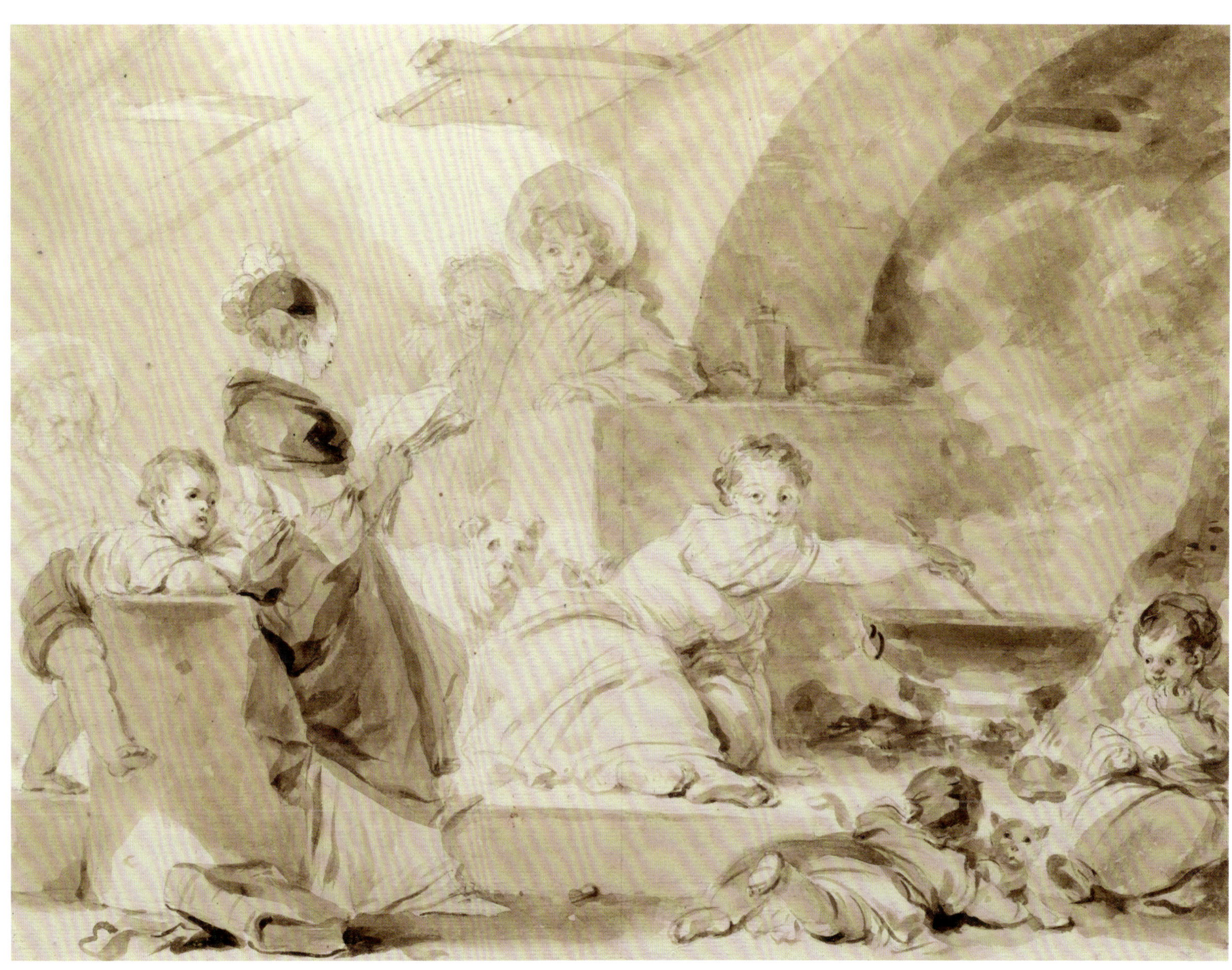

76. *Benevolent Women on Horseback Visiting a Village*

Ca. 1775–80
Black chalk, incised
13¾ × 16¾ in. (34.8 × 42.5 cm)

Many artists put their initial ideas for compositions down on paper in quick sketches called *premières pensées*, or first thoughts. What is unusual about this drawing, indeed what gives it its startling modernity, is the scale of the sheet Fragonard chose for committing these first ideas to paper. One can almost feel the bravado in the rhythm and variety of marks, from the blunt, geometric outlines that render the faces and limbs of the peasant family in the lower left to the emphatic jabs and wiggles that indicate trees and foliage at the upper left. The artist's touch lightens slightly to convey, in more attenuated strokes, the elegant contours of the horses and their female riders.

In style and function, this drawing displays a clear parallel to the Lehman *Children Dancing in a Park* (cat. 77), a sheet of nearly identical dimensions, which features on the verso a similarly broad compositional sketch in black chalk. This one, like the Lehman study, is incised throughout (see p. 65, fig. 56, detail), presumably as a mechanical means to transfer the composition to another sheet. A likely candidate for that second version is a wash and watercolor drawing that appeared at auction in Berlin in 2013 (fig. 116).[1] Having a fully resolved composition with only minimal underdrawing, the finished version uses layers of lightly applied pale gray wash and watercolor to create a delicate aesthetic effect quite distinct from the spirited, quasi-abstract quality of the present sheet. There is no evidence that a painted version ever existed.

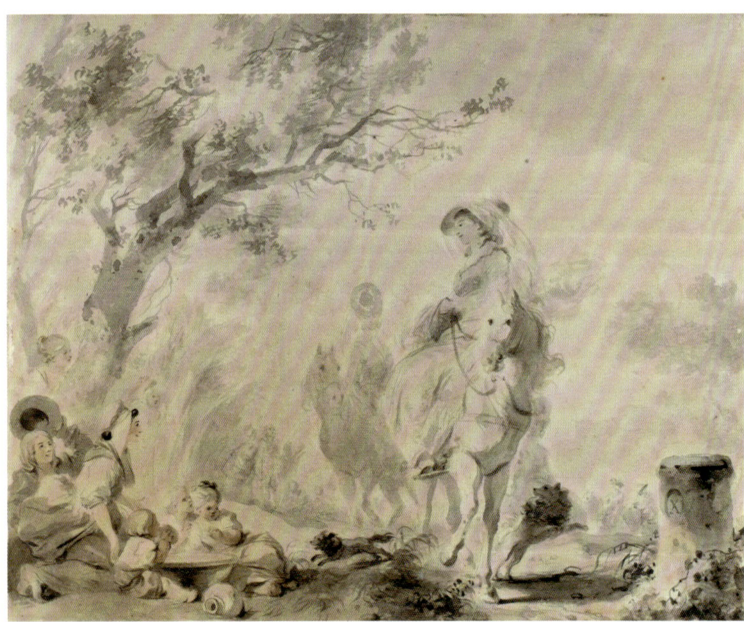

Fig. 116. Jean Honoré Fragonard, *Benevolent Women on Horseback Visiting a Village*, ca. 1780–85. Brush and brown and gray wash with touches of watercolor over black chalk underdrawing, 13⅞ × 17½ in. (35 × 44.4 cm). Private collection, Germany

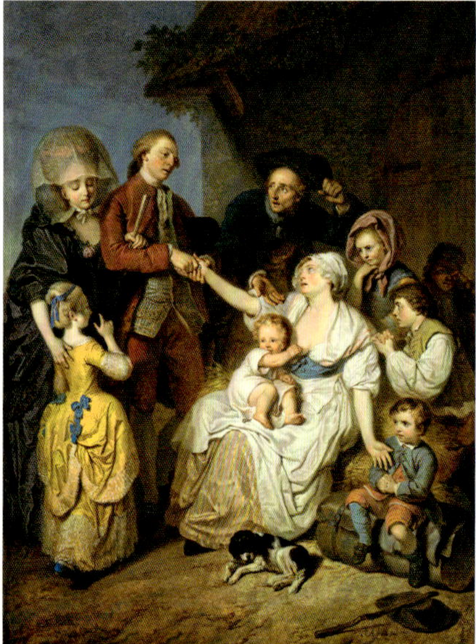

Fig. 117. Pierre Alexandre Wille (French, 1748–1821), *The Alms*, 1777. Oil on canvas, 51¼ × 39 in. (130 × 99 cm). Musée des Beaux-Arts, Angers (MNA 85.11.1)

The subject of the scene has received scant attention. There are no mentions or recorded provenance for any version of the composition before the 1860s. The traditional title, *Cavalcade of Women on Horseback*, was apparently coined by Baron Roger Portalis in 1889.[2] The composition is centered on the encounter between fashionably dressed women on horseback and a peasant family seated at the base of a tree. While no specific charitable act is being depicted, the obvious contrast in their social stations and the clearly legible gestures of gratitude—the father lifting his hat, the mother indicating with an open palm her three children—suggest that the subject is the visit of charitable ladies to a village.

Emma Barker, in her analysis of Jean-Baptiste Greuze's *Lady of Charity* (1775, Musée des Beaux-Arts, Lyon), emphasizes the novelty of the subject and its departure from earlier allegorical images of Christian charity. The popularity of Greuze's painting, exhibited in his studio in 1775 and engraved in 1778 with the title *La dame bienfaisante*, initiated a slew of pictures by a variety of artists depicting charitable acts in contemporary society. Unlike Christian charity, *bienfaisance*, or benevolence, was an Enlightenment concept based on the principle of natural equality. By the late 1770s, charitable acts, often performed by women, grew into what Barker calls a "cult of benevolence," and paintings of such subjects, typically in rural settings, proliferated. Within the social hierarchy, altruism that rewarded peasant virtue was thought to encourage societal harmony and prosperity. In Pierre Alexandre Wille's *The Alms* (fig. 117), for instance, members of a peasant family who are recipients of aristocratic largesse adopt exactly the same poses as those in the present sheet, with the father lifting his hat and the mother gesturing toward her children.[3] The appeal of such subjects to collectors was straightforward. In Barker's words, "a depiction of a member of the elite rewarding peasant virtue [would demonstrate] his own moral worth and social utility."[4] PS

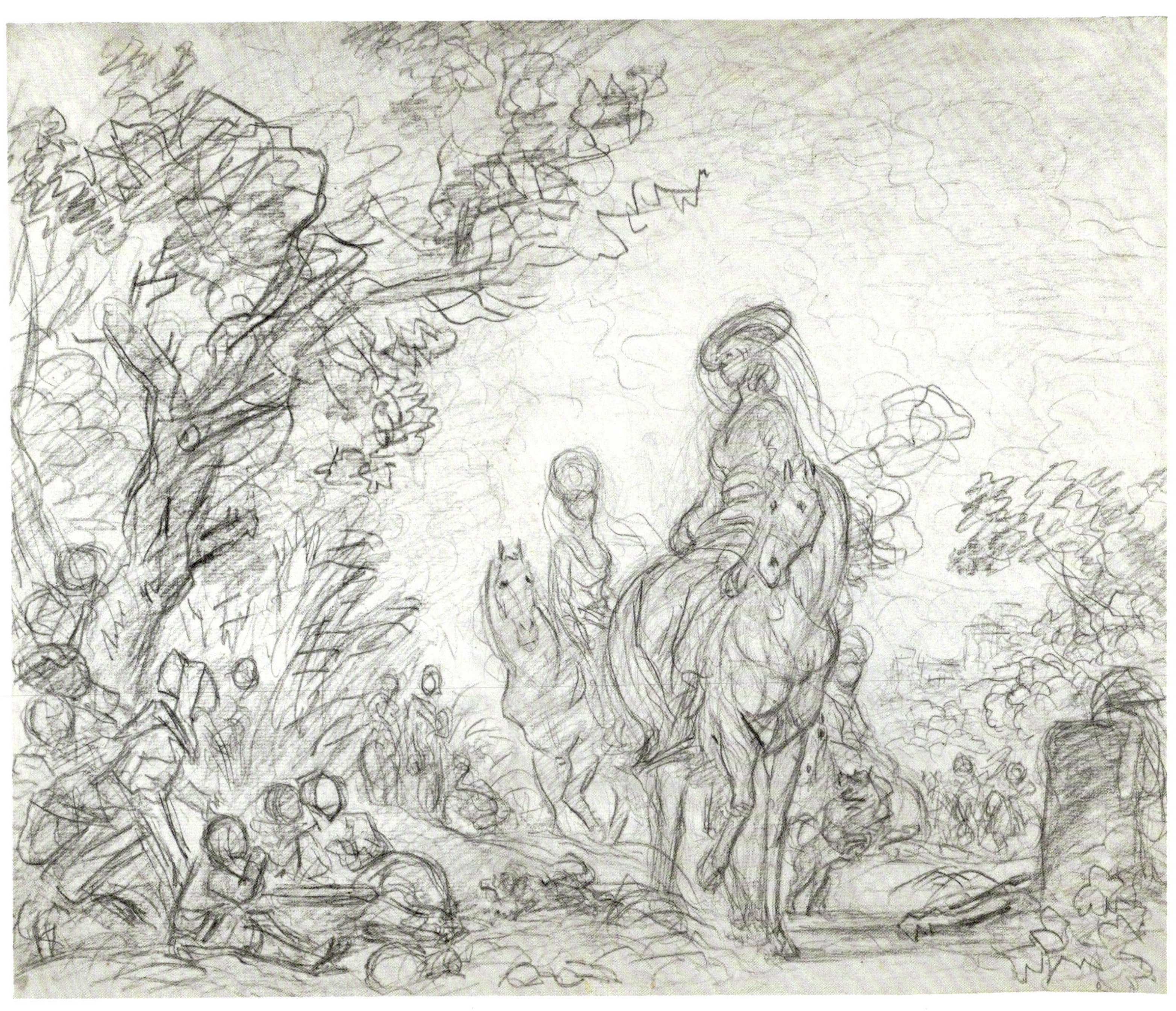

PROVENANCE: Hippolyte Walferdin (1795–1880), Paris; his estate sale, Hôtel Drouot, Paris, April 12–16, 1880 (part of lot 275); acquired at the sale by Madame la Baronne de Ruble; sale, collection of "Madame X," Hôtel Drouot, Paris, May 23, 1928 (lot 53, pl. IX); anonymous sale, Piasa, Drouot Richelieu, Paris, March 22, 2002 (lot 110, ill.); [Wildenstein & Co., Inc., New York, until 2014]; private collection

SELECTED EXHIBITION: New York 2005, pp. 306–7, cat. no. 133.

SELECTED REFERENCES: Portalis 1889, vol. 2, p. 295, ill. on p. 144; Ananoff 1961–70, vol. 4 (1970), p. 81, no. 2117.

77. *Children Dancing in a Park*

Ca. 1775–80
Black chalk with gray wash and touches of pink and green watercolor over graphite underdrawing; verso: *Children Dancing in a Park*, black chalk, incised
14 × 17 in. (35.4 × 43 cm)

One of Fragonard's most ethereal landscapes, *Children Dancing in a Park* is a dreamlike vision of well-heeled leisure in a verdant setting. Constructed in pale and vaporous washes of barely tinted watercolor over the loosest of chalk armatures, the sheet uses the freedom of its technique to evoke the languid pleasures of sunlit gatherings. Two children dance against the backdrop of a balustrade and towering fountain, surrounded by onlookers who recline on the ground or find shade under their elegant parasols. A variation of the composition has been quickly sketched on the verso in black chalk.

In discussing this recto-verso pair of drawings, two questions have occupied scholars: should they be considered studies for the famous Banque de France painting *La Fête à Saint-Cloud*,[1] and how do they relate to the highly finished chalk and brown and gray wash version in the Rijksmuseum, Amsterdam (fig. 118)? The former question resists a definitive answer, as the painting features no direct quotations from the drawings, only a common vocabulary of motifs and a similar subject and mood.[2] We agree with Marie-Anne Dupuy-Vachey's view[3] that even if the drawings do not represent strictly utilitarian stages in the preparation of the *Saint-Cloud* painting, they are interconnected explorations of a theme, part of a constellation of works that contributed to the genesis of one of Fragonard's greatest works—"studies in spirit if not in detail," in the words of Eunice Williams.[4]

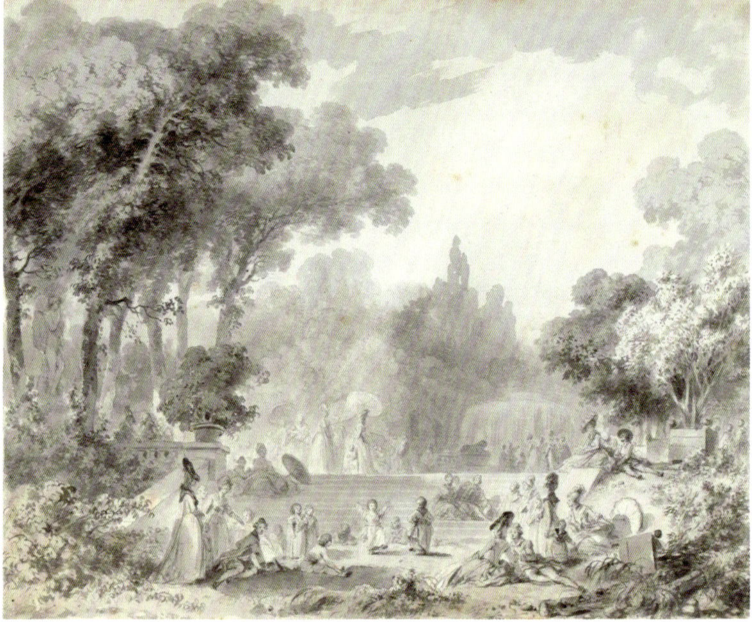

Fig. 118. Jean Honoré Fragonard, *Children Dancing in a Park*, ca. 1775–80. Brown and gray wash over black chalk, 13¾ × 17⅛ in. (34.8 × 43.3 cm). Rijksmuseum, Amsterdam (RP-T-1953-204)

Equally interesting is the relationship of the three drawn versions. It has often been remarked that the sketchier black chalk verso of the Lehman sheet is much closer than the watercolor recto to the Amsterdam drawing. In 1978, Eunice Williams, whose opinion would be followed by Pierre Rosenberg in 1987, proposed the verso as a record drawing of the Rijksmuseum composition precisely because "the details correspond too closely to the finished drawing."[5] However, both of these scholars had known the verso only through a black and white photograph. Recent inspection of the sheet in the Metropolitan Museum's Paper Conservation studio revealed the verso to have been incised throughout.[6] That is, the artist pressed the hard (but not too sharp) point of a stylus or similar tool along the contours of the figures and landscape elements. This incising, which can be seen clearly in the laboratory setting in a network of protruding lines on the front of the sheet, was a standard method of transfer in the eighteenth century. Thus, the highly finished Amsterdam drawing, which has roughly the same dimensions as the Lehman sheet, must have had the basic contours of its composition laid in by Fragonard, in its very initial stages, through a mechanical process of transfer. This observation, for us, firmly establishes the Lehman chalk version as preparatory for the finished drawing. But where does this leave the watercolor version? Both the recto and the verso of the Lehman sheet have elements in common with the Banque de France painting: the placement of the balustrade, the conical shape of the fountain, and the oval forms of the parasols in the case of the watercolor; and the overturned orange tree in the case of the chalk study. The artist chose to elaborate one side in wash and to transfer the other to a new sheet for a more detailed treatment.

Ultimately, questions of anteriority matter less in Fragonard's oeuvre, in which the nonlinear progression of ideas and versions is a natural outgrowth of the evolving importance of drawing as exploration and autonomous artistic expression. For Fragonard, and for the collectors who valued his work, drawings were more than a stepping stone in the creation of a painting. Indeed, Charles Louis François Lecarpentier, who penned the first account of Fragonard's life and work, published just two months after the artist's death,

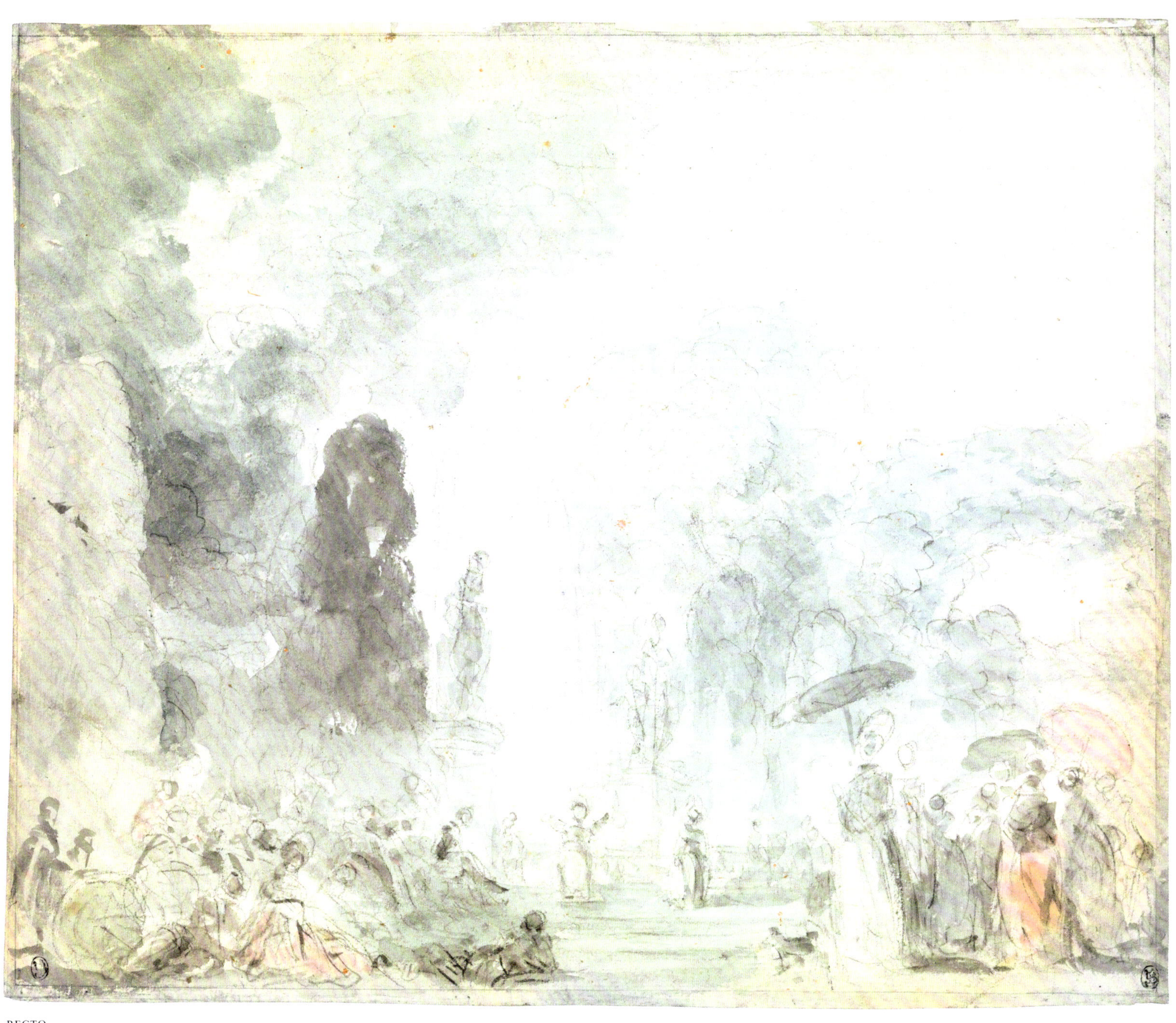

RECTO

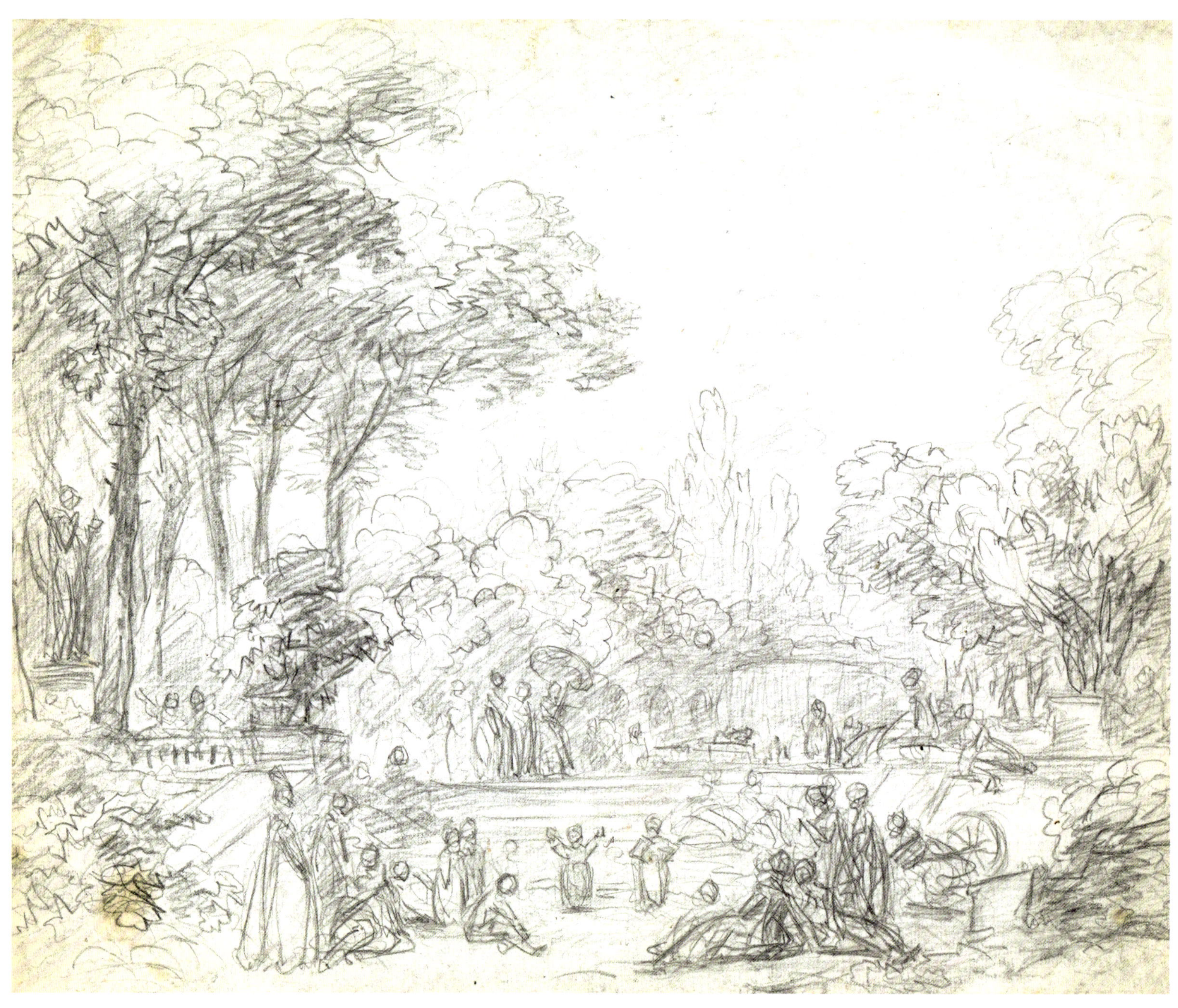

VERSO

could easily have been describing the Lehman watercolor when he singled out for special praise the poetic ambiguity of Fragonard's landscape sketches:

> Born with a natural taste for landscape, he made in this genre an infinite number of studies and drawings of great variety and admirable effect. Of his work, we are familiar with his simple sketches, those that tempt us to feel as if we are beholding beautiful dreams, as, with vague and faint colors, he manages to introduce to the imagination much more than he had originally intended.[7]

PS

PROVENANCE: Baronne de Ruble, Paris (1889); possibly René Gimpel, Paris;[8] Alfred Beurdeley (1847–1919), Paris, his stamp (Lugt 421) in the lower left and right corners on the recto; his collection sale (Lugt 63070), Galerie Georges Petit, Paris, March 13–15, 1905 (lot 80, ill.); Walter Gay, Paris (1856–1937), by 1931; [Galerie André Weil, Paris]; André Seligmann (d. 1945), from whom stolen in 1941 by the Einsatzstab Reichsleiter Rosenberg (no. 166) and restituted to his heirs in 1946; [César de Hauke, Paris]; acquired by Robert Lehman from de Hauke in March 1953; The Metropolitan Museum of Art, New York, Robert Lehman Collection, 1975 (1975.1.628)

SELECTED EXHIBITIONS: Williams 1978, pp. 106–7, cat. no. 39; Rosenberg 1988, pp. 534–35, cat. no. 274; Stein and Holmes 1999, pp. 168–70, cat. no. 72 (entry by Mary Tavener Holmes).

SELECTED REFERENCES: Portalis 1889, vol. 1, p. 81; Ananoff 1961–70, vol. 2 (1963), pp. 86–87, no. 790; Cuzin 2003, pp. 201–2, fig. 248.

78. *The Source*

Ca. 1775–80
Brush and brown and gray wash over black chalk
13⅜ × 18¼ in. (34 × 46 cm)

Following his return from his second Italian trip, Fragonard attained in his handling of brown wash an unprecedented freedom. His drawings from this period, executed on large sheets, have layers of pale brown wash applied with apparent speed and a broad brush over energetic sketches in black chalk. The translucency of the washes contributes to their luminous effect and was presumably intended to allow the vigor and spontaneity of the underdrawing to show through. While we may marvel at these displays of virtuosity, the subjects of this sheet and a number of others from this period are stubbornly enigmatic, even as the figure types, motifs, and stylistic sources remain familiar.

Here, the scene centers on the muscular form of a bearded river god as he presides over a mountaintop, the waters gushing forth from his overturned jar representing the source of a river. A group of at least four men bearing torches have just arrived at the summit, and they gaze in shock in the direction of the river god's gesture. An animal, perhaps a bear or a female lion, warily surveys the scene from the rocky outcropping above, partially obscuring the cloud-veiled disk of the full moon. Virtually the entire sheet has been washed in pale brown, enfolding the scene in shadow and calling attention to the small areas of reserved paper that indicate the flames of the torches.

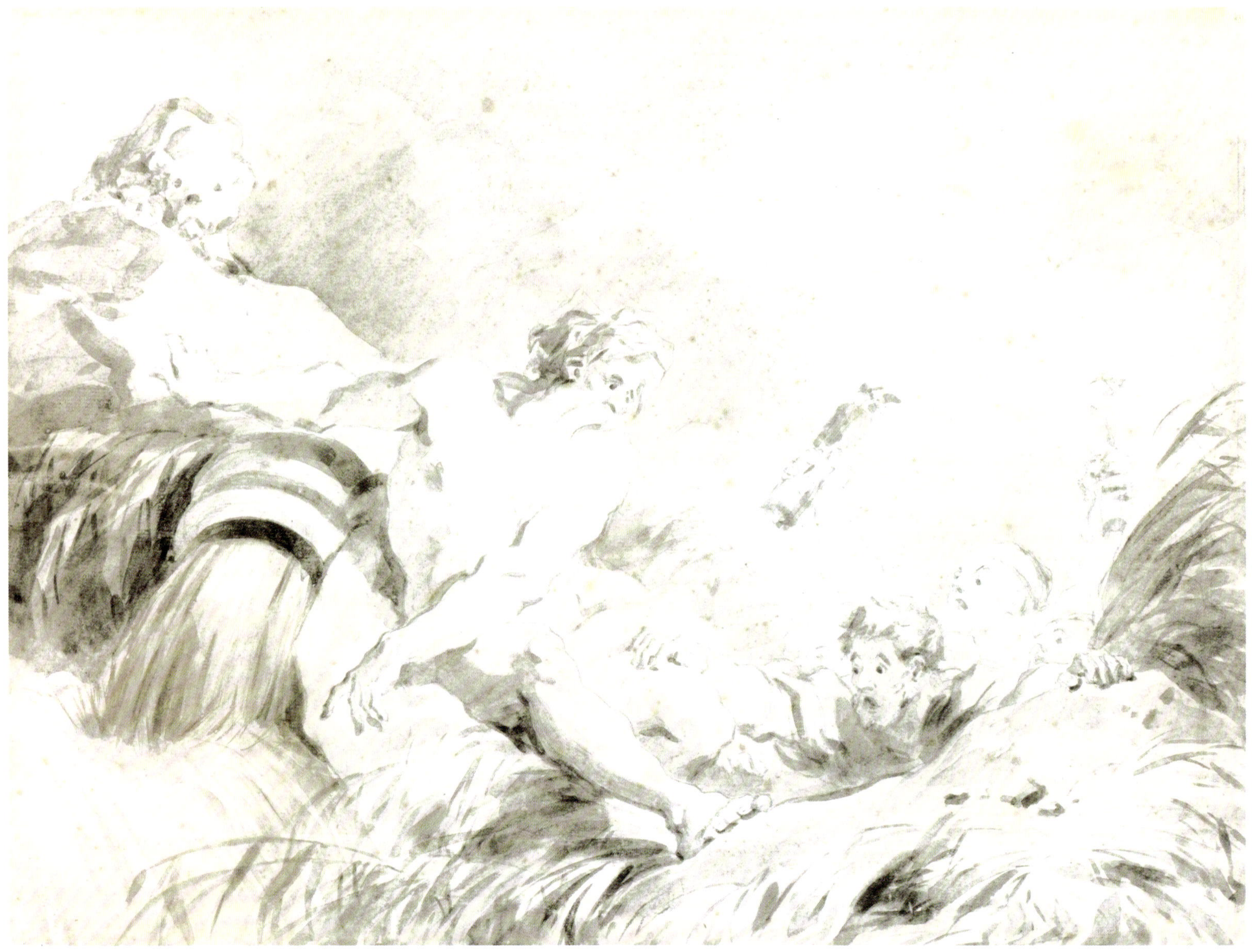

Bearded old men, and river gods in particular, make frequent appearances in Fragonard's oeuvre, in debt and tribute to the Italian masters he so admired, not least of whom Giovanni Battista Tiepolo.[1] Not only the subject but also the freely applied brown wash would have recalled the work of the Venetian master to Fragonard's contemporaries, as we see in the catalogue of the collection of Pierre Jean Mariette, for instance, in which a drawing of the death of a hermit is described as "in the manner of Tiepolo."[2] Such figures were useful for populating biblical and mythological scenes and stories of ancient history, as well as scenes of contemporary genre. Despite the fact that the twisting, pointing pose of the river god and the nighttime setting both recall Salvator Rosa's *Dream of Aeneas* (fig. 119), the subject of the present sheet eludes us. In formal terms, however, it can perhaps be paired with a similarly mysterious drawing in the Albertina (fig. 120). Although their provenances diverged early on, they present themselves visually as pendants, structured around opposing diagonal axes and each featuring an old man, a companion animal, and a clump of male figures seen from the bust up. In other ways, they can be posited as opposites: one is set in a lush landscape of rushing water and bent grasses, while the other occupies an arid landscape, its dryness marked by the rocky setting and the upturned jar. PS

PROVENANCE: Baron Gabriel Benoist-Méchin (1854–1923); his collection sale, Hôtel Drouot, Paris, May 7, 1912 (lot 5, repr.), 12,000 francs; acquired at the sale by the actress and singer Mlle Arlette Dorgère (1880–1965); [acquired in 1965 by Wildenstein & Co., Inc., New York, until 2015]; sale, Sotheby's, New York, January 28, 2015 (lot 104); private collection

SELECTED EXHIBITION: Sutton 1980, cat. no. 126, ill.

SELECTED REFERENCE: Ananoff 1961–70, vol. 1 (1961), p. 166, no. 391, fig. 141.

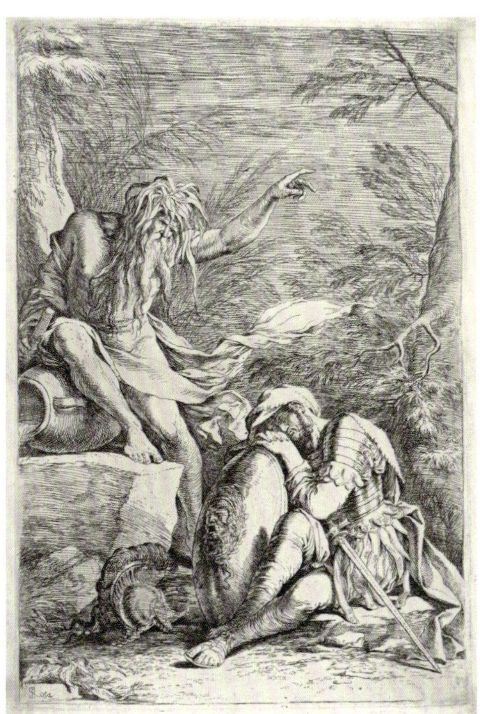

Fig. 119. Salvator Rosa (Italian, 1615–1673), *The Dream of Aeneas,* ca. 1663–64. Etching, 14⅜ × 10 in. (36.3 × 25.3 cm). The Metropolitan Museum of Art, New York, Bequest of Phyllis Massar, 2011 (2012.136.302)

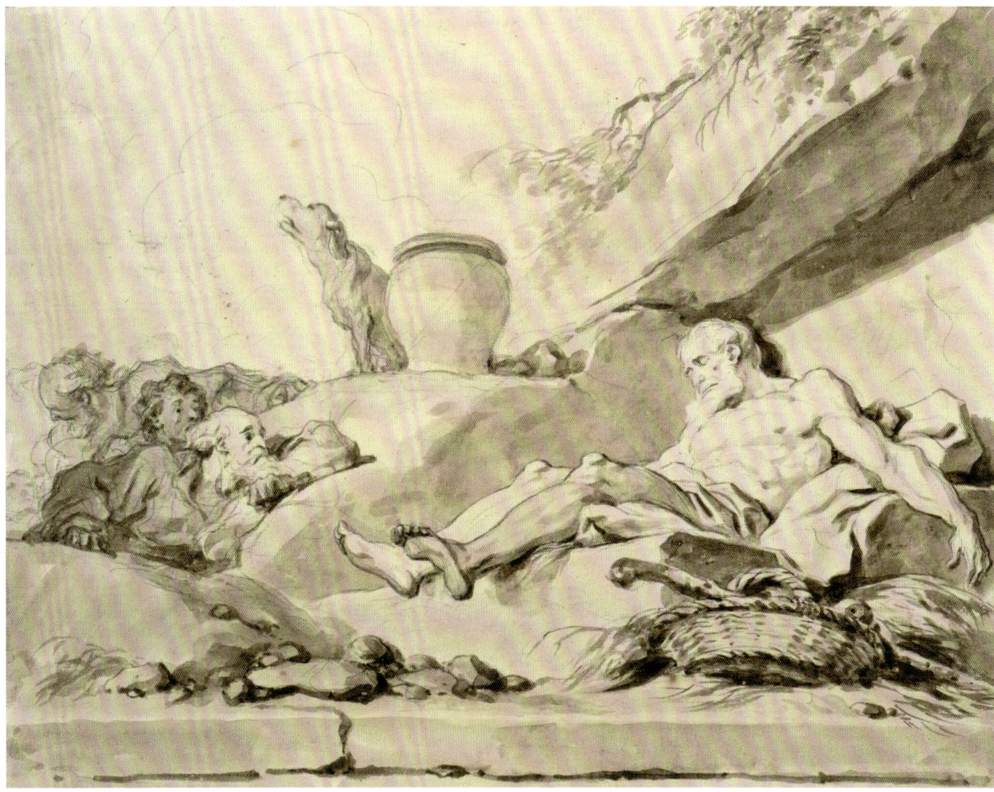

Fig. 120. Jean Honoré Fragonard, *The Death of a Hermit (Diogenes?),* ca. 1775–80. Brush and brown wash over black chalk underdrawing, 13⅜ × 17⅝ in. (33.9 × 44.8 cm). Graphische Sammlung Albertina, Vienna (12730)

79. *An Homage to Gluck*

Ca. 1777–82

Brown wash over black chalk underdrawing

14⅛ × 18⅛ in. (35.8 × 46 cm)

Inscriptions: in pen and brown ink, under each of the three busts, from left to right, "HOMERE," "GLUCK," "VIRgilE"; on the plinth supporting the bust of Gluck, "AMANTI DEGLI ARTI"; on the sheet lying on the desk, "ET MON COEUR / ET MES / OEUVRES"; and at lower left of that sheet, almost illegible, "fragonard"

With the backing of the French queen Marie Antoinette, who had been his pupil in Vienna, the composer Christoph Willibald Gluck enjoyed enormous success in Paris, where several of his operas premiered between 1774 and 1780. Artists rushed to portray him. Thus, at the Salon of 1775, one encountered the musician's likeness in the form of portraits by the painter Joseph Siffred Duplessis and the sculptor Jean Antoine Houdon.[1] To honor the composer, his Parisian admirers desired that a marble version of Houdon's plaster bust be placed in the grand foyer of the Opéra.[2] Toward this end, in July 1776 they launched a subscription to raise Houdon's fee of 4,000 livres. Among the hundred or so subscribers who made contributions appears the name "Fragona," which can only be our artist.[3] However, it seems the painter was not satisfied merely with paying the 12 livres to participate in the subscription and wanted to make a more personal tribute to "the Germanic Orpheus," as shown by this magnificent composition.

Sitting before a sort of large desk, a young man, spellbound with admiration, stares at the bust of Gluck installed, at the top of an odd podium, above the busts of Virgil and Homer. The second of these, with his forehead encircled by a headband, is easily recognizable, as classical depictions have made familiar the image of the mythical blind poet. But we do not know from which portrait Fragonard drew inspiration for the bust the inscription identifies as Virgil. As for the bust of Gluck, it differs clearly from the one by Houdon, in particular in its frontal character and its antique style, which allows it to be in harmony with its neighbors. However, the head, with its broad forehead and tousled hair, recalls the choices made by the sculptor. An epigraph in Italian connects the three busts by designating their subjects "lovers of the arts." This epigraph is presented in somewhat faint capital letters, in the manner of an inscription in stone, which differs from the way the names are marked under each of the busts. They seem to have been put down on the sheet quite quickly, in a darker brown ink, without completely adhering to Roman orthography. These indications suggest that the three names were added later, as the study of the drawing's history invites us to think. In December 1781, a wash sketch of the same dimensions appeared at auction (see "Provenance") with a description corresponding perfectly with ours, except for the identification of the central bust not as Gluck but as Virgil's patron, "Maecenas." This could be another version, but it is not unreasonable to suggest that it was in fact the same drawing, before the inscriptions were added, which would explain the cataloguer's error. The names could have been written afterward, perhaps by Fragonard himself, anxious for his composition to be interpreted correctly. As for the figure who, according to the inscription on the sheet in front of him, dedicates both "his heart and his works" to the composer and to the two poets, no inscription specifies his identity. With his laurel crown, loose clothing, and laced boots in an antique style, he provides a timeless image of the poet. However, in the right foreground, by the lyre leaning against the lovely Louis XVI stool on which he sits, there is a palette. Following the example of the author of the Sireul sale catalogue,[4] it seems fitting to see in this composition an allegory of the inspiration of the painter, that is to say, of Fragonard himself. The visionary character of the scene is accentuated by the clouds that rise up in the background, leaving visible just part of a zodiac arch. It is not easy to interpret the barely sketched sign that appears on the right, but it is tempting to recognize this double circle bristling with claws as Cancer, given that Gluck was born on July 2.

The theme of the inspiration of the artist was especially dear to Fragonard. Tormented visions of the 1760s[5] gave way in the 1770s and 1780s to calmer compositions that combined tributes to writers of the past and metaphorical self-portraits.[6] It is to this later period that our drawing belongs, as is confirmed by its very lively style, with fluid wash underpinned by an emphatic and animated sketch in black chalk. MADV

PROVENANCE: Probably Sireul sale (Lugt 3329), Boileau, Paris, December 3, 1781 (lot 239, "Un superbe Dessin lavé au bistre sur papier blanc. Il représente la Peinture dédiant ses crayons à Homere, Virgile & Mécene. Allégorie ingénieuse présentée sous la figure d'un Peintre dessinant sur une table antique devant les bustes de ces grands Hommes [36 × 48.7 cm]"), sold for 72 livres to de Broc; Norblin de la Gourdaine (according to the present owner's documentation); Mme de Conantré (according to Marianne Roland Michel); Baronne de Ruble (1889); Sigismond Bardac (1856–1919), Paris; Edouard Rahir; Irwin Laughlin of Meridian House, Washington, D.C. (1927); acquired by Hubert Chanler of Geneseo, N.Y.; [Agnew's, London]; Mrs. Hubert Chanler of Geneseo, N.Y.; her sale, Sotheby's, London, June 10, 1959 (lot 20, repr.), sold for £1,100 to Cailleux; [Galerie Cailleux, Paris, gallery stamp (Lugt 4461) at lower right]; Irene Roosevelt Aitken

SELECTED REFERENCES: Oppé 1927, pp. 8–9, pl. 9; Roland Michel 1961, fig. 1; Ananoff 1961–70, vol. 1 (1961), no. 455, fig. 158, vol. 2 (1963), p. 311; Wakefield 1976, p. 15; Rosenberg 1988, p. 506, fig. 2.

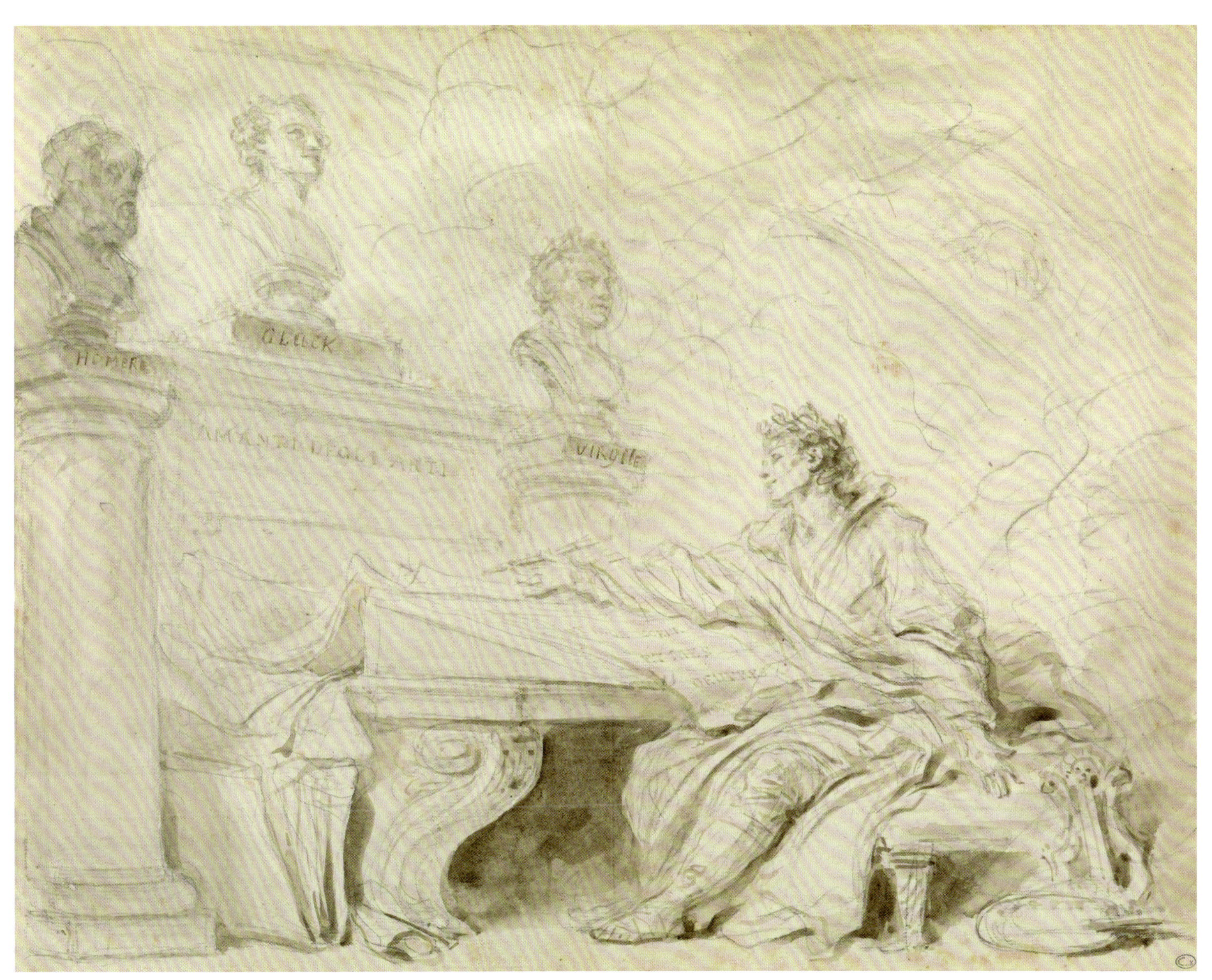
HOMERE
GLUCK
VIRGILE

Etchings with Marguerite Gérard, 1778

Fragonard made etchings during three brief and defined periods. His first foray, while a student in François Boucher's studio, resulted in a single print, made using his master's drawing as a model (cat. 1). His friendship and collaboration with the abbé de Saint-Non provided the context for a second period of activity when, in 1763–64, shortly after his return from Italy, he produced a group of twenty-one small and exquisite etchings after his own drawings, many of them copies after Italian paintings (see pp. 100–101 and cats. 13–25). His third etching campaign yielded his largest and most ambitious plates. These last four prints (cats. 80 and 82–84), all dating to 1778, were again the product of a pedagogical relationship, but this time Fragonard was the master and Marguerite Gérard, his young sister-in-law, was the student.[1]

Gérard had come to Paris from her native city of Grasse in the mid-1770s, and a short time later Fragonard began instructing her in painting and drawing. As part of his tutelage, he also introduced her to the technique of etching. She produced five plates in all, either demonstrably or presumably after brown wash drawings by Fragonard. On the first, *The Swaddled Cat* (p. 62, fig. 53), Gérard proudly inscribed that it was her first plate (*première planche*), made at the age of sixteen. Her progress was appreciable, culminating in a fifth and final print, *The Genius of Franklin* (fig. 121), which was advertised for sale in the *Journal de Paris* in November 1778.[2] When Fragonard picked up the etching needle to demonstrate the technique to his teenage sister-in-law, he must have found himself newly energized by its possibilities, for the project's crowning work, *The Armoire* (cat. 84), a dramatic scene of angry parents interrupting their daughter's tryst, is a great achievement not only of Fragonard's engagement with the medium but also of printmaking in eighteenth-century France. PS

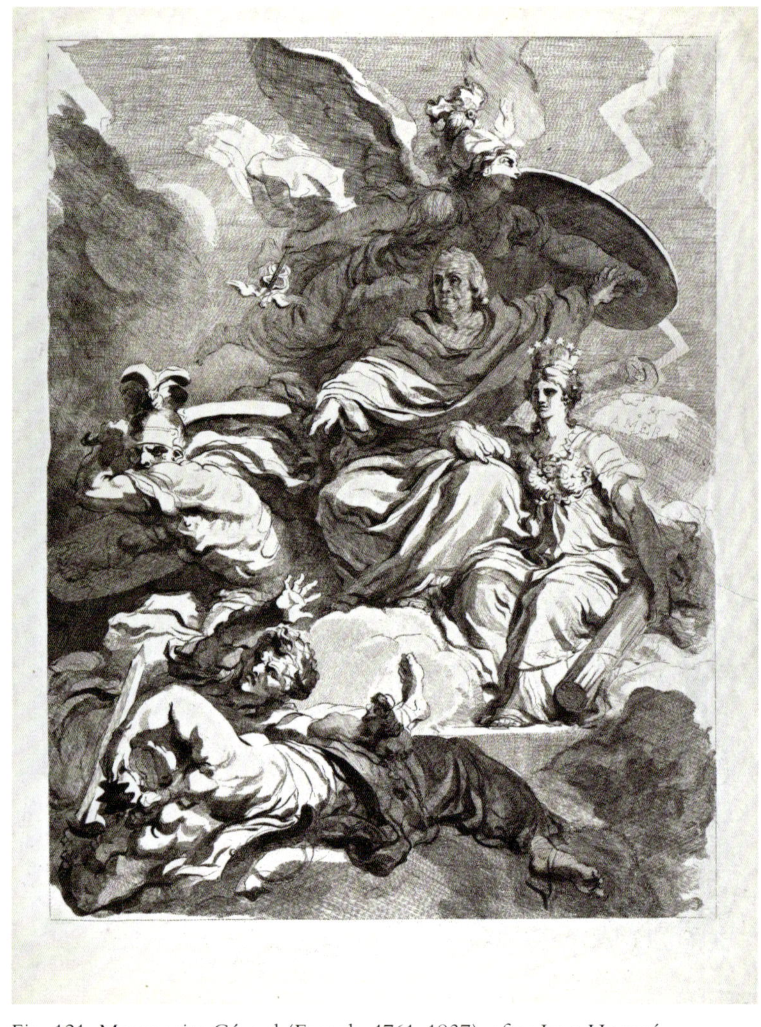

Fig. 121. Marguerite Gérard (French, 1761–1837), after Jean Honoré Fragonard, *The Genius of Franklin*, 1778. Etching printed in brown ink, first state of two, 21⅝ × 16½ in. (54.9 × 41.8 cm). The Metropolitan Museum of Art, New York, Gift of William H. Huntington, 1883 (83.2.230)

80. *The Tax Collectors (Les Traitants)*

1778
Etching
Sheet: 9¼ × 7⅛ in. (23.5 × 18 cm); image: 9⅛ × 6⅞ in. (23.2 × 17.5 cm)
Inscription: in the plate, at bottom center, just inside the framing line, "fragonard 1778"

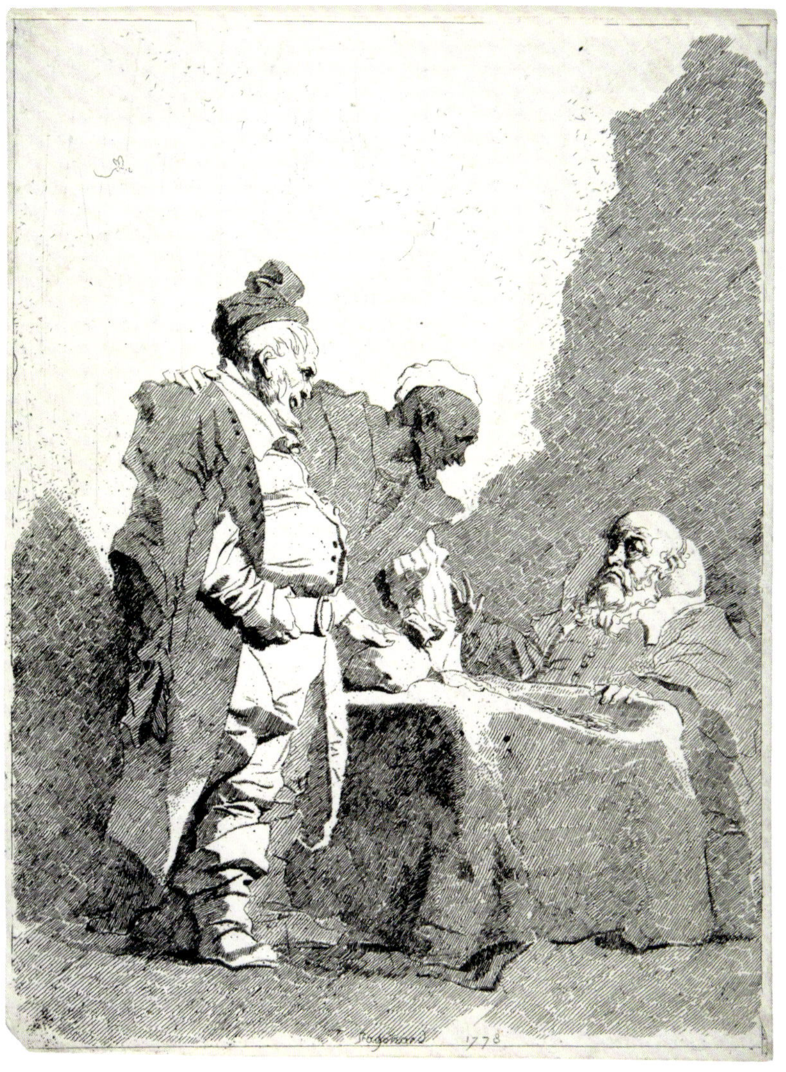

Many unanswered questions surround this print. The drawing on which it is based is lost, and its subject has never been deciphered. Although the hat of the standing figure resembles that of the seated man in *The First Riding Lesson* (cat. 81), the present work suggests a narrative set in an earlier period, unlike the more contemporary and lighthearted genre scenes that Fragonard chose for the other plates he etched during this time. In 1859, Prosper de Baudicour, who was the first to publish the print, described the elements of the composition—two standing men, pushing what appears to be a bag of money toward a seated man—but clearly did not understand the subject Fragonard meant to depict. Baudicour's title, *Les Traitants*, or *The Tax Collectors*, has been used in the literature ever since, without elaboration or verification.

Despite the fact that it bears a signature and date, this print was described as unfinished by Georges Wildenstein when he catalogued Fragonard's etchings in 1956. Victor Carlson in 1984 cast it in a different light, seeing in its stark contrasts of densely worked shading and reserved paper an homage to the prints of the Tiepolos, with their flickering touches and bold expanses of white.[1] Not only would Fragonard have had an opportunity to see prints by members of the Tiepolo family during his two stays in Venice, with Saint-Non in 1761 and with Bergeret in 1774, but he could have easily encountered them in Paris, where each new series issued was avidly sought after by collectors.

If the admiration among contemporary *amateurs* and collectors for the sparkling technique of the Tiepolos provided the context for Fragonard's adoption of a bolder, more simplified style, it was nonetheless a style eminently suited to the pedagogical project at hand: instructing his sixteen-year-old sister-in-law in the rudiments of etching sufficient to translate the nuances of a chalk and wash drawing into printed ink lines. The initial sketching of the figures was done with a simple etched line, the equivalent of the chalk underdrawing that was the basis of his drawn compositions. The heavier lines of the brush were suggested by short perpendicular etched lines, spaced close together, as can be seen in the standing man's collar and sleeve. To create the broad areas of flat tone achieved in a drawing with wash, Fragonard laid down uneven rows of short, broken hatching softened at the edges by sprays of flecks, as if the hatched lines were breaking off and flying away. Aside from occasionally making use of such decorative flourishes to soften transitions from light to shadow, Fragonard's tendency is to distill the faces and clothing of figures into facets, either starkly lit or shaded, which here endows the three men and the draped table with a dramatic monumentality, even if the subject of the scene cannot be identified. PS

PROVENANCE: [M. Knoedler and Co., New York]; The Metropolitan Museum of Art, New York, Purchase, Harris Brisbane Dick Fund, 1946 (46.125.3)

SELECTED EXHIBITIONS: Sutton 1980, cat. no. 171, ill.; Carlson and Ittmann 1984, pp. 230–31, cat. no. 77 (entry by Victor I. Carlson); Rosenberg 1988, p. 490, cat. no. 241.

SELECTED REFERENCES: G. Wildenstein 1956, p. 34, no. XXIV; Hoisington and Stein 2012, pp. 143–47, fig. 119.

81. *The First Riding Lesson*

Ca. 1775–78
Brush and brown wash over black chalk underdrawing
13¾ × 17¾ in. (34.8 × 45.1 cm)

As with many other scenes of genre in Fragonard's oeuvre, an autobiographical reading long dominated the literature on this drawing, beginning with Roger Portalis in 1880, who not only saw the traits of Fragonard's son, Alexandre Evariste, in the baby but also recognized the familiar presence of the family dog.[1] As recently as 1967, the seated man was considered the artist's self-portrait and the young mother a depiction of his wife, Marie Anne.[2] Sally Wells Robertson exposed the fallacy of this tradition when she argued, correctly, for dating the related print by Marguerite Gérard (fig. 122) to 1778, two years before the birth of Fragonard's son.[3] Recognizing the implications of this revised dating, Eunice Williams in 1978 put forward a more nuanced interpretation of the subject, allowing that it likely had roots in his family life while asserting that the figures playing roles in this domestic scene are not portraits but rather simple folk, timeless and universal. Williams proposed dating the Brooklyn sheet to the mid-1770s, based on style and technique, and subsequent scholars have followed suit.[4]

The theme, often playful, of the instruction of young children appears in other large-format drawings of genre scenes datable to the same period, including *A Prayer for Grandpapa* and *The Little Preacher* (both National Gallery of Art, Washington, D.C.).[5] Like *The First Riding Lesson*, they begin with a broadly sketched preliminary design in black chalk. The compositions are further built up with broad strokes of translucent golden brown wash applied with flourishes that Williams likened to "ribbons streaming across the page."[6] It seems clear that the rapid chalk underdrawing was never intended to be hidden; rather, Fragonard meant to leave visible his technique of layering broadly worked media, a process in which forms gradually took on solidity, thus showcasing the artist's inspiration for the collector's delectation.

It is hardly surprising that these familiar motifs—the wiggly child, the attentive mother, and the patient, noble dog (reminiscent of Fragonard's portrayals of standing bulls and lions)—would attract the young Gérard, who went on to make a career out of such appealing

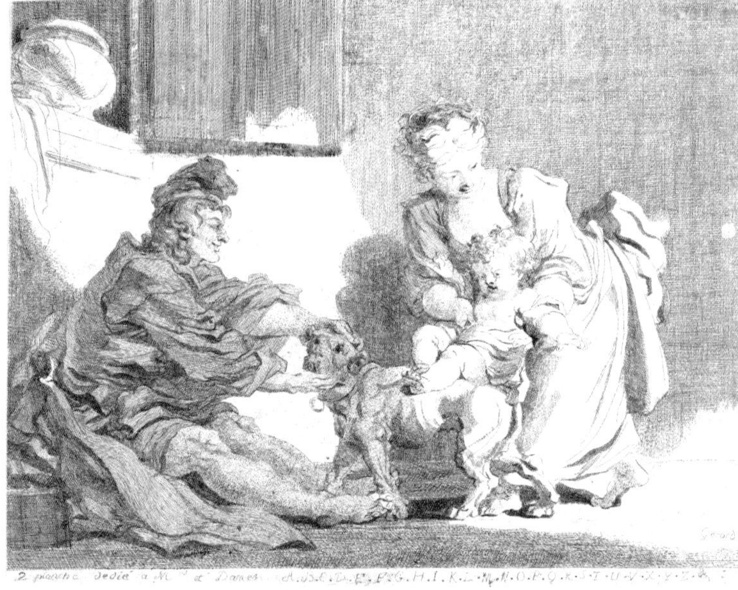

Fig. 122. Marguerite Gérard, *The Child and the Bulldog*, 1778. Etching, second state of three, 6⅞ × 8⅞ in. (17.4 × 22.4 cm). The Metropolitan Museum of Art, New York, Purchase, Phyllis D. Massar Gift, 2011 (2011.279)

domestic subjects. The Brooklyn sheet was one of four she chose (or was assigned) to etch in 1778.[7] Her print, executed on a scale significantly reduced from that of the drawing, faithfully evokes the elegant rhythm of Fragonard's brushstrokes. Biting the plate in acid several times to achieve a broad range of tones,[8] she departed from her model only to strengthen the contrast by darkening areas of the background and foreground. A smaller version of the composition, presumably postdating the Brooklyn sheet, is today in the National Museum of Warsaw.[9] It is this reduced version that was etched, some years later, by the artist, diplomat, and museum administrator Baron Dominique Vivant Denon.[10] PS

PROVENANCE: Duc de Ch *** [Louis Antoine Auguste, duc de Rohan-Chabot (1733–1807), according to the Getty Provenance Index® Databases]; his collection sale (Lugt 4230), Le Brun, Paris, December 10–15, 1787 (lot 274, "c'est une jeune femme qui fait asseoir son enfant sur un dogue qu'un home retient par le museau. Ce dessin est fait avec esprit"), purchased for 60 livres by the comte de Pitignoux, per Getty Provenance Index® Databases; anonymous sale, Paillet, Paris, July 8 and following days, 1793 (part of lot 69, "une jeune femme & son mari promenant leur enfant sur le dos d'un chien"); Baron de Silvestre; his estate sale (Lugt 20547), Hôtel des Ventes, Paris, December 4–6, 1851 (lot 258), purchased by Walferdin for 19 francs 50; Hippolyte Walferdin (1795–1880), Paris, by 1860; his estate sale (Lugt 40074), Hôtel Drouot, Paris, April 12–16, 1880 (lot 224), for 950 francs, to Lacroix; Baron Edmond de Rothschild (1845–1934), by 1889; to his son, Maurice de Rothschild (1881–1957); Mr. and Mrs. Alastair Bradley Martin; Brooklyn Museum, New York, Gift of Mr. and Mrs. Alastair B. Martin, the Guennol Collection, 1957 (57.189)

SELECTED EXHIBITIONS: Williams 1978, pp. 116–17, cat. no. 44; Rosenberg 1988, pp. 492–93, cat. no. 243; Kramer et al. 1993, pp. 62–63, cat. no. 39.

SELECTED REFERENCES: Ananoff 1961–70, vol. 1 (1961), pp. 37–38, no. 12, fig. 2; Hoisington and Stein 2012, pp. 148–52, fig. 123.

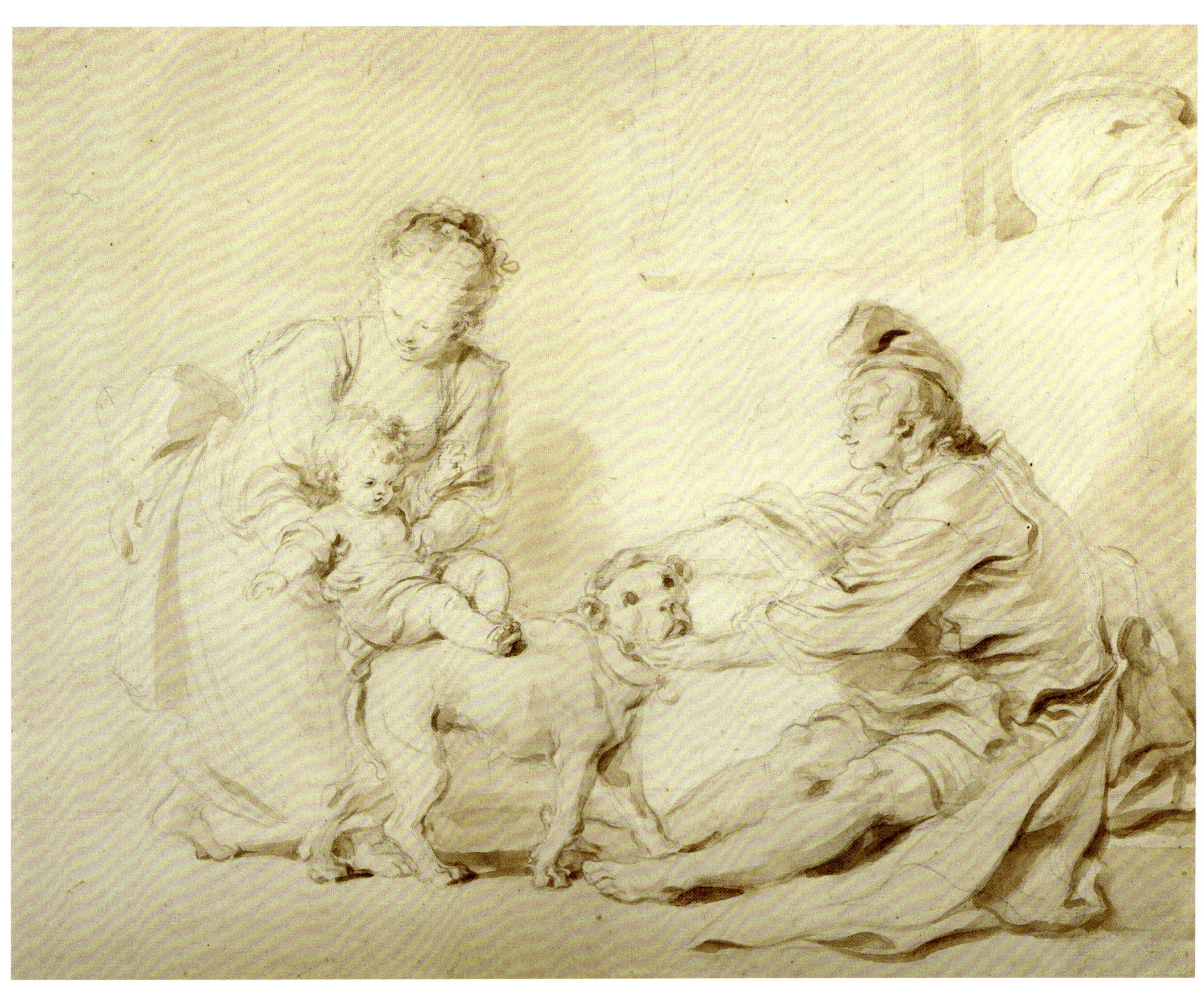

82. *Interior*

1778
Etching
Sheet: 9⅝ × 7 in. (24.5 × 17.6 cm); image: 9⅛ × 6¾ in. (23 × 17 cm)
Inscriptions: in graphite, at lower left, "Gerard," and in the lower margin, at center, "Gerard 1.507."

As with many drawings and paintings of rustic genre scenes going back to Fragonard's first stay in Italy, *Interior* is replete with the vibrant, earthy types—bearded old men, buxom young mothers, and barefoot toddlers—that appealed to French collectors of the time. The traditional title of this print, *Interior*, reflects the lack of evident narrative or theme in so many such works by the artist. Also characteristic is the ambiguous setting, which does not suggest a cottage or farmhouse but rather an undefined cavernous space with arches and high ceilings, as if peasant families have taken up residence in some kind of ruin or communal building (see, for example, cat. 75). Closest to the viewer, a small child seems to savor a snack, while behind him two young women lean toward each other in animated discussion. In another plane, a group of three men, one standing and two sitting, engage in a separate conversation.

Although the lines are less deeply bit in acid and the effect is more delicate, the technique recalls that of *The Tax Collectors* (cat. 80), with its sparkling contrast between areas of tone built of textured hatching and swathes of white paper left in reserve. As in the earlier plate, a broken but lively line lays down the contours of the figures, while the shading is produced by patterns of short, parallel lines, softened by a hand-drawn wobbliness and dissolving into a spray of flecks and dots where the shadows transition into light.

This print is one of two (see also cat. 83) that Fragonard made alongside his young sister-in-law to guide her in learning the process of etching. Gérard's plate, known through a single impression in the Bibliothèque Nationale de France (fig. 123), lacks the three male figures and even the neck of the woman at left, suggesting that Gérard may have become frustrated and left the plate unfinished.[1]

The pedagogical motive of Fragonard's return to printmaking in 1778, and the fact that both teacher and pupil modeled their prints on Fragonard's drawings, led to an entrenched misunderstanding of the authorship of this body of work.[2] In the case of *Interior*, an impression in the Paignon-Dijonval collection had been catalogued in 1810 as being by Gérard, but later scholars considered the two versions to be different states of a single plate, which was considered to be by Fragonard. Georges Wildenstein, in compiling his 1956 catalogue of Fragonard's prints, realized that there were, in fact, two distinct plates but produced a convoluted reasoning to support his attribution of the Bibliothèque Nationale plate to Fragonard, positing that the three background figures had been scraped out and asserting that the present version was a repetition, clearly in the hand of Marguerite.[3] A recataloguing of the 1778 prints was published in 2012 by the present author and Rena M. Hoisington.[4] PS

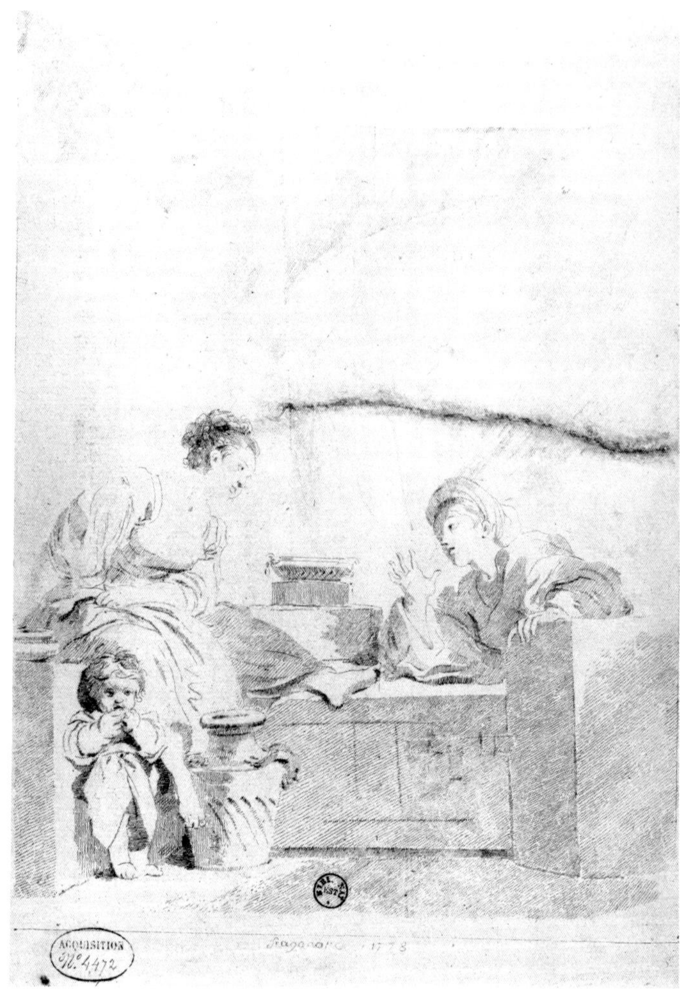

Fig. 123. Marguerite Gérard, *Interior*, 1778. Etching, only state, 10¼ × 7⅝ in. (26 × 19.2 cm). Bibliothèque Nationale de France, Paris

PROVENANCE: François Heugel (1922–2010), his collector's mark (Lugt 3373) in black ink on verso; [Paul Prouté S.A., Paris]; The Metropolitan Museum of Art, New York, Purchase, Susan Schulman Printseller Gift, in honor of Perrin Stein, 2014 (2014.79)

SELECTED EXHIBITION: Rosenberg 1988, p. 491, cat. no. 242.

SELECTED REFERENCES: G. Wildenstein 1956, pp. 35–37, no. XXV (as a "repetition"); Hoisington and Stein 2012, pp. 150–53, fig. 126.

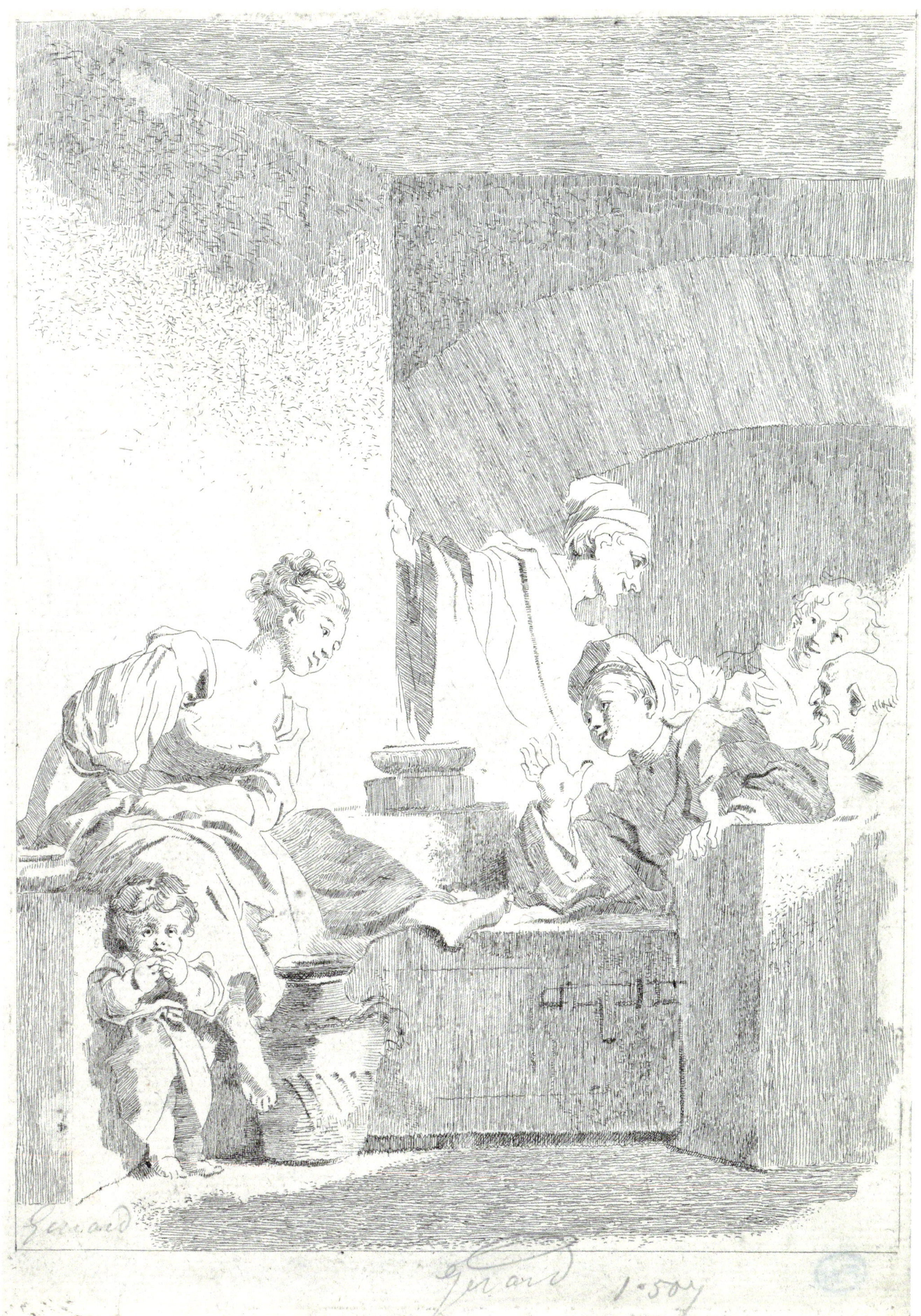

84. *The Armoire*

1778
Etching, first state of four
Sheet: 17 × 22⅜ in. (43 × 56.7 cm); plate: 16⅝ × 22 in. (42.3 × 55.7 cm); image: 13½ × 18¼ in. (34.3 × 46.3 cm)

Profit, for the most part, does not seem to have been the motivating factor behind Fragonard's forays into printmaking. A few plates eventually found their way into the hands of print publishers (see cats. 26–29 and 83) to be printed and sold, but only in one case did he market and sell an etching himself. *The Armoire* was Fragonard's last print; it was his most accomplished, and the culmination of many months of immersion in printmaking. If Fragonard's return to etching in 1778 began with the aim of instructing Marguerite Gérard in the rudiments of the technique, it transformed, along the way, into something more ambitious. After demonstrating in *Fanfan* the range of tone and texture he could achieve simply by scraping ground from a metal plate with a stylus, Fragonard must have decided to go head to head with the reproductive printmakers, choosing to create a large-format, erotic genre scene for the Parisian print market.

The subject was one of his own invention. Angry parents have stormed into a bedroom to interrupt their daughter's tryst. She stands to the side, sobbing into her apron, while they pull open the door of the armoire to reveal the hiding place of the young man, his shame conveyed by his downward glance and the strategically placed hat. A yapping dog and a crowd of curious younger siblings round out the drama.

The drawing that served as Fragonard's model (fig. 125) was first published by Pierre Rosenberg in 1987. Broadly executed in layers of pale brown wash, it is of the same dimensions as the print but in reverse direction. An earlier and smaller study, with a number of differences, was published by Alexandre Ananoff in 1970.[1] The decision to translate the composition into etching gave Fragonard the opportunity to not only introduce greater detail and a more varied sense of texture but also heighten the drama of the scene with theatrical light effects, setting the starkly lit protagonists apart from the shadowy interior. The parents, even more than the sheepish lovers, are a tour de force. They rush forward, their Michelangelesque limbs crisply outlined and economically modeled, drapery flying in their wake. Although his etched lines—as seen in the hair, clothing, and contours of the figures—are clean and decisive, Fragonard must have returned the plate to the acid a number of times to achieve the layers of crosshatching that build up background details, such as the soft folds of the bed linens and the dusky bower of branches atop the armoire.

The advertisement for the print that ran in the *Journal de Paris* on November 27, 1778, made clear that this was not a work executed in the staid hand of a reproductive printmaker; it declared that the creator himself had "etched it with the needle, and applied to it the imprint of his genius,"[2] throwing into it "spice and wit liberally distributed in fistfuls."[3] PS

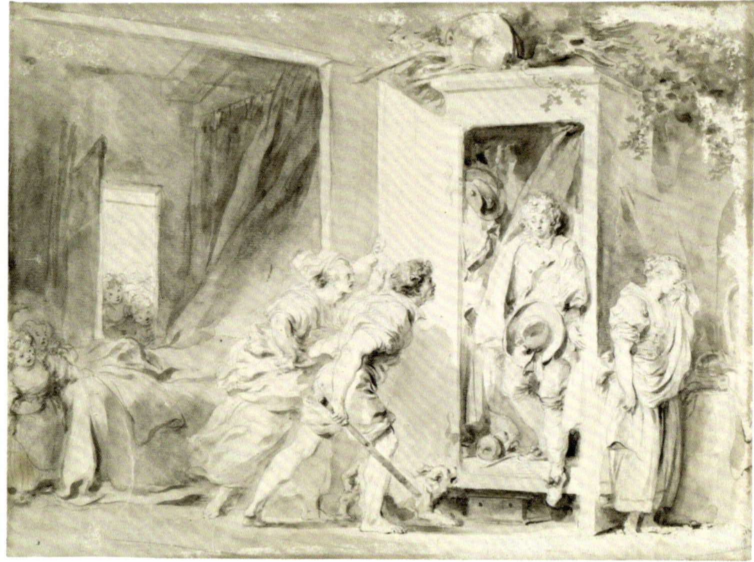

Fig. 125. Jean Honoré Fragonard, *The Armoire*, ca. 1778. Brush and brown wash over black chalk, 13⅜ × 17⅞ in. (34 × 45.4 cm). Hamburger Kunsthalle, Kupferstichkabinett, Hamburg (24005)

PROVENANCE: G. Mühlbacher (d. 1906), Paris, his mark (Lugt 1180) stamped in violet on the verso; his collection sale ["collection de M. G. M★★★" (Lugt 40793)], Hôtel des Commissaires-Priseurs, Paris, February 28–March 5, 1881 (lot 312); The Pierpont Morgan Library, New York; sold in 1972 to The Metropolitan Museum of Art, New York, Purchase, Roland L. Redmond Gift, Louis V. Bell and Rogers Funds, 1972 (1972.539.2)

SELECTED EXHIBITION: Rosenberg 1988, pp. 486–87, cat. no. 238, fig. 2 (the Metropolitan Museum's impression was exhibited *hors catalogue*).

SELECTED REFERENCES: G. Wildenstein 1956, pp. 32–33, no. XXIII; Carlson and Ittmann 1984, pp. 227–29, cat. no. 76 (entry by Victor I. Carlson); Hoisington and Stein 2012, fig. 135; Stein et al. 2013, pp. 37–38, 188, cat. no. 17.

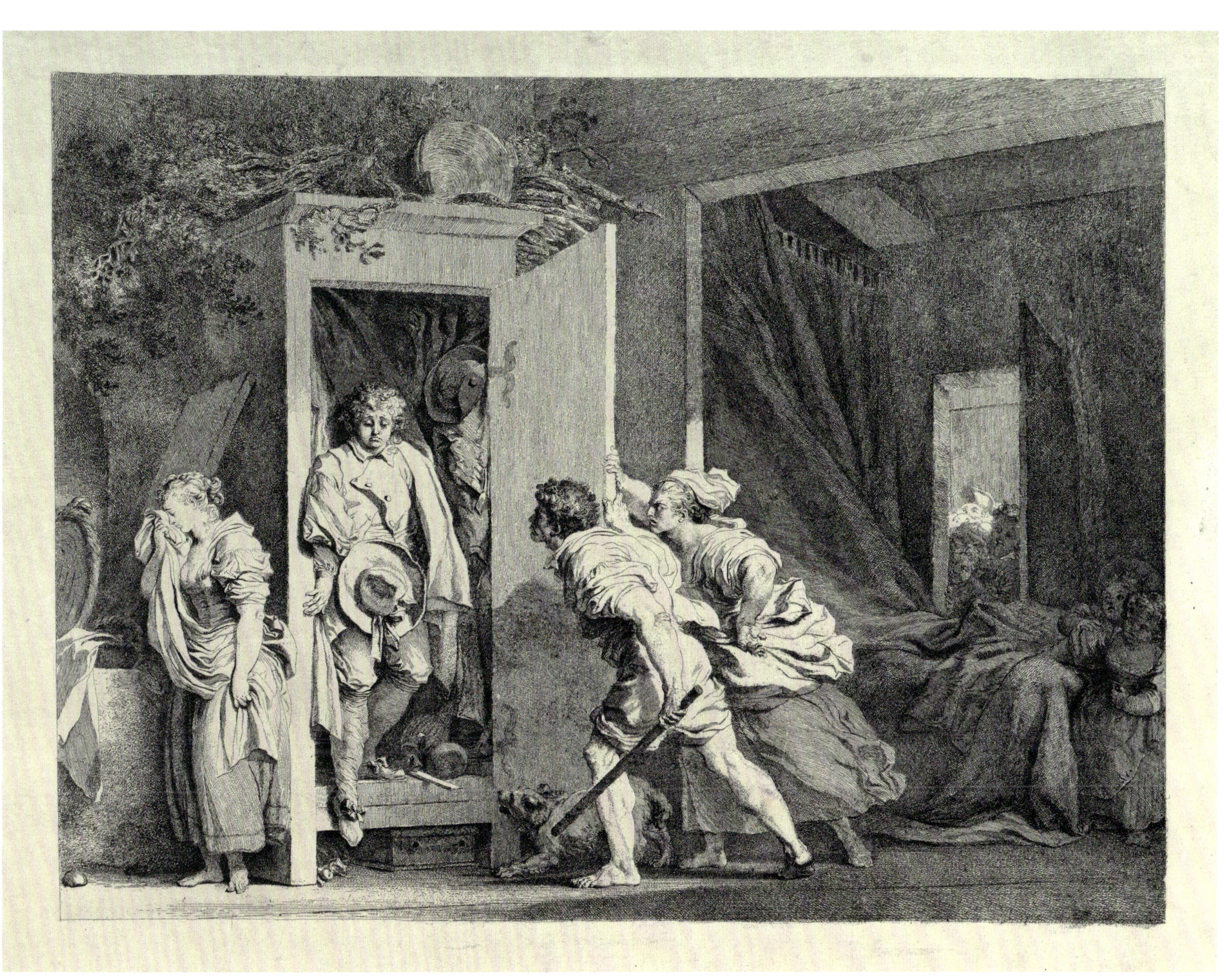

Fragonard as Illustrator

A significant portion of Fragonard's graphic work consists of illustrations of literary texts. That he devoted himself to this activity at several points throughout his career is not at all surprising, given that the eighteenth century was a golden age for the publication of illustrated books. But what is surprising is that none of the projects Fragonard undertook was brought to completion, and we do not know for whom and for what purpose he began these series of illustrations, since no documents relating to any commissions have survived. In any case, Fragonard's interest in this area is far from superficial, as demonstrated by the large number of drawings—nearly three hundred—belonging to this category.

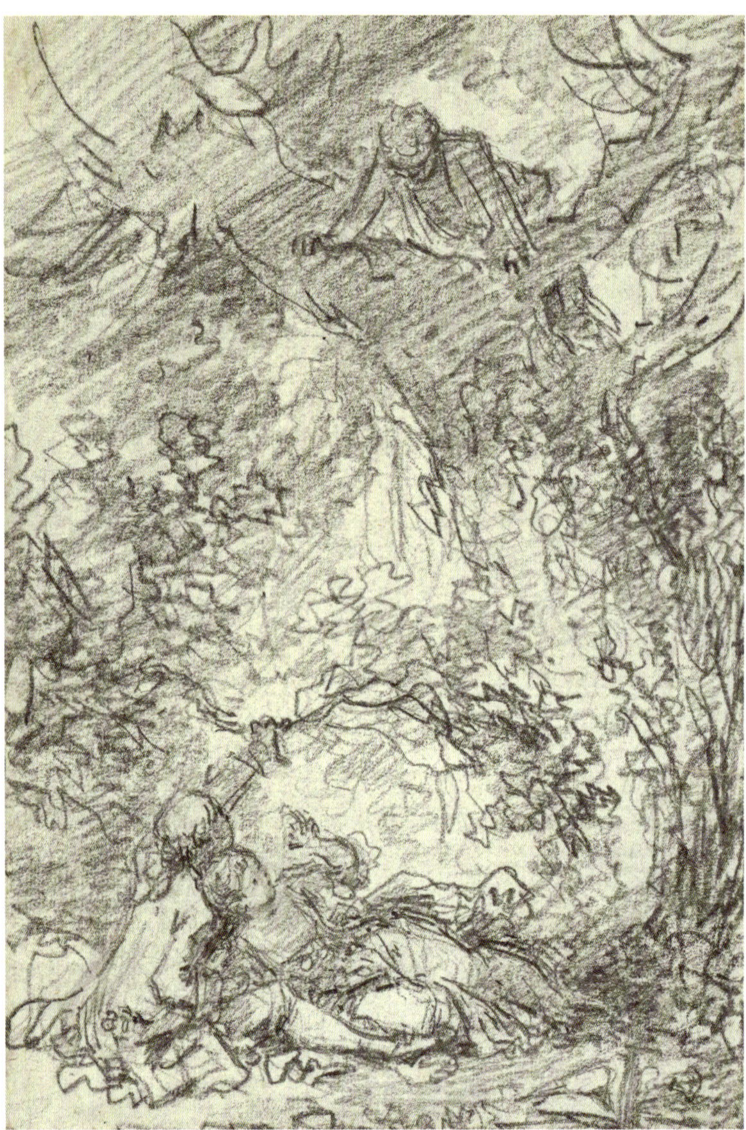

Fig. 126. Jean Honoré Fragonard, *The Villager Searching for his Calf*, ca. 1760. Black chalk, 7⅞ × 5½ in. (20 × 14 cm). Private collection

Nor is the diversity of the authors Fragonard chose to take on insignificant. His first forays in this domain, illustrations for *Les contes* (*The Tales*) of La Fontaine (fig. 126, cats. 85 and 86), were formative, as they allowed him to master the vocabulary of libertinism. Clearly, his work in this light and amusing vein contributed substantially to his reputation. In the final years of his career, he would apply his talents to chivalrous epics and fantastical adventures, such as Cervantes's *Don Quixote* and Ariosto's *Orlando Furioso* (cats. 91–96). Fragonard also engaged with the writing of his contemporaries and produced illustrations inspired by two very different publications, both of which had met with great success: *La reine de Golconde* (1761), by Stanislas Jean de Boufflers (cats. 87–89), and *Tales of the Castle* (1784), by Stéphanie Félicité du Crest, comtesse de Genlis.

Each of these series reveals the artist's intelligence in understanding the spirit of a story in its totality and not simply in terms of specific scenes. Although he faithfully followed the slightest indications given by the authors, his drawings are in every way the opposite of the impeccably composed illustrations produced by specialists in the genre. The skill of the *vignettistes*, as professional illustrators such as Hubert François Gravelot, Charles Dominique Joseph Eisen, and Jean Michel Moreau the Younger were known, lies in their ability to construct a meticulous transcription of the text, despite the sheets' restricted space, in scenes featuring large numbers of figures and details. Fragonard's approach was more one of interpretation than illustration per se. For each story or poem, the artist found a specific style, adapting his manner to that of the writer whom he seemed to want to rival, in particular for Ariosto and *Orlando Furioso*. Lively and informal for La Fontaine, Fragonard's chalk combined vigor and precision to illustrate Boufflers. To echo Don Quixote's madness, the artist used a halting and irregular line. But it is with Ariosto that he reached a pinnacle, achieving a freedom of line that was in pure harmony with the poet's lyricism. MADV

85, 86. ILLUSTRATIONS FOR *LES CONTES* (*THE TALES*) OF LA FONTAINE

Ca. 1770 or 1790(?)

85. *The Fiancée of the King of Garbe: The Tree*

Brown wash over light black chalk underdrawing
8⅛ × 5½ in. (20.4 × 13.9 cm)

86. *The Husband-Confessor*

Brown wash over light black chalk underdrawing
8⅛ × 5⅝ in. (20.4 × 14.1 cm)

Despite an extensive literature, Fragonard's illustrations for *Les contes* (*The Tales*) of La Fontaine still pose many problems for scholars.[1] The issue is all the more complex as each composition gave rise to multiple versions, often including replicas, prints, tracings, and copies, without even mentioning fakes.[2] Fortunately, two series have remained together, offering essential and incontestable starting points for any study. The first comprises forty-two drawings in black chalk alone (private collection, New York). The counterproofs made from this set, retouched with brown wash and pen and brown ink, constitute a second series assembled in two albums now held by the Petit Palais in Paris.[3] Several indications tend to place these two series quite early in Fragonard's career. First, they are executed in a technique quite similar to that the artist perfected in his copies after earlier masters at the end of his first period in Italy (1761). The sheet is covered with a network of rather dense hatching in black chalk, the motifs gone over and made more precise by additional supple, quick lines. Moreover, as Eunice Williams has pointed out,[4] a watermark—"QUARTINO"—which is visible on some copies after the old masters and confirms the Italian origin of the paper, is found on at least one sheet of the first series of the *Contes* and on some pages of a sketchbook that contains studies for what appears to be one of the illustrations.[5] Another argument in favor of an early date lies in the iconography of a large proportion of these illustrations, the settings of which prove that the artist was at the time still deeply influenced by his sojourn in the peninsula, whether in the arrangement of the gardens, the architectural elements, or the reuse of certain classical motifs.[6] The cogency with which the counterproofs were retouched, indeed completed, indicates that the second series was made not long after the first, while the artist still had in his head all the significant elements of the story. The methodical and systematic process by which these three stages were achieved—from black chalk drawing, to counterproof, to reworked counterproof—suggests that the enterprise was undertaken as a commission in view of an eventual publication. From the perspective of contemporary practices, it would be logical for the counterproofs to have been made and retouched to serve as models for a printmaker, with the resulting prints then being in the same direction as the initial series, with the swords and the buttons of the costumes appropriately placed.

But the project produced nothing further until the end of the 1780s. It was at that time that Augustin de Saint-Aubin, Jean-Baptiste Tilliard, and Jean-Baptiste Joseph Delafosse came together to produce a new edition of the *Contes*. The text was published by Pierre Didot in 1795, and the plates, eighty in number, were to appear in several successive editions. The *Mercure de France* specified that the prints were all after drawings by Fragonard, who had created them "in the past . . . in Rome, in the full fire of youth."[7] Fragonard's compositions had to be redrawn, however, to both bring them up to date and provide the printmakers more finished versions that would be suitable for transcription by burin. But no more than about twenty plates were published, of which only seventeen were after Fragonard.[8] Records of payments prove that the artist redrew some of his compositions himself, while others were given to vignette specialists such as Charles Monnet.[9]

But well before Didot's project saw the light of day, Fragonard's compositions were known to collectors, as is proven by the appearance at auction between 1776 and 1786 of several subjects taken from the *Contes*.[10] It is known that La Fontaine's salacious tales enjoyed a renewal of interest during the eighteenth century, in particular due to the illustrated editions by Charles Nicolas Cochin II (1745) and Charles Dominique Joseph Eisen (1762). Fragonard stands apart from his predecessors in both his choice of episodes and their witty compositions, revealing their author's humor and subtlety. So it is not surprising that collectors, who were fond of light and gallant subjects, wished to acquire examples of these illustrations. And rather than giving up sheets from the first or second series, which he probably hoped to be able to use at some point, Fragonard repeated certain subjects. At present only a small number of these autograph replicas are known. Hence, it does not make sense to consider them a homogenous series, especially as they could have been created over several years; it is difficult to determine whether they are repetitions created to be engraved in Didot's publication or made on occasion in response to a commission.

The case presents itself with *The Fiancée of the King of Garbe*. The retouched counterproof (fig. 127) shows Alaciel, daughter of the sultan of Alexandria and destined to marry the king of Garbe, allowing herself to be wooed by a Sudanese lord, Hispal.[11] A great poetic effect emanates from this composition, where the landscape, offering itself

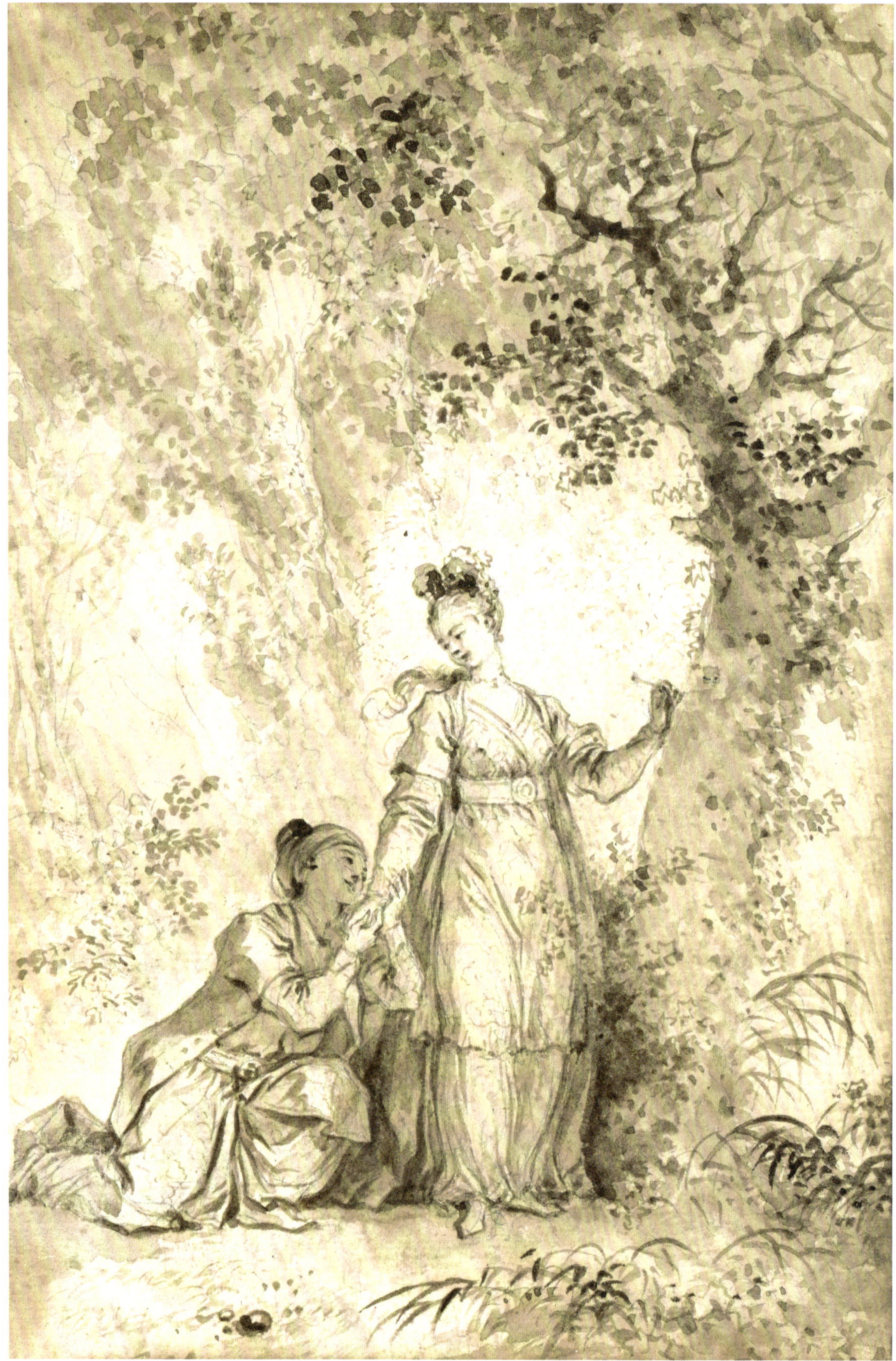

CAT 85

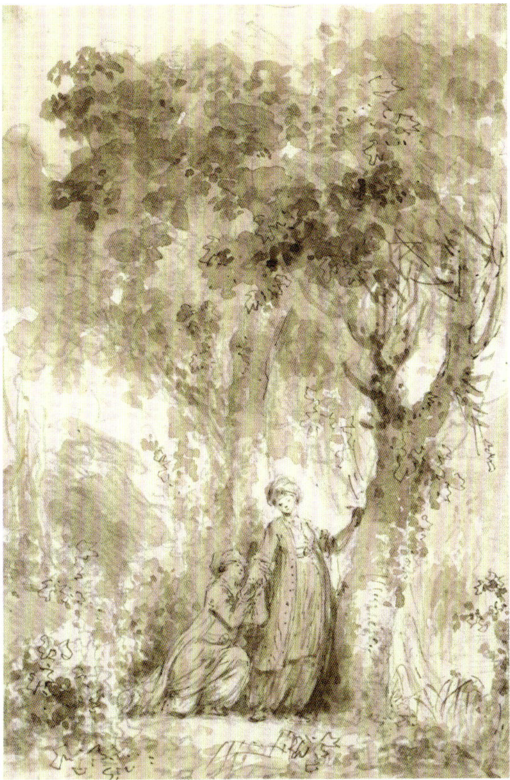

Fig. 127. Jean Honoré Fragonard, *The Fiancée of the King of Garbe*, ca. 1761–63. Brown wash, pen and brown ink over a black chalk counterproof, 8⅛ × 5½ in. (20.5 × 13.9 cm). Petit Palais, Musée des Beaux-Arts de la Ville de Paris (L. Dut. 1173, vol. 1, pl. 13)

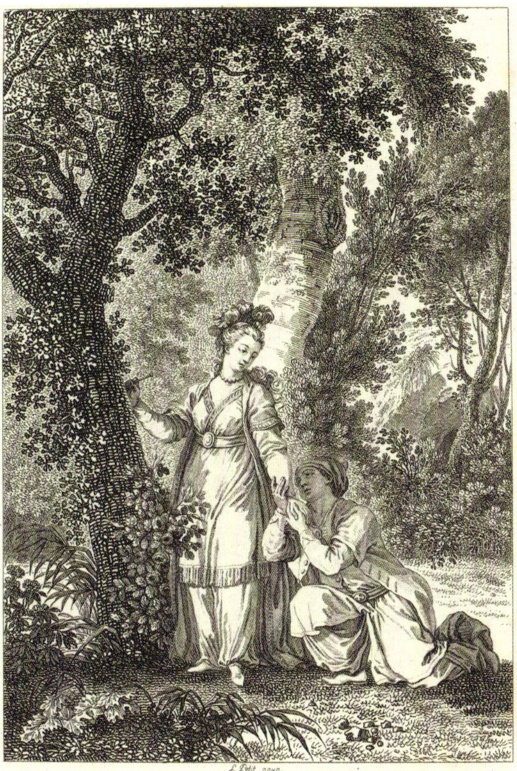

Fig. 128. Louis Jacques Petit, *The Fiancée of the King of Garbe*, after Fragonard, ca. 1790(?). Etching, 7⅞ × 5⅜ in. (19.8 × 13.4 cm). National Gallery of Art, Washington, D.C. (1953.6.195)

as a refuge to the lovers, takes up most of the page. In the Morgan Library version shown here, which is of the same dimensions, the composition is tightened around the couple, and Alaciel, her loosened hair no longer constrained by a turban, sports a costume that better accentuates her femininity. This latter composition was the basis for a print by Louis Jacques Petit (fig. 128), which could date to the end of the 1780s or to the following decade, as Fragonard signed a receipt in 1797 for the payment for two illustrations, including that of "the King of Garbe's fiancée."[12] However, we know from the auction catalogues that at least one other version illustrating this tale existed before Didot's project was embarked upon (see "Provenance").

The question of dating also arises for the Metropolitan's version of *The Husband-Confessor.* It repeats quite precisely the composition in the counterproof version in the Petit Palais, which was based on an initial sketch in black chalk (fig. 129).[13] The changes for the most part move in the direction of greater precision, in particular in the description of the salon where the knight Artus, having returned from war, surprises his wife in gallant company. Large Corinthian capitals crown the pilasters between which medallion portraits are hung. In the background, on the left, can be seen a niche decorated with a shell motif. Although the costumes, like the decor, evoke the era of Louis XV and would have looked old-fashioned at the time, in 1795 the composition was faithfully transcribed in a print by Tilliard.[14] However, the sword of the young man who kisses the fickle wife's hand was added to the present drawing and doesn't appear in the print.[15] We also note somewhat less animation in the drawing, due partly to the ages of the protagonists, who are no longer the adolescents of the earlier versions, and also to the prudent and carefully applied brushwork, worthy of that of a miniaturist. As often with these repetitions, the scene loses in spontaneity what it gains in legibility. MADV

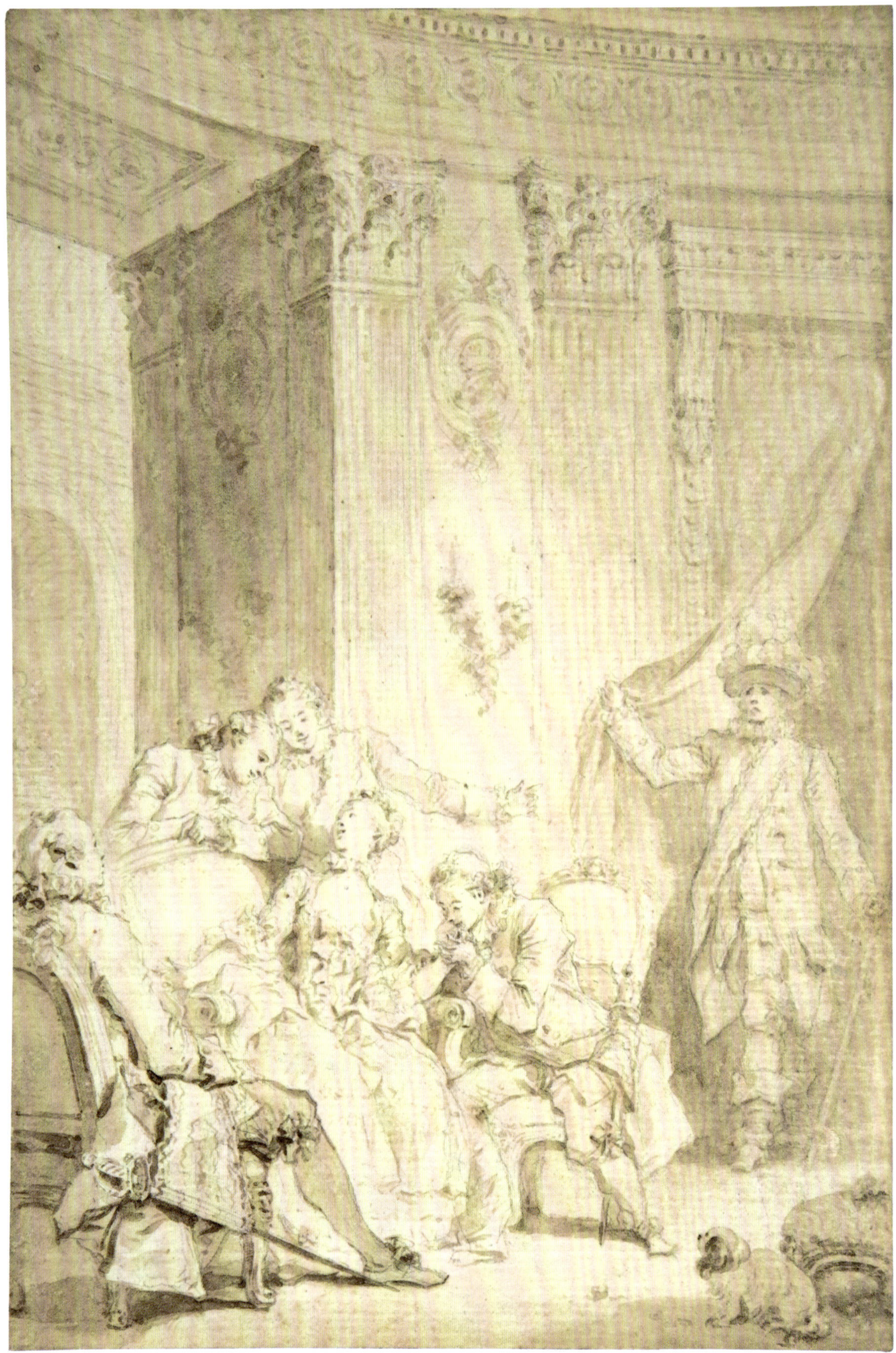

CAT 86

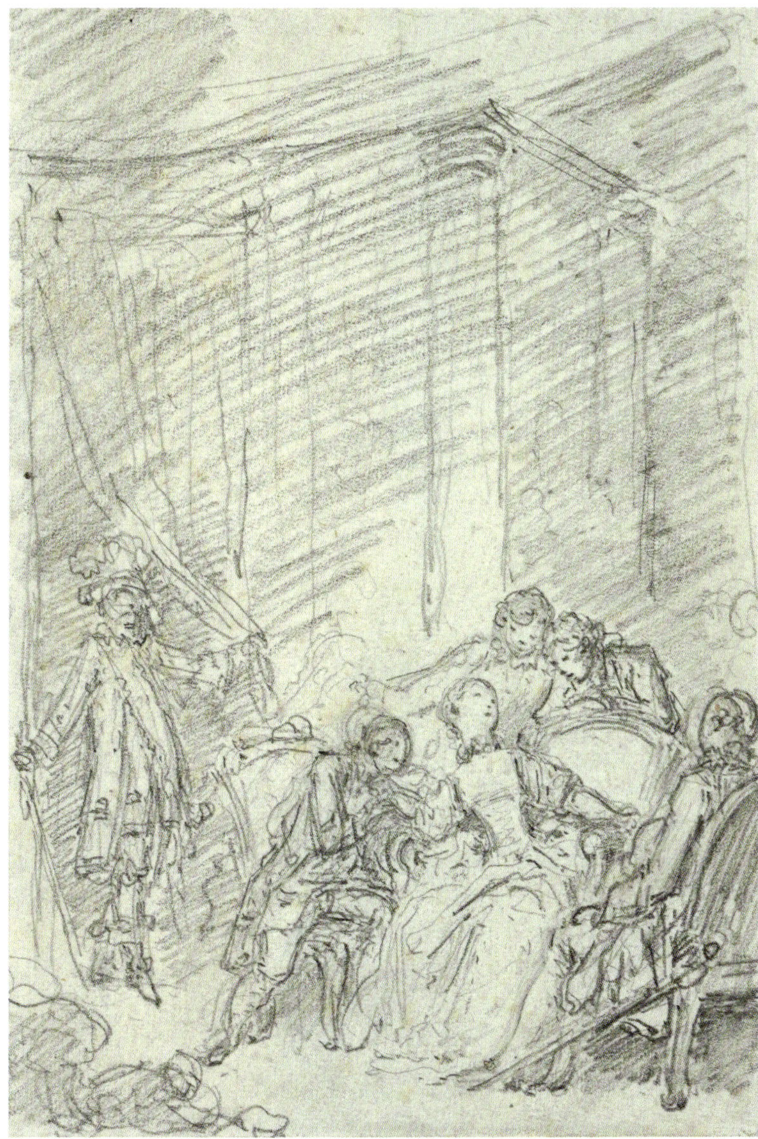

Fig. 129. Jean Honoré Fragonard, *The Husband-Confessor*, ca. 1761–63. Black chalk, 8 × 5½ in. (20.3 × 13.8 cm). Private collection, New York

CAT. 85. PROVENANCE: Possibly sale (Lugt 2533), Chariot and Paillet, Paris, April 22, 1776 (lot 172, "Un jeune Turc aux pieds de sa Maîtresse, dessin au bistre, sur papier blanc"), acquired for 62,19 livres by Jean Antoine Vassal de Saint-Hubert (1741–1782); possibly his collection sale (Lugt 2982), Remy, Paris, March 29–April 13, 1779 (under lot 183, "Quatre sujets tirés des Contes de La Fontaine . . . 7 pouces 9 lignes de haut sur 5 pouces de large [21 × 13.5 cm]"), 181 livres; possibly chevalier de C[lesle] sale (Lugt 4101), Paillet and Boileau, Paris, December 4, 1786 (lot 117, "Un petit Dessin pareillement lavé de bistre, & touché avec esprit; il représente une jeune femme & son amant vus dans un bosquet, & vêtus suivant le costume Turc. Hauteur 7 pouces & demi, largeur 5 pouces 3 lig. [20 × 14 cm]"), 27 livres 12; possibly sale [J. M. des Jamonières], February 24, 1883 (part of lot 13, "la Fiancée du roi de Garbe"); possibly A. Piat estate sale (Lugt 55155), Hôtel Drouot, Paris, March 22–23, 1897 (part of lot 50 [no. 7]); sale, Galerie Charpentier, Paris, June 14, 1955 (lot 73, pl. XXXVIII); private collection (1970); [Thomas Agnew & Sons, Ltd, London (1992)]; The Morgan Library & Museum, New York, Purchased on the Gordon N. Ray Fund (1993.3)

SELECTED REFERENCES: Ananoff 1961–70, vol. 4 (1970), no. 2708, fig. 676, and no. 2720 (for the early provenances); Roland Michel 1970, p. iii, fig. 2b, p. vi n. 16; Dupuy-Vachey 2007, p. 63, fig. 20b.

CAT. 86. PROVENANCE: M. J. D[oucet] sale, Hôtel Drouot, Paris, May 16–17, 1906 (lot 25, "Le mari confesseur. Composition à plusieurs personnages dans un intérieur, pour illustrer un conte de La Fontaine [édition Didot]. Dessin à la sépia. A été gravé par Tilliard [20.5 × 14 cm]"), sold for 2,700 francs to Paulme; Henri Lehmann (1814–1882); Lehmann sale, Paris, June 8, 1925 (lot 154, "Le Mari confesseur. Illustration d'un conte de La Fontaine, pour l'édition Didot, in-4°, 1795. Dessin au lavis de sepia [20.5 × 14.5 cm]"); Marcel Razsovich, Saint-Germain-en-Laye (1931); [A. & R. Ball, New York]; Mr. and Mrs. Lesley Sheafer in 1948; The Metropolitan Museum of Art, New York, The Lesley and Emma Sheafer Collection, Bequest of Emma A. Sheafer, 1973 (1974.356.44)

SELECTED EXHIBITIONS: Paris 1931, cat. no. 113; Williams 1978, cat. no. 53.

SELECTED REFERENCES: Ananoff 1961–70, vol. 4 (1970), no. 2717; Roland Michel 1970, p. vi n. 16; Bean and Turčić 1986, no. 113; Schroder 1996, no. 4, p. 435 n. 5; Schroder 2011, p. 157.

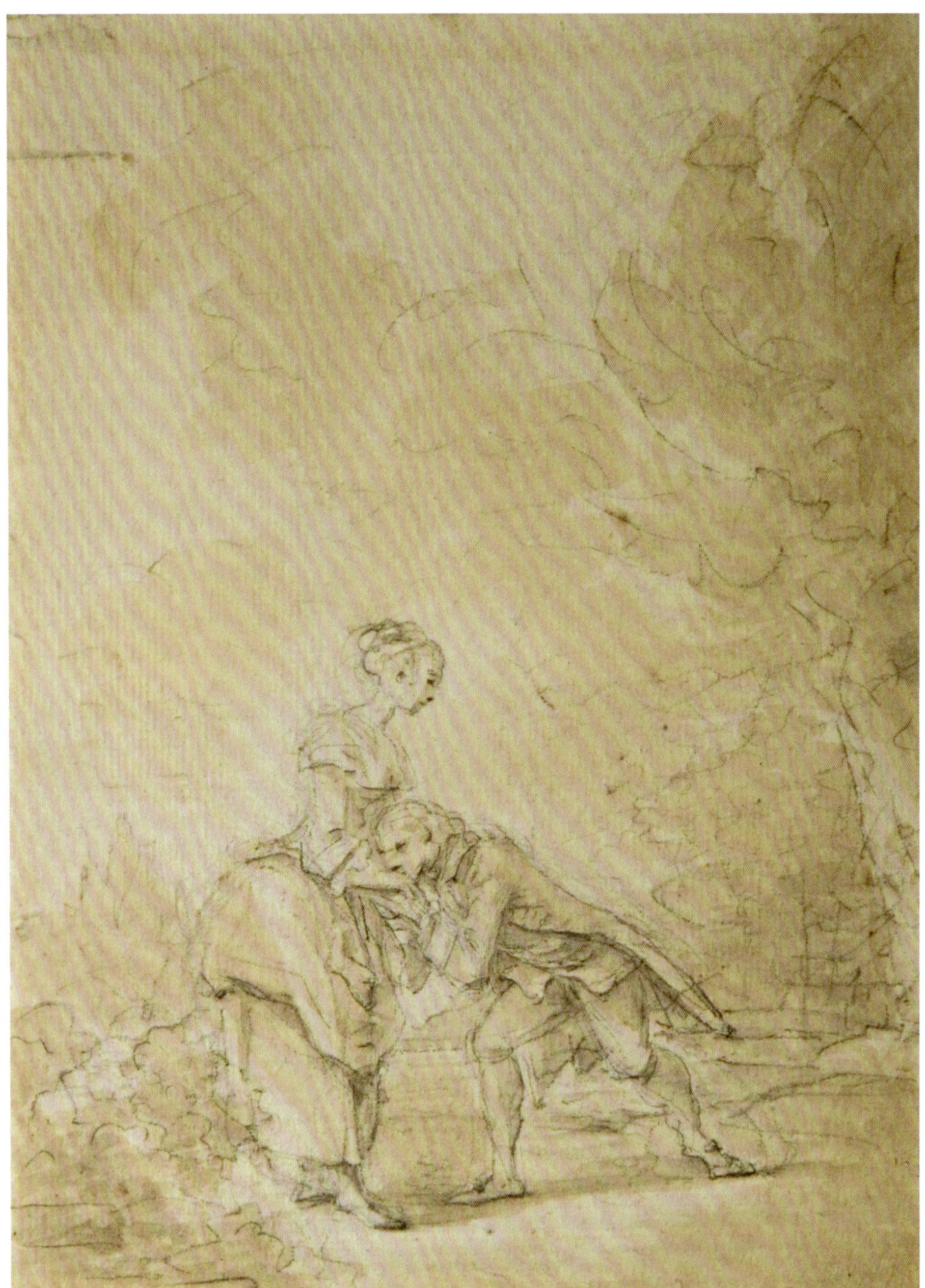

CAT 88

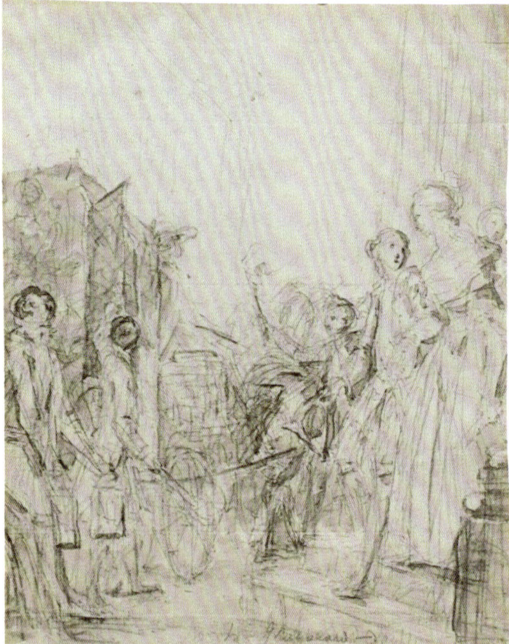

Fig. 131. Jean Honoré Fragonard, *Aline and Saint Phar Leaving the Opera*, ca. 1770–75. Black chalk, brown wash, 8¼ × 6⅝ in. (20.8 × 16.8 cm). Private collection

contours of the natural settings in a way provide a signature for these drawings. The chalk grazes the paper by zigzagging among the foliage and vegetation. On the other hand, the rather light and fairly uniform wash, like the numerous pentimenti that characterize each sheet, could give the impression of a hesitant, even inexperienced hand. The artist seems to be ill at ease in the depiction of the architecture and interiors, as we can see with Aline's salon, where the proliferation of lines constructs quite a confused space. It is possible to make out windows and a tapestry, but the elements do not manage to define a coherent interior. Does the sketch in the upper central area indicate a chandelier or a Rococo boiserie? The position of the chairs and their legs seems also to have caused the draftsman problems. We are similarly surprised by the many pentimenti in the depiction of the figures. The chalk corrects in an almost systematic manner the contours or the expression of a face, the folds in a piece of clothing, the volume of a coiffure. The positions of the arms and legs are also frequently modified, as in the scene showing Saint Phar hanging from the window and twisting his legs in the air. The intention in these cases is obviously to maximize the animation of the compositions, to compete, in a way, with Boufflers's lively and impulsive style. The very lightly sketched nature of the drawings must of course be explained by their status as a project in the process of development. It is likely that it did not go beyond this stage due to the lack of publishing opportunities. Nevertheless, it must have been an important project for the artist, as is demonstrated by a preliminary sketch for the fourth illustration (fig. 131),[4] which is even more schematic. Given the multiple differences compared to a more developed version in Chicago,[5] this one cannot be a copy. No other drawing by Fragonard is known to show such stiff and disproportionate figures, formed by clumsily applied patches of wash. The question of dating for such a series is thus especially complicated to resolve. Without any conclusive evidence, we suggested in 2007 placing the drawings shortly after the publication of the story, attributing their imperfections to the artist's inexperience in regard to illustration. But since that initial

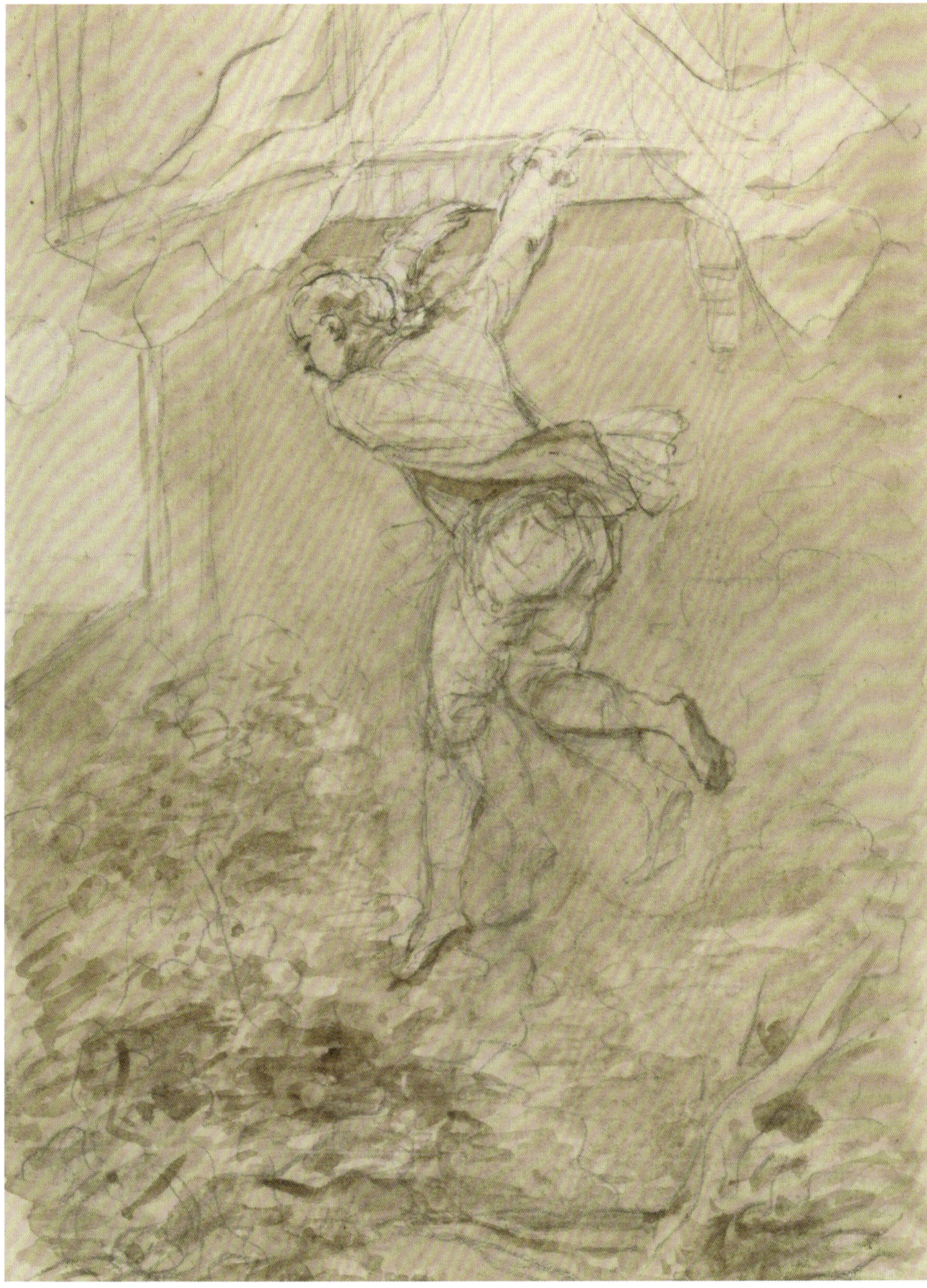

CAT 89

To illustrate La Fontaine's *Contes* (*Tales*) (see cats. 85 and 86), Fragonard relied on a very strong black chalk structure before going over the counterproofs with a pen and brush. Here, he seems to be struggling in search of a style better suited to the illustration of a printed publication. The angular, almost harsh line is in a way intended to be more precise or more descriptive, as if the artist were trying to conform to the standards of professional illustrators. But the result, even at this sketch stage, is a little forced. His imagination and love of movement seem to be restricted. The artist has not succeeded in giving his compositions for Boufflers the spontaneity that emanates from his drawings inspired by La Fontaine. This series with its subtle charm is nonetheless extremely precious, because few studies of this type, showing the artist's work in progress, have survived. MADV

CAT. 87. PROVENANCE: Possibly Jacques de Bryas collection sale (Lugt 56156), Galerie Georges Petit, Paris, April 4–6, 1898 (lot 66, "Scène d'intérieur. Quatre personnages sont groupés auprès d'une table; deux jeunes gens et une jeune femme assis examinent des étoffes. Dessin à la sépia [22 × 17 cm]"), sold for 720 francs to Duval; sale, Hôtel Drouot, Paris, February 22–23, 1905 (lot 58, "[Fragonard?]," "Une famille dans un salon, groupée autour d'une table. Dessin à la mine de plomb rehaussé de sépia, d'une exécution libre, spirituelle et élégante. [23 × 17 cm]"); Serullaz, Paris (according to Henriot); David David-Weill, Neuilly-sur-Seine; private collection

SELECTED REFERENCES: Henriot 1926–28, vol. 3 (1928), pp. 105–7, ill.; Ananoff 1961–70, vol. 2 (1963), no. 643, vol. 3 (1968), no. 1212.

CAT. 88. PROVENANCE: Georges Bourgarel sale (part one, Lugt 83841), Hôtel Drouot, Paris, June 15–16, 1922 (lot 87, repr.), sold for 1,650 francs to M. Kieffer; M. and Mme René Kieffer sale, Paris, May 29, 1969 (lot 16, repr.), sold for 17,000 francs to Cailleux; [Galerie Cailleux, Paris, gallery stamp (Lugt 4461) at lower right, partly effaced, straddling the drawing and the mount]; [Colnaghi, London]; Dr. Mary Tavener Holmes

analysis,[6] it has been possible to link two other drawings to Boufflers's tale, including the one here showing Aline in her salon. The costumes in it are, as is most often the case with Fragonard, quite generic. However, Aline's dress, in its simplicity, can be identified with English-style dresses, which were very fashionable in the 1770s.[7] An even more significant clue is provided by our lovely seductress's medallion chair. Bill Pallot,[8] to whom we are grateful, has indicated that, although oval backs are known from as early as 1765, the fact that the one here is combined with round, tapered legs precludes dating the chair before 1768; a dating of about 1770–75 appears to him more likely.[9]

SELECTED EXHIBITIONS: New York 1983, cat. no. 3; New York 1987, cat. no. 65 (entry by Alan Wintermute); Dupuy-Vachey 2007, p. 170 and cat. no. 39 (not exhibited).

SELECTED REFERENCES: Ananoff 1961–70, vol. 3 (1968), no. 1231, vol. 4 (1970), p. 418; Williams 1978, p. 142, fig. 9.

CAT. 89. PROVENANCE: Walferdin sale, April 12–16, 1880 (lot 217, "La Fuite par la croisée. Dessin à la sépia [22 × 17 cm]"), 265 francs; Hecht, Paris (1889); [Wildenstein (according to information from the owner and from labels on the back of the frame), Pontremoli]; [Rosenberg and Stiebel]; Irene Roosevelt Aitken

SELECTED REFERENCES: Portalis 1889, vol. 2, p. 302; Ananoff 1961–70, vol. 4 (1970), no. 2022.

90. *The Pasha Receiving in His Harem*

Ca. 1776–78(?)
Brush and brown wash over black chalk
6⅞ × 8⅝ in. (17.5 × 21.9 cm)

It would be wrong to underestimate this quick scribble of a sketch, which is not without its charm. Sheets of this type, in which the artist's initial intentions in the development of a composition are expressed so spontaneously, are very rare. Here, a few geometrical lines organize the space succinctly, while the actors are sketched with a nervous hand. The application of the wash is no more meticulous. The brush sweeps large areas of the background and proceeds by daubs and zigzags to model the elliptical forms of the figures. Then slightly thicker and more strongly applied chalk repeats and corrects some forms. The artist juggles his two tools, passing easily from the chalk to the brush to better translate the composition he has imagined, which progressively takes form on the paper. In the same way, he tests different solutions, like, for example, the background of the room broken up with rectangular panels. The broad passages of wash could evoke tapestries or mirrors. The light central area is adorned with a lattice pattern traced with the brush; above emerges a chandelier or sconce drawn in chalk. To the right, the same motif is repeated in wash over a few dancing lines in chalk that could indicate the ornamental design of a boiserie. A simpler solution was finally adopted, as demonstrated by a comparison with the painting (fig. 132) for which our drawing and a few other sketches[1] were preparatory.[2] Large yellow curtains line the background quite uniformly, thus providing a better foil to the main scene. But we also note that all the elements required for the composition are already in place in the rough little sketch, from the arrangement of the trio on the left to the relaxed pose of the sultan reclining upon the cushions of a large sofa. The principal modifications lie in the addition of a second attendant behind the sultan and the omission of the little seated dog seen in profile on the extreme right of the sheet. Although Fragonard enjoyed repeating the image of a beautiful young woman dressed as a sultana during the 1770s,[3] the composition of *The Pasha* is unique in his work. It could have its origin in a story by the writer Jean François Marmontel, an author who had already inspired the painter shortly after his return from Italy, as seen in two canvases based on the story "Annette and Lubin" from Marmontel's *Moral Tales*.[4] About fifteen years after their publication in 1761, his *Moral Tales* were still quite popular, and Fragonard's painting could well be an illustration of an episode from "Soliman the Second," or rather from Charles Simon Favart's theatrical adaptation of that story, *Soliman II, or the Three Sultanas*.[5] In Constantinople, three European slaves were presented to Soliman successively. The sultan tired quickly of Elmire and then of Délia before succumbing to the charms of the cheeky and indomitable Roxelane, whom he ended up marrying. Two of these characters could be represented by the girls that the vizier presents to the pasha in Fragonard's seductive composition. MADV

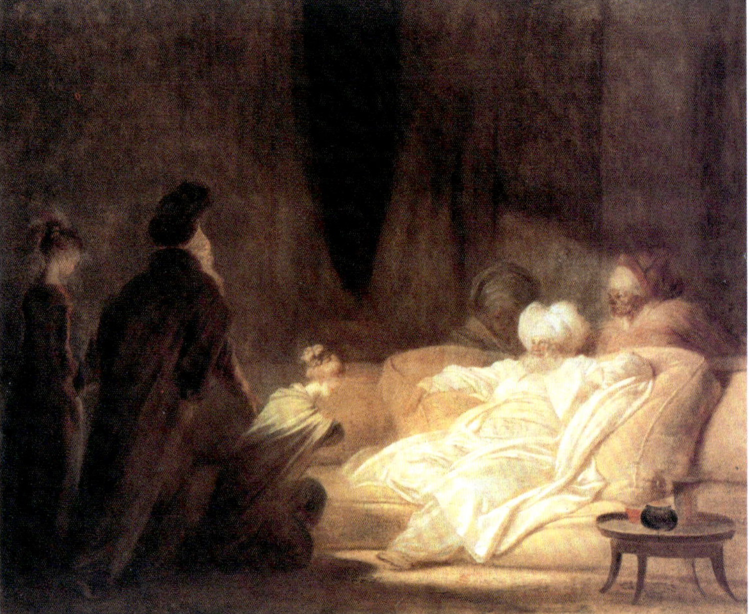

Fig. 132. Jean Honoré Fragonard, *The Pasha*, ca. 1776–78(?). Oil on canvas, 28¾ × 36¼ in. (73 × 92 cm). Private collection

PROVENANCE: [Galerie Glaenzer, Paris]; acquired by Mortimer L. Schiff in 1908; private collection

SELECTED REFERENCES: Rosenberg 1988, pp. 455, 456, fig. 3; Dupuy-Vachey 2007, p. 170, under cat. no. 40, n. 4.

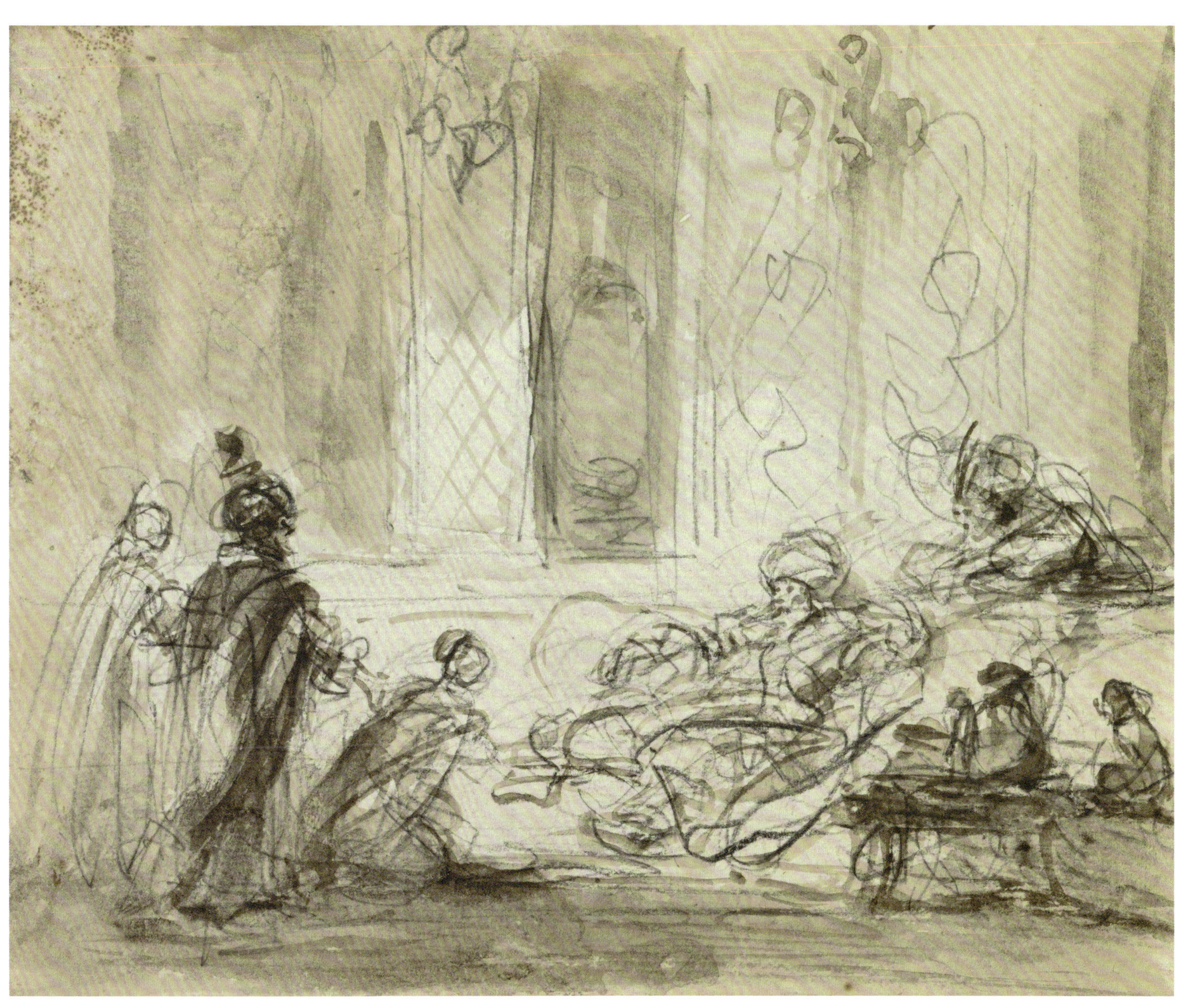

Ariosto's *Orlando Furioso*

Fragonard produced at least 179 drawings inspired by *Orlando Furioso*, an epic poem by Ludovico Ariosto.[1] Written in 1516 for the court of Cardinal Ippolito II d'Este, *Orlando Furioso* details the romantic and chivalric exploits of two heroes, Orlando and Ruggiero. Their adventures unfold against the backdrop of a religious war between the Christian emperor Charlemagne and a fictional Saracen king, Agramante. Orlando, Charlemagne's nephew, abandons his uncle's crusade to pursue Angelica, a pagan princess. When Orlando learns that Angelica has eloped with Medoro, a Saracen soldier, he is driven to madness. Ruggiero, a knight in Agramante's army, is similarly motivated by his impossible love for Orlando's cousin, Bradamante. Though Ruggiero is easily distracted by beautiful maidens, his indiscretions are redeemed when he converts to Christianity and marries the object of his affection.[2]

Replete with violence, magic, and lust, Ariosto's fantastic narrative stimulated the imaginations of several artists in the second half of the eighteenth century.[3] Giovanni Battista Tiepolo, for example, painted a series of frescoes based on *Orlando Furioso* at the Villa Valmarana in Vicenza in 1757,[4] and François Boucher exhibited a canvas depicting the amorous bliss of Angelica and Medoro at the Salon of 1765.[5] Several illustrated editions of *Orlando Furioso* also appeared in the final decades of the century. John Baskerville's edition, published in Paris in 1773, employed forty-six illustrations—one for each of the cantos of the poem—by Giovanni Battista Cipriani, Charles Nicolas Cochin II, Charles Dominique Joseph Eisen, Jean-Baptiste Greuze, Charles Monnet, and Jean Michel Moreau the Younger. A French prose translation by Louis d'Ussieux, published between 1775 and 1783, made use of the same engravings.[6]

These heavy, staid illustrations have little in common with Fragonard's whimsical, ebullient sketches for *Orlando Furioso*, which are traditionally dated to the 1780s on the basis of their loose and confident style (see, for example, fig. 133).[7] This theory seems to be confirmed by Fragonard's grandson, Théophile, who wrote that it was during the final twenty-five years of the artist's career, when "the vogue for Fragonard's work ceased," that he "executed several hundred drawings for *Orlando Furioso* and equally as many large and magnificent drawings for *Don Quixote*."[8]

Unlike Fragonard's illustrations for Jean de La Fontaine's *Contes* (*Tales*) of the 1760s (cats. 85 and 86), however, there is

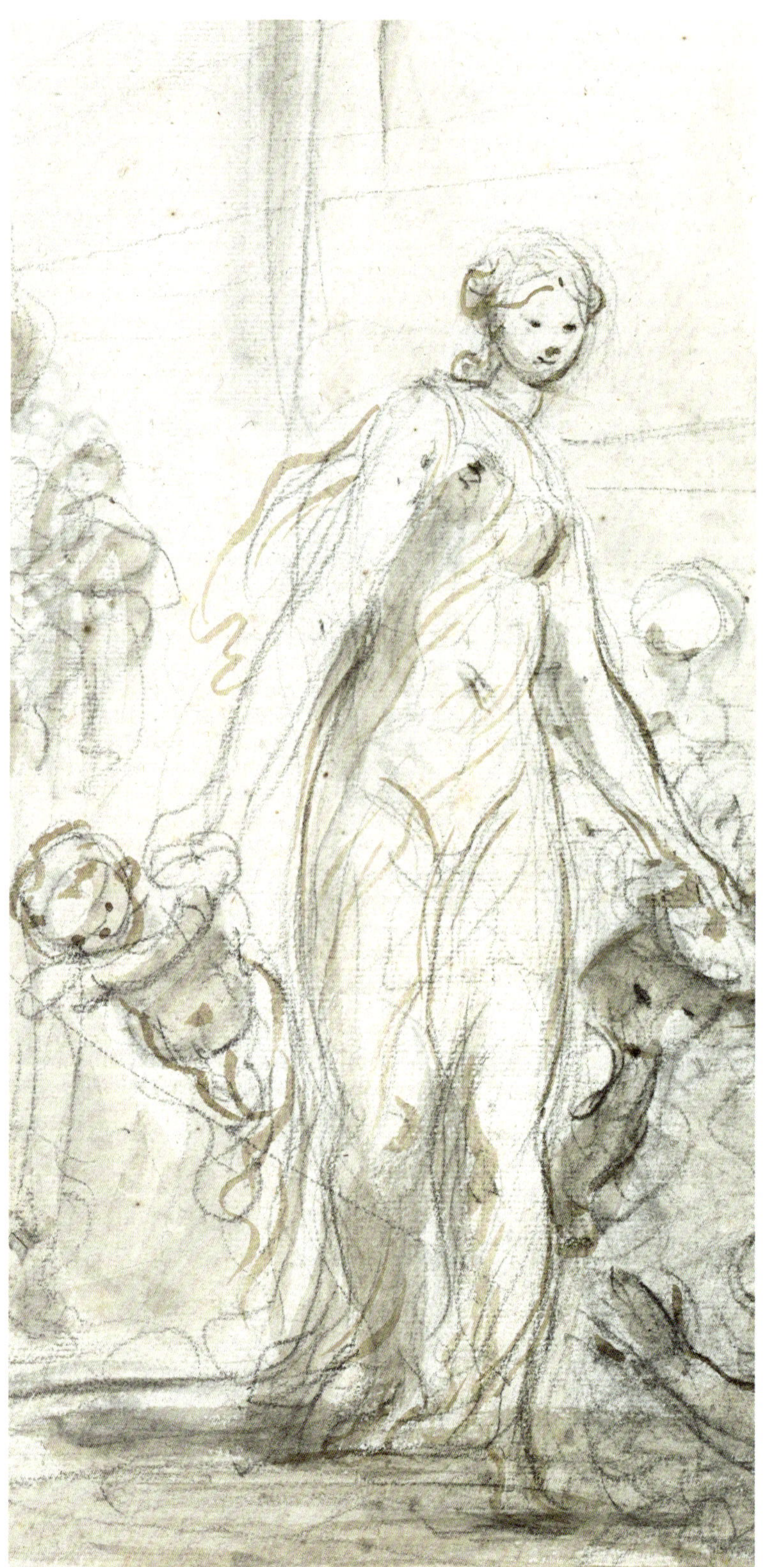

Fig. 133. Detail of *Ruggiero and Alcina at the Bath*, cat. 91

no evidence that his *Orlando Furioso* drawings were meant to be published.[9] Indeed, it would have been impractical to include so many illustrations in a single edition, and Fragonard's chaotic skeins of black chalk and liberal clouds of wash would have been ill suited to reproductive engraving.[10] The drawings may have been *premières pensées* (initial sketches) for a never-realized publication or private commission, yet the sheer number of these impulsive, expressive drawings underscores the personal nature of the project.

Several questions about the *Orlando Furioso* drawings remain. Why did Fragonard choose to represent the scenes that he did? It would seem that, for reasons unknown, Fragonard simply never finished illustrating the text. The drawings illustrate only the first sixteen cantos of the poem, with a handful of drawings tentatively assigned to the last thirty cantos.[11] Furthermore, the distribution of illustrations within those first sixteen cantos is uneven; for example, Fragonard dedicated only two drawings to canto 5, but at least twenty-one drawings to canto 15. This asymmetry may be attributed to the project's incompleteness, or to the artist's discretion.

Fragonard's relationship to the poem is another subject of scholarly debate. The specificity of each drawing suggests a close engagement with the text, whether the artist consulted the original Italian stanzas (as suggested by Marie-Anne Dupuy-Vachey[12]) or an eighteenth-century French prose translation. Endowed with a lyrical theatricality, the drawings may also bear the influence of contemporary opera—for example, *Roland*, a collaboration of French poet Jean François Marmontel and Italian composer Niccolò Piccinni, which was performed by the Académie Royale de Musique at the Théâtre du Palais-Royal in 1778.[13]

Whatever his source, Fragonard translated the frenetic energy of Ariosto's world into a piquant graphic shorthand. Human and animal forms are loosely delineated with black chalk and intuitively embellished with brown wash, ranging from delicate, cursive lines to heavy-handed flourishes. Absent anatomical and facial details, Fragonard's illustrations nevertheless make legible the range of emotions that comprise *Orlando Furioso*. Pleasure, fear, triumph, jealousy, and despair are evoked through bold, dynamic compositions—among the most abstract and imaginative of Fragonard's graphic oeuvre. KB

91. *Ruggiero and Alcina at the Bath*

Ca. 1780–85
Brush and brown wash over black chalk
15½ × 9½ in. (39.4 × 24.1 cm)

In the midst of battle, Ruggiero, a Saracen warrior in King Agramante's army, falls in love with Bradamante, a Christian warrior-maiden in Charlemagne's army. The two are separated, however, when Ruggiero is abducted by a winged hippogriff and transported to the island of a sorceress named Alcina. Ruggiero falls under Alcina's spell and succumbs to the sensual pleasures of her palace, his chaste love for Bradamante forgotten.

In this drawing, one of several that he dedicated to the lovers' idyll, Fragonard evokes the voluptuous languor of the enchanted isle. Alcina steps gingerly into a bath, where Ruggiero waits with open arms. Delicate, cursory strokes of brown wash describe her flowing hair, the curves of her thighs, and the plump winged putti by her side; minimal dots of wash indicate her eyes and nipples. The columned pavilion and attendant members of Alcina's court, however, are only implied with preparatory black chalk lines. The figure of Alcina recalls the elegant female nude in Boucher's *Pygmalion and Galatea* at the State Hermitage Museum in Saint Petersburg (fig. 134), a formal echo that indicates the enduring significance of Fragonard's training in Boucher's studio. KB

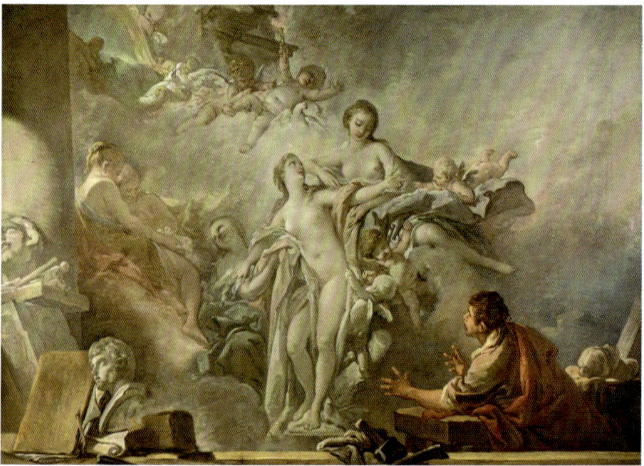

Fig. 134. François Boucher (French, 1703–1770), *Pygmalion and Galatea*, before 1766. Oil on canvas, 7 ft. 8⅛ in. × 13 ft. 1½ in. (2.34 × 4 m). State Hermitage Museum, Saint Petersburg (ГЭ3683)

PROVENANCE: Probably the artist's family; Hippolyte Walferdin (1795–1880), Paris; his estate sale (Lugt 40073), Hôtel Drouot, Paris, April 12–16, 1880 (part of lot 228); Louis Roederer (d. 1880), Reims; Léon Olry-Roederer, until 1922; Abraham Simon Wolf Rosenbach (1876–1952), Philadelphia; John Fleming; private collector in 1955, until 1978; [Agnew's, London]; Mr. and Mrs. Eugene V. Thaw; The Morgan Library & Museum, New York, Thaw Collection (2001.61:1)

SELECTED EXHIBITIONS: London 1978a, cat. no. 9; Denison et al. 1985, pp. 34–35, cat. no. 12; Denison et al. 1994, p. 259.

SELECTED REFERENCES: Mongan et al. 1945, pp. 65–66, no. 34; Dupuy-Vachey 2003, pp. 17, 124–25, 381, no. 47.

92. *With Logistilla's Guidance, Ruggiero Masters the Hippogriff*

Ca. 1780–85
Brush and brown wash over black chalk
15⅜ × 10¼ in. (39.1 × 25.9 cm)

Ruggiero realizes that he has been seduced by Alcina, neglecting both his chaste love for Bradamante and his own sense of chivalric duty. Desperate to escape, Ruggiero solicits the aid of Alcina's sister, Logistilla, the embodiment of wisdom. Logistilla teaches Ruggiero to ride the mythical hippogriff, which serves as a metaphor for reining unbridled passion with reason. He then departs in search of Bradamante.

In Fragonard's illustration, Ruggiero soars into the sky astride the mythical beast, while Logistilla bids him farewell. Fragonard indicates Ruggiero's rapid, triumphant ascent with a quick black chalk sketch and uses a heavier concentration of wash to accentuate Logistilla's billowing robe in the foreground. According to Eunice Williams, this drawing employs the compositional strategies of eighteenth-century history painters such as François Boucher and Charles Joseph Natoire, whose dynamic canvases portray mythological subjects unburdened by gravity and buoyed by clouds.[1] KB

PROVENANCE: Probably the artist's family; Hippolyte Walferdin (1795–1880), Paris; his estate sale (Lugt 40073), Hôtel Drouot, Paris, April 12–16, 1880 (part of lot 228); Louis Roederer (d. 1880), Reims; Léon Olry-Roederer; Abraham Simon Wolf Rosenbach (1876–1952), Philadelphia; John Fleming; private collector in 1955, until 1978; [Agnew's, London]; Mr. and Mrs. Eugene V. Thaw; The Morgan Library & Museum, New York, Thaw Collection (2001.61:2)

SELECTED EXHIBITIONS: Williams 1978, pp. 160–61, cat. no. 65; Denison et al. 1985, p. 36, cat. no. 13; Denison et al. 1994, p. 259.

SELECTED REFERENCES: Mongan et al. 1945, p. 69, no. 65; Ashton 1988, pp. 210, 215; Dupuy-Vachey 2003, pp. 210–11, 384–85, no. 90.

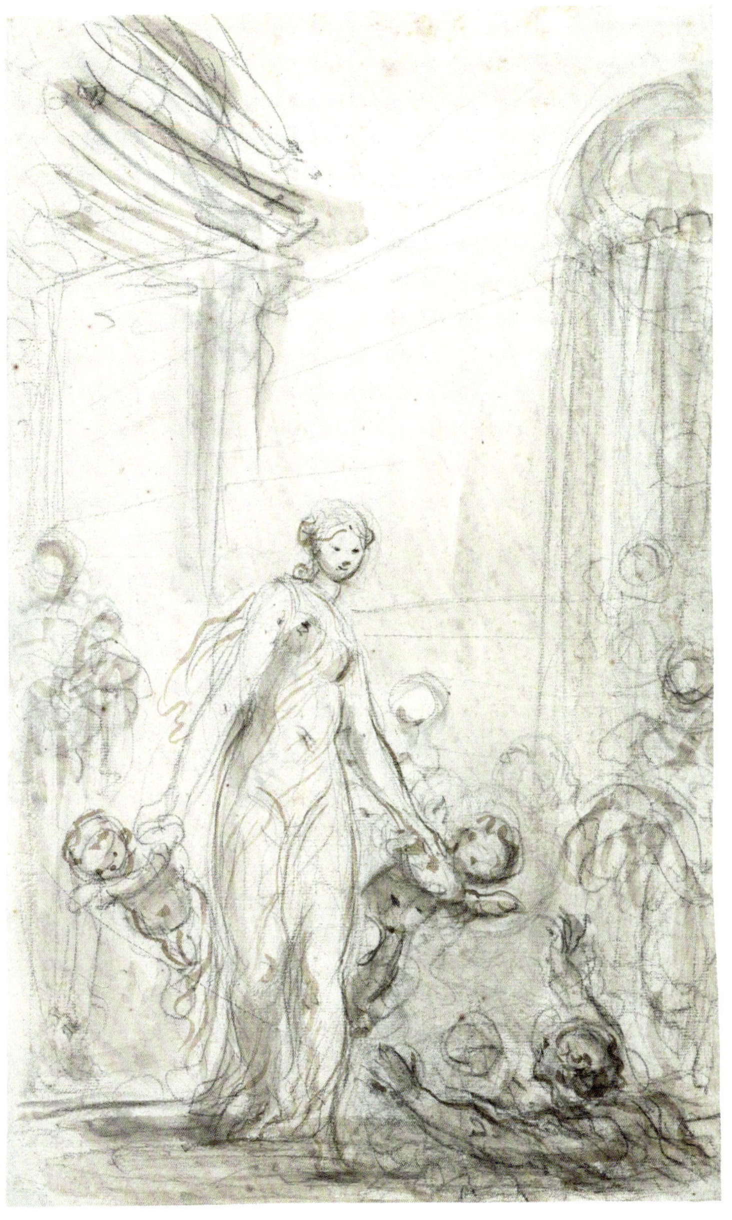

CAT 91

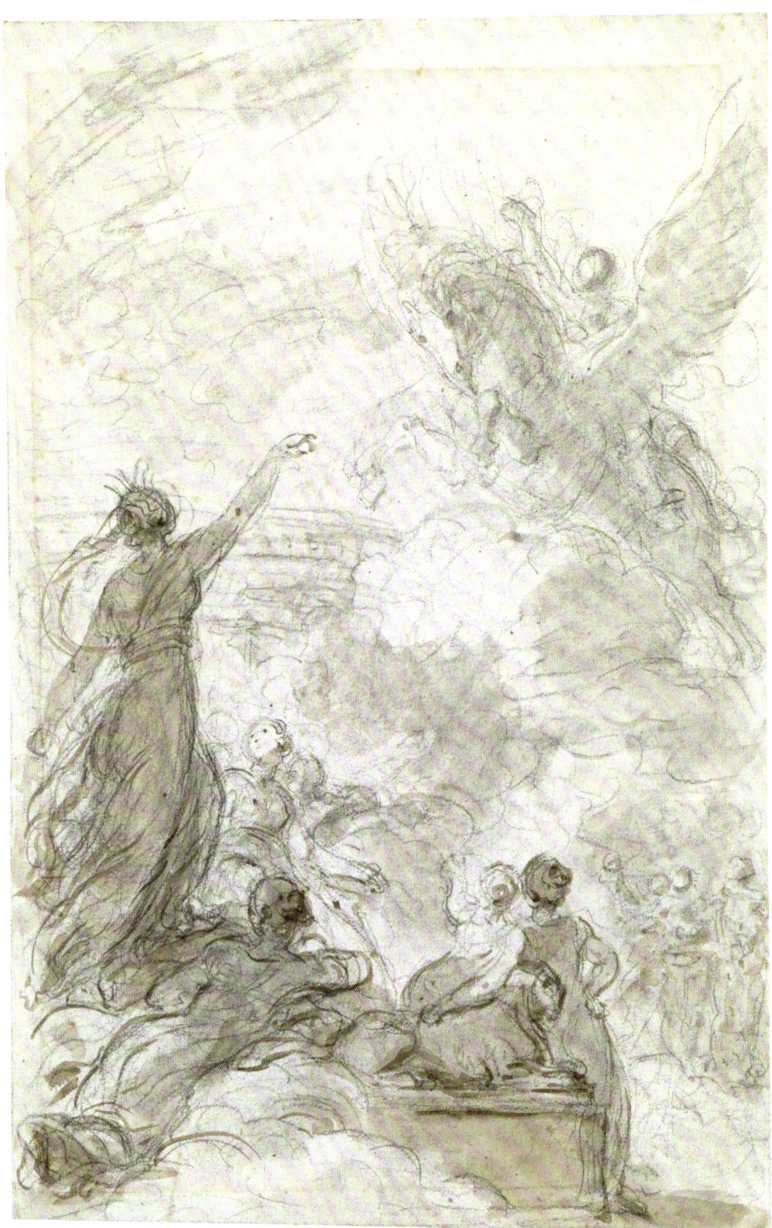

CAT 92

93. *Orlando Leaves Paris in Disguise*

Ca. 1780–85
Brush and brown wash over black chalk
15⅜ × 9⅞ in. (39.1 × 25.1 cm)

Orlando, Charlemagne's nephew and a knight in his court, has fallen in love with Angelica, a pagan princess. One night, while King Agramante lays siege to Charlemagne's Paris, Orlando dreams that Angelica is in mortal danger. Convinced that he must rescue the object of his affection, the warrior quickly dons his armor—with the exception of his family's crest—and steals away from his uncle's palace before the sun rises. This drawing captures Orlando's sense of urgency as he nimbly climbs onto his horse, Brigliadoro. Fragonard also renders the imposing structure of Charlemagne's fortress with an unusual amount of solidity, detailing the heavy, chained wooden portal beneath which Orlando escapes. KB

PROVENANCE: Probably the artist's family; Hippolyte Walferdin (1795–1880), Paris; his estate sale (Lugt 40073), Hôtel Drouot, Paris, April 12–16, 1880 (part of lot 228); Louis Roederer (d. 1880), Reims; Léon Olry-Roederer; Abraham Simon Wolf Rosenbach (1876–1952), Philadelphia, until 1947; Norton Simon Collection, until 1978; [Agnew's, London]; Brooklyn Museum, New York, Purchased with funds given by Karen B. Cohen, 1987 (87.210.1)

SELECTED EXHIBITIONS: London 1978a, cat. no. 9; London 1980, cat. no. 5; Sutton 1980, cat. no. 148; Kramer et al. 1993, pp. 63–64, cat. no. 40.

SELECTED REFERENCES: Mongan et al. 1945, p. 67, no. 45; Dupuy-Vachey 2003, pp. 170–71, 383, no. 70.

94. *Orlando Returns Bireno to Olimpia*

Ca. 1780–85
Brush and brown wash over black chalk
15¾ × 10⅝ in. (40 × 27 cm)

Orlando's tireless pursuit of Angelica gives rise to a number of adventures through which the knight demonstrates his heroic commitment to the virtues of chivalry and love. Soon after he leaves Paris, Orlando encounters Olimpia, the daughter of the Count of Holland, who is grieving the abduction of her lover, Bireno. Orlando is so moved by Olimpia's devotion that he decides to rescue Bireno from the evil King Cimosco.

Fragonard depicts the triumphant moment in which the armored Orlando reunites the two lovers on the threshold of a ship, their joy heralded by a flickering banner. As Marie-Anne Dupuy-Vachey has pointed out,[1] the composition of this drawing bears a strong resemblance to Rubens's *Disembarkation at Marseilles* (fig. 135), from his series of twenty-four paintings for Marie de Médicis. Fragonard, who received permission to copy those paintings at the Palais du Luxembourg in 1767,[2] seems to have recalled several elements from Rubens in this drawing—including the low vantage point, the angled plank, and the rounded arch. Olimpia's regal bearing and Bireno's supplicant posture also find resonance in the figures of Marie de Médicis and the personification of France in Rubens's canvas. KB

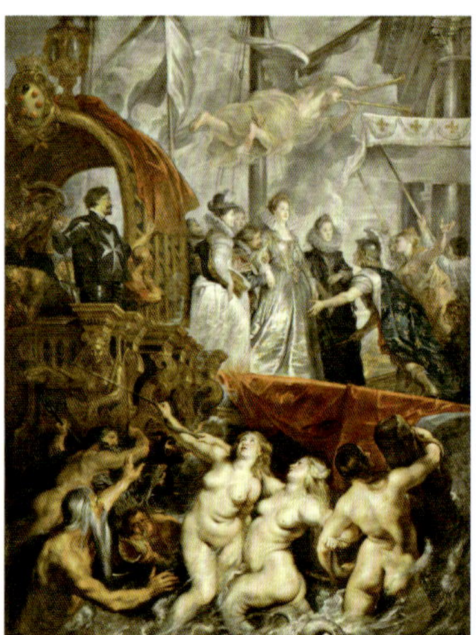

Fig. 135. Peter Paul Rubens (Flemish, 1577–1640), *Disembarkation at Marseilles*, 1622–25. Oil on canvas, 12 ft. 11½ in. × 9 ft. 7 in. (3.94 × 2.95 m). Musée du Louvre, Paris (1774)

PROVENANCE: Probably the artist's family; Hippolyte Walferdin (1795–1880), Paris; his estate sale (Lugt 40073), Hôtel Drouot, Paris, April 12–16, 1880 (part of lot 228); Louis Roederer (d. 1880), Reims; Léon Olry-Roederer, until 1922; Abraham Simon Wolf Rosenbach (1876–1952), Philadelphia, until 1947; Norton Simon Collection, until 1978; [Agnew's, London]; Brooklyn Museum, New York, Purchased with funds given by Karen B. Cohen, 1987 (87.210.2)

SELECTED EXHIBITIONS: London 1978a, cat. no. 13; Sutton 1980, cat. no. 149; Kramer et al. 1993, cat. no. 41.

SELECTED REFERENCES: Mongan et al. 1945, p. 68, no. 51; Dupuy-Vachey 2003, pp. 184–85, 384, no. 77.

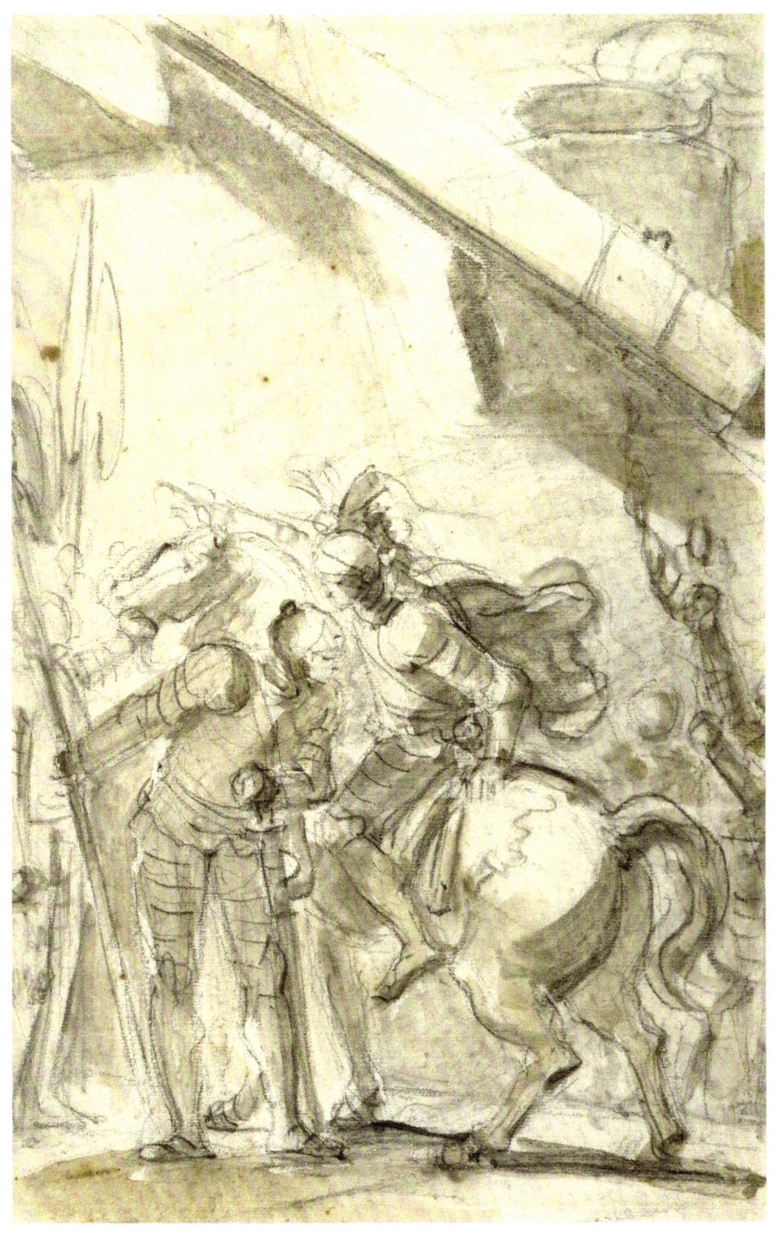

CAT 93

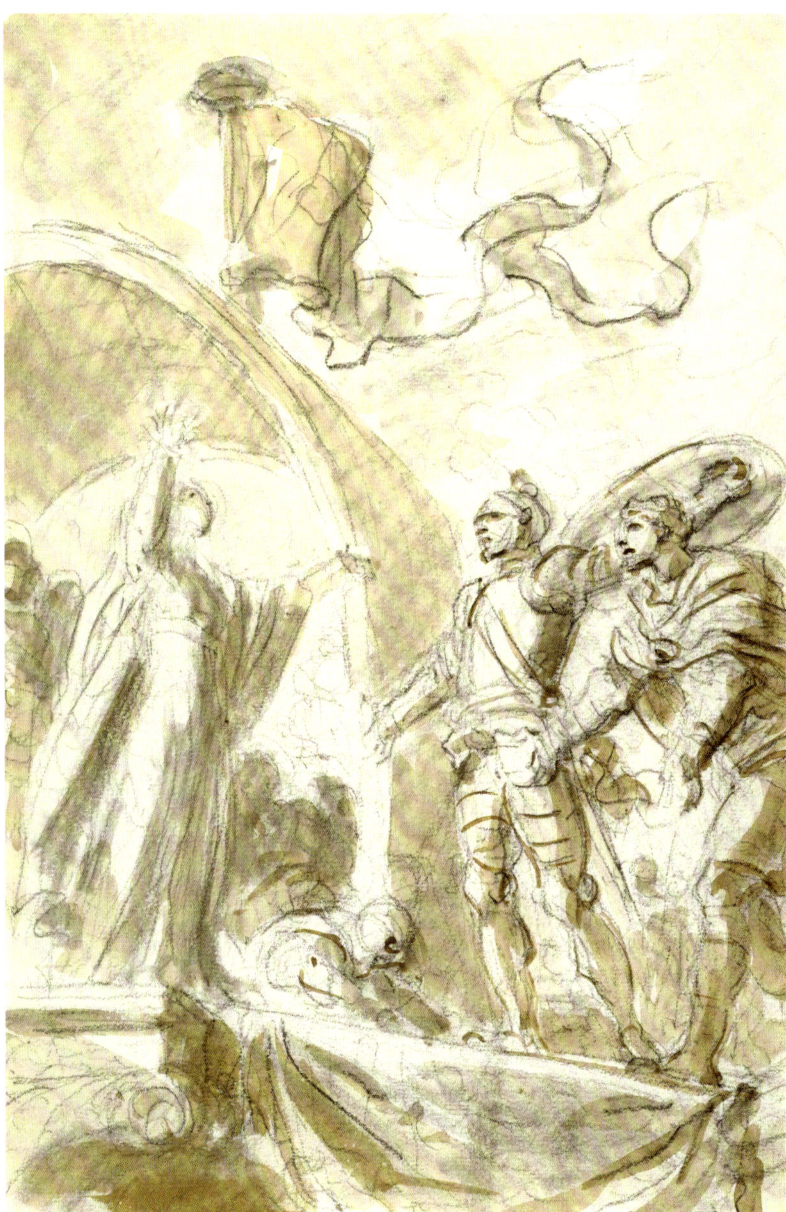

CAT 94

95. *After the Shipwreck, Isabella Is Rowed to Shore*

Ca. 1780–85
Brush and brown wash over black chalk
15½ × 10¼ in. (39.2 × 25.9 cm)

In canto 13, Orlando encounters yet another damsel in distress—Isabella, a princess of Galicia, who recounts to Orlando her own woeful tale of forbidden love. In order to marry the Scottish knight Zerbino, Isabella set sail from her homeland, accompanied by Zerbino's faithful servant, Odorico. When their ship is ravaged by a storm, Odorico saves Isabella from the wreck by rowing her to shore aboard a tiny boat. In his illustration of this scene, Fragonard employs brown wash with a heavy hand to suggest terrific atmospheric turmoil—violent winds, sheets of rain, and surging ocean. The muscular Odorico valiantly battles the elements, plunging his oar into the angry surf, while a limp, ovoid Isabella is born aloft by the crest of the wave. Though their faces are summarized by spare dots and dashes, their peril is palpable. KB

PROVENANCE: Probably the artist's family; Hippolyte Walferdin (1795–1880), Paris; his estate sale (Lugt 40073), Hôtel Drouot, Paris, April 12–16, 1880 (part of lot 228); Louis Roederer (d. 1880), Reims; Léon Olry-Roederer, until 1922; Abraham Simon Wolf Rosenbach (1876–1952), Philadelphia; John Fleming; private collector in 1955; [Agnew's, London, 1978]; Mr. and Mrs. Eugene V. Thaw; The Morgan Library & Museum, New York, Thaw Collection (2001.61:4)

SELECTED EXHIBITIONS: Denison et al. 1985, cat. no. 15; Denison et al. 1994, p. 259.

SELECTED REFERENCES: Mongan et al. 1945, p. 73, no. 92; Ashton 1988, p. 25; Dupuy-Vachey 2003, pp. 18, 272–73, 387, no. 123.

96. *Pinabello Is Drawn to the Light from Merlin's Cave*

Ca. 1780–85
Brush and brown wash over black chalk
15¼ × 9⅞ in. (38.7 × 25.1 cm)

This drawing has long been identified as *Orlando Discovers the Names of Angelica and Medoro*, a climactic moment in canto 23 of *Orlando Furioso*. Orlando's beloved Angelica has fallen in love with a Saracen soldier named Medoro. After nursing his battle wounds, Angelica wanders through the countryside with her new lover, carving their names on trees and rocks. Here, Fragonard's liberal application of dark wash might be interpreted as emotional, rather than atmospheric, tumult, as Orlando discovers the amorous inscription; the hero's shock and despair will soon give way to his titular madness.

More recently, however Marie-Anne Dupuy-Vachey has identified this sheet as an illustration from canto 2, in which Pinabello, a cowardly knight in Charlemagne's army, is drawn toward the light streaming from the wizard Merlin's cavernous lair.[1] Pinabello subsequently lures his rival Bradamante, the Christian warrior-maiden, toward the cave and attempts to kill her by pushing her off a cliff. This sheet is characterized by a virtuosic yet amorphous deployment of wash; a flourish of squiggles denotes Pinabello's horse, as well as the soft mess of foliage in which both the knight and his mount are embedded. Fragonard also makes use of negative space to render the burst of eerie, magical light from the portal. KB

PROVENANCE: Probably the artist's family; Hippolyte Walferdin (1795–1880), Paris; his estate sale (Lugt 40073), Hôtel Drouot, Paris, April 12–16, 1880 (part of lot 228); Louis Roederer (d. 1880), Reims; Léon Olry-Roederer, until 1922; Abraham Simon Wolf Rosenbach (1876–1952), Philadelphia; John Fleming; private collector in 1955, until 1978; [Agnew's, London]; Mr. and Mrs. Eugene V. Thaw; The Morgan Library & Museum, New York, Thaw Collection (2001.61:5)

SELECTED EXHIBITIONS: Denison et al. 1985, cat. no. 16; Denison et al. 1994, p. 260.

SELECTED REFERENCES: Mongan et al. 1945, pp. 77–78, no. 126 (as *Orlando Discovers the Names of Angelica and Medoro Carved in the Rock*); Ashton 1988, pp. 205–6, fig. 57; Dupuy-Vachey 2003, pp. 72–73, 379, no. 21 (as *Pinabel est attirée par la lumière sortant de la grotte de Merlin*).

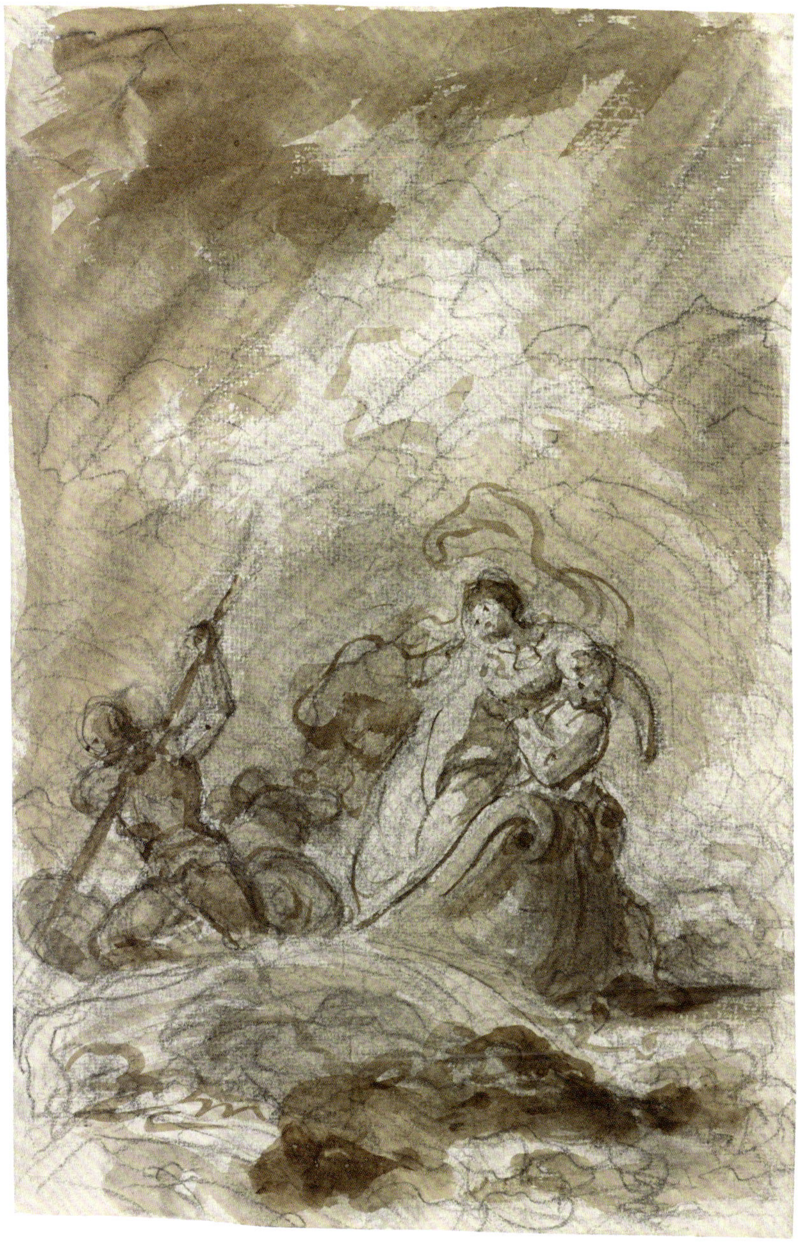

CAT 95

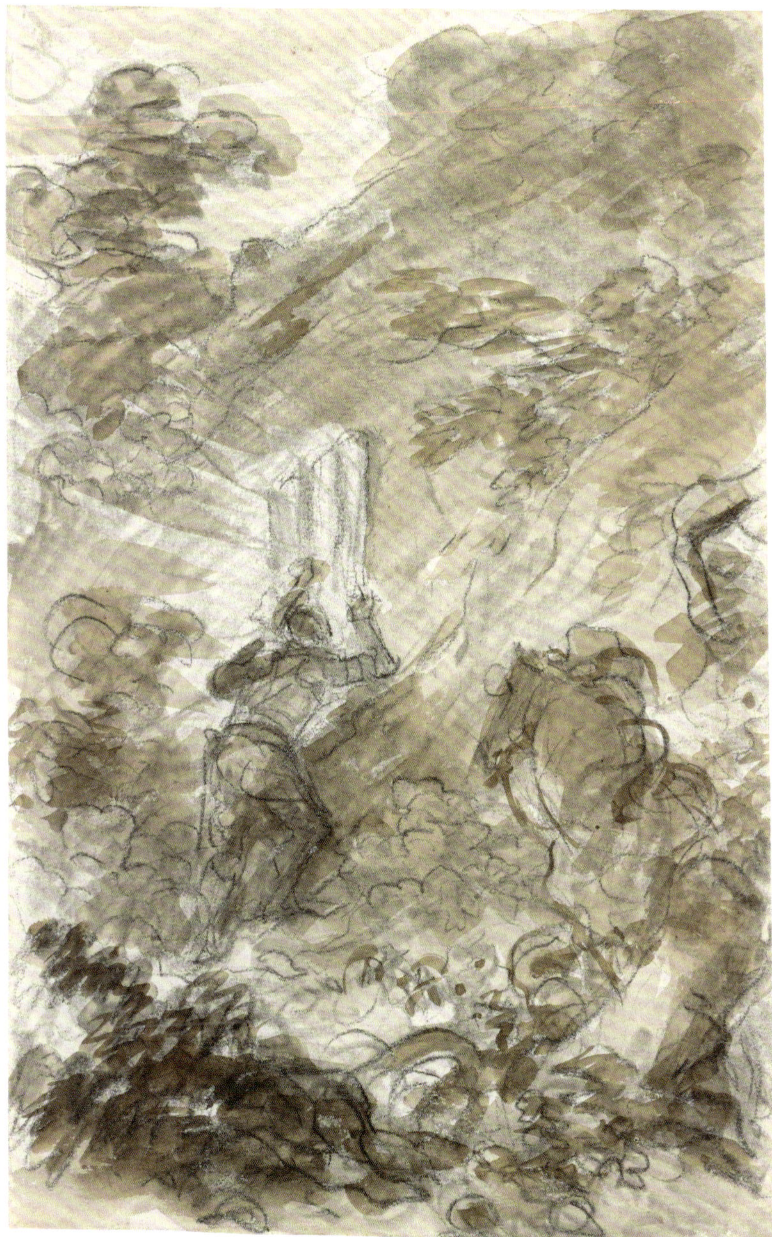

CAT 96

97. *Italian Garden with Cypresses*

Ca. 1775–85
Brush and brown wash with touches of white gouache over black chalk
17½ × 13⅛ in. (44.5 × 33.3 cm)

98. *Landscape with Double Flight of Steps*

Ca. 1775–85
Brown wash over black chalk
12⅞ × 18¾ in. (32.5 × 47.4 cm)

Italian Garden with Cypresses and *Landscape with Double Flight of Steps* belong to a group of wash drawings of lush Italianate gardens. These unidentified landscapes are traditionally associated with Fragonard's second trip to Italy, between September 1773 and October 1774. Unlike the site-specific, red chalk landscapes produced during his first trip, in the 1760s, the present drawings demonstrate Fragonard's new preference for, and increased fluency with, the illusory effects of brown wash in the 1770s and early 1780s.[1]

In many cases, however, it remains uncertain if these late wash landscapes were executed while Fragonard was abroad or sometime after he returned to France.[2] It has been widely suggested that they were reimagined or embellished in the artist's studio, rather than recorded in situ. Indeed, the drawings may not represent real landscapes at all. While the architectural and botanical specificity of the scenes suggests that they are rooted in Fragonard's personal experience of Italy, it is likely that he mined certain elements from his memory (or from his arsenal of sketches) and invented others.[3] Fragonard's supple imagination and deep familiarity with Italian gardens certainly would have enabled him to create such complex, convincing settings.

Fragonard was not alone in privileging formal ingenuity over topographical accuracy. In his *Essay on Gardens* (1774), the *amateur* Claude Henri Watelet described the creative freedoms afforded to artists of picturesque landscapes. According to Watelet, "The painter selects his subjects from nature and combines them pleasingly according to his intended purpose. The designer of a park has no doubt the same goals but is limited in his means. Considerations such as quality of soil, weather conditions, the character and inherent configurations of the terrain present difficulties and often insurmountable obstacles to his art. The canvas, in contrast, is docile and lends itself to all the compositional needs of the painter."[4]

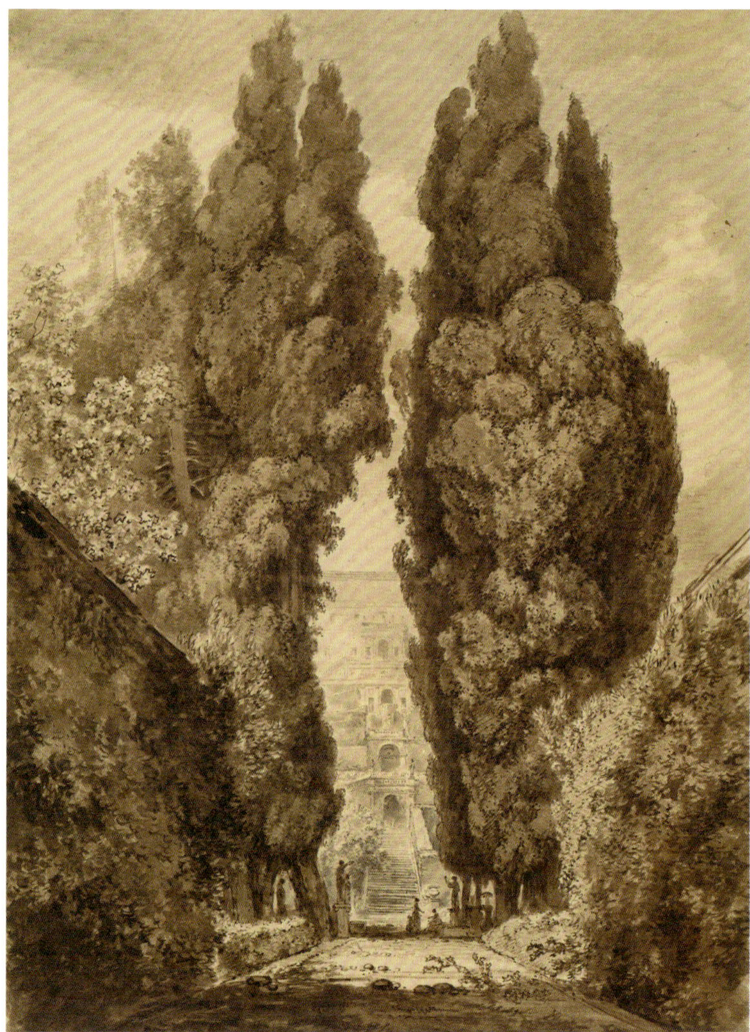

Fig. 136. Jean Honoré Fragonard, *The Avenue of Cypresses at Villa d'Este*, ca. 1765. Pen and brown and gray ink with brown and gray wash over a red chalk counterproof on laid paper, 18 × 13½ in. (45.6 × 34.2 cm). National Gallery of Art, Washington, D.C. (2013.130.3)

Real or imagined (or a combination thereof), the two scenes shown here possess several stylistic and compositional similarities that allow us to discuss them in tandem. These delicate mirages are comprised of translucent veils of brown wash over spare black chalk lines, articulated by squiggles and dots of more concentrated wash. In both drawings, individual leaves of the thick, overgrown foliage

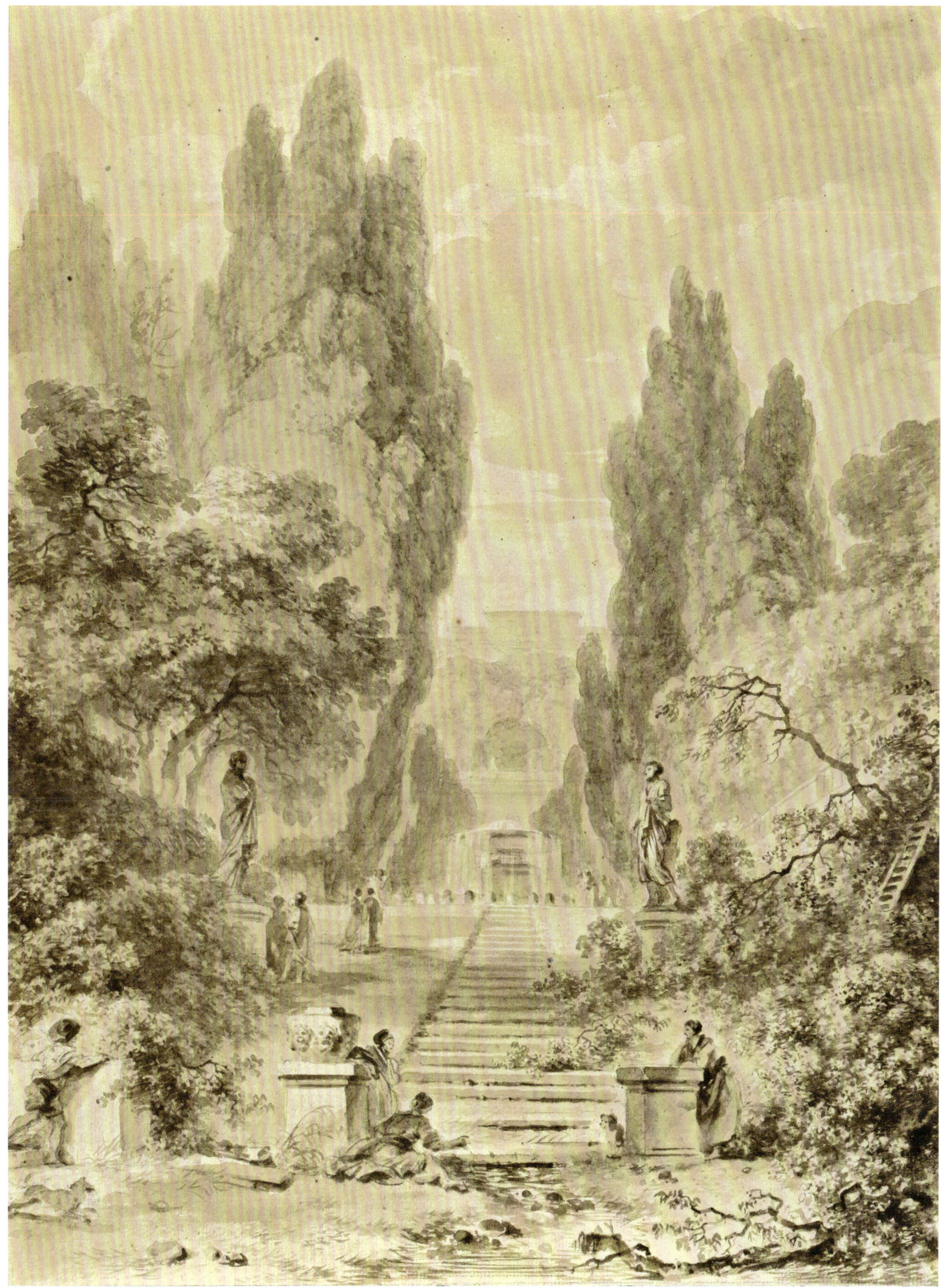

CAT 97

are indicated with dark, staccato flecks—a pointillist shorthand that Fragonard developed during his second Italian trip.[5] *Italian Garden* is further enhanced with spare touches of white gouache, highlighting areas drenched with sunlight.

Both works provide slightly off-center views of symmetrical sets of stairs dwarfed by towering cypress trees. Fragonard populated both gardens with several improvised details, including water fountains, classical statues, and loosely brushed figures—a characteristic mix of elegantly dressed visitors strolling in the background and figures in rural costumes resting in the foreground.[6] Certain elements are familiar motifs borrowed from earlier landscape drawings: for example, *Italian Garden with Cypresses* invokes the cypress avenue at the Villa d'Este in Tivoli (fig. 136), while *Landscape with Double Flight of Steps* recalls the two-tiered landscape shown in *The Little Park* (cats. 30–34).

Far from idealized, Fragonard's brown wash idylls are also characterized by what Richard Rand called "picturesque squalor"—elements of aestheticized disorder and decay.[7] The cypresses in *Landscape with Double Flight of Steps* are irregular and frayed; the titular steps are fringed with sprawling tree limbs; the columns and trellis at the top of the steps are wrapped in ivy. *Italian Garden with Cypresses* is similarly laden with errant, jagged branches; a once-grand cascading fountain now culminates in a gurgling brook choked with pebbles and grass.[8] Rand argued that these calculated imperfections rhymed with the "emerging taste for gardens and, to a certain extent, landscape paintings . . . that celebrated the randomness and haphazard quality of nature through a conscious avoidance of compositional unity and coherence."[9] Fragonard appealed to this unruly, natural aesthetic by summoning the memory of long-abandoned Italian villas—and reinventing them in a pictorial language entirely his own. KB

CAT. 97. PROVENANCE: Eugene Glaenzer (d. 1923, manager of Jacques Seligmann & Co., New York), New York, purchased 1908; Mortimer L. Schiff, New York (as of 1931); private collection

SELECTED EXHIBITION: Paris 1931, p. 47, cat. no. 84 ("Escalier à Tivoli").

CAT. 98. PROVENANCE: In the collection of the same family since the beginning of the 19th century; private collection

SELECTED EXHIBITION: Rosenberg 1988, p. 571, cat. no. 301.

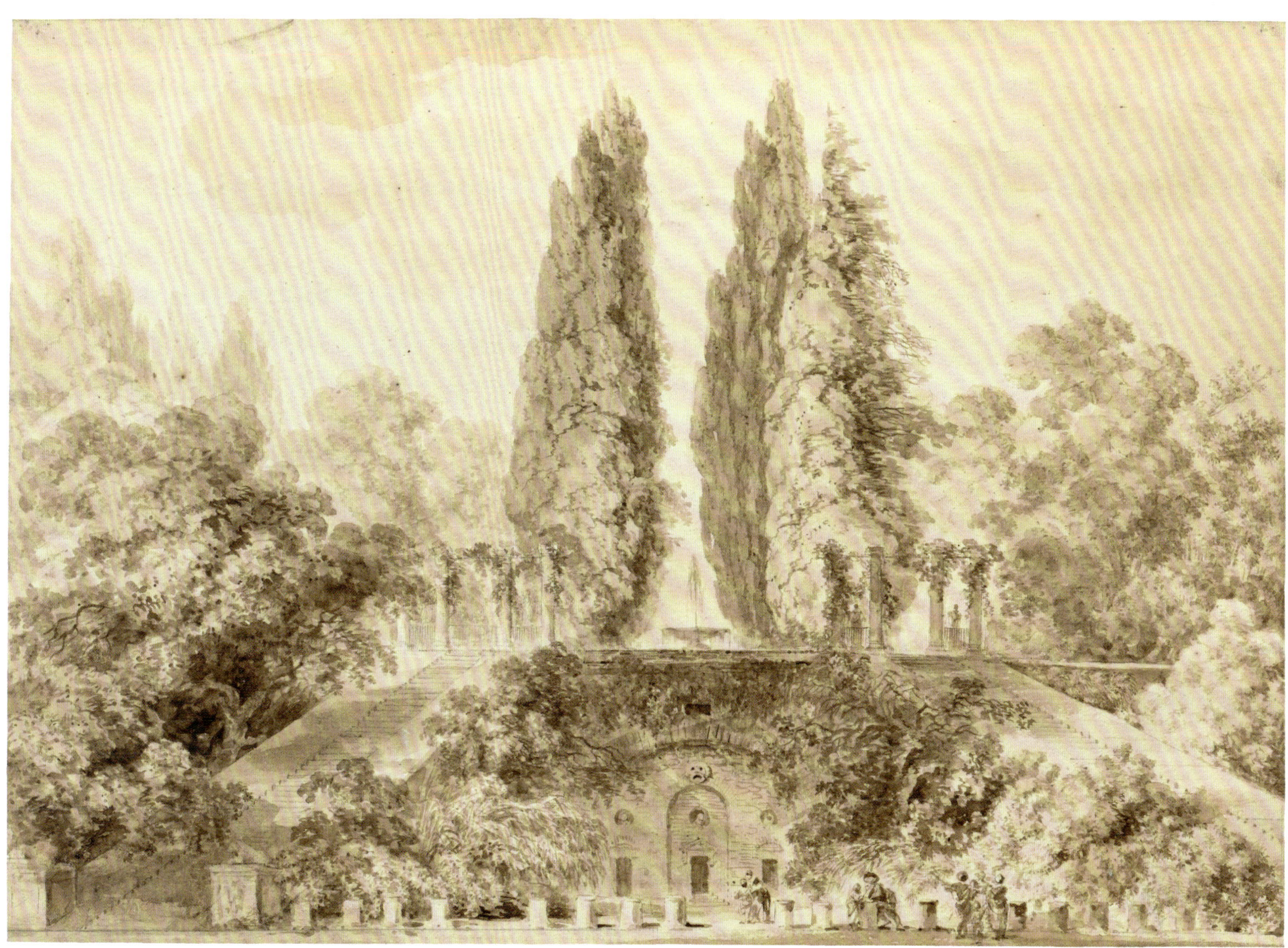

CAT 98

99. *A Boy Carried into a Salon*

Ca. 1780–85

Black chalk, brush and gray wash, incised; verso: faint sketch in black chalk of figures under a tree

16⅞ × 13½ in. (42.9 × 34.2 cm)

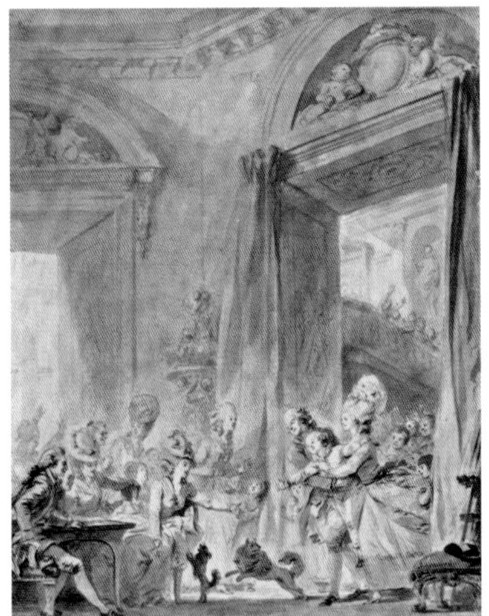

Fig. 137. Jean Honoré Fragonard, *A Boy Carried into a Salon*, ca. 1780–85. Gray wash over black chalk, 17⅛ × 13⅝ in. (43.4 × 34.7 cm). Private collection

In this rapidly sketched scene of daily life writ large, one marvels at Fragonard's virtuosity and inventiveness. In the way the black chalk lines jab and wiggle across the sheet, one can sense the artist's frenzied impatience to capture his ideas on paper. The legibility of the scene is augmented by what Eunice Williams has described as "transparent veils of cool gray wash,"[1] a wash so weakly diluted that it leaves visible for our delectation Fragonard's characteristic web of schematic underdrawing. As with other large-scale preliminary sketches (see, for example, cats. 76 and 77), this study was made in preparation not for a painting but for a highly finished drawing (fig. 137). A loose incising can be seen throughout the sheet, in the figures, animals, furniture, and architecture, indicating the simple mechanical means of transfer by which the artist blocked in the composition on the blank sheet that became the more finished version (fig. 138).

While the technique is clear, the identification of the subject has proven elusive. Neither the Morgan sketch nor the finished version, nor a pendant composition, also known through a sketch and finished version,[2] is documented before the second half of the nineteenth century. As Pierre Rosenberg pointed out in 1987, there is no visual evidence in the drawings to support the traditional titles for the pair, *The Competition* and *The Reward*.[3] Also traditional but lacking in evidence is the theory that the scenes may depict events in the Bergeret household, where Fragonard was a frequent guest in the 1780s.[4] More recent discussions of the group have focused on the burgeoning interest in the nurture and education of children that took root in France in the last decades of the ancien régime, following the publication of Jean Jacques Rousseau's *Emile, ou de l'éducation* in 1762.[5] Pierre Rosenberg drew attention to the inscription on the verso of the mount of the pendant sketch, which describes the subject as the instruction of the children of the duc de Rohan-Chabot;[6] and Marie-Anne Dupuy-Vachey has proposed a possible connection between Fragonard and the comtesse de Genlis, who taught the children of the duc d'Orléans and penned a treatise on education in 1782.[7] For the moment we cannot say whether the Morgan drawing and its pendant depict specific individuals or events, or whether the composition was perhaps intended to illustrate a text. Nonetheless, they show Fragonard's approach to genre subjects as evolving and in step with the cultural concerns of his day. PS

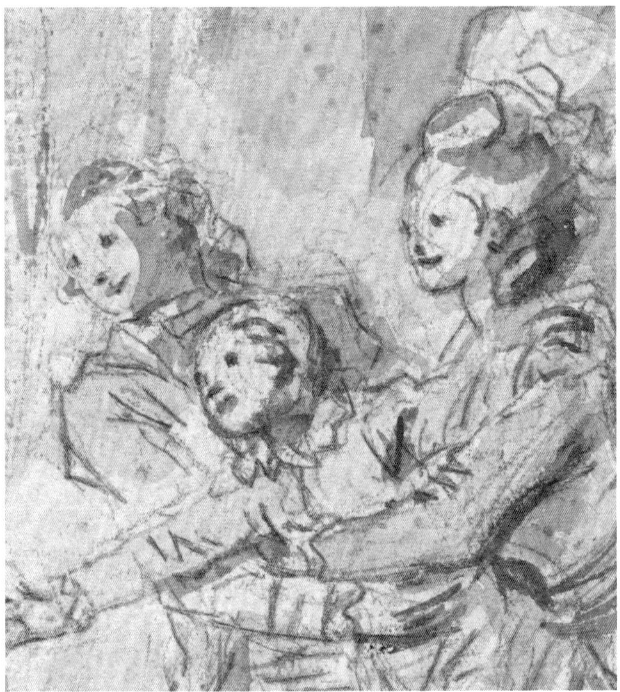

Fig. 138. Detail of cat. 99

PROVENANCE: Hippolyte Walferdin (1795–1880), Paris; his estate sale (Lugt 40073), Hôtel Drouot, Paris, April 12–16, 1880 (part of lot 261); Camille Groult (1832–1908); anonymous sale, Hôtel Drouot, Paris, December 19, 1941 (no. 46, pl. III); acquired by Ancel; Mme Mottart; her estate sale, Galerie Charpentier, Paris, February 8, 1945 (no. 38, pl. XXV), purchased by Mme Rochefort (per Ananoff); Jean Lansade; [Galerie de Bayser, Paris]; The Morgan Library & Museum, New York, Purchased as the gift of the Fellows and with the special assistance of Walter Baker, Mme Renée de Becker, Francis Kettaneh, Mrs. Paul Moore, John S. Newberry, Jr., Mr. and Mrs. Carl Stern, Mrs. Herbert N. Straus, and Forsyth Wickes (1955.5)

SELECTED EXHIBITIONS: Williams 1978, pp. 144–45, cat. no. 58; Rosenberg 1988, p. 539, cat. no. 278; Denison 1993, pp. 160–61, cat. no. 71.

SELECTED REFERENCES: Ananoff 1961–70, vol. 2 (1963), pp. 31–32, no. 605, fig. 193; Reuter et al. 2013, p. 79, fig. 25/1, pp. 82–83.

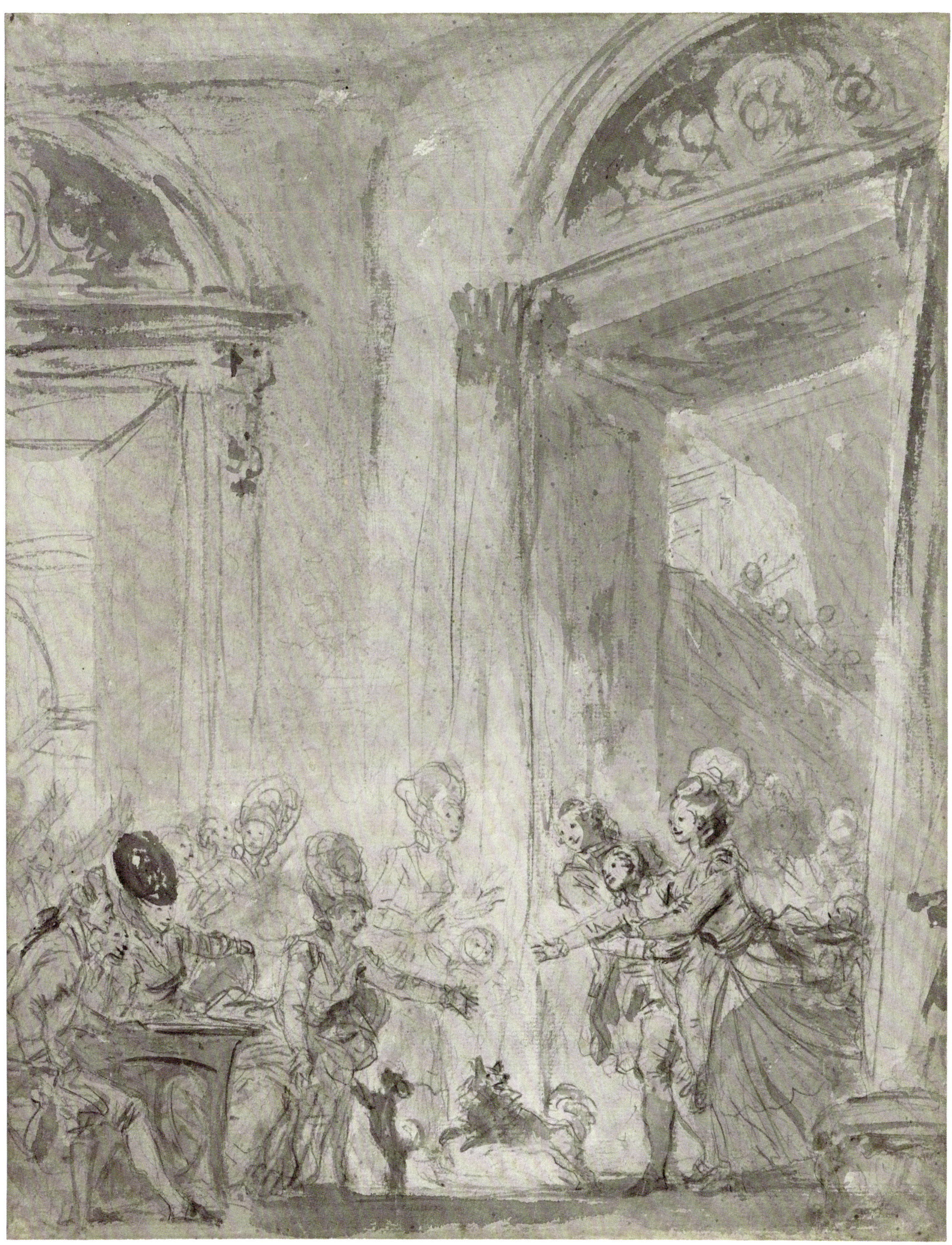

100. *Seated Man, His Elbow Resting on a Book*

Ca. 1785–88
Black chalk
13⅜ × 10⅛ in. (33.8 × 25.6 cm)

Ranging from sober to comical, Fragonard's portrait drawings are not preparatory for paintings; rather, they are studies from life made either for a patron or for the artist's own amusement. He first produced such drawings in earnest on his second trip to Italy in the company of his patron Pierre Jacques Onésyme Bergeret de Grancourt, who presumably requested from Fragonard the series of large, full-length red chalk portraits of his friends made during their stop in Nègrepelisse (see cat. 54). In Rome, the traveling party quickly became integrated into the social milieu of the Académie de France. There, Fragonard was exposed, through the current pensionnaires, to a veritable cult of caricature, as evidenced by the many surviving examples by François André Vincent and others of his cohort.[1] The humor and whimsy of these student caricatures, reflecting the context of social ease and informality in which they were created and shared, must have sowed the seeds for Fragonard's later enjoyment of sketches chronicling the pleasures, pursuits, and mishaps of his friends and family.

Many such informal portraits sketched in black chalk can be dated to the mid- to late 1780s. By this time, the artist had renewed, or perhaps had never interrupted, his friendship with Pierre Jacques Bergeret, whose father he had quarreled with after their return to Paris in 1774.[2] Hippolyte Walferdin's collection alone contained ninety-two sheets catalogued as done for "la famille Bergeret" at the Folie Beaujon, one of Pierre Jacques's various residences; the authenticity of this claim is buttressed by a note in Walferdin's hand, transcribed in the catalogue of his sale, stating that the drawings had been bequeathed to him by M. de la Girennerie, whose mother had married Bergeret in 1796.[3] Nine of these drawings came to light in 2013 and were acquired by the Musée Jean-Honoré Fragonard in Grasse (see, for example, p. 12, fig. 8).[4] The present sheet, in addition to two others of the same technique and dimensions, was probably produced within the same milieu. A sketch of a reclining man with a bandage wrapped around his chin (fig. 139), which appeared at auction with the present sheet in 1995, is in a humorous vein akin to the Grasse caricatures, five of which relay the anecdote of Fragonard falling and injuring his foot. Another sheet, depicting a seated man with a cane,[5] is closer in spirit to this seated man, who pauses in his reading to rest his head upon his hand. Relative to the crisp portraits Fragonard drew in red chalk in Nègrepelisse in 1773, those done in the mid-1780s are softer and more atmospheric. After using a blunt-tipped piece of black chalk to lay parallel hatching in the background and shaded areas, Fragonard added darker flourishes to animate certain areas—the sitter's collar, the edge of the book, the fabric in his lap—without concern for specificity or detail.

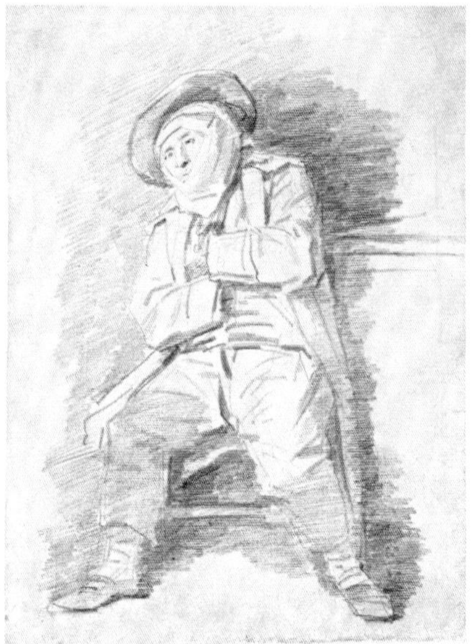

Fig. 139. Jean Honoré Fragonard, *Portrait of a Seated Man*, ca. 1785–88. Black chalk, 13½ × 10¼ in. (34.2 × 25.8 cm). The Horvitz Collection, Boston (D-F-720)

The sitter, a middle-aged man who looks up from his book, has not been identified. His calm and kindly demeanor and the informal technique with which he is rendered support the idea that this is a casual sketch done in one of Pierre Jacques Bergeret's houses, perhaps the château de Cassan, his country estate in L'Isle-Adam, judging from the simplicity of the chair. Just as the elder Bergeret had filled his leisure time abroad with drawing and looking through his portfolios, so, too, the concept of *sociabilité* must have informed the pastimes of his son, and one can imagine a household where such sketches were produced amid gatherings of friends with shared artistic interests. Although the spirit of the drawings is lighthearted, the friendship between the two families was deep; it was to L'Isle-Adam that Fragonard and his wife brought their cherished daughter Rosalie in 1788 when she became ill, and there, a few months later, that she died, at the age of eighteen. This drawing must have been done not long before that devastating event, which was followed less than a year later by the storming of the Bastille, watershed moments that marked the end of a productive phase of Fragonard's career. PS

PROVENANCE: Sale, Hôtel Drouot, Dumousset & Deburaux, Paris, March 13, 1995 (lot 62, as "attributed to Fragonard"); sale, Hôtel Drouot, Dumousset & Deburaux, Paris, October 6, 1995 (lot 44, as "attributed to Fragonard"); sale, Hôtel Drouot, Dumousset & Deburaux, Paris, May 15, 1996 (lot 36, as "attributed to Fragonard"); sale, Paris, June 6, 1997, uncatalogued (as "French school, nineteenth-century"); [Galerie de Bayser, Paris]; private collection

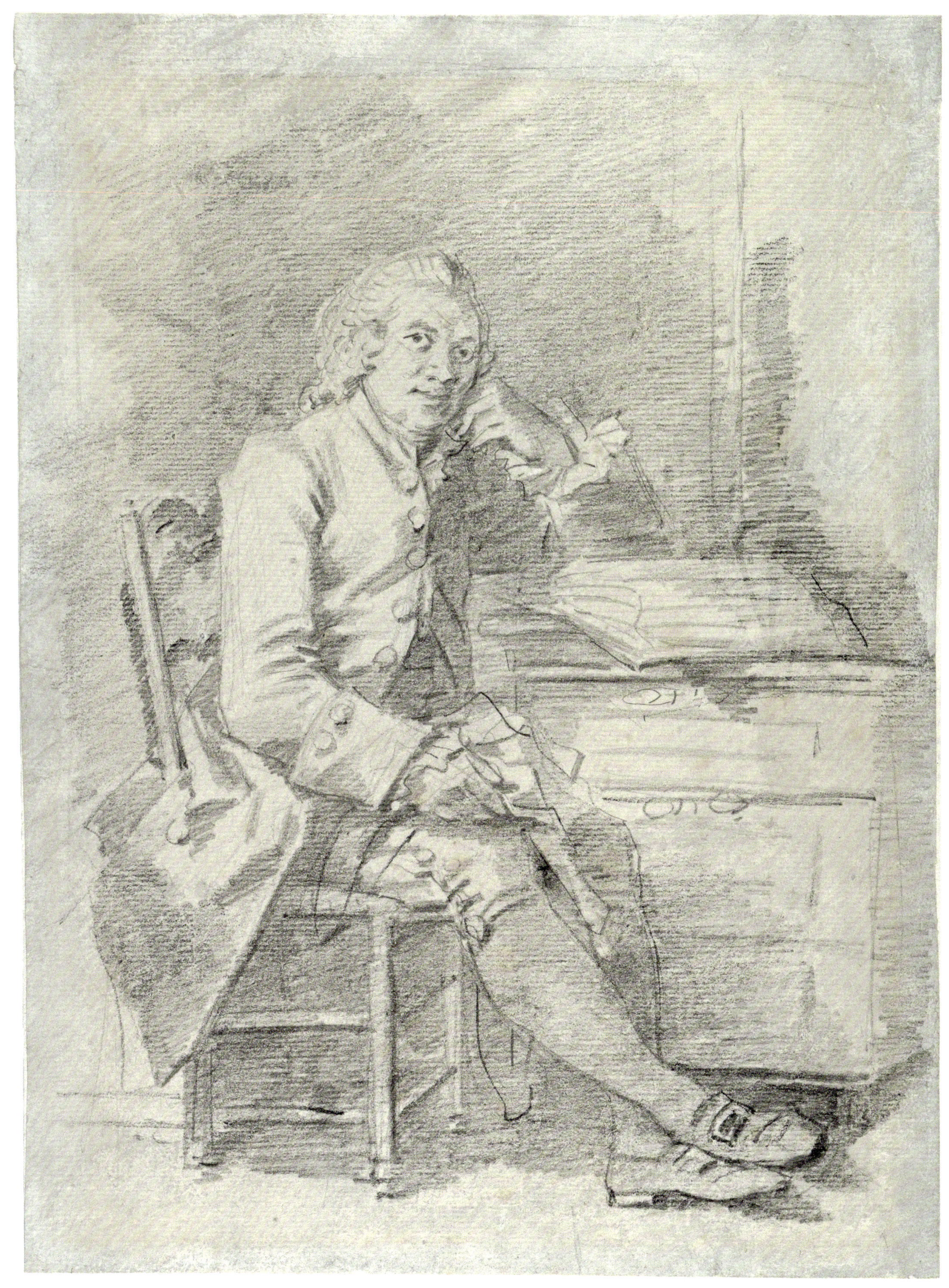

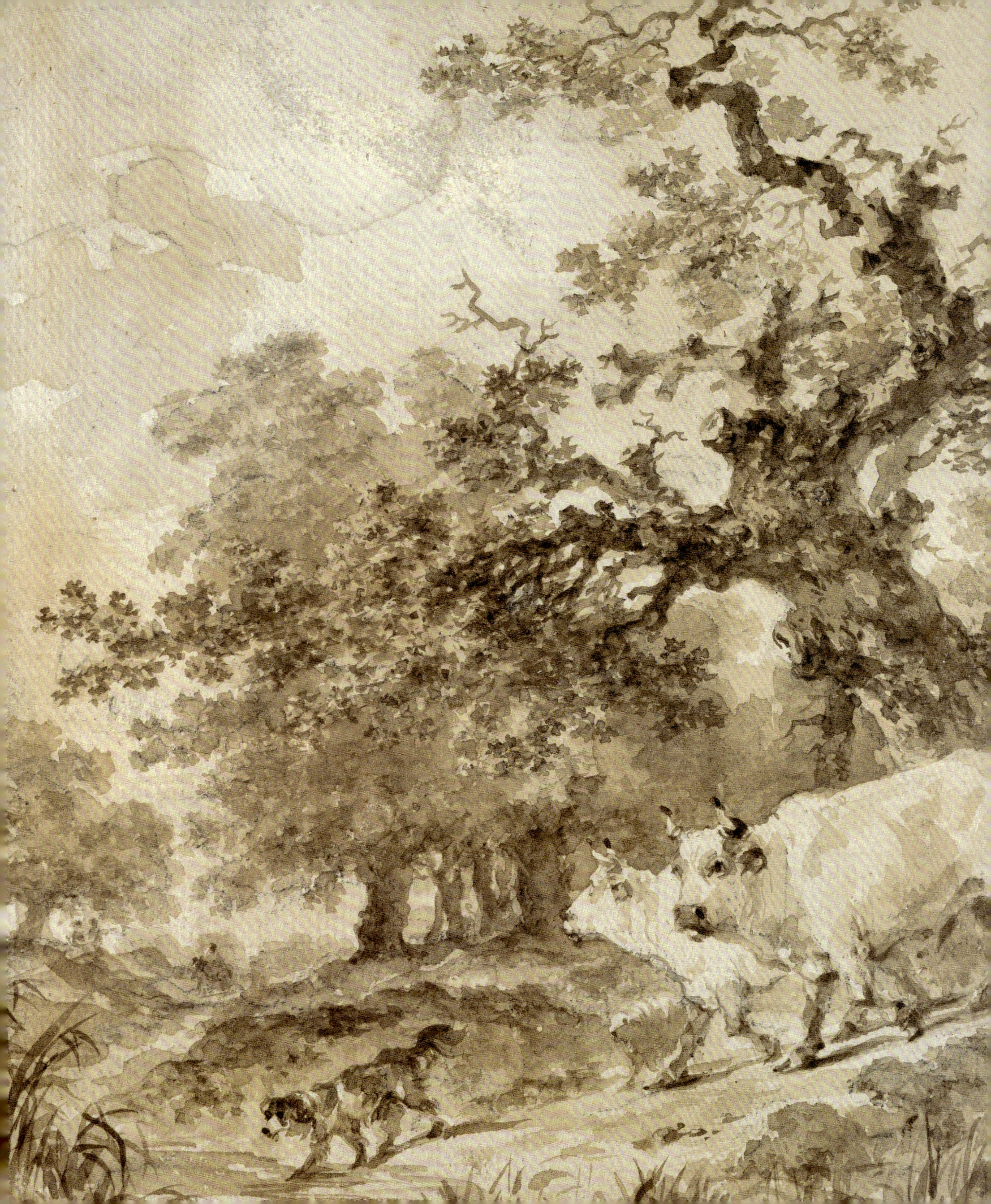

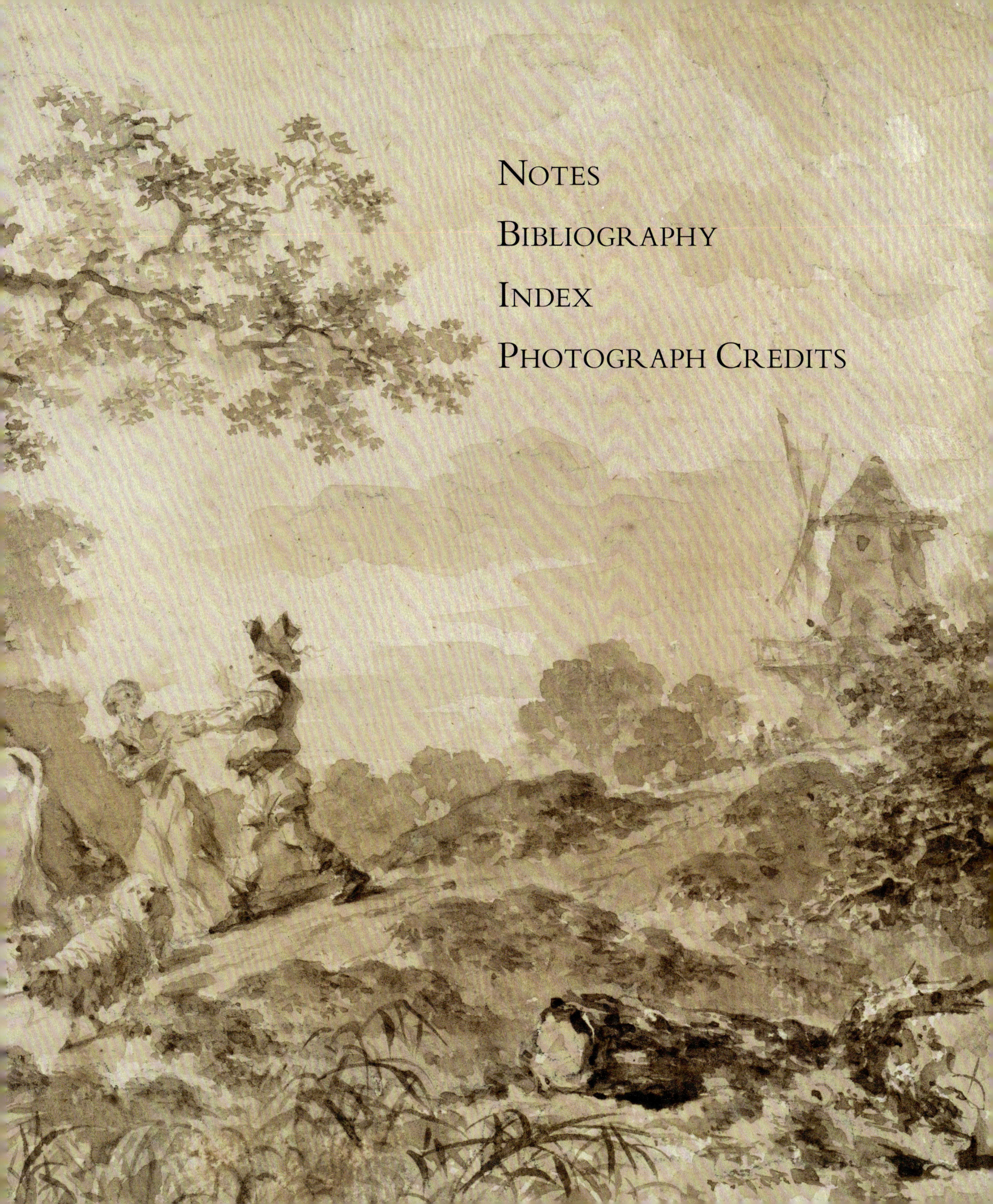

Notes

Bibliography

Index

Photograph Credits

Notes

INTRODUCTION

1. "Le dessin, voilà le triomphe de Fragonard." Portalis 1889, vol. 2, p. 187.
2. Goncourt 1981, p. 276.
3. "[L]e dessin primordial qui a plus d'intimité et moins de prétention." Portalis 1889, vol. 2, p. 202.
4. See Grasselli et al. 2003 and Delapierre et al. 2006.
5. Laing 2003, p. 31.
6. Portalis 1889, vol. 2, pp. 193–95.
7. Smentek 2014, esp. pp. 106–12.
8. "Les grands maîtres finissent peu leurs desseins; ils se contentent de faire des esquisses, ou griffonnemens faits de rien, (*a*) qui ne plaisent pas aux demi-connoisseurs. Ceux-ci veulent quelque chose de terminé, qui soit agréable aux yeux: un vrai connoisseur pense autrement; il voit dans un croquis, la maniere de penser d'un grand maître, pour caractériser chaque objet avec peu de traits; son imagination animée par le beau feu qui regne dans le dessein." Dézallier d'Argenville 1762, vol. 1, p. lxj.
9. "[L]es premières idées d'un peintre, le premier feu de son imagination, son style, son esprit, sa maniere de penser: ils sont les premiers originaux qui servent souvent aux éléves du maître, à peindre les tableaux qui n'en sont pas les copies. Les desseins prouvent encore la fécondité, la vivacité du genie de l'artiste, la noblesse, l'élévation de ses sentimens, & la facilité avec laquelle il les a exprimés." Ibid., vol. 1, p. xxxij.
10. Quoted and translated in Smentek 2014, p. 250.
11. See Stein et al. 2013.
12. Hoisington and Stein 2012.
13. See Rosenberg 2006 and Lorblanchet et al. 2008.
14. Cuzin 2003.
15. Reuter et al. 2013.
16. Réau 1956, pp. 95 ("Pour apprécier à sa mesure le génie de Fragonard, il ne suffit pas de connaître son œuvre de peintre") and 99 ("très amoindries, hélas! par l'exportation aux Etats-Unis, qu'on trouvera les plus beaux dessins de Frago").

FACT, FICTION, FUNCTION, AND PROCESS: TOWARD A MODERN VIEW OF FRAGONARD'S DRAWINGS

1. Sheriff 1986, 1988.
2. Schroder 2001.
3. See Jean-Pierre Cuzin, "Fragonard en 2006," in Cuzin et al. 2006, pp. 194–201, and Guillaume Faroult, "Fragonard amoureux," in Faroult 2015, pp. 17–29.
4. In addition to the evidence of early sale catalogues, Mark Ledbury (2001, p. 197) has drawn our attention to an undated manuscript by Louis-Sébastien Mercier that describes how collectors took advantage of Fragonard in his youth by buying his drawings for pennies and reselling them at a large profit.
5. Excerpts are quoted in Rosenberg 1988, pp. 67–69.
6. Ibid., p. 94.
7. "L'abbé de Saint-Non l'a ramené, avec quantité de desseins qu'il lui a fait faire, et parmi lesquels j'en ai vu plusieurs représentant des veues de Rome, dont la touche et le faire m'ont beaucoup plu." Mariette 1851–60, vol. 2 (1853–54), p. 263. For the drawings owned by Mariette, see Rosenberg and Barthélemy-Labeeuw 2011, vol. 2, pp. 747–49, nos. F2059–F2064.
8. Roland Michel 2003, p. 377 n. 1, and Rosenberg 2006, pp. 56–67, cat. nos. 14–20.
9. Drawings were rarely included in the Salons before 1753 and only began to appear in large numbers in the 1770s and 1780s. In the mid-1760s, it was still rare for painters to exhibit drawings; the majority on view were by sculptors, printmakers, and, increasingly, young artists, who, like Fragonard, were not yet received in the Académie and were referred to as "agréés." These statements are based on data assembled by Harvard PhD candidate Cabelle Ahn while a volunteer in the Metropolitan's Department of Drawings and Prints in 2014–15.
10. Schroder 2001, p. 41.
11. Schroder 2001.
12. Both are quoted and translated in ibid., p. 52.
13. Ibid., p. 53.
14. Blanc 1865, p. 14.
15. Launay 1991.
16. Goncourt 1981, p. 297.
17. Ibid., p. 298.
18. Ibid.
19. Ibid., pp. 301–2.
20. "Le dessin, voilà le triomphe de Fragonard." Portalis 1889, vol. 2, p. 187.
21. Ibid., pp. 293–316.
22. Paris 1931.
23. "Fragonard appartient en effet à cette catégorie d'artistes qui triomphent dans le premier jet, dans le croquis et dans l'esquisse peinte ou dessinée." Ibid., p. 10.
24. "A première vue, il semble qu'il y ait deux sortes de dessin: le dessin d'après nature, d'après un modèle extérieur, et le dessin de mémoire, d'après un modèle intérieur. En fait, la distinction n'est pas si tranchée." Fosca 1954, p. xv.
25. Ibid., p. xvii.
26. Ibid., pp. xxii–xxiv.
27. See Norman 1978a, 1978b, and Stein 2009.
28. Williams 1978, p. 23.
29. Rosenberg 1988. Jean-Pierre Cuzin's monographic study and catalogue of paintings was published in the same year; see Cuzin 1987.
30. Sheriff 1988.
31. Sheriff 1990.
32. Rand 1995.
33. Milam 2006.
34. Lajer-Burcharth 2003.
35. Rosenberg and Brejon de Lavergnée 2000.
36. Dupuy-Vachey 2003.
37. Cuzin 2003.
38. Rosenberg 2006.
39. Pierre Rosenberg in Dupuy-Vachey 2007, pp. 15–17.
40. Rosenberg 1996.
41. Cuzin, "Fragonard en 2006," in Cuzin et al. 2006, p. 194.
42. Schroder 2001. On his accumulated wealth and financial success, and the role of drawings therein, see Rosenberg 2000b, pp. 160–61.
43. Dupuy-Vachey 2007.
44. Raux 2007. See also cat. 52.
45. See Dupuy-Vachey 2012, Blumenfeld 2013, Dupuy-Vachey 2015, and Jackall et al. 2015. A show on the subject is also being planned by the National Gallery of Art, Washington, D.C.
46. "Fragonard a cessé de vivre; mais ses tableaux et ses dessins chers aux amateurs de la peinture, rappelleront toujours ses rares talents. Les charmantes eaux-fortes qu'il a gravées d'un goût exquis, seront placées à côté des Benedette, des Salvator et des meilleurs artistes en ce genre." Lecarpentier 1821, p. 282.
47. Goncourt 1981, p. 269.

48. Ibid.
49. Portalis 1889, vol. 2, pp. 225–26.
50. Quoted in Hoisington and Stein 2012, p. 142.
51. See Faroult 2015, pp. 17–29.
52. G. Wildenstein 1956.
53. Baudicour 1859–61, vol. 1, pp. 159–63.
54. "[L]a 'main' du professeur domine le plus souvent le travail délicat de sa jeune élève." G. Wildenstein 1956, p. 38.
55. Ibid., pp. 35–37, no. XXV and "répétition," and pp. 44–45, nos. XXIX, XXX.
56. Rosenberg 1988, pp. 487–89, 493–94, cat. nos. 239, 240, 244.
57. Hoisington and Stein 2012.
58. Perrin Stein, "Echoes of Rembrandt and Castiglione: Etching as Appropriation," in Stein et al. 2013, pp. 156–83.
59. See Vogtherr et al. 2011; Smentek 2014; Bailey 2011; Guichard 2008; Bailey 2002; Michel 2006; Mickaël Szanto, "La révolution des dessins en France autour de 1750," in Brugerolles et al. 2013, pp. 11–22.
60. See Stein 2000a and Joulie 2004.
61. Caviglia-Brunel 2012, pp. 406–7, nos. D.534–D.537.
62. Cuzin 2013.
63. Guigon 2013; Catala 2014, 2015; and Faroult 2016.
64. Faroult 2015, pp. 122–43.
65. See Pierre Rosenberg, "Un autre Fragonard," in Faroult 2015, pp. 12–13.
66. For the group acquired by Grasse, see Zanella and Dupuy-Vachey 2014. See also Williams 2015.
67. See, for example, Faroult 2015, pp. 244–45, cat. no. 90, fig. 1 (entry by Marie-Anne Dupuy-Vachey).
68. See Jean-Pierre Cuzin, "Marguerite et son maître," and Carole Blumenfeld, "Les tableaux du cardinal Fesch," in Costamagna 2007, pp. 50–97, 98–131.
69. See Williams 1993 and Costamagna 2007, pp. 52–53, figs. 17, 18.
70. See Rosenberg, "Un autre Fragonard," in Faroult 2015, p. 13.

EVERY POSSIBLE COMBINATION:
BETWEEN INSPIRATION AND FINISH IN FRAGONARD'S OEUVRE

1. Ecole Nationale Supérieure des Beaux-Arts, Paris. Cuzin 1987, no. 1; Rosenberg 1989, no. 3. *Mercure de France*, October 1753, p. 165.
2. The poem, which would be published in 1760, allowed its author to enter the Académie Royale the same year.
3. Henriet 1922, p. 179.
4. Gault de Saint-Germain 1808, p. 234; Landon 1808, vol. 1, p. 9.
5. "[S]es bons dessins se payent au poids de l'or et ils le méritent." Letter from F. P. Haudry to A. Th. Desfriches, in Ratouis de Limay 1907, p. 27.
6. Varanchan sale, December 29–31, 1777, lot 66.
7. Sale, December 15, 1777, no. 214.
8. Sale [Vassal de Saint-Hubert], March 29–April 13, 1779, lot 179.
9. Trouard sale, February 22–27, 1779, lot 78. This is probably the painting now at the Real Academia de Bellas Artes de San Fernando in Madrid (p. 142, fig. 87).
10. "Ses dessins sont pleins de feu" (Huber and Rost 1804, pp. 239–40); see also the Huquier sale, November 9, 1772, lot 423.
11. Académie Royale 1765, pp. 30–31.
12. Sale, November 12, 1781, lots 47, 142.
13. Sterling 1964, p. 7: "Agile as a pencil, the brush draws as much as it paints."
14. This issue was first studied by the author in 2013 (see Reuter et al. 2013, pp. 225–39), some of the points of which are repeated here.
15. An interesting comparison of the methods of some artists with those of Fragonard can be found in Rosenberg 2000b.
16. Here reference is made principally to the most recent catalogues of the artist's paintings: Cuzin 1987 and Rosenberg 1989.
17. Sale, November 11, 1784, no. 158. The painting is kept at the Museo Municipal de Vigo "Quiñones de León" (see Dupuy-Vachey 2007, cat. no. 5).
18. *The Swaddled Cat*, ca. 1778, brush and brown wash over black chalk underdrawing, Musée du Louvre, Paris (RF 42670). Cuzin 2003, cat. no. 30.
19. "[U]n enfant tenant entre ses bras un chat emmaillotté." The painting was exhibited at the Salon de la Correspondance (*Nouvelles de la République des Lettres et des Arts*, July 13, 1779, p. 173).
20. Except for light sketching, probably in graphite, visible even in normal light under the painting layer of the little *Blond Child with Flowers*, painted on panel (Cuzin 1987, no. 280; Rosenberg 1989, no. 410), noted by Bergeon et al. 1988, pp. 30 n. 13, 39 n. 80.
21. A summary of analyses of about twenty paintings in the Louvre can be found in Bergeon et al. 1988. See also Cuzin 1988a, pp. 84–85; Leonard et al. 2008; Jackall et al. 2015.
22. "[J]amais content de ses productions, il efface et revient sur lui-même." Mariette 1851–60, vol. 2 (1853–54), p. 263. In 1765, the secretary of the Académie, Charles Nicolas Cochin, noted the artist's "modesty, which goes as far as exaggerated distrust of himself" ("modestie, qui va jusqu'à une défiance outrée de soy-même") (letter to Marigny, April 1, 1765, in Marigny 1905, p. 10).
23. Musée des Beaux-Arts, Angers (MBA J 58 [J.1881] P); Cuzin 1987, no. 118; Rosenberg 1989, no. 114.
24. *The Swing*, Wallace Collection, London (P430); Cuzin 1987, no. 147; Rosenberg 1989, no. 177.
25. *The Progress of Love*, The Frick Collection, New York (1945.1.45-48); Cuzin 1987, nos. 239–42; Rosenberg 1989, nos. 273–76.
26. Musée des Beaux-Arts, Angers (2004.39.1 and 2); Frick Art and Historical Center, Pittsburgh (1973.2); Cuzin 1987, nos. 243, 244; Rosenberg 1989, nos. 277–79.
27. Dupuy-Vachey 2015.
28. This phrase appears on the labels that used to be glued to the reverse of two paintings from this portrait series.
29. According to Théophile Fragonard, the artist's grandson, Paul I of Russia, during a trip to France, visited Fragonard's studio several times, and "one day, curtseyed elegantly to his mannequin, who was dressed as a lady" ("fit un jour une belle révérence à son mannequin, qui était habillé en dame") (letter to Thoré-Burger, November 4, 1847, in Valogne 1955, pp. 1, 9).
30. This comparison was suggested by the fascinating exhibition organized by Jane Munro, "Silent Partners: Artist and Mannequin from Function to Fetish." Information on artist's mannequins in the eighteenth century can be found in the first two chapters of the catalogue. See Munro 2014.
31. Rosenberg 1988, cat. no. 120.
32. Cuzin 1987, no. 28; Rosenberg 1989, no. 19. I have suggested a slightly later date, either at the end of the artist's time in Italy or immediately afterward; see Dupuy-Vachey 2009.
33. Cuzin 1987, nos. 29–31; Rosenberg 1989, nos. 20–23.
34. Ananoff 1961–70, vol. 3 (1968), no. 1775, fig. 439; Rosenberg 1988, pp. 57–58, fig. 7 (Fragonard?). An earlier example of a composition prepared by drawings in a similar style is provided by two sheets showing a sacrificial scene that can be connected to *Jeroboam Sacrificing to the Idols* (sale, Paris, May 3, 1913, lot 84, ill., and sale, Paris, November 30, 1987, lot 1, ill.). As I know these only from reproductions, it is not possible to express a definite opinion about their attribution.
35. Rosenberg (1988, pp. 57–58, fig. 7) "accept[s] [it] with some reservations in spite of its free execution."
36. Cuzin in Cuzin et al. 2006, p. 58, fig. 42; Dupuy-Vachey 2009, p. 51, fig. 10.

36. G. Wildenstein 1956, pp. 15–31, nos. VII–XXII. One of them, moreover, appears to have been left unfinished; see p. 18, no. IX. For an analysis of Fragonard's use of the diminutive "frago" as a signature, its intent, and its social context, see Guichard 2012.
37. "Les charmantes eaux-fortes qu'il a gravées d'un goût exquis, seront placées à côté des Benedette, des Salvator et des meilleurs artistes en ce genre." Lecarpentier 1821, p. 282.
38. This can be difficult to appreciate in Rosenberg and Brejon de Lavergnée 2000, as many of the examples of the *Griffonis* illustrated are from a special set of counterproofs of the aquatints held at the Bibliothèque Nationale de France, Paris, which were subsequently reworked in wash and reinscribed; see pp. 327 and 331, and, for examples, the illustrations of nos. 13 and 14 on p. 338. Thus, they appear in the same direction as Fragonard's drawings, while the conventional printing would have them reversed.
39. Guimbaud 1928, p. 197, no. 56.
40. The full title was *Fragments choisis dans les peintures et les tableaux les plus intéressants des palais et des églises de l'Italie* (fragments chosen from the most interesting paintings and canvases of the palaces and churches of Italy).
41. See, for example, Stein and Holmes 1999, pp. 96–100, cat. nos. 42, 43.
42. "Les grands maîtres finissent peu leurs desseins; ils se contentent de faire des equisses, ou griffonnemens faits de rien, (*a*) qui ne plaisent pas aux demi-connoisseurs. Ceux-ci veulent quelque chose de terminé, qui soit agréable aux yeux: un vrai connoisseur pense autrement; il voit dans un croquis, la maniere de penser d'un grand maître, pour caractériser chaque objet avec peu de traits; son imagination animée par le beau feu qui regne dans le dessein," in Dézallier d'Argenville 1762, vol. 1, p. lxj.
43. See Jombert 1755, pp. 67–68, and Pernety 1757, p. xxiv. For discussions of these sources and others relevant to the practice of counterproofing in the eighteenth century, see Cohn 1987 and Hall 1990. I am indebted to David Pullins for bringing Hall's thesis to my attention.
44. "De plus on en retire une contre-épreuve sur le papier qui étoit blanc, laquelle quoique plus tendre que le dessin original, a encore assez de force, & qui est même plus agréable à la vûe, en ce que les hachures délicates des demi teintes, y sont bien moins dures que dans le dessin," in Jombert 1755, p. 68. "Pour prévenir cet inconvénient on les fait passer à la contr'épreuve, & l'on en a deux pour un," in Pernety 1757, p. xxiv. Both passages are quoted and translated in Cohn 1987, p. 167.
45. Catala 2015, pp. 41–42.
46. See Rosenberg and Barthélemy-Labeeuw 2011, vol. 1, pp. 95–331; for the drawing in the Metropolitan illustrated as fig. 47, see p. 156, no. F461.
47. See sale catalogue F-A391, lot 1150, Getty Provenance Index® Databases, J. Paul Getty Trust.
48. "[L]e crayon rouge était celui dont [Watteau] se servait le plus souvent sur du papier blanc, afin d'avoir des contres-épreuves, ce qui lui rendait son sujet des deux côtés," quoted in Roland Michel 1987, p. 15.
49. Catala 2014, p. 72.
50. See Méjanès 1983, pp. 11, 125, 127; Stein 2000a; and Caviglia-Brunel 2012, pp. 497–507.
51. Caviglia-Brunel 2012, pp. 499–501, nos. R.22–R.37.
52. Ibid., p. 501, no. R.36.
53. It was described in an inventory made by Joseph Marie Vien as "a press for counterproofing the drawings of the *pensionnaires*"; see Stein et al. 2013, pp. 105, 215 n. 8.
54. Alsteens et al. 2009, pp. 197–99, cat. no. 87 (entry by Perrin Stein).
55. Catala 2015, p. 37.
56. Stein 2000b, pp. 179–83, figs. 6, 7.
57. Catala 2014, p. 77.
58. Roland Michel 1987, p. 20.
59. For the La Fontaine series, see, most recently, Faroult 2015, pp. 100–115 (entries by Marie-Anne Dupuy-Vachey).
60. Rosenberg 2006, pp. 64–68, cat. nos. 19, 20. Although not mentioned in the published *livret*, other sources suggest that the entire Tivoli series may have been exhibited at the Salon of 1765; see ibid., p. 52.
61. Rosenberg 1988, p. 150.
62. "Un Paysage contrepreuve à la sanguine, vigoureusement retouchée au bistre, offrant des arcades ruinées & surmontées d'un temple circulaire"; Louis Antoine Auguste, duc de Rohan-Chabot, his collection sale (Lugt 4235), Boileau, Paris, December 17–22, 1787, p. 39, lot 170.
63. On the use of counterproofs to aid in the development of painted compositions, see Marie-Anne Dupuy-Vachey in Reuter et al. 2013, pp. 233–35.
64. See Stein 2004.
65. Raux 2007, p. 18. See also Cuzin et al. 2006, p. 202. According to Raux, Fragonard had likely made other trips to Holland after his return from Italy in 1761.
66. See Szanto 2005 and Michel 2005. On the collecting of northern drawings in particular and the visits of collectors and dealers to Holland and Flanders, see Michel 2006, pp. 195–96, 200–206.
67. Joulie 2004.
68. See sale catalogue F-A244, lots 11, 248, 253, and 316, Getty Provenance Index® Databases, J. Paul Getty Trust.
69. Illustrated in Rosenberg 1988, p. 58, fig. 8. See also Cuzin et al. 2006, pp. 84–85, cat. no. 32 (entry by Jean-Pierre Cuzin).
70. There are exceptions: for example, a copy after Salvator Rosa done in Naples and a pair after Mattia Preti drawn in Rome; see Ananoff 1961–70, vol. 2 (1963), p. 186, no. 1095, fig. 308, and vol. 4 (1970), pp. 196–97, nos. 2576, 2577, figs. 644, 645.
71. Michel 2006, p. 216.
72. Bailey 2002, pp. 123–25, figs. 109, 110.
73. Jean Antoine Gros collection sale (Lugt 2835), Chariot, Paris, April 13, 1778, lots 72–77, 79. For a discussion of the sale and of Gabriel de Saint-Aubin's sketches of lost Fragonard drawings, see Raux 2007.
74. Although they should not necessarily be read as illustrations of Rousseauian ideas, domestic scenes set in humble interiors saw a great popularity in the 1770s. In 1778, the same year Fragonard and Gérard produced this group of etchings, Queen Marie Antoinette gave birth to a daughter and proclaimed, "I want to live like a mother, nurse my child and devote myself to her upbringing." See Barker 2005, pp. 136, 145.
75. For a detailed study of this period, especially the prints of Marguerite Gérard, see Hoisington and Stein 2012.
76. Langlois was a maker of high-quality scientific instruments. An example of one of his pantographs, in the Museum of the History of Science, Oxford, is inscribed "Langlois A Paris aux Galleries du Louvre No 29." See http://www.mhs.ox.ac.uk/collections/imu-search-page/record-details/?TitInventoryNo=40818&querytype=field&thumbnails=on&irn=1935.
77. For both references, see Rena M. Hoisington, "Learning to Etch," in Stein et al. 2013, pp. 33, 36. Pierre Jean Mariette also owned a pantograph and is known to have used it in 1759 to copy a Michelangelo drawing from his own collection; see Smentek 2014, pp. 65, 90 n. 261. For an overview of the mentions of pantographs in contemporary treatises, see Hall 1990, pp. 49–50.
78. This assumption is based on the technique of Gérard's print made after the same drawing. Her technique, which attempted to replicate in etching the appearance of Fragonard's translucent washes and black chalk underdrawing, allows us to form an idea of the lost model drawing. See Hoisington and Stein 2012, pp. 152–57.
79. See, for example, Grasselli et al. 2003, p. 133, cat. no. 73.
80. Jombert 1755, pp. 123–36.
81. See Hall 1990, pp. 33–42.
82. Vogtherr and Holmes 2014, pp. 176–79, cat. nos. 58, 59 (entries by Mary Taverner Holmes).
83. Rand 1995.

84. Goncourt 1981, p. 300; in French, "un peu d'eau, un peu de bistre, un coup de main,—et le tour est fait!"; Goncourt 1882, vol. 2, p. 349.
85. Norman 1978a, 1978b.
86. Stein 2009.
87. Ananoff 1957. In an interview published a year earlier, Ananoff listed multiple methods used by Fragonard to "copy" his own drawings, mentioning copying at the window by transmitted light, pantographs, and tracing; see Ananoff 1956, p. 38.
88. Reuter et al. 2013, p. 235.
89. Lajer-Burcharth 2003, p. 48.

EARLY YEARS: PARIS TO ROME

1. Quoted in Rosenberg 1988, pp. 32–38.

CAT. 1

1. Katie Scott, "Reproduction and Reputation: 'François Boucher' and the Formation of Artistic Identities," in Hyde and Ledbury 2006, pp. 91–132.
2. Couturier 2004, pp. 60–61, cat. no. 20. According to Alastair Laing (correspondence July 20, 2011), Boucher's drawing depicts the prophet Elijah.
3. Jean-Richard 1971, pp. 30–32, cat. nos. 30, 32.
4. Rena M. Hoisington, "Learning to Etch," in Stein et al. 2013, pp. 15–39. On Boucher's *Andromeda*, see especially pp. 21–26, cat. nos. 5, 6.
5. François Boucher estate sale (Lugt 1895), Paris, February 18–March 9, 1771.

CAT. 2

1. *View of a Park*, ca. 1760–67, black chalk and gray wash, Allen Memorial Art Museum, Oberlin College, Ohio (1951.17); Williams 1978, cat. no. 20.
2. Ananoff 1961–70, vol. 4 (1970), no. 2215; Massengale 1979, pp. 271–72; Bean and Turčić 1986, pp. 110–11.
3. McPherson 1985.

CAT. 3

1. "Ça ne fait rien, tu es mon élève." Quoted by the Goncourt brothers (1882, vol. 2, p. 316), who probably learned this from the artist's grandson, Théophile Fragonard.
2. "Lorsque l'artiste est parvenu à bien *dessiner* une figure nue, il pourra la drapper." Diderot and d'Alembert 1754–72, vol. 4, p. 890.
3. Most are kept at the Musée du Louvre, Paris, and the Musée Atger, Montpellier; see, for example, Rosenberg 1988, pp. 72–74.
4. *Jeroboam Sacrificing to the Idols*, 1752, oil on canvas, 43¾ × 56⅜ in. (111 × 143 cm), Ecole Nationale Supérieure des Beaux-Arts, Paris (PRP 7); Cuzin 1987, no. 1; Rosenberg 1989, no. 3.
5. *Christ Washing the Feet of the Apostles*, 1754, oil on canvas, 13 ft. ¾ in. × 6 ft. 6¾ in. (3.98 × 2.92 m), Cathédrale Notre-Dame-du-Puy, Grasse; Cuzin 1987, p. 22; Rosenberg 1989, no. 40.
6. "[D]es habit[s] d'église . . . occasionnent de fort beau[x] plis." Natoire to the marquis de Marigny, October 18, 1758 (Montaiglon and Guiffrey 1901, p. 239).
7. Ananoff 1961–70, vol. 2 (1963), no. 770, fig. 213; Cuzin 1987, p. 42, fig. 45; Pagliano 2005, cat. no. 16. The Orléans museum has another study of the same model, attributed by Eric Pagliano (2005, cat. no. 17) to Charles Monnet (575-427).

CAT. 4

1. "Une étude de différentes plantes groupées, dessein très-brillant à la sanguine"; Jean Denis Lempereur sale, Paris, May 24, 1773, p. 117, no. 736.
2. Cited by Ananoff 1961–70, vol. 4 (1970), under no. 2223: *Paysage imité des jardins d'Italie*.
3. Montaiglon and Guiffrey 1901, pp. 304–5.
4. Drawings inscribed 1759, all in red chalk, include *La Maisonnette*, Musée Jean-Honoré Fragonard, Grasse (Zanella 2011, pp. 52–53); *Interior of a Roman Courtyard*, private collection, London (Ananoff 1961–70, vol. 4 [1970], no. 2313); *Ruins of an Imperial Palace, Rome*, J. Paul Getty Museum, Los Angeles (90.GB.138) (Ananoff 1961–70, vol. 3 [1968], no. 1483; Turner et al. 1998, no. 98, pp. 235–36); and *Monumental Fountain in a Park*, sale, Christie's, Paris, 2013 (Ananoff 1961–70, vol. 3 [1968], no. 1581).
5. See Cayeux 1985, no. 16, ill.

CAT. 5

1. *Le jeu de la bascule*, Städel Museum, Frankfurt (1235); Bauereisen and Stuffmann 1986, cat. nos. 122, 123.
2. Lajer-Burcharth 2003, pp. 36–40.
3. Milam 1999; Cuzin 1986, pp. 58–60.
4. Rosenberg 1988, cat. nos. 13, 14.
5. Rand 1991.

CAT. 6

1. Carlson 1978, p. 19.
2. These early landscapes are discussed in Williams 1978, pp. 34–38, ill.

FRAGONARD AND THE ABBÉ DE SAINT-NON

1. The authoritative study is Rosenberg and Brejon de Lavergnée 2000 (first published 1986). See also Mascoli 1989.
2. Cuzin et al. 2006, p. 195.
3. See Smentek 2014, esp. pp. 101–5, and Stein 2000a, esp. pp. 168–71.
4. Rosenberg and Brejon de Lavergnée 2000, p. 51.
5. "Il fait un magasin pour se nourrir le reste de sa vie. J'éprouve tous les jours que le germe qu'on acquiert à Rome et dans quelques autres villes d'Italie jette des racines si profondes qu'elles survivent pour ainsi dire à celui qui le porte." Caylus 1877, p. 142.
6. See, for example, Rosenberg 2006, pp. 77–108.
7. The counterproofs were almost invariably reworked in black chalk, strengthening their visibility, and their inscriptions were rewritten in pen. It was the opinion of Pierre Rosenberg and Barbara Brejon de Lavergnée in 1986 that, in many cases, the reworking was likely done by Saint-Non. See Rosenberg and Brejon de Lavergnée 2000, p. 326. It is worth noting, however, that, from sketches by Gabriel de Saint-Aubin in the margins of the sale catalogue, it would appear that twenty-eight counterproofs of the black chalk drawings were sold at the sale of the Pigache collection (Lugt 2594), Paris, October 21 and ff., 1776, where they were described simply as drawings by Fragonard. See the page illustrated in Rosenberg and Brejon de Lavergnée 2000, p. 334.
8. Cited in Rosenberg 1988, p. 150, and Rosenberg and Brejon de Lavergnée 2000, pp. 53–54.
9. Quoted and translated in Rosenberg 1988, p. 120.

CAT. 7

1. Montaiglon and Guiffrey 1901, p. 378.
2. For a discussion of the counterproof and a copy of it made by Nicolas Bernard Lépicié to serve as a model for the printmaker, see Stein and Holmes 1999, pp. 96–100, cat. nos. 42, 43.
3. See Rosenberg and Brejon de Lavergnée 2000, p. 344, nos. 34–38. For Preti's series, see De Conciliis and Lattuada 1979.
4. See Rosenberg and Brejon de Lavergnée 2000, p. 326, and Rosenberg 2006, pp. 78–79.

CAT. 8

1. It appears in the 2000 supplement; see Rosenberg and Brejon de Lavergnée 2000, pp. 434, 441, fig. 9.

2. A third factor may have to do with the sheet's dimensions, which are slightly smaller than those of other drawings in the series, raising the possibility that it has been trimmed. This would account for why the hatching appears to go to the edge of the sheet, whereas many other sheets have an irregular white border where the hatching stops before the edge.
3. Titi 1987, vol. 2, pp. 388–89, fig. 1476.
4. D. Wildenstein 1972, p. 86, nos. 7–10.

CAT. 9

1. Brogi 2001, vol. 1, pp. 169–71, no. 56, vol. 2, fig. 141.
2. Rosenberg and Brejon de Lavergnée 2000, p. 83.
3. Ibid., p. 402, nos. 277, 278.
4. "On y voir les beautés & le défaut de couleur ordinaire à ce maître." Cochin 1991, p. 274.
5. Rosenberg and Brejon de Lavergnée 2000, p. 81.
6. The image illustrated in Rosenberg and Brejon de Lavergnée 2000, p. 401, no. 276, is not Saint-Non's aquatint but rather a counterproof of the etching-only state of the print reworked in brown wash (Bibliothèque Nationale de France, Paris). Thus, it appears in the same orientation as Fragonard's drawing, unlike normal impressions of Saint-Non's print, which are in reverse.
7. Rosenberg and Brejon de Lavergnée consider the drawing they catalogued as "unlocated" to be the same as Ananoff 1961–70, vol. 4 (1970), no. 2507. However, the work catalogued by Ananoff, titled *Saint Benoit*, would appear to be a different drawing, as neither the inscription nor the collector's mark nor the provenance seem to correspond to the present sheet.

CAT. 10

1. See Cochin 1991, pp. 284–85; Rosenberg and Brejon de Lavergnée 2000, pp. 81–82.
2. Riccòmini 2006.

CAT. 11

1. Rosenberg and Brejon de Lavergnée 2000, pp. 238–50.
2. Ibid., p. 250.
3. See ibid., pp. 418–19, nos. 341–43. For a discussion of the vantage point of the present drawing, within an essay on the history of the garden, see Magnani 2004. The "S. de" in the inscription stands for "Seconde," meaning that this is the second view, presumably following the one in the British Museum, London; see Rosenberg 1988, p. 137, cat. no. 55.
4. Cochin ca. 1774, pp. 59–60.

CAT. 12

1. Rosenberg and Brejon de Lavergnée 2000, pp. 224–28.
2. Ananoff 1961–70, vol. 1 (1961), no. 345, fig. 123.

ETCHINGS INSPIRED BY ITALY

1. For the prints made during this period, 1763–64, of which most, but not all, are in the present exhibition, see G. Wildenstein 1956, nos. II–XXII.
2. See Charlotte Guichard, "*Amateurs* and the Culture of Etching," in Stein et al. 2013, pp. 136–55. For her longer study on the subject, see Guichard 2008.
3. Rosenberg and Brejon de Lavergnée 2000, pp. 326–33. For the complete catalogue of Saint-Non's etched oeuvre, see Guimbaud 1928.
4. Cayeux 1963, pp. 303, 321–22, and Wiebel 2007. See also Guimbaud 1928, pp. 123–38.
5. Cayeux 1963, pp. 302–3, nos. 31–59.
6. Of the remaining six, three are based on works in Naples, one in Florence, and two in Piacenza.
7. See, for example, Rosenberg 1998.
8. Those that are in the same direction as the original are G. Wildenstein 1956, nos. VII, IX, X, XIII, XVII, XIX, and XX; those that are in reverse direction are nos. VIII, XI, XII, XIV, XV, XVI, XVIII, XXI, and XXII.
9. See Perrin Stein, "Echoes of Rembrandt and Castiglione: Etching as Appropriation," in Stein et al. 2013, pp. 156–83.

CATS. 13 AND 14

1. "L'Eglise des Sts. Apôtres est encore une des plus belles Eglises de Naples; la voûte en est entièrement peinte par le Lanfranc avec une hardiesse et un feu étonnant." Rosenberg and Brejon de Lavergnée 2000, p. 117.
2. "Tous ces morceaux de Lanfranco sont composés avec une hardiesse, un feu & un génie admirables; la maniere en est fiere & terrible." Cochin 1991, p. 158.
3. The drawing of Saint Luke was later mounted on a sheet, perhaps by Saint-Non, together with two copies after Jusepe de Ribera from another church in Naples; see Rosenberg and Brejon de Lavergnée 2000, ill. on p. 338, under no. 12.
4. G. Wildenstein 1956, p. 16, under no. VII.

CAT. 15

1. Stein and Holmes 1999, pp. 98–100, cat. no. 43.
2. The drawing is in the Norton Simon Museum, Pasadena. Rosenberg and Brejon de Lavergnée 2000, p. 344, under no. 34.

CAT. 16

1. In that version, the setting is a moonlit landscape with two additional female onlookers in the left background. See Riccoboni 1947, p. 15, cat. no. 99, pl. 96.
2. For Fragonard's original drawing, today in the British Museum, London, see Stein 2005, p. 142, cat. no. 56, p. 224. The British Museum drawing is in the same direction as the etching, suggesting that in this case Fragonard may have used the counterproof as the model for his print.

CATS. 17 AND 18

1. Rosenberg and Brejon de Lavergnée 2000, p. 214.
2. Ibid., pp. 194–96.
3. Pierre Rosenberg, "Tintoret et Fragonard," in Rossi and Puppi 1996, pp. 27–28.
4. Romanelli 1995, fig. 7.
5. Ibid., p. 377, under no. 176.
6. For the drawing in the Norton Simon Museum, Pasadena, see Rosenberg and Brejon de Lavergnée 2000, p. 378, under no. 179.

CAT. 19

1. Rosenberg and Brejon de Lavergnée 2000, p. 383, under no. 202. The reworked counterproof of the Norton Simon drawing was sold most recently at Sotheby's, New York, January 29, 2013, lot 114. For Ricci's decorations for the church, see Daniels 1976, p. 145, under no. 506.
2. Scarpa 2006, p. 358, under no. P56.
3. G. Wildenstein 1956, p. 27, no. XVIII.
4. Scarpa 2006, pp. 242–43, 494, no. 281, fig. 291.

CATS. 20 AND 21

1. Quoted in Christiansen 1998, p. 11.
2. In addition to the two exhibited here, Fragonard drew and then etched *The Madonna and Child with Saints Catherine of Siena, Rose of Lima, and Agnes of Montepulciano*; see Christiansen 1997, pp. 222–25, cat. no. 35. The drawing is untraced; see Rosenberg and Brejon de Lavergnée 2000, p. 386, under no. 215.

3. See Rosenberg and Brejon de Lavergnée 2000, p. 385, no. 210. For the four other drawings Fragonard made after parts of the Ca' Dolfin cycle, see ibid., p. 385, nos. 207–9, 211.
4. For Jaynie Anderson (2003, pp. 138–41), this grafting of Pluto and Persephone into the scene of the banquet was a "comic but meaningful intrusion," alluding to the lust between Anthony and Cleopatra.

CAT. 22

1. "[C]e morceau est de belle maniere, large, d'un beau pinceau, & plein de goût." Quoted in Cochin 1991, p. 351.

CAT. 23

1. Ugo Ruggeri has put forth the tentative suggestion that it may represent Jupiter in the form of Diana seducing Callisto. See Ruggeri 1996, pp. 57, 185, no. P160, fig. 65.

CATS. 24 AND 25

1. Rosenberg and Brejon de Lavergnée 2000, pp. 234–37.
2. Ibid., p. 411, no. 315.
3. The identification of the figure behind Moses as Hur was first suggested by Carmen Bambach (conversation, February 19, 2015). Moses is sometimes depicted with Aaron and Hur as companions based on the passage in Exodus 17:10–12. In the Piacenza fresco, Aaron, holding the flowering rod, is seen on the other side of Moses. Traditionally, the print has been titled *Two Prophets, after Annibale Carracci*. See G. Wildenstein 1956, p. 28, no. XIX.
4. See Brogi 2001, vol. 1, pp. 207–8, no. 95.1, vol. 2, figs. 199, 200.
5. See Cochin 1991, p. 107.

CATS. 26–29

1. Georges Wildenstein stated in 1956 that the etchings were based on drawings Fragonard had made of bas-reliefs in Herculaneum (G. Wildenstein 1956, p. 12). Pierre Rosenberg and others have accepted Cornelius Vermeule's identification of the source of *Nymph Supported by Two Satyrs* as a relief in the Palazzo Mattei in Rome (Rosenberg 1988, pp. 154–57). It has not been possible to substantiate either of these claims. To the present author, the *Venus Marina* relief then in the Palazzo Mattei has only a superficially similar composition. See Venuti 1776–79, vol. 3, pl. II.1.
2. That the etchings were made in Paris, after Fragonard and Saint-Non returned from Italy, is clear from the dates inscribed on the prints, despite the fact that the inscription on the second state of Fragonard's suite states that they were "gravées en Italie" (engraved in Italy). See G. Wildenstein 1956, p. 11. More puzzling is the inscription in reverse in the uncleaned margin of the first state of *Nymph Supported by Two Satyrs*, which Wildenstein had seen and transcribed as "Bergeret invenit et fecit . . . Frago." If correct, this presents a conundrum, because, even though the two men likely knew each other at this point (Bergeret was a collector of Fragonard's master, Boucher), there is no reason to think Bergeret was involved with the etching of the print. The style is unmistakably the same as that of the other three in the series, and the prints in the series are variously inscribed "Frago," and "1763" within the plate. See G. Wildenstein 1956, p. 11, and L'Isle-Adam 2001, pp. 16–17.
3. See Williams 1978, pp. 44–45, cat. no. 9, and Rosenberg 2006, pp. 87–90, cat. nos. 30, 31. Distinct from these sheets, in which the *mise-en-page* of the sketches anticipates Saint-Non's etchings, a black chalk study for *Nymph Supported by Two Satyrs* (cat. 26) in the reverse direction of Fragonard's etching was sold at Tajan, Paris, November 5, 2014, lot 12.
4. For instance, inscriptions reading "inventé par Robert" appear under individual motifs, while others give the location of the antiquity represented. The fact that each of Saint-Non's etchings, and the drawings that they are based on, contain motifs with a variety of captions suggests that the compositions may have pulled together different sketches made on different days, perhaps by different hands. An exception to this would seem to be two pages removed from the Cambridge album: *Satyr and Maenad with Herm* (1979.70.18) and *Satyr and Maenad Embracing* (1979.70.21), which both appear to be autograph works by Fragonard. I thank Eunice Williams for sharing her thoughts on this group of drawings when we had the opportunity to study them together on March 31, 2015.
5. Faroult 2016, p. 181.

CATS. 30–34

1. "[M]erveilleuse sanguine parmi tant de merveilles de cet artiste si séduisant." See Jacques Victor, comte de La Béraudière (1819–1885) collection sale (Lugt 42893), Hôtel Drouot, Paris, April 16–17, 1883, p. x.
2. For the painting (Wallace Collection, London), the only one of the group not included in the exhibition, see Ingamells 1989, pp. 149–51, no. P379.
3. The first use of the title *Le petit parc* seems to be in Portalis 1889, vol. 1, p. iii, in reference to the etching. In Baudicour 1859–61 (vol. 1, pp. 160–61, no. 4), the title of the print is simply *Le parc*. The print also appeared in an 1855 sale with the title *Le parc*; see the de Vèze collection sale (Lugt 22289), Delbergue Cormont, François, and Vignères, Paris, March 4, 1855, part of lot 271.
4. Without elaborating, Pierre Rosenberg (1988, p. 149) had stated that Fragonard had "adapted a drawing of the Villa d'Este that he had made in Italy for the etching entitled *Le Petit Parc*."
5. See Rosenberg 2006, pp. 64–68, cat. nos. 19, 20. For the possibility that more than two were put on public view, see ibid., p. 52.
6. Carlson and Ittmann 1984, p. 150.
7. Conisbee 1988, p. 320.
8. Wintermute 1990, p. 188, under cat. no. 35 (entry by Eunice Williams).
9. Rosenberg 2006, pp. 71–73, cat. no. 23.
10. Rosenberg 1988, p. 153.
11. "[I]l a privilégié la nature au détriment de l'architecture"; see Rosenberg 2006, p. 54.
12. G. Wildenstein 1956, pp. 8–31, nos. II–XXII. See also Carlson and Ittmann 1984, p. 150, for a discussion of the dating.
13. The fact that the two large trees that structure the scene were borrowed from a drawing made in Italy, rather than drawn after nature, supports the dating of the first sheet in the *Little Park* sequence to after Fragonard's return from Italy.
14. See Salmon 2016.
15. The print also inspired homages from two of Fragonard's contemporaries, his friend the abbé de Saint-Non and the Austrian printmaker living in Paris, Franz Edmund Weirotter (1733–1771); see Stein et al. 2013, pp. 31, 33–35, 187, cat. nos. 12, 13. Interestingly, Saint-Non, like Fragonard, revisited the composition, creating a second state of the print by scraping and burnishing out the statue and niche at the center and adding two dark, partly dead, trees, one at the right and one at the left margin, in much the way Fragonard did in the reworked counterproof, the oil, and the gouache. Impressions of both states are held by the National Gallery of Art in Washington, D.C., both gifts of Gertrude Laughlin Chanler (2000.9.11, 2000.9.12).
16. Making counterproofs and reworking them was an established practice among pensionnaires at the Académie de France in Rome. They were retained by the artist, exchanged as gifts, or sold. Many counterproofs of chalk drawings by Hubert Robert are today in Besançon; see Guigon 2013. For another reworked counterproof by Fragonard, see cat. 35.
17. Scholars have debated the dating of the Wallace picture, vacillating between Fragonard's last year in Rome and the first few years following

his return to Paris. Based on the rough weave of the canvas, more typical of canvases used in Italy, Pierre Rosenberg (2006, p. 52) thinks it more likely that *Le petit parc* and a few other small canvases inspired by Tivoli were painted in Italy. Based on the ordering of the works proposed here, a date of about 1760–61, while not impossible, would move the whole group back to this period and isolate the etching from the twenty plates etched in Paris about 1763–64. Moreover, in 2004, Stephen Duffy and Jo Hedley described the canvas as not being the coarse fabric he used in Italy, leading them to date the painting to about 1762–63; see Duffy and Hedley 2004, p. 152, no. P379.

18. This description could refer to either cat. 30 or cat. 31. Jean Denis Lempereur (1701–1779) was a goldsmith and court jeweler but also a collector, connoisseur, and amateur etcher. He was a friend to many artists, art dealers, and amateurs.
19. The Walferdin provenance is from Ananoff. From the description of lot 188, "*Les Environs de Tivoli*. Paysage, architecture et figures: la Villa d'Este. Dessin à la sanguine. H., 0ᵐ,34. L., 0ᵐ,46," it seems possible but not certain. Ananoff gives the buyer at the Walferdin sale as "Lauverjat," presumably referring to the landscape painter Gaston de Lauverjat (1839–1913).
20. See note 18.
21. Annotations in different copies of the sale catalogue differ. Of the two copies held in the Rijksbureau voor Kunsthistorische Documentatie, one is annotated "Stettiner (Vildenstein)," and the other "Vildenstein." "Stettiner" probably refers to Henri-Julius Stettiner (1842–ca. 1913), who was an art dealer in Paris, and "Vildenstein" to Nathan Wildenstein (1851–1934), the founder of Wildenstein & Co.
22. Philip Conisbee (1988, p. 320) drew attention to it in a review.

CAT. 35

1. Montaiglon and Guiffrey 1901, pp. 334, 339.
2. "[L]a plus délicieuse chose du monde . . . ils sont aujourd'hui dans un délabrement affreux"; Rosenberg and Brejon de Lavergnée 2000, p. 159.
3. *The Avenue of Cypress Trees in the Villa d'Este*, 1760, red chalk, Musée des Beaux-Arts et d'Archéologie, Besançon (D.2842); *The Fountain of Pomona and the Avenue of the Hundred Fountains at the Villa d'Este*, 1760, red chalk, Musée des Beaux-Arts et d'Archéologie, Besançon (D.2845); Salon of 1765, Paris (cat. 178): "Two Drawings: views of the Villa d'Este in Tivoli; they belong to M. l'Abbé de Saint-Non."
4. Rosenberg 2006, pp. 51–75.
5. *The Temple of Vesta, or the Sibyl, in Tivoli*, 1760, red chalk over black chalk sketch, Musée des Beaux-Arts et d'Archéologie, Besançon (D.2839).
6. Giovanni Battista Piranesi, *Another View of the Temple of the Sibyl in Tivoli*, 1761, etching, The Metropolitan Museum of Art, New York (56.581.5); Hind 1922, no. 57.63; Wilton-Ely 1994, no. 239.196.

FRAGONARD AND THE ACADÉMIE ROYALE

1. "[L]égèreté et insouciance"; Rosenberg 1988, p. 430.

CAT. 36

1. *Rinaldo Enters the Enchanted Forest*, ca. 1763, oil on canvas, Musée du Louvre, Paris (RF 2003-11); Cuzin 1987, no. 95; Rosenberg 1989, no. 109; Faroult 2015, cat. no. 81 (entry by Marie-Anne Dupuy-Vachey). *Rinaldo Enters the Enchanted Forest*, 1761–64, brown wash over black chalk underdrawing, Art Gallery of New South Wales, Sydney (485.1993); Beresford and Raissis 2003, cat. no. 22.
2. Cuzin 1987, no. 96; Rosenberg 1989, no. 110.
3. The provenance in this catalogue repeats those in Ananoff 1961–70 and Paris 1951 (cat. no. 35), which more likely featured the drawing that is now in Sydney. Unfortunately, the archives of the Galerie Cailleux do not contain any information that would allow the drawing actually exhibited to be identified precisely.

CAT. 37

1. Pausanias, *Description of Greece* VII, 21:1–5. For a full study of Fragonard's painting, see Rabreau and Henry 2007, more specifically pp. 127–30 for the artist's various possible sources, both ancient and contemporary.
2. Cuzin 1987, no. 117; Rosenberg 1989, no. 113.
3. *Coresus and Callirhoë*, oil on canvas, Musée des Beaux-Arts, Angers (J. 58); Cuzin 1987, no. 118; Rosenberg 1989, no. 113.
4. Cuzin 1988a, pp. 84–85, fig. 2.
5. Cuzin 1987, no. 119; Rosenberg 1989, no. 115.
6. The suggestion, occasionally put forward in the past, that the drawing duplicated the Madrid version of the composition is not convincing.

CAT. 38

1. Exchange of correspondence between Cochin and Marigny, April 1 and 3, August 5 and 8, 1765 (Marigny 1905, pp. 10–12, 27–28).
2. Cuzin 1987, nos. 120, 121; Rosenberg 1989, nos. 117, 116. Ananoff (1961–70, vol. 1 [1961], no. 417, fig. 149, vol. 2 [1963], p. 311) catalogues another drawn version of our composition that is known only from a mediocre photograph.
3. "[J]eunes hommes et jeunes filles à Athènes, tirant au sort pour être livrés au minotaure." Possibly Bruun-Neergaard sale, August 30, 1814 (lot 127).
4. Pausanias, *Description of Greece* XXVII, 10. Plutarch (*Life of Theseus* XV) and Virgil (*The Aeneid* VI, 20–25) also refer to this legend.
5. The Minotaur was the son of Pasiphae and a white bull sent by Poseidon.
6. Williams 1978, cat. no. 19. The scholarly interpretation suggested by Evelyn Harrison (in Stein and Holmes 1999, cat. no. 57) cannot be retained.
7. Several artists interpreted the subject after Fragonard, such as Mathieu van Brée in 1773 (*The Drawings of Lots of the Young Athenian Girls Destined for the Minotaur*, Musées Royaux des Beaux-Arts de Belgique, Brussels) and Pierre Peyron a few years later (Apsley House, Wellington Museum, London; see Rosenberg and van de Sandt 1983, pp. 81–89, nos. 20–31).

CAT. 39

1. *White Bull*, ca. 1763–65, oil on canvas, Musée du Louvre, Paris (RF 1976-10); Cuzin 1987, no. 94; Rosenberg 1989, no. 102.
2. Ananoff 1961–70, vol. 1 (1961), no. 97, fig. 34, vol. 2 (1963), p. 298, vol. 3 (1968), p. 203.
3. The initial sketch in black chalk is in a private collection, New York, and the reworked counterproof is in the Petit Palais, Musée des Beaux-Arts de la Ville de Paris; Faroult 2015, cat. no. 21 (entry by Marie-Anne Dupuy-Vachey).
4. Guillerm 1980.

CAT. 40

1. *The Stalled Cart*, 1759, oil on canvas, Musée du Louvre, Paris (MI 1063); Cuzin 1987, no. 66; Rosenberg 1989, no. 66.
2. *The Stalled Cart*, 1759, red chalk, pen and brown ink, brown, gray, and sanguine wash, Art Institute of Chicago (1936.4); Couturier 2011b, cat. no. 35b (entry by Marie-Anne Dupuy-Vachey).
3. Ananoff 1961–70, vol. 1 (1961), no. 98, fig. 44, vol. 2 (1963), p. 298, vol. 4 (1970), p. 348; sale, Sotheby's, London, July 9, 2014 (lot 82).

CATS. 42 AND 43

1. Saint-Non la Bretèche was a seigneury near the ancient oak forest of Marly. The abbé's father, Jean Pierre Richard, acquired the château in 1736.

2. The duc de Rohan-Chabot sale, December 10–15, 1787, lot 212, expert Le Brun: "La Vue d'un village situé au bord d'un riviere, composition dans le style d'Hobéma."
3. Ananoff 1961–70, vol. 2 (1963), no. 956; and Jacques Wilhelm in Grasse 1957, p. 49.
4. "Dessin d'après nature de Monsieur Fragonard, dont il m'a fait présent 15 septembre 1765—Desfriches." Ananoff 1961–70, vol. 2 (1963), no. 957. Aignan Thomas Desfriches was a draftsman, printmaker, and collector from Orléans. The counterproof was last documented in the E. Calando sale (Lugt 57665), Paris, December 11–12, 1899, lot 54.
5. Stein et al. 2013, p. 34, cat. no. 11.

CAT. 44

1. Collet was the originator of a famous anecdote about the commission for *The Swing* (see most recently Faroult 2015, cat. no. 36).
2. Jean-Baptiste Hilaire, *Travelers Resting at the Entry to an Ottoman City*, signed and dated 1778 (and not 1779, as was stated in the 2013 auction catalogue), black chalk, pen and brown ink, brown wash, 8⅜ × 13¾ in. (21.1 × 34.8 cm), location unknown. Hilaire's drawing was lot 386 in the Collet sale, May 14, 1787 (with dimensions close to the current ones). It then appeared in the sale held on February 9, 1789, lot 549. Since Fragonard's sheet was not included, it can be deduced that the drawings were made pendants at a later date. Hilaire's drawing appeared in the sale at Tajan, Paris, on November 27, 2013, lot 28.
3. Sale, Paris, December 6, 1957, part of lot 139 ("*Le galant berger—Les pêcheurs*, deux sépias [26.5 × 36.5 cm and 28 × 33.5 cm]"). The first drawing was correctly reattributed to Fragonard in Paris 1980, cat. no. 7, and Paris 1987, cat. no. 62. It is not possible to express an opinion on a third version (inscribed "Fragonard"), which is known only from a poor reproduction in the catalogue of the Paulme sale (Paris, May 13–14, 1929, lot 92, pl. 62) and apparently has been destroyed (Réau 1956, p. 225).
4. Cuzin 1987, no. 191; Rosenberg 1989, no. 137.
5. Contrary to what has been said (Near 1981, cat. no. 13) about another drawn version of this composition, X-rays of the painting have not revealed a hat (Rita Albertson, conservator of paintings, Worcester Art Museum, email to the author, August 5, 2015).

CAT. 45

1. *The Pond, or Fishing for Crayfish*, ca. 1766–68, oil on canvas, Kimbell Art Museum, Fort Worth (AP 1968.03). According to Cuzin 1988b, pp. 285–86, no. 136. See Slive 1981.
2. Bjurström 1982, cat. no. 953, ill.; Ananoff 1961–70, vol. 2 (1963), no. 776, fig. 219.
3. Wapler, December 19, 2014, lot 59, R. Millet, expert. Marie-Anne Dupuy-Vachey kindly brought this sale to my attention.
4. Correspondence, November 2015.

CATS. 46 AND 47

1. Burke 1757.
2. As noted by Jean Seznec in Diderot 2011, pp. 22–25; and May 1960.
3. Fried 1980, p. 145.
4. *The Watering Place*, watercolor, private collection, Paris; Ananoff 1961–70, vol. 2 (1963), no. 832. See also Rosenberg 1988, cat. no. 93, ill. on p. 197.
5. Cuzin 1988b, pp. 78–82, nos. 110, 129, ill., pl. 100.
6. Rosenberg 1988, p. 197. He believes they could date as late as 1780.
7. Cuzin 1988b, p. 75.

CATS. 48 AND 49

1. Fragonard would have taken a coach to visit estates and forests; a day trip in contemporary terms would have taken several days in the eighteenth century. His continued friendship with Saint-Non and his brother implies the opportunity to visit their estate.
2. Authors have observed central creases as part of describing a drawing. For example, Rosenberg (1988, cat. no. 36, ill.) reports that a red chalk drawing, *Small Cascades at Tivoli*, is "folded down the middle." See cats. 55 and 56.
3. A sketchbook dating from Fragonard's first stay in Rome belongs to the Harvard Art Museums/Fogg Museum, Cambridge, Mass., Louise Haskell Daly Fund (1968.42). See Williams 1978, cat. no. 15. The second is later and belongs to the Rijksmuseum, Amsterdam (RP-T-1959-538).
4. Ananoff 1961–70, vol. 3 (1968), no. 1617, fig. 421.

CAT. 50

1. Roubo 1775, p. 1038.
2. Dézallier d'Argenville 1747, ch. 8, pp. 92–93: "Des portiques, berceaux, cabinets de treillage & de verdure."
3. See the designs by Gabriel Huquier for interior trompe l'oeil decors in Brugerolles 2003, cat. no. 69.
4. Wilhelm 1975; Cuzin 1987, pp. 137–38, no. 170; Rosenberg 1989, no. 216.
5. We are grateful to Monique Mosser for sharing her informed opinions.
6. Munhall 1971, pp. 406–7.
7. *The Lover Crowned*, 1771–72, oil on canvas, The Frick Collection, New York (1915.1.48); Cuzin 1987, no. 241; Rosenberg 1989, no. 275.

CAT. 51

1. Girouard 2000, pp. 265–79.
2. Eiche 2004, pp. 29, 49.
3. Morin 2008, pp. 379–83.
4. Georges Wildenstein first studied the family and their connections not only to Fragonard but other artists; see G. Wildenstein 1961.
5. Meynard-Villemagne 1995, and verbal communication December 2008.
6. *The Service Yard of a Château, with Poultry*, red chalk counterproof, Rijksmuseum, Amsterdam, Gift of Kunsthandel Bernard Houthakker, 1961 (RP-T-1961-53).

TRAVELS WITH BERGERET, 1773–74

1. Clues to their earliest acquaintance include the purported inscription with Bergeret's name on an early proof of a 1763 etching by Fragonard (see cats. 26–29, n. 2) and the fact that Fragonard's submissions to the Salons of 1765 and 1767 (the only two he exhibited in) included works listed as belonging to Bergeret. See L'Isle-Adam 2001, pp. 28, 31.
2. Raux 2007.
3. L'Isle-Adam 2001.
4. The journal was published in its entirety in 1895; see Tornézy 1895.
5. He had also inherited from his father the office of Receveur générale la Généralité de Montauban.
6. Théophile's letter, dated September 9, 1847, was reprinted in Rosenberg 1989, pp. 12–13. For the dispute more generally, see discussion in Stein 2007.

CAT. 52

1. Tornézy 1895, pp. 89–95.
2. The *Gülich-Bergische* describes the arrival of important figures and travelers, including "vier Franzosen N. Bergeres, Mausion, Lubersalle und Fragonard im 2brückerhof" (*Gülich-Bergische* 1773, p. 232). This inn was the best in Düsseldorf, according to Dr. Carmen Goetz (of the Institut für Geschichte der Medizin der Universität Düsseldorf), to whom we owe the discovery of this mention of Fragonard in Germany (email to the author, November 29, 2012).
3. Raux 2007, pp. 19–20.

4. Liste 1773, no. 35, September 2. We are grateful to Daniel Droixhe for drawing our attention to this reference in which people are referred to with their titles, thus allowing Fragonard's companions to be identified with greater certainty.
5. We are grateful to Dr. Annette Fimpeler-Philippen, Schifffahrtsmuseum, Düsseldorf, for the details she has given us about this subject (email to the author, September 14, 2015). For the cruises along the Rhine at the time and the types of boats taken by Fragonard, see, for example, Fimpeler-Philippen 1987 and Fimpeler-Philippen 2008, pp. 257–63.
6. The name of each of the figures seems to have been inscribed with a pen and in an ink identical to that employed in the drawing itself.
7. There is a preparatory sketch for this figure, sometimes erroneously titled *Hubert Robert Suffering from an Illness*, 1773, brown wash, last known location Albert Meyer sale, Paris, June 15, 1938, lot 9; Ananoff 1961–70, vol. 1 (1961), no. 233, fig. 92.
8. Tornézy 1895, p. 89 n. 1.

CAT. 53

1. Tornézy 1895, pp. 41–42.
2. Ananoff 1961–70, vol. 1 (1961), no. 382, pen and brown wash, shows the roof under repair. Last recorded in a sale at Hôtel Drouot, Paris, December 13, 1995, lot 25, Jean Louis Picard, expert. The other red chalk drawing is a majestic view of the château in Rotterdam (fig. 101); see Ananoff 1961–70, vol. 1 (1961), no. 381, fig. 132.

CAT. 54

1. Lorblanchet et al. 2008, pp. 102–9, cat. nos. 37–41.
2. Another drawing of the same dimensions and technique is in the Horvitz Collection, Beverly Farms, Massachusetts. Eunice Williams in 1995 identified the subject as the astronomer Joseph Jérôme Le Français de Lalande (sale, Christie's, London, July 4, 1995 [lot 134]). In 2006 Jean-Pierre Cuzin put forward the idea that it could represent François André Vincent, then a pensionnaire in Rome. If his hypothesis is correct, the Horvitz drawing would date to a few months later than the New York sheet. See Cuzin et al. 2006, p. 129, cat. no. 71.
3. See Roux 1949, p. 412, no. 251; no. 223 was advertised in May 1770 and no. 263 was exhibited at the Salon of 1771. Marie-Anne Dupuy-Vachey (email to the author, August 18, 2015) points out that although the 1788 catalogue of Demarteau's oeuvre describes the print as a portrait of Bergeret, the inscription on Demarteau's print informs us only that the drawing was owned by Bergeret at the time the print was made. The resemblance to known portraits of Bergeret (see, for example, the portrait by François André Vincent in Besançon in Cuzin 2013, p. 45, cat. no. 148P) is not strong.
4. See Blumenfeld 2013 and Dupuy-Vachey 2015.
5. Lorblanchet et al. 2008, pp. 102–7, cat. no. 38.

CATS. 55 AND 56

1. The vertical fold in Fragonard's large drawings is frequently cited without interpretation in description of media or dimensions. For example, Rosenberg (2006, pp. 56–75) records the vertical fold. Each of the two red chalk landscapes in Frankfurt (see cat. 5) also has a fold and a fine incised line in the center.

CAT. 57

1. See Stein 2009. The forgery (p. 68, fig. 61) was based not on the original drawing but on a lithograph made after that drawing. For a suggestion that Henri Dagneau (active in the nineteenth century) may have been the author of that print, see Dupuy-Vachey 2009, p. 52 n. 17.
2. Stein 2009, pp. 127–28.
3. See Jacquot et al. 2010, pp. 65–79.
4. Rosenberg 2006, pp. 154–56, cat. no. 85.
5. See Jean-Pierre Cuzin, "Vincent et Fragonard: Une émulation," in Cuzin 2013, pp. 76–79.

CAT. 58

1. Correspondence with Eunice Williams, June 4, 2015.
2. See, for example, cats. 54, 57, 59, and 60–63; Rosenberg 2006, pp. 150–54, cat. nos. 83, 84; Rosenberg 1988, pp. 375–79, cat. nos. 174–77.

CAT. 59

1. Rosenberg 1988, p. 438, cat. no. 208. Rosenberg also proposed that the two sheets represent the same sitter.
2. Cuzin et al. 2006, p. 129, cat. no. 71.
3. Several red chalk figure drawings share this uncertainty as to the date and place they were made. In addition to two more loosely executed drawings of anonymous sitters (Musée Atger, Montpellier [MA75 and MA77]), there are two horizontal sheets: one of a young boy with a cat (Musée du Louvre, Paris [RF 40959]) and one of an artist drawing with a female servant (Fine Arts Museums of San Francisco [1975.2.13]), the latter example featuring a tabletop globe seemingly identical to the one in the Horvitz drawing (fig. 104). For the two Montpellier sheets, see Lorblanchet et al. 2008, pp. 108–9, cat. nos. 40, 41; for the Paris and San Francisco sheets, see Rosenberg 1988, p. 449, cat. no. 209 and fig. 1.
4. A counterproof of the drawing, trimmed along the top margin, is in the Ecole Nationale Supérieure des Beaux-Arts, Paris (EBA 911).

CAT. 60

1. Williams 1978, p. 94. See also Rosenberg 1988, p. 396.
2. Williams 1978, p. 94.
3. As suggested in Rosenberg 1988, p. 396, under cat. no. 191. Eunice Williams (1978, p. 94) posited that she may have been a street vendor.
4. Cuzin 2013, p. 49.
5. Ibid., pp. 76–79, and Rosenberg 2006, pp. 150–54, cat. nos. 83, 83bis, 84, 84bis.
6. *A Woman from Santa Lucia*, 1774, brush and brown wash over black chalk, Städel Museum, Frankfurt (1104). Rosenberg 1988, pp. 396–97, cat. no. 191.
7. François André Vincent, *Femme napolitaine*, 1774, brush and brown wash over black chalk, location unknown; François André Vincent(?), *Femme napolitaine*, 1774(?), brush and brown wash, location unknown; and François André Vincent, *La jeune napolitaine*, 1774, oil on canvas, M. and Mme Alain Moatti collection. See Cuzin 2013, pp. 383–84, cat. nos. 179D, 180D, 181P. He also speculates, on p. 78, whether the Thaw drawing might be by Vincent after a lost drawing by Fragonard, pointing to the atypical manner of hatching in the background. His qualms must have been minor, though, for in the caption to the illustration (fig. 18) he still gives the author as Fragonard. It is also on p. 78 that he uses the adjective "fragonardesque" in reference to Vincent's wash drawings.

CATS. 61 AND 62

1. See, for example, Lorblanchet et al. 2008, pp. 102–7, cat. nos. 37–39.
2. Stein 2007, pp. 306–7.
3. For specific parallels, see Wallace 1979, pp. 204, 210, nos. 67, 73.

CAT. 64

1. Tornézy 1895, p. 409.
2. Ibid., pp. 409–10.
3. A horizontal drawing in brown wash in the estate sale of Pierre François Basan (Lugt 5827), Paris, December 1, 1798, lot 93, is described as

Diogenes "entouré du peuple" (surrounded by people) (Ananoff 1961–70, vol. 1 [1961], p. 188, no. 468); another (or the same?) drawing was sold in the M. [François Georges Maréchal, marquis de Bièvre (1747–1789)] sale, Hôtel de Bullion, Paris, March 10 and following days, 1790 (as part of lot 31, "Deux autres [dessins], dont un sujet de Diogène") (Ananoff 1961–70, vol. 4 [1970], p. 171, no. 2488). The term *sujet* (subject) seems unlikely to refer to a bust-length image of a single figure.
4. The visual similarities were first noted in the catalogue of the anonymous sale, Palais Galliera, Paris, December 3, 1966, lot 6.
5. The copy of the sale catalogue held at the Frick Art Reference Library is inscribed "Chabot Duc de La Mure ou Desmarets."

LATE CAREER AND SHIFTING ROLES

1. Williams 2015.
2. Rosenberg 1996.
3. See "Travels with Bergeret, 1773–74" in this volume, pp. 172–73.
4. Rosenberg 1988, p. 581.

CAT. 65

1. *Two Coaches under Tall Trees*, ca. 1773–74, red chalk, Museum Boijmans Van Beuningen, Rotterdam (I-I-155); Ananoff 1961–70, vol. 1 (1961), no. 334.
2. *Cypresses at the Villa d'Este*, ca. 1760, red chalk, Musée des Beaux-Arts et d'Archéologie, Besançon (D.2841); Rosenberg 2006, cat. no. 22, ill.

CAT. 66

1. Goncourt 1981, p. 299.
2. Tornézy 1895, pp. 155, 357.

CAT. 67

1. "[A]près le diné j'ai été passer une heure chez le fameux Piranèze, dessinateur et graveur, qui a un cabinet curieux de toutes sortes d'antiquités en marbre, vases, figures, tombeaux, et des matières précieuses. Il en cède pour le plus d'argent qu'il peut. C'est un homme qui a fait des ouvrages immenses et curieux en gravure," in Tornézy 1895, p. 194.
2. Ibid., p. 195.
3. For an overview of the subject, see Rome 1976.
4. *Entrance to the Villa Adriana*, after 1774, bister wash over black chalk, private collection; Ananoff 1961–70, vol. 3 (1968), no. 1445, fig. 394.

CAT. 68

1. Rosenberg 1988, pp. 355–58, cat. nos. 168, 169.
2. Rand 1995, p. 200.
3. Ibid., p. 197.
4. Ibid., p. 245.
5. Lajer-Burcharth 2003, pp. 40–41.
6. Rand 2001, p. 506.
7. Jean Benjamin Delaborde collection sale, Bizet, Paris, June 14, 1784, lot 10.
8. Rand 2001, pp. 505–6.
9. Ibid., p. 496, although it seems unlikely the commission would have postdated the artist's quarrel in 1773 with Mlle Guimard, for which see Rosenberg 1988, pp. 297–98, 301–2.
10. Quoted in Rosenberg 1988, p. 358, under cat. no. 169.
11. Sale, Chariot, Paris, April 22, 1776, lot 158. The seller is sometimes described as Bache, but for other possibilities, see the Getty Provenance Index® Databases, sale catalogue F-A418.
12. Jean Antoine Hubert, Vassal de Saint-Hubert, collection sale, Paris, March 29–April 13, 1779, lot 209. In this sale, it was described as "d'après un tableau de Fragonard."
13. Williams 1978, pp. 130–31, cat. no. 51.
14. Perhaps the sculpted hedges even recall the repeating arches of the stables of Maecenas. This last point was made by Eunice Williams, email to the author, July 29, 2015.

CATS. 69–71

1. A selection, representative but not exhaustive, is discussed and illustrated in Rosenberg 1988, pp. 432–36, cat. nos. 203–7, figs. 1–8.
2. Paris 2009, p. 18.
3. For recent studies on the subject, see Grasselli et al. 2003 and Delapierre et al. 2006.
4. "Ce sont de vrais dessins au crayon. La belle, l'utile invention que cette manière de graver!" English translation by John Goodman in Diderot 1995, p. 319.
5. Kristel Smentek, "'An Exact Imitation Acquired at Little Expense': Marketing Color Prints in Eighteenth-Century France," in Grasselli et al. 2003, pp. 9–21.
6. Roux 1949, p. 436, no. 351.
7. Hérold 1935, p. 128, no. 201, illustrated in Rosenberg 1988, p. 433, fig. 2.
8. Eunice Williams (1978, pp. 90–91, cat. no. 31) has also drawn a contrast in terms of its somewhat more careful technique relative to the rest of the group.
9. Why the woman is referred to as Italian is unclear.
10. Rosenberg 1988, pp. 432–35, cat. nos. 203–5.
11. Ibid., p. 435, cat. no. 205.
12. See, for example, Rijdt 2003, pp. 230–33, cat. no. 78.
13. Goncourt 1981, p. 302.
14. On the identity of the seller, see http://www.marquesdecollections.fr/detail.cfm/marque/6524/total/1 and the Getty Provenance Index® Databases, sale catalogue F-A377.
15. The drawing, however, does not appear in the sale of Lasquin's eighteenth-century drawings held at Galerie Georges Petit, Paris, June 7–8, 1928.

CAT. 72

1. *The Letter*, ca. 1775–80, brown wash over black chalk sketch, Art Institute of Chicago (1945.32); Ananoff 1961–70, vol. 1 (1961), no. 74, fig. 32.
2. *The Confidence*, ca. 1775–80, brown wash over black chalk sketch, Museum Boijmans Van Beuningen, Rotterdam (F-I-228).
3. These accessories are also found on the wrists of the portrait of a lady, Jeanne Vignier, drawn by Fragonard in Rome in 1774 (Musée des Beaux-Arts et d'Archéologie, Besançon [2013.2.1]).
4. *The Reading*, ca. 1775–80, brown wash over black chalk sketch, Musée du Louvre, Paris (26651).

CAT. 73

1. Ananoff 1961–70, vol. 1 (1961), no. 39, fig. 17, vol. 2 (1963), p. 294; Reuter et al. 2013, cat. no. 40 (entry by Marie-Anne Dupuy-Vachey).

CAT. 74

1. A very similar sketch, featuring the same composition, is in the Villa Musée Jean-Honoré Fragonard, Grasse (2012.0.2673); black chalk, 9½ × 7¼ in. (23.9 × 18.2 cm). It is illustrated in Ananoff 1961–70, vol. 2 (1963), no. 801, fig. 221.

CAT. 75

1. *The Beggar's Dream*, ca. 1769, wash over black chalk underdrawing, sale, Artcurial, Paris, December 13, 2005, lot 24; Rosenberg 1988, cat. no. 123.
2. *Making Fritters*, ca. 1780, wash over black chalk sketch, J. Paul Getty Museum, Los Angeles (2012.4).

3. *Reading on the Farm*, ca. 1775–80, wash over black chalk underdrawing, location unknown; Ananoff 1961–70, vol. 2 (1963), no. 640, vol. 3 (1968), p. 324, fig. 518, vol. 4 (1970), p. 373; and *The Family Reading Together*, ca. 1775–80, wash over black chalk underdrawing, location unknown; Williams 1978, cat. no. 59.
4. *Reading to the Children*, ca. 1775–80, black chalk, wash, sale, Sotheby's, New York, January 28, 2015, lot 110, location unknown; Ananoff 1961–70, vol. 1 (1961), no. 45, fig. 22.
5. *The Fritters*, ca. 1780, wash, private collection; Ananoff 1961–70, vol. 1 (1961), no. 52, fig. 26, vol. 4 (1970), p. 346; Rosenberg 1988, p. 540, fig. 2.

CAT. 76

1. Sale, Villa Grisebach, Berlin, November 28, 2013, lot 313. Ananoff did not know this drawing but catalogued three other treatments of the subject; see Ananoff 1961–70, vol. 1 (1961), pp. 128–29, nos. 274, 277, and vol. 4 (1970), pp. 81–82, no. 2118.
2. Portalis 1889, vol. 2, p. 295. The title given the Berlin version when it was sold in 1867 (estate sale of the duc de Feltre, Hôtel des Commissaires Priseurs, Paris, May 6–9, 1867, lot 90) was *Jeunes dames se promenant à cheval à l'entrée d'un village*.
3. This discussion of Greuze's *Lady of Charity* and the cult of benevolence is drawn from "Social Hierarchy in Sentimental Painting: *Le trait de bienfaisance*," in Barker 2005, pp. 177–204.
4. Ibid., p. 196.

CAT. 77

1. Rosenberg 1988, pp. 338–43, cat. no. 161.
2. For an analysis of these subjects in which people, either aristocratic or of mixed classes, enjoyed entertainments and games in parks, and a discussion of their social context, see Milam 2006, pp. 139–73.
3. Reuter et al. 2013, p. 235.
4. Williams 1978, p. 106.
5. See ibid., pp. 106–7, cat. no. 39, and Rosenberg 1988, pp. 534–35, cat. no. 274.
6. I would like to thank Marjorie Shelley, head of Paper Conservation at The Metropolitan Museum of Art, for examining and discussing the drawing with me.
7. "Né avec un goût naturel pour le paysage, il fit en ce genre une infinité d'études et de dessins d'une variété et d'un effet admirables. On connaît de lui de simples ébauches, que l'on serait tenté de prendre pour de beaux rêves, quand, avec des couleurs vagues et indécises, il trouve le moyen de presenter à l'imagination bien plus qu'il n'a eu intention de faire." Lecarpentier's eulogy, given on October 16, 1806, was initially published as a four-page pamphlet (according to Schroder 2001, p. 57 n. 103); it was later reprinted in Lecarpentier 1821, pp. 280–81.
8. Haverkamp-Begemann 1999, p. 339 n. 2 (entry by Mary Tavener Holmes).

CAT. 78

1. See, for example, Rizzi 1971, pp. 274–75, cat. no. 124.
2. The page of the Mariette catalogue is illustrated in Rosenberg 1988, p. 419, fig. 1. See also Rosenberg ca. 2001.

CAT. 79

1. Joseph Siffred Duplessis, *Portrait of Christoph Willibald Gluck*, 1775, oil on canvas, Kunsthistorisches Museum, Vienna (GG 1795).
2. Houdon's plaster bust for the 1775 Salon is lost; the marble version made for the Opéra was destroyed by fire in 1873 but is known from reproductions. For the various versions of Houdon's bust of Gluck, see Poulet et al. 2004, cat. no. 10 (entry by Ulrike D. Mathies).
3. For information on this subscription, see Prod'homme 1928. We have found the document cited by Prod'homme at the Archives Nationales, Paris (MC/ET/III/1079).
4. "A superb Drawing washed in bister on white paper. It shows Painting dedicating its pencils to Homer, Virgil and Maecenas. Ingenious allegory presented under the figure of a Painter drawing on a classical table in front of the busts of these great Men."
5. *The Inspiration of the Artist*, ca. 1760–63, pen and brown ink, brush and brown wash over black chalk underdrawing, Museum Boijmans Van Beuningen, Rotterdam (F.I.182); Ananoff 1961–70, vol. 2 (1963), no. 987, vol. 4 (1970), p. 386, fig. 720. *The Inspiration of the Poet*, ca. 1761–63, pen and brown ink, brush and brown wash over black chalk underdrawing, private collection; Ananoff 1961–70, vol. 1 (1961), no. 454, fig. 155, vol. 3 (1968), p. 303. The latter drawing recently appeared at auction; sale, Sotheby's, London, July 5–6, 2016 (lot 231).
6. *The Inspiration of the Poet*, ca. 1770–76, brown wash over black chalk underdrawing, location unknown; Ananoff 1961–70, vol. 1 (1961), no. 456. *Ariosto Inspired by Love and Folly*, ca. 1775–80, brown wash over black chalk underdrawing, Musée des Beaux-Arts et d'Archéologie, Besançon (D.2862); Rosenberg 2006, cat. no. 93.

ETCHINGS WITH MARGUERITE GÉRARD, 1778

1. For a discussion of these four prints in relation to the prints of Marguerite Gérard, with which they have been confused in the past, see Hoisington and Stein 2012.
2. See Rena M. Hoisington, "Learning to Etch," in Stein et al. 2013, pp. 37–39.

CAT. 80

1. Carlson and Ittmann 1984, pp. 230–31, cat. no. 77. In an insightful mistake, Louis Guimbaud had believed in 1928 that *Les Traitants* was "probably by" Tiepolo. See G. Wildenstein 1956, p. 34.

CAT. 81

1. Portalis 1880, p. 313.
2. Brooklyn 1967, p. 378.
3. Robertson 1978, pp. 723–24, no. 2. The present author and Rena M. Hoisington, in cataloguing the prints of Gérard in 2012, concurred with this dating; see Hoisington and Stein 2012.
4. Williams 1978, p. 116.
5. Grasselli 2009, pp. 202–5, cat. nos. 89, 90.
6. Williams 1978, p. 116.
7. These were long, and incorrectly, considered to be collaborations between the two artists. See Hoisington and Stein 2012.
8. For a discussion of the states, see ibid., pp. 151–52.
9. Kozak and Monkiewicz 1993, pp. 48–49, cat. no. 26 (entry by Justyna Guze).
10. Rosenberg 1988, p. 493, fig. 4.

CAT. 82

1. A related drawing in brown wash, last recorded in the collection of Mme Seymour de Ricci, Paris, and in reverse direction to the etching, was published in Ananoff 1961–70, vol. 2 (1963), p. 88, no. 795, vol. 4 (1970), p. 378, fig. 704.
2. See "Originals, Copies, Mirrors, and Multiples" in this volume, pp. 47–69.
3. G. Wildenstein 1956, pp. 35–37. The Gérard version is inscribed "fragonard" along the lower center margin, but this must have been done either in a gesture of playfulness or in emulation of the conventions of reproductive printmakers, who inscribed their plates with the name of the artist whose work they reproduced.
4. Hoisington and Stein 2012.

CAT. 83

1. For the copy, see Rosenberg 1988, p. 494, fig. 1.
2. Wildenstein catalogued this print in his section on collaborations between Fragonard and Gérard. He illustrated only the version that we consider to be by Gérard and described Fragonard's version as a "second plate."

CAT. 84

1. Rosenberg 1988, pp. 486–87, cat. no. 238. It was published more recently, and illustrated in color, in Reuter et al. 2013, pp. 110–13, cat. no. 36. For the smaller version, see Ananoff 1961–70, vol. 4 (1970), pp. 35–36, no. 1987, fig. 542.
2. "[Q]u'il a gravée lui-même à la pointe, y a bien mis le cachet de son génie." The full text, along with an English translation, can be found in Hoisington and Stein 2012, pp. 158–59.
3. Rosenberg 1988, p. 487.

CATS. 85 AND 86

1. For the bibliography, see most recently José-Luis de Los Llanos in Paris 1992, pp. 191–275, and Los Llanos 1994. Schroder 2011 should also be consulted, even though I do not agree with all the opinions and attributions.
2. On this subject, see Norman 1978a and 1978b.
3. Since this series contains fifty-seven sheets, it should be noted that fifteen drawings from the first series have not survived.
4. Williams 1978, pp. 46, 58, 134, 178.
5. This is *Féronde, or Purgatory*; see, for example, Dupuy-Vachey 2007, pp. 54–55.
6. Faroult 2015, cat. no. 24 (entry by Marie-Anne Dupuy-Vachey).
7. "[A]utrefois . . . à Rome, dans toute la chaleur de la jeunesse," *Mercure de France*, September 6, 1796, no. 44, p. 83.
8. Wolf 1949, pp. 9–16.
9. For records of payments and the titles of the compositions redrawn by Monnet, see Archives INHA, Paris, carton 35.
10. We have noted for this decade about a dozen sales in which drawings illustrating *Les contes* of La Fontaine appear. The title of the story illustrated is rarely specified; when the technique is, it is always described as a drawing "in bister."
11. Paris 1992, cat. no. 140. The initial version, in black chalk only, is not known.
12. Fondation Custodia, Paris, reproduced in Rosenberg 1988, p. 592, fig. 9.
13. Paris 1992, cat. no. 130.
14. Jean-Baptiste Tilliard, *The Husband-Confessor*, 1795, etching and engraving, The Metropolitan Museum of Art, New York (33.104.17).
15. The sword does appear in a version in chalk alone, in the same direction as the engraving (ca. 1790[?], Bibliothèque Royale, Brussels, Réserve précieuse, F.S. XI 12, vol. I), which Anne Schroder (2011, pp. 157–58, fig. 8) thought to be the version redrawn by Augustin de Saint-Aubin in view of the print.

CATS. 87–89

1. For a study of the various versions of the story and its illustrations, see Boufflers 1995.
2. The second drawing of the series, *Saint Phar Grasping Aline, Who Has Fallen to the Ground* (private collection; Faroult 2015, cat. no. 28), was attributed by Ananoff (1961–70, vol. 4 [1970], no. 2029) to Alexandre Evariste, Fragonard's son, with the title *Young Man in Pursuit of a Girl*. The fourth drawing of the series, *Aline and Saint Phar Leaving the Opera*, was for a time attributed to Jean Michel Moreau the Younger with the title *The Departure by Coach*; ibid., no. 29, see note 5 below.
3. Sale, Christie's, New York, January 30, 1998, lot 259.
4. Dupuy-Vachey 2007, cat. no. 37.
5. *The Departure by Coach*, 1780–89, black chalk, brown wash, Art Institute of Chicago (1960.825).
6. Dupuy-Vachey 2007, pp. 84–89.
7. I am grateful to Catherine Join-Dieterle for sharing her considerable knowledge about this.
8. Email to the author, September 10, 2015. I am grateful to Perrin Stein for drawing our attention to this issue, as well as to Daniel Alcouffe and Danielle Kisluk-Grosheide.
9. For comparison, see the chairs depicted in the drawing by Moreau the Younger showing the inauguration of Madame du Barry's pavilion at Louveciennes in September 1771 (*Fête donnée à Louveciennes, le 2 septembre*, 1771, pen and ink, brush and gray wash, watercolor, touches of white chalk, Musée du Louvre, Paris [31360]).

CAT. 90

1. The figure of the pasha seems to have been the subject of a painted study that appeared at auction (Leroy de Senneville, Paris, April 5–11, 1780, lot 218, "Une charmante Etude, & de l'effet le plus piquant par la magie de la couleur: elle représente un Sultan assis sur un sopha. H. 5 po. 9 lig. L. 4 po. 3 lig. [16 × 11 cm]") and at the sale of July 8, 1793, lot 18 ("Deux petites Etudes touchées avec intelligence; l'une offre la figure d'un Sultan assis sur des coussins . . . Haut. 6 p. larg. 4.T"). The drawing of the sale of April 22, 1829, lot 94 ("Des jeunes femmes esclaves, présentées à un vieux pacha. Dessin capital exécuté avec beaucoup de talent") corresponds in its description to ours, but given its characterization as "major," it is probably a more finished version, possibly repeating the painting rather than preparing it. It differs from the drawing in the Walferdin sale (Paris, April 12–16, 1880, lot 222 [21 × 30 cm]), known from a mediocre reproduction (Ananoff 1961–70, vol. 1 [1961], no. 50, fig. 24, vol. 4 [1970], p. 346). Another version, smaller in size, in red chalk and wash, seems to have existed (M[athey] sale, Paris, May 15, 1897, lot 66).
2. Cuzin 1987, no. 362; Rosenberg 1989, no. 329.
3. Cuzin 1987, nos. 266–68, 325; Rosenberg 1989, nos. 330–33.
4. Cuzin 1987, no. 106; Rosenberg 1989, no. 124.
5. For the reasons we lean toward the Favart version, see Dupuy-Vachey 2007, pp. 90, 170, cat. no. 40, n. 4.

ARIOSTO'S *ORLANDO FURIOSO*

1. In 2003, Marie-Anne Dupuy-Vachey catalogued 176 *Orlando Furioso* drawings, including the 137 first published by Elizabeth Mongan, Philip Hofer, and Jean Seznec (Dupuy-Vachey 2003; Mongan et al. 1945). Several other drawings have recently surfaced, indicating that other illustrations belonging to the series have yet to be identified. See, for example, Dupuy-Vachey 2007, pp. 122, 136, cat. no. 70.
2. Ariosto 2008.
3. Marie-Anne Dupuy-Vachey, "Le Roland Furieux au siècle des lumières: L'Arioste à la folie?," in Paoli and Preti 2012, pp. 237–51.
4. Fragonard may have seen Tiepolo's frescoes when he passed through the city in the summer of 1761 (Rosenberg 1988, p. 69). However, Dupuy-Vachey (2003, p. 15) has argued that this is unlikely, because Saint-Non did not mention the Villa Valmarana in his journal. See also Broude 2009.
5. Linsky Collection 1984, pp. 121–25, no. 47.
6. Griffiths 2004, pp. 121–23, 177.
7. Williams 1978, p. 159.
8. Quoted in Rosenberg 1988, p. 508.
9. On Fragonard's illustrations for La Fontaine's *Contes*, see Schroder 2011 and Paris 1992, pp. 191–200.
10. Dupuy-Vachey 2003, p. 23. She notes (pp. 24–25) that at the Salon of 1787, Jean Philippe Guy Le Gentil, comte de Paroy, exhibited at least two engravings after Fragonard's Ariosto drawings. The location of these

Brooks et al. 2012
Brooks, Julian, et al. *Drawn to Excellence: Renaissance to Romantic Drawings from a Private Collection*. Exh. cat. Northampton, Mass.: Smith College Museum of Art, 2012.

Broude 2009
Broude, Norma. "G. B. Tiepolo at Valmarana: Gender Ideology in a Patrician Villa of the Settecento." *Art Bulletin* 91 (June 2009), pp. 160–83.

Brugerolles 2003
Brugerolles, Emmanuelle. *François Boucher et l'art rocaille dans les collections de l'Ecole des Beaux-Arts*. Exh. cat. Paris: Ecole Nationale Supérieure des Beaux-Arts, 2003.

Brugerolles et al. 2013
Brugerolles, Emmanuelle, et al. *De Poussin à Fragonard: Hommage à Mathias Polakovits*. Exh. cat. Paris: Ecole Nationale Supérieure des Beaux-Arts, 2013.

Brunel 2007
Brunel, Georges, ed. *Pagodes et dragons: Exotisme et fantaisie dans l'Europe rococo, 1720–1770*. Exh. cat. Paris, Musée Cernuschi. Paris: Paris-Musées, 2007.

Burke 1757
Burke, Edmund. *A Philosophical Inquiry into the Origin of Our Ideas of the Sublime and Beautiful*. London, 1757.

Cailleux et al. 1978
Cailleux, Jean, Annette Rambaud, and Marianne Roland Michel. *Sanguines: Dessins français du dix-huitième siècle*. Exh. cat. Paris: Galerie Cailleux, 1978.

Carlson 1978
Carlson, Victor I. *Hubert Robert: Drawings & Watercolors*. Exh. cat. Washington, D.C.: National Gallery of Art, 1978.

Carlson and Ittmann 1984
Carlson, Victor I., and John W. Ittmann, eds. *Regency to Empire: French Printmaking, 1715–1814*. Exh. cat. Baltimore Museum of Art; Minneapolis Institute of Arts. Minneapolis: Minneapolis Institute of Arts, 1984.

Catala 2014
Catala, Sarah. "Hubert Robert et l'usage de la contre-épreuve: De la création à la reproduction." In *Espaces dessinés / Espaces du dessin*, edited by Alexandre Holin and Nathalie Poisson-Cogez, pp. 71–83. Villeneuve-d'Asq: Presses Universitaires du Septentrion, 2014.

Catala 2015
Catala, Sarah. "Les usages de la contre-épreuve dans le dessin français au XVIIIe siècle." *Cahiers d'Histoire de l'Art*, no. 13 (2015), pp. 35–43.

Caviglia-Brunel 2012
Caviglia-Brunel, Susanna. *Charles-Joseph Natoire, 1700–1777*. Paris: Arthena, 2012.

Cayeux 1963
Cayeux, Jean de. "Introduction au catalogue critique des 'Griffonis' de Saint-Non." *Bulletin de la Société de l'Histoire de l'Art Français* (1963), pp. 297–384.

Cayeux 1985
Cayeux, Jean de. *Les Hubert Robert de la collection Veyrenc au Musée de Valence*. Valence: Musée de Valence, 1985.

Caylus 1877
Caylus, Anne Claude Philippe, comte de. *Correspondance inédite du comte de Caylus avec le P. Paciaudi, Théatin (1757–1765)*. Vol. 1. Edited by Charles Nisard. Paris: L'Imprimerie Nationale, 1877.

Caylus 1910
Caylus, Anne Claude Philippe, comte de. *Vies d'artistes du XVIIIe siècle: Discours sur la peinture et la sculpture*. Edited by André Fontaine. Paris: H. Laurens, 1910.

Chanson 1998
Chanson, Hubert. "Le développement historique des cascades et fontaines en gradins." *La Houille Blanche: Revue Internationale de l'Eau* 7 (1998), pp. 76–84.

Chiarini 2000
Chiarini, Marco. *Livio Mehus: Un pittore barocco alla corte dei Medici, 1627–1691*. Exh. cat. Florence, Galleria Pallatina. Livorno: Sillabe, 2000.

Christiansen 1997
Christiansen, Keith, ed. *Giambattista Tiepolo, 1696–1770*. Exh. cat. New York: Metropolitan Museum of Art, 1997.

Christiansen 1998
Christiansen, Keith. *The Ca'Dolfin Tiepolos*. New York: Metropolitan Museum of Art, 1998.

Chu 1985
Chu, Petra ten-Doesschate. *French Masters of the Nineteenth Century: Dominique Vivant Denon*. The Illustrated Bartsch, vol. 121. New York: Abaris Books, 1985.

Cochin ca. 1774
Cochin, Charles Nicolas. *Lettres à un jeune artiste peintre, pensionnaire à l'Académie Royale de France à Rome*. Paris, ca. 1774.

Cochin 1991
Cochin, Charles Nicolas. *Le Voyage d'Italie de Charles-Nicolas Cochin, 1758*. Edited by Christian Michel. Rome: Ecole Française de Rome, 1991.

Cohn 1987
Cohn, Marjorie B. "Red Chalk: Historical and Technical Perspectives, Part 1: Aspects of Historical Usage." In *Drawings Defined*, edited by Walter Strauss and Tracie Felker, pp. 165–70. New York: Abaris Books, 1987.

Conisbee 1988
Conisbee, Philip. "New York: Fragonard at the Metropolitan." *Burlington Magazine* 130 (April 1988), pp. 319–21.

Conisbee 2009
Conisbee, Philip. *French Paintings of the Fifteenth through the Eighteenth Century*. Washington, D.C., and Princeton: National Gallery of Art and Princeton University Press, 2009.

Copenhagen 1935
Exposition de l'art français au XVIIIe siècle. Copenhagen, Palais de Charlottenburg. Paris: Frazier-Soye, 1935.

Costamagna 2007
Costamagna, Philippe, ed. *Le cardinal Fesch et l'art de son temps*. Exh. cat. Ajaccio, Musée Fesch. Paris: Gallimard, 2007.

Couturier 2004
Couturier, Sonia. *French Drawings from the National Gallery of Canada*. Exh. cat. Ottawa: National Gallery of Canada, 2004.

Couturier 2011a
Couturier, Sonia, ed. *Drawn to Art: French Artists and Art Lovers in 18th-Century Rome*. Exh. cat. Ottawa, National Gallery of Canada; Caen, Musée des Beaux-Arts. Milan: Silviana Editoriale, 2011.

Couturier 2011b
Couturier, Sonia, ed. *Pour l'amour de l'art: Artistes et amateurs français à Rome au XVIIIe siècle*. Exh. cat. Ottawa, National Gallery of Canada; Caen, Musée des Beaux-Arts. Milan: Silviana Editoriale, 2011.

Cuzin 1986
Cuzin, Jean-Pierre. "Fragonard dans les musées français: Quelques tableaux reconsidérés ou discutés." *Revue du Louvre* 36, no. 1 (1986), pp. 58–66.

Cuzin 1987
Cuzin, Jean-Pierre. *Jean-Honoré Fragonard, vie et oeuvre: Catalogue complet des peintures.* Paris: Editions Vilo, 1987.

Cuzin 1988a
Cuzin, Jean-Pierre. "Fragonard, un nouvel examen." *Revue de l'Art* 80 (1988), pp. 83–87.

Cuzin 1988b
Cuzin, Jean-Pierre. *Jean-Honoré Fragonard, Life and Work: Complete Catalogue of the Oil Paintings.* New York: Abrams, 1988.

Cuzin 2003
Cuzin, Jean-Pierre. *Fragonard.* Exh. cat. Paris, Musée du Louvre. Milan: 5 Continents, 2003.

Cuzin 2013
Cuzin, Jean-Pierre. *François-André Vincent, 1746–1816: Entre Fragonard et David.* Exh. cat. Tours, Musée des Beaux-Arts; Montpellier, Musée Fabre. Paris: Arthena, 2013.

Cuzin et al. 2006
Cuzin, Jean-Pierre, Katharina Schmidt, and Sophie Raux. *Jean-Honoré Fragonard (1732–1806): Orígenes e influencias de Rembrandt al siglo XXI.* Exh. cat. Barcelona: Caixa Forum, 2006.

Daniels 1976
Daniels, Jeffery. *Sebastiano Ricci.* Hove: Wayland, 1976.

Daulte 1954
Daulte, François. *Fragonard.* Exh. cat. Bern: Kunstmuseum, 1954.

De Conciliis and Lattuada 1979
De Conciliis, Domenico, and Riccardo Lattuada. "Unpublished Documents for Mattia Preti's Paintings in San Pietro a Maiella in Naples." *Burlington Magazine* 121 (May 1979), pp. 294–301, 303.

Delapierre et al. 2006
Delapierre, Emmanuelle, et al. *Quand la gravure fait illusion: Autour de Watteau et Boucher, le dessin gravé au XVIIIe siècle.* Exh. cat. Valenciennes, Musée des Beaux Arts. Montreuil: Gourcuff-Gradenigo, 2006.

Denison 1993
Denison, Cara D. *French Master Drawings from the Pierpont Morgan Library.* Exh. cat. Paris, Musée du Louvre. New York: Pierpont Morgan Library, 1993.

Denison et al. 1985
Denison, Cara D., et al. *Drawings from the Collection of Mr. & Mrs. Eugene V. Thaw.* Vol. 2. Exh. cat. New York: Pierpont Morgan Library, 1985.

Denison et al. 1994
Denison, Cara D., et al. *The Thaw Collection: Master Drawings and New Acquisitions.* Exh. cat. New York: Pierpont Morgan Library, 1994.

Denison et al. 1995
Denison, Cara D., et al. *Fantasy and Reality: Drawings from the Sunny Crawford von Bülow Collection.* Exh. cat. New York: Pierpont Morgan Library, 1995.

Denison et al. 1996
Denison, Cara D., et al. *From Mantegna to Picasso: Drawings from the Thaw Collection at the Pierpont Morgan Library, New York.* Exh. cat. London, Royal Academy of Arts. New York: Pierpont Morgan Library, 1996.

Dézallier d'Argenville 1747
Dézallier d'Argenville, Antoine Joseph. *La théorie et la pratique du jardinage.* Paris, 1747.

Dézallier d'Argenville 1762
Dézallier d'Argenville, Antoine Joseph. *Abrégé de la vie des plus fameux peintres.* 4 vols. Paris: De Bure, 1762.

Diderot 1995
Diderot, Denis. *Diderot on Art*, vol. 2, *The Salon of 1767.* Translated and edited by John Goodman with an introduction by Thomas Crow. New Haven: Yale University Press, 1995.

Diderot 2011
Diderot, Denis. *On Art and Artists: An Anthology of Diderot's Aesthetic Thought.* Edited by Jean Seznec. New York: Springer, 2011.

Diderot and d'Alembert 1754–72
Diderot, Denis, and Jean Le Rond d'Alembert. *Encyclopédie, ou, Dictionnaire raisonné des sciences, des arts et des métiers.* Paris: Chez Briasson, 1754–72.

Duffy and Hedley 2004
Duffy, Stephen, and Jo Hedley. *The Wallace Collection's Pictures.* London: Unicorn Press and Lindsay Fine Art, 2004.

Dupuy-Vachey 2003
Dupuy-Vachey, Marie-Anne. *Fragonard et le Roland furieux.* Paris: Editions de l'Amateur, 2003.

Dupuy-Vachey 2007
Dupuy-Vachey, Marie-Anne. *Fragonard: Les plaisirs d'un siècle.* Exh. cat. Paris, Musée Jacquemart-André. Gand: Snoeck, 2007.

Dupuy-Vachey 2009
Dupuy-Vachey, Marie-Anne. "Un nouveau tableau de Fragonard identifié au musée d'Amiens." *Revue des Musées de France: Revue du Louvre* 5 (December 2009), pp. 46–53.

Dupuy-Vachey 2012
Dupuy-Vachey, Marie-Anne. "Fragonard and the Fantasy Figure: Painting the Imagination." *Tribune de l'Art*, July 19, 2012, at http://www.latribunedelart.com/fragonard-and-the-fantasy-figure-painting-the-imagination-article003885.html.

Dupuy-Vachey 2015
Dupuy-Vachey, Marie-Anne. "Fragonard's 'Fantasy Figures': Prelude to a New Understanding." *Burlington Magazine* 157 (April 2015), pp. 241–47.

Eiche 2004
Eiche, Sabine. *Presenting the Turkey: The Fabulous Story of a Flamboyant and Flavourful Bird.* Florence: Centro Di, 2004.

Eitel-Porter et al. 2006
Eitel-Porter, Rhoda, et al. *From Leonardo to Pollock: Master Drawings from the Morgan Library.* Exh. cat. New York: Pierpont Morgan Library, 2006.

Eouzan 2013
Eouzan, Fanny. "Le fou et la magicienne: Réécritures de l'Arioste à l'opéra (1625–1796)." PhD diss., Aix-Marseille Université, 2013.

Faroult 2015
Faroult, Guillaume, ed. *Fragonard amoureux, galant et libertin.* Exh. cat. Paris, Musée du Luxembourg (Sénat). Paris: Réunion des Musées Nationaux, 2015.

Faroult 2016
Faroult, Guillaume, ed. *Hubert Robert, 1733–1808: Un peintre visionnaire.* Exh. cat. Paris, Musée du Louvre. Paris: Somogy, 2016.

Fimpeler-Philippen 1987
Fimpeler-Philippen, Annette. *Fürstliches Reisen auf dem Rhein*. Exh. cat. Düsseldorf: Stadtmuseum Düsseldorf, 1987.

Fimpeler-Philippen 2008
Fimpeler-Philippen, Annette. *Die Schiffahrt und ihre Fahrzeuge auf dem Niederrhein vom späten Mittelalter bis ins 18. Jahrhundert*. Düsseldorf: Droste, 2008.

Fosca 1954
Fosca, François. *Les dessins de Fragonard*. Paris: D. Perret, 1954.

Fried 1980
Fried, Michael. *Absorption and Theatricality: Painting and Beholder in the Age of Diderot*. Berkeley: University of California Press, 1980.

Gault de Saint-Germain 1808
Gault de Saint-Germain, Pierre Marie. *Les trois siècles de la peinture en France, ou Galerie des peintres français depuis François Ier jusqu'au règne de Napoléon, empereur et roi*. Paris: Belin, 1808.

Genlis 1782
Genlis, Stéphanie Félicité. *Adèle et Théodore, ou, Lettres sur l'éducation*. Paris: M. Lambert, 1782.

Girouard 2000
Girouard, Mark. *Life in the French Country House*. New York: Knopf, 2000.

Goncourt 1882
Goncourt, Edmond de, and Jules de Goncourt. *L'art du dix-huitième siècle*. 2 vols. Paris: A. Quentin, 1882.

Goncourt 1981
Goncourt, Edmond de, and Jules de Goncourt. *French Eighteenth-Century Painters, 1856–1875*. Ithaca, N.Y.: Cornell University Press, 1981.

Grasse 1957
Oeuvres de Fragonard. Exh. cat. Grasse: Musée Jean-Honoré Fragonard, 1957.

Grasse 2006
Jean-Honoré Fragonard, peintre de Grasse. Exh. cat. Grasse, Musée Jean-Honoré Fragonard. Paris: Somogy, 2006.

Grasselli 2009
Grasselli, Margaret Morgan, ed. *Renaissance to Revolution: French Drawings from the National Gallery of Art, 1500–1800*. Exh. cat. Washington, D.C.: National Gallery of Art, 2009.

Grasselli et al. 2003
Grasselli, Margaret Morgan, et al. *Colorful Impressions: The Printmaking Revolution in Eighteenth-Century France*. Exh. cat. Washington, D.C.: National Gallery of Art, 2003.

Grasselli et al. 2007
Grasselli, Margaret Morgan, et al. *Private Treasures: Four Centuries of European Master Drawings*. Exh. cat. New York, Morgan Library & Museum; Washington, D.C., National Gallery of Art. London: Lund Humphries, 2007.

Griffiths 2004
Griffiths, Antony. *Prints for Books: Book Illustration in France 1760–1800*. London: British Library, 2004.

Guichard 2008
Guichard, Charlotte. *Les amateurs d'art à Paris au XVIIIe siècle*. Seyssel: Champ Vallon, 2008.

Guichard 2012
Guichard, Charlotte. "Fragonard et les jeux de la signature au XVIIIe siècle." *Revue de l'Art* 177, no. 3 (2012), pp. 47–55.

Guigon 2013
Guigon, Emmanuel, ed. *Les Hubert Robert de Besançon*. Exh. cat. Besançon, Musée des Beaux-Arts et d'Archéologie. Milan: Silvana, 2013.

Guillerm 1980
Guillerm, Alain. "Le système de l'iconographie galante." *Dix-huitième Siècle* 12 (1980), pp. 177–94.

Guimbaud 1928
Guimbaud, Louis. *Saint-Non et Fragonard, d'après des documents inédits*. Paris: Le Goupy, 1928.

***Gülich-Bergische* 1773**
"Arrivée de personnalités et voyageurs . . . quatre Français, N. Bergeres, Mausion, Lubersalle et Fragonard à l'auberge du 2weibrückerhof." *Gülich-Bergische Wochentliche Nachrichten*, no. 35, August 31, 1773, at http://digital.ub.uni-duesseldorf.de/ihd/periodical/zoom/4487455.

Hall 1990
Hall, Lisa E. "Counterproofs: An Investigation into the History, Materials, Techniques, and Uses of Red Chalk Counterproofs with an Examination of Other Methods of Copying." MA thesis, Center for Conservation and Technical Studies, Harvard University Art Museums, Cambridge, Mass., 1990.

Hammer 1977
La Collection Armand Hammer. Exh. cat. Paris, Musée du Louvre and Musée Jacquemart-André. Los Angeles: Armand Hammer Foundation, 1977.

Haverkamp-Begemann 1999
Haverkamp-Begemann, Egbert, ed. *Fifteenth- to Eighteenth-Century European Drawings, Central Europe, The Netherlands, France, England*. New York: Metropolitan Museum of Art, 1999.

Henriet 1922
Henriet, Maurice. "Un amateur d'art au XVIIIe siècle: L'académicien Watelet." *Gazette des Beaux-Arts* (September–October 1922), pp. 173–94.

Henriot 1926–28
Henriot, Gabriel. *Collection David Weill*. 3 vols. Paris: Braun, 1926–28.

Hérold 1935
Hérold, Jacques. *Louis-Marin Bonnet (1736–1793): Catalogue de l'oeuvre gravé*. Paris: M. Rousseau, 1935.

Hind 1922
Hind, Arthur Mayger. *Giovanni Battista Piranesi: A Critical Study*. New York: E. Weyhe, 1922.

Hoisington and Stein 2012
Hoisington, Rena M., and Perrin Stein. "*Sous les yeux de Fragonard*: The Prints of Marguerite Gérard." *Print Quarterly* 29 (June 2012), pp. 142–62.

Huber and Rost 1804
Huber, Michael, and Carl C. H. Rost. *Manuel des curieux et des amateurs de l'art*. Vol. 8. Zurich: Orell, 1804.

Hyde and Ledbury 2006
Hyde, Melissa, and Mark Ledbury, eds. *Rethinking Boucher*. Los Angeles: Getty Publications, 2006.

Ingamells 1989
Ingamells, John. *The Wallace Collection: Catalogue of Pictures*, vol. 3, *French before 1815*. London: Trustees of the Wallace Collection, 1989.

L'Isle-Adam 2001
Fragonard et le voyage en Italie 1773–1774: Les Bergeret, une famille de mécènes. Exh. cat. L'Isle-Adam, Musée d'Art et d'Histoire Louis-Senlecq; Grasse, Musée Jean-Honoré Fragonard. Paris: Somogy, 2001.

Jackall et al. 2015
Jackall, Yuriko, John K. Delaney, and Michael Swicklik. "'Portrait of a Woman with a Book': A 'Newly Discovered Fantasy Figure' by Fragonard in the National Gallery of Art, Washington." *Burlington Magazine* 157 (April 2015), pp. 248–54.

Jacquot et al. 2010
Jacquot, Dominique, et al. *Jean Barbault (1718–1762): Le théâtre de la vie italienne.* Exh. cat. Strasbourg, Galerie Heitz. Strasbourg: Musées de la Ville de Strasbourg, 2010.

Jean-Richard 1971
Jean-Richard, Pierette. *François Boucher, gravures et dessins provenant du Cabinet des Dessins et de la Collection Edmond de Rothschild au Musée du Louvre.* Exh. cat. Paris, Musée du Louvre. Paris: Réunion des Musées Nationaux, 1971.

Jombert 1755
Jombert, Charles Antoine. *Méthode pour apprendre le dessein, ou l'on donne les regles générales de ce grand art, & des préceptes pour en acquérir le connoissance, & s'y perfectionner en peu de tems.* Paris: L'Imprimerie de l'Auteur, 1755.

Joulie 2004
Joulie, Françoise. *Boucher et les peintres du nord.* Exh. cat. Dijon, Musée Magnin; London, The Wallace Collection. Paris: Réunion des Musées Nationaux, 2004.

Kozak and Monkiewicz 1993
Kozak, Anna, and Maciej Monkiewicz, eds. *Master European Drawings from Polish Collections.* Exh. cat. Kansas City, Mo., Nelson-Atkins Museum of Art. Washington, D.C.: Trust for Museum Exhibitions, 1993.

Kramer et al. 1993
Kramer, Linda Konheim, Karyn Zieve, and Sarah Faunce. *French Nineteenth-Century Drawings and Watercolors at the Brooklyn Museum.* Exh. cat. Brooklyn Museum of Art. New York: Hudson Hills, 1993.

Laing 1999
Laing, Alastair. "New York: French Eighteenth-Century Drawings." *Burlington Magazine* 141 (June 1999), pp. 378–80.

Laing 2003
Laing, Alastair. *The Drawings of François Boucher.* Exh. cat. New York, The Frick Collection; Fort Worth, Kimbell Art Museum. New York: American Federation of Arts, 2003.

Lajer-Burcharth 2003
Lajer-Burcharth, Ewa. "Fragonard in Detail." *Differences* 14 (Fall 2003), pp. 34–56.

Lamers 1995
Lamers, Petra. *Il viaggio nel sud dell'abbe de Saint-Non: Il "Voyage pittoresque à Naples et en Sicile": Le genesi, i disegni preparatori, le incisioni.* Naples: Electa Napoli, 1995.

Landon 1808
Landon, Charles Paul. *Salon de 1808.* 2 vols. Paris: C. P. Landon, 1808.

Launay 1991
Launay, Elisabeth. *Les frères Goncourt: Collectionneurs de dessins.* Paris: Arthena, 1991.

Lecarpentier 1821
Lecarpentier, Charles-Louis-François. "Fragonard (Honoré)." In *Galerie des peintres célèbres*, vol. 2, pp. 279–83. Paris: Treuttel et Wurtz, 1821.

Ledbury 2001
Ledbury, Mark. "The Hierarchy of Genre in the Theory and Practice of Painting in Eighteenth-Century France." In *Théories et débats esthétiques au dix-huitième siècle: Elements d'une enquête*, edited by Elisabeth Décultot and Mark Ledbury, pp. 187–209. Paris: H. Champion, 2001.

Leonard et al. 2008
Leonard, Mark, Ashok Roy, and Scott Schaefer. "Two Versions of *The Fountain of Love* by Jean-Honoré Fragonard: A Comparative Study." *National Gallery Technical Bulletin* 29 (2008), pp. 31–45.

Leribault 2002
Leribault, Christophe. *Jean-François de Troy (1679–1752).* Paris: Arthena, 2002.

Linsky Collection 1984
The Jack and Belle Linsky Collection in The Metropolitan Museum of Art. New York: Metropolitan Museum of Art, 1984.

Liste 1773
"Liste des Seigneurs et Dames Venus aux Eaux Minérales de Spa, l'an 1773," at http://www.swedhs.org/visiteurs/spa1773.pdf.

London 1978a
Fragonard Drawings for Orlando Furioso. Exh. cat. London: Thomas Agnew and Sons, 1978.

London 1978b
18th Century French Paintings, Drawings and Sculpture. Exh. cat. London: David Carritt, 1978.

London 1980
Old Master Paintings and Drawings. Exh. cat. London: Thomas Agnew and Sons, 1980.

Lorblanchet et al. 2008
Lorblanchet, Hélène, et al. *Chefs-d'oeuvre d'une collection: Dessins du Musée Atger.* Exh. cat. Musée de Lodève. Bes-et-Esparon: Etudes et Communications, 2008.

Los Llanos 1994
Los Llanos, José-Luis de. "Les *Contes* et Nouvelles de La Fontaine et l'art galant au XVIIIe siècle." In *Jean de La Fontaine, Contes, illustrés par Jean-Honoré Fragonard*, pp. 299–346. Paris: Edition Diane de Selliers, 1994.

Louis 1994
Louis, François. "'L'âme de l'homme de génie': Fragonards Rinaldo-Pendants im literarischen Kontext." *Georges-Bloch-Jahrbuch des Kunstgeschichtlichen Seminars der Universität Zürich* 1 (1994), pp. 191–202.

Magnani 2004
Magnani, Lauro. "Storia di un giardino." In *Il Palazzo del Principe: Genesi e trasformazioni della villa di Andrea Doria a Genova*, edited by Laura Stagno, pp. 39–54. Rome: Carocci, 2004.

Mariette 1851–60
Mariette, Pierre Jean. *Abécédario de P. J. Mariette et autres notes inédites de cet amateur sur les arts et les artistes.* Edited by Charles Philippe de Chennevières-Pointel and Anatole de Montaiglon. 6 vols. Paris: Dumoulin, 1851–60.

Marigny 1905
Marigny, Abel François Poisson, marquis de. *Correspondance avec Coypel, Lépicié et Cochin.* Edited by Marc Furcy-Raynaud. Paris: Schemit, 1905.

Martine 1927
Martine, Charles. *Honoré Fragonard*. Paris: Helleu et Sergent, 1927.

Mascoli 1989
Mascoli, Laura. "Le 'Journal de voyage en Italie' de l'abbé de Saint-Non." *Dix-huitième Siècle*, no. 21 (1989), pp. 423–38.

Massengale 1979
Massengale, Jean Montague. "Current and Forthcoming Exhibitions: Drawings by Fragonard in North American Collections." *Burlington Magazine* 121 (April 1979), pp. 268, 270–74.

Massengale 1980
Massengale, Jean Montague. "Fragonard Elève: Sketching in the Studio of Boucher." *Apollo* 112 (December 1980), pp. 392–97.

Massengale 1993
Massengale, Jean Montague. *Jean-Honoré Fragonard*. New York: Abrams, 1993.

May 1960
May, Gita. "Diderot and Burke: A Study in Aesthetic Affinity." *Proceedings of the Modern Language Association of America* 75 (December 1960), pp. 527–39.

McPherson 1985
McPherson, Heather. "Jean-Baptiste Greuze's Italian Sojourn." *Studies in Eighteenth-Century Culture* 14 (1985), pp. 93–107.

Méjanès 1983
Méjanès, Jean-François. *Les collections du comte d'Orsay: Dessins du Musée du Louvre*. Exh. cat. Paris, Musée du Louvre. Paris: Editions de la Réunion des Musées Nationaux, 1983.

Meynard-Villemagne 1995
Meynard-Villemagne, Nanou. *N comme Nointel*. Nointel, 1995.

Michel 2005
Michel, Patrick. "La peinture 'flamande' et les goûts des collectionneurs français des années 1760–80: Un état des lieux." In *Collectionner dans les Flandres et la France du Nord au XVIIIe siècle: Actes du colloque international organisé les 13 et 14 mars 2003*, edited by Sophie Raux, pp. 289–306. Villeneuve-d'Ascq: Université Charles de Gaulle–Lille 3, 2005.

Michel 2006
Michel, Patrick. "Collection de dessins et marché de l'art en France au XVIIIe siècle." In *Liber memorialis Erik Duverger: Bijdragen tot de kunstgeschiedenis van de Nederlanden*, edited by Henri Pauwels et al., pp. 169–220. Wetteren: Universa, 2006.

Milam 1999
Milam, Jennifer D. "Fragonard's 'Le Furet.'" *Burlington Magazine* 114 (September 1999), pp. 542–43.

Milam 2006
Milam, Jennifer D. *Fragonard's Playful Paintings: Visual Games in Rococo Art*. Manchester: Manchester University Press, 2006.

Molotiu 2007
Molotiu, Andrei. *Fragonard's Allegories of Love*. Exh. cat. Los Angeles: J. Paul Getty Museum, 2007.

Mongan et al. 1945
Mongan, Elizabeth, Philip Hofer, and Jean Seznec. *Fragonard Drawings for Ariosto*. New York: Pantheon Books, 1945.

Montaiglon and Guiffrey 1901
Montaiglon, Anatole de, and Jules Guiffrey, eds. *Correspondance des directeurs de l'Académie de France à Rome avec les surintendants des Bâtiments, publiée d'après les manuscrits des Archives Nationales*, vol. 11, *1754–1763*. Paris: Charavay, 1901.

Morgan Collection 1912
J. Pierpont Morgan Collection of Drawings by the Old Masters Formed by C. Fairfax Murray. Vol. 3. London, 1912.

Morin 2008
Morin, Christophe. *Au service du château: L'architecture des communs en Île-de-France au XVIIIe siècle*. Paris: Publications de la Sorbonne, 2008.

Mulherron 2016
Mulherron, Jamie. "François Boucher and the Art of Conchology." *Burlington Magazine* 158 (April 2016), pp. 254–63.

Munhall 1971
Munhall, Edgar. "Fragonard's Studies for 'The Progress of Love.'" *Apollo* 93 (1971), pp. 400–407.

Munich 1991
Einige Neuerwerbungen. Exh. cat. Munich: Galerie Arnoldi-Livie, 1991.

Munro 2014
Munro, Jane. *Silent Partners: Artist and Mannequin from Function to Fetish*. Exh. cat. Cambridge, Fitzwilliam Museum; Paris, Musée Bourdelle. New Haven: Yale University Press, 2014.

Near 1981
Near, Pinckney L. *Three Masters of Landscape: Fragonard, Robert, and Boucher*. Exh. cat. Richmond: Virginia Museum of Fine Arts, 1981.

New York 1914
Exhibition of Paintings and Drawings by Fragonard. Exh. cat. New York, E. Gimpel & Wildenstein, 1914. New York: Hill-Matthews, 1914.

New York 1983
18th Century French Drawings. Exh. cat. New York: Colnaghi, 1983.

New York 1984
French Master Drawings. Exh. cat. New York: Didier Aaron, 1984.

New York 1987
François Boucher: His Circle and Influence. Exh. cat. New York: Stair Sainty Matthiesen, 1987.

New York 1996
Master Drawings. Exh. cat. New York, Brame & Lorenceau, Kate de Rothschild, Didier Aaron, 1996. New York: Didier Aaron, 1996.

New York 2000
Old Master Drawings. Exh. cat. New York and London: W. M. Brady & Co. and Thomas Williams Fine Art, 2000.

New York 2003
Old Master Drawings. Exh. cat. New York: Artemis Fine Arts, 2003.

New York 2005
The Arts of France from François 1er to Napoléon 1er: A Centennial Celebration of Wildenstein's Presence in New York. New York: Wildenstein & Co., 2005.

Niemeijer 1974
Niemeijer, Jan W. *Franse tekenkunst van de 18de eeuw uit nederlandse verzamelingen / French Drawings of the 18th Century from Dutch Collections*. Exh. cat. Amsterdam: Rijksmuseum, 1974.

Nolhac 1906
Nolhac, Pierre de. *J.-H. Fragonard, 1732–1806*. Paris: Goupil, 1906.

Norman 1978a
Norman, Geraldine. "More Than 30 'Fragonard' Drawings May Be Fakes." *Times* (London), March 8, 1978, pp. 1–5.

Norman 1978b
Norman, Geraldine. "When a Fragonard Copy Looks Just Too Good to Be True." *Times* (London), March 9, 1978, p. 12.

Ongpin 1997
Ongpin, Stephen. *An Exhibition of Master Drawings.* Exh. cat. New York: Colnaghi, 1997.

Oppé 1927
Oppé, Adolf P. "Honoré Fragonard." *Old Master Drawings* 2 (June 1927).

Pagliano 2005
Pagliano, Eric. *Plis & drapés dans les dessins français des XVIIe et XVIIIe siècles du Musée des Beaux-Arts d'Orléans.* Exh. cat. Orléans: Musée des Beaux-Arts, 2005.

Paoli and Preti 2012
Paoli, Michel, and Monica Preti, eds. *L'Arioste et les arts.* Paris: Musée du Louvre, 2012.

Paris 1879
Catalogue descriptif des dessins de maîtres anciens exposés à l'Ecole des Beaux-Arts, mai–juin 1879. Exh. cat. Paris: G. Chamerot, 1879.

Paris 1907
Exposition Chardin et Fragonard. Exh. cat. Paris: Galerie Georges Petit, 1907.

Paris 1921
Exposition d'oeuvres de J.-H. Fragonard. Exh. cat. Paris: Musée des Arts Décoratifs, 1921.

Paris 1931
Exposition de dessins de Fragonard. Exh. cat. Paris, Jacques Seligmann & Fils, Hôtel de Sagan, 1931. Paris: Fondation de la Maison de Santé du Gardien de la Paix, 1931.

Paris 1934
Les artistes français en Italie: De Poussin à Renoir. Exh. cat. Paris: Musée des Arts Décoratifs, 1934.

Paris 1951
Dessins français de Watteau à Prud'hon. Paris, Galerie Cailleux, 1951.

Paris 1980
Des monts et des eaux: Paysages de 1715 à 1850. Exh. cat. Paris: Galerie Cailleux, 1980.

Paris 1983
Rome 1760–1770: Fragonard, Hubert Robert et leurs amis. Exh. cat. Paris: Galerie Cailleux, 1983.

Paris 1987
Aspects de Fragonard: Peintures–Dessins–Estampes. Exh. cat. Paris: Galerie Cailleux, 1987.

Paris 1992
Fragonard et le dessin français au XVIII siècle dans les collections du Petit Palais. Exh. cat. Paris, Musée du Petit Palais. Paris: Paris-Musées, 1992.

Paris 2009
Marguerite Gérard, artiste en 1789, dans l'atelier de Fragonard. Exh. cat. Paris, Musée Cognacq-Jay. Paris: Paris-Musées, 2009.

Percival 2012
Percival, Melissa. *Fragonard and the Fantasy Figure: Painting the Imagination.* Farnham: Ashgate, 2012.

Pernety 1757
Pernety, Antoine Joseph. *Dictionnaire portatif de peinture, sculpture et gravure.* Paris: Bauche, 1757.

Portalis 1880
Portalis, Roger. "La Collection Walferdin et ses Fragonards." *Gazette des Beaux-Arts* 21 (April 1880), pp. 297–322.

Portalis 1889
Portalis, Roger. *Honoré Fragonard, sa vie et son oeuvre.* 2 vols. Paris: J. Rothschild, 1889.

Portalis and Béraldi 1880–82
Portalis, Roger, and Henri Béraldi. *Les graveurs du dix-huitième siècle.* 3 vols. Paris: Morgand et Fatout, 1880–82.

Poulet et al. 2004
Poulet, Anne L., et al. *Houdon, sculpteur des Lumières, 1741–1828.* Exh. cat. Château de Versailles. Paris: Réunion des Musées Nationaux, 2004.

Prod'homme 1928
Prod'homme, Jacques Gabriel. "A propos du centenaire de la mort de Houdon: Gluck et Houdon, histoire d'un buste." *Mercure de France* (July 1928), pp. 67–83.

Rabreau and Henry 2007
Rabreau, Daniel, and Christophe Henry. *Corésus et Callirhoé de Fragonard: Un chef d'oeuvre d'émotion.* Bordeaux: Arts & Arts, 2007.

Rand 1991
Rand, Richard. "Two Landscapes by Fragonard from Saint-Non's Collection." *Burlington Magazine* 133 (December 1991), pp. 246–48.

Rand 1995
Rand, Richard. "Representing the Picturesque Garden: The Landscapes of Fragonard." PhD diss., University of Michigan, 1995.

Rand 2001
Rand, Richard. "Fragonard dans le jardin d'amour." In *L'art et les normes sociales au XVIIIe siècle,* edited by Thomas W. Gaehtgens et al., pp. 493–508. Paris: Editions de la Maison des Sciences de l'Homme, 2001.

Rand 2008
Rand, Richard. "Fragonard: Paris." *Burlington Magazine* 150 (February 2008), pp. 124–26.

Ratouis de Limay 1907
Ratouis de Limay, Paul. *Un amateur orléanais au XVIIIe siècle: Aignan-Thomas Desfriches (1715–1800), sa vie, son oeuvre, ses collections, sa correspondance.* Paris: Librairie H. Champion, 1907.

Raux 2007
Raux, Sophie. "Le voyage de Fragonard et Bergeret en Flandre et Hollande durant l'été 1773." *Revue de l'Art* 156, no. 2 (2007), pp. 11–28.

Réau 1956
Réau, Louis. *Fragonard, sa vie et son oeuvre.* Brussels: Elsevier, 1956.

Reuter et al. 2013
Reuter, Astrid, et al., eds. *Fragonard, Poesie & Leidenschaft.* Exh. cat. Staatliche Kunsthalle Karlsruhe. Munich: Deutscher Kunstverlag, 2013.

Riccoboni 1947
Riccoboni, Alberto. *Quattrocento pitture inedite.* Exh. cat. Venice: Stampa Editrice Già Zanetti, 1947.

Riccòmini 2006
Riccòmini, Eugenio. *L'ercole trionfante: I tre Carracci a casa Sampieri.* Argelato: Minerva Edizioni, 2006.

Rijdt 2003
Rijdt, Robert-Jan te, ed. *De Watteau à Ingres: Dessins français du XVIIIe siècle du Rijksmuseum Amsterdam*. Exh. cat. Amsterdam, Rijksmuseum; Paris, Institut Néerlandais. Paris: Fondation Custodia, 2003.

Rizzi 1971
Rizzi, Aldo, ed. *Mostra del Tiepolo: Udine, Celebrazioni tiepolesche*. Exh. cat. Villa Manin di Passariano. Milan: Electa, 1971.

Robertson 1978
Robertson, Sally Wells. "Marguerite Gérard, 1761–1837." PhD diss., Institute of Fine Arts, New York University, 1978.

Roland Michel 1961
Roland Michel, Marianne. "The Themes of 'the Artist' and of 'Inspiration' as Revealed by Some of Fragonard's Drawings." *Burlington Magazine* 103 (November 1961), suppl. no. 9, pp. i–iii.

Roland Michel 1970
Roland Michel, Marianne. "Fragonard—Illustrator of the 'Contes' of La Fontaine." *Burlington Magazine* 112 (October 1970), suppl. no. 25, pp. i–vi.

Roland Michel 1987
Roland Michel, Marianne. *Le dessin Français au XVIIIe siècle*. Paris: Editions Vilo, 1987.

Roland Michel 2003
Roland Michel, Marianne. "Fragonard: Du dessin à la gravure." In *Dessins français au XVIIe et XVIIIe siècles: Actes du colloque, Ecole du Louvre, 24 et 25 juin 1999*, edited by Nicolas Sainte Fare Garnot, pp. 377–94. Paris: Ecole du Louvre, 2003.

Romanelli 1995
Romanelli, Giandomenico. *Scuola grande di San Rocco*. Milan: Electa, 1995.

Rome 1976
Piranèse et les Français, 1740–1790. Exh. cat. Rome, Villa Medici; Dijon, Palais des Etats de Bourgogne; Paris, Hôtel de Sully. Rome: Edizioni dell'Elefante, 1976.

Rosenberg 1987
Rosenberg, Pierre. "Ce qu'on disait de Fragonard." *Revue de l'Art* 78, no. 1 (1987), pp. 86–90.

Rosenberg 1988
Rosenberg, Pierre. *Fragonard*. Exh. cat. Paris, Galeries Nationales du Grand Palais; New York, The Metropolitan Museum of Art. New York: Abrams, 1988.

Rosenberg 1989
Rosenberg, Pierre. *Tout l'oeuvre peint de Fragonard*. Paris: Flammarion, 1989.

Rosenberg 1993
Rosenberg, Pierre. "Fragonard at the Fogg." *Burlington Magazine* 135 (November 1993), p. 787.

Rosenberg 1996
Rosenberg, Pierre. "De qui sont les miniatures de Fragonard?" *Revue de l'Art* 111, no. 1 (1996), pp. 66–76.

Rosenberg 1998
Rosenberg, Pierre. "Fragonard et Venise." In *Parigi-Venezia: Cultura, relazioni, influenze negli scambi intellettuali del Settecento*, edited by Carlo Ossola, pp. 383–88. Florence: L. S. Olschki, 1998.

Rosenberg 2000a
Rosenberg, Pierre. "Eighteenth-Century French Drawings in New York Collections." *Master Drawings* 38 (Summer 2000), pp. 187–90.

Rosenberg 2000b
Rosenberg, Pierre. *From Drawing to Painting: Poussin, Watteau, Fragonard, David & Ingres*. Princeton: Princeton University Press, 2000.

Rosenberg 2001
Rosenberg, Pierre. *Du dessin au tableau: Poussin, Watteau, Fragonard, David et Ingres*. Paris: Flammarion, 2001.

Rosenberg ca. 2001
Rosenberg, Pierre. "Un tableau de Tiepolo, un dessin de Fragonard, Algarotti et Mariette." In *Per l'arte da Venezia all'Europa: Studi in onore di Giuseppe Maria Pilo*, edited by Mario Piantoni and Laura De Rossi, vol. 2, pp. 469–70. Monfalcone: Laguna, ca. 2001.

Rosenberg 2006
Rosenberg, Pierre. *Les Fragonard de Besançon*. Exh. cat. Besançon, Musée des Beaux-Arts et d'Archéologie. Milan: 5 Continents, 2006.

Rosenberg and Barthélemy-Labeeuw 2011
Rosenberg, Pierre, in collaboration with Laure Barthélemy-Labeeuw. *Les dessins de la collection Mariette*. 2 vols. Milan: Mondadori Electa, 2011.

Rosenberg and Brejon de Lavergnée 1986
Rosenberg, Pierre, and Barbara Brejon de Lavergnée. *Saint-Non—Fragonard. Panopticon italiano: Un diario di viaggio ritrovato, 1759–1761*. Rome: Edizioni dell'Elefante, 1986.

Rosenberg and Brejon de Lavergnée 2000
Rosenberg, Pierre, and Barbara Brejon de Lavergnée. *Saint-Non—Fragonard. Panopticon italiano: Un diario di viaggio ritrovato, 1759–1761*. 2d ed. Rome: Edizioni dell'Elefante, 2000.

Rosenberg and Prat 1994
Rosenberg, Pierre, and Louis-Antoine Prat. *Nicolas Poussin, 1594–1665: Catalogue raisonné des dessins*. 2 vols. Milan: Leonardo Editore, 1994.

Rosenberg and Prat 1996
Rosenberg, Pierre, and Louis-Antoine Prat. *Antoine Watteau, 1684–1721: Catalogue raisonné des dessins*. 3 vols. Milan: Leonardo Arte, 1996.

Rosenberg and van de Sandt 1983
Rosenberg, Pierre, and Udolpho van de Sandt. *Pierre Peyron, 1744–1814*. Neuilly-sur-Seine: Arthena, 1983.

Rossi and Puppi 1996
Rossi, Paola, and Lionello Puppi, eds. *Jacopo Tintoretto nel quarto centenario della morte*. Padua: Il Poligrafo, 1996.

Roubo 1775
Roubo, André Jacob. *L'art du treillageur, ou Menuiserie des jardins: Quatrième et derniere partie de L'art du menuisier*. Paris, 1775.

Roux 1949
Roux, Marcel. *Inventaire du fonds français: Graveurs du XVIIIe siècle*. Vol. 6. Paris: Bibliothèque Nationale, 1949.

Ruggeri 1996
Ruggeri, Ugo. *Pietro e Marco Liberi: Pittori nella Venezia del Seicento*. Rimini: Stefano Patacconi, 1996.

Saint-Non 1781–86
Saint-Non, Jean Claude Richard de. *Voyage pittoresque, ou description des royaumes de Naples et de Sicile*. 4 vols. Paris: Imprimerie de Clousier, 1781–86.

Salmon 2002
Salmon, Xavier, ed. *Madame de Pompadour et les arts*. Exh. cat. Château de Versailles. Paris: Réunion des Musées Nationaux, 2002.

Salmon 2016
Salmon, Xavier, ed. *A l'ombre des frondaisons d'Arcueil: Dessiner un jardin du XVIIIe siècle*. Exh. cat. Paris, Musée du Louvre. Paris: Editions du Musée du Louvre, 2016.

Scarpa 2006
Scarpa, Annalisa. *Sebastiano Ricci*. Milan: Bruno Alfieri, 2006.

Schroder 1996
Schroder, Anne L. "Compte rendu de l'exposition Fragonard et le dessin français au XVIIIe siècle dans les collections du Petit Palais." *Master Drawings* 34, no. 4 (1996), pp. 430–35.

Schroder 2001
Schroder, Anne L. "Reassessing Fragonard's Later Years: The Artist's Nineteenth-Century Biographers, the Rococo, and the French Revolution." In *Art and Culture in the Eighteenth Century: New Dimensions and Multiple Perspectives*, edited by Elise Goodman, pp. 39–58. Newark: University of Delaware Press, 2001.

Schroder 2011
Schroder, Anne L. "Fragonard's Later Career: The 'Contes et Nouvelles' and the Progress of Love Revisited." *Art Bulletin* 93 (June 2011), pp. 150–77.

Senior 1936–37
Senior, Elizabeth. "Drawings Made in Italy by Fragonard." *British Museum Quarterly* 11 (1936–37), pp. 5–9.

Shelley 2009
Shelley, Marjorie. "A Tale of Two Sultans, Part II: The Materials and Techniques of an Original Drawing by Fragonard and a Copy." *Metropolitan Museum Journal* 44 (2009), pp. 130–37.

Sheriff 1986
Sheriff, Mary D. "For Love or Money? Rethinking Fragonard." *Eighteenth-Century Studies* 19 (Spring 1986), pp. 333–54.

Sheriff 1988
Sheriff, Mary D. "Fragonard." *Art Journal* 47 (Winter 1988), pp. 368–72.

Sheriff 1990
Sheriff, Mary D. *Fragonard: Art and Eroticism*. Chicago: University of Chicago Press, 1990.

Sjöberg 1977
Sjöberg, Yves. *Inventaire du fonds français: Graveurs du XVIIIe siècle*. Vol. 14. Paris: Bibliothèque Nationale, 1977.

Slive 1981
Slive, Seymour. "A Fragonard Landscape after Jacob van Ruisdael's 'Wooded Landscape with a Pond.'" In *The Shape of the Past: Studies in Honor of Franklin D. Murphy*, edited by Giorgio Buccellati and Charles Speroni, pp. 267–76. Los Angeles: Institute of Archaeology, University of California, 1981.

Smentek 2014
Smentek, Kristel. *Mariette and the Science of the Connoisseur in Eighteenth-Century Europe*. Farnham: Ashgate, 2014.

Stampfle and Denison 1975
Stampfle, Felice, and Cara D. Denison. *Drawings from the Collection of Mr. & Mrs. Eugene V. Thaw*. Exh. cat. New York: Pierpont Morgan Library, 1975.

Stein 1996
Stein, Perrin. "Boucher's Chinoiseries: Some New Sources." *Burlington Magazine* 138 (September 1996), pp. 598–604.

Stein 2000a
Stein, Perrin. "Copies and Retouched Drawings by Charles-Joseph Natoire." *Master Drawings* 38 (Summer 2000), pp. 167–86.

Stein 2000b
Stein, Perrin. "Drawings by Hubert Robert in The Metropolitan Museum of Art: Some Restored Attributions." *Metropolitan Museum Journal* 35 (2000), pp. 179–91.

Stein 2004
Stein, Perrin. "Notes on the Boucher Exhibitions Marking the Tercentenary of the Artist's Birth." *Burlington Magazine* 146 (March 2004), pp. 169–73.

Stein 2005
Stein, Perrin. *French Drawings from the British Museum: Clouet to Seurat*. Exh. cat. New York, The Metropolitan Museum of Art; London, The British Museum. London: British Museum Press, 2005.

Stein 2007
Stein, Perrin. "Fragonard in Naples: Two Rediscovered Drawings." *Burlington Magazine* 149 (May 2007), pp. 305–8.

Stein 2009
Stein, Perrin. "A Tale of Two Sultans, Part 1: Fragonards Real and Fake." *Metropolitan Museum Journal* 44 (2009), pp. 121–29.

Stein and Holmes 1999
Stein, Perrin, and Mary Tavener Holmes. *Eighteenth-Century French Drawings in New York Collections*. Exh. cat. New York: Metropolitan Museum of Art, 1999.

Stein et al. 2013
Stein, Perrin, et al. *Artists and Amateurs: Etching in 18th-Century France*. Exh. cat. New York: Metropolitan Museum of Art, 2013.

Sterling 1964
Sterling, Charles. *Portrait of a Man (the Warrior), Jean Honoré Fragonard*. Exh. cat. Williamstown, Mass.: Sterling and Francine Clark Art Institute, 1964.

Sutton 1980
Sutton, Denys. *Fragonard*. Exh. cat. Tokyo, National Museum of Western Art; Kyoto Municipal Museum. Tokyo: Yomiuri Shimbun, 1980.

Szabó 1980
Szabó, George. *Seventeenth and Eighteenth Century French Drawings from the Robert Lehman Collection*. Exh. cat. New York: Metropolitan Museum of Art, 1980.

Szabó et al. 1988
Szabó, George, et al. *Landscape Drawings of Five Centuries, 1400–1900, from the Robert Lehman Collection of the Metropolitan Museum of Art*. Exh. cat. Evanston, Ill.: Mary and Leigh Block Gallery, Northwestern University, 1988.

Szanto 2005
Szanto, Mickaël. "La peinture du Nord et sa réception en France au XVIIIe siècle: Réflexions sur l'accrochage des tableaux de Madame de Verrue." In *Collectionner dans les Flandres et la France du Nord au XVIIIe siècle: Actes du colloque international organisé les 13 et 14 mars 2003*, edited by Sophie Raux, pp. 221–50. Villeneuve-d'Ascq: Université Charles de Gaulle–Lille 3, 2005.

Thuillier 1967
Thuillier, Jacques. *Fragonard: Biographical and Critical Study*. Geneva: Editions d'Art Albert Skira, 1967.

Titi 1987
Titi, Filippo. *Studio di pittura, scoltura, et architettura, nelle chiese di Roma (1674–1763).* 2 vols. Florence: Centro Di, 1987.

Tornézy 1895
Tornézy, Albert. *Bergeret et Fragonard: Journal inédit d'un voyage en Italie, 1773–1774.* Paris: May et Motteroz, 1895.

Turner et al. 1998
Turner, Nicholas, Lee Hendrix, and Carol Plazzotta, eds. *European Drawings 3: Catalogue of the Collections.* Malibu: J. Paul Getty Museum, 1998.

Valogne 1955
Valogne, Catherine. "Fragonard, mon grand-père, par Théophile Fragonard." *Les Lettres Françaises*, February 17, 1955, pp. 1, 7, 9.

Venuti 1776–79
Venuti, Ridolfino. *Vetera monumenta quae in hortis Caelimontanis et in aedibus Matthaeiorum adservantur.* 3 vols. Rome: Monaldini, 1776–79.

Vichy 1943
Exposition de Dessins de maîtres français du XVIIIe siècle. Exh. cat. Vichy: Galerie Sévigné, 1943.

Virch 1960
Virch, Claus. "The Walter C. Baker Collection of Master Drawings." *The Metropolitan Museum of Art Bulletin* 18 (June 1960), pp. 309–17.

Virch 1962
Virch, Claus. *Master Drawings in the Collection of Walter C. Baker.* Exh. cat. New York: Metropolitan Museum of Art, 1962.

Vogtherr and Holmes 2014
Vogtherr, Christoph Martin, and Mary Tavener Holmes. *De Watteau à Fragonard: Les fêtes galantes.* Exh. cat. Paris, Musée Jacquemart-André. Brussels: Fonds Mercator, 2014.

Vogtherr et al. 2011
Vogtherr, Christoph Martin, et al. *Jean de Jullienne, Collector & Connoisseur.* Exh. cat. London: Wallace Collection, 2011.

Wakefield 1976
Wakefield, David. *Fragonard.* New York: Jupiter Books, 1981.

Wall 2014
Wall, Anthony. *La place du lecteur: Livres et lectures dans la peinture française du XVIIIe siècle.* Rennes: Presses Universitaires de Rennes, 2014.

Wallace 1979
Wallace, Richard W. *The Etchings of Salvator Rosa.* Princeton: Princeton University Press, 1979.

Watelet 2003
Watelet, Claude-Henri. *Essay on Gardens: A Chapter in the French Picturesque, 1774.* Translated and edited by Samuel Danon. Philadelphia: University of Pennsylvania Press, 2003.

Wiebel 2007
Wiebel, Christiane. "Jean-Claude Richard, abbé de Saint-Non." In *Aquatinta, oder, "Die Kunst mit dem Pinsel in Kupfer zu stechen": Das druckgraphische Verfahren von seinen Anfängen bis zu Goya*, pp. 134–49. Berlin: Deutscher Kunstverlag, 2007.

D. Wildenstein 1972
Wildenstein, Daniel. *L'opera completa di Fragonard.* Milan: Rizzoli, 1972.

G. Wildenstein 1921
Wildenstein, Georges. *Exposition d'oeuvres de J.-H. Fragonard.* Exh. cat. Paris: Musée des Arts Décoratifs, 1921.

G. Wildenstein 1956
Wildenstein, Georges. *Fragonard, aquafortiste.* Paris: Les Beaux-Arts, 1956.

G. Wildenstein 1959
Wildenstein, Georges. "L'Abbé de Saint-Non, artiste et mécène." *Gazette des Beaux-Arts* 54 (1959), pp. 225–44.

G. Wildenstein 1960
Wildenstein, Georges. *The Paintings of Fragonard.* London: Phaidon, 1960.

G. Wildenstein 1961
Wildenstein, Georges. "Un amateur de Boucher et de Fragonard, Jacques-Onésyme Bergeret, 1715–1785." *Gazette des Beaux-Arts* 58 (1961), pp. 39–84.

Wilhelm 1975
Wilhelm, Jacques. "Le salon du graveur Gilles Demarteau peint par François Boucher et son atelier avec le concours de Fragonard et de J. B. Huet." *Bulletin du Musée Carnavalet* 28, no. 1 (1975), pp. 6–19.

Williams 1978
Williams, Eunice. *Drawings by Fragonard in North American Collections.* Exh. cat. Washington, D.C., National Gallery of Art; Cambridge, Mass., Fogg Art Museum; New York, The Frick Collection. Baltimore: Schneidereith & Sons, 1978.

Williams 1987
Williams, Eunice. "Drawings for Collaboration." In *Drawings Defined*, edited by Walter Strauss and Tracie Felker. New York: Abaris Books, 1987.

Williams 1993
Williams, Eunice. *"Gens, Honorez Fragonard!" Works from the Collections of Harvard University and Harvard Friends.* Exh. cat. Cambridge, Mass.: Harvard University Art Museums, 1993.

Williams 2015
Williams, Eunice. "Jean-Honoré Fragonard: Two Drawings from the 1780s in the Fogg." *Master Drawings* 53 (Winter 2015), pp. 503–6.

Wilton-Ely 1994
Wilton-Ely, John. *Giovanni Battista Piranesi: The Complete Etchings.* San Francisco: Alan Wofsy Fine Arts, 1994.

Wintermute 1990
Wintermute, Alan, ed. *Claude to Corot: The Development of Landscape Painting in France.* Exh. cat. New York, Colnaghi. Seattle: University of Washington Press, 1990.

Wolf 1949
Wolf, Edwin. *Fragonard Plates for the Contes et Nouvelles de La Fontaine.* New York: New York Public Library, 1949.

Wright 1986
Wright, Beth. "New (Stage) Light on Fragonard's Corésus." *Arts Magazine* 60 (Summer 1986), pp. 54–59.

Zanella 2011
Zanella, Andrea. *Trois peintres grassois: Jean-Honoré Fragonard, Marguerite Gérard, Jean-Baptiste Mallet.* Grasse: Musée Fragonard, 2011.

Zanella and Dupuy-Vachey 2014
Zanella, Andréa, and Marie-Anne Dupuy-Vachey. *Les dessins oubliés de Fragonard.* Exh. cat. Grasse: Musée Jean-Honoré Fragonard, 2014.

Index

Italic page numbers refer to illustrations.

This catalogue is published in conjunction with "Fragonard: Drawing Triumphant—Works from New York Collections," on view at The Metropolitan Museum of Art, New York, from October 6, 2016, through January 8, 2017.

The exhibition is made possible by the Gail and Parker Gilbert Fund and the Diane W. and James E. Burke Fund.

This publication is made possible by the Drue E. Heinz Fund.

Published by The Metropolitan Museum of Art, New York

Mark Polizzotti, Publisher and Editor in Chief
Gwen Roginsky, Associate Publisher and General Manager of Publications
Peter Antony, Chief Production Manager
Michael Sittenfeld, Senior Managing Editor

Edited by Elisa Urbanelli
Designed by Laura Lindgren
Production by Peter Antony with Lauren Knighton and Megan Kincaid
Bibliography edited by Philomena Mariani
Image acquisitions and permissions by Josephine Rodriguez-Massop
Translations from the French by Jane MacAvock

Typeset in Bembo
Printed on 135 gsm Perigord
Color separations, printing, and binding by
Conti Tipocolor, S.p.A, Florence, Italy

Details: jacket front: *Rinaldo in the Enchanted Forest* (cat. 36); jacket back: *Draftsman in a Trellised Garden* (cat. 50); p. ii: *Young Athenian Women Drawing Lots* (cat. 38); p. iv: *Study of Plants, Including Acanthus* (cat. 4); p. vi: *A Fisherman Pulling a Net* (cat. 61); p. viii: *A Gathering at Wood's Edge* (cat. 49); pp. xx–xxi: *Landscape with Stormy Sky* (cat. 47); p. xxii: *The Little Park* (cat. 34); p. 14: *Reading in the Kitchen* (cat. 75); p. 46: *The Little Park* (cat. 32); pp. 70–71: *View of the Temple of Vesta at Tivoli* (cat. 35); pp. 270–71: *The Return of the Herd* (cat. 44)

First printing

The Metropolitan Museum of Art
1000 Fifth Avenue
New York, New York 10028
metmuseum.org

Distributed by
Yale University Press, New Haven and London
yalebooks.com/art
yalebooks.co.uk

Cataloguing-in-Publication Data is available from the Library of Congress.

ISBN 978-1-58839-601-3

Photographs of works in The Metropolitan Museum of Art's collection are by the Imaging Department, The Metropolitan Museum of Art, unless otherwise noted.

Additional photography credits: Courtesy Didier Aaron & Cie: fig. 16; Ananoff 1961–70: figs. 11, 30, 42; Photography © The Art Institute of Chicago: figs. 17, 53; © Ashmolean Museum, University of Oxford: fig. 73; Photo by Marco Baldassari / Electa / Mondadori Portfolio via Getty Images: fig. 79; Photo by Karen Bartsch: fig. 116; © Beaux-Arts de Paris, Dist. RMN-Grand Palais / Art Resource, N.Y.: p. xvi; © Besançon, Musée des beaux-arts et d'archéologie, photo by Charles Choffet: fig. 100; © Besançon, Musée des beaux-arts et d'archéologie, photo by Pierre Guenat: figs. 1, 21, 83, 102; bpk, Berlin / Hamburger Kunsthalle / Christoph Irrgang / Art Resource, N.Y.: fig. 125; © The Calouste Gulbenkian Foundation / Scala / Art Resource, N.Y., photo by Catarina Gomes Ferreira: fig. 109; Cameraphoto Arte, Venice / Art Resource, N.Y.: fig. 76; © The Cleveland Museum of Art: figs. 32, 51; Christiansen 1997, p. 282: fig. 77; Cuzin 1988, p. 88: figs. 88, 89; De Agostini Picture Library: fig. 80; Faroult 2015, pp. 171, 226: figs. 24, 86; Courtesy of Fine Arts Museums of San Francisco: fig. 111; Photo by Fine Art Images / Heritage Images / Getty Images: fig. 87; © The Frick Collection: p. xviii; Galleria dell' Accademia, Venice, Italy / Bridgeman Images: fig. 44; Gemäldegalerie Alte Meister, Staatliche Kunstsammlungen Dresden, photo by Elke Estel, Hans-Peter Klut: fig. 107; Photo by Michael Gould: figs. 7, 104, 139; © Cecilia Heisser / Nationalmuseum, Stockholm: figs. 12, 96; Imaging Department © President and Fellows of Harvard College: figs. 27, 28, 124; Photo by Alex Jamison: cats. 68, 75, 98; Erich Lessing / Art Resource, N.Y.: fig. 135; © Musée Carnavalet / Roger-Viollet: fig. 99; ©Musées de Chambéry, photo by D. Gourbin: fig. 38; © Musée Cognacq-Jay / Roger-Viollet: figs. 34, 90; © Musée de Grasse, photo by Carlo Barbiero: fig. 93; Musée Grobet-Labadié, Marseille / photo by David Giancatarina: fig. 13; Photograph © 2016 Museum of Fine Arts, Boston: fig. 112; Courtesy of National Gallery of Art, Washington, D.C.: fig. 128; Photo © National Gallery of Canada: fig. 63; © National Gallery, London / Art Resource, N.Y.: p. vi; © The National Trust, Waddesdon Manor: fig. 31; Orléans, Musée des beaux-arts, photo by François Lauginie: fig. 3; Paris 1980: fig. 94; © Petit Palais / Roger-Viollet: figs. 35, 91, 127; The Pierpont Morgan Library, New York: cats. 34, 37, 45, 60, 67, 69, 71, 85, 91, 92, 95, 96, 99, figs. 57, 74, 133, 138; © Polo Museale del Lazio, Archivio Fotografico: fig. 69; Royal Collection Trust / © Her Majesty Queen Elizabeth II 2016: fig. 78; © RMN-Grand Palais / Art Resource, N.Y.: fig. 71; © RMN-Grand Palais / Art Resource, N.Y., photo by Daniel Arnaudet: fig. 18, p. xvii; © RMN-Grand Palais / Art Resource, N.Y., photo by Michele Bellot: p. xix; © RMN-Grand Palais / Art Resource, N.Y., photo by Jean-Gilles Berizzi: fig. 52; © RMN-Grand Palais / Art Resource, N.Y., photo by Gérard Blot: p. xviii, xix; RMN-Grand Palais / Art Resource, N.Y., photo by Agence Bulloz: fig. 29; © RMN-Grand Palais / Art Resource, N.Y., photo by Stéphane Maréchalle: figs. 20, 26; © RMN-Grand Palais / Art Resource, N.Y., photo by R. G. Ojeda: fig. 85; © RMN-Grand Palais / Art Resource, N.Y., photo by Franck Raux: fig. 25, p. xix; © RMN-Grand Palais / Art Resource, N.Y., photo by Benoit Touchard: figs. 15, 117; © The Samuel Courtauld Trust, The Courtauld Gallery, London: fig. 3; © Städel Museum, U. Edelmann, ARTOTHEK: fig. 37; Photograph © The State Hermitage Museum, photo by Vladimir Terebenin, Pavel Demidov: figs. 70, 134; Sterling and Francine Clark Art Institute, Williamstown, Massachusetts / Bridgeman Images: fig. 62; Photo by Studio Tromp, Rotterdam: figs. 9, 101; By kind permission of the Trustees of the Wallace Collection, London / Art Resource, N.Y.: fig. 84, p. xvii; Image © Worcester Art Museum: fig. 95